Imagined Histories

Imagined Histories

AMERICAN HISTORIANS

INTERPRET THE PAST

EDITED BY ANTHONY MOLHO
AND GORDON S. WOOD

PRINCETON UNIVERSITY PRESS

PRINCETON, NEW JERSEY

Library of Congress Cataloging-in-Publication Data

Molho, Anthony, and Wood, Gordon S.
Imagined histories : American historians interpret the past / edited by Anthony Molho
and Gordon S. Wood.
p.   cm.
Includes bibliographical references and index.
ISBN 0-691-05810-5 (alk. paper). — 0-691-05811-3 (pbk. : alk. paper)
1. Historiography—United States.   2. Historians—United States.
I. Molho, Anthony   II. Wood, Gordon S.
D13.5.U6157   1998
907'.2073—dc21   98-10246

This book has been composed in Berkeley Book

Princeton University Press books are printed
on acid-free paper and meet the guidelines for
permanence and durability of the Committee on
Production Guidelines for Book Longevity
of the Council on Library Resources

http://pup.princeton.edu

Printed in the United States of America

1   3   5   7   9   10   8   6   4   2

3   5   7   9   10   8   6   4   2
(Pbk.)

• CONTENTS •

THIS BOOK is based on the proceedings of a conference held at the University of the Republic of San Marino in June of 1995. The object of the conference was to examine the different ways historians in the United States have viewed the pasts of both their country and other peoples. An organizing committee invited to the conference thirty speakers, all of whom teach in colleges and universities in North America. At the same time, sixteen European scholars were invited to attend the meetings of San Marino as discussants. The result was a week of intense and enlightening discussions that revealed the often peculiar perspective that Americans have had on the past—their own and those of other peoples. Following the conference, we selected eighteen of the thirty essays presented there (one was later added) and asked the authors to reflect upon the observations raised in our discussions. In some cases, the essays included in this volume differ substantially from their previous versions. Other essays have been changed only slightly.

The San Marino meeting was planned by a group of Brown University historians who regularly met for nearly two years to discuss both the substance and the logistics of the conference. During our meetings we reached a number of decisions that were discussed and basically confirmed in December 1994, when most of the speakers gathered in Providence, Rhode Island, for two days to exchange ideas on how best to cast their papers. The most important of these decisions was that our collective aim should be to present a sustained though multivoiced reflection on how American historians over the previous century or so have thought about—indeed, how they have imagined—the past. Our objective was to survey the period from the beginnings of the historical profession in the latter part of the nineteenth century to the present in order to uncover the conventions, assumptions, and convictions that shaped the work of America's professional historians. We hoped too to understand how our profession's various fields evolved in the ways they did over the past three or four scholarly generations. Crucial to our goal was development over time. Our interest in the history of history-writing, in other words, took precedence over the dilemmas and epistemological doubts facing the profession today.

Although many of our authors bring their analyses up to the present, their essays are not designed to be surveys of current historiographical debates. Nor is this collection of essays intended to focus on postmodern developments such as the "linguistic turn" or on the current fascination of historians in the United States and elsewhere with memory and agency. Many of the authors, of course, do address these issues, but that is not their main objective. All are primarily interested in the ways American historians imagined the past. Of course, to imagine the past is not to write fiction, for the histories American historians of the past century imagined were continually measured against an always elusive but still real and objective past.

A problem continually faced by the organizers of the conference and the editors was one of coverage. What fields ought to be selected to survey and on the basis of what criteria ought this selection to take place? It turned out that we had many more excellent papers on relevant subjects than we could reasonably put together in one volume, and regrettably we have had to leave many important pieces out. The resultant collection is therefore highly selective and partial. Although we are keenly aware of many more subjects and fields that ideally ought to have been included, nevertheless we believe that the present collection, selective as it may be, is an important contribution to an understanding of history-writing in America.

History-writing at present seems to be changing in fundamental ways, which suggests that this is an especially appropriate moment for exploring the unusual ways Americans have conceived of their past and the pasts of other nations. Although only time will tell whether or not American history-writing is actually at a crossroads, we believe that there is a pervasive sense in the historical profession that important changes are taking place in American culture that are affecting the ways Americans have thought about the past. The long-standing assumption that America has a unique destiny and a unique role in the world seems at last to be dissipating. Older ideas of the relationship between America and the world are now being questioned, and a new transoceanic cosmopolitanism is emerging. All these changes make it increasingly difficult today to isolate a distinctively American voice in historical writing.

We thus believe that that this is the right moment to look at the ways American historians have conceived of various pasts—before these imagined pasts fade from memory and we forget how distinctively American they once were.

ACKNOWLEDGMENTS

Aldo Schiavone, president of the School of Historical Studies of the University of San Marino in the early 1990s, was the first to suggest that we should organize the conference on which this book is based. To him, to his colleagues in San Marino, most especially Maurice Aymard and Corrado Vivanti, and to the staff of the school, especially Signora Laura Dolcini, we extend our warm thanks for their help, encouragement, and hospitality. Once the idea of the conference was launched, Vartan Gregorian, then president of Brown University, and Thomas Biersteker, director of Watson Institute at Brown University, gave us their full and enthusiastic support.

A number of friends and colleagues helped in the organization and success of the conference. Among colleagues at Brown, Stephen Graubard and Tom Skidmore were immensely helpful with their advice. We wish to formally acknowledge their support and friendship. In addition, Willi Paul Adams, Maurice Aymard, Tiziano Bonazzi, Glen Bowersock, Roger Chartier, David William Cohen, Emilio Gabba, Giuseppe Galasso, Juan Carlos Garavaglia, William Harris, Thomas Haskell, David Hollinger, Christopher Jones, James McPherson, Gian

Giacomo Migone, Peter Novick, Luisa Passerini, Silvana Seidel Menchi, Giuliano Procacci, Jacques Revel, James Sheehan, Maurizio Vaudagna, and Roberto Vivarelli participated in the conference as paper writers and commentators. Their enthusiastic and always helpful engagement in the discussions at San Marino served as stimulus to all those present to rethink and refine their ideas on American historiography.

We wish to thank Dr. Giovanni Ciappelli and Ms. Anna Rosa Muller for their excellent work in preparing the book's comprehensive index. We also wish to thank members of the staff of the Princeton University Press most specially Brigitta van Rheinberg, Molan Chun Goldstein, and Will Hively for their encouragement, patience, and good sense.

Finally, we wish to single out the contribution of our extraordinary secretary and assistant. Cherrie Guerzon's intelligence, commitment, and constant enthusiasm were essential for the completion of the manuscript. We are immensely grateful to her.

Imagined Histories

ANTHONY MOLHO AND
GORDON S. WOOD

A VAST and unsettling transformation in the writing of history is taking place in America. During the past several decades we seem to be experiencing nothing less than what Daniel Rodgers, in chapter 1, calls "a historiographical revolution."[1] The historical landscape seems to be shifting, and only now are we beginning to assess the implications of this shift. This volume, which explores many of the various ways American historians have imagined the pasts of their own country as well as other nations, is part of the assessment.

American historians have traditionally brought to bear on the past a perspective often strikingly different from that of historians of other nations. None of the major European countries, for example—neither France, Italy, Germany, nor England—has shared America's idiosyncratic conception of Western civilization. But America's unusual perspective on the past, both of Europe and of itself, is changing and changing radically, and these changes make this volume possible. Only at this moment—when the identity of the United States and the discipline of history are shifting in profound ways—are we able to perceive clearly the peculiar ways Americans have written about the past. Only now, it seems, could the papers included in this book have been written.

Although Americans are supposed to be a notoriously unhistorically minded people, they have always spent a great deal of time and energy writing histories of themselves and of other peoples. The United States today has a huge and diverse historical profession, and much of that profession has developed in the past thirty or forty years. In 1950 the American Historical Association had about 5,500 members. By 1960 the number had jumped by half, to more than 8,200. Ten years later it more than doubled, to about 18,000. Although by the mid-1990s membership had dramatically declined, suggesting the economic uncertainties that presently plague the American academy, the American Historical Association today still has nearly 13,000 members, with many more thousands of professionally trained historians choosing for one reason or another not to join. In addition, of course, there are many amateur historians, genealogists, and antiquarians. It is hard to imagine that many other nations produce as many history books; probably none devotes as many resources to generate historical knowledge. What is more, Americans do not study merely their own country's past. Two out of three professional historians in the United States actually work on the histories of other societies and cultures. In fact, 590 out of the 800 Ph.D.s in history awarded by American universities in 1994—nearly three out of four— were in fields other than American history.[2]

This breadth of interest in other peoples' pasts is not new; it goes back at least to the beginning of professional history writing at the end of the nineteenth century. Indeed, from the very beginning of the nation Americans have been fascinated with the history of Europe and their peculiar relationship to it. That relationship, more than any other single thing, has decisively affected the character of nearly all American history writing, about both the nation itself and other nations. From the very outset the perception of a contrast with the Old World created that peculiar sense of American difference and distinctiveness which some recent historians, including some in this volume, have labeled American "exceptionalism."[3]

Until quite recently many Americans thought of their history and their role in the world as not merely different from those of other nations but as "exceptional"—as a beacon or model for other nations, with a special and unique destiny to lead the rest of the world to freedom and democracy. Many historians shared this view. For more than two centuries, much of the interest Americans have had in the pasts of other peoples and other cultures—in Antiquity, the Middle Ages, the Renaissance, the Reformation, in what came to be called "Western Civilization"—grew out of their desire to bolster and make sense of their "exceptionalist" destiny in the world. Surely every nation has its own peculiar view of its role in the world, but few have equaled America in promoting the claim of its special destiny. In the second half of the twentieth century only the Soviet Union could advance claims as sweeping as those of the United States about its peculiar historical mission.

In one way or another, this theme—the long-held notions nurtured by Americans and American historians about their nation's allegedly exceptional history—links the papers that follow and gives this volume a measure of its unity. As Dorothy Ross notes in chapter 4, exceptionalism for Americans has generally meant a New World that was "antithetical to the Old," an America that was different from Europe, inferior in many ways, but at least free from Europe's ills and an exemplar or model for the future progress of liberty and democracy. Exceptionalism has been a resilient long-term constant in American culture, as a number of American historians, including John Higham, Michael Kammen, and Jack P. Greene, have recently noted.[4] Greene, in his book *The Intellectual Construction of America*, traced the term exceptionalism back to Tocqueville's statement about Americans being "quite exceptional." After surveying American thinking over the past three centuries, Greene concluded that the concept of exceptionalism was "present at the very creation of America."[5] By the time of the Revolution this belief in its exceptionalism and its special place in the world had become an integral part of America's identity. Always underlying this belief, of course, was a sense of difference from Europe. Generation upon generation of intellectuals and members of the general public shared this conviction.

During the colonial era that sense of difference was usually one of inferiority. Most colonists realized only too keenly that they were simply British provincials living on the very edges of Christendom. They were awed and mortified by the contrast between their own seemingly trivial world and that of the great British metropolis three thousand miles away. The Revolution changed much of this sense of inferiority. At a stroke, what had been seen as deficiencies for the colonists—their lack of a royal court, a hereditary aristocracy, and an established church—were transformed into advantages for the new republican government. Americans now saw their country possessing a freer, more prosperous, more egalitarian society than any in Europe; America had become for them a beacon and an asylum for the oppressed of the Old World. Americans in 1776 may have felt culturally inferior to Britain and to Europe; but they were a rising people, and they believed that sooner or later they would become the greatest nation in the world.

This belief by Americans that, in the words of President James K. Polk, their history lay ahead of them colored much of their national history-writing in the nineteenth century and gave it much of its teleological and exceptionalist character—its sense that the United States was the fulfillment of all that was great and progressive in the past. In chapter 7 Gordon Wood shows that if a history of the colonial period did not point to the future greatness of the United States, then few people were interested in it. It has been the same with the Civil War, which, as George Fredrickson says, "has inspired more scholarship than any other nineteenth-century subject" precisely because it defined the nation as no other nineteenth-century event did. Indeed, the subject of the Civil War is especially attractive in the present, writes Fredrickson, in that "it provides a persuasive argument for the uniqueness of American history that is not based on some claim to special virtue."

Despite this celebration of their national history, Americans never lost sight of their history's rootedness in the European past. Sometimes they stressed the contrast of America with Europe. Their fascination, for instance, with what Richard Kagan calls "Prescott's paradigm"—"an understanding of Spain as America's antithesis"—grew out of their need for an example of what they must avoid if they were to remain free and grow and prosper. The early nineteenth-century historian William Prescott, writes Kagan, "sought to determine the forces that destined certain societies for greatness, others to decadence and decay." Americans were convinced that their republican government, liberal Protestantism, and bold commercial spirit gave their country a huge moral advantage over Spain, saddled as it was with royal absolutism, Inquisition-dominated Catholicism, and economic backwardness. In responding to this gloomy assessment of Spain, however, Americans never forgot that they were as liable to corruption and decay as the Spanish or as any people; their experiment in free government was always problematic, always capable of failing.

The New World may have been different from the Old World, but few Americans ever doubted that they were linked to that older civilizaton and had something to learn from it. Although they were confident that they were in the vanguard of history and were leading a corrupt monarchical world toward free republican government, they always retained a pervasive sense of their cultural inferiority to Europe. They tried to tell themselves that the arts and sciences were sooner or later destined to cross the Atlantic and flourish in the New World. In the eighteenth century they had thrilled to Bishop George Berkeley's conventional notion of the westward movement of the arts from the Near East to Greece, from Greece to Rome, from Rome to western Europe, and from western Europe eventually across the Atlantic to their New World. They had believed, as Philip Freneau and Hugh Henry Brackenridge declared in their 1771 Princeton commencement poem, "The Rising Glory of America," that they would in time have their own Homers and Miltons and their own achievements "not less in fame than Greece and Rome of old."[6] They had hoped that the torch of Western civilization would be passed to them, where it would shine with new brilliance.[7] But many of them soon came to realize that the torch was not crossing the Atlantic and that amid the crass money-making of American society they would have to struggle to keep alive any semblance of the lights of European art and culture.

Whatever else the American Revolution was, it was not a repudiation of European culture. The revolutionary leaders never intended to reject the Western republic of letters; rather, they aimed to embrace it and fulfill its highest cultural aims. In later generations, however much Americans might set themselves apart from Old World politics, they never imagined that their culture was separate from that of the Old World. In his textbook, written in the early years of this century, Carlton Hayes expressed this very idea when he wrote that Europe was "the seat of that continuous high civilization which we call 'western'—which has come to be the distinctive civilization of the American continents as well as of Europe."[8] Indeed, Eugen Weber in his chapter on the cult of "Western Civ" in American higher education writes that Americans in a peculiar manner made the Old World part of their national past. Like Europeans, writes Weber, Americans teach and write a great deal about their own national history. But unlike Europeans, Americans spend much time and energy on other peoples' histories as well. They "conceive and present the national past as prolonged backward not into the British past alone, but into a broader Western tradition, originating in the Fertile Crescent, and the Mediterranean of Greece and Rome, where the groundwork was laid for references and memories that resurface in the conflicts and creations of the Middle Ages, Renaissance, Reformation, Enlightenment, and so on." American historians invented the conception of "Western Civilization" and made it "the inescapable background" of their national history. Always American scholars have had a sense of their nation as the culmination of a long and great Western tradition, and this sense has underlain their extraordinary efforts to attach the history of the Old World to their national history. Witness an example cited by Philip Benedict in chapter 14—the course taught by Herbert Darling Foster at Dartmouth for many years: "The Puritan State in Geneva, England, and Massachusetts Bay."

Despite their differences of approach and interpretation, the authors in this volume who write on the history of Europe show that most prominent American historians over the past century have always believed that the study of the European past illuminated some aspect of American history. It did not matter whether they studied Antiquity, the Middle Ages, the Renaissance, the Reformation, or the Ancien Régime. Europe was the ground where ideas vital to America originated and were first tested. In some cases, Americans looked to the European past for inspiration and for lessons crucial to their moral, political, and aesthetic well-being. In others, the study of Europe's history could impart cautionary lessons, tell of ideals and revolutions gone astray, of morally robust societies undermined by wrong political turns, or of economies corrupted by the excessive selfishness of individuals or classes. In all cases these American images of Europe dwelled upon America's deep European roots. Believing that they belonged to the same moral universe, were bound by the same historical rules, and were subject to the same rewards and penalties as other peoples, these American historians sought to derive both positive and negative lessons from the study of Europe. They imagined themselves not only to be a part of Western civilization but to be its fulfillment. Europe had created Western civilization. America had the responsibility of helping it survive and flourish.

Many of the essays in this book point to the intensity with which the history of Europe was studied in America, and to the link—often drawn explicitly, but nearly always implicit in historians' questions and approaches—between the European past and American society. Early in the twentieth century, as Richard Saller shows in chapter 11, Tenney Frank, the first eminent professional American historian of ancient Rome, thought that Americans and the early Romans of the republic "were kindred spirits." Since Rome's and America's moral destinies were inextricably intertwined, Frank was understandably curious about the reasons for the Roman republic's decline. He attributed that decline to the migration into freedom-loving Italy of "impulsive and passionate races that had never known self-government." It was an explanation that came right out of the anti-immigrant atmosphere of early twentieth-century America. It was as if ancient Rome and twentieth-century America were not separated by two millennia.

In her chapter devoted to the Middle Ages, Gabrielle Spiegel stresses a similar sense of connectedness between America and the distant Western past. Precisely because the United States had no medieval past, American medievalists, she writes, insisted "in a highly overdetermined fashion" on the importance of the Middle Ages to "the origin of the modern, hence American, world." From Charles Homer Haskins to Joseph Strayer, a distinguished line of American historians of the Middle Ages resolutely stressed "the continuity of the American present with past medieval institutions." In an address to the American Historical Association in 1923, Haskins argued that European history is "of profound importance to Americans. . . . We cannot ignore the vital connections between Europe and America, their histories [are] ultimately but one."[9]

This theme of America's close involvement with Europe is captured in several other chapters in this volume. Anthony Molho shows that for well over a century the Renaissance has held "a place of special honor" within the long tradition of Western civilization. Not only did Americans believe that their country could learn from fifteenth-century Florence how to convert its mercantile energies into artistic beauty, but, as Molho says, they came to see the Renaissance "as the key, pivotal moment in the unfolding of that historical process which culminated in the creation of the United States." Those Americans searching for the sources of individualism and other modern forces that defined the special character of American society inevitably looked back to the Renaissance. It is thus not surprising that within a little more than a year of its English translation in 1878 Jacob Burckhardt's *Civilization of the Renaissance in Italy*, which set forth the clearest and most authoritative claim regarding the modernity of the Renaissance, was being used in the classrooms of Brown University.[10]

The Reformation was thought to be even closer still to America's spirit. Indeed, in perhaps no other field of European historiography was the sense of an intimate moral community between America and Europe more explicit and persistent than in Reformation history. Philip Benedict writes that "to this day, a powerful impetus attracting scholars to this subject remains the concern of Christian believers [in America] to explore the roots of their diverse traditions." Just as social, political, and aesthetic considerations dominated in American historiography of Antiquity, the Middle Ages, and the Renaissance, so did powerful confessional interests affect American historiography of the Reformation. As Benedict writes, more than a few American historians were willing to follow Preserved Smith in imagining the Reformation as "the origin of the modern world," whose most magnificent and accomplished product, of course, was America.

Until recently American historians have treated the French Revolution differently from the way they have treated the Renaissance and the Reformation. They have generally pictured it negatively, as something uncongenial to the American spirit. Many American historians, as Keith Baker and Joseph Zizek point out in chapter 16, have tended to draw implicit or explicit contrasts between the excesses of the French Revolution and the moderation of the American Revolution. Still, even in the case of the French Revolution some Americans wanted to place the event into some larger progressive scheme in which America was the leader. Thus as early as 1906 James Harvey Robinson urged Americans to view the French Revolution as an aspect of the great reformation that brought the world into modernity. Early twentieth-century champions of the "new history" like Robinson wanted their historical knowledge to be socially useful: this view of the Revolution as a reformation, said Robinson, would help in "our great contemporaneous task of human betterment." And that task of human betterment would best be carried out in America.

Many of this book's chapters describe the intense interest of American historians both in the distinctiveness of America and in the pasts of European countries and peoples. Since the nineteenth century, American historiography has played many variations on these two themes—America's distinctiveness from and connectedness to Europe. But the twentieth century has seen American involvement in two world wars that have complicated these themes and challenged America's older provincial sense of its relationship to Europe.

As Volker Berghahn and Charles Maier point out in chapter 17, America's participation in World War I and the subsequent debate over "war guilt" divided the American historical profession and raised questions about America's traditional connection with Europe. In the 1920s, as Philip Gleason indicates in chapter 6, American professional historians first began devoting serious attention to immigration, which further unsettled conventional attitudes toward America's ties to Europe. Most important, however, in broadening America's mental horizons was the great "intellectual migration" of the 1930s that led thousands of European scholars to seek refuge in the United States from the horrors of racial persecution and war. Although the story of this migration has often been told, its effects appear to be no less astonishing in its retelling by several of the writers in this book.

All aspects of American life felt the impact of these European exiles. They enriched everything they touched, including historical scholarship. They not only profoundly transformed fields such as Medieval and Renaissance history and the history of modern Germany, but they affected history-writing in many other areas as well, including American history: think, for example, of Felix Gilbert's important book on Washington's Farewell Address.[11] Because they were not emigrants but exiles, forced to flee from the evils of Nazism, most of these scholars could at first only admire the country that had given them refuge and emphasize its exceptionalist difference from a brutal and corrupted Europe. But in the end all their intellectual training, all the sources of their outlook on the world, were based in Europe; and thus eventually they could not help but erode American parochialism and enlarge the perspectives of American historial scholarship.

World War II itself had a broadening effect. Of the many soldiers returning home to complete their education, many chose to study the history of countries and cultures they had encountered during the war. If the First World War had brought Germany within America's orbit of historical interest—as Berghahn and Maier's chapter demonstrates—then the Second World War brought in the entire world. America's triumphant position at the end of World War II and its new global responsibilities emphasized the two themes of distinctiveness and connectedness in American history-writing in new ways. The well-being of the country, its ability to discharge its new international responsibilities, its willingness to dedicate huge quantities of material resources to strengthening friendly "democratic" governments in all corners of the world—all required scholarly support and explanation.

America's strategic interests demanded that historians now study parts of the world they had rarely studied before. They did so with remarkable energy, enthusiastically shouldering the responsibilities they were convinced the world had thrust upon them. Centers for the study of the Soviet Union, Latin America, East Asia, Africa, and, more recently, the Middle East were set up, with each center inevitably engaging the services of one or more historians. Although small beginnings had been made before or during the war, only in the immediate postwar decades did Americans devote large intellectual energies and material resources to studying the pasts of these distant and alien cultures, all generally in the name of current policy interests.

While Martin Malia's chapter deals only with the development of Russian and Soviet history in the post–World War II United States, what he says about his subject seems to hold for American history-writing about other non-European regions as well. Certainly Carol Gluck's account of the rapid expansion of Japanese studies in the 1950s and '60s suggests as much. Despite the strenuous efforts in the postwar era to investigate non-European history, both Malia's and Gluck's chapters also show that American historians were not always successful in fully understanding the new foreign pasts they had set out to study. But at least they had begun to break out of their earlier exclusive embrace of the western European past. Prior to the Second World War American historians had imagined their country connected in direct and indirect ways only to the history of Europe. In the past half century, they have greatly increased the links between the United States and the world beyond Europe. Indeed, American historians virtually invented the concept of "world history."

America's direct twentieth-century involvement in the world had other broadening effects on the historical profession. The postwar period was awash with social science theories that had their origins in the Old World. As the several reports of the committees of historiography of the Social Science Research Council issued in 1945 and in 1954 indicated, many distinguished members of the historical profession were eager to use "ideas and methods dominant in the various social sciences" in order to further cooperation between history and the other social sciences and thus promote "greater understanding of how men and societies change and develop through time."[12]

Although some historians, notably Charles Beard, had long been interested in European social science theories, it was only in the immediate postwar years that the American historical profession became widely and deeply engaged in these theories, especially in the ideas of Marx, Max Weber, and the Annales school.[13] Many historians responded to the reports of the committees set up by the Social Science Research Council and became preoccupied with the ways social science theories might be used in history. Both Dorothy Ross and Naomi Lamoreaux discuss the rich theoretical experiments of the American historical profession in those years. The story of the Social Science History Association described by Ross exactly parallels the story of the Econometric Society described by Lamoreaux. In both cases young historians launched highly focused professional associations to promote what they believed were better, more scientific and technical approaches to the study of history. With the aid of sociologists, economists, political scientists, and anthropologists, they hoped to experiment with social theories and build economic models and thus make history quantitative, objective, and scientific. It did not take long, however, for these scientifically minded historians to realize that their organizations had become what Lamoreaux calls "intellectual ghettos" cut off from the mainstream of American history-writing.

Despite the extraordinary influence of a variety of European and cosmopolitan theories and perspectives, however, the mainstream of American historiography in the 1950s and early 1960s remained obsessed with Cold War ideas of American exceptionalism. As James Patterson notes in chapter 9, American historians of that time "tended to celebrate the stability of America's institutions, to extol its courageous role in the world wars and the Cold War, and to imagine that social 'consensus' was blurring age-old divisions of race, class, ethnicity, and religion in the nation." Ultimately their wider involvement in the world was not enough to break Americans free from their deeply rooted belief in their own uniqueness. It took a series of fundamental changes in the nation's society itself to destroy the "consensus" that Patterson speaks about and to shake historians out of their traditional conceptions of America and its relationship to the rest of the world.

These changes first became manifest in the 1960s. The civil rights movement allowed the voices of black Americans to be heard in increasing numbers. This together with the remarkable growth of immigrants from non-European areas of the world—from Mexico, other parts of Latin America, and Asia—created a new sense of American diversity and pluralism that have brought into question older conceptions of America's identity. These changes in turn have contributed to a dramatic democratization of higher education. Never before have so many Americans from so many different social and ethnic backgrounds gone to college, earned higher degrees, and studied history.

The women's movement has had equally powerful effects on the history profession. The number of new female Ph.D.s in history steadily grew through the decade of the sixties and the decades following. In 1970, 13 percent of new Ph.D.s were awarded to women; by 1989 that had increased to 37 percent. As the character of the history profession has become more diverse, so have the subjects about which historians write. Between 1958 and 1978 the proportion of doctoral dissertations written on social history quadrupled, and social history surpassed political history as the primary area of historical research.[14]

With these changes in the character of the nation and the historical profession it was natural therefore for historical perspectives to shift. Many historians in the 1960s and 1970s were excited by the Annales school and the scientific possibilities of quantification and set about writing a new kind of social history, "history from the bottom up." Instead of focusing on statesmen, generals, diplomats, and elite institutions, these new social historians, themselves often members of ethnic and racial groups newly entered in the profession, concentrated on ordinary folk and marginal people—the poor, the oppressed, the silent. Since few of these forgotten people left letters, memoirs, or the usual kind of literary documents, their stories, which tended to be group stories, had to be painstakingly extracted from the most intractable and impersonal sorts of sources—birth records, probate inventories, land titles, and tax assessments. More important than the innovative historical methods of this new social history was its significance for the traditional triumphal and exceptionalist conception of American history. The histories of outsiders, marginal people, and women could scarcely be celebrations of heroic achievements and patriotic glory; indeed, most of them were stories of frustration, despair, and defeat. The nation's history could no longer be a simple story of the triumph of liberty and democracy. In his essay Philip Gleason discusses how new accounts of immigration and ethnic interaction led historians to imagine a new and different American past and new and different ways of thinking about the country's collective identity. All the contributors to this volume are keenly aware of the profound and exciting effects the entrance of women and new ethnic and racial groups into the profession has had on the writing of history. In the past thirty years this larger and more diverse historical profession has asked new questions of the past and has revealed a new sensibility to the historical experiences of a wide variety of hitherto neglected individuals and groups.

Dealing with large groups of ordinary people in this way increasingly led historians to imagine that there was no universal human nature that explained motivations and ascribed meanings. Consequently, they came to believe that the societies they were studying were culturally constructed, mere assemblages of meanings. This conviction in turn led in the 1980s to the adoption of a new kind of history called cultural history, which gained a widespread following among historians. Borrowing heavily from anthropology and literary theory, cultural historians tended to break up the past into discrete ethnographic moments, imagining that cultures could be studied as if they were texts, with no more than a tenuous relationship to anything outside themselves. Even Marxist historians, under the influence of theorists like Antonio Gramsci and Raymond Williams, distanced themselves from old-fashioned economic materialism and drew their inspiration from the new cultural history.

All the essays in this volume attest to the recent significance of this new social and cultural history. In its attempts to supplant the older narrative histories the new social and cultural history suggested that those narratives had been partial and propagandistic and even mythical. Some historians even ventured the thought—heretical by the standards of the profession even a quarter of a century ago—that past historical accounts were not all that different from fiction. Consequently, one of the implications of the new history was to bring the reliability and impartiality of traditional history-writing into question. As Joyce Appleby, Lynn Hunt, and Margaret Jacob point out in their book *Telling the Truth about History*, the work of the new social and cultural historians "fostered the argument that history could never be objective."[15] The women historians who were entering the profession in increasing numbers were especially attracted to the new social and cultural history; and because they were only too keenly aware of the ways in which claims of objectivity had been used to exclude them and other marginal groups from public life and indeed from history itself, they were more than willing to challenge those traditional claims of objectivity.[16] Some feminist historians found in the epistemological skepticism of new literary theories a means of demonstrating the social constructiveness of gender distinctions that in turn, as Linda Kerber points out, allowed for the transformation of women's history into the history of gender.

This emergence of epistemological skepticism is just the latest in the series of changes that have affected the writing of history during the last half of the twentieth century. But, as Dorothy Ross points out in her chapter, this "postmodern" relativism does not run deep in the profession, and because it is so destructive of all historical reconstruction it is not likely to have a lasting effect on the writing of history in the United States. What does run deep and what does seem likely to have a profound effect on American history-writing is the fundamental transformation Americans are experiencing in their sense of national identity and their place in the world. Because the character of the nation itself is radically changing, something momentous seems to be happening to America's historical consciousness.

American historians are developing a new moral perspective, a new way of looking at the world. The distinguished medievalist and president of the American Historical Association, Caroline Walker Bynum, recently expressed some of the significance of this shift in perspective. Having been born shortly before the outbreak of the last world war, she felt that she belonged to the last American "Eurocentric generation." Consequently, "in these days of multiculturalism and postcolonial studies," she argues, "it is the task of my generation of historians to find ways of turning, responsibly and wisely, from the Eurocentric history into which we were born to the more global history our children will inherit." Bynum regards her conclusion as an "obvious insight about my scholarly generation." With Europe and America no longer at "the center of history," the American historical profession is bound to become different from what it used to be.[17]

American historians now seem to have a broader, more cosmopolitan sense of their country's relationship to the world. They have become involved in the world beyond their country's frontiers as never before. As Berghahn and Maier point out, American historians have become "fully integrated contributors to a broad international research community," a cosmopolitan community initially encompassing historians of North America and Western Europe, but more recently embracing Asian, African, Australian, and Latin American scholars as well. Many foreign historians now hold joint or part-time appointments in American universities, while at the same time American scholars are being invited to lecture or teach abroad. International conferences—of which the meeting in San Marino was but one example—offer new and unprecedented possibilities for scholarly communication and exchange.

Evidence that the American historical profession is becoming more international in outlook is everywhere. The works of American historians are now translated into other languages and reviewed in foreign journals with surprising rapidity. But since English has become the lingua franca of the contemporary world, even translations are not always necessary for the spread of American historical writings abroad. Whether in English or in translation, the works of American historians, perhaps for the first time ever, are being taken seriously by foreign scholars. American specialists in French history, for example, no longer have to wonder if French scholars are reading their works or if their books are in the Bibliothèque Nationale; some of them, as Baker and Zizek point out, now even find themselves equal participants in the debates with French historians over France's past. Sometimes it has even been American historians who first raised issues that transformed the history-writing of other countries. There are, for example, Eugen Weber's analysis of the social transformation of French society in the nineteenth century, Robert Paxton's studies of Vichy France, or the American examinations of the history of the Holocaust. In short, a new modern republic of historical letters has come into being, with American historians, as a recent reviewer in *Le Monde* rather glumly noted, standing at its center.[18]

This broadening of perspective is changing the definition of the nation's history. Historians of colonial America no longer focus exclusively on the thirteen continental British colonies that became the United States; they now have to take account of the entire Atlantic world involving western Europe, West Africa, South America and the Caribbean, and the rest of North America.[19] We are now beginning the history of American immigration from where the people came, in Europe or Africa or Asia, instead of starting the story at the docks of North America, a point of view that, as the Canadian historian J. M. Bumsted points out, "stressed, explicitly or implicitly, the unique and exceptional nature of immigration to North America."[20] Consequently, we now know that European and Asian emigrants went to many more places than the United States. In this new cosmopolitan atmosphere comparative studies are flourishing as never before. The history of slavery is now being viewed within the largest possible perspectives, comparing North American slavery not with just that in Latin America but, as Peter Kolchin has done, with Russian servitude as well. George Fredrickson has compared race relations in the United States and South Africa.[21] Common circumstances and common experiences in the modern world suggest more and more comparisons between histories of the United States and other nations; involving everything from the demilitarization of economies after the world wars to the movement of people from the countryside to the cities and the development of mass politics.[22] All this seems to suggest that the United States is not an exceptional place with an exceptional role in history after all.

The demise of the Soviet Union in 1989 should have left the way open for the triumphant assertion of American uniqueness and particularity. Ironically, at the very moment when their nation emerged as the world's dominant economic and military power, American historians have appeared reluctant to make such claims. American exceptionalism is losing much of its earlier resonance, and thus Europe no longer has the same meaning for Americans as it once did. The American nation does not seem to be the same either. For good or ill, the increasingly multicultural diversity of the United States is diluting and blurring an old-fashioned unified sense of American identity. Some American intellectuals are promoting a new intellectual globalism that seeks to transcend all national loyalties and even the idea of national citizenship. Some, like the philosopher Martha Nussbaum, argue for a civic education that cultivates a citizenship of all humanity, not of a particular nation. Since national identity is "a morally irrelevant characteristic," students should be taught that their "primary allegiance is to the community of human beings in the entire world."[23] With such sentiments in the air it is not surprising that some historians have difficulty holding on to traditional conceptions of the American nation.

Since the late 1960s, many political commentators, intellectuals, and historians have concluded that the United States no longer has the special, historically sanctioned role to be the path setter of humanity. The country is not exceptional after all; it does not seem exempt from the constraints and contingencies of history. If nothing else, the conflict in Vietnam convinced many Americans that the moral character of the United States is not different from that of other nations, that they, as a people, have no specially transcendent part to play in the world. At the same time European nations have attained standards of living and degrees of freedom and democratic political stability that are equal to, if not higher than, those of the United States. Even such a conservative celebrator of America as Irving Kristol admits that America now is "a middle-aged nation," not all that different from the older nations of England and France. "American exceptionalism," he says, is virtually over. "We are now a world power, and a world power is not 'city on a hill,' a 'light unto the nations'—phrases that, with every passing year, ring more hollow."[24] For the first time in their history Americans are confronting the fact that the United States may be just another nation among nations without any messianic destiny. It seems just yesterday that President Kennedy told the world that "we shall pay any price, bear any burden, meet any hardship, support any friend, oppose any foe to assure the survival and success of liberty."[25] Today, we cannot imagine any president promising to pay any price to promote liberty in the world. To many of its own citizens, America no longer appears to be a special nation with a special destiny in the world.

It is in this context that Daniel Rodgers's chapter on the idea of exceptionalism becomes especially meaningful. For Rodgers, American exceptionalism is not mere difference. Every nation sees itself as different. Exceptionalism for him means exception from a rule, from the common tide of change, from time itself, and for Americans it has meant excepting their nation "from the universal tendencies of history, the 'normal' fate of nations, the laws of historical mechanics itself." According to Rodgers, even if the germ of the idea of exceptionalism can be traced back to the beginning of American history, most historians in the nineteenth and early twentieth centuries, including George Bancroft, Charles M. Andrews, and Charles Beard, managed to avoid being infected by it. Although Frederick Jackson Turner can be charged with the taint of exceptionalism, "the generation which launched its work in the 1940s," says Rodgers, "was the first to take exceptionalism as an American given." Indeed, "exceptionalism would not call the tune in professional historical scholarship until after the Second World War." The term itself, writes Rodgers, was coined by Stalinists in the 1920s unhappy with the heretical thinking of the American Communist Party. It then "unexpectedly found its way after the Second World War into the core vocabulary of American historical writing." Only then was an American ideology "saturated with exceptionalist convictions" able to seep into the minds of the historical profession. America's powerful Cold War culture proved capable of creating among professional historians "a desire not merely for difference but for a particularity beyond all other nations' particularities: a yearning for proof of its own uniqueness so deep that it tied every other nation's history in fetters." Only now, in the midst of profound changes in the historical profession and in America's sense of itself, suggests Rodgers, are we able to see the limitations of this exceptionalist conception of America's past.

Yet, as Rodgers notes, in the absence of this exceptionalist conception, it is hard to find a unifying historical theme for Americans. Those who would escape from exceptionalism, he suggests, have been unable or perhaps reluctant to present "an overarching conceptual framework for a nonexceptionalist history of the United States." The profession is increasingly fragmented and turning out more and more complex, technical, and specialized renditions of the past that fewer and fewer people read.[26] Consequently, there has been a weakening of the earlier support that the study of the past found in American society. From 1970–71 to 1985–86, years when there was a boom in student enrollments, the number of history degrees granted by all American colleges and universities declined almost by two-thirds, from 44,663 to 16,413.[27] The decline of the American Historical Association membership in the 1970s and 1980s is itself a sign of this weakening of the profession. The evidence compiled by Peter Novick in *That Noble Dream* reinforces the impression conveyed by these figures. He argues that the historical profession during the past several decades seems to have lost a unified sense of purpose; without a clear sense any longer of the United States's role in history the discipline seems to be coming apart. "In no other field was there such a widespread sense of disarray; in no other discipline did so many leading figures express dismay and discouragement at the current state of their realm."[28] Many historians see themselves as only congeries of specialists solving technical problems and talking mostly to each other.[29]

Perhaps "the death of the past" that J. H. Plumb foresaw nearly three decades ago has come about faster than he anticipated. By "the past" Plumb meant the "created ideology," the "mythical, religious, and political interpretations" with which humans have sought to sanctify their societies, buttress their institutions, and invest their lives and their nations with a sense of destiny—interpretations, in other words, that resemble the imagined histories described in this volume. Such imagined pasts, said Plumb, should never be identified with critical history. "True history," he wrote, is basically "destructive"; "for by its very nature it dissolves those simple, structural generalizations by which our forefathers interpreted the purpose of life in historical terms." Its role is to eliminate those simple generalizations and "to cleanse the story of mankind from those deceiving visions of a purposeful past."[30] During the past three decades historical scholarship apparently has fulfilled its destructive role only too well, and not just in America. As Carl Schorske has pointed out, "history, conceived as a continuous nourishing tradition," no longer has the same meaning for us.[31]

Modern history-writing in the Western world, says Pierre Nora, has broken the "ancient bond of identity" with what he calls "memory," something that seems very similar to Plumb's "past." This "critical history" has ended what hitherto "we had experienced as self-evident—the equation of memory and history." History has now clearly become the enemy of memory. "History," says Nora, "is perpetually suspicious of memory, and its true mission is to suppress and destroy it."[32] But of course it cannot; it just forces memory to take different forms, to become what David Lowenthal recently has called "heritage." Heritage may by a worthless sham, its credos fallacious, even perverse; but, writes Lowenthal, "heritage, no less than history, is essential to knowing and acting." It fosters community, identity, and continuity, and in the end makes possible history itself. "By means of it we tell ourselves who we are, where we came from, and to what we belong." We thus tamper with our heritage, our memory, our past at our peril.[33]

Be that as it may, the dynamics of historical scholarship and the demands of seeing the past as it really was can scarcely be stopped. Despite the consequent fragmentation and apparent disarray, the writing of history over the past several decades has enabled us to see more clearly than we ever could before the unusual ways we Americans have remembered the pasts not only of our own nation but of other nations as well. This volume is perhaps the best evidence of this. Probably only at this moment—when the idea of American "exceptionalism" is being seriously challenged and America's tradition of memory has become increasingly self-conscious and historical—could this collection of papers be assembled. Just as French historians are now undertaking their own systematic investigations into the history of their profession, so too is the present an opportune moment for American historical introspection.[34] Only now can we fully appreciate our peculiarly American manner of conceiving of the histories of Spain, the Middle Ages, the Renaissance, or Western civilization. Only now can we understand the unusually American modes of using various theories to explain the economy, society, race, or the role of women in the past. Some, such as Carol Gluck in chapter 19, are optimistic about the recent turn of events; in her words, "with a heightened sense of historicity, a greater epistemological sensitivity, and an array of new methodological options, historians are better prepared to ask big questions without trumping them with prefabricated big answers." Others are more cautious in their assessments of the present historiographic moment. Everyone would nonetheless agree that we may be at the end of an era.[35]

We believe therefore that this is a particularly appropriate moment for seeing American history-writing over the past century or so in a new and fresh light. A long exceptionalist tradition in American historical thinking seems to be drawing to a close, and historians are now able to perceive with greater clarity the peculiarities of approach and interpretation that defined that tradition. This volume thus can be seen as a kind of requiem to an older provincial tradition of American historical writing.

All the scholars participating in the book were asked to reflect upon the peculiarly American approaches characterizing the study of their subjects. What did American historians in the past deem to be worthy of study? How did these preferences change over time? Is the peculiarly American historiographic perspective to be found in the subject matter, the questions asked, the approaches taken, or the assumptions brought to bear in these studies? What links did American historians make between the foreign cultures they studied and their own American culture? These are some of the issues addressed by the participants in this volume.

Although all the contributors were given the freedom to define the chronological boundaries of their essays, in most cases the authors begin their accounts at the opening of this century and carry them up to our own day. Out of these nineteen chapters emerges a fascinating and complicated picture of America's intellectual life over the past hundred years. These wide-ranging studies of American historiography not only reveal the tensions and contrasts that existed between a learned and popular culture and between the open-minded and provincial members of the historical profession, but they bring to light the Americans' often intense struggle to accommodate their study of the past to the needs of their present. In the end this collection of essays tells us as much about America as about American history-writing.

NOTES

1. For similar sense of a historiographical revolution in France see the recently published *L' histoire et le métier d'historien en France 1945–1995*, sous la direction de François Bédarida (Paris, 1995).

2. Robert O. Simmons and Dolores H. Thurgood, eds., *Summary Report 1994: Doctorate Recipients from United States Universities*, National Research Council (Washington, D.C., 1995), 49.

3. Byron Shafer, ed., *Is America Different? A New Look at American Exceptionalism* (Oxford, 1991); Seymour Martin Lipset, *American Exceptionalism: A Double-Edged Sword* (New York, 1996). For criticism of American exceptionalism see Ian Tyrrell, "American Exceptionalism in an Age of International History," with a critique by Michael McGerr and a rejoinder by Tyrell, *American Historical Review* 96 (1991): 1031–72. For a sympathetic view of America's uniqueness see Michael Kammen, "The Problem of American Exceptionalism: A Reconsideration," *American Quarterly* 45 (1993): 1–43.

4. John Higham, "The Future of American History" *Journal of American History* 80 (1994): 1289–1309; Kammen, "American Exceptionalism"; Jack P. Greene, *The Intellectual Construction of America: Exceptionalism and Identity From 1492 to 1800* (Chapel Hill, 1993).

5. Greene, *Intellectual Construction of America*, 4, 6.

6. Freneau and Brackenridge, "The Rising Glory of America" (1772), in Fred Lewis Pattee, ed., *The Poems of Philip Freneau: Poet of the American Revolution* (Princeton, 1902), I, 74, 78.

7. Kenneth Silverman, *A Cultural History of the American Revolution: Painting, Music, Literature, and the Theater in the Colonies and the United States from the Treaty of Paris to the Inauguration of George Washington, 1763–1789* (New York, 1976), 9–11, 228–35.

8. Quoted in Gilbert Allardyce, "The Rise and Fall of the Western Civiliation Course," *American Historical Review* 87 (1982): 709.

9. Charles H. Haskins, "European History and American Scholarship," *American Historical Review* 87 (1923): 215–27.

10. Not until well after World War II did American historians of the Renaissance begin to emphasize the negative valences in Burckhardt's concept of modernity. Until recently then this concept provided a bridge between fifteenth-century Italy and modern America.

11. Felix Gilbert, *To the Farewell Address: Ideas of Early American Foreign Policy* (Princeton, 1961).

12. "Theory and Practice in Historical Study: A Report of the Committee on Historiography," *Social Science Research Council Bulletin* 54 (New York, 1946); "The Social Sciences in Historical Study—a Report of the Committee on Historiography," *Social Science Research Council Bulletin* 64 (New York, 1954). An excellent survey of this question is found in

Lawrence Stone, "History and the Social Sciences in the Twentieth Century," in Charles F. Dalzell, ed., *The Future of History: Essays in the Vanderbilt University Centennial Symposium* (Nashville, 1977).

13. R. Bendix, *Max Weber—An Intellectual Portrait* (New York, 1960), xx–xxiii. See also the "Bibliography on Max Weber" in *Social Research* 16 (1949): 70–89.

14. Joyce Appleby, Lynn Hunt, and Margaret Jacobs, *Telling the Truth about History* (New York, 1994), 147–48.

15. Appleby, Hunt, and Jacob, *Telling the Truth about History*, 200.

16. Appleby, Hunt, and Jacob, *Telling the Truth about History*, 2.

17. Caroline Walker Bynum, "The Last Eurocentric Generation," *Perspectives: American Historical Association Newsletter* 34, 2 (Feb. 1996): 3–4.

18. Nicolas Weill, "L' histoire s'est arrêtée à Montréal," *Le Monde*, 8 Sept. 1995, viii: "Au Québec, et quarante ans plus tard, l' histoire sociale existe encore, à côté d' autres écoles. Montréal marquera-t-il aussi une consécration? Si tel est le cas, ce sera, à n' en pas douter, celle de ce que l'on qualifiera peut-être, en 2035, d' 'école américaine.' " . . . These are the concluding sentences of a long article devoted to the Congress of Historical Studies held in Montreal at the end of August 1995.

19. Bernard Bailyn, "The Idea of Atlantic History," *Itinerario* 20 (1996): 1–27.

20. J. M. Bumsted, Book Review, *Journal of American History* 82 (1995): 1181.

21. Peter Kolchin, *Unfree Labor: American Slavery and Russian Serfdom* (Cambridge, Mass., 1987); George Fredrickson, *White Supremacy: A Comparative Study of American and South African History* (New York, 1981); Fredrickson, *Black Liberation: A Comparative History of Black Ideologies in the United States and South Africa* (New York, 1995). For another recent comparative study see Colleen Dunlavy, *Politics and Industrialization: Early Railroads in the United States and Prussia* (Princeton, 1994).

22. Of course, comparative history may not lead at all to less emphasis on America's exceptionalism. As Marc Bloch pointed out long ago, and Michael Kammen and others have recently underlined, people often suppose "that the [comparative] method has no other purpose than hunting out resemblances." "On the contrary," said Bloch, "correctly understood, the primary interest of the comparative method is . . . the observations of differences." Quoted in Kammen, "American Exceptionalism," 19. This has been borne out by recent comparative studies, which often begin by emphasizing America's similarity to other cultures but usually end in highlighting its differences. American historians, for example, working in comparative race relations, have eventually come to appreciate the peculiarity of the American theory of race—"that each person has a race but only one." Gary B. Nash, "The Hidden History of Mestizo America," *Journal of American History* 82 (1995): 960.

23. Nussbaum, quoted in Michael J. Sandel, *Democracy's Discontent: America in Search of a Public Philosophy* (Cambridge, Mass., 1996), 341.

24. Irving Kristol, "America Dreaming," *On the Issues: American Enterprise Institute* (Sept. 1995).

25. Quoted in James T. Patterson, *Grand Expectations: The United States, 1945–1974* (New York, 1996), 486.

26. Paula Baker, "The Fragmentation of the Profession and Its Class Culture," *Journal of American History* 81 (1994): 1148–49.

27. C. Vann Woodward, *The Future of the Past* (New York, 1989), 26–27.

28. Peter Novick, *That Noble Dream: The "Objectivity Question" and the American Historical Profession* (Cambridge, 1988), 578.

29. David Thelen, "The Practice of American History," *Journal of American History* 81

(1994), 933–60; Thomas Bender, "'Venturesome and Cautious': American History in the 1990s," *Journal of American History* 80 (1994): 997.

30. J. H. Plumb, *The Death of the Past* (Boston, 1970), 11–17.

31. Carl Schorske, *Fin-de-Siecle Vienna: Politics and Culture* (New York, 1980), xvii.

32. Pierre Nora, "Between Memory and History: Les Lieux de Mémoire," in Jacques Revel and Lynn Hunt, eds., *Histories: French Constructions of the Past* (New York, 1995), 632–36. For nearly a decade Nora has been assembling seven volumes of Les lieux de mémoire, which was designed, said Nora, to "decompose the unity" of the French nation. A first volume of an English translation was recently published with the title *Realms of Memory: The Construction of the French Past* (New York, 1996).

33. David Lowenthal, *Possessed by the Past: The Heritage Crusade and the Spoils of History* (New York, 1996), ix–xiii.

34. See the papers in the *American Historical Review* 100, 2 and 3 (1995), which attempt, as do the essays in this volume, to describe the peculiar ways Americans have written about the pasts of themselves and of other peoples.

35. It is only this sense of being at the end of an era in American history that makes possible a book like that of the late Dutch historian Jan Willen Schulte Nordholt, *The Myth of the West: America as the Last Empire* (Grand Rapids, Mich., 1995).

Exceptionalism

DANIEL T. RODGERS

"Is AMERICA different?" a recent collection of scholarly essays undertook to inquire.[1] One might have thought it a puzzling question, so rhetorically framed, the implied comparison so remarkably vague, and yet the answer, whatever the comparative yardstick should turn out to be, so patently "yes." And, indeed, "yes" even if another subject were to be introduced in the place of "America," so that the question came to read "Is Argentina different?" or Afghanistan. One might have thought it a remarkable question, that is, had it not been asked so often before in the American past and with such intense hunger for an affirmative answer.

To the question "Is America different?" the professional historian is expected to respond with a list of the circumstances and exemptions which have distinguished the history of the United States: a land radically underpopulated by European standards and (given the vast inequalities in biological immunities and technological inheritances between its inhabitants and its invaders) relatively costlessly conquered, abundant in readily exploitable natural resources, far from the great powers and the central cockpit of great-power warfare, without an hereditary aristocracy monopolizing landed property and the offices of the state and therefore (in contrast to the *anciens régimes* of Europe) relatively costlessly democratized, all in a period of modern world history when economic growth came relatively easily to nations close to the western European core, and so on. All (and more) are true, and all important.

But if the answers matter, so at a deeper level does the inquiry itself. It was an odd question, so timelessly phrased, to have lodged itself in a discipline in which possession of the Ph.D. putatively certified an expert sensitivity to time and mutability. At the height of the Cold War, American "exceptionalist" history bore, through a curious kind of political cross-dressing, a Stalinist neologism for a name. Of the controlling themes in contemporary United States history writing, however, none were pressed more urgently upon professional historians by the surrounding culture than a desire not merely for difference but for a particularity beyond all other nations' particularities: a yearning for proof of its own uniqueness so deep that it tied every other nation's history in fetters. What was the historiographical past of that conceit? What are its current historiographical tendencies?

•

In a debate in which substance so often slides into wordplay, let us start with the terms themselves. Whatever the argument about American differentness may have been about, it was not about difference in itself. In difference, pure and simple, nothing special or distinguishing is to be found. "All nations are different," Joyce Appleby puts the common sense of the matter in a recent essay; "and almost all national sentiments exploit those differences."[2] Both in mind and in fact, uniqueness is every nation's lot. Around so bare a tautology, the rhetorical and analytical heat sufficient to kindle an historiographical controversy could never have been collected.

In the skein of tropes which, from the seventeenth century forward, Euro-Americans wove around that part of the Americas which became the United States, difference, in fact, was only one of several strands, and neither the most distinctive nor the most important. The New World's "newness" was a more striking metaphor. First used to represent the Europeans' surprise at the unexpected inaccuracy of their geographic knowledge of the world, it became, in the revolutionary atmosphere of the 1770s and 1780s, the marker for a claim much headier still, the opening in British North America of an era in social and political relations unknown to history before: a "new order of the ages."[3] Yet a third thread has been the providential one. From John Winthrop to Oliver North, the "rituals of God's country" (as Sacvan Bercovitch once called them) have run: a sense of God acting within and through the history of His specially chosen land.[4] Not the least, difference in American national culture has meant "better": the superiority of the American way. The distinctions merge and tangle. To be different is to be best, to claim membership in a new and uniquely blessed society.

Little in this bundle of sentiments, however, is as peculiar to the United States as Americans tend to imagine. If the Americans are "different," the British have their treasured peculiarities, the French their *génie français*, nineteenth-century Germans their distinctive *Kultur*. Americans have not been the only people to imagine restarting the clock of time or to know the euphoria of thinking, in Thomas Paine's words, that the "birthday of a new world" was at hand. Pride and providentialism are too widely spread to imagine them American peculiarities. If European visitors to the nineteenth-century United States suffered under the self-importance of the Americans, American travelers to Wilhelmine Germany and late-Victorian England suffered under a sense of national superiority no less overweening and self-satisfied. Throughout history armies have assembled with God as their marshal, and statesmen have plotted foreign policy as if they were agents of Destiny itself. These are not accidental similarities. Cultivation of sentiments of difference and superiority has been, from the early modern era to the postcolonial present, at the heart of the project of nation-state formation. To make a peasant think like a Frenchman (or an Indian or Iraqi) nothing matters more than clapping on that citizen's head a sense of national uniqueness.

Within these common terms, however, there has run a thread which, if not wholly distinct to the American complex, carries there a peculiarly striking weight. That is the idea of "exceptionalism." Exceptionalism differs from difference. Difference requires contrast; exceptionalism requires a rule. Difference claims feed on polarities and diversity; exceptionalist claims pin one's own nation's distinctiveness to every other people's sameness—to general laws and conditions governing everything but the special case at hand. Exceptionalism, Appleby writes, posits "deliverance from a common lot. There are no exceptions without well-understood generalizations or norms in contrast to which the exception commands attention."[5] When difference is put in exceptionalist terms, in short, the referent is universalized. Different from what? Different from the universal tendencies of history, the "normal" fate of nations, the laws of historical mechanics itself.

The term "exceptionalism" was a latecomer to American historical and political analysis, a Stalinist coinage of the 1920s which unexpectedly found its way after the Second World War into the core vocabulary of American historical writing. The term was bound up from the first in what Marx himself called the general "laws of historical motion"—the world historical movement toward ever more intense forms of capital accumulation, immiseration, proletarianization, and class conflict which would ultimately bring down the house of capital. A theoretical issue for turn-of-the-century Marxian intellectuals—not the least with regard to the United States, whose development was not always easy to fit into the general line—the idea of universal history had become by the late 1920s a club to beat deviant national communist parties into submission. Among those was the American Communist Party of the late 1920s. Overwhelmed by the difficulties of organizing in the era of Henry Ford and Herbert Hoover, its leaders resisted the Comintern's pronouncement that a "third period" in modern world history had begun in early 1929, insisting that the American economy, not yet having reached the point of "collapsing stabilization," remained stuck in capitalism's upward phase. Worse, they asked for greater autonomy in day-to-day tactics and strategy. Summoned to Moscow for a laboriously contrived airing of the "American" question, the American party leaders made the mistake of linking their cause to that of Nikolai Bukharin just as Stalin was arranging his coleader's deposition. Branded with the heresy of "exceptionalism," the Americans were ejected from the party and a rival cadre installed in their place. Stalin, who engineered the event, had no interest in the historical issues at stake. The ejected Lovestoneites, for their part, had neither used the term "exceptionalism" nor claimed that American economic developments were of a different order than economic developments elsewhere—only that they lagged behind.[6]

From such profoundly inauspicious beginnings, the idea of exceptionalism might have been expected to die a quick conceptual death. Had it not been for a set of powerful homologies with other currents in the national culture, it could hardly have slipped the peculiar circumstances of its birth. In other keys and other registers, however, exceptionalist history had roots in America deeper and firmer than Marxism. Protestant Americans had long had their own universal history, written in the language of eschatology and millennialism, their own basic law of sinward historical motion from which a special people might be chosen out, a nation "elected." "Republican" versions of exceptionalist history secularized the terms of Protestant history but kept the exceptionalist structure intact.

Nations rose in bursts of power and fortune, but the general drag of history was downward as morals and manners decayed under the temptations of private wealth and self-regarding egoism. Let the general tendencies of time go unresisted, and the normalization, the "Europeanization," of the American republic was its expected fate—unless, through virtue, a nation should hoist itself free of the common tide of change, elect itself out of time.[7] Rule and exception: into the pattern which smelled so heretical to the American commission in Moscow, earlier and later variations on the exceptionalist theme have run, homogenizing in the very act of differentiating, laying down universal law in the very act of claiming, but only for the United States, a special escape clause.

In all these formulations, it has never been easy to distinguish where analysis halted and exhortation began. From John Winthrop's assertion forward—not that God had set the Puritan project "upon a hill" but that his company, quarreling in mid Atlantic, should conduct themselves in hope that He might—the conditional and the factual in exceptionalist rhetoric have been exceedingly difficult to pry apart. In the United States, however, exceptionalism has drawn on wells of pride as deep as those of anxiety. The especially exempt nation might default on its freedom from all other nations' lot, but the terms of the proposition were not widely doubted. Exceptionalist rhetoric in the United States differs in that regard from the exceptionalism of most of the other nations—materially so similar—formed on the edges of the early modern European empires. There, too, one finds strong assumptions of normal national development. But in Canada and Latin America, observers stress, the rhetoric of exceptionalism is one of estrangement from the normal, of absence, loss, and regret. They are lands on the margins, their identities still partly colonial, their mythology, as Sacvan Bercovitch writes of Canada, "elsewhere."[8]

In the United States, by contrast, exceptionalism is accepted not as a deficit but as a gift. It, too, is a rhetoric of absences, but the absences are the ills and defects of a universalized external world. Still, having posited its identity in difference, and its difference in exemption from the rule, the American myth lies, in its own way, "elsewhere." A nation which conceives of itself in exceptionalist terms is fated to spend at least as much of its popular historical energy imagining everyone else's history as in writing its own. That is one of the unrecognized ironies of American history.

•

Though they wrote within a national culture steeped in exceptionalist convictions, the historians who shaped the professional writing of American history in its formative years did not always keep in step. Inhabiting scholarly worlds which were as Atlantic as they were American, they were better trained to see the history of the United States as proceeding within world history than outside it. Their America answered less often to historical necessities all its own than to broader, transcultural historical forces: the progress of nations, the rise of Europe or the West, or the updraft of civilization itself. Arguments coming in family clusters, exceptionalism entailed in its very frame its antitheses and alternatives: connectedness, complicity, embeddedness. As the historical profession gathered itself together in the 1880s and 1890s, it would be fair to say that the latter had the upper hand.[9]

These took a number of different forms. In George Bancroft's *History of the United States*, brought to completion in 1882, the prime mover was the "world spirit" of liberty taking up, for a moment, its abode in America. That was what made the American Revolution not merely a national affair for Bancroft but "an assertion of rights . . . for the entire world of mankind and all coming generations, without any exceptions whatsoever."[10] By the end of the nineteenth century, Bancroft's faith in the "unity of mankind" had worn thin, replaced in the Eastern gentry social circles, from which the new university faculty were being heavily recruited, by a much more cramped and constricted belief in something they alternatively called the Teutonic or the Anglo-Saxon heritage. A handy device to extract the essence of American history from the possibility that immigrant and nonwhite Americans might lay serious claim to it, Anglo-Saxon historiography nonetheless made no illusions of national self-sufficiency. "No nation has a history disconnected from that of the rest of the world," Harvard's Albert Bushnell Hart began his list of the "fundamental principles of American history" in 1883. "Our institutions are Teutonic in origin; they have come to us through English institutions."[11]

The heaviest opposing gun on the exceptionalist side was Frederick Jackson Turner's. In his emphasis on "perennial rebirth" as the defining American experience and his explicit sense of deviation from the norms of social development which held sway everywhere else, Turner gathered the tropes of exceptionalist history into particularly powerful form. The spatial vagueness of Turner's frontier has often been noted, for it was never so much a place on the map as the site of Europe's negation. Arriving on the margin of settlement "European in dress, industries, tools, modes of travel, and thought," Turner wrote in one of the most famous passages of his 1893 essay, the pioneer fell out of history's normally irreversible necessities to be rebaptized as an American. No less than Marx, Turner had his laws of historical motion: from simple to complex, from primitive to manufacturing economies, from savagery to civilization, all the usual social-evolutionary baggage of a well-educated late Victorian. But the frontier was America's emancipator; there the general laws of historical motion were turned back. The frontier was America's "gate of escape from the bondage of the past," Turner wrote: from the gentry-historians' Teutonic germs, from Europe, indeed from history itself.[12]

How so metaphoric an essay as Turner's "The Significance of the Frontier in American History" should have established itself as the most important single piece of historical writing to come out of the late nineteenth-century United States can scarcely be comprehended outside the popular convictions Turner's word pictures caught so well. Pitching camp at the intersection of academic scholarship and Chautauqua culture, Turner's frontier thesis became, in truth, all but immobilized there. Turner's was a boundary-condition form of exceptionalism, written in full, nervous awareness that the material conditions he held responsible for everything exceptional about the United States were now exhausted. If the frontier held the exceptionalist key Turner posited for it, there was no way, with the frontier's passing, to prevent the New World from growing old. But the line between history and faith has always been thin in the exceptionalist camp, and never thinner than with Turner. For the next twenty years in, the face of his own environmental materialism, Turner could not resist exhorting his countrymen to make their "stand against the tendencies to adjust to a European type" by an act of will alone.[13]

For all of Turner's prominence, however, exceptionalism did not yet call the tune in professional historical scholarship. The biggest and most ambitious collective work of historical scholarship of its time, Harper and Brothers's twenty-eight volume history of the United States, published between 1904 and 1918, opened not with the frontier but with William Cheyney's *European Background of American History*, followed, remarkably enough, by Livingston Farrand's detailed ethnographic account of the American Indian peoples, before settling into what American historians of the 1940s and 1950s were to think of as the beginnings of American history proper, the English settlement of the Atlantic seaboard.[14] Under the leadership of Charles M. Andrews, the most authoritative students of the American Revolution withdrew the inflated patriotism from that event to redescribe it as a series of misunderstandings within an Atlantic, English-speaking empire.[15] As for the giants of early twentieth-century American history writing—Charles Beard and W. E. B. Du Bois—they had absorbed too much of class and economic analysis and instinctually thought on too large, world canvases to be exceptionalists. "The discovery, settlement, and expansion of America form merely one phase in the long and restless movement of mankind on the surface of the earth," Charles and Mary Beard began the most influential American history book of the early twentieth century. The twist of the knife came, of course, in that gratuitous word "merely." In the Beards' *Rise of American Civilization* (1927), economic processes heaved and strained, empires rose, and interests clashed, but the hand of special destiny was not in American history.[16]

Writing in a culture saturated with exceptionalist convictions, in short, professional historians did not unquestionably swallow the exceptionalist premises. They did not because they were Hegelians (like Bancroft), or elitists (like Hart), because they knew worlds far beyond America (Oxford radicalism for Beard, student Berlin for Du Bois), or because (like Andrews, burrowing deep in English sources) the facts did not seem to add up for them in exceptionalist patterns.

It was the second shattering of Europe in the late 1930s, the "suicide" of the Old World, as many Americans were calling it in the 1940s, that changed the historiographic mood. The generation which launched its work in the 1940s was the first to take exceptionalism as an American given. In retrospect it seems clear that they did so, not because the phenomena they stressed in the American past had gone unnoticed before, but because their understanding of Europe had been so dramatically shaken. One had to read between the lines to see it, but what was being rewritten was not so much the special history of the United States but, in a newly tragic key, the general laws of historical motion themselves.

Among the several telltale marks of the new historiographical turn a particularly striking one was the sudden ubiquity of references to that failed eighteenth-century French expatriate and travel writer, J. Hector St. John de Crèvecoeur. Virtually unread in the United States before the twentieth century, Crèvecoeur's lyric passage on the transforming effects of American society on its immigrant newcomers, its "melting" of persons of all nations into "a new race of men," extracted from context, retitled as "What Is the American, This New Man?" now seemed to appear everywhere.[17] Arthur Schlesinger, Sr., made it the motif of his presidential address to the American Historical Association in 1942.[18] The literature of the new American Studies movement was saturated with Crèvecoeur references. They led off that catalyst for revisionist histories of the Revolution, Robert E. Brown's *Middle-Class Democracy and the Revolution in Massachusetts*, in 1955.[19] It was scarcely possible to write about the relationship between American and European history without them. That so liminal a figure as Crèvecoeur, neither of France nor of British North America but stranded in between by a Revolution whose rationale he professed himself ignorant, whose "innovations" he distrusted, and whose violence he detested,[20] should have come to hold the key to the land from which, in 1780, he had fled suggests how deep the historians' stake in an America broken free of Europe's past had suddenly become.

The Crèvecoeur revival was a surface symptom of deeper shifts in intellectual foundations. From the wartime morale projects, studies of national character and personality moved into the forefront of postwar social science. References to the "American national character" sprouted in the "soft" multidisciplinary eclecticism of the new American Studies programs and in the "hard" social sciences alike.[21] David Riesman subtitled his *Lonely Crowd* in 1950 a study in "the changing American character." David Potter, in a revision and extension of the Turnerian frame, used it to suggest abundance as the key to the special history of the United States.[22] Through the work of Perry Miller and others, the providential strain in the American past was drawn into the center of historical scholarship. Extracting New England Puritanism from the aspersions into which the prohibition-baiters of the 1920s had thrown it—as the sin-obsessed, pleasure-denying shadow on the American psyche—Miller and his students held up New England separatist utopianism as the key to the national mind and culture. John Winthrop's "city upon a hill," beacon to a world whose fate it had escaped, was no longer a mid-Atlantic hope, or even Boston; it was now America itself.[23]

The need to articulate a distinctive "American way" for the war and Cold War played a central role in these exceptionalist projects. But a less overtly political necessity drove them as well: the need, in the face of traditional Europe's collapse, to explain how it had come about that the United States seemed to have skated unscathed past the disasters of the mid twentieth century, past the revolutions of the left in Russia and of the right in Italy, Germany, and Spain, the inner collapse of 1940s France, the bankruptcy of Britain, the perilous instabilities of central and southern Europe. If these were the tendencies of history—a Marxian world of upheaval and revolution, of sustained and brutal class conflicts but stripped of Marx's illusions about their happy outcome—then the history of the United States was truly exceptional.

In this rethinking of the general tendencies of history, the American Revolution occupied a specially important place. Where Andrews had told a tale of an empire torn apart by miscalculation, where the Beards had seen economic universals at work, and where Crane Brinton had discerned the general shape of revolution itself,[24] the postwar historians of the American Revolution reformulated the event as an extraordinary historical anomaly. In a world haunted by the destabilizing effects of revolution, the American case seemed sui generis: a popular revolution which had remained within moderate, Lockean bounds, a revolution without its Jacobins or Bolsheviks, without its reign of terror, without its Lenin or Robespierre. A European historian like Robert Palmer might write of a general age of eighteenth-century revolution,[25] but for American historians the upheavals of 1776 and 1789 were, symbolically and historically, worlds apart. The American Revolution was "anything but revolutionary," Robert Brown wrote with a piece of his mind, like that of so many of his fellow historians, on Paris. It was "unique," as he tried to show from the distribution of property in the Massachusetts colony on the eve of independence, because social stratification of the North American colonies was, itself, uniquely foreshortened into a structure "almost the exact opposite of European society."[26]

Starting there, the rest of American politics unfolded. Where the Revolution was reconceptualized as an extraordinary break in the normal laws of revolution, the subsequent course of politics was remade as a triumph of classlessness. Only after the radical fires of the 1930s had cooled, only with the incorporation of the CIO into the coprosperity spirit of postwar economic growth, and, most importantly, only against the background of Europe's catastrophe could such a reading of American politics have taken hold. Arthur Schlesinger, Jr.'s, *The Age of Jackson* (1945) still breathed the spirit of prewar history writing, but that spirit was rapidly thinning out.[27] Extracting "exceptionalism" from Communist Party jargon, scholars moving centerward from the anti-Stalinist left injected it into the central vocabulary of American social and political science. An absence—the relative failure of socialism in the United States—became the defining point of the nation's history, a ratification of the special dispensation of the United States in a revolutionary world where Marx still tempted.

No book brought together the themes of postwar exceptionalist history more influentially than Louis Hartz's *The Liberal Tradition in America* in 1955. Hartz, to be sure, was a student of political theory not an historian. Beyond early nineteenth-century Pennsylvania, whose political economy he knew intimately, his history was never more than schematic; but he put in vivid form what postwar Americans wanted to hear: that the laws of historical motion which held Europe by the throat did not run in the United States. Like Turner's, Hartz's was a boundary condition form of exceptionalism. Starting without a feudal past, a bourgeois "fragment" of European society, American history could not but unfold differently. But unlike Turner's exceptionalism, in which the general forces of history retained their sway behind the moving frontier, in Hartz's exceptionalism time itself in America came to a halt. Without a feudal past, the inner, dialectical engine of history had no purchase. No Robespierre, no de Maistre, no Marx, no Goebbels, no Stalin, only (in the shorthand Hartz affected) an eternal Locke. Other nations went through the throes of the twice-born, but the Americans, by the chance conditions of their founding, had slipped free of the underlying motor of historical change. Starting differently, they were fated to be eternally the same—and eternally different from everyone else.[28]

The "storybook truth about America," as Hartz called it, was that of a people who, in escaping Europe's past, had found their own exceptional future, freer and yet more stable than Europe's. So self-evident did that tale seem that the historians who contributed to it would have found it hard to recognize how strikingly, in their anti-Marxism, they had reimagined Marx's general laws of historical motion applied everywhere but to their own national case. The revolutionary instability which, projected elsewhere, seethed between the lines of United States history writing had hardly been absent, of course, from the history of the United States itself. In another setting, the combustible elements of race and slavery, the thirty-year struggle over section, and the cataclysm of the Civil War might have rattled the assumptions at the core of exceptionalist history. But where the Paris Commune was France, the Civil War, though an incomparably larger historical event, was somehow beside the point which was America. The exceptionalist historians' hands might be deep in the archives in America, but a part of their mind was fixed elsewhere: on Paris in 1793 with its guillotine working at fever pitch, Leningrad as the Winter Palace was stormed in 1917, or Berlin with its streets full of brownshirts in 1933. It was only against this selective history of Europe, amalgamating other nations' histories into a single theme that proved the distinctiveness of their own, that the American past seemed stable, "seamless" (as Daniel Boorstin called it), an exemption from the rule.[29]

Exceptionalist American history, even at its height, never controlled the entire terrain any more than had the cosmopolitan history before it. Courses in Western Civilization, designed to glue the aspirations of the American present to the best of the European past, proliferated in the 1940s and 1950s—though historians of the United States rarely taught in them, not merely because they had other work to do but because the conceptual moat remained too large.[30] Other historians sounded the call for American leadership of the Atlantic community or the "free world." But nothing showed the massive presence of exceptionalist assumptions more than the difficulty critical historians in the 1960s and 1970s had in surmounting them. The "new" diplomatic historians trained in William A. Williams's workshop recovered an empire which had been all but suppressed from political memory, but only to explain it as a projection of uniquely American forces and values.[31] A new generation of immigration historians showed assimilation to be much more difficult and incomplete than regenerative or melting pot accounts had had it; but starting their stories where exceptionalist histories had begun them, with the immigrants' moment of entrance to the New World, they found it far easier to qualify the master trope of acculturation than to overturn it.[32]

The new social historians, setting out to show the hollowness of the core premises of exceptionalist history—to demonstrate empirically that social mobility in the United States had never been as far-reaching as the rags-to-riches myth had supposed, that the early democratization of American politics had failed to penetrate beyond a privileged circle of white male citizens, that class and racial divisions ran too deep in the United States's past to ignore, that the American working class had not played passively into the emerging capitalist and wage-labor regime but had resisted it, more violently, indeed, than the working classes in Europe—even they did not ultimately escape exceptionalist history's structures. The vigor of this recovery of an authentic history of working people in the United States, slave and free, immigrant and American-born, female and male, can hardly be exaggerated. But though these historians dramatically complicated the story of class relations in the United States, they did not escape the question the exceptionalists had made the central one: why normative, European-style socialism sank such shallow roots in the United States. As long as the only effective negation of exceptionalist history was to find a radical tradition, an autonomous working-class culture conscious of its own self and political interests, equal in historical centrality to the prewar German Social Democrats or the postwar British Laborites, the dissenting historians' quest was doomed to frustration. The narrative thread of the new social history unrolled as a string of heroic failures and frustrated opportunities. Its bottom line was not fundamentally different from Hartz's; there was not enough socialism in America after all.[33]

•

To challenge the exceptionalist frame of postwar American history writing would take more fundamental recasting of the image of world history in the American historians' minds' eye. Within the last decade, however, it is clear that something of that sort has begun to appear across a broad historiographic front. Albeit dogged with controversy, a postexceptionalist American history has come into view.[34]

One of the key events in this regard has been the fading away of the exceptionalists' imagined Europe and, with it, the imagined rules of other nations' histories. Fifty years after the end of the Second World War, the inherent instability of western European society no longer seems an historical given. With Communist Europe in disarray, the teleological engine of Marxist history has likewise broken down. Neither Marx's conviction that the common forces of capitalism would strip the proletariat "of every trace of national character" nor the alternative, liberal theories of convergence on a common modernity command assent. Throughout the modern world, economic integration and national particularization both proceed at once. The imagined central tendencies of history no longer hold. But in a world without rules there can be no exceptions—only an infinite regress of differences.

The fading of the teleological arrow of exceptionalist history has had its most striking impact on American labor history. Sean Wilentz's "Against Exceptionalism," roughly handled a decade ago, now speaks the field's conventional wisdom. No historic model of working-class organization, it is now clear—not German social democracy, not French radical syndicalism, not Scandinavian farmer-labor welfarism, nor British Lib-Laborism—captured that Hegelian will-o'-the-wisp: consciousness of class in and for itself. There have been virtually as many socialisms as there have been European nations.[35] Acceptance of a world without a normative path of working-class development has freed American labor historians to focus less on absences than on presences in the American past. It is now possible to write about the Populist movement and the Knights of Labor without apologizing for their insufficient socialism. The old structural arguments for the failure of working-class politics in the United States—the lure of cheap land and high wages, the ethnically fractionated character of the labor force and the racialization of its inner identities, the early incorporation of white working-class males into electoral politics, the antistatist animus in the political culture at large, and the particularly inhibiting constraints of two-party, majoritarian politics—have not disappeared. But one now hears less about permanent structural deterrents and more about contingency and history, about particular, fortuitous convergences of forces and events.[36] The return of contingent history does not yield a working class in the United States like that of other working classes. But the question of difference was, from the beginning, false and tautological. The antithesis at the core of exceptionalist history was never that between difference and sameness but between autonomy and connection.

In that sense, the less heralded aspect of the emerging historiographic revolution has been more far-reaching: a recognition of American complicity in larger world historical forces. Abandonment of dichotomous for connected development has gone farthest in the writing of colonial American history. In a recent historiographical overview, Joyce Appleby has stressed the colonial social historians' embrace of the techniques of the Annales school and the Cambridge demography group as the moment when American historians rediscovered the Europeanness of colonial America. Immerse oneself in the early records of a New England town, Kenneth Lockridge had reported in 1970, and one found not the American "national character" but a strain of that same peasant culture, wedded to "ancient, universal patterns of rural life," which permeated early modern Europe.[37] But in retrospect the more transformative event was not the new techniques—which just as often skittered away from Lockridge's conclusion—but the rediscovery of the Atlantic economy. A key moment in this regard was Philip Curtin's census of the Atlantic slave trade. In the efflorescence of comparative slavery studies Curtin's work helped to fuel, it was possible to read an exceptionalist moral for the American case. Only in British continental North America did slave populations sustain themselves demographically against the economic advantages which ran everywhere else toward extremely high ratios of male to female slaves: toward a familyless labor force of young, expendable, repurchasable human resources. But the larger implication of Curtin's work was to bring back into focus the extraordinary dimensions of the Atlantic trade in human bodies between Europe, Africa, and the Americas. If slavery was central to American history, as a spate of books was arguing eloquently and irrefutably by the 1970s, then the forces of the Atlantic economy were inextricable from its core dynamics.[38]

Where Curtin filled in the Atlantic with enslaved Africans, others began to fill in the seventeenth-century and eighteenth-century Atlantic in other ways. Alfred Crosby revealed an Atlantic filled with plants, food crops, and pathogens—not a barrier at all but a broad highway of biological exchange. Historians of American Indian–European relations refound a world trade in furs whose fingers reached, with profoundly destabilizing effects, deep into the continent. Bernard Bailyn filled the Atlantic with migrants and land speculators, David Hackett Fischer with folkways in transit, Richard Bushman with the material goods of fashion. Even the British empire has begun to turn up again as an object of historical inquiry.[39]

This repositioning of colonial British America at the western rim of a vast Atlantic economy was abetted by the movement of the center of interest in colonial American history out of New England—where Miller, Bailyn, and Edmund Morgan had helped fix it in the 1950s—to the Chesapeake. That movement, visible by the mid 1970s, had as much to do with the diminishing returns of an overcrowded historiography as any broader agenda. But it soon became clear that reintegration of the South into the core American story meant substituting for stories of boundedness (as in Lockridge's "closed, corporate community") stories of instability and penetration, in a region as porous as its estuaries were to the sea itself. The contrast to the New England studies, framed within localistic, Durkheimian narratives of the accretion and release of social strain, was sharp and far-reaching. Tobacco, slaves, servants, goods, elites, and ideas passed too quickly through the Chesapeake settlements to make even the very boundaries of an American history distinct.[40]

The colonial British America which emerged from these studies remained profoundly different from Britain itself; but it was the difference of a periphery to its center, the extractive edge of a commercial empire to its core. In a world of unequal and specialized distribution of functions and labor, connection proves, in fact, to be a far more powerful explanation for difference than mere distance. As the metaphors of isolation melt away, it has begun to be possible to see on the western edge of the Atlantic not "America" but British (and Spanish) North America, embedded in larger imperial projects and world systems of commerce, labor, and power.

This notion of an Atlantic system has not yet transformed the history of the Revolution as profoundly as the period preceding it, but here, too, the effects of a changed point of view can no longer be dismissed. Whatever causes may be adduced for the breakup of the empire, it is clearly no longer possible to describe it as the estrangement of two increasingly dissimilar peoples. From the work of Bailyn, Gordon Wood, Jack Greene, and many others, it is now clear that when it came to mobilizing opposition to British colonial policy—to putting words on the colonists' opposition to taxation and trade restrictions, to an occupying and expensive army, to the usual concomitants of imperial administration—the patriots borrowed heavily from the political language of British radical Whiggism and the precedents of British parliamentarianism. Knowing London better than they knew each other (as Garry Wills notes in a striking passage in *Inventing America*), the very ability of the delegates to the Continental Congresses to mount a common cause was rooted in their Britishness. Different settings put sharply different spins on common ideas and slogans. But the ability of a Thomas Paine, scarcely off the boat from artisan radical London, to tap the core of the Americans' grievances and the long and intimate connection between English and colonial American radicals have brought back to currency Robert Palmer's notion of an age of Atlantic revolution, in which ideas, aspirations, and republican and democratic heresies passed freely between Britain, France, the Americas, and still farther afield.[41]

It cannot be said that nineteenth-century United States history has yet been remade in the same way. But some critically important phases of it have already been transformed. Turner's West, for instance. Of the all the contributions of the "new" Western history of the 1980s, the most important has been the insistence on the West, not as a place of escape or rebirth, but as an arena for the projection of metropolitan economic and political power. In Donald Worster's West, the forces of agrarian capitalism call the tune; in William Cronon's, the forces of commodification. In Richard White's recent synthesis, the American West swarms with advance agents of the federal government: military expeditionaries, federal land agents, geological surveyors, and territorial administrators. "Frontier" is not in White's index; one does not meet a homesteader, sodbuster, or farmer until almost a third of the way into the book. The new Western historians' West is fundamentally a place of extraction and exploitation, its mines, forests, animals, and croplands inextricably mixed in a world economy. Its cowboys were ethnically international; its vaunted self-sufficiency was a myth. The American West was not where world systems of economy and politics petered out in virgin emptiness but where, to the contrary, they were etched most clearly.[42]

As the West has been drawn into global history, so have Crèvecoeur's new immigrant Americans. It had always been a peculiarity of exceptionalist history to imagine immigration as an American-centered story. Even the critical historians had difficulty moving the United States out of the narrative's vital center, reaching deep into a slumbering, tradition-bound, peasant world with promises it would not keep. Within the last decade, however the field has been recast as a phase in the history of global labor migration. In the newest paradigm, the key is not movement to the United States but movement itself in an international labor market of ever enlarging scope. "For America as the special haven of the downtrodden," Virginia Yans-McLaughlin writes, the new immigration histories "substitute America as one point on the periphery of an expanding system of world capitalism."[43]

The special immigrant character of the United States has all but disappeared. Argentina, Canada, and Brazil were American magnets in their own right; during the classic period of immigration, 1870–1914, though in raw numbers their immigrant streams never matched those of the United States, both Argentina and Canada had much higher percentages of immigrant to native-born persons in their populations than the United States. The European nations were immigrant nations too, far more porous than conventionally described. Thus between 1876 and 1915, while some eight million Italians left for the Americas, over six million uprooted themselves for other European nations. By the end of the nineteenth century, there were workers on the move everywhere: across Europe, throughout the Atlantic, up and down the Americas, through the Pacific, and virtually everywhere within the great Indian Ocean basin. In this global labor market, a world of diasporas, ghettos, and borderlands, the processes of migration and adaptation did not make the United States different but the same.[44]

More slowly, other parts of nineteenth-century United States history have begun to reflect these broader horizons. Historians of social movements have begun to remap a world of international influences and borrowings, in which the movement of any one country within the Atlantic system could not but leave the others changed. Since publication of the second volume of David Brion Davis's grand work on the history of antislavery, it has been clear that American antislavery cannot be adequately fathomed outside its complicated reciprocal relations with antislavery in Britain and elsewhere.[45] The history of American religion is an Atlantic history (and by the twentieth century a Pacific history as well); one finds British Methodists in Kentucky, Mormons in London, Zionists in Boston, Presbyterians in China, Buddhists in Chicago.[46] The nineteenth-century women's movement was an international movement with far-flung international structures and a heavy traffic in aspirations and tactics.[47] The labor movement, too, can hardly be comprehended except in global terms. Throughout the Atlantic economy, sojourning artisans brought the threads of a recognizable artisan radicalism together; Marxian socialism came to the United States in the heads of German immigrant workers; craft unionism was a successful British importation. The project of establishing the distinctive social origins of American movements of social reform is now being challenged at dozens of sites by a frame of analysis which sees social movements as passed back and forth between interrelated social and cultural systems.

American economic history, long absorbed in the project of understanding the distinctive factor shares in the processes of American economic growth, is ripe for similar reconfiguration: as the story of continuous international flows of capital, technology, skills, labor, raw materials, and manufactured goods into and out of the United States.[48] The history of foreign policy formation holds out—but with steadily diminishing territory—against international history, where even national boundaries and identities are not always clear.[49]

Of all the aspects of American history, political history clings most strongly to the old exceptionalist story line. Atlantic political-culture studies on the lines of Robert Kelley's *Transatlantic Persuasion* or James Kloppenberg's *Uncertain Victory* remain rare.[50] Even the political centuries are not the same in and outside American history writing. The European historian's twentieth century is a short one, from 1914 to 1989; the Americanist's, beginning somewhere in the 1890s, still stretches on past the horizon. But the library of comparative work from which historians of American politics may now draw has expanded dramatically—the best of it blending common and differential threads in designs which confound any simple exceptionalist paradigm. Whether it is the processes of racial segregation in Alabama and South Africa, the conditions of public and private railroad finance in the United States and Prussia, strategies in big business regulation and macroeconomic crisis management, blue- and white-collar political formation, or even social welfare policy development, an American politics isolated from external tendencies and influences becomes ever harder to find.[51] The common forces of politics were not lost to consciousness. American political developments were keenly watched by nineteenth-century Europeans for their portents of the times. In the early years of the twentieth century, American progressives returned the curiosity, scouring Europe for social-political borrowings.[52]

An overarching conceptual framework for a nonexceptionalist history of the United States is not yet in place. Between the rigidity of Immanuel Wallerstein's world system and the looseness of Michael Geyer's and Charles Bright's, there are conceptual worlds to choose.[53] But whatever shape that overview will take, markets and empires (formal and informal) will figure in it far more strongly than they have figured in United States history in the past. Beginning on the rim of an expanding Europe, the trading outpost of distant, commercial empires, the United States grew to preside over a world-spanning commercial empire of its own. Between these beginnings and this destination, the splendid isolation which Americans have wrapped around their history is no longer to be easily found.

The future of such a reading of United States history in a culture still deeply, passionately wedded to exceptionalism is, nonetheless, not easy to predict. The new Western history is bathed in controversy both generational and professional. In the discipline's core journals, as the recent articles by Michael McGerr and Michael Kammen demonstrate, challenges to the exceptionalist paradigm generate sharp, visceral reactions. McGerr worries that the price of the transnational history will be "an estrangement from our audiences." Kammen, in an acerbic rhetoric that belies his moderate conclusion, pits "the newly orthodox homilies" of transnational history against "the solid work . . . [of] judicious and conscientious practitioners." John Higham worries about a history in which the "nation" no longer acts, in which America becomes merely a mere geographic container for processes within and beyond it. "Contrary to much current academic opinion, Ann Douglas opens her recent book, "I believe . . . that America is a special case in the development of the West."[54]

Within a political culture which has pinned so many of its ideals to faith in its own uniqueness, there has been a quickness to read challenges to the exceptionalist character of the United States as challenges to those ideals themselves. There ensues a clinging to difference, as if difference were the point in question, a clinging to the terms of exceptionalism even as the conditions which framed exceptionalist historiography pass away. Americans are fond of "the splendid misery of uniqueness," J. G. A. Pocock once wrote with an immigrant scholar's irony;

they might be "happier if they shared their history with other people."[55] To give up the imagined rules of everyone else's history which set off, with artificial brilliance, the uniqueness of American history, to re-embed the history of the United States within a world of transnational historical forces, will not erase the "differentness" of American history—only its imputed immunities and dispensations.

NOTES

1. Byron E. Shafer, ed., *Is America Different? A New Look at American Exceptionalism* (Oxford, 1991).

2. Joyce Appleby, "Recovering America's Historic Diversity: Beyond Exceptionalism," *Journal of American History* 79 (1992): 419.

3. J. H. Elliott, *The Old World and the New, 1492–1650* (Cambridge, England, 1970); C. Vann Woodward, *The Old World's New World* (New York, 1991); Jack P. Greene, *The Intellectual Construction of America: Exceptionalism and Identity from 1492 to 1800* (Chapel Hill, 1993); Karen Ordahl Kupperman, ed., *America in European Consciousness, 1493–1750* (Chapel Hill, 1995).

4. Sacvan Bercovitch, *The Rites of Assent: Transformations in the Symbolic Construction of America* (New York, 1993), p. 30.

5. Appleby, "Recovering America's Historic Diversity," pp. 419–20.

6. Robert J. Alexander, *The Right Opposition: The Lovestoneites and the International Communist Opposition of the 1930s* (Westport, Conn., 1981); Bertram D. Wolfe, *A Life in Two Centuries: An Autobiography* (New York, 1981).

7. Michael Lienesch, *New Order of the Ages: Time, the Constitution, and the Making of Modern American Political Thought* (Princeton, 1988).

8. Bercovitch, *Rites of Assent*, p. 8.

9. In an argument which places an "ideology of American exceptionalism" at the very core of the emerging social sciences, Dorothy Ross has emphasized the timeless optimism, the quick and unproblematic extrapolation from present to future tense, the "prehistoricist" understandings of progress and social processes which held in their grip nineteenth- and early twentieth-century history writing. But while the characterizations fit, Ross overdraws their peculiarly American character. Dorothy Ross, *The Origins of American Social Science* (Cambridge, England, 1991). Cf. Daniel T. Rodgers, "Fine for Our Time," *Intellectual History Newsletter* 13 (1991): 41–44.

10. George Bancroft, *History of the United States, from the Discovery of the Continent* (New York, 1890), vol. 4, p. 450.

11. John Higham with Leonard Krieger and Felix Gilbert, *History* (Princeton, 1965), p. 161.

12. Frederick Jackson Turner, *The Frontier in American History* (New York, 1921), pp. 2, 4, 38.

13. Ibid., p. 281.

14. Edward P. Cheyney, *European Background of American History, 1300–1600* (New York, 1904); Livingston Farrand, *Basis of American History (1500–1900)* (New York, 1904). Turner was assigned *The Rise of the New West, 1819–1829* (New York, 1906).

15. Charles M. Andrews, *The Colonial Background of the American Revolution* (New Haven, 1924).

16. W. E. B. Du Bois, *Black Reconstruction* (New York, 1935); Charles A. and Mary R. Beard, *The Rise of American Civilization*, rev. ed. (New York, 1940), p. 3.

17. Crèvecoeur's own title was more modest: "What Is an American?" J. Hector St. John de Crèvecoeur, *Letters from an American Farmer* (1782; reprint ed., Garden City, N.Y., n.d.). Crèvecoeur's short passage was only one of the canonical texts of the new exceptionalist historiography. Werner Sombart's *Why Is There No Socialism in the United States?* was another—not the text Sombart himself wrote, in the which the special conditions of cheap land and artificially high real wages only temporarily stayed the general forces he saw pressing, in the United States as elsewhere, toward a common working-class politics, but a rather different one, in which Sombart's temporary condition became inherent in the nation's special fortune. Even Tocqueville, whose entire interest in the United States drew on his sense of the interconnectedness of the democratic impulse on both sides of the Atlantic, who saw in Jackson's America not the exception but the rule, the face of France's future, was rewritten, through selective quotation, as a seer of American exceptionalism. Seymour Martin Lipset, "American Exceptionalism Reaffirmed," in Shafer, *Is America Different?* p. 2.

18. Arthur M. Schlesinger, "'What Then Is the American, This New Man?'" *American Historical Review* 48 (1943): 225–44.

19. Robert E. Brown, *Middle-Class Democracy and the Revolution in Massachusetts, 1691–1780* (Ithaca, 1955).

20. Crèvecoeur, *Letters from an American Farmer*, Letter XII; Thomas Philbrick, *St. John de Crèvecoeur* (New York, 1970).

21. Michael McGiffert, "Selected Writings on American National Character," *American Quarterly* 15 (summer 1963, supplement): 271–88; Michael McGiffert, "The Uses of National Character Studies," ibid., 21 (1969): 330–49; Luther S. Luedtke, "Introduction: The Search for American Character," in Luedtke, ed., *Making America: The Society and Culture of the United States* (Chapel Hill, 1992).

22. David Riesman, *The Lonely Crowd: A Study of the Changing American Character* (New Haven, 1950); David M. Potter, *People of Plenty: Economic Abundance and the American National Character* (Chicago, 1954).

23. "Chronologically speaking," Miller wrote in 1954, "Smith and a few others in Virginia, two or three in Plymouth, published works on America before [Winthrop's] 'Modell,' but in relation to the principal theme of the American mind, . . . Winthrop stands at the beginning of our consciousness." Perry Miller, *Nature's Nation* (Cambridge, 1967), p. 6.

24. Crane Brinton, *The Anatomy of Revolution* (New York, 1938).

25. R. R. Palmer, *The Age of Democratic Revolution: A Political History of Europe and America, 1760–1800* (Princeton, 1959, 1964).

26. Brown, *Middle-Class Democracy*, pp. 368, 401.

27. Arthur M. Schlesinger, Jr., *The Age of Jackson* (Boston, 1945).

28. Louis Hartz, *The Liberal Tradition in America: An Interpretation of American Political Thought since the Revolution* (New York, 1955); Louis Hartz et al., *The Founding of New Societies: Studies in the History of the United States, Latin America, South Africa, Canada, and Australia* (New York, 1964).

29. Daniel J. Boorstin, *The Genius of American Politics* (Chicago, 1953), p. 30.

30. Eugen Weber, "Western Civilization," chapter 10 in this volume.

31. William Appleman Williams, *The Tragedy of American Diplomacy* (Cleveland, 1959); William Appleman Williams, *The Roots of the Modern American Empire* (New York, 1969); Lloyd C. Gardner, ed., *Redefining the Past: Essays in Diplomatic History in Honor of William Appleman Williams* (Corvallis, 1986).

32. Philip Gleason, "Crèvecoeur's Question," chapter 6 in this volume.

33. Among many others in this vein: David Montgomery, *Beyond Equality: Labor and the Radical Republicans, 1862–1972* (New York, 1967); Alan Dawley, *Class and Community: The*

Industrial Revolution in Lynn (Cambridge, 1976); John H. M. Laslett and Seymour Martin Lipset, *Failure of a Dream? Essays in the History of American Socialism* (Garden City, N.Y., 1974); David R. Roediger, *The Wages of Whiteness: Race and the Making of the American Working Class* (London, 1991); Kim Voss, *The Making of American Exceptionalism: The Knights of Labor and Class Formation in the Nineteenth Century* (Ithaca, 1993).

Nor, in an historiography which was slow to penetrate American professional circles, was there enough socialism in Britain either—for different, though equally persuasive, reasons. E. P. Thompson, "The Peculiarities of the English" (1965), in his *The Poverty of Theory and Other Essays* (London, 1978); Ross McKibbin, "Why Was There No Marxism in Great Britain?" *English Historical Review* 99 (1984): 297–331.

34. Essential in this regard are Laurence Veysey, "The Autonomy of American History Reconsidered," *American Quarterly* 31 (1979): 455–77; Ian Tyrrell, "American Exceptionalism in an Age of International History," *American Historical Review* 96 (1991): 1031–55; David Thelen, "Of Audiences, Borderlands, and Comparisons: Toward the Internationalization of American History," *Journal of American History* 79 (1992): 432–62.

35. Sean Wilentz, "Against Exceptionalism: Class Consciousness and the American Labor Movement," *International Labor and Working Class History* 26 (1984): 1–24; Aristide R. Zolberg, "How Many Exceptionalisms?" in *Working-Class Formation: Nineteenth-Century Patterns in Western Europe and the United States*, ed. Ira Katznelson and Aristide R. Zolberg (Princeton, 1986); Jean Heffer and Jeanine Rovet, eds., *Why Is There No Socialism in the United States?* (Paris, 1988); James E. Cronin, "Neither Exceptional nor Peculiar: Towards the Comparative Study of Labor in Advanced Society," *International Review of Social History* 38 (1993): 59–75.

36. Leon Fink, *In Search of the Working Class: Essays in American Labor History and Political Culture* (Urbana, 1994), esp. p. 28.

37. Joyce Appleby, "A Different Kind of Independence: The Postwar Restructuring of the Historical Study of Early America," *William and Mary Quarterly* 50 (1993): 245–67; Kenneth A. Lockridge, *A New England Town. The First Hundred Years: Dedham, Massachusetts, 1636–1736* (New York, 1970), p. 78.

38. Philip D. Curtin, *The Atlantic Slave Trade: A Census* (Madison, 1969); Philip D. Curtin, *The Rise and Fall of the Plantation Complex: Essays in Atlantic History* (Cambridge, England, 1990).

39. Alfred W. Crosby, *The Columbian Exchange: Biological and Cultural Consequences of 1492* (Westport, Conn., 1972); Alfred W. Crosby, *Ecological Imperialism: The Biological Expansion of Europe, 900–1900* (Cambridge, England, 1986); D. W. Meinig, *The Shaping of America*, Vol. 1, *Atlantic America, 1492–1800* (New Haven, 1986); Bernard Bailyn, *Voyagers to the West* (New York, 1986); David Hackett Fischer, *Albion's Seed: Four British Folkways in America* (New York, 1989); Richard L. Bushman, *The Refinement of America: Persons, Houses, Cities* (New York, 1992); Jack P. Greene, *Peripheries and Center: Constitutional Development in the Extended Polities of the British Empire and the United States, 1607–1788* (Athens, Ga., 1986).

40. Edmund S. Morgan, *American Slavery, American Freedom: The Ordeal of Colonial Virginia* (New York, 1975); T. H. Breen, *Tobacco Culture: The Mentality of the Great Tidewater Planters on the Eve of Revolution* (Princeton, 1985); Lois Green Carr, Philip D. Morgan, and Jean B. Russo, eds., *Colonial Chesapeake Society* (Chapel Hill, 1988); Jack P. Greene, *Pursuits of Happiness: The Social Development of Early Modern British Colonies and the Formation of American Culture* (Chapel Hill, 1988). Cf. John M. Murrin, "The Irrelevance and Relevance of Colonial New England," *Reviews in American History* 18 (1990): 177–84.

41. Bernard Bailyn, *The Ideological Origins of the American Revolution* (Cambridge, 1967); Gordon S. Wood, *The Creation of the American Republic, 1776–1787* (Chapel Hill, 1969); Eric Foner, *Tom Paine and Revolutionary America* (New York, 1976); Garry Wills, *Inventing America: Jefferson's Declaration of Independence* (Garden City, N.Y., 1978); Margaret Jacob and James Jacob, eds., *The Origins of Anglo-American Radicalism* (London, 1984); and, bridging British, North American, and Latin American history, Peggy K. Liss, *Atlantic Empires: The Network of Trade and Revolution, 1713–1826* (Baltimore, 1983).

42. Donald Worster, *Under Western Skies: Nature and History in the American West* (New York, 1992); Donald Worster, "Transformations of the Earth: Toward an Agroecological Perspective in History," *Journal of American History* 76 (1990): 1087–1106; William Cronon, *Nature's Metropolis: Chicago and the Great West* (New York, 1991); Richard White, *"It's Your Misfortune and None of My Own": A History of the American West* (Norman, 1991); Patricia Nelson Limerick, Clyde A. Milner II, and Charles E. Rankin, eds., *Trails: Toward a New Western History* (Lawrence, Kan., 1991).

43. Virginia Yans-McLaughlin, ed., *Immigration Reconsidered: History, Sociology, and Politics* (New York, 1990), p. 6.

44. Walter Nugent, *Crossings: The Great Transatlantic Migrations, 1870–1914* (Bloomington, 1992); "Transatlantic Migration in Comparative Perspective," *American Historical Review* 88 (1983): 251-346; Mark Wyman, *Round-Trip to America: The Immigrants Return to Europe, 1890–1930* (Ithaca, 1993); John Bodnar, *The Transplanted: A History of Immigrants in Urban America* (Bloomington, 1985). Unlike other phases of the "Europeanization" of American history, this one was deeply affected by the work of European scholars from Frank Thistlethwaite's paradigm-setting essay of 1960 to the recent work of Dirk Hoerder and his collaborators at the University of Bremen. Frank Thistlethwaite, "Migration from Europe Overseas in the Nineteenth and Twentieth Centuries," in XIe Congrès International des Sciences Historiques, *Rapports* (Uppsala, 1960), vol. 5, pp. 32–60; Dirk Hoerder, ed. *American Labor and Immigration History, 1877–1920s: Recent European Research* (Urbana, 1983); Dirk Hoerder, ed., *Labor Migration in the Atlantic Economies: The European and North American Working Classes during the Period of Industrialization* (Westport, Conn., 1985); Dirk Hoerder and Horst Rössler, eds., *Distant Magnets: Expectations and Realities in the Immigrant Experience, 1840–1930* (New York, 1993).

45. David Brion Davis, *The Problem of Slavery in the Age of Revolution, 1770–1823* (Ithaca, 1975).

46. Richard Carwardine, *Trans-atlantic Revivalism: Popular Evangelicalism in Britain and America, 1790–1865* (Westport, Conn., 1978); Mark A. Noll, David W. Bebbington, and George A. Rawlyk, eds., *Evangelicalism: Comparative Studies of Popular Protestantism in North America, the British Isles, and Beyond, 1700–1990* (New York, 1994); Thomas A. Tweed, *The American Encounter with Buddhism, 1884–1912: Victorian Culture and the Limits of Dissent* (Bloomington, 1992).

47. Richard J. Evans, *The Feminists: Women's Emancipation Movements in Europe, America, and Australia, 1840–1920* (London, 1977); Seth Koven and Sonya Michel, "Womanly Duties: Maternalist Policies and the Origins of Welfare States in France, Germany, Great Britain, and the United States, 1880–1920," *American Historical Review* 95 (1990): 1076–1108; Ian Tyrrell, *Woman's World/Woman's Empire: The Women's Christian Temperance Union in International Perspective, 1880–1930* (Chapel Hill, 1991).

48. Tyrrell, "American Exceptionalism," pp. 1044–48.

49. "Writing the History of U.S. Foreign Relations: A Symposium," *Diplomatic History* 14 (1990): 554–605; Thomas J. McCormick, "The State of American Diplomatic History," in *The State of American History*, ed. Herbert J. Bass (Chicago, 1970).

50. Robert Kelley, *The Transatlantic Persuasion: The Liberal-Democratic Mind in the Age of Gladstone* (New York, 1969); James T. Kloppenberg, *Uncertain Victory: Social Democracy and Progressivism in European and American Thought, 1870–1920* (New York, 1986).

51. John W. Cell, *The Highest Stage of White Supremacy: The Origins of Segregation in South Africa and the American South* (Cambridge, England, 1982); Colleen A. Dunlavy, *Politics and Industrialization: Early Railroads in the United States and Prussia* (Princeton, 1994); Tony Freyer, *Regulating Big Business: Antitrust in Great Britain and America, 1880–1900* (Cambridge, 1992); Peter Gourevitch, *Politics in Hard Times: Comparative Responses to International Economic Crises* (Ithaca, 1986); Margaret Weir and Theda Skocpol, "State Structures and the Possibilities for 'Keynesian' Responses to the Great Depression in Sweden, Britain, and the United States," in *Bringing the State Back In*, ed. Peter B. Evans, Dietrich Rueschemeyer, and Theda Skocpol (Cambridge, England, 1985); Jürgen Kocka, *White-Collar Workers in America, 1890–1940: A Social-Political History in International Perspective* (London, 1980); Gary Marks, *Unions in Politics: Britain, Germany, and the United States in the Nineteenth and Early Twentieth Centuries* (Princeton, 1989); John Myles, *Old Age in the Welfare State: The Political Economy of Public Pensions* (Boston, 1984); Gøsta Esping-Andersen, *The Three Worlds of Welfare Capitalism* (Cambridge, England, 1990). Cf. George M. Fredrickson, "From Exceptionalism to Variability: Recent Developments in Cross-National Comparative History," *Journal of American History* 82 (1995): 587–604.

52. R. Laurence Moore, *European Socialists and the American Promised Land* (New York, 1970); Henry Pelling, *America and the British Left: From Bright to Bevan* (New York, 1957); Melvyn Stokes, "American Progressives and the European Left," *Journal of American Studies* 17 (1983): 5–28; Benjamin R. Beede, "Foreign Influences on American Progressivism," *Historian* 45 (1983): 529–49; Kenneth O. Morgan, "The Future at Work: Anglo-American Progressivism, 1890–1917," in *Contrast and Connection: Bicentennial Essays in Anglo-American History*, ed. H.C. Allen and Roger Thompson (Athens, Ohio, 1976); Daniel T. Rodgers, *Atlantic Crossings: Social Politics in a Progressive Age* (Cambridge, 1998).

53. Immanuel Wallerstein, *The Modern World System* (New York, 1974–89); Charles Ragin and Daniel Chirot, "The World System of Immanuel Wallerstein: Sociology and Politics as History," in *Vision and Method in Historical Sociology*, ed. Theda Skocpol (Cambridge, England, 1984); Michael Geyer and Charles Bright, "World History in a Global Age," *American Historical Review* 100 (1995): 1034–60.

54. Michael McGerr, "The Price of the 'New Transnational History,'" *American Historical Review* 96 (1991): 1066; Michael Kammen, "The Problem of American Exceptionalism: A Reconsideration," *American Quarterly* 45 (1993): 6; John Higham, "The Future of American History," *Journal of American History* 80 (1994): 1289–1309; Ann Douglas, *Terrible Honesty: Mongrel Manhattan in the 1920s* (New York, 1995), p. 3.

55. J. G. A. Pocock, "Between Gog and Magog: The Republican Thesis and the *Ideologia Americana*," *Journal of the History of Ideas* 48 (1987): 325.

CHAPTER 2

Gender

LINDA K. KERBER

THE WORD "gender" itself is an old word; it came into use in late Middle English, and was used to describe grammatical distinction and the state of being one sex or the other. Only in the last third of the twentieth century has its meaning expanded to encompass, as the *Oxford English Dictionary* puts it, "sex as expressed by social or cultural distinctions." Yet what is meant by gender analysis is still so new that it is not always clear what is syntactically correct, or, if syntactically correct, meaningful. The recent proliferation of books and articles whose titles depend on the the gerund form "engendering" can be confusing; what it means "to engender" is often sensed but not always clear.[1]

A decade ago, my assignment would most assuredly have been "Women" or "Women's History." Women's history as a topic has been addressed at least since the days of Christine de Pisan, and has been formally addressed in doctoral dissertations in the United States since the 1920s. Women's history has regularly flourished in times of progressive and feminist politics and regularly declined in periods of repression; activists are hungry for their history. The revitalized feminist movement of the early 1970s and thereafter sustained its own demand and its own audience for women's history. When established historical fields—economic history, political history, social history—proved slow to welcome the new work, the structure of the academy was gradually reshaped to accommodate women's history as a distinctive field of historical practice. As historical *inquiry*, fresh subjects of study have been identified, new questions have been asked, and fresh criticism of traditional writing has been developed. As academic *practice*, new fields were named (history departments added specialists in U.S. women's history, European women's history, and more recently in gender studies and in the history of sexuality); new units in colleges and universities have been established (notably departments or programs in women's studies in which women's historians participated); new research tools have been developed (manuscript guides, bibliographies, biographical dictionaries). Endowed chairs in women's studies and women's history buttress the field against ebbs and flows of administrative confidence.

These developments now seem to have been necessary precursors to the conceptualization of gender as, in Joan Scott's graceful phrase, "a useful tool of historical analysis."[2] "Gender" can not be contemplated as a historical construction until women are first understood to figure consequentially in historical narratives, whether in relationship with each other or in relationship to men. In effect every successful investigation into the distinctive historical experience of women carries with it an implicit criticism of traditional narratives that float on what Mary Beard called the "opinionative assurance" that "woman throughout long ages of the past [was] . . . a being always and everywhere subject to *male* man, or . . . a ghostly creature too shadowy to be even that real."[3] Women's history sought to undermine the confidence that change over time happens as a result of men's choices; as J. H. Hexter so memorably put it, "Columbus's voyage to America, the College of Cardinals, the Constitutional Convention have been pretty much stag affairs."[4] Before it is possible to think about, say, the frontier as a site of gendered negotiation, it is first necessary to undermine the generic claims of the assumptions and indeed the language in which virtually all historical prose has been written. For example, Frederick Jackson Turner's classic sentences, "The wilderness masters the colonist. . . . It strips off the garments of civilization and arrays him in the hunting shirt and the moccasin," not only evacuated Native Americans from the wilderness but also made assumptions about maleness which could not be interrogated until the gendered language was itself recognized as significant. Turner wrote in 1893, but the first explicit attack on his argument as inaccurate for women was not published until seventy years later.[5]

Embedded in the generic "he" was a denial—what Beard called "opinionative assurance"—all the more aggressive because it was unacknowledged, of the significance of women as historical actors. If women are part of the history of "universal man," then living women are marginalized into consumers of or supplements to other peoples' stories; an analogous process is at work when Africans are made into a chapter in the history of imperialism or Jews a chapter in the history of heresy. If Heroes and Villains are necessarily male, then women enter the classic narrative primarily as spoilers. From the witches of Salem to Ethel Rosenberg, from the women who marched on Versailles in October 1789 to Marie-Louise Giraud, who, for performing abortions, was the last victim of the guillotine in metropolitan France in 1943, women have figured in the standard narratives as disruptive. They were rarely evaluated for complexity, either in their thoughts, deeds, or relationships. Without women as actors, there was no need for gender as a historical category.

The first generation of professional women's historians in the United States emerged from the first substantial cohort of women graduate students in history departments in the 1920s; their dissertations and first books were published in the late 1920s to the mid-1930s. This line of work was silenced—a victim of the Depression-era concerns to sustain the "virility" of American economy and culture, of World War II anxieties that new opportunities for women not undermine the traditional family as a source of social stability, and of Cold War fears. During the "long 1950s" that stretched from the mid-1940s until deep into the 1960s, political anxieties were translated into an absence of hospitality in universities for women, as embodied in the refusal of fellowship support (especially for married women in an era which enthusiastically sustained early marriage) and skepticism about women as subjects of historical inquiry (the knowledge that publishers would not welcome books on women as historical agents undermined even powerful ideas and wishes of students and advisers alike). Significant dissertations (among them Janet Wilson James's on women in the era of the American Revolution, and Elizabeth Warbasse's on women and early American law, both from Harvard) could not find publishers.[6] Other graduate students, learning from their colleagues' bitter experience, avoided writing about women. The economic prosperity of the period made possible great institutional expansion, not least of rare-book and manuscript collections, but manuscripts of women were not aggressively collected; when collected, they were often not catalogued. No basic guide to U.S. women's manuscripts would be published until 1979.[7]

But at the same time that the academic practice of women's history was being extinguished, profound questions were being raised outside the academy, in the communities of the political Left, flowing out from explicitly Marxist, socialist, and Communist circles. Socialist women's organizations, notably the Congress of American Women and Emma Lazarus Clubs, sustained in the 1940s a linkage between praxis and theory, calling attention to women as historical actors as part of a Marxist vision of the connections between economic forces and historical change. The hospitality of socialists and the Communist Party to women's history—indeed, to an interracial women's history—may be part of what made women's history problematic in the Cold War academy.[8]

The most significant books to inspire a reconceptualization of women's history and to point to the possibilities of an analysis of gender appeared outside the academy in the postwar years. Perhaps the most potent book emerging from the nonacademic Left was Simone de Beauvoir's *The Second Sex*. Published in France in 1949, it appeared in English translation in the United States four years later and quickly achieved best-seller status.[9] Both profound and suggestive, *The Second Sex* was a tour de force, making grand sweeping generalizations, carrying complex learning lightly—sprinkled with quotations from the classics, from philosophers, anthropologists, novelists, poets, but, at least in its American edition, lacking complex and detailed footnotes.

Beauvoir used the phrase "oppression of women" repeatedly as something deeply embedded in and characteristic of Western culture. Blending elements of Marxist thought with elements of psychoanalytic teaching, Beauvoir injected into mainstream, middle-class conversation a host of ideas which had not been so sharply articulated in the United States since Elizabeth Cady Stanton's day. Significantly, Beauvoir maintained that the very idea of "man" virtually required the construction of an "other" who would represent what "man" is not. She was interested in the components of subjectivity and of citizenship, and in the deep ways in which women were denied the one and excluded from the other. This exclusion was not simply a matter of sloppy legislation, of ignorance, or of distractions; it was, Beauvoir insisted, powerfully intentional, part of the very fabric of Western thought.

> For the male it is always another male who is the fellow being, the other who is also the same, with whom reciprocal relations are established. The duality that appears within societies under one form or another opposes a group of men to a group of men; women constitute a part of the property which each of these groups possesses and which is a medium of exchange between them.[10]

These were harsh assertions; they were surely difficult for most of her American readers to hear in the Cold War period.

In developing the argument about the way in which women's alterity functioned, Beauvoir was startling. She drew on Gunnar Myrdal to analogize sex difference and race difference. At a time when most Americans interpreted women's difference as privileged or at least benign, Beauvoir insisted that difference was the sign of an intentionally maintained inferiority. "There is this great difference," she wrote: "the Negroes submit with a feeling of revolt, no privileges compensating for their hard lot, whereas woman is offered inducements to complicity. . . ."[11]

The Second Sex is a capacious book, offering sections focusing on mythology, anthropology, literature, and political science as well as history. Politically the book aligned itself with Marxist critics of American capitalism, as Beauvoir was herself aligned with Marxist critics of French imperialism in Indochina and Algeria, but in the United States it was absorbed by a liberal center. It is always hard to measure the impact of a book; especially this one, long and dense, which many people bought but did not read, or did not read carefully, while at the same time many people borrowed copies from public and commercial lending libraries and may have read them with great intensity. But like Betty Friedan's *The Feminine Mystique*, which commanded an even larger audience in the United States a decade later, *The Second Sex* was recognized by thousands who had not read it, and many of its ideas began to seep, slowly and in ways we cannot measure, into informal conversation, into the popular culture of middle-class and educated women.

For historians, perhaps the most significant book of the postwar period has been Eleanor Flexner's *Century of Struggle*. Although it was published in 1959 by a university press, Flexner held no formal academic positions, and she possessed, as Ellen DuBois has put it, "a very mixed attitude to academic historians, whom she aspired to influence but who caused her considerable bitterness when they ignored her contributions."[12] Based on remarkable archival research, and on a left-feminist social critique, Flexner wrote the first serious history which understood black women and working women to be essential to the narrative of social movements in American history. She understood women as political actors in struggle with each other as well as with men of different class and political positions. Her attention to class and race as well as to sex is now standard among social historians; her narrative has not yet been superseded.

Betty Friedan's book itself formed something of a bridge between the Marxist/ psychoanalytical reflections of Beauvoir and the archival scholarship of the left-feminist displayed by Flexner.[13] Historian Daniel Horowitz has found Flexner influenced in the early 1950s in part by her reading of Betty Friedan's work as a reporter and writer for the publications of the UE, the United Electrical, Radio, and Machine Workers of America, one of the largest labor unions of its day and one most linked to the Communist Party.[14] We know that Betty Friedan read *The Second Sex* in the early 1950s and found it profoundly depressing; she would count it a central moment in the raising of her own consciousness.[15] Friedan also read and was greatly indebted to Flexner. *The Feminine Mystique* offers its readers a shortened version of *Century of Struggle* as a historical base. By the 1960s, women's history was reengaged by British Marxist-feminists, imported into the United States by an international community of socialist scholars. These feminist critics, notably Sheila Rowbotham, were less abstract than Beauvoir often was; they were more likely to challenge the exclusion of unwaged domestic labor from analyses of capitalist modes of production. In *Women, Resistance and Revolution*, Rowbotham embedded women into the master narrative of European history; women were, she argued, indispensable to the history of the French Revolution, the revolutions of 1848, the Paris Commune.[16] This was a sharp challenge to those historians who had more comfortably located women in settings— domestic life, family relations—already part of the traditional account of where women were to be found. Although they did not always use the term, Marxist-feminists were engaged in tracing hierarchical gender relations within working-class households, and insisting that patriarchy and domination could be found within those households as well as outside them.[17]

Thus when a revitalized feminist movement burst on the scene in the late 1960s, historical reconstruction was already part of the activists' agenda. It was part of the vision of those who came to feminism from the New Left, familiar as they were with a linkage of the oppression of women to capitalism, racism, and sexual repression. *Sisterhood Is Powerful*, an expression of radical feminist ideas published in 1970, included essays by historians.[18] That the intellectual roots of women's history are planted in the Left probably exacerbated the skepticism with which conservatives, even right-of-center-liberals, often regarded it, even though feminism had its enemies in the Left as well. This skepticism was visible even when, as in the publication of the biographical dictionary *Notable American Women*, books and courses offered themselves as apolitical contributions to knowledge. Liberal activists also constructed their agendas with an eye toward the past; liberal feminist lawyers developed a historical vision, as civil rights lawyers had done before them. Ruth Bader Ginsberg, for example, who would in the early 1970s successfully argue before the Supreme Court that discrimination on the basis of sex was a denial of the Fourteenth Amendment's guarantee of equal protection under the law, repeatedly listed the three (sometimes four) judicial precedents stretching back to the era of Reconstruction that she and her colleagues were determined to overturn.

Political activity in the streets and in legislatures was accompanied by an inventive wave of new college and university courses in 1969–73. That these courses could be taught at all was dependent on the extent to which women historians had entered the profession in the United States, for with very few exceptions—Carl Degler, then of Vassar, was one—it was the rare man who engaged the growing feminist scholarship. Though located at the margins—in women's colleges, as teaching assistants, in extension and evening schools—women had earned 13 percent of the Ph.D.s awarded in history in the 1960s, and there were women in positions in which they had not been in the late 1940s.[19] Feminist historians inherited the Berkshire Conference of Women Historians, organized in

1929 by Jeannette Nicols and Mary Beard at a time when women historians were unwelcome at the "smokers" to which male historians repaired in the evenings at conventions. In the late 1960s the "Berks," whose membership had declined in the 1950s and 1960s—perhaps a dozen historians actually came to the annual informal meetings in the Berkshires or at country inns elsewhere—was greatly invigorated by a younger generation that found it to be, in effect, a profession-specific consciousness-raising group. Simultaneously dozens of feminist historians organized themselves as the Coordinating Committee on Women in the Historical Profession (still flourishing as the Coordinating Committee of Women Historians), a caucus of activists who successfully demanded that the historical learned societies—the American Historical Association, the Organization of American Historians—establish standing committees on the status of women. Sustained in these ways by national and regional communities of women historians, and urged on by feminist students who perceived that their courses were conceptually old-fashioned, feminist historians agressively changed college curricula. The syllabi and bibliographies and collections of primary sources developed for the women's history courses of the early 1970s are themselves significant historiographical documents. By 1975 several now-classic theoretical essays of the new departure had already appeared, notably Gerda Lerner's prediction of four historigraphical stages for women's history, Carroll Smith-Rosenberg's historicization of sexuality, Natalie Zemon Davis's perception that "the relation of the wife—of the potentially disorderly woman—to her husband was especially useful for expressing the relation of all subordinates to their superiors," and Joan Kelly's argument that women's history was in fact about "the social relations of the sexes"—that is, about gender.[20]

•

U.S. historians of women and gender relations have generally cherished their political engagement, a consciousness which, because it was associated with the revitalization of research in the 1970s, is somewhat more marked than in most other fields, and which has contributed to the intensity of argument within it. Perhaps the most notable characteristic of recent U.S. historical writing in this field is the insistence that sites which had once been assumed to be empty of women, innocent of gender, instead are not only inhabited by women as well as men but also are permeated with assumptions, ideas, and visions about gender relations. As we have learned to treat (or at least learned that we ought to treat) class and race as fluid *formations* rather than as static constructions, we are learning now to treat gender as itself a formation, fluidly formed, historically and spatially located.[21] For more than a generation, historians of women have been engaged in the effort to understand the political, legal, and cultural work that has been invested in forming and sustaining particular gender relations and managing them as natural, rather than social, formations.[22] (There is an analogy to be drawn with contemporary efforts to comprehend race formation, and the political, legal, and cultural work that it takes to sustain racial hierarchies.) This has never been easy to do, in large part because before World War II, with the notable exception of Marxist analysis, most historical writing about women had tended toward the anecdotal. Inheriting a subject that had for the most part been treated only descriptively, grounded in a limited historiographical analytic tradition, historians of women struggled to create concepts that would enable them to impose order on the confusion of the quotidian. In the late 1960s, a number of historians embarked on a discussion of the concept of "separate spheres" inhabited by women and men, a concept traceable in much nineteenth-century writing. Historians' analysis of how ideas about separate spheres were put in practice guided them toward a recovery of homosocial relationships, new understandings of the meanings of domesticity, and revised evaluations of the meaning of marriage in the nineteenth century.[23] But the language of "separate spheres" easily drifted toward concepts of a distinctive "women's culture" and then on to an essentialist definition of the difference between women and men.[24] By the early 1980s many historians were sending cautionary signals, and by the 1990s it was generally conceded that the concept of "separate spheres" for men and women was itself an inscription of difference on complex relationships between men and women, and among women, which were characteristic of and enforced by a particular social, racial, and political culture, not a "natural" sorting out of social responsibilities and roles.[25] Indeed, by the beginning of the decade it had become clear that masculinity was also a socially constructed concept, and an explosion of new scholarship in that vein was heralded by the appearance of volumes edited by Mark Carnes and Ava Baron, each including selections from work in progress that within a few years would appear in book form.[26] In 1995, Gail Bederman's *Manliness and Civilization* offered a carefully crafted analysis of the ways "anatomy, identity and authority" were linked in the Progressive era in ways that tied male power to white racial dominance. "[B]etween 1890 and 1917," Bederman argues, "as white middle-class men actively worked to reinforce male power, their race became a factor which was crucial to their gender . . . whiteness was both a palpable fact and a manly ideal. . . ."[27]

In order to reach this understanding, it was necessary to destabilize not only the concept of "woman"—the abstraction that Simone de Beauvoir had used as frequently as her nineteenth-century counterparts, but which the writers of the mid-1970s had long since repudiated—but also the plural form "women." Severe critiques launched by African American feminists in the late 1970s challenged efforts to gather all women, whatever their class, racial, or sexual identity, into a single category. This work was made possible in part by the recuperation of the historical experiences of African-American women, a research enterprise marked in the late 1960s by Gerda Lerner's documentary history *Black Women in White America* and continuing through the 1990s, notably by the enterprising work of activists like the Combahee River Collective who demanded the construction of their history. Challenges to synthesizing histories of slavery which omitted women emerged from the the painstaking research of Jacqueline Jones and Deborah Gray White.[28] A revitalized scholarship on Reconstruction, energized in part of by the new accessibility of the massive archives of the Freedmen's Bureau,[29] had by the late 1990s provided underpinning to a new line of scholarly argument that insisted that gender relations had shaped the outcome of the Civil War in unexpected ways in which relations between men and women, black and white, were central.[30] A new generation of reference materials, notably *Black Women in America: An Historical Encyclopedia*, edited by Darline Clark Hine and others, was appearing at the end of the decade, sustaining ever more complex understanding of the history of African American women.[31]

Also in the early 1970s, lesbians sharply challenged heterosexual historians for evacuating sexual difference from synthesizing narratives. Whether left or liberal, most of the new scholarship had carried the implicit assumption that "women" were heterosexual; perhaps restless in their marriage or in their work, but not in their sexuality. Anthropologist Gayle Rubin's influential essay, "The Traffic in Women: Notes on the 'Political Economy' of Sex"—begun as a senior honors thesis at the University of Michigan in 1972, and published in 1975—situated heterosexuality firmly in socially constructed kinship relations; as Lisa Duggan would felicitously put it some years later, "sexual representations construct identities (they do not merely reflect preexisting ones)."[32] Historians seeking a holistic understanding of women's experience were challenged to destabilize traditional assumptions of heterosexuality and to interrogate the sexual representations on which they relied. The development of a vision of the past which made space for erotic homosocial relations and challenged what Blanche Wiesen Cook called "the historical denial of lesbianism" occurred simultaneously with a gay and lesbian civil rights movement.[33] By the late 1980s, postmodern theorists were problematizing bodies, following Michel Foucault in making sex itself a system which, as Judith Butler puts it, "imposes a duality and a uniformity on bodies in order to maintain reproductive sexuality as a compulsory order." In this vision, "gender reality is created through sustained social performances." The challenge to historians, that they consider as performance much that they had taken to be biological in social relations, would be taken up in the following decade.[34]

The plural noun *women* absorbs or leaves implicit differences among women which could be quite as consequential as differences between women and men. Extinguishing difference made it impossible to understand occasions when race interacted with gender (as it often did in the choices African American women made in solidarity with African American men, or when, as Atina Grossman has carefully reported, German women responded to Nazi demands by expelling Jewish women from feminist organizations) or when class identity interacted with gender (as it often has done for working-class women, black and white).[35]

The calibration of how much to emphasize equality with men or difference from them locates women themselves on a political continuum in relation to each other. Jane De Hart has emphasized the characteristics that cultural or "difference" feminists may share with antifeminists. While the first "challenge patriarchal privilege" and the latter "seek protection within patriarchy," both groups, she writes, "are convinced of the importance of differences between the sexes, whether biologically or culturally based, and both wish to preserve rather than diminish those differences. Affirming 'female' values and women's culture and community, both see value in separatism and danger in assimilation." On this ground, feminism shades imperceptibly into antifeminism.[36] "[T]he dominant motif in U.S. women's-studies scholarship and feminist theory," Linda Gordon has observed, "has been 'difference.'"[37]

But if attention to difference expands the categories open for research, analysis, and narrative, it can also be set to the service of normalizing white, middle-class, heterosexual practice, marginalizing lesbians, women of color, women of some ethnicities.[38] These latter groups enter the "women's" narrative only to destabilize it, much as, in the older practices, women derailed men's narratives. Thus accounts of women's liberation or second-wave feminism still rarely make space for attention to the National Welfare Rights Organization, although it was the site of the most vigorous working-class black women's energies; histories of the struggle for access to abortion center on *Roe v. Wade* (1973) but rarely give substantial attention to *Harris v. McRae* (1980), which denied public funding for abortions, deepening a health care gap between rich and poor women. The relationship between "women" and sexuality, once treated as a relatively simple matter of relations between heterosexual and lesbian women, is understood as a complex site, itself a historical subject, on which not only heterosexuals, gay men, bisexuals, and lesbians are formed but on which the understanding of gay/lesbian gives way to queer, itself the center of new critical theoretical ventures.[39] Categories implode.

The solution to that implosion, and to the threat that attention to matters of specific difference will play into the arguments of those who are content to let straight women and queers make their own arguments in their own corner of Clio's closet, is to widen the context in which gender relations are studied. And indeed, in this decade, historians in the United States who take gender for their subject are likely to inquire into the ways in which concerns about normative masculinity, femininity, and effeminacy have sustained public institutions and social relationships. They are likely to think about the dynamic flow of power between weak and strong (sometimes with explicit reference to Foucauldian analysis, sometimes not). In explicit or implicit criticism of the absence of gender relations in Jurgen Habermas's conceptualization of the public sphere, historians have engaged in redefinitions of what activities count as "public" and are significant in the creation of the realm in which public opinion is formed.[40]

One result is that fields of historical inquiry which had once seemed gender-neutral—state formation, intellectual history, the history of crime, the history of violence, the history of medicine and public health, the history of social security legislation, postwar Reconstruction, diplomatic history, the history of imperialism, urban history—are now added to older sites (the history of suffrage, the history of education, family history, the history of immigration, the history of race relations, working-class history, and the history of sexuality) as locations in which gender is formed and contested.[41] In this work, the construction of normative institutions and the power they exert have come under fresh scrutiny. The state in its various forms is central, writes Michel Foucault, to the "relations of power which permeate, characterize and constitute the social body. . . . [and which in turn] cannot themselves be established, consolidated, nor implemented without the production, accumulation, circulation and functioning of a discourse." This insight into the power/knowledge nexus has supported what has been called a "linguistic turn" in historical scholarship. The purpose of continually analyzing language is to assure that we give power no place to hide; the paths of postmodernism on the one hand and social history on the other both lead to heightened attention to language and to legal form. Wherever we start on our bookshelves, if the publication date is in the 1990s, attention to the role of public authority and of language itself in the shaping of gender is likely to be salient in the author's agenda.

Whether as legislation or as embodied in policing agencies of the state, law shapes the terrain on which gender systems are established and contested. For western European democracies and the United States, a good starting point is Carole Pateman's *The Sexual Contract* (1988), which argues that historical and political understanding of the Enlightenment and the Age of the Democratic Revolution has been deeply flawed by a failure to understand that the new social contract which infused democratic constitutionalism itself continued to rest on unacknowledged and ancient assumptions about family hierarchy, especially the continuing patriarchal right of husband over wife. Even in the new liberal republics of the late eighteenth century, civil freedom would be, Pateman argues "a masculine attribute" dependent on patriarchal right.[42] In that context, continuing resistance to absorbing adult women into "universal" suffrage becomes reasonable rather than anachronistic; the difficulty of the struggle to reform liberalism to include women as political actors turns out to be preordained.

Implicit in most choices that individuals make—social, economic, political— is generally a judgment about whether an action is likely to be understood as legal or illegal; if legal, whether it is likely to be easy or hard to accomplish. Statutes and legal practice define what counts as privacy, what counts as rape, what counts as queer.[43] When women behave differently than men (just as when poor behave differently than rich, when blacks behave differently than whites), it is often because they are making reasonable deductions about how to live under the laws they encounter, which in turn define the gender system within which they live. Many of the most powerful historical studies of the last decade have understood this. Indeed attention to law—construed broadly enough to encompass revolutions against old regimes, the construction of new constitutional settings, and including not only submission to the law but also efforts (sometimes individual, sometimes collective) to resist and overthrow legal authority—has been a primary characteristic of the new historical scholarship on gender.

In this process, citizenship is coming to be understood less as a mark of fixed status and more as distinctive practices. As legal codes specifying women are changed, their meaning for men simultaneously changes. Laws which regulate black women's behavior have implications for the behavior of *all* others in their community, male and female, black or white; politics, as Glenda Gilmore has written, "includes those who are made its objects [even when they] cannot participate in elections."[44] One approach is work which engages legal codes directly. This work includes Martha Howell's consideration of the exclusion of women from civic roles when feudal patterns of authority broke down in early modern European cities; Sarah Hanley's analysis of the way in which family formation was tightly linked to state building in early modern France; Marilyn Lake's wide-ranging studies of the conceptualization of female citizenship in Australia; Steve J. Stern's reconstruction of the social relations between the sexes in late colonial Mexico drawing heavily on lawsuits and other court records; and Glenda Gilmore's carefully nuanced account of black women's resistance to segregation and violence during the "Progressive" era in the United States.[45] Moreover, social historians increasingly write with attentiveness to the ways in which legal codes lurk under the "free" choices which individuals and groups make. Lizabeth Cohen's subtle analysis of the relationship between female authority, shoppping centers, and "a huge expansion of consumer credit in the postwar era" is a good example of this, as are the essays collected by Joanne Meyerowitz in *Not June Cleaver: Women and Gender in Postwar America, 1945–1960.*[46]

Another approach is to seek gender relations as they are in tension with, and reshaped by, the actual policing practices of state authorities. Victoria de Grazia has written a powerful social history of the way Mussolini's dictatorship claimed to be restoring the old when in fact it was not only "recasting economic and political institutions" but also "restructuring . . . gender relations"; it was "nationalizing" Italian women as, in the nineteenth century, the modern bourgeois state had nationalized men.[47] In a wide-ranging examination of society and culture in fin-de-siècle Russia, Laura Engelstein finds in criminal codes a detailed map of the boundaries between the normative and the deviant, which guide her through the complex terrain of the Russian encounter with modernity.[48] In *Heroes of Their Own Lives*, Linda Gordon focuses on the clients of social work agencies, discerning the force with which women whom historians have generally treated as silent and weak were engaged in active and creative struggle to define wife beating as violence and to insist that regulating agencies defend them against it.[49] Reconstructing a century of prostitution in Buenos Aires, a sexual commerce fueled by an international traffic, Donna Guy has argued forcefully that the "politics of social control in modern Argentina . . . rested upon the relation of gender and class to concepts of citizenship."[50] Beth Bailey and David Farber found that the civilian police of Honolulu and the military police of the U.S. Army bases there competed vigorously to regulate servicemen's access to prostitutes during World War II, but neither group cared to rectify the conditions which had driven the women into prostitution.[51] Elsa Barkley Brown has taken the Habermas agenda to the post–Civil War South; tracing with precision the modes by which black women and men in Richmond enacted their freedom, she destabilizes older assumptions that women were silenced and invisible.[52] In her analysis of city life in the nineteenth century, Mary Ryan concludes that gender "supplied the sexual prohibitions, codes of segregation and rhetorical power with which to mortar the rising wall of racial segregation."[53] And George Chauncey's *Gay New York* turns out to be inhabited not only by straight men and homosexuals but also by the

agents of Anthony Comstock's Society for the Suppression of Vice and the New
York City Police, who, in monitoring citizens' sexual practices, provide the official accounts which make much of Chauncey's book possible.[54]

    A third characteristic of the new work on citizenship is that historians of gen-
der are bringing together questions about how national loyalties are constructed
(questions initiated by postcolonial intellectuals of the subaltern studies movement) and the strategies for analyzing visual and verbal texts pioneered by
postmodern critics. Although Benedict Anderson nowhere deals with women in
his influential *Imagined Communities*, the implications of that book—that nation-
states are made not only by force but by loyalties, which in turn have to be
constructed, often out of gendered materials—have infused much recent work.
Much of this work is driven, as Antoinette Burton has put it, by "the conviction
that all modernities have been produced through colonialism" and that central to
the imperial project has been the construction of a contrast between "manly" and
"effeminate" men.[55] Carroll Smith-Rosenberg's "Dis-Covering the Subject of the
'Great Constitutional Discussion,' 1786–1789," is a tour de force which argues
that the virtuous and independent white male citizen was constructed on a conceptual base which "fused masculinity and republicanism as the defining characteristics of the new American subject," and positioned him against "discursively
constructed negative others[:] . . . the white middle-class woman, the American
Indian warrior, and the enslaved African American." The evidence for her argument includes a critical analysis of the female images—Columbia, Minerva—
which ambivalently embodied gendered anxieties as well as claims to nationhood.[56] In *The Family Romance of the French Revolution*, Lynn Hunt interrogates
psychopolitical transformations that accompanied regicide and then the Napoleonic empire that followed it. Hunt argues that family relationships—between
fathers and sons, mothers and children, husbands and wives—are "critical to the
founding of social and political authority"; she finds clues to these transformations in the personal, familial and sexual, even pornographic imagery spawned by
the Revolution.[57] In *Taste and Power: Furnishing Modern France*, Leora Auslander
links the construction of national identity and the sustaining of patterns of consumption; "French taste," she writes, not only signaled class location but also
"was to assure continuity of society and Frenchness." The result is that the choice
of objects which women purchased for their homes carried political frieght, as it
still does throughout the developed world; "furniture and homes [and clothing
choices, I would add] represented their owners." Auslander emphasizes that the
rise of "this particular form of commodity fetishism coincided [not only] with the
establishment in France of universal manhood suffrage" but also the continued
exclusion of women from suffrage. "In late nineteenth-century France the responsibility for the representation of the nation through consumption was attributed largely to women, and the responsibility for the representation of the state
through citizenship was attributed to men."[58] Women's role as constructors of
social identity through their behavior as consumers continued, even strengthened, long after the achievement of suffrage.

    National loyalties are always, however, constructed in tension with competing
national identities and also with international efforts to shape a peaceful world.

Leila Rupp's recent rich account of the many transnational women's organizations which struggled to bring to life an imagined international community in the first half of the twentieth century challenges historians to develop fuller studies of these societies and their members.[59] As the 1990s draw to a close, as political boundaries to international travel fade, and as internet communications make international exchange easier, more and more historians are addressing multinational subjects in their research.

•

Douglas Moore's American opera *Carrie Nation* opens with a scene in which Carrie Nation and her colleagues are wreaking havoc on a barroom. Through the noise and chaos booms the voice of the sheriff: "Madam, I arrest you!!" Carrie Nation responds, "On what grounds?" and he says, "For defacing private property." And her alto voice declaims, emphasizing the last word, "I'm not defacing, I'm *destroying!*" We are still destroying the large narratives built around structures which deny women's subjectivity, which suffocate knowledge of same-sex love, which reify patriarchy in the process of describing it. But the task of historians of women and of gender has also been, and will continue to be, constructive. Our own historiographical moment requires that we reimagine narratives capable of capturing the dynamic tensions between and among men and women over time. We are still searching the past, like Diogenes with a lantern, looking for women, looking for the myriad ways in which people shaped their sexualities. It is not necessary that what we learn be pleasing or flattering; it is necessary that the history we write name and interrogate hidden structures of power which would prefer to remain hidden.

NOTES

I am grateful to Linda Gordon for a helpful conversation at a critical time in the development of this essay.

1. Recent examples include Arnaldo Testi, "The Gender of Reform Politics: Theodore Roosevelt and the Culture of Masculinity," *Journal of American History* 81 (1995): 1509–34; Ruth Feldstein, "'I Wanted the Whole World to See': Race, Gender and Constructions of Motherhood in the Death of Emmett Till," in Joanne Meyerowitz, ed., *Not June Cleaver: Women and Gender in Postwar America, 1945–1960* (Philadelphia, 1994); Toni Morrison, ed., *Race-ing Justice, En-gendering Power: Essays on Anita Hill, Clarence Thomas, and the Construction of Social Reality* (New York, 1992); Martha Minow, "Justice Engendered," *Harvard Law Review* 101 (1987), 10–95; Anna Clark, *The Struggle for the Breeches: Gender and the Making of the British Working Class* (Berkeley, 1995); Barbara Melosh, *Engendering Culture: Manhood and Womanhood in New Deal Public Art and Theater* (Washington, D.C., 1991); *Gendered Domains: Rethinking Public and Private in Women's History: Essays from the Seventh Berkshire Conference on the History of Women* (Ithaca, 1992).

2. Joan W. Scott, "Gender: A Useful Tool of Historical Analysis," *American Historical Review* 91 (1986): 1053–75.

3. Mary Beard, *Woman as Force in History: A Study in Traditions and Realities* (New York, 1946), p. 77.

4. Review of Beard, *Woman as Force in History*, *New York Times Book Review*, March 17, 1946.

5. Turner's essay is "The Significance of the Frontier in American History" (1893), in *The Frontier in American History* (New York, 1920), p. 4. David Potter challenged Turner in "American Women and the American Character" (1962), in Don Fehrenbacher, ed., *History and American Society: Essays of David Potter* (New York, 1973), pp. 278–303.

6. Decades later the unmodified dissertation texts were issued, without copy-editing or revision, as Janet Wilson James, *Changing Ideas about Women in the United States 1776–1825* (New York, 1981), and Elizabeth Bowles Warbasse, *The Changing Legal Rights of American Women, 1800–1861* (New York, 1987). For similar exclusionary processes in the sciences, see Margaret W. Rossiter, *Women Scientists in America: Before Affirmative Action 1940–1972* (Baltimore, 1995), chap. 1.

7. Andrea Hinding, ed., *Women's History Sources: A Guide to Archives and Manuscript Collections in the United States* (New York, 1979). This guide is now deeply outdated; at this writing it is not clear what may replace or supplement it.

8. See Amy Swerdlow, "The Congress of American Women: Left-Feminist Peace Politics in the Cold War," in Linda K. Kerber, Alice Kessler-Harris, and Kathryn Kish Sklar, eds., *U.S. History as Women's History: New Feminist Essays* (Chapel Hill, 1995), esp. pp. 305–06, 309–11, and 432–33, n.35; and Joyce Antler, "Between Culture and Politics: The Emma Lazarus Federation of Jewish Women's Clubs and the Promulgation of Women's History, 1944–1989," ibid., pp. 267–95.

9. Simone de Beauvoir, *The Second Sex*, trans. H. M Parshley (New York, 1953).

10. Beauvoir, *Second Sex*, pp. 70–71.

11. Beauvoir, *Second Sex*, pp. 297–98; see also comments on pp. 116 and 259.

12. Eleanor Flexner, *Century of Struggle: The Woman's Rights Movement in the United States* (Cambridge, 1959); Ellen DuBois, "Eleanor Flexner and the History of American Feminism," *Gender and History* 3 (1991): 82.

13. DuBois, "Eleanor Flexner," pp. 81–90.

14. Daniel Horowitz, "Rethinking Betty Friedan and *The Feminine Mystique:* Labor Union Radicalism and Feminism in Cold War America, *American Quarterly* 48 (1996): 1–42. On the UE and its politics, see Gerald Zahavi, "Passionate Commitments: Race, Sex, and Communism at Schenectady General Electric," *Journal of American History* 83 (1996): 514–48.

15. Friedan, *It Changed My Life*, pp. 304–05, quoted in Toril Moi, *Simone de Beauvoir: The Making of an Intellectual Woman* (Cambridge, Mass., 1994), p. 181. For the appeal of Friedan's book to women who did not share the left politics of Flexner or Beauvoir, see the memoir of Mary Louise Smith, who chaired the Republican National Committee, 1974–77, in Louise R. Noun, *More Strong-Minded Women: Iowa Feminists Tell Their Stories* (Ames, 1992), pp. 148–49.

16. Sheila Rowbotham, *Women, Resistance and Revolution: A History of Women and Revolution in the Modern World* (New York, 1972).

17. Important contributions in this vein are Juliet Mitchell, "Women: The Longest Revolution," *New Left Review*, no. 40 (1966): 11–27; Margaret Benston, "The Political Economy of Women's Liberation," *Monthly Review* (September 1969), 13–27; and Heidi I. Hartmann, "Capitalism, Patriarchy, and Job Segregation by Sex," *Signs* 1 (1976): 137–70.

18. Robin Morgan, ed., *Sisterhood Is Powerful* (New York, 1970). On the history of radical feminism, see Alice Echols, *Daring to Be Bad: Radical Feminism in America 1967–1975* (Minneapolis, 1989).

19. Indeed, one of the sharpest contrasts between the practice of the history of women

and of gender formation between the United States and Europe may well be the strength of the senior professoriate in the United States, which in turn is linked to the decentralized forms of U.S. higher education. Substantial journals devoted to women's studies were quickly established in the United States, and they have multiplied; in contrast, there are no journals fully devoted to women's history in France, and one of the most distinguished of the Italian journals, *Memoria*, has recently died. Academics who teach women's history and gender outside the United States have tended to have appointments as social historians, with somewhat less ability to set their own teaching agendas.

20. This argument was the more important because it engaged those who still conceptualized women's history as primarily a branch of family history. See, for example, Michael Kammen, ed., *The Past before Us: Contemporary Historical Writing in the United States* (Ithaca, 1980).

Gerda Lerner, "Placing Women in History: Definitions and Challenges" (1974), reprinted in *The Majority Finds Its Past: Placing Women in History* (New York, 1979), pp. 145–49; Carroll Smith-Rosenberg, "The Female World of Love and Ritual: Relations between Women in Nineteenth Century America," *Signs* 1 (1975): 1–30; Natalie Zemon Davis, *Society and Culture in Early Modern France* (Stanford, 1975), p. 127; Joan Kelly, "The Social Relations of the Sexes: Methodological Implications of Women's History," *Signs* 1 (1976): 809–23. "Our goal," Natalie Zemon Davis wrote, "is to understand the significance of the *sexes* of gender groups in the historical past."

21. I am indebted for this shrewd observation to Alice Kessler-Harris; see her contribution to *New Viewpoints in Women's History: Working Papers from the Schlesinger Library 50th Anniversary Conference* (Cambridge, 1994). For her own work in this vein, see Alice Kessler-Harris, "Gender Identity: Rights to Work and the Idea of Economic Citizenship," *Schweizerische Zeitschrift fur Geschichte* 46 (1996): 411–26, and *A Woman's Wage: Historical Meanings and Social Consequences* (Lexington, 1990). See also Elizabeth Faue, *Community of Suffering and Struggle: Women, Men and the Labor Movement in Minneapolis, 1915–1945* (Chapel Hill, 1991). For further reflections on the interaction of concepts of class and race, see Gerda Lerner, "Rethinking the Paradigm," *Why History Matters: Life and Thought* (New York, 1997), pp. 146–98.

22. One sign of this expansion is the growth of new journals, notably *Feminist Studies*, first published in 1972, and *Signs: A Journal of Women in Culture and Society*, founded by Catharine Stimpson and the University of Chicago Press in 1975. By the late 1980s the well-established journals—both disciplinary and interdisciplinary—were insufficient to handle the new scholarship; the *Journal of Women's History* was initiated by Indiana University Press, and a new international journal, *Gender and History*, quickly established itself.

23. See, for example, Carroll Smith-Rosenberg, "The Female World of Love and Ritual"; Blanche Weisen Cook, "Female Support Networks and Political Activism: Lillian Wald, Crystal Eastman, Emma Goldman," *Chrysalis* 3 (1977): 43–61; Nancy F. Cott, *The Bonds of Womanhood: "Woman's Sphere" in New England 1780–1835* (New Haven, 1977); and Carl Degler, *At Odds: Women and the Family in America from the Revolution to the Present* (New York, 1980).

24. For argument on this point, see Ellen DuBois, Mari Jo Buhle, Temma Kaplan, Gerda Lerner, and Carroll Smith-Rosenberg, "Politics and Culture in Women's History: A Symposium," *Feminist Studies* 6 (1980): 26–64. This drift was encouraged by the popularity of Carol Gilligan, *In a Different Voice: Psychological Theory and Women's Development* (Cambridge, Mass., 1982); see comments on Gilligan in Linda K. Kerber et al., "Forum," *Signs* 12 (1986): 304–10.

25. I've discussed this point at some length in "Separate Spheres, Female Worlds, Woman's Place: The Rhetoric of Women's History," *Journal of American History* 75 (1988): 9–39.

26. Mark Carnes, ed., *Meanings for Manhood: Constructions of Masculinity in Victorian America* (Chicago, 1990); Ava Baron, *Work Engendered: Toward a New History of American Labor* (Ithaca, 1991).

27. Gail Bederman, *Manliness and Civilization: A Cultural History of Gender and Race in the United States, 1880–1917* (Chicago, 1995), pp. 4–5.

28. Gerda Lerner, *Black Women in White America* (New York, 1972); Jacqueline Jones, *Labor of Love, Labor of Sorrow: Black Women, Work and the Family from Slavery to the Present* (New York, 1985); Deborah Gray White, *Ar'n't I a Woman? Female Slaves in the Plantation South* (New York, 1985).

29. Edited at the University of Maryland by a staff headed by Leslie Rowland. The founding editor was Ira Berlin.

30. Victoria Bynum, *Unruly Women: The Politics of Social and Sexual Control in the Old South* (Chapel Hill, 1992); Drew Gilpin Faust, *Mothers of Invention: Women of the Slaveholding South in the American Civil War* (Chapel Hill, 1996); Leslie Schwalm, *"A Hard Fight for We": Women's Transition from Slavery to Freedom in Low Country South Carolina* (Urbana, 1997); Laura Edwards, *Gendered Strife and Confusion: The Politics of Reconstruction* (Urbana, 1997).

31. Darline Clark Hine et al., eds., *Black Women in America: An Historical Encyclopedia* (Brooklyn, 1994).

32. Gayle Rubin, "The Traffic in Women: Notes on the 'Political Economy' of Sex," in Rayna Reiter, ed., *Toward an Anthropology of Women* (New York, 1975), pp. 157–210; Lisa Duggan, "Introduction," in Duggan and Nan D. Hunter, *Sex Wars: Sexual Dissent and Political Culture* (New York, 1995), p. 5.

33. *Radical History Review*, no. 20 (1979): 60–65.

34. Judith Butler, "Contingent Foundations: Feminism and the Question of "Postmodernism," in *Feminists Theorize the Political*, ed. Judith Butler and Joan W. Scott (New York, 1992), p. 17; Butler, *Gender Trouble: Feminism and the Subversion of Identity* (New York, 1990) p. 141. For recent discussion of these issues, see "More Gender Trouble: Feminism Meets Queer Theory," special issue of *differences: A Journal of Feminist Cultural Studies* 6 (summer–fall 1994).

35. Atina Grossmann, "Abortion and Economic Crisis: The 1931 Campaign against Paragraph 218," in *When Biology Became Destiny: Women in Weimar and Nazi Germany* (New York, 1984), pp. 66–86.

36. Jane De Hart, "Gender on the Right: Meanings Behind the Existential Scream," *Gender and History* 3 (1991): 248.

37. Linda Gordon, "On 'Difference,'" *Genders*, no. 10 (1991): 91–111. For her own work on the marginalization of a group marked as "different," see Linda Gordon, *Pitied but Not Entitled: Single Mothers and the History of Welfare, 1890–1935* (New York, 1994).

38. On this, see Gordon, "On 'Difference,' " and also Elsa Barkley Brown, "'What Has Happened Here': The Politics of Difference in Women's History and Feminist Politics," *Feminist Studies* 18 (1992): 295–312.

39. Henry Abelove, "The Queering of Lesbian/Gay History," *Radical History Review*, no. 62 (1995): 44–57; Donna Penn, "Queer: Theorizing Politics and History," ibid., 24–42; Elizabeth Young, "Confederate Counterfeit: The Case of the Cross-Dressed Civil War Soldier," in *Passing and the Fictions of Identity*, ed. Elaine K. Ginsberg (Durham, 1996) pp. 181–217; Bernice Hausman, *Changing Sex: Transsexualism, Technology and the Idea of Gender* (Durham, 1996).

40. The basic response to Habermas on this issue is by the philosopher Nancy Fraser: "Rethinking the Public Sphere: A Contribution to the Critique of Actually Existing Democracy," in Craig Calhoun, ed., *Habermas and the Public Sphere* (Cambridge, Mass., 1992), pp. 109–42. See also Mary Ryan's essay in the same volume, "Gender and Public Access: Women's Politics in Nineteenth-Century America," pp. 259–88. For an eloquent narrative of the ways in which women of different religiosities shaped their lives, see Natalie Zemon Davis, *Women on the Margins: Three Seventeenth-Century Lives* (Cambridge, Mass., 1995).

41. Examples: intellectual history, Charles Capper, *Margaret Fuller: An American Romantic Life* (New York, 1992); crime, Judith Walkowitz, *City of Dreadful Delight: Narratives of Sexual Danger in Late-Victorian London* (Chicago, 1992); violence, Richard Maxwell Brown, *No Duty to Retreat* (New York, 1991); diplomatic history, symposium in winter 1994 issue of *Diplomatic History*; social security systems, Gordon, *Pitied But Not Entitled*, and Susan Pedersen, *Family, Dependence, and the Origins of the Welfare State: Britain and France 1914–1945* (Cambridge, 1993); urban history, Mary Ryan, *Women in Public: Between Banners and Ballots 1825–1880* (Baltimore, 1990); sweatshops, Eileen Boris, "'A Man's Dwelling House Is His Castle': Tenement House Cigarmaking and the Judicial Imperative," in Baron, ed., *Work Engendered*; war, Margaret Higgonet et al., eds., *Behind the Lines: Gender and the Two World Wars* (New Haven, 1987).

Unlikely subjects turn out to be deeply gendered, e.g., tort law (Barbara Welke, "Gendered Journeys," unpublished Ph.D. dissertation, University of Chicago, 1995); criticism of the Book of the Month Club (Janice Radway, "On the Gender of the Middlebrow Consumer and the Threat of the Culturally Fraudulent Female," *South Atlantic Quarterly*, fall 1994); the displays in natural history museums (Donna Haraway, *Primate Visions: Gender, Race and Nature in the World of Modern Science*, New York, 1989, chap. 1, pp. 20–64); civil defense (Laura McEnaney, "He-Men and Christian Mothers: The America First Movement and the Gendered Meanings of Patriotism and Isolationism" *Diplomatic History* 18 [1994]: 47–57).

42. Carole Pateman, *The Sexual Contract* (Stanford, 1988), pp. 2–3.

43. Miscegenation statutes in the United States, which were not declared unconstitutional until 1966, made it illegal for people of European descent to marry African-Americans, Native Americans, or Asians. These statutes not only, as Nancy Cott has put it, outlined "a map of marriage" but also placed severe constraints on the descent of property. Peggy Pascoe's work in progress makes clear that the management of what counted as legal marriage also "guarded the junction between marriage and economic privilege." For Cott, see "Giving Character to Our Whole Civil Polity: Marriage and the Public Order in the Late Nineteenth Century," in Kerber, Kessler-Harris, and Sklar, eds., *U.S. History as Women's History*, pp. 107–21; for Pascoe, see "Race, Gender and the Privileges of Property: On the Significance of Miscegenation Law in United States History," in *New Viewpoints in Women's History*, p. 103. The practices of law enforcers also define the boundaries of gender: for example, for many years the rumor persisted in urban areas of the United States that it was not cross-dressing unless three garments identified with the opposite sex were worn. See Elizabeth Lapovsky Kennedy and Madeline D. Davis, *Boots of Leather, Slippers of Gold: The History of a Lesbian Community* (New York, 1993) pp. 411–12, n. 29.

44. Glenda Gilmore, "'We Can Go Where You Cannot Afford to Go': Intersections of Gender and Race in New South Political Praxis," in *New Viewpoints in Women's History*, p. 159.

45. Martha C. Howell, "Citizenship and Gender: Women's Political Status in Northern Medieval Cities," in *Women and Power in the Middle Ages*, ed. Mary Erler and Maryanne Kowaleski (Athens, Ga., 1988), pp. 37–60; Sarah Hanley, "Social Sites of Political Practice in France: Lawsuits, Civil Rights and the Separation of Powers in Domestic and State

Government, 1500–1800," *Americas Historical Review* 102 (1977): 27–52; Marilyn Lake, "The Inviolable Woman: Feminist Conceptions of Citizenship in Australia, 1900–1945," *Gender and History* 8 (1996): 197–211; Steve J. Stern, *The Secret History of Gender: Women, Men and Power in Late Colonial Mexico* (Chapel Hill, 1995); Glenda Gilmore, *Gender and Jim Crow: Women and the Politics of White Supremacy in North Carolina, 1896–1920* (University of North Carolina Press, 1996).

46. Lizabeth Cohen, "From Town Center to Shopping Center: The Reconfiguration of Community Marketplaces in Postwar America," *American Historical Review* 101 (1996): 1073 ff.; Meyerowitz, *Not June Cleaver.* See also Victoria de Grazia, ed., *The Sex of Things: Gender and Consumption in Historical Perspective* (Berkeley, 1996).

47. Victoria de Grazia, *How Fascism Ruled Women: Italy, 1922–1945* (Berkeley, 1992), pp. 3, 6.

48. Laura Engelstein, *The Keys to Happiness: Sex and the Search for Modernity in Fin-de-Siècle Russia* (Ithaca, 1992).

49. Linda Gordon, *Heroes of Their Own Lives: The Politics and History of Family Violence, Boston, 1880–1960* (New York, 1988).

50. Donna Guy, *Sex and Danger in Buenos Aires: Prostitution, Family and Nation in Argentina* (Lincoln, 1991).

51. Beth Bailey and David Farber, *The First Strange Place: The Alchemy of Race and Sex in World War II Hawaii* (New York, 1992).

52. Elsa Barkley Brown, "Negotiating and Transforming the Public Sphere: African American Political Life in the Transition from Slavery to Freedom," *Public Culture* 7 (1994): 107–46.

53. Mary P. Ryan, *Civic Wars: Democracy and Public Life in the American City during the Nineteenth Century* (Berkeley, 1997), p. 296.

54. George Chauncey, *Gay New York: Gender, Urban Culture and the Making of the Gay Male World 1890–1940* (New York, 1994). See also Angus McLaren, *The Trials of Masculinity: Policing Sexual Boundaries 1870–1930* (Chicago, 1997).

55. Antoinette Burton, "Remapping Colonial Culture: Feminist Perspectives," *Radical History Review,* no. 66 (1996): 220–28, and *Burdens of History: British Feminists, Indian Women, and Imperial Culture, 1865–1959* (Chapel Hill, 1994). See also Lata Mani, "Contentious Traditions: The Debate on Sati in Colonial India," *Cultural Critique* 7 (1987): 119–56; and Mrinalini Sinha, *Colonial Masculinity: The 'Manly Englishman' and the 'Effeminate Bengali' in the Late Nineteenth Century* (Manchester, 1995). For a fine example of a feminist subaltern approach, see Florencia E. Mallon, "The Promise and Dilemma of Subaltern Studies: Perspectives from Latin American History," *American Historical Review* 99 (1994): 1491–1515. Especially instructive are two special issues of *Gender and History*: "On Gender, Nationalisms and National Identities" 5 (summer 1993), and "Gendered Colonialisms in African History" 8 (November 1996).

56. Carroll Smith-Rosenberg, "Dis-Covering the Subject of the 'Great Constitutional Discussion,' 1786–1789," *Journal of American History* 79 (1992): 841–73.

57. Lynn Hunt, *The Family Romance of the French Revolution* (Berkeley, 1992).

58. Leora Auslander, *Taste and Power: Furnishing Modern France* (Berkeley, 1996), pp. 174, 408–10.

59. Leila Rupp, *Worlds of Women: The Making of an International Women's Movement* (Princeton, N.J., 1997).

Economic History and the Cliometric Revolution

NAOMI R. LAMOREAUX

DURING THE 1960s there was a sharp increase in interest within the American historical profession in borrowing theory and analytical techniques from the social sciences. In part, the motivation for this change was a complementary surge of interest in the experience of "common" people. Because ordinary men and women typically did not leave written accounts of their lives, historians had to learn to extract useful information from dry quantitative sources like vital records and census returns, and they turned to the social sciences for guidance. American historians were by no means unique in this kind of borrowing; indeed, they often consciously followed in the footsteps of their Annalist colleagues in France and of historical demographers in England. More than scholars in Europe, however, historians in the United States turned to the social sciences for a second reason as well—to make the study of the past more systematic and objective, less subject to ideological contamination or bias. As political historian Lee Benson complained, the "profusion of varying interpretations" of American history owed more than anything else to the "near-universal dependence upon impressionistic techniques and data." He called for historians to formulate "potentially verifiable hypotheses" and engage in the quantitative research needed to test them.[1]

Nowhere was this search for rigor pushed further in the 1960s than in the field of economic history. There a small group of economists launched a veritable revolution, seizing control of the discipline's organizations and using them to build a coherent and uniquely American body of scholarship based on the application of economic theory and econometric techniques to the study of the past.[2] The new economic historians, or cliometricians as they quickly became known, saw their mission as improving the practice of history by making the articulation of clear, testable hypotheses central to scholarly inquiry. Robert W. Fogel, who received the Nobel Prize in economics for his role in the cliometrics revolution, claimed that traditional economic history was "permeated with untested covert models and subliminal mathematical assumptions." He was joined by Douglass C. North, the other recipient of the prize, in arguing that economic history should "meet of necessity the same set of standards that we attempt to impose by the use of scientific methods in economics."[3]

Although the cliometric revolution initially attracted an enormous amount of attention in the United States and abroad, and in both the disciplines of economics and history, over the long term its impact has been relatively limited. Until very recently, new economic historians have had few imitators abroad, whereas at home they have become increasingly isolated from the intellectual mainstream in both the economics and historical professions. The aim of this essay is to trace the history of the movement and explore the reasons for its relative lack of influence. Although my narrative will focus as a matter of course on developments specific to economic history, the main outlines of the story can be generalized to other historical fields. The increasing availability of funds for higher education and research, especially in the third quarter of the twentieth century, made it possible for energetic scholars in the United States to build organizations that promoted their particular intellectual visions. Although the resulting associations and journals fulfilled the expectations of their founders by providing support for the new kinds of scholarship they were advancing, these organizations also divided the profession in ways that, in the end, imposed high intellectual costs. The current fragmentation of the American historical profession is the unhappy result.

ECONOMIC HISTORY BEFORE CLIOMETRICS

Economic history as a subject in its own right emerged out of the critique of classical economics posed by members of the (largely German) school of historical economics. Members of this school deplored the deductive methods of modern economics, proposing instead an inductive approach whereby scholars would infer the laws and principles of economic life through careful historical study. Economic history, as opposed to historical economics, was actually a compromise position worked out in Britain during the late nineteenth century, at the same time as marginalists like Alfred Marshall were reformulating classical economics. The compromise in effect recognized the superiority of neoclassical economics for the study of economic choices within a given institutional setting, but left to economic history the study of changes in that setting over time.[4]

The field of economic history had its formal beginning in the United States in 1892 when Harvard created a chair in economic history and appointed British scholar William J. Ashley to fill it.[5] A number of other universities followed Harvard's lead and established similar chairs during the last decade of the nineteenth century. But though these chairs were situated within the discipline of economics, economic history never gained a solid beachhead in that field. Guy S. Callender complained in 1913 that economists were so absorbed with current events that "topics in economic history found no place upon their programme."[6] His statement was something of an exaggeration. Most economics departments included at least one economic historian on their faculties, and most required their graduate students to take courses in the field. Nonetheless, economic history clearly occupied a peripheral position in the discipline. During the interwar period, the annual meetings of the American Economic Association rarely included papers on economic history, but instead relegated practitioners to a "roundtable" discussion each year. Nor did the leading journals (the *American Economic Review*, the *Journal of Political Economy*, and the *Quarterly Journal of Economics*) publish much economic history. Even if one defines the subject matter of the field broadly to include articles on current topics that contain statistical series going back at least twenty years, manuscripts in economic history accounted for only 10 to 15 percent of the articles in the journals. Moreover, the vast majority of the contributions included in this count dealt with very recent topics and contemporary policy issues—not with history proper.[7]

The position of economic history within the historical profession was similarly marginal, but for different reasons. In the same article in which Callender complained about economists' lack of interest in economic history, he commented favorably on developments within the historical profession: "No one who attended the meeting of the American Historical Association in Boston last winter could fail to be impressed by the interest which its members manifested in the economic side of history."[8] Callender was referring to the newfound preoccupation of Charles Beard and other so-called progressive historians with economic self-interest as a force in historical development. But progressive historians were primarily interested in the connection between economic interests and political events; they were relatively uninterested in studying the economy in its own right. Moreover, there were important ideological differences between the two groups of scholars. Progressive historians typically focused on the negative, exploitative aspects of capitalism, whereas economic historians were more likely to appreciate the material gains that economic development brought and to seek to understand the institutional foundations of that improvement. Consequently, economic history never really found a comfortable home in history departments either.[9]

Despite the lack of a disciplinary home, economic history expanded in the United States during the interwar period and developed its own debates and controversies. Members of the first generation of economic historians—Ashley is a good example—had been trained mainly in constitutional, legal, and political history. Research along these lines continued, but there was also a new effort to expand the use of quantitative economic analysis in historical study. British scholar J. H. Clapham was an important leader of the movement, but in the United States this view was pushed even further by scholars such as Abbott Payson Usher, who argued for a more explicit use of statistics in historical research. Others whose work acquired a quantitative dimension included Wesley Mitchell, who pioneered the study of business cycles, Leland Jenks, who analyzed the migration of British capital to the United States in the nineteenth century, Norman J. Silberling, whose *Dynamics of Business: An Analysis of Trends, Cycles, and Time Relationships in American Activity Since 1700* was, after many years of effort, finally published in 1943, and Arthur D. Gayer, Walt W. Rostow, and Anna Jacobson Schwartz, who launched a study of the British economy comparable to Silberling's.[10] New and existing organizations provided critical financial support. The Rockefeller Foundation granted $250,000 to form an International Committee to study changes in price levels over time. Edwin F. Gay and Wesley Mitchell jointly organized and headed the National Bureau of Economic

Research, whose founding principle was the belief that research in economic history, particularly the careful collecting of long-term quantitative data sets, provided a vital foundation for policy making. The newly created Commission on Recent Economic Changes, the Commission on Recent Social Trends, and the Social Science Research Council had similar motivations.[11]

Despite this activity, the American branch of the field was still largely dependent on European scholarship for ideas and support. Many of the nation's early practitioners had been trained abroad. William J. Ashley, the first occupant of Harvard's chair in economic history, was, of course, English. Edwin F. Gay, Ashley's successor and a leader of the field in the interwar period, had studied in Germany. These men, and others like them, introduced American scholars to German stage theories of economic development and to the English idea that the modern era of economic growth had originated in a "take-off" which Arnold Toynbee called the "industrial revolution." The interwar generation of quantifiers were similarly inspired by the work of Clapham and also by the founders of the Annales school on the Continent.[12] Indeed, the prestige of European scholarship was so pronounced that, as late as 1940, one major scholar (quoting another prominent economic historian) was able to declare that "American economic history . . . has been less interesting to read than European economic history."[13]

One could argue, in fact, that the dominance of European scholarship delayed the formation of a disciplinary apparatus in the United States. Many American scholars were members of the Economic History Society, which was organized in Britain in 1926, and they contributed actively to that society's *Economic History Review*. Although some scholars, especially those working on American topics, began to argue in the 1930s that the United States should have its own professional organization and journal, others thought that the resulting fragmentation would weaken the discipline, and this position easily carried the day during the Great Depression, when resources for new academic initiatives were scarce.[14]

Ultimately, however, the outbreak of war in Europe provided the impetus for change. As Herbert Heaton later explained, "If research, monographs, and periodicals were doomed to be blacked out in Europe, the lights must burn more brightly in America; and if old lamps were not to be re-lit, new ones must be made."[15] The Economic History Association was the product of two separate initiatives in 1939—one by historians who took the opportunity afforded by the American Historical Association (AHA) meeting of that year to organize an Industrial History Society, the other by economists associated with the American Economic Association (AEA). The latter group, whose executive committee consisted of Arthur H. Cole, Herbert Heaton, Earl J. Hamilton, and Anne Bezanson, proved the more energetic. They polled the membership of the two larger associations (getting more than 400 positive responses to 500 mailings) and arranged for joint meetings of the proposed Economic History Association with both the AHA and AEA in 1940, at which gatherings the new organization was ratified. The Economic History Association claimed 361 members at its first meeting.[16]

The formation of an American association was accompanied by a burst of related activity involving many of the same leading scholars. One of the most important results was the creation of the Committee for Research in Economic History (CREH) in the winter of 1940–41 with the support of the Rockefeller Foundation.[17] The committee determined to play an active role in the profession by channeling research funds to projects it commissioned. Its first major effort was to fund a series of studies on the role of government in American economic development, a project that generated Oscar Handlin and Mary Flug Handlin's *Commonwealth: A Study of the Role of Government in the American Economy: Massachusetts, 1774–1861* (New York University Press, 1947) and Louis Hartz's *Economic Policy and Democratic Thought: Pennsylvania, 1776–1860* (Harvard University Press, 1948). The committee also became the locus of planning for a new Research Center in Entrepreneurial History, which was founded, again with Rockefeller seed money, at Harvard in 1948. The center became a magnet for scholars interested in understanding the sources of entrepreneurship and why certain societies are more innovative than others.[18]

Although the scholars who organized both the Economic History Association and the Committee for Research in Economic History were mainly economists, the studies sponsored by the latter group in particular brought in a wide range of other participants and moved the discipline away from its original location in economics departments. The project on the role of government in the economy attracted historians like the Handlins and political scientists like Hartz, who had the training and inclination to delve minutely into the policy debates of the early nineteenth century. The effect of the Research Center in Entrepreneurial History was even more profound. Although many of the scholars at the center were economists, others felt that neoclassical theory had little to contribute to the study of entrepreneurship. After an active search for a usable alternative, they turned to Parsonian sociology instead. The work of some of the most important scholars associated with the center—good examples are David Landes, Thomas Cochran, and Alfred D. Chandler, Jr.—consistently employed concepts and addressed debates at the heart of this sociological literature, even when they did not make extensive use of its rather arcane vocabulary and categories of analysis.[19] As a result, then, of the committee's activities, by the mid 1950s—that is, by the eve of the cliometric revolution—many of the field's most active practitioners no longer retained close intellectual ties to the discipline of economics.

The Cliometric Revolution

The cliometric revolution would have been impossible without this period of organization building, for otherwise there would have been nothing for the "Young Turks" who launched the movement to take over. It is also difficult to imagine the revolution occurring without the increased flow of research funds, from both governmental and private sources, that occurred in the post-Sputnik period. Moneys were suddenly available to support initiatives in the hard social sciences, and the early cliometricians made effective use of them. Lance Davis, Jonathan R. T. Hughes, and Duncan McDougall, all young faculty members at

Purdue, took the lead and secured funding in 1960 for a series of cliometrics conferences held annually at that institution for the next nine years. After the three original organizers left Purdue, the conference moved to the University of Wisconsin, then to the University of Chicago, and then to other locations. In 1985 participants in a "World Congress" held at Northwestern University ratified the creation of a permanent association, the Cliometric Society, to promote econometric history. The society continues to hold annual meetings funded by the National Science Foundation.[20]

The first few Purdue meetings were extraordinarily important in forging cliometricians into a cohesive group. The meetings quickly became known for both their feisty criticism and their camaraderie. As Jonathan Hughes later recollected, at Purdue "all the best parties took place when the economic historians were in town. . . . [I]t was New Year's Eve for several days."[21] Fogel, who was just beginning his first teaching appointment (and still writing his dissertation) when he attended the first (1960) meeting, recalled the "tremendous excitement and exhilaration on the part of everybody" who was present.[22] According to Robert Gallman, it was these events that created "a special cliometrics group with a sense of identity." The meetings transformed his career: "Before I went to the first Purdue meeting, I thought of myself as a development economist of a Kuznetsian variety." But his self-definition changed after attending a couple of the "clio" sessions: "Discovering that there was a group of scholars who were interested in the full range of issues that had captured my imagination and who were at work on really creative, useful research along these lines was the most exciting discovery of my scholarly career."[23] In actuality, the participants already had much in common. Most had been heavily influenced by the growth economics literature associated with Simon Kuznets, and many had been Kuznets's students.[24] But the Purdue meetings created a heightened "sense of intellectual communion," to use William Parker's phrase, that carried over into other projects—for example, the multiauthor textbook *American Economic Growth: An Economist's History of the United States*, published by Harper & Row in 1972. By the time of that collaboration, Parker felt "we really were quite a little group."[25]

Like all revolutionaries, the cliometricians advanced a narrative of their origins that denigrated the achievements of their predecessors and exaggerated the intellectual distance they had come. In a 1963 communication published in the *American Economic Review* Douglass C. North proclaimed that "a revolution is taking place in economic history in the United States" and went on to justify in sweeping terms the overthrow of the old regime. "Even a cursory examination of accepted 'truths' of U.S. economic history suggests," he asserted, "that many of them are inconsistent with elementary economic analysis and have never been subjected to—and would not survive—testing with statistical data."[26] Two years later he elaborated the point, summarizing the "deficiencies of economic history" as previously practiced:

(1) Vast areas of economic history have not been treated at all; that is, treated in the sense that economic theory and statistics have been used to examine the past.

(2) Many writings in economic history are loaded with statements which have economic implications and imply causal relationships which are not only not supported in the research but which run counter to basic economic propositions. In fact, in most such cases, the author appears to be completely unaware of these implications. (3) Even more conspicuous is the character of the evidence advanced to support propositions. In good part it consists of a mishmash of quotations and oddly assorted statistics which do not provide any support or test for the propositions developed. (4) A good deal of economic history draws broad welfare conclusions which are by no stretch of the imagination warranted from the evidence cited. In fact, a general characteristic of economic history is that the treatment of propositions with broad welfare implications is typically undertaken without even a token acquaintance with welfare economics.[27]

Both North and Fogel showed their contempt for earlier work by playing "games" in their classes. North would ask his students to develop explicit models to capture the arguments made by traditional economic historians, and claimed that "even by plugging into each model the most favorable possible implicit assumptions, most of the resultant models turn out either to be internally inconsistent or to run counter to the most fundamental propositions in economics."[28] Fogel would challenge his students "to pick any page at random from whatever history book they had at hand. The odds were . . . that there'd be either an explicit or implicit quantitative statement that needed to be measured." Fogel later claimed that "the challenge was often taken up and I was never shown up."[29]

Most of the early leaders have since moderated their views, and indeed, more than a third of a century after the fact, the elements of continuity between the "old" economic history and the "new" appear much more important than they undoubtedly did to contemporaries. For example, one of the hallmarks of cliometrics was the rigorous quantitative testing of hypotheses, but, as we have seen, the interwar generation of economic historians had already moved a long way in this direction. Paraphrasing Clapham, Herbert Heaton complained at the time of the founding of the Economic History Association that the field "in its early stages . . . [had] suffered from an overdose of generalizations based on scanty data." By contrast, he claimed, the "urge . . . to answer such questions as How much? How many? How quickly? or How representative? is perhaps the outstanding characteristic of our generation."[30] Similarly, E. A. J. Johnson, first editor of the *Journal of Economic History*, used the bully pulpit associated with his position to call for more explicit use of economic theory in historical work and urged economic historians to use theory as a defense against the "fascination of antiquarian details."[31]

John Meyer, recalling the reaction to his and Alfred Conrad's controversial "The Economics of Slavery in the Antebellum South," presented in 1957 at a joint meeting of the Economic History Association and the Conference on Research in Income and Wealth, cautioned that "it's easy to overestimate the hostility of it. The hostility was fairly limited. Most [of the old economic historians] were really quite open-minded and responsive."[32] As Robert Gallman recalled that meeting and another joint undertaking the next year, there was no "general division between cliometricians and traditionalists," and several of the latter gave "thoughtful and friendly reviews" of cliometric papers.[33] Certainly, some of the leading members of the profession actively encouraged the young cliometricians. Arthur Cole offered the position of director of the Research Center in Entrepreneurial History to Douglass North in 1954, and tapped John Meyer for the role of acting editor of *Explorations in Entrepreneurial History* (the journal started by the Research Center) in 1957. In 1959 Frederick C. Lane put North on the council that replaced the Committee on Research in Economic History, and the traditional economic historians who constituted the board of trustees of the Economic History Association chose North and William Parker to be coeditors of the *Journal of Economic History* in 1960.[34]

There is no doubt, however, that others were much less tolerant of the new work. Lance Davis later recalled, "It certainly was difficult to get quantitative work published; and I had my share of losing bouts with George Rogers Taylor," then editor of the *Journal of Economic History*.[35] Fogel has similarly claimed that journals "initially refused to accept articles with complex tables, and even after such articles began to be accepted, equations were forbidden."[36] At a conference at the Hagley Museum and Library, Fritz Redlich ranted to Gallman about "that madman Fogel," who "plans to build canals across the Appalachian Mountains."[37] Redlich was not alone in his view of Fogel's work, and after North and Parker began publishing cliometric work in the *Journal of Economic History*— particularly a Fogel article on railroads—several of the trustees of the Economic History Association moved to get them fired. Parker appeared before the trustees to explain the editors' decisions, and the outcome, as North recollected later, was "we got impeached but we didn't get fired; finally, they went back and agreed to continue us, even though with some reluctance on quite a number of the trustees' parts."[38]

Claudia Goldin has argued that the opposition of traditional economic historians to the new economic history arose in large measure because the conclusions of early cliometric work ran counter to orthodoxy. As she put it, "there was already a huge fossilized stock of accepted wisdom concerning major projects, figures, and events of the past," and as a result, cliometrics inevitably involved "a major challenge to an entire field."[39] Such a view, however, overstates the coherence of the discipline of economic history before cliometrics—divisions between quantifiers and institutionalists went back at least as far as Clapham and Usher's interwar salvos.[40] In addition, much of the conventional wisdom that cliometricians attacked was not in fact the work of economic historians but instead of progressives and other mainstream historians. One of the primary targets of Peter Temin's *The Jacksonian Economy*, for example, was Arthur Schlesinger, Jr.'s, *Age of Jackson*.[41] Similarly, it was the progressive view of the Populists that North critiqued in *Growth and Welfare in the America Past*.[42] Moreover, even when cliometricians clearly targeted the work of older economic historians, there were often other traditionalists who held views comparable to their own. For example, though the "axiom" of indispensability that Fogel attacked in *Railroads and American Economic Growth* could be attributed to W. W. Rostow and Leland Jenks, contrary views (to which Fogel himself was intellectually indebted) had been promoted by earlier scholars such as Kent T. Healy and Carter Goodrich.[43]

Historians like Redlich were less enraged by Fogel's attack on the conventional wisdom than they were by his method—in particular, his notion of the counter-factual.[44] Fogel argued that anyone who asserted the indispensability of the rail-road to American economic development was implicitly rejecting the hypothesis that the American economy could have attained essentially the same level of economic well-being in the absence of this particular transportation innovation. His aim was to test the counterfactual hypothesis explicitly by calculating the social savings of the railroad over alternative means of transportation that already existed or alternatively could have been built. To Redlich, this was a wrong-headed exercise. Fogel was investigating "what would have happened in the event that something else had happened which . . . *could* not have happened." In his view, there was a logic, a direction, to technological change: "Once the atmo-spheric engine had been developed into an efficient steam engine and the steam engine had successfully been put into boats, . . . it was only a question of when the steam engine would be put on wheels, particularly as the railroad minus locomotive had existed for a long time." Fogel was not contesting the idea that cheap transportation was necessary for the economic development of the United States; so it was a rather silly exercise, Redlich thought, to question the impor-tance of the particular form of cheap transportation that technological logic had produced.[45]

Other historians accepted the validity of Fogel's notion of the counterfactual hypothesis, but looked askance at the comparative static methodology he used to test it. What Fogel did, in effect, was compare the costs of shipping various goods by railroad and water in 1890, after making some clever adjustments for the greater speed and safety of shipment by rail. As Fogel himself admitted, the calcu-lation ignored possible dynamic consequences of the innovation: "the model [was] not designed to deal with other important issues such as the effect of trans-portation improvements on the spatial location of economic activity, induced changes in the industrial mix of products . . ., induced changes in the aggregate savings rate, and possible effects on either the rate of technological change in various industries or on the overall supplies of inputs."[46] Yet it was changes like these that the historians who rallied to reassert the railroads' role in American economic development thought were important. Reviewing Fogel's book, for ex-ample, Louis Hacker questioned whether water transportation rates would have declined as dramatically as they actually did in the absence of the railroad over-building: "If . . . the bitter struggle for markets of the railroad promoters had not occurred through building and overbuilding, would water rates have gone down so sharply?" He then moved on to bigger issues. "Only railroads," he suggested, "could carry swiftly public supplies and personnel (soldiers) into and across the vast unsettled country. . . . [H]ow could the continental United States have be-come a single, unified nation?"[47]

Perhaps more important, the debate over Fogel's work highlighted real and important differences in approach between the old and new economic historians that were obscured by all the rhetoric about formal testing of hypotheses. Although Redlich himself was not theoretically oriented, most of the historians at the Harvard Research Center were. Their starting point was Joseph Schumpeter's concept of entrepreneurship as a creative act that in discontinuous fashion altered—shifted outward—the economy's production possibility frontier.[48] Entrepreneurship was important to study, they argued, because these discontinuous creative acts were the key to greater social well-being. As already discussed, many of them found conventional neoclassical price theory to be of limited utility in this endeavor, and they turned instead to role theory and other sociological models of human behavior in order to understand what motivated entrepreneurs. By contrast, Fogel and other new economic historians subscribed to the neoclassical view that technological innovation was induced by changes in relative prices—that is, by market-driven opportunities for profit. Thus Fogel not only postulated that the canal system would have (and could have) expanded to meet the demand for transportation services; he also raised the possibility that automobiles would have been developed earlier in the absence of railroads. Inventors had been experimenting with steam-powered carriages in the 1820s, and the theory of both the internal combustion and diesel engines had been published by 1824. As Fogel pointed out, "The axiom of indispensability proceeds on the implicit and unverified assumption that the success of railroads did not choke off the search for other solutions to the problem of overland transportation."[49]

Other leading cliometricians shared Fogel's view that technological innovation was largely a response to demand-side stimuli. As William Parker later explained, a good part of "what the new economic history is about . . . is a gigantic test of the hypothesis of economic rationality. . . . There is not much room here for good and bad entrepreneurs, leaders and followers."[50] Despite his position as editor of *Explorations in Entrepreneurial History*, John Meyer was, to use his own recent characterization, "very skeptical of the importance of any intangible, such as entrepreneurship" and committed "some of that skepticism to paper."[51] Similarly, Douglass North explicitly downgraded the role of the entrepreneur in his *Economic Growth of the United States*, arguing instead "that productivity changes stemming from technological innovations are, in part at least, a nearly automatic response to successful expansion of industries in an acquisitive society under competitive market conditions." Although North qualified his generalization by emphasizing its application to "economies which: (1) followed in the process of industrial development, and (2) were acquisitively oriented under competitive market conditions," the central point was clear. He saw no reason to devote time or resources to studying the entrepreneurial function in American business. For example, though the cotton gin was in North's view "unquestionably the most significant invention during the years between 1790 and 1860," one could learn little by studying Eli Whitney. The cotton gin was the product of a "concerted search" for a solution to the South's economic dilemma "that the demand for its traditional staples was no longer increasing and its heavy capital investment was in slaves." If Whitney had not invented it, someone else would have.[52]

What the new economic historians did, in a nutshell, was to upset the long-standing division of labor between economics and economic history—a division of labor that relegated marginalist (neoclassical) economics to the study of short-term phenomena.[53] Not all traditional economic historians had been atheoretical; on the contrary, many of them had devoted their lives to studying theory and developing systematic ways of understanding the long-term changes with which they concerned themselves. They had simply turned to other bodies of theory besides neoclassical economics for their models. By contrast, cliometricians consciously aimed to expand the domain of neoclassical economics by emphasizing the pervasiveness of the market processes that this brand of theory was so well suited to analyze. They even formulated a new theory of institutional change in which rational economic actors would organize to secure change if the benefits promised to outweigh the costs of the organizational effort.[54]

In subsequent years, more and more cliometricians would become dissatisfied with this expansive approach and again proclaim the limitations of neoclassical economics for the study of institutional change. North dubbed the earliest of these critics the "Harvard Wing" because many members of the group had studied with Alexander Gerschenkron at that institution. By the early 1970s, however, North himself had joined their ranks. As he stated in his 1974 address as president of the Economic History Association, "Neo-classical economic theory has two major shortcomings for the economic historian. One, it was not designed to explain long-run economic change; and two, even within the context of the question it was designed to answer, it provides quite limited answers since it is immediately relevant to a world of perfect markets."[55] Reviewing two decades later the achievements of cliometrics, North admitted, "What we did then was impressive enough to be called a revolution, but the failure to go on to deal with the two major shortcomings of neoclassical theory applied to history have aborted the revolution."[56] From the early seventies on, North for the most part abandoned cliometric work and devoted his energies to developing a general theory of institutional change that would transcend the limits of neoclassical economics.[57]

Boundaries of Cliometric Influence

The iconoclasm of the cliometricians attracted new practitioners to the field and inaugurated a period of rapid growth for the Economic History Association. As late as 1959, the association's individual members numbered 476, only 32 percent more than in 1941. By 1965, however, the number had grown to more than 800.[58] Most of the new members were economists, and the association took on an increasingly cliometric tone. As Robert Whaples's quantitative analysis of the *Journal of Economic History* has shown, the cliometric revolution was accompanied by a dramatic shift in the subject matter of the journal away from business history, the history of economic thought, and banking, in favor of studies of economic growth, trade, and industrialization. The proportion of the journal devoted to cliometric-type articles also increased—from 10.2 percent in 1956–60 to 42.8 percent in 1966–70 to 71.8 percent in 1971–75.[59] At the same time, the cliometricians gained control of *Explorations in Entrepreneurial History*, which they renamed *Explorations in Economic History* in 1969, and which now defined its target audience to be scholars trained in economics.

While all this was going on, economic historians trained in history increasingly retreated to a new organization called the Business History Conference. The conference had its origin in a series of meetings (the first was at Northwestern in 1954) that brought together economic and business historians who were rebelling against the atheoretical type of scholarship promoted by N. S. B. Gras at the Harvard Business School. The group met twice in 1954, once in 1956, once in 1958, and then yearly thereafter, and in 1971 it transformed itself into a fullfledged professional association with dues, officers, a board of trustees, and a journal (albeit one that published only a single issue a year). Although many of its original members were economists, during the 1970s the conference increasingly provided historians fleeing the cliometric revolution with an intellectual home. To the present day, the Business History Conference is dominated by scholars trained in history, whereas the Economic History Association is controlled by economists; only a small number of scholars attend both meetings.[60]

Outside the United States there was no comparable transformation in the practice of economic history. The overwhelming majority of participants in the Purdue conferences had appointments in American academic institutions, so the movement never produced a sizable cadre of foreign scholars who could go back to their home countries and influence the direction of research there. Instead the spread of cliometrics abroad depended in large measure on its intellectual appeal, which in turn was limited by the perceived narrowness and conservatism of the neoclassical models on which it was based. Latin American economists, for example, were subjecting neoclassical theory to extended critical attack at the very moment that cliometrics was gaining ground in the United States. The result was the rise of dependency theory, whose fundamental tenet that capitalist exchange was the source of underdevelopment in the Third World—that is, that markets do *not* work for the greater good of all—was diametrically opposed to the assumptions of cliometrics.[61] Similarly, as George Grantham has pointed out, cliometricians' emphasis on economic rationality may have limited its appeal in France, where academics typically had more training in philosophy than was common in the United States and where more philosophically sophisticated disciplines like structural anthropology consequently had greater influence. But it is also important to recognize that economic history never had had much of a presence in France—as late as 1960 there was only one chair in the field—and the dominance of the more eclectic Annales school may have stymied its development thereafter.[62] In Germany, the antitheoretical bias that derived from historical economics was a continuing factor inhibiting the spread of cliometric work there. As Richard Tilly put it, "German economic historians, increasingly producing economic history without economics, have been playing Hamlet without the

Prince." He also pointed out that economic historians in Germany had largely transformed themselves into social historians, and that little economic history was actually being written at the time of the cliometric revolution in the United States.[63] In Britain, the situation was somewhat different. The Clapham tradition of empirical research continued strong, but by the time of the cliometric revolution most practitioners were trained as historians rather than as economists and were predisposed to regard cliometric work as narrow. For example, although Peter Mathias recognized the validity of Fogel's call for rigorous testing of hypotheses, including implicit counterfactual ones, he argued that the inevitable narrowing of focus that such a pursuit of rigor required would "paradoxically" strengthen the position of historians like himself who aim "to see things in the round."[64]

This is not to say that cliometrics had no early followers abroad. Roderick Floud proselytized for the new economic history in Britain with modest success, and Maurice Lévy-Leboyer's experiments with econometric techniques stimulated a minor wave of interest in France.[65] Although the immediate impact in both cases was limited, in recent years as American-style neoclassical economics has increasingly spread internationally, so has cliometrics. The second "World Congress" of cliometrics held in Santander, Spain, in 1989 still attracted nearly two-thirds of its attendees from the United States and Canada, but there were thirteen participants from Spain and sixteen others from Western Europe. The growth of interest since then, moreover, has been impressive, and the Cliometric Society now claims forty-one European members, up from six in 1990.[66] The expansion has been particularly marked in Great Britain, where approximately 50 percent of the articles published by the Economic History Review in 1994 could be considered cliometric.[67] French academia has been enlivened by rising new economic historians such as Jean-Michel Chevet, Gilles Postel-Vinay, and Pierre Sicsic, and the University of Munich attracted John Komlos from the United States in order to develop a cliometric presence in Germany. In the mid-1990s, moreover, European cliometricians took steps to organize their own association and scholarly journal.[68]

Ironically, within the United States, the trend in the influence of cliometrics has been just the opposite, with both economists and historians loosing interest in the new economic history. Economists had originally found the cliometric revolution intriguing. The breakdown of the traditional division of labor between economics and economic history awoke their interest in historical topics. In addition, economics was itself undergoing an econometric revolution at the same time, and cliometricians' demonstration of the utility of new techniques for historical research suited the imperialism of the econometricians. By the mid-1970s, however, economics as a discipline had become more theoretical and mathematical in its orientation, and applied work in general suffered a decline in influence and in resources. Because they had to devote a great deal of their training to acquiring historical knowledge and research skills, few economic historians were able to remain at the cutting edge of quantitative work. As a result their studies held less and less interest for econometricians. Compared with other applied fields like labor economics, moreover, research in economic history appeared to have fewer direct policy implications. As a result, economic history increasingly came to be seen as an unaffordable luxury, and departments began to cut positions and eliminate required courses from the curriculum.[69]

There has been a similar loss of interest on the historical side, although for very different reasons. Initially, many mainstream historians—like many of the traditional economic historians in the Economic History Association—regarded the work of cliometricians with guarded interest. Worried about a lack of rigor in historical research, they applauded the attempt to import research methods and theories from the other social sciences. From their perspective, the new economic history was not fundamentally different in thrust from the new social history or the new political history that were flourishing at the same time. Moreover, the assumptions about economic rationality that most cliometricians shared were not seriously at variance with the assumptions about the popular acceptance of capitalism that underpinned consensus history, the dominant intellectual tradition at the time. Because, however, the theories and quantitative techniques employed by economists were more difficult to master than those of the other social sciences, few historians attempted this kind of work themselves. In effect, they abandoned the field to scholars whose training was primarily in economics.[70]

The regard in which many historians initially held cliometric work was undermined, however, by developments within the historical profession during the 1960s, particularly the growth of "bottom up" and "New Left" history. Those who wrote about the "underside" of history started from the premise that economic development had dire consequences for the bulk of the laboring population. They had little sympathy for the idea that the market works for the general good. Similarly, those who wrote history from the New Left perspective focused on exposing ways in which business interests (with the help of government) had manipulated the market for their own ends. Perhaps more important, the attack that historians of both these schools launched against consensus history inevitably undermined faith in historical objectivity, and with it the belief that social science methods could make the research process more rigorous. Neither careful research nor borrowings from social science theory, these scholars claimed, had prevented consensus historians from infusing their work with their own political preferences and class biases. Moreover, consensus historians could respond in kind, accusing their challengers of "present-mindedness" and pursuing a political agenda in their scholarship.[71]

The idea of historical objectivity suffered further assaults with the rise of black and women's history, and it was just when all these new movements were peaking that Robert Fogel and Stanley Engerman came out with *Time on the Cross*.[72] The authors made broad claims for the book's scientific character. Following the formula that Fogel had used so successfully in his railroad study, the book began with a dramatic list of "principal corrections" to the "traditional characterization of the slave economy" that had emerged as a result of the application of "mathematics and statistics in historical analysis."[73] However, the authors' strategy for presenting their findings seemed to belie their claim to the mantel of science.

Time on the Cross was published in two volumes. The first consisted of a summary of the authors' findings, written for maximum popular impact and lacking the scholarly edifice of notes and documentation that other historians would need to begin the scientific process of verification. The authors claimed that such documentation was contained in the second volume, but historians were dismayed to find not only that "the arrangement demand[ed] inordinate time and patience of the reader" but that, in fact, it was "extraordinarily difficult to associate the argument with the proof on which it rest[ed]."[74] Moreover, to many historians the ideological biases of the book appeared to be, if anything, more pronounced in *Time on the Cross* than in other cliometric work. Once again, Fogel and Engerman asserted, systematic hypothesis testing confirmed that the market worked: slave-based agriculture was a profitable, efficient system; economic incentives encouraged planters to provide adequate food, clothing, shelter, and medical care to their slaves, and, as a result, the proportion of the slaves' product expropriated by their masters "was much lower than has generally been presumed"; "it was to the economic interest of planters to encourage the stability of slave families and most of them did so," limiting slave sales largely to whole families or to ages when it would have been "normal" for children to leave home; finally, planters recognized the value of (and used) positive incentives to induce their slaves to labor more intensely, and slaves responded to these carrots with greater effort.[75]

Although most historians found at least some of these claims objectionable, for the most part they were acquiescent in their reviews of the book. How, after all, could they help but be intimidated by Fogel and Engerman's references to hoards of research assistants "searching out and systematically sifting through huge quantities of data" using new "advances in economics, statistics, and applied mathematics, together with the availability of high-speed computers."[76] Fogel and Engerman's fellow cliometricians were not so reticent, however. In a series of meetings and conferences, new economic historians like Paul David, Richard Sutch, Peter Temin, and Gavin Wright mounted a critique that challenged the book on every level—from its philosophical underpinnings to the correctness of its economic theory to the appropriateness of its quantitative tests to its handling of historical data.[77]

The cliometricians offered their critique "as a scientific contribution to the writing of American history"—that is, as an exercise in "replication" that fulfilled the scientific injunction to subject the work of colleagues to the "recognized methodological standards of the discipline"—but many historians drew a very different lesson from the exercise.[78] After watching cliometricians rip the book apart, they concluded that the new economic history was no more or less scientific or objective than any other kind of history. Kenneth Stampp underscored the lessons to be drawn from the debate: "History is not an exact science—not even the 'New Economic History' with its immensely valuable methods of quantification and data analysis. Ultimately the most meticulously weighed and finely measured data, both numerical and literary must be subjectively interpreted by the historian, for historical facts do not speak for themselves."[79]

Some of the critics of *Time on the Cross* feared that the problems they had uncovered in Fogel and Engerman's work would provide "a perfect foil for those
skeptical of efforts to employ techniques and methods of the social sciences in the
reconstruction of the past."[80] Their worry turned out largely to be correct. Historians generally missed the fact that it was precisely Fogel and Engerman's careful
framing of hypotheses and use of quantitative data—and their generous willingness to make their research available to critics—that made it possible for other
economic historians to test their views. They also missed the point that even a
cursory comparison of the literature before and after the *Time on the Cross* debate
shows how much our understanding was advanced by the whole process.[81] Instead, when news of the cliometricians' attack on *Time on the Cross* spread
through the profession, historians tended to throw up their hands and turn their
backs on the discussion. Historical work on slavery was already moving in the
direction of cultural studies, and from this point on historians displayed very
little interest in the economic dimensions of the institution of slavery.

This reaction itself cries out for explanation, however. After all, debates over
interpretation and even substance are staples of historical scholarship, and typically fuel more discussion rather than generate silence. Why in this case were the
consequences so dire for interdisciplinary dialogue? Thomas L. Haskell's assessment of the debate in the pages of the *New York Review of Books* offers important
clues. What bothered Haskell in particular was the contrast between the surface
impression that cliometrics was "an austere and rigorous discipline that mini-
mizes the significance of any statement that cannot be reduced to a clear empirical test" and what he called its "soft, licentious side." This contrast, he believed,
owed "paradoxically" to cliometricians' reliance on mathematical equations. Although this reliance enabled economic historians to give precise expression to
their hypotheses, it also forced them, in the face of a necessarily incomplete
historical record, to estimate missing data by making a variety of assumptions
that ultimately depended on the same kind of intuitive feel for the data as traditional historical research. Moreover, although cliometric methods required that
these assumptions be made explicit, they set no limits on the number of assumptions that could be made or how high they might be piled.[82]

So long as historians had faith that cliometricians' methods were more objective than those of other historians, they had willingly allowed the new economic
historians to specialize in topics for which their training gave them a comparative
advantage and then incorporated the results into their own view of history. The
Time on the Cross debate, however, convinced many historians not only that this
faith had been misplaced but that the mathematical expressions in which many
cliometric findings were couched were particularly misleading. Because they did
not themselves have the knowledge or skills to determine the effect on the models of changing assumptions they found unreasonable, they tended to dismiss the
whole literature as suspect, a reaction that was reinforced by the underlying ideological divisions between cliometricians, on the one hand, and most historians,
on the other. Now, moreover, the negative side of the cliometricians' institution
building became strikingly apparent. Because economic historians had organized

themselves so effectively into a separate subdiscipline, their mainstream colleagues in history had to make a conscious effort to follow developments in the field. After the mid-1970s historians, convinced that cliometrics had little to offer them and increasingly preoccupied with building up their own subdisciplinary organizations, stopped making the effort—stopped reading the *Journal of Economic History* and stopped following developments in the field.

The gulf that resulted between economic history and history proper has clearly been detrimental to scholarship. Not only have the two groups of academics deprived themselves of the benefits of cross-fertilization of ideas, but because practitioners on either side of the divide have failed to keep abreast of developments on the other, they have not upheld the profession's minimal standards of scholarly competence. Because keeping up with the economic history literature required more effort for historians than the reverse did for cliometricians, the negative consequences have been particularly apparent on the historical side. Thus many historians of the United States continue to teach the view of the Great Depression that John Kenneth Galbraith popularized in his 1955 book *The Great Crash*, complacently ignoring the voluminous literature on Federal Reserve monetary policy and the banking crises of the early 1930s that has accumulated since then and seemingly unaware that a powerful new interpretation connects the depth and severity of the depression to adherence to the gold standard.[83] Similarly, most historians seem to be completely unaware that the optimistic consensus about standards of living during the industrial revolution has been seriously challenged by new work on nutrition and mortality stimulated by Fogel.[84] Historians, moreover, continue to evince an often painful naiveté about economic concepts, equating, for example, market behavior with the narrow pursuit of profits and suggesting that the mere existence of markets can somehow force a supply response from unwilling participants.[85]

THE "LINGUISTIC TURN" IN HISTORY AND ECONOMICS

In recent years this gulf has grown even wider as a result of a shift in intellectual fashions in favor of cultural, as opposed to social and economic, history. This shift has effectively redefined historical studies "as the investigation of the contextually situated production and transmission of meaning" and inspired historians to take a "linguistic turn"—that is, to turn to literary theory rather than the social sciences for inspiration and guidance.[86]

Ironically, the discipline of economics has also recently been transformed by a series of theoretical developments that parallels in intriguing ways the emergence of critical theory in the humanities. Abandoning the convenient but unrealistic assumptions of traditional neoclassical theory—in particular the assumption that all economic actors make decisions on the basis of perfect information—economists have begun to reconceptualize the world as a place where information is scarce, imperfect, and costly, where people build institutions in order to cope with problems of imperfect information, where human beings' "bounded rationality" affects their economic decision making, and where economic processes can have multiple outcomes depending on participants' perceptions of each other's actions.[87]

The questions at the heart of this new work—how do economic actors know what (they think) they know, and how does what (they think) they know affect their behavior?—are remarkably similar to those that inform the work of the new cultural historians. But, of course, the theorists who are participating in this intellectual movement are interested, as is their wont, in developing general economic models that capture the new assumptions about information and in exploring the implications of these models under a variety of circumstances. The models they build are highly abstract and mathematical and, to the uninitiated observer, appear to bear little or no connection to actual circumstances, whether current or historical. The purposes of these scholars are thus very different from those of historians, who are more interested in understanding specific historical phenomena. Indeed, the intellectual agendas of the two disciplines appear to be so dissimilar that it might seem doubtful whether, on their own, practitioners could ever come to appreciate, let alone learn anything, from each other's work.

Economic historians are well positioned, however, to bridge the gap, and in recent years there has been an outpouring of work that applies the new economics of information to historical problems. For example, Avner Greif has applied game theoretic models to the problem of overseas trade in the medieval period and to the development of stable political institutions in twelfth- and thirteenth-century Genoa.[88] Margaret Levenstein has researched the accounting techniques adopted by American businesses during the late nineteenth century and explored the ways in which managers decided what information to collect about their enterprises' internal operations and how the kinds of information they collected in turn affected their decision making.[89] Kenneth Snowden has demonstrated that the peculiar information problems inherent in the interregional mortgage market caused lenders to suffer repeated cycles of organizational innovation, overexpansion, and crisis that were finally ended only by the development of federal mortgage guarantees.[90] To give one last example, Peter Temin has argued that the impact of government actions during the Great Depression was determined by the "policy regime" within which people perceived them to occur. Thus open-market purchases by the Federal Reserve Bank had very different macroeconomic effects during Herbert Hoover's presidency than precisely the same actions did under Franklin D. Roosevelt.[91]

All these economic historians are well read in the historical literature, and many of them have done extensive archival research. Their studies are of high quality and should be of great interest to historians working in related areas. Whether, however, it is possible to communicate this relevance over the wall that currently divides economic history from the rest of the historical profession is a matter of serious concern. Several efforts are now under way to encourage interdisciplinary discussion. For example, scholars associated with the National Bureau of Economic Research have sponsored a series of conferences to bring together economic historians, business historians, and economic theorists.[92] Similarly, Judith Miller of Emory University has spearheaded an effort to encourage participation by historians in the Economic History Association and economic historians in the American Historical Association. Partly as a result of Miller's efforts, EHA president Deirdre McCloskey proclaimed the theme of the association's 1997 meeting to be "interdisciplinary conversations." There are also a large number of local and regional economic history seminars that provide opportunities for economists and historians interested in a common set of problems to mix. One of the largest and best organized, the All-University of California Economic History Conference, has been promoting interdisciplinary exchanges at its twice yearly meetings since the 1970s.

Nonetheless, the struggle is an uphill one. Funding to attend national conferences is limited, so many scholars go only to one or two professional meetings a year and are unlikely to use their scarce travel dollars to cross disciplinary boundaries. At the same time, the expansion both of higher education and of the number of subdisciplines over the last quarter century has resulted in a multiplication of the number of academic books and journals being published. Scholars are finding it increasingly difficult to keep up with the literature in their own fields, let alone follow developments in other areas. Moreover, anyone who, in the last few years, has attended one of meetings devoted to bringing together scholars with different academic backgrounds will recognize that over time the various fields have developed such separate vocabularies, concerns, and research agendas that it can be painfully difficult to conduct interdisciplinary conversations.

Despite recent efforts, therefore, the organizations that cliometricians built so assiduously to promote their work during the early sixties now increasingly demarcate an intellectual ghetto. So, of course, do the many associations that the various other historical subdisciplines—from labor history to African-American and women's history to queer studies—have constructed over the past quarter century. Because, however, the cliometric revolution has largely run its course, it highlights in an especially clear way the double-edged character of these organizations. In particular, it highlights the intellectual costs that disciplinary fragmentation can entail.

NOTES

I have greatly benefited in writing this article from the comments of Jeremy Atack, Roger Chartier, Louis Cain, Jan De Vries, Stanley Engerman, Anthony Molho, Dorothy Ross, Frank Smith, Kenneth Sokoloff, Gordon Wood, Mary Yeager, and participants in the Conference on the State of Historical Writing in North America, held at the University of San Marino in June 1995, and in the All-University of California Conference on the Comparative Economic History of Latin America and the United States, held at Stanford University in November 1996. I am also indebted to Deborah Morner, John Lyons, and Samuel Williamson of the Cliometric Society for providing me with membership figures and back issues of the society's newsletter, and to William J. Hausman for a videotape of the "Heritage Session" of the 34th Annual Meeting of the Business History Conference.

1. Lee Benson, "Research Problems in American Political Historiography," in Mirra Komarovsky, ed., *Common Frontiers of the Social Sciences* (Glencoe, Ill., 1957), pp. 113–14. See also the essays collected in Robert P. Swierenga, ed., *Quantification in American History: Theory and Research* (New York, 1970). For a long-term perspective on American historians' relations with the social sciences, see chapter 4 by Dorothy Ross in this volume.

2. For an excellent survey of the fruits of this revolution, see Jeremy Atack and Peter Passell, *A New Economic View of American History from Colonial Times to 1940*, 2nd ed. (New York, 1994). For earlier assessments by participants and disciples, see Lance E. Davis, "'And It Will Never Be Literature': The New Economic History: A Critique," in Ralph L. Andreano, ed., *The New Economic History: Recent Papers on Methodology* (New York, 1970), pp. 67–83; Albert Fishlow and Robert W. Fogel, "Quantitative Economic History: An Interim Evaluation: Past Trends and Present Tendencies," *Journal of Economic History* 31 (Mar. 1971), pp. 15–42; and Donald N. McCloskey, "The Achievements of the Cliometric School," *Journal of Economic History* 38 (Mar. 1978), pp. 13–28.

3. Robert William Fogel, "The Specification Problem in Economic History" *Journal of Economic History* 27 (Sept. 1967), p. 284; Douglass C. North, "Economic History: Its Contribution to Economic Education, Research, and Policy," *American Economic Review* 55 (May 1965), p. 86. See also John R. Meyer and Alfred H. Conrad, "Economic Theory, Statistical Inference, and Economic History," *Journal of Economic History* 17 (Dec. 1957), pp. 524–44.

4. Guy S. Callender, "The Position of American Economic History," *American Historical Review* 19 (Oct. 1913), pp. 80–81; Edwin F. Gay, "The Tasks of Economic History," *Journal of Economic History* 1 (Dec. 1941), supplement, pp. 9–16; Steven A. Sass, *Entrepreneurial Historians and History: Leadership and Rationality in American Economic Historiography, 1940–1960* (New York, 1986), pp. 15–19; Robert William Fogel, "The Reunification of Economic History with Economic Theory," *American Economic Review* 55 (May 1965), pp. 94–95. For an excellent example of the "compromise" position as it was worked out in British economic history, see J. H. Clapham, "The Study of Economic History," in N. B. Harte, ed., *The Study of Economic History: Collected Inaugural Lectures, 1893–1970* (London, 1971), pp. 57–70.

5. Sass, *Entrepreneurial Historians and History*, p. 15; Arthur H. Cole, "Economic History in the United States: Formative Years of a Discipline," *Journal of Economic History* 28 (Dec. 1968), pp. 558–59.

6. Callender, "The Position of Economic History," p. 80.

7. I sampled one out of every five volumes of the *American Economic Review* and *Journal of Political Economy* and two out of every five of the slimmer *Quarterly Journal of Economics*.

8. Callender, "The Position of Economic History," p. 80.

9. Sass, *Entrepreneurial Historians and History*, pp. 24–26. Lack of a clear disciplinary home was a common refrain among British economic historians as well. See the inaugural addresses given by British chair holders in economic history. They are collected in Harte, ed., *The Study of Economic History*. Many British universities later coped with this problem by setting up separate departments of economic history.

10. Abbott Payson Usher, "The Application of the Quantitative Method to Economic History," *Journal of Political Economy* 40 (Apr. 1932), pp. 186–209; Herbert Heaton, "Recent Developments in Economic History," *American Historical Review* 47 (July 1942), pp. 727–46; Cole, "Economic History in the United States," pp. 571–79.

11. Cole, "Economic History in the United States," pp. 573–75, 579; Sass, *Entrepreneurial Historians and History*, pp. 29–34.

12. Gay, "The Tasks of Economic History," p. 9; Cole, "Economic History in the United

States," pp. 559, 560–61, 565–67. Cole, a student of Gay's, worked on the American woolen industry, but even here he felt the influence of European scholarship. As Cole put it, "It was perhaps a reflection of Gay's thorough training in German materials that he was annoyed with me for failing to find evidences of the appearance of a putting-out stage" (p. 567). This is not to say, however, that there were no American antecedents for these intellectual movements. For example, the experience of American scholars (including Gay) who collected statistics for government planning agencies during World War I helped spur interest in quantification.

13. John U. Nef, "The Responsibility of Economic Historians," *Journal of Economic History* 1 (Dec. 1941), supplement, p. 7. He was quoting Herbert Heaton.

14. Herbert Heaton, "The Early History of the Economic History Association," *Journal of Economic History* 1 (Dec. 1941), supplement, p. 107.

15. Ibid., p. 107.

16. Ibid., pp. 107–9; and Herbert Heaton, "Twenty-Five Years of the Economic History Association: A Reflective Evaluation," *Journal of Economic History* 25 (Dec. 1965), p. 470.

17. Sass, *Entrepreneurial Historians and History*, pp. 54–59.

18. Ibid., pp. 53–106; Hugh G. J. Aitken, "Entrepreneurial Research: The History of an Intellectual Innovation," in Aitken, ed., *Explorations in Enterprise* (Cambridge, 1965), pp. 3–19; Arthur H. Cole, "The Committee on Research in Economic History: An Historical Sketch," *Journal of Economic History* 30 (Dec. 1970), pp. 723–41.

19. This search for theory often took the form of written scholarly debate in the pages of the center's in-house journal, *Explorations in Entrepreneurial History*. For an excellent analysis of the process by which participants turned to Parsonian sociology, see Sass, *Entrepreneurial Historians and History*, pp. 107–223. For an analysis of the utility of this body of theory from someone associated for a time with the center, see Louis Galambos, "Parsonian Sociology and Post-Progressive History," *Social Science Quarterly* 50 (June 1969), pp. 25–45. I am also indebted for this account to Louis Cain, E-mail communication of Jan. 18, 1996.

20. "An Interview with Lance Davis," *Newsletter of the Cliometric Society* 5 (Feb. 1990), pp. 9–10; Samuel H. Williamson, "The History of Cliometrics," in *Two Pioneers of Cliometrics: Robert W. Fogel and Douglass C. North* (Oxford, Ohio, 1994), pp. 119, 124–26.

21. "An Interview with Jonathan R. T. Hughes," *Newsletter of the Cliometric Society* 6 (Oct. 1991), p. 24.

22. "An Interview with Robert W. Fogel," *Newsletter of the Cliometric Society* 5 (July 1990), p. 6.

23. "An 'Interview' with Robert E. Gallman," *Newsletter of the Cliometric Society* 7 (Feb. 1992), pp. 5–6.

24. See Stephen Haber, "Introduction: Economic Growth and Latin American Economic Historiography," in Haber, ed., *How Latin America Fell Behind: Essays on the Economic History of Brazil and Mexico* (Stanford, 1997), pp. 5–9.

25. "An Interview with William N. Parker," *Newsletter of the Cliometric Society* 6 (July 1991), pp. 23–24.

26. Douglass C. North, "Quantitative Research in American Economic History," *American Economic Review* 53 (Mar. 1963), pp. 128–29.

27. North, "Economic History," p. 87. Similarly, Lance E. Davis, Jonathan R. T. Hughes, and Stanley Reiter ended their milder plea for quantitative economic history with the warning: "if the discipline chooses to remain completely in the literary tradition, we can see small hope for anything but a continual rehashing of the already existing sources and a continuation of the century-long cleavage between economics and economic history."

"Aspects of Quantitative Research in Economic History," *Journal of Economic History* 20 (Dec. 1960), p. 547.

28. North, "Economic History," p. 90.

29. "An Interview with Robert W. Fogel," p. 28.

30. Heaton, "Recent Developments in Economic History," p. 735.

31. E. A. J. Johnson, "New Tools for the Economic Historian," *Journal of Economic History* 1 (Dec. 1941), supplement, p. 38. Fogel recognized that traditional economic historians had done quantitative work, but he claimed that they "limited themselves primarily to the presentation, in more or less original form, of data found in standard historical sources." See his comment on papers by Peter Temin, Albert Fishlow, and Roger L. Ransom, "Discussion," *American Economic Review* 54 (May 1964), p. 378. See also Lance Davis, "Professor Fogel and the New Economic History," *Economic History Review*, 2nd ser., 19 (Dec. 1966), p. 658.

32. "An Interview with John Meyer," *Newsletter of the Cliometric Society* 10 (Feb. 1995), p. 4. The Conrad and Meyer paper is generally regarded as the first major cliometrics paper.

33. "An 'Interview' with Robert E. Gallman," p. 4. These meetings preceded the Purdue conferences and were important in attracting attention to the earliest cliometric work.

34. Sass, *Entrepreneurial Historians and History*, p. 245; "An Interview with John Meyer," p. 22; Cole, "The Committee on Research in Economic History," p. 738; Williamson, "The History of Cliometrics," p. 116; Claudia Goldin, "Cliometrics and the Nobel," *Journal of Economic Perspectives* 9 (spring 1995), pp. 193–94.

35. "An Interview with Lance Davis," p. 7. Apparently Taylor would reject Davis's submissions out of hand, without even sending them out for review. Conversation with Davis, May 17, 1995.

36. Robert William Fogel, "A Life of Learning," *ACLS Occasional Paper*, no. 34 (1996 Charles Homer Haskins Lecture), p. 8.

37. "An 'Interview' with Robert E. Gallman," p. 5. Meyer also remarked on Redlich's hostility. See "An Interview with John Meyer," p. 5.

38. "An Interview with Douglass C. North," *Newsletter of The Cliometric Society* 8 (Oct. 1993), p. 11.

39. Goldin, "Cliometrics and the Nobel," p. 194.

40. The divisions are eloquently captured in the ambivalence with which the institutionalist Cole wrote about developments in the field during the interwar period. Although he labeled this period "The Efflorescence," his description of scholarly trends contains words like "devastating" and "misfortune." See "Economic History in the United States," pp. 571–79. In a conciliatory moment Fogel himself admitted that "the discipline of economic history was no more monolithic in the past than it is at present" and that "every one of the elements which taken together serve to define the new economic history can be found in one or another of the classics of the past." See his comment on papers by Temin, Fishlow, and Ransom, "Discussion," p. 388.

41. Peter Temin, *The Jacksonian Economy* (New York, 1969), pp. 15–22. Only one of the scholars whom Temin lists as prominent sources of the traditional view could be considered an economic historian. That was Bray Hammond. The others, Richard Hofstadter and Marvin Meyers, were mainstream historians of the consensus school, who had acquired from the progressives much of their sense of economic history.

42. Douglass C. North, *Growth and Welfare in the American Past: A New Economic History* (Englewood Cliffs, N.J., 1966), Chap. 11.

43. Robert W. Fogel, "A Quantitative Approach to the Study of Railroads in American Economic Growth: A Report of Some Preliminary Findings," *Journal of Economic History* 22

(June 1962), pp. 163–97; Fogel, *Railroads and American Economic Growth: Essays in Econometric History* (Baltimore, 1964), pp. 1–9. Goodrich advised Fogel's master's thesis on the Union Pacific Railroad. See Fogel, "A Life of Learning," pp. 5–6.

44. On this point, see also Goldin, "Cliometrics and the Nobel," p. 195.

45. Fritz Redlich, "'New' and Traditional Approaches to Economic History and Their Interdependence," *Journal of Economic History* 25 (Dec. 1965), p. 486.

46. Robert William Fogel, "Notes on the Social Saving Controversy," *Journal of Economic History* 39 (Mar. 1979), p. 5.

47. Louis M. Hacker, "The New Revolution in Economic History: A Review Article Based on *Railroads and Economic Growth: Essays in Econometric History* by Robert William Fogel," *Explorations in Entrepreneurial History*, 2nd ser., 3 (spring 1966), pp. 166–69. It is doubtful, however, that historians like Hacker would have formulated their views so explicitly without Fogel's demonstration that the actual cost savings of railroads over canals were so minimal.

48. See Joseph A. Schumpeter, *The Theory of Economic Development: An Inquiry into Profits, Capital, Credit, Interest, and the Business Cycle* (Cambridge, 1934).

49. Fogel, *Railroads and American Economic Growth*, pp. 14–15.

50. Parker was critical of this tendency to produce "simply a kind of hymn to what really happened." William N. Parker, "From Old to New to Old in Economic History," *Journal of Economic History* 31 (Mar. 1971), pp. 6–7.

51. Meyer has since changed his mind about the importance of entrepreneurship. See "An Interview with John Meyer," pp. 22–23.

52. Douglass C. North, *The Economic Growth of the United States, 1790–1860* (Englewood Cliffs, N.J., 1961), pp. 8, 52.

53. On this point, see Fogel, "The Reunification of Economic History with Economic Theory."

54. See for example, Lance E. Davis and Douglass C. North, *Institutional Change and American Economic Growth* (Cambridge, 1971).

55. Douglass C. North, "Beyond the New Economic History," *Journal of Economic History* 34 (Mar. 1974), p. 2. On North's transformation, see Richard C. Sutch, "Douglass North and the New Economic History," in *Two Pioneers of Cliometrics*, pp. 77–79.

56. "An Interview with Douglass C. North," p. 9.

57. See especially his *Institutions, Institutional Change, and Economic Performance* (New York, 1990). Other new economic historians who have attempted to broaden their analysis beyond the basic neoclassical model include Paul David, Peter Temin, and Gavin Wright. See, for example, David, "CLIO and the Economics of QWERTY," *American Economic Review* 75 (May 1985), pp. 205–20; Wright, *The Political Economy of the Cotton South: Households, Markets, and Wealth in the Nineteenth Century* (New York, 1978); and Temin, *Taking Your Medicine: Drug Regulation in the United States* (Cambridge, 1980). Fogel has also recently broadened his work to include, for example, the qualitative analysis of religious beliefs. See *Without Consent or Contract: The Rise and Fall of American Slavery* (New York, 1989), part 2. See, in addition, Alexander J. Field, "The Future of Economic History," in Field, ed., *The Future of Economic History* (Boston, 1987), pp. 1–41.

58. Heaton, "Twenty-Five Years of the Economic History Association," p. 472.

59. Robert Whaples, "A Quantitative History of the *Journal of Economic History* and the Cliometric Revolution," *Journal of Economic History* 51 (June 1991), pp. 291–94. Whaples defined a cliometric article as one that had both a theoretical and a quantitative dimension.

60. Alfred D. Chandler, Jr., opposed the move to transform the Business History Conference into a formal organization because he did not want to abandon the Economic

History Association to the cliometricians. His point of view did not prevail, however. Videotape of "Heritage Session," consisting of informal remarks by Harold F. Williamson, Sr., Donald Kemmerer, Alfred D. Chandler, Jr., and Wayne Broehl (reading comments from Thomas Cochran), 34th Annual Meeting of the Business History Conference, Atlanta, Ga., 1988. I am also basing this account on the recollections of Louis Cain, communicated to me in an E-mail message of Jan. 18, 1996. Members of the Business History Conference also typically subscribed to and published in the *Business History Review*, which came out of the Harvard Business School but over time came to represent the same style of business history as the conference.

61. See Haber, "Introduction."

62. George Grantham, "Cliometrics in France: A Revolution Manquée?" unpub. paper, Department of Economics, McGill University, 1994. The chair was held by C. E. Labrousse, whose brand of economic history was similar to that of quantifiers in the United States during the interwar period.

63. Richard Tilly, "Soll und Haben: Recent German Economic History and the Problem of Economic Development," *Journal of Economic History* 29 (June 1969), pp. 298–319. See also Donald N. McCloskey, "Editor's Introduction," in McCloskey, ed. *Essays on a Mature Economy: Britain after 1840* (Princeton, 1971), p. 3.

64. Mathias, "Living with the Neighbours: The Role of Economic History," in Harte, ed., *The Study of Economic History*, pp. 369–83. On the lukewarm reception of the new economic history in Great Britain, see Jonathan R. T. Hughes, "Is the New Economic History an Export Product?" R. M. Hartwell, "Is the New Economic History an Export Product? A Comment on J. R. T. Hughes," Barry Supple, "Can the New Economic History Become an Import Substitute?" and R. C. O. Matthews, "The New Economic History in Britain: A Comment on the Papers by Hughes, Hartwell, and Supple," in McCloskey, ed., *Essays on a Mature Economy*, pp. 401–33. See also McCloskey, "Editor's Introduction," p. 3

65. See Roderick Floud, ed., *Essays in Quantitative Economic History* (Oxford, 1974); Floud, *An Introduction to Quantitative Methods for Historians* (London, 1973); Maurice Lévy-Leboyer and François Bourguignon, *L'économie française au xixe siècle: Analyse macro-économique* (Paris, 1985); Grantham, "Cliometrics in France."

66. There are now also sixteen members from Asia (including Russia) and seven from Australia and New Zealand. Cliometric Society membership figures.

67. I am using Robert Whaples's definition for this calculation. See note 59 above and Whaples, "A Quantitative History of the *Journal of Economic History* and the Cliometric Revolution." On the growth of cliometric work in Britain, see also Grantham, "Cliometrics in France."

68. Grantham, "Cliometrics in France"; conversation with Tim Hatton of Essex University, who is to be one of the editors of the new journal, Sept. 8, 1995.

69. See Field, "The Future of Economic History," pp. 1–2, 14–16.

70. For a discussion of the mood of the historical profession during this "Era of No Hard Feelings," see Peter Novick, *That Noble Dream: The "Objectivity Question" and the American Historical Profession* (New York, 1988), pp. 321–411. See also John Higham, *History: Professional Scholarship in America* (Englewood Cliffs, N.J., 1965), pp. 132–44, 212–32.

71. Novick, *That Noble Dream*, pp. 424–26, 437–38.

72. Ibid., Chap. 14.

73. Robert William Fogel and Stanley L. Engerman, *Time on the Cross: The Economics of American Negro Slavery* (Boston, 1974), pp. 4–6.

74. Oscar Handlin, "The Capacity of Quantitative History," *Perspectives in American History* 9 (1975), pp. 7–8. On this point, see also Norman R. Yetman, "The Rise and Fall

of *Time on the Cross*," *Reviews in American History* 4 (June 1976), pp. 196–97; and Kenneth M. Stampp, "Introduction: A Humanistic Perspective," in Paul A. David et al., *Reckoning with Slavery: A Critical Study in the Quantitative History of American Negro Slavery* (New York, 1976), pp. 9–10.

75. Fogel and Engerman, *Time on the Cross*, pp. 4–6.

76. Ibid., pp. 4, 7. On this point, see C. Vann Woodward, "The Jolly Institution," *New York Review of Books* 21 (May 2, 1974), p. 3. For notable exceptions, see Handlin, "The Capacity of Quantitative History"; and the review of *Time on the Cross* by Frank B. Tipton, Jr., and Clarence E. Walker, published in *History and Theory* 14 (Feb. 1975), pp. 91–121.

77. Some of the most important criticism has been collected in David et al., *Reckoning with Slavery*.

78. Ibid., pp. vi–vii.

79. Stampp, "Introduction," in ibid., pp. 1–2.

80. Yetman, "The Rise and Fall of *Time on the Cross*," p. 202. Herbert G. Gutman worried about this effect as well. See *Slavery and the Numbers Game: A Critique of Time on the Cross* (Urbana, 1975), p. 13.

81. This can easily be confirmed by a quick glance at Atack and Passell, *A New Economic View of American History*, chaps. 11 and 12. The debate also spilled over to stimulate new work on the postbellum South.

82. Thomas L. Haskell, "The True & Tragical History of 'Time on the Cross,'" *New York Review of Books* 22 (Oct. 2, 1975), p. 34.

83. John Kenneth Galbraith, *The Great Crash, 1929* (Boston, 1955); Milton Friedman and Anna Jacobson Schwartz, *The Great Contraction, 1929–1933* (Princeton, 1965); Peter Temin, *Did Monetary Forces Cause the Great Depression?* (New York, 1976); Barry Eichengreen, *Golden Fetters: The Gold Standard and the Great Depression, 1919–1939* (New York, 1992); Peter Temin, *Lessons from the Great Depression* (Cambridge, 1989). For a survey of the voluminous article literature on this subject, see Atack and Passell, *A New Economic View of American History*, chap. 21.

84. See, for example, Robert W. Fogel et al., "Secular Changes in American and British Stature and Nutrition," *Journal of Interdisciplinary History* 14 (autumn 1983), pp. 445–81; and Fogel, "Nutrition and the Decline in Mortality Since 1700: Some Preliminary Findings," in Stanley L. Engerman and Robert E. Gallman, eds., *Long-Term Factors in American Economic Growth* (Chicago, 1986), pp. 439–555. For a survey of this literature, see Richard H. Steckel, "Stature and the Standard of Living," *Journal of Economic Literature* 33 (Dec. 1995), pp. 1903–40.

85. The whole literature on the mentalité of farmers is riddled with such errors. See, for example, Michael Merrill, "Cash Is Good to Eat: Self-Sufficiency and Exchange in the Rural Economy of the United States," *Radical History Review* 4 (winter 1977), pp. 42–71; and James A. Henretta, "Families and Farms: Mentalité in Pre-Industrial America," *William and Mary Quarterly* 35 (Jan. 1978), pp. 3–32. Although Christopher Clark has read some economic history, he does not completely escape the errors of his predecessors. See *The Roots of Rural Capitalism: Western Massachusetts, 1780–1860* (Ithaca, 1990).

86. See John E. Toews, "Intellectual History after the Linguistic Turn: The Autonomy of Meaning and the Irreducibility of Experience," *American Historical Review* 92 (Oct. 1987), 879–907. The quote is from p. 882. On this point, see also chapter 4 by Dorothy Ross in this volume.

87. For an introduction to this literature, see Daniel M. G. Raff and Peter Temin, "Business History and Recent Economic Theory: Imperfect Information, Incentives, and the Internal Organization of Firms," in Temin, ed., *Inside the Business Enterprise: Historical*

Perspectives on the Use of Information (Chicago, 1991), pp. 7–35. See also Oliver E. William-son, *The Economic Institutions of Capitalism: Firms, Markets, Relational Contracting* (New York, 1985); Jean Tirole, *The Theory of Industrial Organization* (Cambridge, 1988); John Eatwell, Murray Milgate, and Peter Newman, eds., *The New Palgrave: Allocation, Information, and Markets* (New York, 1989); Richard Schmalensee and Robert Willig, eds., *Handbook of Industrial Organization* (Amsterdam, 1989); and Thrainn Eggertsson, *Economic Behavior and Institutions* (Cambridge, 1990).

88. Avner Greif, "Reputation and Coalitions in Medieval Trade: Evidence on the Ma-ghribi Traders," *Journal of Economic History* 49 (Dec. 1989), pp. 857–82; and Greif, "On the Political Foundations of the Late Medieval Commercial Revolution: Genoa During the Twelfth and Thirteenth Centuries," *Journal of Economic History* 54 (June 1994), pp. 271–87.

89. Margaret Levenstein, "The Use of Cost Measures: The Dow Chemical Company, 1890–1914," in Temin, ed., *Inside the Business Enterprise*, pp. 71–112; and Levenstein, *Accounting for Growth: Competition, Information Systems, and the Creation of the Large Corporation* (Stanford, in press). See also H. Thomas Johnson and Robert S. Kaplan, *Relevance Lost: The Rise and Fall of Management Accounting* (Boston, 1987).

90. Kenneth A. Snowden, "The Evolution of Interregional Mortgage Lending Channels, 1870–1940: The Life Insurance–Mortgage Company Connection," in Naomi R. Lamoreaux and Daniel M. G. Raff, eds., *Coordination and Information: Historical Perspectives on the Organization of Enterprise* (Chicago, 1995), pp. 209–47.

91. Temin, *Lessons from the Great Depression*.

92. The proceedings of the first two conferences have been published in Temin, ed., *Inside the Business Enterprise*, and Lamoreaux and Raff, eds., *Coordination and Information*. Papers given given at a third conference on learning by firms, organizations, and nations will appear in a forthcoming volume edited by Lamoreaux, Raff, and Temin.

CHAPTER 4

The New and Newer Histories:
Social Theory and Historiography
in an American Key

DOROTHY ROSS

DURING THE TWENTIETH CENTURY, historians in Europe and the United States have repeatedly revised their historical programs to make greater use of social theory. Beginning early in the century with the American Progressives' "New History" and the French Annales, there has been a succession of "new histories" based on alliance with the social sciences. Instead of writing narrative accounts of political events, the new historians used social theory to analyze the social and economic forces within and structures beneath the course of national politics. Using the Annales as his prime example, Georg Iggers links the rise of new history and its more structural understanding of historical process to the decline of belief in progress around the time of the First World War. "Exactly because the societies and cultures of the past are no longer seen as stages in a linear progression, they are now viewed not merely diachronically but also synchronically as structures possessing a degree of integrity and stability in time." As such, they invited analysis rather than narrative, and attention to collectivities and their material, social, and cultural conditions rather than individual actions.[1]

These new histories of the twentieth century thus stand at the intersection of two larger histories. One is the history of historicism, defined broadly as that "historical-mindedness" which began in the eighteenth century: a recognition of the qualitative difference, the "otherness," of the past, which mandated that human affairs be understood historically.[2] While abandoning or attenuating the conception of linear progress and the focus on political events that gave shape to nineteenth-century historicism, the new histories of the twentieth century retained the grounding in temporality.[3]

The new histories also belong to the history of the social sciences, studies that grew out of the Enlightenment effort to understand modernity. In their belief that the West had embarked on a novel course of historical development that was still unfolding, early social scientists shared the historicism of the eighteenth century. But unlike the historians, their focus was on the social and economic dimensions of civil society that modernity disclosed. Using analogues of scientific method, they produced social theories rather than political narratives.[4] During the nineteenth century history and the social sciences diverged and intertwined in a number of ways, although it was not until the twentieth century that a succession of new historians made a concerted effort to use social theory in their practice.

At first glance, the relation between historiography and social theory in the United States seems to follow a different path from that Iggers laid out. The New History that was announced in the United States in 1912 did not abandon, but emphasized, the liberal narrative of Western progress. When American historians finally turned to analytic, structural history and a full alliance with the social sciences in the decade after World War II, it was during a moment of American triumphalism. On closer examination, however, the United States proves to be a variant, rather than an exception. Both historicism and social science have had somewhat different histories in the United States, producing differences in the character and timing of anxieties about the course of history and the uses of social theory. In the American case, too, new historians used social theory to stabilize an increasingly uncertain narrative of Western history. The newer histories that make use of postmodern theories both extend and alter that story.

•

What accounts for the American variation on this Western theme is historical consciousness, shaped in the United States, as it was in the other countries of Europe, by the understanding of national history. The writers, politicians, and clergymen who constructed that national self-understanding in the decades after the American Revolution located the United States within the story of Western progress, a liberal story of growing commercial development, representative political institutions based on democratic consent, and the advance and diffusion of knowledge, processes that were projected to remake the entire world. They seated world progress not in Europe, where a class-ridden feudal past and industrial future distorted history, but in the American nation. The special place of the United States in this story was attributed in part to favorable historical conditions that allowed it to form a New World antithetical to the Old: the heritage of Anglo-Saxon institutions, the republican frame of government, the continent of uncultivated land, the opportunity offered by a free market of small producers. But specialness derived fundamentally from divine favor, a favor that began with the Puritan mission to New England and was sealed in the Revolution and Constitution. The country's unique foundation located it in millennial as well as historical time, freeing it from the ills of Europe and guaranteeing it an ideal future, exemplary for the world. In this view, American progress would be a quantitative multiplication and elaboration of the country's founding institutions, not a process of qualitative change. George Bancroft gave this exceptionalist historical consciousness its most popular form in the nineteenth century, while his contemporaries J. L. Motley and William H. Prescott set the pattern for American historians of Europe, who found there histories of decline that proved the rule of American progress. American exceptionalism was thus one variant among many nationalist versions of special destiny derived from a Christian heritage.[5]

During the Gilded Age, roughly from the late 1870s to late 1890s, the weakening of religious belief and the industrial transformation of society called American exceptionalism into question. The Gilded Age was also the period in which history and the new social sciences established disciplinary identities in the universities. The historians wanted to separate history from its divine background and turn it into an historical science on the Rankean model. The central figures in the movement to professionalize history, however, like Andrew Dickson White, John W. Burgess, and Herbert Baxter Adams, also believed that history and political science were part of the same large field. Their double enterprise of historico-politics was linked by a common task: amidst rapid industrial development, fierce social conflict, and widespread political corruption, they wanted to strengthen established historical principles so as to guide political action in a conservative direction. They sought this structural support in political principles and institutions: Adams's tracing of Teutonic "germs" from old to New England communities was one contribution to this program, as was the importation of Germanic conceptions of the "State."

At the same time, however, they were cognizant of the economic and social upheavals around them and of the new social science disciplines competing for academic space; they opened their field outward and laid the groundwork for the New History. They often spoke of the historical and political sciences in the plural and took under their wings historical jurisprudence, economics, and sociology. Adams's students, among them Frederick Jackson Turner, quickly developed social and economic dimensions in their work. At Columbia, the interdisciplinary environment Burgess established was the seedbed for James Harvey Robinson's announcement of a New History in 1912 and for Charles Beard's economic interpretation of history.[6]

Taking over from historico-politics the desire to link historical knowledge to present politics and to widen attention to economic and social history, this younger generation also had a deeper appreciation of historicism. The Gilded Age crisis had opened the way to a full recognition of the difference of the American past and the country's dependence on the contingent forces of history. To secure the ideal American future, the New Historians fully attached American history to Western liberal history and its progressive motors of capitalism, democracy, and science. The New History turned to the social sciences because those studies show us not accidental events, Robinson said, but "the general trend of development and progress."[7] European history was no longer seen as a realm of failure that proved American success, but as a realm of progress continuous with that of the United States and moving toward a common goal.[8] Exceptionalism was retained by placing the United States at the forefront of the movement and by casting progress in American shapes.

Turner was a transitional figure in this New History. Deeply committed to the old exceptionalist ideal, he located the source of American democracy in the vanishing frontier rather than in the new industrial process. He then tried to translate the frontier thesis into sectional analysis, in the vain hope that the continued diversity of sections and the democratic character of the American West would provide a continuing basis for American democracy. Geography and comparative geography were tools in this project and had some influence on the school of Western history founded on his work but never became a major source of social-theoretical interest in American historiography.[9] Geography, as Annales history confirms, is best suited to provide continuity, and in American historiography political principles continued to serve that purpose until after World War II.

In contrast, Robinson and Beard were driven by their liberal reformist politics to look forward: the ideal American democracy had yet to be achieved, and they were impatient with the slow pace of reform. Their models were the progressive European evolutionary theories of the nineteenth century and the adaptations of them American social scientists had already begun to make in the 1890s. In *The New History* Robinson borrowed Thorstein Veblen's evolutionary concept of institutions as "habits of thought," but his major focus was on social psychology. An intellectual historian and latter-day *philosophe*, he believed that advances in science and knowledge were the chief factor in progress. The social psychologies of James Mark Baldwin, Gabriel Tarde, and Sigmund Freud explained the irrationality of the masses of humanity, the inertial force that progress must overcome. Robinson never inserted such social psychological analysis into his textbooks or articles but elaborated it only in his popular book *The Mind in the Making* (1921), where it remained programmatic.[10]

Beard's economic interpretation of history was by far the most influential form of the New History. He learned it from his exposure to socialism in England and from his Columbia colleague, the historical economist E. R. A. Seligman, who had transformed Marx's historical materialism into a liberal theory of capitalist progress. Beard's focus was on the economic basis of politics and the construction of American democracy. But Seligman's theory did not offer much guidance on the specific links between economic conditions, politics, and ideas. Beard chronicled the conflict between social-economic classes, but dealt with them most often as economic interest groups rather than structural classes.[11] Politics and ideas were generally treated as derivative of economic and social "forces" and perpetually lagging behind technological and industrial advance. This view of historical change, formalized by the sociologist William Ogburn in the 1920s as "cultural lag," ran all through Progressive social science and historiography. It configured social conflict not as structural contradiction but as a partiality in historical advance that progress would resolve.[12]

Still, lagging progress exposed the dependence of the American ideal on the contingencies of history. After World War I and the conservative reaction of the 1920s, the New Historians' anxiety was palpable. It was reflected in Robinson's stress on irrationality in *The Mind in the Making* and in the textbook he titled *The Ordeal of Civilization* (1926). In the companion volume by Charles and Mary Beard, *The Rise of American Civilization*, progress operated as the regulative principle of the narrative, but it was now a question that had to be explicitly asked and answered. The uncertainties of history drove a wedge between the New History and the social sciences. During the Progressive era, Robinson and Beard had based the historical alliance with the social sciences on a common genetic viewpoint, and a younger generation of historians continued that project during the

interwar decades. Social scientists, however, soon broke with historical and evolutionary theory in order to form instrumental sciences that would enable them
to predict and control the uncertain course of human affairs.[13]

It was not until the decades after World War II that American social science
and historiography joined again, this time around a more structural, analytic
model of historiography. During this period the social sciences were in command
of growing resources and intellectual authority in academia, government, and
popular culture. Over the course of the 1930s and 1940s they had absorbed new
influences from European social theory. Talcott Parsons brought into American
social theory a Durkheimian sense of the reality of social norms. The work of Max
Weber also had a major impact on the structural understanding of society. Although Marx was largely proscribed in American universities, his work nonetheless influenced social thinkers in and out of academia. American social science
thus greatly expanded its conceptual repertoire.

At the same time, it shifted from a focus on socializing individuals to a concern
for integrated social systems. Society was still presumed to consist of aggregated
individuals, but the statistical analysis of collective behaviors and the functional
constituents of society that ruled behavior became the focus of analysis. System
norms were assumed to achieve social cohesion and equilibrium. In politics,
too, American democracy was configured as a pluralist system of competing interest groups that tended toward an equilibrium of justice and order. These
functionalist theories incorporated the description of modernity found in earlier
evolutionary theories, but functionalism assumed a static society, removed from
history. It often identified the social systems actually at work in contemporary
American society with the exceptionalist ideal. Older theories of liberal progress,
recast as modernization theory, were applied to the world outside the United
States and measured the distance still to be traversed to achieve the American
norm.[14]

The social sciences thus participated in the construction of a newly static historical consciousness. During the decade after World War II, the country was
experiencing the "American Moment" of the "American Century," when the
United States seemed already to stand at the summit of world power and already
to embody the values its exceptionalist history promised.[15] At the same time,
however, Cold War abroad and McCarthyism at home created a new sense of
anxiety about the exceptionalist triumph. To some critical intellectuals, the dominant position of the United States in the world quickly raised questions about
the limits of American power and the American example. The possibility that
America's unique consensus had disabled the country from effectively playing its
leading role in the world—a possibility soon reinforced by widespread criticism
of the United States—threatened the universal consummation of exceptionalist
history.[16] It was in this context that the historians Richard Hofstadter, H. Stuart
Hughes, David Potter, and Edward N. Saveth, among others, called for a new
alliance with the social sciences.[17] The static structuralism of the postwar/Cold
War social sciences, with their sense of liberal progress achieved, promised to
stabilize the disorientation in time of a less than perfect triumph.

The social sciences at the same time promised relief from historians' epistemological problems. In the 1930s Beard and Carl Becker led historians into a debate on whether the historian could ever reach objective knowledge of history. Much of the profession eventually took a compromise position, concluding that certainty was possible with regard to facts but that interpretation was necessarily subjective.[18] Recognizing that history was at bottom an imaginative "representation of the human situation," Hofstadter turned to social science concepts as a way of deepening the historical imagination. Potter, on the other hand, believed social science theory would remedy "the historian's lack of systematic procedure in the practice of generalization," making history more scientific.[19]

One consequence of both disorientation in time and the turn to social science was the demotion of narrative. The books written by these postwar/Cold War historians were what Hofstadter called "the new genre of analytical history . . . part narrative, part personal essay, part systematic empirical inquiry, part speculative philosophy."[20] Analytical history is framed by the historian's argument; the chronological time of its story can be interrupted or obscured to fit the purposes of argument.

Another consequence was the construction of an ironic version of exceptionalist history that reflected contemporary postwar/Cold War concerns.[21] Social theory helped to conceptualize American failings as inevitable aspects of success. Ironic historians argued that the achievement of egalitarian democracy led to a harmonious pluralist order, but this very success and the consequent absence of real ideological conflict and debate led to inflated expectations and a conformist, absolutist mentality. Drawing on Marxist influences of the 1930s that had criticized the monolithic liberalism of American society,[22] this analysis centered after the war in Tocqueville's consensual understanding of American society. As Wilfred McClay has shown, a host of social scientists in the 1950s from Erich Fromm to David Riesman were finding a "soft" totalitarianism in the United States parallel to the "hard" totalitarianism attributed to Nazi Germany and the Soviet Union, an idea rooted in the critique of atomized mass society that had originated with conservative thinkers after the French Revolution, including Tocqueville. The theory was revived by the Frankfurt critics of modern society and culture, many of whom had emigrated to the United States, and then taken up by American social theorists.[23] This theoretical apparatus allowed American historians to configure American vices as the unfortunate product of consensual virtues.

The social sciences were also used extensively in historical analysis. Historians paid particular attention to concepts like status, role, culture, and personality—theories of the middle range that could specify the social, economic, and psychological relations left inchoate by the New History. These concepts were understood by many American historians to operate within a liberal functionalist theoretical framework.[24] Status anxiety, deviance, relative deprivation, and a host of psychological disorders defined the tensions emerging from society understood in a functionalist way. Static "social strains" replaced progressive "cultural lag" as a focus of historical/social scientific explanation.[25] The irrational, dysfunctional processes of history were also important for American historians of Europe, who looked to European theorists like Freud and Pareto. As Leonard Krieger has pointed out, postwar historians of Europe, continuing on a well-worn American path, were attracted to the lost causes, the failed rationality, and the reactionary episodes that marked a counterpoint to the larger story of Western and American progress.[26]

•

The postwar/Cold War alliance of historiography and the social sciences around an ironic revision of American exceptionalism and its middle-range conceptual apparatus turned out to be unstable. It became the opening wedge in a proliferating series of historiographical programs making use of social science and social theory.

By the late 1950s a number of political and economic historians began to argue that it was scientific method that produced novel findings and reliable generalizations, not borrowed concepts. Although they made use of theory, they chiefly urged that historians adopt scientific methods, particularly quantitative methods. They launched a new social history "from the bottom up" that aimed to correct the impressionistic, overgeneralized stories previous historians told by using large data sets and statistical correlations.[27]

That history was no sooner begun, however, when the political conflict of the 1960s created new historiographical energies and directions. The concatenation of the civil rights movement, the war in Vietnam, youth rebellion, and the women's movement decisively ended the "American Moment" and its consensual explanation of American virtues and vices. What has been called the "New Left" drew into political debate and then into the historical profession a range of radical views, based in liberal democratic, populist, Marxist, and feminist traditions as well as in contemporary radical movements. It produced a social-cultural history that focused on the "inarticulate," the working class, racial minorities, and women, those who had been marginalized in American history and left out of its historiography.[28] Both these new social histories "from the bottom up" were heavily influenced by the achievements of European historiography, particularly the social-cultural history of the Annales group in France and the English historians associated with *Past and Present* and the History Workshop, themselves influenced by Marxism and the Annales.[29] And fueling all these political and historiographical trends was the changing composition of the profession, as the postwar democratization of higher education opened a historical vocation to men and—after the mid-1960s—women from a wider spectrum of American society.[30]

Many varieties of historiography flowed from these influences. I would like to look at three variants of new history that developed in these post-sixties decades: the social science history that formed in the mid-1970s around the Social Science History Association (SSHA), the historiography that has made use of modernization theory, and the social-cultural history of marginalized groups that was influenced by the activism of the 1960s. All three categories overlap, and I can only touch on them here, but I will try to suggest some of the characteristic ways these American new histories used social theory and how those uses have changed in recent years. All three set out to remake American historiography on terms suggested by social theory; all have enriched historiography, but none has succeeded in its imperialist ambition.

The movement for social science history was spearheaded by a group of historians in the late 1950s who responded to the instability of historical interpretation and the heated ideological climate of the Cold War by trying to make history into a science. The ambitions of these pioneers varied from William Aydelotte's modest desire to improve the way historians generalize to Lee Benson's effort to turn history into a science that generates general laws of human behavior.[31] They were joined by pioneer economic historians like Robert Fogel and Stanley Engerman, and in the late 1960s and 1970s by younger historians who were drawn into social science methods through their work on new social history topics, such as studies of voting behavior and demography. Their model of science was most often the empirical, behaviorist, quantitative social science practiced in the United States.[32]

Some of the social scientists who joined the SSHA in the mid-1970s shared the historians' scientific aspirations, but most had a very different agenda: while retaining the goal of a generalizing science, they wanted to move beyond a narrow positivism in social science and import some of the hermeneutic understanding and contextual richness of historiography. Charles Tilly, influenced by the Annales, and Theda Skocpol, influenced by Barrington Moore, along with their students and allies were early participants, as were scholars of historical demography and the sociology of the family. The social science participants were chiefly political scientists, sociologists, and economists; a small group of anthropologists appeared but virtually no psychologists.[33]

The social science history that resulted thus represented a number of theoretical strains, but quantitative American social science predominated. One of its most characteristic products were the voting-behavior studies that developed an ethnocultural interpretation of American politics. Like the Annales "serial history," these studies used numerical series to find continuous or changing patterns over time. However, the Annalistes took their patterns as clues to a qualitative analysis of underlying social structural conditions, while the behaviorist historians of voting submitted their numbers to statistical analysis in the hope of producing a causal account of political behavior; they largely ignored the structural features of American politics and society that shaped both political behavior and ethnocultural identity.[34]

During the 1980s, the scientific fervor of the social science history program receded, the victim of powerful critiques of the results of quantitative history and the broad attack on positivism.[35] At the SSHA, the balance between historians and social scientists has shifted: in recent years social scientists have come to comprise 60 percent of the program participants.[36] Among social scientists the interest in history has grown, but those committed to historicism are still marginalized in their own disciplines, making the SSHA a welcome venue. The reverse is true among historians: committed scientism has declined, while an eclectic interest in social theory is welcomed throughout the discipline.[37] Moreover, the array of interests represented in the SSHA has broadened. Gender has become an important area of interest, as has culture, and even narrative—the enemy against which the association originally formed—has established a beachhead.[38]

As a result, those involved in SSHA's original aims tend to be disappointed, whether historians devoted to the original quantitative scientific program or social scientists who wanted to transform the social sciences into genuinely historicist disciplines.[39] The SSHA nonetheless remains one of the few forums where historians, sociologists, political scientists, and historical economists can listen to one another on topics of overlapping—if not quite mutual—interest. The joint venue also attracts European scholars. *Social Science History* now prints articles that self-consciously test the power of social theories in historical contexts, often concluding that the theories do not adequately capture the complexity of history. That exercise can be illuminating, but it is a long way from the original effort to reconstitute American historiography.

Another kind of new history emerged from efforts to use modernization theory as the narrative and analytical spine of American historiography. Modernization theory descends from ideas of liberal progress that have been powerful since the eighteenth century and from the sociological theories of Ferdinand Tönnies and Max Weber. In the version formulated by 1950s American social scientists, modernization was understood as synonymous with Westernization and, particularly in the United States, Americanization; it was designed to provide a counterideology to Marxism that would enlist the "Third World." It cast economic development as the prime motor of progress, to which were linked changes in personality and politics. Inscribing the structural-functionalist assumptions of 1950s sociology, it tended to view modernization as an integrated, deterministic process but allowed for failure, particularly through the semiautonomous sphere of politics.[40]

Modernization theory provided a social-theoretical replacement for discredited ideas of progress, but its ideological use, reductionism, and historical determinism made historians wary of it from the start. Few historical studies have in fact openly claimed modernization as the theoretical basis of their work.[41] Perhaps the most influential instance of modernization theory in American historiography was Robert Wiebe's *The Search for Order, 1877–1920*, published in 1967. Applying the theory to the developing United States, Wiebe analyzed the transformation of a decentralized, agrarian-commercial society constructed around "island communities" into a nationalized, industrial capitalist, urban, bureaucratic society.[42] While his prose sometimes hinted at distress over the impersonality of this process, what he wanted was a smoothly running, integrated bureaucratic order of the kind theorists imagined to exist in the postwar United States. Wiebe's emphasis was on the disorder of the transitional process: by 1920 the decisive turn had been taken, but there were still only "separate bureaucracies, barely joined in some areas, openly in conflict elsewhere."[43] What almost all readers of Wiebe failed to notice was that after the upheavals of the late 1960s, he lost faith in the ability of the modernization process to achieve unassisted a harmonious bureaucratic order in modern America. Instead he attempted to construct a uniquely American order that was only partially modernized, but that had, in exceptionalist fashion, turned persisting conflict into harmony.[44]

The Search for Order was nonetheless a major starting point for the attempt to formulate an "organizational synthesis" of modern American history around the formation of large-scale bureaucratic organizations. Drawing on Weber, the new political science of the American state, and Alfred Chandler's pioneer work in business history, it has attempted to draw together the expanding historiography of professions, business corporations, and the intersection of state and private institutions in United States political economy. It is not clear that these historiographies, written by both liberal modernists and left critics of "corporate liberalism," constitute a "synthesis." One of its principal architects, Louis Galambos, notes that it often ignores crucial issues of conflict, power, and the distribution of resources. He also carefully disconnects his discussion of modern organizations from modernization as a necessary process. The "organizational synthesis" nonetheless assumes such a single, interconnected process, while historicizing the different forms that it takes in different locales.[45]

If organizations have not provided a new master narrative of American history, modernization continues to reappear, in part as a foil against which more complex historical accounts are written, in part as the narrative line around which stories are silently told. It also reappeared with its valences reversed. Although modernization theory was resolutely progressive, it incorporated the theory of traditional society as gemeinschaft and thus could be turned to express ambivalence about modernity.[46] Numerous studies in American history, often elegaic in tone, chart the movement from gemeinschaft to gesellschaft, starting with the early social histories of New England communities and stretching through the twentieth century. New Left historians of working-class and popular culture, lamenting the loss of community, have found this framework particularly congenial.[47] In part as a reaction to the historiography of community, social and economic historians have begun to reexamine the early development of the capitalist market and to reaffirm the progressive course of capitalism, a line of analysis that establishes ideological as well as analytical links to modernization theory and which may take on new life with the resurgence of market economics.[48]

Finally I want to discuss the social-cultural historians who were energized by the activism of the 1960s and have hoped to rewrite history on the basis of race, gender, class, and ethnicity. Rebelling against the consensus historiography of the postwar/Cold War era, they argued that workers, immigrants, racial minorities, and women had resisted domination and maintained their own group identities. Among the leaders of this compound movement, a number came from backgrounds that had exposed them to the orthodox Marxism that had survived in the United States and to Marxist theory. Rejecting orthodox Marxism but remaining attuned to Marxist theory, they and others from different backgrounds were then influenced by the broader antiauthoritarian, antiracist, and feminist currents of the 1960s.[49] As a result, Marxist theory was modified by an eclectic and culturally oriented mix of social theory: revisionist Marxism, particularly Gramsci and the English historians Raymond Williams and E. P. Thompson; the symbolic anthropology of Clifford Geertz, Victor Turner, and others; and most recently poststructural literary theories. The implications of this last influence—poststructural literary theory—are complex, and I will return to them shortly, but on one level the view of language as hegemonic yet broken, contradictory, and open to reconstruction by its speakers reinforced both the Gramscian critique and pluralist reconfiguration of American culture already underway in social-cultural historiography.

Moved by populist, socialist, and/or feminist political sympathies, social-cultural historians often valorized their subjects' resistance to oppression and sturdy survival, or conversely, their victimization by oppressors.[50] Using a symbolic anthropology that depicted culture as the primary realm of integration and meaning in peoples' lives, these historians viewed culture as the site of indigenous strength.[51] This romantic tendency has been both accentuated and made more difficult with the increase in historical sophistication, egalitarian sensitivity to each historical subject, and the poststructuralist valorization not simply of differences but of difference, with its fear of essentializing any category. Because racial, ethnic, class, and gender identities crosscut each other, sometimes supporting and sometimes contradicting other identities, historians have been pushed to an increasingly atomized level of analysis. At the same time they strove to maintain the conceptual and moral integrity of social-cultural groups.[52]

These historians nonetheless expressed the ambition to reconfigure all of American or Western history on the basis of the social-cultural history of the dispossessed. They brought with them progressive narratives of history that might effect such integration, derived from Marxism, feminist theories of patriarchy, and liberal/social democratic hybrids. While the politics of the 1960s had regenerated these progressive historical hopes, the political weakness of Marxism in the United States and the recent retreat of socialism and collapse of communism around the world have made progressive narratives difficult to sustain. At the same time, the romantic current in the social-cultural enterprise, the determination that those who have, by some standards, lost in life will not lose in historiography, makes it difficult to plot a narrative that leaves the subjects of social history undiminished. Herbert Gutman, for example, in 1981 quoted T. S. Eliot's Christian imagery of redemption, and thereby the mythic basis of both Marxist and American history, when he called for "a new synthesis . . . that incorporates and then transcends the new history" of blacks, the working class, and women.[53] In his own work on labor history, however, unlike his model E. P. Thompson, Gutman was unable to achieve a Marxist-like synthesis that would sustain a progressive history of the American working class.[54]

Increasing disillusion with liberal politics and the liberal state has taken a heavy toll on liberal proposals for reintegration as well. Thus Thomas Bender has suggested that a synthetic history of the United States could be written around the idea of the civic sphere, developed by Jurgen Habermas and others, "as an arena for the play of cultures and interests in society and the product of that play." But his proposal was immediately met with criticism of the structural constraints on that civic "arena" and of the hierarchical premise of civic culture as "core" and social-cultural life as "periphery."[55]

So the progressive narratives of American and Western history promised by social theory have remained elusive. Nonetheless, the social-cultural history of the dispossessed has had a major impact on the practice of historiography in the United States, more so than that of social science history or modernization theory. The relatively decentralized university system and the conjunction of 1960s politics with the opening of academic careers to women, African-Americans, and the children of immigrants swept this new history rapidly through the discipline. Grounding their work in the accepted scholarly standards of the profession and showing that agency—and with it, politics—operates at all levels of society and culture, the social-cultural historians succeeded in multiplying the subjects of historiography and revising traditional topics.[56]

If we step back for a moment to compare the new histories of the last three decades with Annales historiography, we can see that in many ways they have followed similar paths.[57] Like Annales historiography, American new histories entered into a "dialogue between history and the social sciences" that looked for the social-cultural structures and processes at work beneath the level of political events. Especially among the social science historians and modernizationists, that dialogue included the adoption of formal social scientific theories and methodologies. Most often, however, both American historians and Annalistes have borrowed questions, approaches, and techniques less formally. Working eclectically to suit the needs of their empirical data, they have brought multiple dimensions of analysis to bear on their studies. That loose and eclectic mode of operation often reflects historians' superficial engagement with social theory, but it also follows from their preference for empirical richness and complexity.[58] On both sides of the Atlantic, the new histories are now less driven by their original programmatic intentions, and—as historiography has multiplied—less by theory than historiography.[59]

There are also distinct differences between Annales historiography and the American new histories. The Annales emphasis on the *longue durée* has suited the French national temper far better than the American.[60] The *longue durée* focuses on the structural conditions that constrain human action, while American social thought, even in the truncated form of behaviorism, has tended to assume voluntarism. Social-cultural historians in the United States have tried to show how even ordinary people construct their own lives. The *longue durée* in France is also an alternative to progress, while American new histories have at least hoped to reestablish a sense of progress, whether the progress of a genuine historical science, or the progress inscribed in the middle-range theories of American social science, or the narratives of American and Western progress provided by Marxist and liberal social theory. It is indicative of that difference that the Annales program of "total" history has moved in recent years away from global ambitions to emphasize depth within a smaller compass, while many social-cultural historians in the United States have moved in the other direction, calling for larger narrative syntheses or, in Charles Tilly's terms, analyses of "big structures, large processes, huge comparisons."[61]

The hallmark of post-sixties historiography in the United States, however, is the social-cultural history of dispossessed groups. And here, of course, is a major difference from Annales historiography. If French historians recovered the social experience and mentalité of the peasantry and *marginaux*, American historians focused specifically on women, the working class, and the diverse racial and ethnic groups that compose American society. When we move from the social-cultural history of the dispossessed to the newer cultural history that has formed in its wake, the difference is even more striking. A principal catalyst of that new cultural history is poststructural literary theory that originated in France, but given its emphasis on discontinuity and the fragmentary, it has influenced American rather than French historiography.

•

The newer histories of culture, gender, race, and postcolonialism enact an alliance with the humanities rather than the social sciences, a shift in alliance linked to the declining fortunes of positivism just as historicism and theories of language were gaining new philosophical stature.[62] The theories that have influenced these newer histories are—roughly speaking—postmodern: anti-foundationalist philosophies and poststructural literary theories that examine the linguistic construction of reality.[63] In the American academy, language and texts have generally come to be understood as products of history, but postmodern theory embraces a radical historicism. It pushes the qualitative difference of the past to the point of discontinuity, leading the historian to look for breaks and fissures that have been glossed over by previous historiography and to show how historical forms are at every moment produced and reproduced. Radical discontinuity also means radical contextualism. Not only are there no transcendental or natural kinds embedded in history that persist through time, there are no "historical individuals," no self-acting, holistic historical entities such as stages, nations, classes, intellectual disciplines, or selves. Like the "natural" categories of race and sex, these too are held to be discontinuous social-cultural constructions whose fissures and reproduction must be disclosed.[64]

Postmodern theories found a welcome audience among social-cultural historians of the dispossessed who were already studying culture and already becoming self-critical about their historical categories. Through work in anthropology, particularly Geertz's textualization of culture, they were prepared for a view of culture as a system of signs.[65] The new theory encouraged them to go beyond the separate histories of groups to the social-cultural conventions or codes of gender, race, class, and ethnicity that define those groups. As a result postmodern theory has helped to catalyze an explosion of new historical energies. Women's history, already the most innovative sector of social-cultural history, was reenergized by the study of gender.[66] Gender and race became major categories of analysis, to be applied not only to women and people of color but to the white race and the male gender.[67] New topics emerged that drew on the methods and perspectives of postmodern theory, such as the body, time, and postcolonial experience. And cultural history, including the study of popular culture, became a fast-growing frontier of historical investigation.[68]

Postmodern theory also found an audience among intellectual historians. During the 1970s, intellectual historians had felt challenged by the new social history to defend their focus on elites and on ideas that seemed to float free of concrete social realities.[69] In a variety of efforts to rethink the basis of their practice, they drew on Collingwood, speech-act theory, and Kuhn's historical theory of science to argue that actions and social formations are inseparable from their meanings and that meanings are produced by speakers and writers engaged in a social enterprise. As a result of this work, intellectual historians in the United States began to think of their subject less as "ideas" than as the collective enterprise that shaped them. David Hollinger described that enterprise as the discourse of intellectuals and the term discourse was adopted by others, though it could mean a variety of things. Hollinger urged that discourses centered on questions. Others applied the term to J. G. A. Pocock's historical languages, paradigms, and traditions, and still others to looser connections of ideas and metaphors. Michel Foucault's understanding of discourse, with its emphasis on the linguistic construction of experience as an exercise of power, both reinforced and altered historians' use of the term.[70] The interest in the social construction of meanings that drew American intellectual historians toward discourse could also draw them toward the study of culture. The new cultural history was formed as both social and intellectual historians converged on the importance of culture and began to explore postmodern methods of analysis.[71]

Postmodern theories thus originate in different intellectual territory from the social theories we considered earlier. On one level, postmodern theories extend deeper into the historian's hermeneutic realm the structural elaboration of historicism that has been going on since early in the twentieth century. They insert into language and culture the structuralist concern with power: their interest is in how linguistic codes and systems construct subjectivity; they prefer spacial metaphors that make abstract linguistic and cultural phenomena concrete. Yet on another level, these poststructural theories move in a profoundly different direction from the global theories of progress and the analytical theories of structure and process that previously have been employed to stabilize the uncertainties of modern history. In postmodern theories, it is precisely the structural element, the constructed character of all texts and linguistic categories, that make them unstable. In this view, the social-theoretical narratives of progress and fixed theoretical categories like class and culture, by their normative inclusive character, deny their own fictionality and instability and thereby distort the creative possibilities of the present and future.[72]

There are good reasons for the special appeal of postmodern theory in the United States. The twentieth century's brutalities and the inchoate condition of the contemporary world have stunned without entirely banishing the deep reserve of liberal faith in America. The political tendency of postmodernism is individualistic and pluralistic, if not anarchistic, motivated by fear of the monolithic social order it locates in modernity.[73] Such a fear has deep roots in the ambivalent American individualism analyzed by Tocqueville. Since the postwar/ Cold War decade, an important segment of American social thinkers and new historians have mobilized against similar threats to individual freedom, first in the form of a "soft totalitarianism" and then, on the New Left, the cultural hegemony exerted by capitalism.[74] The fear of a monolithic social order leads postmodernists toward liberal and radical versions of individualistic, pluralist politics. It also leads toward the realm of culture, a prime contemporary site of contestation between individual freedom and social constraint. Postmodern theory can thus express both the uncertainties of the present and deeply ingrained political impulses. It is no accident that in concluding her introduction to the new cultural history, Lynn Hunt asked playfully, "Are we headed here for a 'comic' ending in literary terms? An ending that promises reconciliation of all contradictions and tensions in the pluralist manner most congenial to American historians?"[75]

How postmodern theory will play itself out in American historiography is an open question. Decentralization and specialization give academic disciplines in the United States enormous power to absorb and disarm disruptive innovations. Indeed, these theories have not yet penetrated very deeply into the historical profession; even those areas most strongly affected, like women's history and cultural history, are only partially shaped by them.[76] Unlike earlier social theories that provided historians with useful and reassuring tools, the tools of postmodern theory carry with them epistemological burdens. Social theory attacked the epistemological doubt that had been an undercurrent in the discipline since the 1920s, strengthening the historian's authoritative claim to discover what really happened. Postmodern theory questions that claim and urges the historian to examine doubt in her text. Social theory helped stabilize the uncertainties of twentieth-century history and of historical interpretation. Postmodern theory urges that these uncertainties be acknowledged and creatively magnified. To date, intellectual historians are more cognizant of these issues than others; many in the discipline have been scared off by a political attack on postmodern theory that caricatures its most radical implications. However, American historians who have made use of poststructural theories show no inclination to accept the reduction of all experience to textuality or of all narrative to fiction. On the contrary, most have argued that experience remains a viable category apart from textuality and that their constructed narratives produce warrantable knowledge.[77]

Just as American new historians and Annalistes used social theory loosely and eclectically and stopped short of the point at which historical values would be threatened, a similar outcome is likely for postmodern theories. Most historians will be more interested in reaping the empirical harvest of this new perspective than in facing or resolving its epistemological dilemmas. Nor is it likely that the focus on language and culture will eclipse all other approaches to history. Rich veins of structural analysis and social history are still productive, and social theorists themselves are exploring postmodern theories, reconfiguring what has been sharply separated as "social" and "cultural."[78] Again it is noteworthy that Lynn

Hunt has already voiced regret at the absence of social theory from new works in cultural history.[79]

Postmodern theory nonetheless contributes to a new kind of alliance between history and neighboring disciplines, a process foreshadowed in the transformation of the SSHA. What is happening in the United States is not a partnership of the sort forecast by the new historians of 1912 or 1950, nor the Annales model of an integration of other perspectives within the master discipline of history. Rather it is the diffusion of historicism across disciplinary boundaries into the humanities and social sciences, producing works that are recognizably historicist yet recognizably different in aproach. American historians are increasingly conscious of these historical works as well as the theory being produced in adjacent disciplines.[80] Historians' special authority may, of course, disperse along with the diffusion of their outlook.[81] Yet a common, if variegated, allegiance to historicism could allow the human sciences and humanities to function more like the natural sciences, where the assurance of a common approach allows researchers to follow their problems across disciplinary lines. In either case, this new alliance between history and theory promises again to reshape the writing of history in the United States.

NOTES

I want to thank my colleagues at the San Marino conference for their stimulating comments, particularly Roger Chartier and Jacques Revel. I am also grateful for the excellent suggestions offered by Orest Ranum and Lynn Hunt and by the members of the Washington Seminar on American History and Culture, particularly James Gilbert and James Banner; and for the thoughtful comments of John R. Hall, who responded to my brief paper on this topic at the SSHA meeting in 1994.

1. This understanding of the twentieth-century new histories is derived from Georg G. Iggers, "Historicism (a Comment)," *Historia Historiographie* 10 (1986): 131–44, and Ignacio Olabarri, "'New' New History: A *Longue Durée* Structure," *History and Theory* 34 (no. 1, 1995): 1–29. Following an earlier suggestion of Iggers in *New Directions in European Historiography*, Ian Tyrrell has developed the comparison between the first New History in the United States and Annales historiography in *The Absent Marx: Class Analysis and Liberal History in Twentieth-Century America* (New York, 1986), chap. 2. See also Ernst A. Breisach, "Two New Histories: An Exploratory Comparison," in *At the Nexus of Philosophy and History*, ed. Bernard P. Dauenhauer (Athens, Ga., 1987). The quotation is from Iggers, "Historicism," 140.

2. There are a number of definitions of historicism. Karl Popper identified historicism as a hybrid of naturalistic conceptions of law and historicist conceptions of change in *The Poverty of Historicism* (Boston, 1957). Maurice Mandelbaum limited historicism to teleological doctrines of historical development and specifically excluded the historian's "historical sense," in *History, Man, and Reason: A Study of Nineteenth Century Thought* (Baltimore, 1971). My view of historicism follows one usage common in intellectual history and draws from Iggers, "Historicism," 131–40; Friedrich Meinecke, *Historism*, trans. J. E. Anderson (London, 1972); Hayden V. White, "On History and Historicisms," introduction to Carlo Antoni, *From History to Sociology: The Transition in German Historical Thinking* (Detroit, 1959), xv–xxviii; and J. G. A. Pocock, *Politics, Language and Time* (New York, 1973).

3. This point is implied in Iggers, "Historicism," 141–42, and developed in Olabarri, "'New' New History," 4–11.

4. Dorothy Ross, *The Origins of American Social Science* (Cambridge, 1991), chap. 1.

5. In calling the view of American history that Bancroft exemplified "exceptionalism," I resist the argument of the admirable essay by Daniel Rodgers in chapter 1 of this volume. To limit the term to Turner and post-1945 histories misses the way in which Bancroft, as well as many Teutonist historians, understood American history as an exception from salient, universal processes of history. Precisely because America gathered in the historical seeds of liberty from around the world and enacted the ideal toward which universal history moved, it was exempt from the destructive historical forces that shaped the histories of all other countries. I believe it is more than homology that links the millennial identification of the American republic with Turner's seating of the universal frontier process in the United States, and Bancroft's Hegelianism with the American historical dynamics inspired by Marx. For this more expansive view of American exceptionalism, see Ross, *Origins*, pt. 1; Dorothy Ross, "Historical Consciousness in Nineteenth-Century America," *American Historical Review (AHR)* 89 (October 1989): 909–28, and "Grand Narrative in American Historical Writing: From Romance to Uncertainty," *AHR* 100 (June 1995): 651–77. On Motley and Prescott as well as Bancroft, see David Levin, *History as Romantic Art* (Stanford, 1959).

6. This view of historico-politics as the context for the founding of the historical discipline in the United States and seedbed for the New History is set out in Ross, *Origins*, chaps. 3 and 8.

7. James Harvey Robinson, *The New History: Essays Illustrating the Modern Historical Outlook* (New York, 1912), 14.

8. Although he does not link it to a revision of American exceptionalism under the deeper influence of historicism, Leonard Krieger notes this shift in American historians' treatment of European history, in "European History in America," in John Higham, Krieger, and Felix Gilbert, *History* (Englewood Cliffs, N.J., 1965), 241, 263, and chaps. 2–3, passim.

9. Ross, *Origins*, 270–74.

10. Dorothy Ross, "The 'New History' and the 'New Psychology': An Early Attempt at Psychohistory," in *The Hofstadter Aegis*, ed. Stanley Elkins and Eric McKitrick (New York, 1974), 207–34. In Robinson, *New History*, see particularly chaps. 1 and 3.

11. For illuminating discussions of Beard and the New History, see Tyrrell, *The Absent Marx*, chaps. 1–2, and Ernst A. Breisach, *American Progressive History* (Chicago, 1993). On Beard's influence, see also Terrence J. McDonald, "Theory and Practice in the 'New' History: Rereading Arthur Meier Schlesinger's *The Rise of the City, 1878–1898*," *Reviews in American History* 20 (1992): 432–45. McDonald shows that Arthur M. Schlesinger used Beard and Seligman's economic interpretation in his urban history, but at such a low level of specificity that it was taken for no theory at all. As McDonald points out, Beard's reputation as a radical also probably helped to blur Schlesinger's analysis.

12. Ross, *Origins*, chap. 9 and 442–44.

13. Ibid., chap. 10.

14. The key text in the structural transformation of postwar/Cold War American social science is Talcott Parsons, *The Structure of Social Action* (New York, 1937). For surveys of the structural movement in a number of social sciences, see Fred Matthews, "Social Scientists and the Culture Concept, 1930–1950: The Conflict between Processual and Structural Approaches," *Sociological Theory* 7 (1989): 87–101, and Dorothy Ross, "Social Science," in *A Companion to American Thought*, ed. Richard Wightman Fox and James T. Kloppenberg (Oxford, 1995), 634–37.

15. Edward A. Purcell, Jr., *The Crisis of Democratic Theory: Scientific Naturalism and the Problem of Value* (Lexington, Ky., 1973), pt. 4. For liberals, this shift in historical consciousness was prepared by the depression and theories of a mature economy; for the left, by the stalemate between the discredited alternatives of Marxism and liberalism. See Howard Brick, *Daniel Bell and the Decline of Intellectual Radicalism: Social Theory and Political Reconciliation in the 1940s* (Madison, 1986).

16. This theme is implicit and explicit in many texts of this period. Among historians, see Louis Hartz, *The Liberal Tradition in America* (New York, 1955), chap. 11; C. Vann Woodward, "The Irony of Southern History" (1953), in *The Burden of Southern History* (New York, 1960).

17. Richard Hofstadter, "History and the Social Sciences," in *Varieties of History*, ed. Fritz Stern (New York, 1956); Richard Hofstadter, "History and Sociology in the United States," in *Sociology and History: Methods*, ed. Hofstadter and Seymour Martin Lipset (New York, 1968); H. Stuart Hughes, "The Historian and the Social Scientist," *AHR* 60 (1960): 20–46; David M. Potter, *People of Plenty: Economic Abundance and the American Character* (Chicago, 1954), introduction; Edward N. Saveth, ed., *American History and the Social Sciences* (Glencoe, 1964).

18. On the response to Beard's and Becker's relativism, see Tyrrell, *The Absent Marx*, 22–23, 36–39, 93–95, although, unlike Tyrrell, I believe this uncertainty was only partially contained and never vanquished; on Becker, Carl L. Becker, *The Heavenly City of the Eighteenth-Century Philosophers* (New Haven, 1932); Burleigh Taylor Wilkins, *Carl Becker: A Biographical Study in American Intellectual History* (Cambridge, 1961).

19. Hofstadter, "History and the Social Sciences," 370; Potter, *People of Plenty*, xii. For Hughes, the social sciences also offered to make generalization more precise, as well as to make historians' weakly conceptualized fields of economic, social, and cultural history more coherent. Hughes, "The Historian and the Social Scientist."

20. Richard Hofstadter, "History and Sociology in the United States," in *Sociology and History*, 18.

21. For a view of postwar/Cold War historiography as more complacent and monolithic than I suggest here, see Peter Novick, *That Noble Dream: The 'Objectivity Question' and the American Historical Profession* (Cambridge, 1988), pt. 3.

22. For example, Richard Hofstadter's *American Political Tradition* (New York, 1948). See Hofstadter, "The Importance of Comity in American History," *Columbia University Forum*, 13 (winter 1970): 9.

23. This connection is drawn by Wilfred M. McClay in *The Masterless: Self and Society in Modern America* (Chapel Hill, 1994), chaps. 6–7, a superb study of the symbiotic relationship between autonomous individualism and social absorption in the nineteenth and twentieth centuries.

24. Saveth, *American History and the Social Sciences*, 17–18. On theories of the "middle range," see Robert Merton, *Social Theory and Social Structure*, rev. ed. (New York, 1963).

25. Examples are Richard Hofstadter, *The Age of Reform* (New York, 1955) and *The Paranoid Style in American Politics* (New York, 1965); David Donald, "Toward a Reconsideration of Abolitionists," in *Lincoln Reconsidered* (New York, 1956); Marvin Meyers, *The Jacksonian Persuasion* (New York, 1960). William H. Sewell, Jr., remarks on this cast of 1950s social science history in "Introduction: Narratives and Social Identities," *Social Science History* (*SSH*) 16 (fall 1992): 487.

26. Krieger, "European History in America," chaps. 4–5. Examples are Franklin L. Ford, *Robe and Sword: The Regrouping of the French Aristocracy after Louis XIV* (Cambridge, 1953), and H. Stuart Hughes, *Consciousness and Society: The Reconstruction of European Social Thought 1890–1930* (New York, 1961 [1958]).

27. For an early sampling, see Robert P. Swierenga, ed., *Quantification in American History: Theory and Research* (New York, 1970).

28. Novick, *That Noble Dream*, chap. 13.

29. Lynn Hunt, ed., *The New Cultural History* (Berkeley, 1989), introduction and pt. 1.

30. Novick, *That Noble Dream*, 362–67, 470.

31. See the selections in Swierenga, ed., *Quantification in American History*, and Lee Benson, *Toward the Scientific Study of History* (Philadelphia, 1972).

32. My account of the social science history that formed around the SSHA draws largely on Andrew Abbott, "History and Sociology: The Lost Synthesis," in *Engaging the Past: The Uses of History across the Social Sciences*, ed. Eric H. Monkkonen (Durham, 1994), 77–112, an excellent account of the movement. On this model of American social science, see Christopher G. A. Bryant, *Positivism in Social Theory and Research* (New York, 1985), chap. 5.

33. The information on relative participation comes from Donna Gabaccia, "Interdisciplinary Communication and SSHA Annual Conferences: A Program Chair's Perspective," *SSHA News* (winter 1995): 8–10.

34. For an excellent account of the Annales method of "serial history," see Robert Forster, "Achievements of the Annales School," *Journal of Economic History* 38 (March 1978): 58–76. Ronald P. Formisano, "The Invention of the Ethnocultural Interpretation," *AHR* 99 (April 1994): 453–77, is a revealing history and defense of ethnocultural voting studies; the best critique is still Richard L. McCormick, "Ethno-cultural Interpretations of Nineteenth-Century American Voting Behavior," *Political Science Quarterly* 89 (June 1974).

35. One obstacle faced by social science history—the time-consuming difficulty of gathering data—speaks to the difference between the individualistic and decentralized historical discipline in the United States and the centralized historical program of the Annales. See Forster, "Achievements of the Annales School."

36. Gabaccia, "Interdisciplinary Communication," 9.

37. As Edward Berkowitz tells me, political historians who feel marginalized in an historical profession predominantly devoted to social and cultural history continue to find the SSHA a welcome venue for meeting the historically oriented political scientists who share their interests.

38. Sewell, "Introduction: Narratives and Social Identities."

39. Thus Abbott regards the SSHA alliance as a mismatched failure, in "History and Sociology"; for an historian's disappointment, see Allan G. Bogue, "Great Expectations and Secular Depreciation: The First Ten Years of the Social Science History Association," *SSH* 11 (fall 1987): 329–42, and Eric H. Monkkonen, "Lessons of Social Science History," *SSH* 18 (summer 1994): 161–68.

40. The best introduction is the long entry on "modernization" written by two architects of the theory, Daniel Lerner and James S. Coleman, in *International Encyclopedia of the Social Sciences*, 10:386–402.

41. Peter Burke, *History and Social Theory* (Ithaca, 1992), 132–41.

42. Robert Wiebe, *The Search for Order* (New York, 1967). Wiebe reported in a talk at the American Historical Association, December 3, 1996, that he had known the work of Max Weber and Robert Merton but not the work of 1950s theorists of "third world" modernization. See also Kenneth Cmiel, "Destiny and Amnesia: The Vision of Modernity in Robert Wiebe's *The Search for Order*," *Reviews in American History* 21 (1993): 352–68.

43. Wiebe, *Search for Order*, 300.

44. Robert Wiebe, *The Segmented Society: An Historical Preface to the Meaning of America* (New York, 1975). The subtitle is revealing. Wiebe argued for "the persisting segmentation of American society" and relocated the source of harmony to a "unique pattern of relationships" among those segments, which constitute a "consistent, interdependent system"

based on "widespread agreement on certain fundamentals" (x–xi, 13). Alan Brinkley noted that Wiebe had retreated to a position of incomplete modernization, in "The Problem of American Conservatism," *AHR* 99 (April 1994): 427.

45. Louis Galambos, "The Emerging Organizational Synthesis in Modern American History," *Business History Review* 44 (1970): 279–90, and "Technology, Political Economy, and Professionalization: Central Themes of the Organizational Synthesis," ibid., 57 (1983): 471–93.

46. Harry Liebersohn, *Fate and Utopia in German Sociology, 1870–1923* (Cambridge, 1988).

47. See Thomas Bender, *Community and Social Change in America* (Baltimore, 1982 [1978]).

48. For a sympathetic review of some of this literature, see Gordon S. Wood, "Inventing American Capitalism," *The New York Review of Books* (June 9, 1994), 44–49.

49. Henry Abelove et al., eds., *Visions of History* (New York, 1983), particularly the interviews with Linda Gordon, Natalie Zemon Davis, and Herbert Gutman; Warren I. Susman, *Culture as History: The Transformation of American Society in the Twentieth Century* (New York, 1984), introduction and headnotes.

50. Michael Kammen, ed., *The Past before Us: Contemporary Historical Writing in the United States* (Ithaca, 1980), particularly Peter N. Stearns, "Toward a Wider Vision: Trends in Social History."

51. Lawrence W. Levine, "Clio, Canons, and Culture," *Journal of American History (JAH)* 93 (1993): 864; Suzanne Desan, "Crowds, Community, and Ritual in the Work of E. P. Thompson and Natalie Davis," in Hunt, ed., *New Cultural History*, 47–71; Ira Berlin, "Introduction: Herbert G. Gutman and the American Working Class," in Gutman, *Power and Culture: Essays on the American Working Class*, ed. Berlin (New York, 1987), 36–45; Carroll Smith-Rosenberg, "The Female World of Love and Ritual: Relations between Women in Nineteenth Century America," *Signs* 1 (1975): 1–29.

52. See, for example, David Roediger, "Race and the Working-Class Past in the United States: Multiple Identities and the Future of Labor History," *International Review of Social History* 38 (supplement, 1993): 127–43.

53. Herbert G. Gutman, "The Missing Synthesis: What Ever Happened to History?" *Nation* (November 21, 1981), 554. For other calls for a new synthetic history based in working-class history, gender, and race, see J. Carroll Moody and Alice Kessler-Harris, eds., *Perspectives on American Labor History: The Problems of Synthesis* (DeKalb, Ill., 1990), and Roediger, "Race and the Working-Class Past."

54. On the comparison of Gutman and Thompson, see also Tyrrell, *The Absent Marx*, 146–54.

55. Thomas Bender, "Wholes and Parts: The Need for Synthesis in American History," *JAH* 73 (June 1986): 120–36, and "A Round Table: Synthesis in American History," *JAH* 74 (June 1987): 107–30.

56. The massive publication of the Freedmen's Bureau papers, edited and interpreted by a team under Ira Berlin, for example, has both enlarged and shifted the focus of Reconstruction historiography: *Freedom: A Documentary History of Emancipation, 1861–1867* (Cambridge, 1982–); see also Eric Foner, *Reconstruction: America's Unfinished Revolution, 1863–1877* (New York, 1988). The ways in which women's civic participation reconfigured politics and shaped the welfare state is now a major topic in the study of the United States and of Europe: Mary Ryan, *Women in Public: Between Ballots and Banners, 1825–1880* (Baltimore, 1990); Paula Baker, *The Moral Frameworks of Public Life: Gender, Politics, and the State in Rural New York, 1820–1930* (New York, 1991); Linda Gordon, *Pitied but Not En-*

titled: *Single Mothers and the History of Welfare* (New York, 1994); Seth Koven and Sonya Michel, eds., *Mothers of a New World: Maternalist Politics and the Origins of Welfare States* (London, 1990).

57. My comparisons here are drawn against Forster, "Achievements of the Annales School."

58. For an excellent analysis of historians' failures in this regard, see Terrence J. McDonald, "Faiths of Our Fathers: Middle Range Social Theory and the Remaking of American Urban History, 1940–1985," in *American City History: Modes of Inquiry*, ed. Kathleen Neils Conzen, Michael H. Ebner, and Russell Lewis (Chicago, 1992).

59. Galambos makes this point for the organizational synthesis, but it is also true of the other new histories. Galambos, "Technology, Political Economy, and Professionalization," 471, 493.

60. As Gordon Wood points out in chapter 7 of this volume, only the colonial period of American history provided American historians with something like a *longue durée* of a century or more.

61. Charles Tilly, *Big Structures, Large Processes, Huge Comparisons* (New York, 1985). On the reformulation of total history, see Olabarri, "'New' New History," 17–18. On differences between American New History and the Annales school, Breisach, "Two New Histories," finds interesting lapses in Annales historians' rejection of progress.

62. A good way to track this shift is through the work of Richard J. Bernstein: *The Restructuring of Social and Political Theory* (New York, 1976); *Beyond Objectivism and Relativism: Science, Hermeneutics, and Praxis* (Philadelphia, 1985), and *The New Constellation: The Ethical-Political Horizons of Modernity/Postmodernity* (Cambridge, 1992).

63. Introductions to this body of theory that are especially useful in this context are Allan Megill, *Prophets of Extremity: Nietzsche, Heidegger, Foucault, Derrida* (Berkeley, 1985); Bernstein, *The New Constellation*; Lynn Hunt, "Introduction: History, Culture, and Text," in Hunt, ed., *New Cultural History*; Terry Eagleton, *Literary Theory* (Minneapolis, 1983), chap. 4.

64. The historicist direction of American literary theory is exemplified in Frank Lentricchia, *After the New Criticism* (Chicago, 1980). See also Brook Thomas, *The New Historicism and Other Old-Fashioned Topics* (Princeton, 1991). On radical historicism, see Michel Foucault, "Nietzsche, Genealogy, History," in *Language, Counter-Memory, Practice*, ed. Donald Bouchard (Ithaca, 1988).

65. Hunt, "Introduction: History, Culture, and Text," and Aletta Biersack, "Local Knowledge, Local History: Geertz and Beyond," in Hunt, ed., *New Cultural History*.

66. Historians of women, for example, quickly found it useful to discuss the way culture "constructs" gender differences and the way women refigure those differences in their own lives. See, for example, Joan Scott, *Gender and the Politics of History* (New York, 1988).

67. David Roediger, for example, has convincingly shown that male gender and white race-consciousness were crucial to the forging of the antebellum working class in the United States. David Roediger, *The Wages of Whiteness: Race and the Making of the American Working Class* (London, 1991).

68. Hunt, ed., *New Cultural History*.

69. See John Higham and Paul Conkin, eds., *New Directions in Intellectual History* (Baltimore, 1979).

70. This history is reviewed in David A. Hollinger, "Running To and Fro: Discourse, Historians, and Daniel's Dream," paper delivered at the San Marino conference, June 1995. See also Hollinger, "Historians and the Discourse of Intellectuals," in Higham and Conkin, eds., *New Directions*, 42–63; J. G. A. Pocock, "Introduction: The State of the Art," in *Virtue,*

Commerce, and History (Cambridge, 1985); Jan Goldstein, "Foucault among the Sociologists: The 'Disciplines' and the History of the Professions," *History and Theory* 23 (1984): 170–92.

71. That joint convergence is visible in Hunt, ed., *New Cultural History*, and Richard Wightman Fox and T. J. Jackson Lears, eds., *The Power of Culture: Critical Essays in American History* (Chicago, 1993).

72. Terry Eagelton, *Literary Theory* (Minneapolis, 1983), chap. 4.

73. On the centrality of this fear in postmodern theory, see John McGowan, *Postmodernism and Its Critics* (Ithaca, 1991).

74. McClay, *The Masterless*. See note 23 above.

75. Hunt, ed., *New Cultural History*, 22.

76. The distinction often made between cultural history and cultural studies, for example, marks a line most historians are reluctant to cross into a fuller embrace of postmodern theory.

77. See, for example, John E. Toews, "Intellectual History after the Linguistic Turn: The Autonomy of Meaning and the Irreducibility of Experience," *AHR*, 92 (1987): 879–907; Gabrielle M. Spiegel, "History, Historicism, and the Social Logic of the Text in the Middle Ages," *Speculum* 65 (1990): 59–86; Nancy Partner, "History without Empiricism/Truth without Facts," in *Transformations: The Languages of Culture and Personhood after Theory*, ed. Christie McDonald and Gary Wihl (State College, Pa., 1994), 1–10. This can be said even of Hayden White and Dominick LaCapra, who go furthest in acceptance of the theoretical claims of postmodernism but continue to produce historical narratives that follow the conventional rules of the profession's realist historiography. See LaCapra, *Rethinking Intellectual History: Texts, Contexts, Language* (Ithaca, 1983).

78. The works of sociologists Pierre Bourdieu and Richard Harvey Brown and of the social theorist Richard J. Bernstein point in this direction.

79. Lynn Hunt, "History Beyond Social Theory," in *The States of 'Theory': History, Art, and Critical Discourse*, ed. David Carroll (New York, 1993).

80. One sign is the books being reviewed in the leading reviewing journal in American history. In a recent number singled out by Morton Keller as indicative of the new orientation of American historiography, at least ten of the forty-three books reviewed were by scholars in disciplines other than history. *Reviews in American History* 21 (December 1993); Morton Keller, "Reviews in American History," *Times Literary Supplement* (March 18, 1994), 22.

81. For example, in a recent survey of the historical work being done in the social sciences, the authors found that historical social scientists looked to each other rather than to historians for their authorities, creating subfields within rather than across disciplinary borders. Monkkonen, ed., introduction to *Engaging the Past*.

CHAPTER 5

Explaining Racism in American History

THOMAS C. HOLT

In 1940, the African-American intellectual and political activist W. E. B. Du Bois described in *Dusk of Dawn* his intellectual odyssey of fifty-odd years. He noted that upon his graduation from Harvard in the 1890s, he had thought of "[t]he Negro problem [as] a matter of systematic investigation and intelligent understanding. The world was thinking wrong about race, because it did not know. The ultimate evil was stupidity. The cure for it was knowledge based on scientific investigation." Consequently, he decided to address the problem by studying "the facts, any and all facts, . . . and by measurement and comparison and research, work up to any valid generalization which I could." But soon "there cut across this plan which I had as a scientist, a red ray which could not be ignored. . . . a poor Negro in central Georgia, Sam Hose, had killed his landlord's wife. I wrote out a careful and reasoned statement concerning the evident facts and started down to the Atlanta *Constitution* office, . . . I did not get there. On the way news met me: Sam Hose had been lynched, and they said that his knuckles were on exhibition at a grocery store farther down on Mitchell Street, along which I was walking. . . . I turned back to the University. I began to turn aside from my work."[1]

Much like Du Bois, we—scholars and laypersons alike—are still frustrated by our continuing incapacity to explain racism or most racial phenomena. Indeed, our intellectual problems are not unlike those Du Bois confronted almost a century ago: Is racism a phenomenon best understood as caused by misinformation and ignorance or by deep irrational urges and psychological dysfunction? Or more precisely, perhaps: we have made some progress in explaining the origins of racism, but not its reproduction. There is a growing consensus that the origins of racism are linked with the advent of modernity; that is, to developments in the aftermath of European overseas expansion and colonization in the fifteenth and sixteenth centuries.[2] Thus we have come to understand racism not as something "transhistorical" or "epiphenomenal," something outside normal historical and social processes, but as social creations under determinate historical circumstances.[3] But even as the concepts of race and racism have become thus historicized, our notions of racism—in historical literature as well as in lay thought—remain in many other respects stubbornly naturalized. Even some of the best historical literature and some of the more prominent historical treatments of America's racial history written since 1960 illustrate the intellectual difficulties we confront. That is to say, very often they offer insightful, sometimes subtle, and potentially illuminating examinations of the development of racial ideas, of the "historical" determination of racial phenomena, and even of the "social construction" of racial concepts, only to regress to forms of explanation that are at their core often functionalist, occasionally reductionist, and sometimes even biologistic.

Indeed, explaining racist phenomena confronts contemporary social theory with some of its most profound challenges, intellectual and political. It puts in play some of the crucial issues we confront in attempting to elaborate a social theory adequate to contemporary society. It illuminates especially our difficulty in reconciling materialist with symbolic/discursive approaches to explaining social phenomena, and of determining the locus and nature of their interaction or fit. It exposes a fundamental discontinuity between most behavioral explanations sited at the individual level of human experience and those at the level of society and social forces.

Obviously these intellectual problems are neither exclusively American nor distinctively the province of historians. Indeed, many of our key insights into strategies of explanation for racial phenomena come from social scientists other than historians, or historians other than Americans.[4] Nonetheless, national historiographies of racism are in some respects quite divergent. British, French, German, and Brazilian discussions of race, for example, have developed very differently, with different objects of study, prompted by different political and social concerns, and informed perhaps by different historical and intellectual trajectories. A thorough comparative examination of these distinctive national discussions is beyond the capacity of this—and perhaps any—brief paper to undertake, but even cursory, selective observations on some of the differences and similarities might be suggestive of the distinctive intellectual and institutional terrain on which the American historiography has flourished.

Formal discussion of the problem of race in America, dating at least since Thomas Jefferson's *Notes on the State of Virginia* (1785), has from the start carried a certain concreteness, wherein the social history of settlement, nation building, and public policy were explicitly and inextricably linked to issues of racial identifications and distinctions *within its own national territory*. This has given a kind of prominence, even urgency to American discussions of race throughout its history that one finds among European scholars largely in the post–World War II era.

Consequently, perhaps, race in America has acquired heretofore—for Europeans no less than for Americans—a kind of "exceptionalist" character; exceptionally rigid, pervasive, and violent. As with most "exceptionalist" assumptions, the notion that American racism was somehow unique rested on a very selective parsing of the historical record. Although American racism was profoundly shaped by the existence of slavery on its own soil, for example, European societies were also thoroughly implicated in colonial slave regimes that strained their laws, their politics, and their social mores. As decolonized subjects have sought refuge in their respective metropoles in the post–World War II era, those repressed historical issues have also emerged—and with a vengeance. In America, the land of immigrants, race relations have been indelibly marked by successive waves of white and nonwhite immigration, with each wave redefining the meaning of "race" or provoking new episodes of "racial" tension or both. But similar phenomena—of guest workers and ex-colonials—have stimulated re-examinations of race and immigration among European scholars in the late twentieth century that raise analytic problems comparable to the older American discussions.[5] In the *longue-durée*, therefore, European and American race relations may well reveal more convergence than divergence; America may be less the unique exemplary of the profound analytic difficulties Du Bois sketched almost a century ago than simply the earliest.

It is true, nonetheless, that the historiographical trajectory of the American discourse on race has been shaped by its distinctive history. Slavery, the sectional controversy it gave rise to, and the Civil War that destroyed it have defined decisively America's history and American historical studies. Despite their best efforts historians could never completely segregate race from these fundamental issues of national integrity. The issues raised by African-Americans were present, even when they themselves were invisible. Arguably this was less true for other victims of American racism, such as Native Americans, Mexican-Americans, and Asian-Americans, notwithstanding the clear importance of their respective histories in the formation of the American nation. For this reason, perhaps, the African-American experience has formed the template—rightly or wrongly—for studies of all other racializing experiences in America. For much the same reason, successive African-American movements for civil rights and cultural revival in the 1960s and 1970s laid the basis for the reexamination of race and racism in American historical scholarship. Since the 1960s, studies of slavery have focused much less on the traditional issues of sectional politics and southern nationalism than on the institutional and experiential qualities of slavery itself. Studies of emancipation and its aftermath now focus much less on arcane struggles among national legislative factions than on the evolution of repressive social and economic systems. As a result of these trends, the African-American experience—especially their racial victimization—has emerged at center stage in the larger national historical experience.

Recapturing the experience of racialized groups is not synonymous, however, with an explicit examination of racism as such. Thus the *explanation* of racial phenomena remains largely implicit in much of the historical literature on African-Americans, Native Americans, Mexican-Americans, and Asian-Americans. Rather than attempt a broad survey of the American historiography as such, therefore, I will focus on some of the major texts that have addressed the problematic of racism explicitly and that have deployed exemplary strategies of explanation. For our purposes the major approaches or paradigms for explaining racism can be effectively summarized under four rough headings: (1) an idealist paradigm, that is, the notion that racism is a consequence of racist ideas, a product of thought; (2) an economistic or materialist paradigm, the notion that racism is a function of economic exploitation or competition; (3) a psychological paradigm, that racism arises from pathologies in the unconscious and/or conscious minds of individuals; and (4) a cultural paradigm, that racism is an aspect of specific cultural formations in a given society. Since these approaches are not mutually exclusive, any given explanation may rely on combinations of more than one or even all of them. But their separation allows for a clearer picture of how the "triggering mechanism" of race is envisioned in each.

The Idealist Paradigm. The simplicity of the syllogism that racist ideas lead to racist actions is powerful and ubiquitous. It has provided the most common analytic framework for both popular and academic analyses of racism. As Du Bois explained, before the Sam Hose incident he, too, had been convinced that racism was simply a matter of ignorance and its solution required only new and better information and right thinking. In short, people had the wrong ideas about race, and they could simply be educated out of those ideas. The problem is that the exact causal relationship between ideas and behavior is not nearly as uncomplicated as this argument assumes. Ideas are not autonomous but mediated by social structures and processes.

One of the more comprehensive studies of this genre is Reginald Horsman's *Race and Manifest Destiny*.[6] Horsman traces the evolution of racist ideas from European originators of Aryan and Anglo-Saxon myths of racial superiority to their descendants in America. He shows rather convincingly how various intellectual and political leaders took up or rediscovered elements of the old myths and rearticulated them in the new American context. The ideas of a great westward march of progress out of India and across the seas, of the need for racial purity, and so forth all found utility and resonance as justifications for enslaving Africans, exterminating Native Americans, and taking the land of Mexicans.

But there is an almost studied ambiguity in Horsman's discussion of historical causality. He seems on the mark when describing the very plasticity of European intellectual traditions that permitted "re-inventions" of those traditions in the Americas. The Irishman, for example, "a lazy, ragged, dirty Celt when he landed in New York," would become "the vanguard of the energetic Anglo-Saxon people" once he reached California.[7] But at other moments it is not entirely clear just what the explanatory status of "ideas" is. They appear at times to be nearly autonomous entities, nourished by—but not created by—historically specific social contexts. They are utilitarian, integral, and self-contained; they "fell," they were "used," they could "assuage."

> The new [racial] ideas *fell* on fertile ground in the 1830s and 1840s. In a time of rapid growth and change, with its accompanying insecurities and dislocations, many Americans found comfort in the strength and status of distinguished racial heritage. The new racial ideology could be *used to force* new immigrants to conform to the prevailing political, economic, and social system, and it could also be *used to justify* the sufferings or deaths of blacks, Indians, or Mexicans. Feelings of guilt could be *assuaged by* assumptions of historical and scientific inevitability.[8]

At times they are plastic ideological instruments consciously deployed to achieve certain political and material objectives—like Indian removal or the conquest of Mexico. And yet again, they sometimes appear to arise out of individual psychological needs, to be projections of and deflections from guilty consciences pursuing a not-so-manifest destiny.

But even as Horsman demonstrates how preexisting racist ideas rationalized racial oppression and inequality in nineteenth-century America, his evidence also reveals how new ideas or new twists on old ideas developed out of particular ideological conjunctures and historical confrontations—in other words, in some instances the inequality and oppression came first. For example, Indians were seen as *potentially* white by Thomas Jefferson; they represented not savagery but innocence, an enduring emblem of nature and the wilderness Euro-Americans wanted to tame. Thus, in marked contrast with his ideas about Africans, Jefferson could urge a government policy designed to encourage Indians to be civilized and assimilated. With the growth of the cotton trade, however, other southerners came increasingly to see Indians as barriers to economic progress because they occupied some of the best cotton lands of the South. So under Andrew Jackson they were forcibly removed from these lands, many of them—like the Seminoles in Florida—with great violence and brutality. Concurrent with this expulsion there developed a strikingly different view of Indians: not natural but savage, not candidates for eventual assimilation but for extermination.[9]

Ideas, then, are not autonomous from material and political realities. In some instances they shape our behavior; in others they are altered in response to what we do. In still other cases they appear to have no relation at all to what we do. They are certainly relevant to any explanation of racism, but seem not *in themselves* to be adequate explanations for racist phenomena.

The Economistic Paradigm. At first blush, the brute realities of economic interests appear to offer a more reliable explanation of racist behavior. These are what Du Bois, referring to African-Americans, called the "rational, conscious determination of white folk to oppress us." Simply stated, it is in the clear economic interest of some people to oppress or discriminate against other people, and such economic oppression lies at the root of racial oppression more generally.

There are two basic forms of this argument, however: one blames the ruling classes as cynical exploiters; another blames the white working class as vicious reactionaries to black competition. In the first case, the argument goes, it is in the interest of a ruling class to exploit a "racialized" workforce because the workers are less able to fight back, either because racism rationalizes or justifies their exploitation (slavery for example), or because they are divided from and against other workers and therefore become easier to control. In the second case white workers become the main oppressors because in a racially divided society the racial Other offers direct or potential competition for jobs and other economic resources and a vulnerable target for attack.

There is little doubt that there are specific historical and contemporary situations in which these explanations are especially powerful in explaining racist tensions and outbursts, but generally they offer unsatisfactory or incomplete accounts of either the original process of differentiation or its reproduction over time. Alexander Saxton's examination of white workers' reaction to Chinese labor in California is a case in point.[10] The role of wealthy capitalists in the creation and manipulation of a racially segmented labor force is convincingly demonstrated, as are the lines of ethnic cleavage and hostility among the working class. But confronting the questions of why Asians were singled out as the "racial" Other (rather than Irishmen or other "benighted" Europeans as found at various moments in the Northeast), and how the system reproduced itself once the original cause was no longer relevant, Saxton turns to political and ideological domains. As he notes at one point in concluding the narrative: "Entanglement of an economic conflict over contract labor with older ideological and organizational cleavages precluded any single or simple solution."[11]

Examining economic forces and structural contexts is essential to understanding how a racialized social order is constituted; how, for example, those Euro-American and Asian-American workers were brought into an arena of conflict in the first place. But once the precipitating economic cause or friction is removed, why does racism continue to be reproduced in the society? Once Africans or Asians or Mexicans cease to be an important reservoir of labor—as slaves, sharecroppers, or cheap industrial workers—why does racial hostility continue and in fact often increase? These questions cannot be answered by analyses that simply *reduce* race to class. For most of the nineteenth century certainly the competition blacks posed to "white" jobs was not proportionate to the violent responses of white workers—at least not in the Northeast, where African-American workers were few in number and largely excluded from growth industries.[12] And clearly, all groups who are economically exploited or economic competitors are not thought of or treated the same. As Du Bois observed bitterly in the early 1930s, whites as well as blacks were attacked for being scabs and strikebreakers, but the white scabs were attacked to scare them off or recruit them into the unions; the black scabs were attacked to kill them.[13]

Edmund S. Morgan's explanation of the development of slavery and racism in colonial Virginia represents a more subtle model for integrating materialist and ideological analyses to explain racist phenomena. In addressing that perennial chestnut of which came first, racism or slavery, Morgan argues convincingly that whatever the racial attitudes or prejudices of white planters in seventeenth-century Virginia, their actual treatment of African and white labor was not nearly so differentiated as it would become in the late colonial period. The transformation in their attitudes and treatment he traces to material and demographic changes in the colony. Africans were reduced to slavery when the life expectancy of workers increased to a point where it was *profitable* to own a slave for life as opposed to an indentured servant for a term of years; *and* when the political and military pressure exerted on the colony by a growing (longer-living) sector of landless white ex-indentured servants made it safer to subjugate Africans to slavery than to hire more white laborers.[14]

But although Morgan successfully explains the differential treatment of white and black labor and the origins of slavery and racism, an argument of this form will not explain why and how the system reproduced itself throughout another century of slavery, through another half century of sharecropping, through wage-labor in the twentieth century, down to the late twentieth century when black labor has become increasingly redundant. Again, no effective explanation can exclude the linkage between racial thought and practice and the changes in material and economic life, but that alone is inadequate to a full explanation of racism's development or its maturity. Again, after conceding the reasons for the original sin—the actions that marked and institutionalized the difference between white and black—how do we explain Sam Hose's broken and dismembered body?

The Psychological Paradigm. In his dissatisfaction with the inadequacy of both idealist and materialist explanations for "the red ray" that crossed his path, Du Bois turned to what he called "age-long complexes sunk now largely to unconscious habit and irrational urges." The unconscious and the "irrational" fall within the province of psychological explanations, and most of the most prominent historical works drawing on this approach to explain racism have emphasized some variant of Freudian analysis.[15] In its general form, as found in historical studies, the psychological argument is that personal anxieties produced in individual human beings are evaded by projecting them onto an object of aggression, an outsider. Thus the common causal triad runs: "repression," "projection," "oppression."

One influential example of the direct application of such a psychological analysis to the history of racism in America is the work of Joel Kovel. Although not a historian, Kovel makes explicit much of the analytical apparatus many historians employ. He argues, among other things, that the "natural" association of blackness with dirt and excrement together with sexual anxieties stemming from our childhood development—if unresolved—will be projected onto black people as objects of fantasy and invention, and that this helps explain racist impulses.[16]

Although Kovel goes on to attempt to relate these purely individual traumas to the larger social and cultural orders, the latter appear to be mere metaphorical extensions to the social level of individual-level, psychological traits. As such, Kovel's explanation exposes one of the biggest hurdles for all such explanations—how does one use individual-level phenomena to explain social-level behaviors? The only answer—usually implicit—is that the social is merely an aggregate of the individual; ergo, a sick society is merely a collection of sick individuals.

There is reason to doubt that this particular image of the connection between individual and social phenomena actually works. In fact, it is more persuasive that *the social* forms the individual rather than the other way around. The other major problem is that purely psychological approaches tend to naturalize racist behavior; that is, the psychological mechanisms described in child development theories are generalized over all times, peoples, and places. As such, they become in reality (or function) like biological explanations.[17] So in a period where we have finally come to see race as socially constructed rather than biological, we are asked to reverse field and explain racism in terms of innate human processes. Although Kovel and other proponents of such approaches would not deny that social structures shaped individual psychologies, their explanations do not explain the exact relation between these two levels and thus imply a psychoanalytical remedy for racial ills. The implications of this for any theory of social change and for any effort to change society are very discouraging, to say the least.

Winthrop Jordan's *White over Black*, which attempts to explain the origins of American racism, reflects some of the conceptual and analytical difficulties encountered in the historical application to racial phenomena of the typical psychological approach.[18] Much like Kovel, Jordan locates racism's origins in the derogatory attitudes that white people had toward blackness long before they encountered Africans. These attitudes were reflected in their language, which was emotionally coded to denigrate anything dark or black, and in the formation of their sexual personalities, whereby repressed fantasies were projected onto blacks. Thus the Elizabethan Englishmen's sexual anxieties and guilt, projected onto West Africans, gave shape to racial "attitudes," which were passed on to their English and American descendants. But since the subsequent generations, like Thomas Jefferson's, appear to have reproduced the original racist ideas in strikingly similar ways to the Elizabethans, history becomes more a backdrop for than a factor in the process Jordan describes.

As with other psychological explanations, Jordan's suffers from a lack of clarity as to the exact connection between the individual pathologies and the social action they purport ultimately to describe and explain. Jordan attempts to get around the problem by invoking parallel economic and social developments: that is, that Africans were enslaved because they were needed to work American sugar and cotton plantations; that English psychological pathologies regarding race were exacerbated or stimulated by societywide cultural anxieties during the age of discovery, and so forth. But in his explanatory schemes, all these phenomena are largely peripheral to and certainly are not the driving force behind the development of racist thought and action. Thus time and time again Jordan resorts to the sheer shock effect that the African's color purportedly excited and its resonance at the deepest levels of white psyches.[19] This has the effect of "naturalizing" the process and thus cuts against his otherwise commendable efforts to historicize it. Consequently, despite his gestures toward material or sociological explanations, Jordan's analysis relies at its base on the mechanism of differentiation and projection found in individual, unconscious minds, that is, on their innate properties. We are left with the inference, for example, after the long exploration of Thomas Jefferson's psychosexual problems, that we need only project Jefferson's mind onto a larger screen to have the American mind, or at least the white male version of it.

How then do we get from the individual to the social level of analysis? Clearly the kind of structural analyses necessarily involved in any economic or materialist explanation tend to rely too much on rational-conscious motivations, or they downplay human agency and become too schematic, even deterministic. Also, such approaches cannot account for the irrational, the unconscious aspects so prevalent in the long history of race in America. Psychological explanations, on the other hand, can be enlightening about how racial notions function in individual pathology but seem incapable of explaining collective acts, except as aggregates of individual tendencies. In either form, deterministic schemes lose contingency and complexity, a sense of historical development, and racism tends again to become naturalized. What is needed, then, are explanations that are symmetrical at both levels—that is, where the connections between individual thought, belief, and action can be related to or explained in relation to societywide phenomena and vice versa.

The Cultural Paradigm. My notion of a "cultural paradigm" is a loosely framed scaffolding over a broad terrain. By this rubric I intend to convey some sense of works that share certain premises: Racism is a product of historically specific social formations. It is neither exogenous to the society (i.e., coming from the outside) nor reducible to or the effect of something else (like class). Rather it is a part of a given culture, often in some sense, simultaneously a product of the culture and producing that culture. (Indeed, one of the dangers of some variants of this approach is that they tend to totalize racial phenomena or culture or both).[20]

Ronald Takaki's *Iron Cages* is one of the more stimulating and provocative early works within this genre. Takaki attempts to locate the development of mature American racism in the evolution of American culture during the nineteenth century. The American Revolution ruptured the moorings that held the former British colonists to a secure sense of self, place, and destiny, even as it freed them to pursue their manifest destiny of material and geographical expansion. In the absence of aristocratic hierarchies, social relations were more thoroughly mediated by the market, which allocated assessment of spiritual value and self-worth as well as material rewards and punishment. Material and moral success now depended transparently on self-discipline and self-denial. Drawing on Max Weber, Takaki argues that such a social regime must perforce foster repressed anxieties and guilt, the outlet for which was projection onto the colored minorities, who were deemed to harbor all the repressed sins of the white Other.

> In the North and the South, the racial ideology of the black "child/savage," in its emphasis on the need to develop self-restraint and accumulate goods, complemented the ideology of capitalism and gave specific support to Jacksonian individualism and enterprise. . . . [T]he black "child/savage" represented what whites thought they were not, and more importantly—what they must not become. . . . In the total structure of American society, racial and class developments interpenetrated each other. White over black had an organic relationship to class divisions and conflicts forming within white society.[21]

Although the structure of Takaki's argument is very similar to that within the psychological paradigm, its substance and media are less psychological than cultural. Culture spawns and sustains political, economic, and social institutions; it is also the product of such institutions. Indeed, Takaki conflates culture with ideology, defining it as "a shared set of ideas, images, values, and assumptions about human nature and society," and his access to it is through the cultural productions of the elite, what he calls "the culture-makers."[22] Thus the problems raised by Takaki's analysis are general to this genre of historical explanation.[23] What is the relation between culture and material life? Indeed, just what is culture? What is ideology—and its relation to culture and material life? How can we most usefully think about the nature of hegemony and agency, or the roles of elites and masses in shaping racial phenomena?

In sorting out these questions as they emerge in the historiographical literature on race, it might be useful to recognize the distinctions between and the interdependence of the three concepts: culture, ideology, and discourse. Although there are many possible definitions of these concepts, for our purposes *culture* might be taken quite simply as the way we live, or rather the practices by which we live (doing); *ideology* as the way we understand how we live (knowing); and *discourse* as the way we communicate those understandings (making known). The cultural is intimately linked to both our material and nonmaterial lives—our economy, our various power structures, our technologies, as well as our social and spiritual life. It involves all those systems that mediate our relations with other human beings and with the natural world. The ideological comprehends all the ways in which we understand, mentally order and reorder, manipulate, or visualize those dense systems or webs of interrelationships. The discursive invokes that complex system of symbols by which we code and thus are able to transmit what we know and what we feel. As such it is an essential window onto the ideological and the cultural landscape. It not only reflects meaning but creates it by forging new connections, metaphorical associations, and so forth. And most important, it is not just the language or verbal system but includes a whole array of nonverbal signs and symbols as well. All three concepts, then, are social and collective as well as individual. Without the individual level, they are deprived of life; without the social level, they are deprived of meaningful effect.[24] All three are connected in complex ways, therefore, but should not be conflated.

Some of the most recent work on racial and class formation in nineteenth-century America has begun to approach this more complex level of discussion.[25] In *Wages of Whiteness*, for example, David Roediger has demonstrated how "whiteness" and "blackness" were mutually constituted within the selfsame process by which a white working class was formed in nineteenth-century America. Although Roediger's analysis bears a family resemblance to Takaki's of that same period, in Roediger's story the culture of white workers is not simply the artifact or by-product of white elite hegemony. White workers were subject to stresses and strains imposed by economic transformations raining down from above, but they also made their own decisions, adjustments, and mistakes. They created a vibrant vernacular language, lively popular theater, and street parades that were democratic outlets for their joys and grievances. But these same forms of discourse, culture, and ideology demeaned and stigmatized blacks—and often fostered direct physical attacks upon them. Most demeaning of all, perhaps, was blackface minstrelsy, which constituted at once a cultural institution, an ideological production, and a set of discursive practice that would stretch well into the twentieth century.[26]

What Roediger's work—and the work of others along similar lines—suggests, therefore, are the ways that race and rascism might be comprehended historically; that is to say that they are not just socially constructed but are historical processes as well. Humans make race, to paraphrase Marx, but they are not free to make it in any old way they please. The constraints within and the givens with which they construct racial meanings are not biological but historical, including the material conditions that history fashions. An historicized, social process allows space for agency and choice at the individual level, yet individual behavior does not arise out of some naturalized psychological processes but is "determined" in the arena of social relations.

Furthermore, this approach suggests that we need to conceptualize racist practice in relation to all manner of other ordinary human intellectual, cultural, and social practices. Thus racism is not seen simply as some kind of abnormality, outside the realm of ordinary affairs, a historical wrong turn. Produced in the social world, its potential is ever present. Recognition of all this might displace the persistent tendency to biologize race and the reaction to race, locating both somehow in our genetic makeup. To say that these phenomena are profoundly historical is also to attempt to reconcile constraint with volition, and the ideological with the material.

What the historiography of racism in American history suggests, therefore, is that an effective analysis of racial phenomena must be at once psychological and sociological, material and nonmaterial. This is not to suggest some mere eclectic mix of approaches, however, but a reconceptualization of the very meaning of individual action, that under certain circumstances the dichotomies between individual and social, material and nonmaterial are false ones. Individual preferences, values, ideas, behaviors have meaning only in a social context; they are constituted out of the social and are in large measure the effects of relations of power. Put another way, the multiple exercises of power create the individual; and individual subjects are both the objects of power and its conduits. Thus how we understand—and explain—racism depends very much on how we understand social action more generally; and how we understand social action in general will be powerfully informed by how we understand racial phenomena.

Notes

1. W.E.B. Du Bois, *Dusk of Dawn: An Essay toward an Autobiography of a Race Concept* (1940; reprint, New York, 1975), 51, 58, 67.

2. This chronology is implicit, if not explicit, in most contemporary analyses of racism. For its most explicit form, see Ivan Hannaford's *Race: The History of an Idea in the West* (Baltimore, 1995), which argues the thesis of racism's modernity in exhaustive detail.

3. For a sharp critique of these tendencies, see especially Barbara Fields, "Ideology and Race in American History," in *Region, Race and Reconstruction: Essays in Honor of C. Vann Woodward*, ed. J. Morgan Kousser and James McPherson (New York, 1982); and idem, "Racism in America," *New Left Review* 181 (May/June 1990): 95–118.

4. Here I am thinking in particular of the work, among others, of Stuart Hall's "Race, Articulation and Societies Structured in Dominance," in *Sociological Theories: Race and Colonialism* (Paris, 1980); Paul Gilroy's *'There Ain't No Black in the Union Jack'* (Chicago, 1991); David Theo Goldberg, *Racist Culture: Philosophy and the Politics of Meaning* (New York, 1993); and Michael Omi and Howard Winant, *Racial Formation in the United States: From the 1960s to the 1980s* (New York, 1986).

5. For examples in the recent literature on France, see Pierre-André Taguieff, *La force du préjuge: essai sur le racisme et ses doubles* (Paris, 1987); Maxim Silverman, ed., *Race, Discourse and Power in France* (Aldershot, 1991); idem, *Deconstructing the Nation: Immigration, Racism and Citizenship in Modern France* (London, 1992); Colette Guillaumin, *Racism, Sexism, Power and Ideology* (London, 1995); and Etienne Balibar and Immanuel Wallerstein, *Race, Nation, Class: Ambiguous Identities* (London, 1991).

6. Reginald Horsman, *Race and Manifest Destiny: The Origins of American Racial Anglo-Saxonism* (Cambridge, 1981).

7. Ibid., 4.

8. Ibid., 5 (emphasis added).

9. Ibid., 189–207. Cf. Ronald Takaki, *Iron Cages: Race and Culture in Nineteenth-Century America* (New York, 1979), 55–65, 80–107.

10. Alexander Saxton, *The Indispensable Enemy: Labor and the Anti-Chinese Movement in California* (Berkeley, 1971).

11. Ibid., 261.

12. Ironically, in parts of the postbellum lower South—where they were a plurality or even majority in some instances—blacks were sometimes able to forge temporary alliances with white worker organizations in shipyards and plantations. For example, Eric Arnesen, *Waterfront Workers of New Orleans: Race, Class and Politics, 1863–1923* (New York, 1991).

13. Cited in Thomas C. Holt, "The Political Uses of Alienation: W. E. B. Du Bois on Politics, Race, and Culture, 1903–1940," *American Quarterly* 42 (June 1990): 313.

14. Edmund S. Morgan, *American Slavery, American Freedom: The Ordeal of Colonial Virginia* (New York, 1975).

15. I do not mean to deny the potential usefulness of psychoanalytic paradigms as such. Indeed, some feminist theory may yet demonstrate the general applicability, for example, of Lacanian thought to problems of difference, which might include race. But these perspectives have not to my knowledge been systematically and effectively applied to racial phenomena as yet.

16. Joel Kovel, *White Racism: A Psychohistory* (New York, 1971), 46–105.

17. For examples, see Colette Guillaumin, "'Race' and Discourse," trans. Claire Hughes, in Silverman, ed., *Race, Discourse and Power in France*, 5–13; and George W. Stocking, Jr., "Essays on Culture and Personality," in *Malinowski, Rivers, Benedict and Others: Essays on Culture and Personality*, ed. George W. Stocking, Jr. (Madison, 1986), 5.

18. Needless to say, perhaps, this is not a claim that Jordan was influenced by Kovel; Jordan's book was published first. Winthrop Jordan, *White over Black: American Attitudes toward the Negro, 1550–1812* (Chapel Hill, 1968).

19. For examples, see Jordan, *White over Black*, 5–7, 95–97, 142–44, 257, 341, 458–59, 475.

20. An example of this totalizing effect is Omi and Winant's *Racial Formation*, in which we are told to think of "race as an unstable and 'decentered' complex of social meanings constantly being transformed by political struggle," and told at the same time that "the racial dimension [is] present to some degree in every identity, institution and social practice in the United States" (68). In short, the racial formation appears to include everything

and to be everywhere. Thus it becomes just a covering term, not an explanation of relationships or processes.

21. Takaki, *Iron Cages*, 126, 127.

22. "What white men in power thought and did mightily affected what everyone thought and did." Ibid., xiv–xv.

23. Another notable work within this genre is Joel Williamson's *Rage for Order: Black-White Relations in the American South since Emancipation* (New York, 1986). Williamson explains the resurgence of what he calls southern "white radicalism" in the 1890s by a combination of political and economic interests that blacks directly or indirectly threatened and the conjuncture of general social and psychological anxieties in which sexual and racial fears were aroused by the sudden inability of white men to fulfill their gender roles as economic providers for their women and families. There followed what might be best described as a generalized social psychosis in which "the rage against the black beast rapist was a kind of psychic compensation." A more subtle and nuanced elaboration of the general scheme Williamson frames can be found in Glenda Elizabeth Gilmore, *Gender and Jim Crow: Women and the Politics of White Supremacy, 1896–1920* (Chapel Hill, 1996). See also Nancy MacLean, *Behind the Mask of Chivalry: The Making of the Second Ku Klux Klan* (New York, 1994).

24. Cf. Henri Lefebvre, *Critique de la vie quotidienne: Fondements d'une sociologie de la quotidienneté* (Paris, 1961), 143–44. See discussion of this text in Thomas C. Holt, "Marking: Race, Race-Making, and the Writing of History," *American Historical Review* 100 (February 1995): 1–20.

25. The works I have in mind are David R. Roediger, *The Wages of Whiteness: Race and the Making of the American Working Class* (London, 1991); Alexander Saxton, *The Rise and Fall of the White Republic: Class Politics and Mass Culture in Nineteenth-Century America* (London, 1990); and Eric Lott, *Love and Theft: Blackface Minstrelsy and the American Working Class* (New York, 1993). My discussion of these texts will be brief and wholly inadequate here, but I have discussed them at greater length and more critically in Holt, "Marking," and in "Racism and the Working Class," review essay, *International Labor and Working-Class History* 45 (spring 1994): 86–95.

26. Holt, "Marking," 16–18.

CHAPTER 6

Crèvecoeur's Question

HISTORICAL WRITING ON
IMMIGRATION, ETHNICITY,
AND NATIONAL IDENTITY

PHILIP GLEASON

THE STUDY of immigration and ethnic groups in the United States, as John Higham observed in 1982, "has long been an expression of a fundamental debate over the nature of American society." Thanks to the renewal of large-scale immigration in the past thirty years, and to the recent emergence of "multiculturalism" as a way of understanding American society, we are now in the midst of a particularly intense phase of that debate. But the basic issue was formulated as a question more than two centuries ago. In his *Letters from an American Farmer* (1782), J. Hector St. John de Crèvecoeur asked, "What then is the American, this new man?" Today, we would use gender-inclusive language, and speak perhaps of "identity," but the same underlying question fuels the debate: "What does it mean to be an American?"[1]

Immigration figured prominently in Crèvecoeur's treatment of the question, and he gave it a very definite answer. The favorable conditions that obtained in American society—most notably, freedom and material well-being—were, he asserted, "melting" European newcomers of diverse backgrounds into a "new race of men" which was destined to achieve great things. This optimistically assimilationist interpretation of American nationality, though challenged by Know-Nothing nativism in the 1850s, dominated American thinking on the subject for a century. By 1900, however, immigration was widely regarded as a major social problem, and a movement to restrict it had come into being. After World War I, immigration was cut back sharply by the passage of laws that embodied invidious racial assumptions about the intrinsic worth of different nationality groups and whether they were "assimilable"—that is, whether they had it in them to become real Americans. From the midtwenties, when restriction took effect in earnest, until 1965, when a new law changed the basis of American policy, immigration seemed a thing of the past. Since then, it has come back strongly as a social reality and an issue of public policy.

Our concern in this essay is with the way professional historians have dealt with immigration, and (implicitly if not explicitly) with its relation to American national identity. The subject can be divided into four chronological phases, the opening and closing dates of which are of course somewhat arbitrary. The first period begins with the founding year of the American Historical Association and ends with the appearance of the first general history of American immigration written by a professional historian.

THE PREHISTORY OF IMMIGRATION HISTORIOGRAPHY, 1884–1926

It is a striking coincidence that history established itself as a professional academic discipline at roughly the same time the "immigration problem" became a significant policy issue. Even more striking is the fact that professional historians paid almost no attention to immigration, either as an area of research or as a contemporary social problem. Only forty-nine doctoral dissertations on matters related to immigration were written between 1885 and 1920, and students of history produced less than a third of this meager total. Edward N. Saveth, who wrote the standard work on the subject, says that the first two generations of professional historians either passed over immigration in silence or "treated it as a sort of historiographic hangnail."[2]

Preoccupied in the post–Civil War years with the theme of national unification, historians of that era focused on the nation as a whole, giving special attention to the constitutional and political aspects of national development. This helps explain why immigration seemed to them a side issue, but their attitude was surely reinforced by the fact that they were themselves of "old American stock" and took it for granted that the Anglo-Saxon or (in Henry Adams's case) Norman strains were the ones that really counted in the making of America. Looking back on their work from the perspective of the 1990s, one might say that their outlook implicitly betrayed something of the "filiopietism" for which Saveth reproached the "amateur" (i.e., nonprofessional) historians of the day, who, along with social scientists, produced most of what was written on immigration, but who wrote as more or less militant champions of the ethnic groups whose stories they were telling. Saveth did not take note of filiopietistic tendencies on the part of mainstream historians. The reason, perhaps, was that though he lamented their neglecting immigration, he shared the academic professionals' conviction that the national story constituted the larger whole into which subsidiary reports on the place of immigrants in American life were to be fitted.[3] However that may be, we must postpone further discussion of filiopietism lest we get ahead of our own story.

After the turn of the century, historians' work reflected in an incidental way the prevailing concern about immigration as a social problem, but the most explicit discussion by a leading historian, Frederick Jackson Turner, was confined to a series of newspaper articles that were largely descriptive in nature. Except for a book by the labor economist-cum-historian John R. Commons (who is not included among the professionals discussed by Saveth), they did not make extended contributions to the discussion. The same is true of the racialist assumptions so prevalent among commentators on the immigration problem—

historians may have accepted racialism, but they were not the leaders in elaborating or promoting it. Elsewhere on the conceptual front, new terms of discourse were introduced that have retained their prominence to the present day, most notably "melting pot" and "cultural pluralism." Neither was introduced by a historian. The playwright Israel Zangwill put the first in circulation; the social philosopher Horace Kallen, the second.[4]

None of the general histories of immigration appearing in those years was written by a professional historian; a social worker, Edith Abbott, edited the most important collections of documents; and the best known studies of individual groups were done by nonhistorians. Consider three books that merit being called classics: *Our Slavic Fellow Citizens* (1910) was written by Emily Greene Balch, an economist and social worker; *The Italian Emigration of Our Time* (1919), by Robert F. Foerster, an economist; and *The Polish Peasant in Europe and America*, 5 vols. (1918–20), by W. I. Thomas and Florian Znaniecki, two sociologists. It is true that Arthur M. Schlesinger, the pioneer of American social history, published an essay in 1921 calling his colleagues' attention to the importance of immigration as a factor in the nation's development. But it is revealing that the article appeared in the *American Journal of Sociology* before being included in Schlesinger's *New Viewpoints in American History* (1922).[5]

Schlesinger's being of immigrant background himself perhaps had something to do with his conviction that the Anglo-Saxon heritage was giving way to "a new composite American type now in the process of making." The experience of World War I also played a role in alerting historians of the United States to its connections with the larger world. Even Turner expanded his horizons, "dimly discern[ing]," as Moses Rischin puts it, "a pattern that would place the immigration story within an international framework of frontier and section. . . ." As we have seen, Turner was not altogether unmindful of immigration before the war. He had, after all, grown up among immigrants in Wisconsin and often referred to the frontier as a crucible of assimilation. One of his early graduate students, Kate A. Everest, researched the coming of the Germans to Wisconsin in a dissertation that was the second immigration-history Ph.D. ever done at an American university. It should also be noted that Turner was *Doktorvater* to two other key figures in immigration historiography—George M. Stephenson, whose general history marks the end of the first phase of our story, and Marcus L. Hansen, the giant of the next phase, who encountered Turner just as the war opened the latter's eyes to the possibility of "national cross-fertilization."[6]

Stephenson launched his career with a doctoral dissertation on a classically Turnerian topic, public land policy. It was published as a book the year the United States entered the war, and the wartime experience probably helped to turn Stephenson's attention to immigration. The nationalistic passions it aroused, among old-stock Americans as well as those of immigrant background, brought out with unprecedented clarity what he called the "problems of a composite citizenship." He devoted two chapters of his *History of American Immigration* (1926) to the war and its effects, one being the Johnson-Reed Act of 1924, which ended a century of largely unrestricted immigration and thereby, as Stephenson put it in the first sentence of the book, "closed a momentous chapter in American and European history, and indeed in world history."[7]

Apart from its landmark status, Stephenson's book holds up moderately well as a first effort to synthesize the history of immigration. It is very sketchy by later standards, but does include a relatively full and sympathetic discussion of "oriental immigration," which, as Stephenson acutely observed, "profoundly affected our whole immigration policy."[8] By far the most striking feature of the book is its narrowly political focus. Aside from brief remarks on old-country backgrounds in Europe, Stephenson did not discuss immigrant groups as entities in themselves, focusing rather on how they impinged on U.S. national politics. Besides the participation of immigrants in party battles, he covered nativist reactions and the evolution of immigration policy. But only in respect to politics did immigration seem to function as a factor in American life. Stephenson, who was of immigrant background himself, did not lack interest in the internal history of immigrant groups, nor in the nonpolitical dimensions of their experience. Indeed, his next book was a detailed analysis of the religious history of his own group, Swedish Americans. But when he undertook to synthesize the history of immigration as a whole, his approach resembled that of earlier scholars who had neglected the subject, in the sense that he cast the story in terms of American political history as traditionally understood.

IMMIGRATION HISTORY BECOMES A FIELD OF SPECIALIZATION, 1926–1940

The first group of professional historians to specialize in immigration history were midwesterners of northern European derivation.[9] Stephenson belonged to the group, as did his Norwegian-American colleague Theodore C. Blegen; together they made the University of Minnesota a major institutional center for immigration history. Carl Wittke, who was of German background, had a Harvard degree but spent his career as a teacher, writer, and administrator in his home state of Ohio. Marcus Hansen, whose father was Danish and mother Norwegian, was born in Wisconsin and educated in Iowa before going off to Harvard to study with Turner in 1917; he taught at the University of Illinois for the last ten years of his tragically short life, dying in 1938 at the age of forty-five. These were not the only historians interested in the subject, but aside from W. F. Adams's book on emigration from Ireland and R. A. Billington's study of antebellum nativism, they produced the outstanding works of the period in question.[10]

The social and cultural context within which they worked had changed notably from that of the preceding period.[11] The "immigration problem" had disappeared as a public issue; nativist fears evaporated after the religiously divisive presidential campaign of Al Smith in 1928; and "culture" (as anthropologists used the term) replaced "race" as the key to understanding human groups. Among second- and third-generation immigrants—that is, the children and grandchildren of those who actually immigrated—assimilation seemed to contemporary observers to be proceeding very rapidly. After the depression hit, economic and political issues dominated the scene, but Franklin D. Roosevelt's New Deal encouraged a spirit of social liberalism and tolerance. Although intellectuals deprecated nationalism, by the late thirties the mounting threat of totalitarianism in Europe sparked an ideological revival of democracy that reinforced preexisting currents of interest in the roots of American culture and its manifestations in art, literature, and folklore. Social history, which had gained at least a foothold among professionals, reflected something of the same spirit, since its devotees sought to illuminate the ways of life of ordinary Americans.

Though immigration history was still a very minor theme, these developments created a more favorable climate for its reception. Three of its four major practitioners focused on the internal history of immigrant groups. Stephenson's 1932 study, which concentrated on the "religious aspects" of Swedish immigration, went far toward providing an overall history of the group, including the old-country background. Blegen's two-volume work on Norwegian immigration was even more comprehensive, and the publications of the Norwegian-American Historical Association, of which he was the driving force, set a new standard of scholarly excellence for such organizations.[12] Wittke, the most prolific immigration historian of his generation, was an indefatigable researcher who mined the ethnic press as no one had before. Though he devoted most of his scholarly attention to German-Americans, his published work covered a broad range and included a general history of immigration that served for two decades as the standard survey of the subject.

The appearance of Wittke's We Who Built America (1939) coincided with the reawakening of democratic nationalism set off by the outbreak of war in Europe, and its very title claimed for immigrants a place of honor in the making of America. Like his contemporaries, Wittke believed large-scale immigration was over, and he anticipated continued "fusion of [the] immigrant strains" already present in American society. But this basically assimilationist outlook did not justify overlooking the historic significance of immigration. Adducing a personal example, Wittke spoke movingly of his father, who had immigrated from Germany in 1889 and lived for almost half a century in the United States. The elder Wittke was a "thoroughly trained mechanic," whose simple but productive life, along with his devotion to American ideals, enabled him to "blend into the American stream" and provide for his children advantages he had not himself enjoyed. Of such "humble but honorable fragment[s]," his son declared, "the real Epic of America must eventually be written."[13]

Wittke disclaimed doing more than sketching the broad outlines of that epic story, but what he really supplied was an anthology of ethnic sub-epics. His book provides a great wealth of information on a score of immigrant nationalities. It is richest for the "old immigrants," especially the Germans and Irish, much thinner on Asians and the "new immigrants" from southern and eastern Europe whose history had not yet been studied in detail. The approach is, however, purely descriptive. *We Who Built America* has no overarching interpretive scheme or principle of structural unity. Although he assumed, "of course," that "our American civilization is basically Anglo-Saxon" and that the great majority of the people were English in derivation, Wittke nevertheless confined his attention to "non-English immigrants."[14] By doing so he presumably meant to highlight the role of these groups and compensate for their previous neglect. But since the Anglo-Saxons had supposedly shaped American civilization, omitting them left Wittke without a framework of national development into which "the saga of the immigrant" could be integrated. The result is a series of disconnected stories that fails to cohere as a unified narrative and leaves the reader without the sense of having grasped the subject as an intelligible whole.

Wittke's attempt to write a comprehensive history of immigration by telling the story of one group after another dramatized the limitations of the internalist approach. Marcus Hansen had already expressed his dissatisfaction with it, even when restricted to the history of only one immigrant nationality. Reviewing Blegen's first volume on Norwegian immigration in 1932, Hansen praised its merits and then went on to say: "But the student of American history is not interested primarily in nationalities. The significance of the movement [immigration] is broader than the experience of detached groups." Historians should seek rather to understand "the mysterious forces that, disregarding political boundaries, operated to set mankind in motion" all across Europe, in one region after another.[15] Precisely this was the task that Hansen set for himself, first in his doctoral dissertation, then in three additional years of research in Europe. Death intervened before he was able to finish even the first of the three volumes he envisioned. *The Atlantic Migration, 1607–1860* (1940), which appeared posthumously thanks to the editorial work of Arthur M. Schlesinger, is thus but a fragment of the full project.[16]

Truncated though it is, Hansen's work constituted a monumental conceptual breakthrough. Prescinding altogether from nationalities as such, Hansen linked the whole phenomenon of immigration to broader historical developments affecting both Europe and America. Moreover, he showed that the forces at work in the migration of English settlers to America as "colonists" were the same as those that moved non-English "immigrants" in the colonial era and in the nineteenth century.[17] By framing the story of colonial beginnings in this manner, and by showing that a sharp falling off of immigration between 1789 and 1815 hastened the assimilation of the immigrants already here, Hansen succeeded in linking immigration to the narrative core of American history as it had never been done before—and this despite his book's being much more a study of emigration from Europe than of immigration to America. For Hansen perceived that immigration *connected* America to Europe and had to be studied at both ends. Since the process began with people being set in motion from somewhere, one should begin at that beginning, asking what unsettled them. From there, one followed along, inquiring what attracted them elsewhere, how they learned about such possibilities, how a multitude of political, economic, commercial, and technological factors interacted in their movement and in their resettlement and adjustment in new homes. All this is now familiar, as is Hansen's sketch of demographic, agrarian, and industrial change moving across Europe from west to east, affecting one national group after another and sending them in successively mounting waves to the shores of America. But by comparison to the existing literature on immigration when his book appeared, it was a novelty of Copernican proportions.

Besides his pathbreaking analysis of the process of migration and the "mysterious forces" that shaped its operation, Hansen is also remembered for a collection of interpretive essays entitled *The Immigrant in American History* (1940). Since it appeared, two other essays have come to light, one of which was not uncovered until 1979 and not published until 1990.[18] The essays sound more than one theme, to be sure, but they also establish pretty clearly that Hansen shared the liberal assimilationist outlook that characterized enlightened commentary on intergroup relations in the 1930s. According to this view, which was really a generous version of the melting pot, the existence of a distinctive American national culture is taken for granted. It had been shaped in fundamental ways by its English founders, but non-English ethnic groups had made their own unique contributions to it, even as they were being blended into it. Like other observers, Hansen lamented that the pragmatic and unimaginative host society had not absorbed many of the artistic and cultural riches the immigrants had to offer. But he was under no illusion that immigrant cultures were going to survive in America.

It is true that Hansen speculated that "the principle of third generation interest" might lead the grandchildren of the immigrants, who felt at home in America, to identify more closely with their ancestral heritage than did their second-generation parents, who (it was thought) were intent on throwing off the taint of foreignness. But he did not speak of third-generation interest as a force that could perpetuate the culture of the group as a coherent entity in itself. Rather, he asserted, "men of insight . . . understand that it is the ultimate fate of any national group to be amalgamated into the composite American race. . . ." All that could be hoped for was that third-generation interest might be directed toward a selective retrieval of "those features of [the immigrant group's] cultural life that should be added to the heritage of America." The most concrete form such a contribution could take was in the writing of history, and Hansen laid down firm guidelines for how it should be done. To bear good fruit historically, the third generation's delving into the ethnic past must follow two fundamental principles: first, the history of the group must be written without "self-laudation" and on "broad impartial lines"; secondly, it must be "made to fit in as one chapter in the larger volume that is called American history. . . ."[19]

Had he lived longer, Hansen's thought might have moved in more up-to-date "multicultural" directions.[20] As matters stand, however, we can confidently conclude that he accepted the benign version of melting-pot assimilationism characteristic of his day. And he obviously endorsed the idea of a "master narrative" for American history, though he did not, of course, call it that. We must, however, add that his own historical work served not merely to enrich "the heritage of America" but also to reshape our understanding of "the larger volume that is called American history."

THE HANDLIN EPOCH, 1941–1964

The next phase of immigration historiography is dominated by one man to a greater degree than any other period. Oscar Handlin gained instant visibility in the profession with the publication in 1941of his doctoral dissertation, *Boston's Immigrants*, which won a major prize from the American Historical Association. Ten years later, *The Uprooted*, a Pulitzer prize winner, gained a wide general readership and made Handlin one of the best-known American academics of his time.[21] He attracted a galaxy of brilliant graduate students and made Harvard *the* center for the historical study of immigration (though many of his students wrote on other subjects, for Handlin was very much a generalist). His influence continued long after the date given above as marking the end of the Handlin epoch. Indeed, a paperback edition of *Boston's Immigrants* went through nine printings between 1968 and 1974. But the publication in 1964 of Rudolph J. Vecoli's critique of *The Uprooted* foreshadowed the opening of a new era in immigration historiography in which Handlin's approach was, if not flatly rejected, at least severely discounted.[22]

Of course everything was changing by the midsixties, when a new generation of young people rejected the world of their parents.[23] Handlin was very much part of that parental world—the world usually labeled "Cold-War America." The label is misleading, because the defining experience for that generation of Americans was not the "Communist threat," despite the disproportionate anxieties it aroused. The Cold War was but a protracted sequel to the real war—World War II—in which the United States was actively engaged for four years and the coming of which affected society and thought even before hostilities broke out in 1939. The experience of World War II was what shaped the thinking of Handlin's generation and carried over into the presidential administration of the navy veteran John F. Kennedy.

The awakening of national feeling and the ideological revival of democracy already discernible in the late 1930s were powerfully reinforced by the attack on Pearl Harbor and America's active entry into the struggle against totalitarian aggression. National unity became a wartime imperative, but it was to be based on the commitment of all Americans to a commonly held set of ideas. Because they all believed in freedom, equality, and the dignity of the individual—the most basic elements of the "American creed," as Gunnar Myrdal called it—Americans were *one people* no matter what their race, religion, or national origin. These factors were, or should be, irrelevant to one's being an American. And since "tolerance for diversity" was a major corollary to the democratic creed, failure to regard racial, ethnic, or religious differences as irrelevant constituted a deviation from true Americanism, which, if it translated into prejudiced attitudes and discriminatory behavior, amounted to a betrayal of democracy itself—a point driven home by the monstrous example of Nazi racism.

Besides defining wartime unity, democratic universalism underlay the postwar campaign to improve intergroup relations, the most significant aspect of which was the drive for desegregation and civil rights for African-Americans. It likewise played a role in the anticommunist hysteria, since communism represented a challenge to the very core of American national identity, that is, agreement on basic political principles. And it was obviously central to the "consensus" mentality said to characterize so much historical work of the 1950s, including that of Oscar Handlin. From the viewpoint of immigration historiography, however, the main point is that democratic universalism tacitly assumed a degree of immigrant assimilation that approached total absorption.

For if, despite our much-valued diversity, we were really "One America,"[24] it had to be because diversity didn't cut very deep. And where it did cut deep, it created problems. Why, otherwise, was "divisiveness" such a pejorative term if "pluralism" was such a good thing? Actually, "cultural pluralism" as it was understood at midcentury differed little in substance from the traditional assimilationist belief that many ethnic elements had contributed to, and were blending together in, a composite American nationality. In fact, the individualistic basis of democratic universalism implicitly required assimilation. The connection was not developed at the time; perhaps it was not even recognized in the rhetorical climate of tolerance-for-diversity. But to improve intergroup relations one had to eliminate sharp group differences, whether based on race, religion, or some other cultural feature. Racial integration was a goal clearly assimilationist in tendency; Nazi racism, of which Jews were the principal victims, dramatized how religious divisions could be exploited. Group consciousness and group pride, far from being prized as healthy signs of "ethnicity" (a term that had not yet come into general use), were branded "ethnocentric"—an attitude that, according to one influential school of thought, reflected a fascist mindset.

In its linkage with democratic universalism and desirable social goals, assimilation was tacitly accepted as a good thing. But it was not an unmixed blessing. Indeed, it was more likely to be thought of in connection with something that aroused widespread concern at midcentury—the fear that America was fast becoming a "mass society," whose remaining diversity was destined to disappear in a sea of bland "conformity." Mass society had many sources. At bottom were the dislocations brought on by industrialization, urbanization, and modernization. However, Tocqueville (who enjoyed a great revival in these years) had pointed out a century earlier that democracy itself contributed to the process. Equality, which it prized above all, eroded traditional social groupings and nurtured a spirit of individualism that isolated people from one another. A society reduced to nothing but a dust of individuals could hardly resist what Tocqueville called the tyranny of the majority. Since his time, new media of communication made the problem more urgent, for Hitler had shown how easily the deracinated masses could be manipulated. Hitlerism had been defeated, but the war left deep psychic scars—to which were added the Cold War and the prospect of nuclear destruction as sources of continuing anxiety. Small wonder that postwar commentators found many disturbing symptoms of anomie, alienation, and need-for-belonging in the "lonely crowd" that constituted American society.

Against this complex background—an "American celebration" troubled by undercurrents of ambivalence, irony, and ambiguity—*The Uprooted* appeared in 1951. Its title immediately contributed a new metaphor for the prevailing sense of malaise, to which Handlin was keenly attuned. The book likewise reflected his sophisticated acquaintance with the social sciences, something already evident in *Boston's Immigrants*, which was subtitled "a study in acculturation." Having grown up in New York City, the son of Russian Jewish immigrants, Handlin brought to his work a perspective derived from personal experience quite different from that of the midwestern pioneers of immigration historiography. But like Wittke and Hansen, he wanted to tell the full story of immigration and demonstrate its centrality to American history. "Once I thought to write a history of the immigrants in America," reads the first line of *The Uprooted*. "Then I discovered that the immigrants *were* American history."[25]

To illuminate the nation's past by following the single strand of immigration, Handlin essayed an interior history of the phenomenon, focusing his attention on the experience of the immigrants themselves. In telling the story, he drew at least as much on humanistic empathy as on his knowledge of social psychology, but to give it breadth of scope he generalized freely, adopting at times the sociologist's ideal-typical approach. The latter method is most evident in chapter one, "Peasant Origins," but Handlin aims throughout to capture the typical experience of immigration, merely taking note of the most significant variations. In this manner he moves from European background, through the ordeal of the ocean crossing, to a series of chapters covering the manifold dimensions of the immigrant's adaptation to life in the New World. The book also describes the host society's reaction to immigration and concludes with a meditation on the larger meaning of the immigrant experience.

The most striking feature of the book is the elegiac, almost lugubrious, tone that results from Handlin's unremitting emphasis on alienation, separation, sadness, and loss. Interpreting immigration as "a history of alienation and its consequences" spoke poignantly to the sensibilities of literate Americans at midcentury and shaped that generation's understanding of the immigrant experience. More than that, it opened a new perspective on the spiritual inquietude of the day because the immigrant's alienation was, in greater or lesser degree, the experience "of all those whom the modern world somehow uproots."[26]

Unlike its transparent relevance to this dimension of the prevailing mentality, *The Uprooted* related more subtly to the contemporary emphasis on democracy with its tacit assumption of assimilation. Uprootedness as Handlin described it certainly ruled out the survival of coherent and permanently distinctive ethnic cultures in American society. He was, in that sense, an assimilationist. But he took assimilation as a given; he did not celebrate it. On the contrary, his book is an inventory of its psychic cost in "broken homes, interruptions of a familiar life, separation from known surroundings, the becoming a foreigner and ceasing to belong."[27] Yet there is a still deeper ambivalence, for the shock of alienation was at the same time a radical *liberation* which opened the way to existential nobility. Being torn from the nest of ancestral security and required to overcome one obstacle after another awakened in those who were uprooted a new consciousness of self. Though infinitely painful, their struggles drove them back upon themselves, thereby bestowing upon them "the human birthright of . . . individuality." This experience prepared them for life in America, for displacement was a characteristic feature of this "land of separated men" and the immigrants had already learned that freedom exacted its price in personal suffering.[28]

Handlin's assimilationism was thus deeply ambivalent, his Americanism embedded in a tragic sense of life. But despite its pervading melancholy, *The Uprooted* affirmed the basic national values, freedom and the dignity of the individual. The same critically positive stance toward American life may be found in Handlin's other works, but they are too numerous and wide-ranging for discussion here. Concentrating on *The Uprooted* is justified because it was so widely read at the time and because it is the book later critics have singled out as epitomizing the mistaken assumptions governing immigration historiography at midcentury. That does not mean of course that all other scholars patterned their studies upon it. The only other work of the fifties on immigration to attain classic status, John Higham's *Strangers in the Land* (1955), approached the subject from a very different angle, using the prism of nativism to analyze its significance in American history. The British scholar Maldwyn Allen Jones's admirable survey *American Immigration* (1960) owes at least as much to Hansen as it does to Handlin.[29] Even Handlin's own students, who dominated the field, produced works too fresh and original to be thought of as mere repetitions of a model. It is, however, fair to say that immigration historians of that era accepted the view that assimilation was inevitable and had in fact taken place. They likewise tended to regard it benignly because "Americanization" (as it was often called) meant that the immigrants had been absorbed into a nation whose essential identity derived from common acceptance of praiseworthy social and political ideals. All these assumptions were to be called into question in the next epoch.

IMMIGRATION HISTORY IN ERUPTION, 1964–1997

Unparalleled growth in the number of works produced, in addition to sharp shifts in interpretive stance, make it only mildly hyperbolic to call the last three decades a revolutionary epoch in immigration history. When Rudolph J. Vecoli published the first of his valuable historiographic surveys of the subject in 1970, he reproached historians for having neglected immigration; before the decade ended, he found himself "inundated by a virtual flood" of new publications on race and ethnicity.[30] In 1970, Jones's brief survey was the only thing approximating a suitable classroom text; since then, upward of a dozen textbooks or general syntheses have appeared—along with hundreds of monographs, major reprint series, new scholarly journals, a new professional association, several centers devoted to research an immigration, and the landmark *Harvard Encyclopedia of American Ethnic Groups* (1980). Dramatic increases in the number of doctoral dissertations tell the same story: 314 were written on immigration or ethnicity in the 1950s; 677 in the 1960s; and 1,813 in the 1970s.[31] Given the scale and complexity of the phenomena in question, what follows must be not only schematic but also somewhat speculative in character. Before turning to immigration historiography as such, however, we must look briefly at the larger context.

It is, in the first place, quite clear that the race issue and the Vietnam War, which together dominated the American scene in the 1960s, influenced the outlook of scholars interested in immigration.[32] The middecade shift of emphasis from civil rights to black power coincided with large-scale American military involvement in Vietnam and the growth of a widespread and passsionate antiwar movement at home. This combination—along with urban riots, campus disorders, the New Left, the counterculture, the women's movement, and a series of political assassinations—fueled a deep and pervasive radicalization of feeling. In the atmosphere of crisis that accompanied these developments, two shifts in perspective stand out as influences on subsequent historical scholarship. On the one hand, particularistic group consciousness, group pride, and group assertiveness—hitherto deprecated as ethnocentrism—were now *legitimated* as ethnicity. On the other hand, Americanism as it had been understood since World War II was *delegitimated*—discredited because racism at home and imperialism abroad persuaded the most radical critics that the "American creed" was a mere smoke screen for oppression, and left more moderate observers shaken and uncertain whether the nation's historic principles would endure.

Just before the midsixties shift in feeling took hold, a new immigration law abandoned the system in place for forty years whereby "national-origins quotas" determined the number of entries allocated to various countries. The rejection of this system, which was based on the invidious racialist assumptions of the 1920s, paralleled the civil rights legislation passed at the same time and represented the high-water mark of the democratic universalist outlook of the post–World War II era. It also opened the way to an enormous expansion of immigration which, for the first time in the twentieth century, included Asians on the same basis as immigrants from the Western Hemisphere. The new law, along with several major refugee flows and heavy migration from Latin America, resulted in unanticipated changes in the ethnic composition of the immigrant population as well as its vast enlargement. Of the almost twelve million immigrants who entered the country between 1971 and 1990, over 70 percent were either Asian or Latin American; only about 13 percent were European. (These figures do not include an unknown but significant number of illegal, or "undocumented," immigrants.)[33]

By the 1980s, these developments made immigration and multiculturalism important matters of public policy; in the 1960s, however, the most obvious immigration-related issue involved Mexican-Americans. For despite their historic roots in the Southwest, and a vast increase in their numbers brought about by immigration after 1910, Mexican-Americans did not gain real visibility on the national scene until the 1960s, when the agricultural workers' strike led by Cesar Chavez associated their cause with the broader civil rights movement. The subsequent emergence of a more militant "Chicano" movement reflected the midsixties shift. Thanks to the religious idealism of the earlier crusade led by Martin Luther King, Jr., "minorities" already held the high ground morally. In that context, the interrelated legitimation of ethnicity and discrediting of Americanism encouraged a new spirit of militance all along the line. "Black Power" gave rise to "Brown Power" and "Red Power," and eventually to a generalized "revival of ethnicity." The latter, also called the "new pluralism," drew upon residual group feeling among the descendants of European immigrants but was also to some extent a consciously devised strategy aimed at defusing the "backlash" thought to be building up among "white ethnics" resentful of the gains made by other minority groups, especially African-Americans.[34]

Along with these societywide developments, revisionist stirrings in the academic world gave early warning of the coming historiographic upheaval. Even before the civil rights/black power shift, two books by social scientists—Nathan Glazer and Daniel P. Moynihan's *Beyond the Melting Pot* (1963) and Milton M. Gordon's *Assimilation in American Life* (1964)—challenged earlier views about the degree and depth of immigrant assimilation.[35] In 1964, Vecoli's previously mentioned critique of *The Uprooted* focused that challenge on the regnant historical paradigm. A revitalized labor history soon discovered the relevance of immigration, and the New Left perspective, which was strong among labor historians, made the unmasking of Americanist pretensions a congenial task. Political historians had begun to explore "ethnocultural" influences on voting behavior, while social historians—among whom Handlin's student, Stephan Thernstrom, was a pioneer—revealed that ethnicity was a significant variable in social mobility. Social mobility as a contemporary reality figured in the picture more directly, for the vast postwar expansion of higher education brought into academic life unprecedented numbers of graduate students of immigrant background. As this ethnically diverse cohort took its place in history departments, the combination of intradisciplinary and broader cultural shifts created the most favorable climate for the study of immigration history that had ever existed.

The outpouring of scholarship that followed defies comprehensive summary; its very richness makes any effort to identify the leading trends a risky business, for in expanding so rapidly immigration history lost much of its conceptual tidiness. The growing importance of Hispanics and Asians has added distinctive new elements; the refugee issue demands greater attention than in the past, as do considerations of gender and class. Topics hitherto regarded as belonging to specialists in other fields (e.g., African-American and Native-American history) are now often included in treatments of immigration history. This is most notable in works that make ethnicity their central organizing principle, for "ethnic history" is a more inclusive category than "immigration history." Indeed, the compilers of a recent collection of course syllabi characterize the difference between the two approaches as "a central tension within the field" and hint at epistemological profundities.[36]

Further conceptual ambiguities lurk in the terms "race" and "ethnicity"—and in the relationship between them. As a scientific idea, race has supposedly been discredited for more than half a century. David Hollinger accepts its discrediting but insists that "racism" is still a viable concept, though "race" isn't—which hardly simplifies matters. And even if race is interpreted as a cultural construct rather than a biological reality, the question remains how it differs from ethnicity, the constructed nature of which has been emphasized by writers who speak of "the invention of ethnicity" and the process of "ethnicization." The two concepts obviously cover much the same ground, but there is no theoretical consensus about their respective boundaries. Thus the *Harvard Encyclopedia of American Ethnic Groups* treated race as a dimension of ethnicity, but a reviewer prominent in the study of plural societies branded this a "monumental confusion" because it subsumed race under a conceptual category trivial by comparison.[37]

Assigning greater theoretical importance to race is certainly in line with recent developments in the "real world," the most important of which is affirmative action. This complex of policies, as it evolved in the late sixties, was designed with African-Americans in mind, yet the term used to designate those to whom it would apply was "minorities" (and under a separate provision, women). Because a multitude of groups had previously been included under that rubric, a short list of minorities eligible for affirmative action benefits had to be drawn up. What ultimately emerged from the bureaucratic mazes where this process was carried out was the now-familiar list—African-Americans, Native Americans, Asians and Pacific Islanders, and Hispanics. Since these groups were generally identifiable by physical differences popularly thought of as "racial," and since African-Americans had unquestionably suffered from "racism," the practical logic of the situation enforced the conclusion that something called "race" really existed. The corollary, upon which government policy seemed clearly to be premised, was that victims of "racism" deserve special status in the polity because the wrongs visited upon them were *different in kind* from the prejudice and discrimination suffered by others in American society. In the quarter century it has been in force, affirmative action has thus lent powerful impetus to the racialization of American thought—a fact illustrated by recent efforts by Mexican-Americans to get themselves explicitly classified as a *racial* group in the next federal census, and by the rise of "whiteness studies."[38]

Besides adding to the conceptual ambiguities of the field, affirmative action figures in another way in the complications that beset historians of immigration and ethnicity—it is highly controversial. So also is immigration policy itself, to say nothing of multiculturalism and associated issues of "political correctness."[39] This does not mean that historians cannot continue their work; indeed, controversy makes their studies more timely and relevant. Yet the distortion and oversimplification unavoidable in an atmosphere of controversy exacerbated by partisan politics cannot help but affect the realm of discourse in question. This might not turn historians themselves into partisans—although the ideal of scholarly detachment is not as robust as it used to be—but it will not lighten their task.

Despite all these ambiguities and complications, certain features of the new historiographic landscape stand in sharp contrast to what had gone before. The most striking is a twofold reversal of opinion on the subject of assimilation. *Sociologically*, according to the revisionists, the concept of assimilation is fundamentally flawed because the process it refers to didn't happen; *ideologically*, it must be rejected because it embodies an unacceptable vision of American society. These positions are not uniformly held by all historians, or equally emphasized by those who do, and several scholars have recently reaffirmed the reality of assimilation as a social process. Although the U.S. Commission on Immigration Reform has undertaken to rehabilitate "Americanization," its ideological status remains deeply suspect, and if we consider the last quarter-century as a unit, the twofold revision of the concept of assimilation has enjoyed hegemonic status. Both of its aspects were reflected in the all-but-universal execration of melting-pot symbolism, and the talismanic quality taken on by the terms "cultural pluralism" and, more recently, "multiculturalism" and "diversity."[40]

Explicit discussion of interpretive issues, along with pejorative or honorific use of symbolic language, is most likely to be found in journalistic, polemical, or programmatic contexts, but the revisionist stance also shaped more technical scholarly work in immigration history. The title of a much-admired synthesis, John Bodnar's *The Transplanted* (1985), suggests the way Handlin's *Uprooted* has served as a foil in this regard. Handlin erred, say the revisionists, in portraying the immigrants as deracinated individuals, buffeted by impersonal forces beyond their control, whose pain and suffering in an alien land were prospectively redeemed by the better American future the more assimilated second generation would inherit. Actually, according to the new view, the immigrants were prepared for change by prior Old-World experience; their decision to emigrate was rational, freely undertaken, and occurred within a framework of family and communal support, as did the process of migration and resettlement. Far from being first uprooted and then assimilated, immigrants brought most of their ancestral culture with them, preserved their ethnic identity, and perpetuated their distinctive culture as part of the mosaic of a pluralistic society. So dominant had this revision become by 1990 that Vecoli, who first adumbrated it in 1964, warned historians not to substitute a new stereotype for the old "caricature of uprooted, oppressed, traumatized victims," and Jon Gjerde's recent study of nineteenth-century immigrants in the Midwest is, indeed, far more nuanced.[41]

The revisionist interpretation is based on thorough research and corrects exaggerations in the older view, especially Handlin's almost melodramatic emphasis on alienation. But as Vecoli's remarks suggest, it is subject to its own exaggerations, and it reflects changes in the overall ideological climate at least as much as it reflects the unearthing of new information or advances in analytical understanding. We may grant, for example, that simplistic versions of assimilation went too far. But could the perduring quality of ethnic culture, which was treated as virtually axiomatic in the seventies and eighties, have attained that theoretical status absent the legitimation of ethnicity that took place in the sixties? And since assimilation implies identification by immigrants with the host nation's ideals and institutions, the discrediting of old-fashioned Americanism was a necessary precondition to the celebration of "unmeltable ethnicity." Thus Nathan Glazer could speak in 1975 of a situation in "the ecology of identities" that made it more advantageous to claim an ethnic identity than to affirm that one was simply an American.[42] And though "multiculturalism" can mean many things, the strongest versions of the 1990s interpret traditional Americanism as oppression and deny that a straightforwardly "American" national identity even exists.

Another revision closely related to the uprooted-to-transplanted shift is the insistence that American immigration must be viewed within the context of larger international (primarily European) migration patterns. Though Hansen's work pointed in this direction, the decisive stimulus came from a paper delivered at the International Congress of Historical Sciences in 1960. There Frank Thistlethwaite, a British scholar who spent two years at the University of Minnesota in the late thirties, drove home the point that overseas migration had to be set against the background of intense prior and contemporaneous *intra-European* migration.[43] It took time to lift what Thistlethwaite called the "salt-water curtain," but by the mid-1970s several European-based migration research projects were under way, and American studies like Josef Barton's *Peasants and Strangers* rested on intensive analysis of the old-country matrix from which overseas migration sprang. Several more recent works demonstrate that the transatlantic perspective is now firmly established and illustrate the ways it has enriched our understanding of migration as an international phenomenon.[44]

Stressing as it does the back-and-forth flow of people and information between the United States and Europe, the internationalist perspective reinforces the emphasis on cultural continuity that figures so prominently in the critique of Handlinesque uprootedness. It likewise resonates with the ideological dimension of postsixties revisionism. Merely placing "immigration" to the United States within the larger context of transnational "migration" in itself reduces the nationalistic overtones of the earlier strictly American focus. The ideological element is more evident in transnational studies that reflect a Marxian orientation. This is strongest in European-based work, some of which, according to a leading practitioner, is animated by a vision of international working-class solidarity.[45] Yet a generally New Left outlook is also discernible in the emphasis American scholars place on class and economic issues. In Bodnar's synthesis, for example, "capitalism" explains virtually everything; indeed, he originally planned to call his book "Children of Capitalism" rather than *The Transplanted.*[46] Still another connection with ideology has to do with "American exceptionalism," a term deriving from the Marxist tradition which scholars influenced by the New Left employ pejoratively, especially in reference to the "consensus" historians' emphasis on American uniqueness. The expression has not figured prominently in immigration historiography, but one of the purposes of Walter Nugent's *Crossings* (1992) was to test the exceptionalist hypothesis by comparing European immigration to the United States with the same phenomenon in Argentina, Brazil, and Canada.[47]

Not enough study has been devoted to multiculturalism as an object of analysis to permit confident generalization about it.[48] My own impression is that virtually all historians of immigration would accept it in the broadest (and weakest) sense, that is, as meaning that American society contains within itself a multitude of subgroups with distinctive cultural features, whether defined by race, ethnicity, religion, gender, language, or something else. But they have not played a prominent role in theorizing about it, especially by comparison to writers on education, literature, and the arts. More robust versions of multiculturalism, which tend to portray "America" as *nothing but* a collocation of culturally autonomous groups, perhaps exert greater appeal among historians who derive from ethnic groups officially designated as "minorities." Rodolfo Acuña, Ronald Takaki, and Gary Okihiro, for example, emphasize the racist oppressiveness of "Euro-Americans" and other themes characteristic of strong multiculturalism.[49] Historical work on women in immigration is still generally traditional in approach, but the powerful theoretical bent of women's studies could well move it too toward the stronger versions of multiculturalism.[50]

Two features of recent work hark back to the prehistory of immigration historiography. The first is that today social scientists dominate the study of the immigration that is actually taking place just as they did in the opening decades of the century. Even the new historical work on Hispanics and Asians concentrates on the earlier phases of those groups' experience. Only David Reimers, Reed Ueda, and Elliott Barkan have written general historical accounts of the most recent immigration, and the leading book on the refugee issue since 1945 was coauthored by a political scientist and a lawyer.[51]

That historians should prefer a longer time-perspective, while social scientists devote themselves to contemporary phenomena, is a finding unlikely to generate much controversy. The second resemblance to the prehistory era will perhaps seem less bland, for it concerns the filiopietistic strain to be found in not a little of the newer work. As noted earlier, Edward Saveth—who put "filiopietism" into circulation and loaded it with pejorative connotations—had no patience with in-group historians who demanded "just recognition" for this or that immigrant people, claiming for them equal standing with "Anglo-Saxons in the soil of American nationality." Nor could he approve the notion that American history "should be re-written along 'racial or ethnic' lines"; on the contrary, ethnic cultures were to be understood, not as "separate entitites," but as "aspects of a larger whole." Saveth also complained that filiopietistic accounts glorified outstanding individuals but paid little attention to ordinary folk.[52] That's about the only part of his critique today's revisionists would agree with, for much of their own work— especially in its polemical and programmatic forms—is shot through with moral indignation at the prior historiographic neglect and social oppression suffered by whatever group is under consideration. Moreover, the demand for "just recognition" underlies the whole ethnic studies movement, and the goal of rewriting

American history with greater attention to racial and ethnic goups—and women—has guided the textbook industry since the late 1960s.

Because filiopietism has been academically disreputable for fifty years, no historian of immigration is likely to espouse it.[53] Indeed, one occasionally runs across a disclaimer to the effect that something just said, or about to be said, is "not filiopietistic"—which betrays a certain uneasiness about the applicability of the term. But perhaps it is time to reexamine the whole issue, which is at bottom a subspecies of the larger issue of historical objectivity. For it was, after all, professional historians' putative commitment to objectivity that crucially distinguished them from "amateurs" and allowed them to avoid filiopietistic distortions. And in Saveth's mind at least, professionalism entailed the assumption that American history had a master narrative, a national history to which the histories of the various ethnic groups must be related. These positions are no longer tenable as unanalyzed assumptions. The status of the objectivity question is very different now from what it was when Saveth wrote, to say nothing of what it was in the period of classical filiopietism; and many multiculturalists deny the existence of anything real to which a master narrative could refer. This is obviously not the place to undertake a rethinking of filiopietism. But it is perhaps apposite to note that historians must confront the existence of the filiopietistic strain in recent work before any such project can be carried out.

CONCLUSION

What has been concluded that we can draw conclusions about it? That rhetorical question—once addressed, I believe, to William James—fits our situation admirably, for everything touched on in this survey is still in process. History offers no more clear-cut lessons here than in most other areas. Our survey does, however, highlight recurrent themes that might repay further investigation.

One such theme is the relationship between changes in the overall intellectual climate and interpretive shifts in immigration history. Congruence between the two stands out most vividly in the 1960s, but it is discernible over the whole century under review. The influence of war as a factor in these concurrent changes might also be noted—most obviously in connection with World War II and Vietnam, but also in lesser degree in the case of World War I. Another kind of recurrent connection has to do with the ethnic composition of the historical profession and the attention devoted to immigration by different cohorts of historians. Here we find a positive correlation between what might be called the ethnic democratization of the profession and the degree and range of interest in ethnic subjects—with the present and recent past being most inclusive in both senses.

Another theme has to do with the relationships that exist between immigration historiography and the way American identity is understood. Conclusions here cannot help being impressionistic, but it seems clear that historians of different eras understood the relationship differently. Saveth established that the earliest professional historians regarded immigration as incidental to national development. His book also suggests that their understanding of American identity was more ethnic than ideological, in the sense that it was shaped by the prevailing racialism of the times. It was also ethnic in the sense that it reflected their own "old American" derivation, which probably disposed them to agree with their fellow citizens of like background that unrestricted immigration could not continue indefinitely without imperiling the fabric of American society.

The first generation of professionals to make immigration history their specialty were of different ethnic background, and immigration was no longer a live issue politically when they wrote. Unlike their predecessors, they believed immigration was a significant historical subject; they were interested in the immigrant story for its own sake, and they stressed the contributions immigrants made to national development. But they, too, were assimilationists who accepted the view that in becoming Americans the immigrants were becoming part of a nation which had an identity of its own compounded of the various elements that went into it as they developed together over time. The terminology of race was still employed in discussions of immigration, but it was less determinative than formerly, and immigrant groups were more apt to be referred to as "nationalities." Conceptual issues of this sort were not, however, discussed systematically by historians.

By the Handlin era, immigration had become an even more strictly "historical" topic. Assimilation, it was thought, had all but completed its work so far as immigrant "nationality" was concerned, although religious differences remained and racial boundaries were even more resistant to change. Moreover, alienation and the mass society problem rendered assimilation a culturally ambiguous process. The penetration of social scientific thought made immigration historiography more conceptually sophisticated than before, one result of which was the discrediting of race, an effect massively reinforced by the counterexample of Nazism. The kind of group consciousness we now think of as "ethnic" was likewise discredited, for Nazism illustrated the grotesque extremes to which such *völkisch* thinking could be carried. For these reasons, and because national ideals were so stongly stressed in the war years, ethnicity was quite recessive and ideology quite dominant in the way midcentury historians of immigration thought of American identity.

That situation has been reversed in the most recent epoch. Immigration has returned with a vengeance, both as social reality and public issue. The ethnic and racial dimensions of group identity are more prominently featured than at any time since before World War I. Particularism enjoys a premium intellectually; universalism is at a severe discount. The ideological understanding of American national identity, though not driven completely from the field, is regarded by most as naive or even hypocritical. But those who champion some version of the ethnic perspective do not reject the basic values that constitute the core of the American ideology; on the contrary, they honor freedom, equality, and the dignity of the individual (although their emphasis on the group makes the latter problematic). Their claim is that Americanism as traditionally understood failed to embody these values effectively—or, in some versions, was never intended to embody them.

Assuming that what has just been said about the presently dominant view is correct, it follows that the ideological element is still a vital constituent in the understanding of American identity, although it is much obscured by clamorous ethnic claims and recriminations about oppression. Contestation is the order of the day. From it, we may hope, there will eventually emerge a deeper and more satisfactory common understanding of what it means to be an American.

NOTES

1. John Higham, "Current Trends in the Study of Ethnicity in the United States," *Journal of American Ethnic History* [hereafter *JAEH*] 2 (fall 1982): 6–7; J. Hector St. John de Crève-coeur, *Letters from an American Farmer* (New York, 1957), chap. 3. For discussion, see Moses Rischin, "Creating Crèvecoeur's 'New Man': He Had a Dream," *JAEH* 1 (Fall 1981): 26–42. Gary Gerstle, "Liberty, Coercion, and the Making of Americans," *Journal of American History* [hereafter *JAH*] 84 (September 1997): 524–58, which offers a different interpretation of immigration historiography, appeared too late to be considered here.

2. A. William Hoglund, *Immigrants and Their Children in the United States: A Bibliography of Doctoral Dissertations, 1885–1982* (New York, 1986), viii–ix; Edward N. Saveth, *American Historians and European Immigrants, 1875–1925* (New York, 1948), 9.

3. Saveth, *Historians and Immigrants*, 202–15.

4. Turner's articles appeared in the *Chicago Record-Herald*, August 28, September 4, 18, and 25, and October 9 and 16, 1901. His comments, especially in the fourth and sixth of these articles, reveal that Turner was troubled by the coming of the "new immigrants" around the turn of the century. For John R. Commons, see his *Races and Immigrants in America* (New York, 1907); for Zangwill and Kallen, see Arthur Mann, *The One and the Many: Reflections on the American Identity* (Chicago, 1979), chaps. 5–6.

5. Edith Abbott, *Immigration: Select Documents and Case Records* (Chicago, 1924); Abbott, *Historical Aspects of the Immigration Problem: Select Documents* (Chicago, 1926); Emily Greene Balch, *Our Slavic Fellow Citizens* (New York, 1910); Robert F. Foerster, *The Italian Emigration of Our Time* (Cambridge, Mass., 1919); W. I. Thomas and Florian Znaniecki, *The Polish Peasant in Europe and America*, 5 vols. (Boston, 1918–20); Arthur M. Schlesinger, *New Viewpoints in American History* (New York, 1922).

6. Schlesinger, *New Viewpoints*, 16; for Turner, see Saveth, *Historians and Immigrants*, 122–37; Theodore C. Blegen, ed., *Land of Their Choice: The Immigrants Write Home* (Minneapolis, 1955), ix–x; Moses Rischin, "Marcus Lee Hansen: America's First Transethnic Historian," in Richard L. Bushman et al., *Uprooted Americans: Essays to Honor Oscar Handlin* (Boston, 1979), 333–38; and Frederick C. Luebke, "Turnerism, Social History, and the Historiography of European Ethnic Groups in the United States," in Luebke, *Germans in the New World* (Urbana and Chicago, 1990), 138–56.

7. George M. Stephenson, *Political History of the Public Lands* (Boston, 1917); Stephenson, *A History of American Immigration, 1820–1924* (Boston, 1926), 3, and chaps. 16–17.

8. Ibid., 264.

9. For discussion of this group, see O. Fritiof Ander, "Four Historians of Immigration," in Ander, ed., *In the Trek of the Immigrants: Essays Presented to Carl Wittke* (Rock Island, Ill., 1964), 17–32.

10. William Forbes Adams, *Ireland and Irish Emigration to the New World from 1815 to the Famine* (New Haven, 1932); Ray Allen Billington, *The Protestant Crusade: A Study of the Origins of American Nativism* (New York, 1938).

11. See Philip Gleason, *Speaking of Diversity: Language and Ethnicity in Twentieth-Century America* (Baltimore, 1992), chaps, 6–7, and the literature cited there.

12. George M. Stephenson, *The Religious Aspects of Swedish Immigration* (Minneapolis, 1932); Theodore C. Blegen, *Norwegian Migration to America*, 2 vols. (Northfield, Minn., 1931–40). See also John Higham, "The Ethnic Historical Society in Changing Times." *JAEH* 13 (winter 1994): 30–44.

13. Carl Wittke, *We Who Built America: The Saga of the Immigrant* (New York, 1939), 518, v. In the last-quoted passage, Wittke was probably alluding to, and implying the incompleteness of, James Truslow Adams's widely read book, *The Epic of America* (Boston, 1931).

14. Wittke, *We Who Built*, xviii.

15. This review (*American Historical Review* 37 [April 1932]: 572–73), which also covered a book on Swedish immigration by Florence E. Janson, did not endear Hansen to Blegen's friends. It still rankled with Carlton Qualey more than thirty years later; others expressed skepticism that Hansen had full mastery of the Scandinavian languages. See Qualey, "Marcus Lee Hansen," *Midcontinent American Studies Journal* 8 (fall 1967): 18–25; and Rischin, "Hansen," 328–29.

16. Marcus L. Hansen, *The Atlantic Migration, 1607–1860* (Cambridge, Mass., 1940); for discussion, see Rischin, "Hansen," 319–47, and Moses Rischin, "Just Call Me John: Ethnicity as *Mentalité*," in Peter Kivisto and Dag Blanck, eds., *American Immigrants and Their Generations* (Urbana and Chicago, 1990), 64–82.

17. For discussion of the relationship between immigrants and members of the founding "charter group," see John Higham, *Send These to Me: Jews and Other Immigrants in Urban America* (New York, 1975), chap. 1.

18. Marcus L. Hansen, *The Immigrant in American History* (Cambridge, Mass., 1940); the other two essays, "The Problem of the Third-Generation Immigrant," and "Who Shall Inherit America?" are both reprinted in Kivisto and Blanck, eds., *Immigrants and Their Generations*, 191–203, 204–13.

19. Ibid., 201–2, 210, 198–201.

20. See Rischin , "Just Call Me John," 69–71, 76–77.

21. Oscar Handlin, *Boston's Immigrants: A Study in Acculturation* (Cambridge, Mass., 1941); Handlin, *The Uprooted: The Epic Story of the Great Migrations That Made the American People* (Boston, 1951).

22. Rudolph J. Vecoli, "*Contadini* in Chicago: A Critique of *The Uprooted*," *JAH* 51 (December 1964): 407–17. Bushman et al., *Uprooted Americans*, includes a sketch of Handlin's career, a bibliography of his writings, and a listing of the doctoral students he directed up to the date of publication (1979); see also Maldwyn Allen Jones, "Oscar Handlin," in Marcus Cunliffe and Robin W. Winks, eds., *Pastmasters: Some Essays on American Historians* (New York, 1969), 239–77; David J. Rothman, "*The Uprooted*: Thirty Years Later," *Reviews in American History* 10 (September 1982): 311–19; and Reed Ueda, "Immigration and the Moral Criticism of History: The Vision of Oscar Handlin," *Canadian Review of American Studies* 21 (fall 1990): 183–201.

23. Fuller development of, and documentation for, the interpretation advanced in this and following paragraphs may be found in Gleason, *Speaking of Diversity*, chaps. 3–9.

24. It is revealing that the main title, *One America*, was added to the 1946 and 1952 editions of the miniencyclopedia of American minorities edited by Francis J. Brown and Joseph S. Roucek, which appeared before the war under the title *Our Racial and National Minorities* (New York, 1937).

25. Handlin, *Uprooted*, 3 (quotations are from the Grosset and Dunlap paperback edition [New York, n.d.]).

26. Ibid., 4, 6.

27. Ibid., 4.

28. Ibid., 304–5.

29. John Higham, *Strangers in the Land: Patterns of American Nativism, 1860–1925* (New Brunswick, N.J., 1955); Maldwyn Allen Jones, *American Immigration* (Chicago, 1960).

30. The following essays, all by Rudolph J. Vecoli, provide an excellent guide to the explosion of research: "Ethnicity: A Neglected Dimension of American History," in Herbert J. Bass, ed., *The State of American History* (Chicago, 1970), 70–88; "European Americans: From Immigrants to Ethnics," in W. H. Cartwright and R. L. Watson, eds., *The Reinterpretation of American History and Culture* (Washington, D.C., 1973), 81–112; "The Resurgence of American Immigration History," *American Studies International* 17 (Winter 1979), 46–66; "Return to the Melting Pot: Ethnicity in the Eighties," *JAEH* 5 (fall 1985): 7–20; "From *The Uprooted* to *The Transplanted*: The Writing of American Immigration History 1951–1989," in V. G. Lerda, ed., *From 'Melting Pot' to Multiculturalism* (Rome, 1990), 25–53; "An Inter-Ethnic Perspective on American Immigration History," *Mid-America* 75 (April–July 1993): 223–35. For Vecoli's more recent substantive contributions, see "Ethnicity and Immigration" in Stanley Kutler, ed., *Encyclopedia of the United States in the Twentieth Century*, vol. 1 (New York, 1996), 161–93; and "The Significance of Immigration in the Formation of an American Identity," *The History Teacher* 30 (November 1996): 9–17.

31. Hoglund, *Immigrants and Their Children*, xxiii. Approximately 30 percent of the dissertations were in history in the 1950s; approximately 20 percent in the 1970s. Immigration-related dissertations in education and English increased the most in those two decades.

32. For more on the interpretation advanced here, see my essay "American Identity and Americanization," in Stephan Thernstrom, Ann Orlov, and Oscar Handlin, eds., *Harvard Encyclopedia of American Ethnic Groups* (Cambridge, Mass., 1980), 52–55.

33. Statistics derived from U.S. Bureau of the Census, *Statistical Abstract of the United States: 1993* (Washington, D.C., 1993), 11, table 8. For discussion, see David Reimers, *Still the Golden Door: The Third World Comes to America*, 2nd ed. (New York, 1992); Reed Ueda, *Postwar Immigrant America* (Boston, 1994).

34. Carey McWilliams, *North From Mexico*, rev. ed. (New York, 1990), esp. chaps. 17–18, written by Matt S. Meier; David R. Colburn and George E. Pozzetta, "Race, Ethnicity, and the Evolution of Political Legitimacy," in David Farber, ed., *The Sixties: From Memory to History* (Chapel Hill, 1994), 119–48; Perry L. Weed, *The White Ethnic Movement and Ethnic Politics* (New York, 1973); Mann, *One and Many*, chaps. 1–2.

35. Nathan Glazer and Daniel P. Moynihan, *Beyond the Melting Pot* (Cambridge, Mass., 1963); Milton M. Gordon, *Assimilation in American Life* (New York, 1964); for historiographical developments, see John Higham, *History* (Baltimore, 1989), 235–64; Higham, "The Future of American History," *JAH* 80 (March 1994): 1289–1309; and Peter Novick, *That Noble Dream: The 'Objectivity Question' and the American Historical Profession* (Cambridge, 1988), part 4.

36. See Donna Gabaccia and James Grossman, "Introduction: The Teaching of Immigration History," in Gabaccia and Grossman, compilers, *Teaching the History of Immigration and Ethnicity: A Syllabus Exchange* (Chicago, mimeo., 1993).

37. David Hollinger, *Postethnic America: Beyond Multiculturalism* (New York, 1995), chap. 2, esp. 38–39; Werner Sollors, ed., *The Invention of Ethnicity* (New York, 1989); Kathleen N. Conzen et al., "The Invention of Ethnicity: A Perspective from the USA," *JAEH* 12 (fall 1992): 3–63; M. G. Smith, "Ethnicity and Ethnic Groups in America: The View from Harvard," *Ethnic and Racial Studies* 5 (1982): 1–22.

38. For Mexican-American efforts to be classified as a race, see Hollinger, *Postethnic America*, 33; for whiteness, David R. Roediger, *The Wages of Whiteness* (London, 1991), and Noel Ignatiev, *How the Irish Became White* (New York, 1994); for the development of affirmative action categories, Gleason, *Speaking of Diversity*, 102 ff., and the literature cited there; for operation of the policy, Lawrence H. Fuchs, *The American Kaleidoscope: Race, Ethnicity, and the Civic Culture* (Middletown, Conn., 1990), 381–457.

39. For a sampling of views on these matters, see Russell Nieli, ed., *Racial Preference and Racial Justice* (Washington, D.C., 1991); John Higham, "Multiculturalism and Universalism: A History and Critique [and comments thereon]," *American Quarterly* 45 (June 1993): 195–256; Harold K. Bush, Jr., "A Brief History of PC, with Annotated Bibliography," *American Studies International* 33 (April 1995): 42–64; and Nathan Glazer, *We Are All Multiculturalists Now* (Cambridge, Mass., 1997).

40. See Russell A. Kazal, "Revisiting Assimilation: The Rise, Fall, and Reappraisal of a Concept in American Ethnic History," *American Historical Review* 100 (April 1995): 437–71; U.S. Commission on Immigration Reform, *Becoming an American: Immigration and Immigrant Policy* (Washington, D.C., 1997); and Gleason, *Speaking of Diversity*, chap. 2.

41. Vecoli quoted from his "Introduction" to Rudolph J. Vecoli and Suzanne M. Sinke, eds., *A Century of European Migrations, 1830–1930* (Urbana and Chicago, 1991), 11; John Bodnar, *The Transplanted: A History of Immigrants in Urban America* (Bloomington, Ind., 1985); Jon Gjerde, *The Minds of the West: Ethnocultural Evolution in the Rural Middle West, 1830–1917* (Chapel Hill, 1997). For general discussion of the interpretive shift, see Peter Kivisto, "The Transplanted Then and Now: The Reorientation of Immigration Studies from the Chicago School to the New Social History," *Ethnic and Racial Studies* 13 (October 1990): 455–81; and Ewa Morawska, "The Sociology and Historiography of Immigration," in Virginia Yans-McLaughlin, ed., *Immigration Reconsidered* (New York, 1990), 187–238.

42. Nathan Glazer, *Affirmative Discrimination: Ethnic Inequality and Public Policy* (New York, 1975), 177–78.

43. Thistlethwaite's 1960 paper is reprinted, with interesting retrospective comments by the author, in Vecoli and Sinke, *Century of European Migrations*, which is the best introduction to this literature.

44. Josef J. Barton, *Peasants and Strangers* (Cambridge, Mass., 1975); Dirk Hoerder, ed., *"Struggle a Hard Battle": Essays on Working Class Immigrants* (De Kalb, Ill., 1986); Walter Nugent, *Crossings: The Great Transatlantic Migrations, 1870–1914* (Bloomington, Ind., 1992); Mark Wyman, *Round-Trip to America: The Immigrants Return to Europe, 1880–1930* (Ithaca, N.Y., 1993); H. Arnold Barton, *A Folk Divided: Homeland Swedes and Swedish Americans, 1840–1940* (Carbondale, Ill., 1994).

45. See, for example, Dirk Hoerder, *American Labor and Immigration History, 1877–1920s: Recent European Research* (Urbana and Chicago, 1983), 3–15.

46. For this point, see Kivisto, "Transplanted Then and Now," 472, 477; see also the comments on Bodnar's book by James R. Barrett and John J. Bukowczyk in *Social Science History* 12 (fall 1988): 221–31, 233–41.

47. Nugent, *Crossings*, 5–6, 164–65.

48. For a variety of perspectives, see Hollinger, *Postethnic America*; Higham, "Multiculturalism and Universalism"; Werner Sollors, "E Pluribus Unum; or Matthew Arnold Meets George Orwell in the 'Multiculturalism Debate'" (working paper no. 53/1992 of the John F. Kennedy Institute for North American Studies, Freie Universität Berlin); the chapters by Reed Ueda ("Ethnic Diversity and National Identity in Public School Texts") and Gary B. Nash ("American History Reconsidered: Asking New Questions about the Past") in Diane Ravitch and Maris Vinovskis, eds., *Learning from the Past: What History Teaches Us about School Reform* (Baltimore, 1995), 113–34 (Ueda), 135–63 (Nash); and Avery F. Gordon and Christopher Newfield, eds., *Mapping Multiculturalism* (Minneapolis, 1996).

49. Rodolfo Acuña, *Occupied America: A History of Chicanos*, 3rd ed. (New York, 1988); Ronald T. Takaki, *A Different Mirror: A History of Multicultural America* (Boston, 1993); Gary Okihiro, *Margins and Mainstreams: Asians in American History and Culture* (Seattle, 1994).

50. For a recent synthesis, see Donna Gabaccia, *From the Other Side: Women, Gender, and Immigrant Life in the U.S., 1820–1990* (Bloomington, Ind., 1994); for a more theoretical emphasis, see Sydney Stahl Weinberg, "The Treatment of Women in Immigration History: A Call for Change," in Donna Gabaccia, ed., *Seeking Common Ground: Multidisciplinary Studies of Immigrant Women in the United States* (Westport, Conn., 1992), 3–22.

51. Reimers, *Still the Golden Door*; Ueda, *Postwar Immigrant America*; Ueda, *The Permanently Unfinished Country* (forthcoming); Elliott Robert Barkan, *And Still They Come* (Wheeling, Ill., 1996); Gilburt D. Loescher and John A. Scanlan, *Calculated Kindness: Refugees and America's Half-Open Door, 1945-Present* (New York, 1986). See also Francesco Cordasco, *The New American Immigration: Evolving Patterns of Legal and Illegal Emigration: A Bibliography of Selected References* (New York, 1987).

52. Saveth, *Historians and Immigrants*, 202–15.

53. Critical attention to filiopietism in recent works is extremely rare, but its presence is noted in Oscar Handlin, *The Uprooted*, 2nd ed., enlarged (Boston, 1973), 330, note 53; David Noel Doyle and Owen Dudley Edwards, eds., *America and Ireland, 1776–1976: The American Identity and the Irish Connection* (Westport, Conn., 1980), 313–14; Diane Ravitch, "Multiculturalism: E Pluribus Plures," *American Scholar* 59 (summer 1990): 341, 346; and Ueda, "Ethnic Diversity and National Identity," in Ravitch and Vinovskis, eds., *Learning from the Past*, 126.

CHAPTER 7

The Relevance and Irrelevance of American Colonial History

GORDON S. WOOD

AMERICANS have always had a special problem relating to the colonial period of their history. Although nearly as many years separate the first European explorations of North America from the beginning of the United States as separate the beginning of the United States from the present, Americans have often thought the earlier colonial period to be less relevant, less historically significant than the later national period of American history. For many Americans the colonial era has lacked seriousness; it seems trivial and antique and shrouded in nostalgia. For much of American history popular opinion has considered the century and a half of the colonial period to be simply a quaint prologue to the main national story that followed the American Revolution.

In part this is because the colonial period has become the Americans' natural source of folklore and myth-making. Since Americans, unlike other Western nations, lack a misty past where the historical record is remote and obscure, they have tended to turn authentic historical figures and events of their colonial past into mythical characters and legends. In America there are no King Canutes, no King Arthurs, no Robin Hoods to spin tales and legends about. Instead, Americans have transformed John Smith and Pocahontas, the Pilgrim Fathers and Squanto—historical figures about whom we know a good deal—into fanciful and fabulous characters.[1] As a consequence of this kind of myth-making, time does not have the same meaning in the seventeenth and eighteenth centuries as it does in the nineteenth and twentieth centuries. Even modern professional historians, who presumably should know better, have tended to foreshorten and telescope the colonial period in strange ways. Twentieth-century textbook writers, for example, have squeezed into a single paragraph accounts of Bacon's Rebellion in 1676 and the uprising of the Paxton Boys in 1763–64 as incidents of colonial violence.[2] Of course, they would never think of doing the same thing in the national period: they would never lump together discussions of the Whiskey Rebellion in 1794 with the march of Coxey's Army on Washington in 1894 or place in the same paragraph the draft riots of the 1860s with the black riots of the 1960s. Apparently time in the colonial period is considered shorter and more compressible.

Events in the colonial period often seem less real and less significant than those in the national period. In school children are taught about Columbus and the discovery of America, and then around Thanksgiving they learn about the Pilgrims and Plymouth Rock and the feast with the Indians at the end of the first difficult year in the New World. Two centuries are often collapsed into a few quasimythical events preceding the Revolution, when the real history of the United States presumably begins. Thus it is not surprising that the colonial period has often appeared remote and detached from the rest of American history. As the repository of America's myths and legends and the source for schoolchildren's sentimental stories, the colonial period has often seemed to modern Americans to be irrelevant and unconnected to the national history of the United States and not an object of serious historical study.

But this has not always been the case. In the decades following the Revolution the colonial period was very much an integral and important part of American history. The Revolutionary leaders took the colonial period seriously indeed. They tended to look back to the seventeenth-century settlements, in John Adams's words, "as the opening of a grand scene and design in Providence for the illumination of the ignorant and the emancipation of the slavish part of mankind all over the earth."[3] In such Revolutionary sentiments lay the sources for the emerging notion of America as an exemplary nation. The United States, the revolutionaries declared, was a new kind of nation and the best hope for saving the world from corruption and tyranny.[4] But America's special role in the world could not be appreciated properly by focusing exclusively on the Revolution. Full understanding of America and its unique place in the world required going back to the original settlements of the seventeenth century or earlier. Right from the beginning of the United States historians and fiction writers began using the colonial period to work out problems of national identity.[5] For the citizens of the early republic America's colonial origins thus could not be simply a source of folklore and romantic legends; the colonial era was essential to an understanding of the whole progressive story of the United States. The founding of the nation lay not with the Declaration of Independence in 1776 but with the early explorations or, more often, with the earliest settlements and events of the seventeenth century—with Jamestown in 1607, John Winthrop and the Puritans in 1630, and Lord Baltimore's statute of religious toleration in 1649.

New Englanders of the early republic in particular celebrated the achievements of the Massachusetts Puritans in creating the sense of America as "a city upon a hill," as an exemplar for the world and as an asylum for religious liberty. In the 1820s citizens of the early republic reprinted numerous seventeenth-century Puritan texts, including Cotton Mather's *Magnalia Christi Americana* in 1820, John Winthrop's *History of New England* in 1825, and Nathaniel Morton's *New England's Memorial* in 1826.[6] But important as the Puritans as a special godly people were in the founding of the nation, their story could not compare in poignancy with that of the simple Pilgrims of Plymouth Colony, as told by their leader William Bradford. This was the story of a small band of English refugees, numbering only a hundred or so, driven from their homes for their religious views, journeying first to Holland and then to the New World, binding themselves together with their "Mayflower Compact" in 1620 in an apparently democratic

fashion, suffering terrible losses their first year in Plymouth, and all along want-
ing nothing more than to be left alone to practice their "Separatist" religion. As
one-time New Hampshire congressman Salma Hale pointed out in his *History of
the United States* (1826), the experience of these Pilgrim immigrants offered a
lesson to the new republic on how to build "a body politic, for the purpose of
making equal laws for the general good."[7] In celebrating the special role of the
Pilgrims and Puritans in the messianic founding of the United States, New Englanders and other Americans of the early nineteenth century never lost the sense
that these seventeenth-century stories were integrally related to the subsequent
history of the country. Indeed, wrote David Ramsay in his posthumously published *History of the United States* (1818), the seventeenth-century New England
Puritans "were advanced a century a-head of their contemporaries, in the school
of republicanism and the rights of man."[8]

In his 1802 commemoration of the landing of the Pilgrims on Plymouth rock
John Quincy Adams tried to expand the number of founders, and he listed Sir
Walter Raleigh, John Smith, George Calvert, William Penn, and George Ogle-
thorpe as men who "excite in our minds recollections equally pleasing, and grat-
itude equally fervent" with those of Bradford and Winthrop.[9] Although orators
and writers like Adams and others described these seventeenth-century founders
in heroic and filiopietistic terms, they nevertheless did not mythologize them but
treated them as authentic and significant historical figures whose stories necessarily made up the first stage in the development of the later United States.

Historians in the early years of the nation's existence had little doubt of the
relevance of the colonial period to the story of America. Professor Samuel Williams of Harvard writing his *History of Vermont* in 1794 had no doubt that the
foundations of American freedom were laid in the social developments of the
colonial era. Jeremiah Belknap believed that he had to begin at the very beginning
of exploration for his biographical dictionary of important individuals in American history. He thus devoted two volumes to the original explorers and settlers,
ranging from the Phoenicians and Columbus to George Calvert and William
Penn; he died in 1798 before he could get out of the seventeenth century. John
Marshall likewise thought that American history necessarily began with the earliest colonial settlements. He therefore spent the entire first volume of his five-
volume biography of George Washington (1804–7) describing the history of the
colonies before he even got to Washington's birth.[10]

It is not surprising then that when George Bancroft, the young nation's first
significant historian, sought in the 1830s to tell the complete story of America he
would go back to its early colonial beginnings. Bancroft declared that he "dwelt
at considerable length" on the seventeenth century in his great history of America
"because it contains the germ of our institutions."[11] He began his history with the
Icelandic voyages and Columbus's discovery and intended to bring it up to his
own time, but in the end he carried his ten-volume history only through the
peace with England in 1783. (Only later did he add the formation of the Constitution.) For Bancroft and his fellow Americans the colonial period was the
natural source of the whole of American history. It was the nation's youth. It

flowed naturally into the national history that followed and was intimately connected with it. After all, "the maturity of the nation is but a continuation of its youth." Of course, that youth did not know all that the mature nation knew. The early colonists did not know about religious freedom and democracy as people of the nineteenth century did, but the seeds of these developments were planted in the colonial period. The American people had gradually learned about these principles and had progressed and developed into a more free and democratic nation than any people before them had known. More than any other work, Bancroft's *History of the United States* contributed to the belief that the American republic was showing the world the way toward true liberty and democracy.[12]

Bancroft's view of the colonial past was highly whiggish; he saw the past as simply an anticipation of the present and future. In volume one of his history of the nation, even in the fifteenth edition, he entitled the chapter describing the early English voyages to North America, including the Roanoke settlement in the 1580s, as "England takes possession of the United States."[13] The colonies were already the nation in embryo; the United States and the spirit of freedom were present from the earliest beginnings of exploration and settlement. Since history for Bancroft was just the realization of these earliest beginnings, his readers could have no doubt of the relevance of colonial history: it had to be an essential part of the history of the United States, and all Americans had a stake in it.

Yet this Bancroftian conception of the colonial past as an integral part of the whole of American history did not last. Americans of the later nineteenth century did not continue to regard the colonial period as relevant and essential to the rest of American history as they had at the beginning of the century. Even as early as the middle decades of the nineteenth century many Americans began viewing the colonial period in very different ways and gradually separating it from the rest of American history. The sectional conflict that led to the Civil War resulted in the increasing divergence of the South from the mainstream of American history.

In his *History of the United States* Bancroft had labored to portray seventeenth-century Virginia's being as devoted to liberty and the Parliamentary cause in the English Civil War as Puritan Massachusetts had been. But some southern critics balked at Bancroft's interpretation. As early as 1835 southerners rejected what they called Bancroft's "strange attempt to pervert the truth of history" by identifying Virginia's history with that of Massachusetts; and they refused to "acquiesce in the new notion 'that the people of the colonies, all together, formed one body politic before the Revolution.'" Instead of emphasizing its common colonial beginnings with the rest of the United States, the South now began claiming its special aristocratic origins. The southern colonies, especially Virginia, it was said, had been settled by royalist Cavaliers, that is, by supporters of Charles I in England. In contrast, the northern colonies had been settled by Roundhead Puritans, by narrow-minded plebeian people who had no aristocratic taste or grace. That may have been true, retorted some New England writers, but at least New Englanders were the ones who had "the exclusive honour of having *originated* the free principles" that had come to characterize the United States. At the very moment the Virginians were "importing into the country a cargo of negroes, to entail the curse of slavery on their remotest posterity, . . . our first fathers were founding the liberties of America on the Plymouth rock."[14]

These different sectional conceptions of the colonies' origins contributed to the Cavalier myth of the South and helped to justify what seemed by the 1840s and '50s to be the very distinctive aristocratic southern culture.[15] A nation that was coming apart could no longer have a colonial past that belonged equally and uniformly to all parts of it. As the sectional crisis deepened, Bancroft's view that the colonial period was essential to the subsequent democratic story of the United States lost much of its significance.

There were other reasons too for the repudiation of Bancroft's interpretation and the gradual separation of the colonial era from the rest of American history. During these same mid–nineteenth-century decades patrician elites in the North began looking to their colonial roots as a means of distinguishing themselves from the common people who were gaining increasing authority in democratic America, and in the process they gradually cut many of the ties that had hitherto bound the colonial past to the national history of the country. Through genealogical investigations they sought to assert their pride of ancestry and their special relationship to the colonial period. In 1844 the New England Historic-Genealogical Society was founded, followed in 1869 by a similar organization in New York. Everywhere in the Northeast state and local historical societies tended to become centers for genealogical and antiquarian interest. In the decades following the Civil War, these tendencies were accentuated. As the United States became more urbanized and industrialized, with ever increasing numbers of new non–Anglo-Saxon and non-Protestant immigrants, many old-stock Yankees organized a variety of societies designed to establish the priority of their ancestors as Americans. These included the Sons of the American Revolution (1889), the Daughters of the American Revolution (1890), the Colonial Dames of America (1890), the Society of Mayflower Descendants (1897), and many others. Members of these societies claimed that they had a special connection to the colonial past, that it was peculiarly their preserve and not, as it had been earlier, an integrated part of the rest of American history.[16]

At first the New England Historic-Genealogical Society had been concerned only with those ancestors who had come to America before 1700. But perhaps because of the need to expand the subscription rolls, this date was eventually moved forward to 1776. By the late nineteenth century many members of these various genealogical and antiquarian societies were claiming that any ancestor who settled in America before the Declaration of Independence should be included among the nation's founders.[17] They implied that those citizens whose ancestors came to the New World after 1776 were something less than full Americans.

Various ethnic groups responded to these implications by establishing their own patriotic societies in order to throw out their own lifelines to the colonial past and to document their particular ancestors' contributions to America's heritage. Thus was organized the Huguenot Society (1883), the Holland Society (1885), the Scotch-Irish Historical Society (1889), the American Jewish Historical Society (1892), the American-Irish Historical Society (1897), and the German-American Historical Society (1897).[18] All these ethnic groups sought, sometimes desperately, to establish some sort of historical relationship with the colonial era.

Despite these efforts, however, many Americans increasingly regarded the colonial period as something detached and separate from the rest of American history, as something that did not belong equally to all Americans. It was at the time of the centennial celebrations of the Revolution and especially of the formation of the Constitution that the designation of "founding fathers" was shifted from the seventeenth-century settlers to the Revolutionary leaders of 1776 and the Constitution-makers of 1787. Influential members of the Massachusetts Historical Society began calling for less attention to be paid to colonial origins and more to the national period of American history. What had gone on before the Revolution was no longer as important to the history of the United States as it once had been.[19]

Developments in American popular culture contributed to that view. During the latter part of the nineteenth century the colonial past became less and less a period of authentic historical actors and events and more and more a nostalgic repository of an imagined and mythic America—a simple bucolic world that was free of the sprawling slums and ethnic diversity of a modern urban society. Instead of seeing, as Bancroft had, the colonial era as containing the seeds of later American democracy and being a continuous and integral part of the whole story of the republic, many late nineteenth-century Americans saw it as unrelated to subsequent American history, indeed, as a point of contrast to the more complicated and sordid world that had followed. Painters like Francis David Millet and writers like Alice Morse Earle portrayed clean and cosy colonial scenes that appealed deeply to the longings of late nineteenth-century Americans. In 1896 Henry Wadsworth Longfellow's poetic depiction of seventeenth-century Plymouth, *The Courtship of Miles Standish*, was republished and built into the curriculums of many of the nation's schools.

The colonial period seemed more and more to belong to American folklore and the story-telling of elementary school, and not to serious historical study. Everywhere colonial antiques and old-country furnishings told Americans of a lost past. The "clear white houses" of an old New England village were to a character in Henry James's novel *Roderick Hudson* (1875) representations of "kindness, comfort, safety, the warning voice of duty, the perfect absence of temptation." Much of the colonial revival movement in art, architecture, and literature that took place at the end of the nineteenth century and the beginning decades of the twentieth was designed to Americanize the new immigrants and teach them what the first curator of the American Wing of the Metropolitan Museum of Art in 1925 called the ideals and values "held by the men who gave us the Republic."[20] Yet the colonial revival movement had the effect of sentimentalizing the colonial period and making it seem irrelevant to the lives of the new and recent immigrants. These developments reached their peak during the first four decades of the twentieth century, expressed most remarkably perhaps by the restoration of

Colonial Williamsburg in the 1930s and '40s. As this popular and sentimental interest in the colonial period grew, however, not only was the period further separated from the rest of American history, but professional historical interest in it gradually declined.

At the time of the founding of the *American Historical Review* in 1895 and the beginnings of the American historical profession the colonial period still dominated the writing of American history just as it had for Bancroft's generation. Not only did the amateur antiquarians centered in the state and local historical and genealogical societies continue to focus on the colonial sources of America, but Herbert Baxter Adams, often considered, perhaps mistakenly, to be the first of American professional historians, devoted most of his energies in the 1870s and '80s to promoting the study of local institutions in the colonial period, including the New England town. Adams and many of his students were obsessed with continuities between Europe and America, with what has been called a "germ theory," and they reached back for the origins of America's local institutions not just to the the colonial period but all the way back to Anglo-Saxon England and the Teutonic forests of Germany.[21]

The new professional historians quickly showed that the Teutonic germ thesis was improbable and undemonstrable and already undermined by English scholars. J. Franklin Jameson, the first Ph.D. under Adams at Johns Hopkins University, continually moaned over the unscientific character of the local studies, especially over having to trace institutions "back *nearly* to when our ancesters chattered in the tree tops."[22] But these complaints were nothing compared with the scorn the new professionals directed at the parochialism and mindless fact-collecting of most colonial scholarship. They were desperate to escape from what Jameson sneeringly called "the local and antiquarian details of the colonial period."[23] Some of their frustration with the triviality of colonial scholarship was captured by a young Hopkins graduate student, Woodrow Wilson, who complained in 1884 of going into his colonial history examination "crammed with one or two hundred dates and one or two thousand minute particulars about the quarrels of nobody knows who with an obscure Governor, for nobody knows what. Just think of all that energy wasted! The only comfort is that this mass of information won't long burden me. I shall forget it with great ease."[24]

It was not that the new professionals wished to ignore the colonial period; quite the contrary. But they wanted a much more cosmopolitan and more professional perspective brought to bear on it. They aimed to study the colonial period seriously and scientifically. They were disgusted with the way colonial America had been romanticized and littered with myths and false legends. They were determined to clean up this mythical litter and to set straight the history of the colonial past. Ironically, however, these efforts by the new professional historians to write a more scientific history of early America in the end only contributed further to detaching the colonial period from the subsequent national history of the United States.

At the beginning of the twentieth century there were three major emerging schools of professional historians concerned with early America—the imperial historians, the Progressive historians, and those historians connected with Frederick Jackson Turner and his frontier thesis. Although each of these schools began by studying early America, each of them inadvertently helped to set the colonial period apart from the rest of American history. Each of them suggested in different ways that the colonial era was not naturally connected with the national history of the United States, and each implied that the colonial period had not fundamentally contributed to the making of what was distinctive or unique about American institutions and culture. The work of these several schools of professional historians eventually undermined all that Bancroft and his generation had believed about the continuity and relevance of the colonial period to the subsequent history of America.

The so-called imperial school, led by Herbert Osgood and Charles McLean Andrews, thought that nineteenth-century historians had been much too parochial and antiquarian in their attitude toward early American history. The nineteenth-century historians had too often viewed the "colonial era as a tangled mass of genealogical tree roots." They had focused too narrowly on the states and localities and had been unable to distinguish between "the really important and the insignificant." Previous historians had concentrated on each of the thirteen colonies at the expense of the whole and had ignored the other British colonies in the Western Hemisphere. They had enveloped "men and events connected with our colonial past in an atmosphere of piety, patriotism, and perfection." Both Osgood and Andrews, as good professionals, wanted colonial history to escape from its previous triviality and parochialism and become more impartial and cosmopolitan. Early American history, they said, ought to be looked at "not only from the colonial but from the British standpoint."[25]

The result was a half century or more of important studies of the American colonies that tended to view them from the vantage point of London. The history of the thirteen continental colonies became less the history of the origins of the United States and more the history of some of the outposts of the expanding first British empire. In fact, the imperial scholars argued that their history should not confine itself to the thirteen colonies that became the United States but should embrace all the western hemispheric colonies of the British empire, the West Indian and Canadian as well as the mainland colonies. The breadth and depth of this imperial scholarship was truly remarkable. However rich and significant, however, it had the ultimate effect of separating the colonial period from the rest of American history. In the hands of the imperial historians the history of the colonies became largely a branch of British history, not the first stage in the development of the American nation. As Andrews put it, "The years from 1607 to 1783 were colonial before they were American or national, and our Revolution is a colonial and not an American problem."[26]

The work of Frederick Jackson Turner and his followers, writing more or less at the same time during the first half of the twentieth century, accentuated this detachment of the colonial period from the national history of the United States. Unlike the imperial historians, Turner was exclusively and unequivocally interested in the roots of Americanism. Indeed, probably no historian has contributed more to the myth of American exceptionalism. Above all, Turner sought to explain what he saw as the peculiarities of the American character—the democratic and individualistic tendencies of the American people. He saw the source of that character in the availability of free virgin land. The West for Turner was not important for its own sake. Rather, he said, "the distinctive thing about the West is its relation to free lands; and it is the influence of her free lands that has determined the larger lines of American development" and has set "the evolution of American and European institutions in contrast."

Turner saw three phases of American growth. The first ran from the first European settlements to the time of the Revolution. The second, the golden age of frontier history, went from the Revolution to 1890. The third, in which Turner now lived, saw the end of free lands and the beginnings of an entirely new phase of American history. "With conditions comparable to those of Europe," he wrote in 1895, "we have to reshape the ideals and institutions fashioned in the age of wilderness-winning to the new conditions of an occupied country."

In Turner's opinion the first phase of the colonial period—"the application of European men, institutions, and ideas to the tide-water area of America"—did not have much influence on the peculiar development of America. Although some modification of European culture took place during this colonial period, "English traits and institutions preponderated." During most of the first century and a half of colonial history the colonists remained confined to a several-hundred-mile or so strip of the eastern coast of North America. "The constant touch of this part of the country with the Old World prevented the modifying influences of the new environment from having their full effect, and the coast area seemed likely to produce institutions and men that were but modified shoots from the parent tree." Even the physical features of the colonists, he said, were still English: the colonists remained ruddy in appearance and without the nervous energy or expressiveness of later Americans. During the first phase of American development—the colonial period—the settlers, according to Turner, remained still essentially Europeans.

Only during the second phase of American growth, at the end of the eighteenth and the beginning of the nineteenth centuries, did the "process of Americanization" really take place. This phase began after the Seven Years' War "with the spread of this colonial society towards the mountains; the crossing of the Alleghenies, and the settlement upon the Western Waters. . . . As each new advance occurred, the process was repeated with modifications. In this reaction between the West and the East, American society took on its peculiar features." Thus only when Americans had broken free of the British imperial shackles and entered the trans-Appalachian west did the free lands and open environment of America begin to have decisive effects on the American character.[27]

Since what was uniquely American did not develop during the seventeenth and first half of the eighteenth centuries, Turner and his followers never had much interest in the colonial period; it seemed irrelevant to the process of Americanization. In the colonial era the settlers remained essentially Europeans; only with the Revolution did the settlers become Americans and experience the effects of the frontier. Consequently Turner's frontier history tended to concentrate in the nineteenth century, especially in the period from 1800 to 1850 when the Midwest was settled. The Turnerite school of history thus effectively intensified the remoteness and irrelevance of the colonial period to the history of America. The colonial period seemed to have little to say about the sources of what was peculiarly American.

The work of the third and most important school of professional historians writing during the first half of the twentieth century, the Progressive historians, had similar unintended effects. These historians, led by Carl Becker, Charles Beard, and Arthur Schlesinger, Sr., unlike the imperial historians, were interested in the origins and character of the United States. But they stressed the discontinuity of American history and were preoccupied with the ways in which the colonial era was different from subsequent American history. For them the Revolution marked a real turning point in American history, the uprising of popular forces against conservative aristocracies and the beginning of American democracy. In this perspective the colonial period that preceded the Revolution was not really American in character; it was instead English or European—a kind of ancien régime, undemocratic and quasifeudal and marked by elite rule, established churches, and a limited suffrage. In the eyes of the Progressive historians little that was truly American came out of the colonial era. They became interested in the period only so far as it helped to explain the Revolution, which they saw as a radical break from the past, and they consequently wrote very little about the seventeenth and early eighteenth centuries. Their writings suggested that anyone who wanted to understand the roots of American liberty and democracy really ought to begin with the Revolution. It was the Revolution that destroyed the older aristocratic order, expanded the suffrage and popular participation in government, and created the nation. When Charles McLean Andrews once reproached the Progressive historian Arthur Schlesinger, Sr., for ignoring the colonial era, Schlesinger in reply made just this point: the origins of the United States, he said, really lay with the Revolution, not with the colonial period.[28] With such a viewpoint the Progressive historians could not help but further separate the colonial period from what they took to be the real history of America.

All these developments during the first half of the twentieth century—the myth-making and sentimentalizing of the colonial era, the efforts by old-stock Anglo-Saxons to make the colonial period their special preserve, and the peculiar perspectives of the various schools of professional historians—all these led to a diminishing of professional interest in early American history. In their search for the roots of the nation, historians did not believe the colonial period had much to offer them.

This waning of interest did not show up at once. In the 1890s, at the beginning of professional history-writing in the United States, the colonial period still absorbed the attention of many scholars; but over the next half century it gradually gave way to other fields of interest, particularly to the more recent periods of United States history. More and more young talented researchers saw the colonial period as unimportant for what they wanted to say. In the first six volumes of the

American Historical Review between 1895–96 and 1900–1901 there were fifteen articles dealing with the colonial period of American history. The next six volumes between 1901–2 and 1906–7 saw this number drop to nine. Thereafter, despite all the substantial work of the imperial scholars like Osgood and Andrews, there began an irregular but unmistakable decline in the concern for early America as a subject of professional teaching and research. In the six volumes of the *American Historical Review* between 1907–8 and 1912–13 there were only five articles dealing with the colonial era. After a brief flurry of early American papers between 1914 and 1916, the number of articles on colonial history in the *American Historical Review* declined to one a year; in 1920–21 there were none. Over the next two decades the situation never really improved. By the time of World War II the colonial period was attracting very little of the historical profession's attention; in the six volumes of the the *American Historical Review* between 1941–42 and 1946–47 there was only one article concerned with the first 150 years of American history.

This decreasing professional interest in early American history finally reached the point in 1948 where historian Carl Bridenbaugh felt compelled publicly to lament "the neglected first half of American history." Survey courses and textbooks in American history spent less and less time on the colonial period, sometimes omitting the first century and a half entirely. The numbers of new dissertations and publications in early American history had declined. Fewer young scholars were being trained in the subject. Most universities and colleges did not even offer courses in early American history. By the 1940s Johns Hopkins University, which had been the center of colonial studies in the late nineteenth century, no longer even had a historian working in the field. The same was true of other important graduate training centers such as Princeton, Pennsylvania, Chicago, and Berkeley.

Bridenbaugh blamed a number of developments for this neglect of early America, including an increased interest in presentism and relevance, lopsided textbooks, and the influence of Turner and the trans-Appalachian frontier at expense of the Atlantic seaboard. He hoped that the formation of the Institute of Early American History and Culture, of which he was then director, and the establishment of the third series of the *William and Mary Quarterly* in 1944 would help to turn things around. He and nine other distinguished scholars of early America met at Princeton in the spring of 1947 to devise ways and means for stimulating professional interest in colonial and Revolutionary history.[29] If what happened over the next several decades is any measure, they succeeded beyond their wildest dreams.

In the decades following 1947 everything changed. Colonial history became an important and flourishing field, not just of American history but of early modern Western history in general. Most universities and colleges now have courses in early American history, and some of the most distinguished historians in the country are specialists in the subject. In fact, three out of the past five presidents of the Organization of American Historians have been early Americanists, at least for a good part of their careers. Much of the most significant and pathbreaking historical scholarship in America over the past generation has focused on the colonial period. In 1980 the principal journal in the field, *The William and Mary Quarterly*, was judged to be the most frequently cited historical journal in the world.[30]

Following World War II many of the conditions that had existed at the beginning of the twentieth century were transformed. Most impotant in revitalizing colonial scholarship in the 1950s was the reemergence of a whiggish or Bancroftian view of American history. Amidst the Cold War atmosphere of the decades following World War II many Americans once again celebrated the long-existing role of the United States as the leader of the free world, destined by history to show people everywhere the way to liberty and democracy. What has been called an "exceptionalist" conception of America was never more widely proclaimed, as American historians, like Bancroft before them, began to see the whole of America's past pointing toward this providential role. All at once the first century and a half of American history became an integral part of the whole national story; the colonial past was relevant once again.

The historiography that had inhibited serious consideration of the colonial era was now evaded or overturned. One by one the works of historians written during the first half of the twentieth century were either bypassed or refuted. In the exceptionalist climate of the Cold War years Americans wanted to see their colonial past from their own side of the Atlantic; and the broad imperial perspective of Andrews and Osgood had to give way to newer, narrower, nationalist viewpoints. America was once again different from Europe, and it had been different from the beginning. The frontier theory of Turner that ignored the colonial era was attacked and modified out of importance; if it still had any meaning, that meaning was now made applicable to the colonial period as well as later periods of American history. And, most important, the works of the Progressive school of historians were undermined in dozens of different ways. Colonial society was not an ancien régime after all. There was no aristocracy in colonial America worthy of the name. The established churches were never as strong as the state churches in England or Europe. White male colonists could vote in larger proportions than any people in the world. Eighteenth-century America, historians of the 1950s like Robert E. Brown claimed, was already a middle-class democracy; the Revolution was merely a colonial rebellion, designed simply to preserve what had developed during the previous 150 years of colonial history. America, as Louis Hartz put it, echoing Tocqueville, had become free and equal in the migrations of the seventeenth century; it was liberal from the beginning of the colonial period. Suddenly the first half of American history was important once again in creating the sources of American democracy and nationhood.[31]

At the same time as the work of earlier schools of historians—work that had prevented serious consideration of the colonial period—was being dismantled, other circumstances that had cut the colonial era off from the rest of American history changed as well. The increasing ethnic diversity of the United States became such that efforts by a few Anglo-Saxons to claim some sort of special tie to the colonial era seemed more and more ludicrous. Organizations like the DAR now had none of the importance in American life they had had during the early decades of the twentieth century. Antiquarian and colonial historical societies still existed, but many of them, such as the American Antiquarian Society, the Colonial Society of Massachusetts, and the Massachusetts Historical Society, were invaded by professional historians who had no genealogical roots in the colonial past or even in rural America. In the face of these changes the notion that the colonial period was simply a repository of old Yankee ancestors and customs could not be sustained.

Ironically, this emergence of the children and grandchildren of recent immigrants into the historical profession was lamented by Bridenbaugh in his presidential address to the American Historical Association in 1962. These urban-bred scholars, he said, were trying to write about a rural colonial past that they had no inherited connectedness with.[32] It was a foolish lament. Not only was Bridenbaugh denying the very premise of all imaginative historical recovery, but he was ignoring the fact that it was precisely the post–World War II appearance in the profession of new historians without Anglo-Saxon backgrounds that was important to the revival of interest in early American history that Bridenbaugh himself had called for a decade and a half earlier. These new historians with varying ethnic backgrounds had no personal or emotional stake in the colonial period except as Americans, and therefore they tended to approach it disinterestedly and dispassionately.

As the character of the history profession changed and became more diverse in the decades following World War II, traditional political history gave way to social and cultural history, for which the colonial period had a natural receptivity. Indeed, much of the new American social and cultural history of the past thirty years was born in the colonial period. In the seventeenth and eighteenth centuries there are few headline political events to hang a conventional narrative line on: no presidents, no congresses, no supreme court decisions, no national elections to write about, which is one reason why the colonial period usually has seemed so mythical and free-floating, so easily telescoped and foreshortened. Yet during the past generation in which modern social and cultural history has flourished this lack of palpable political events and national institutions in the colonial period has become an advantage. The headline events and political institutions that preoccupied historians of the national period were not present to divert the attention of social and cultural historians. Colonial historians therefore were freer than national historians to concentrate on the *longue durée*, on social and cultural developments that go on longer than a few years or even a few decades. Only in the colonial period could historians of America have the long sweep of a century or more, uninterrupted by political events, in which to lay out long-term social and cultural developments. It is not coincidental that the modern study of American demographic and family history began first in the colonial period; or that one of the earliest studies of American attitudes toward death concentrated on the colonial period.[33] Historians could not trace such enduring social and cultural subjects over only a decade or two; they needed long stretches of time. Colonial historians, unlike national historians, had been used to dealing with long periods of time and thus were more likely to be attracted to the new social and cultural history.

But the revival of interest in early American history was more than a matter of its being especially receptive to the new social and cultural history. Over the past thirty years the field has erupted and expanded in all directions. Early American history, according to Bernard Bailyn, the historian who over the past generation has dominated the period as much as any single scholar could, has experienced a "creative ferment of scholarship," resulting in "a wealth of research and writing concentrated on a relatively short period of time that is perhaps unique in western historiography."[34] The changes in the writing of colonial history have been phenomenal.

The impulses that initially lay behind the revival of early American history in the 1950s and early '60s have been transformed. Since the late 1960s American historians have become less and less interested in celebrating the uniqueness of the United States. The war in Vietnam if nothing else convinced many Americans that the moral character of the United States was not different from that of other nations and that the nation had no special transcendent role to bring liberty and democracy to the world. During the past several decades many American historians, if not the general public, have shed whatever faith they might once have had in the traditional idea of American exceptionalism.

These changes in outlook have been matched by equally important changes taking place in the society of the United States and in its historical profession. The new emphasis on diversity and the new racial, ethnic, and gender consciousness have tended to dilute a unified sense of American identity and have led to less and less emphasis on the nation as a whole in historical research and writing. All these changes have resulted in a shift in perspective on the colonial past; they have, in John Higham's words, "disconnected the colonial era from the narratives of American uniqueness or identity."[35]

Once again the colonial period has lost much of its relevance for those historians looking for the origins or roots of the nation. But it has gained new relevance for those who have other questions or interests in mind. Recent historians, as Joyce Appleby says, have found it "easy to abandon the idea that what was truly important about the colonies was their contribution to American nationhood."[36] The consequence of this "gradual liberation from the nationalist paradigm" has been a fundamental shift in the nature and purposes of colonial historiography.[37]

Most obvious has been a reappreciation of the discontinuity between the colonial and national periods of American history. The roots of modern democratic America cannot be found in the colonial era after all. America, it seems, was not born free, equal, and liberal in the seventeenth century; like the nations of Europe, it had to become so, and this apparently did not happen until the nineteenth century. Some colonial historians like James Horn and David Hackett Fischer have explicitly challenged the "paradigm of exceptionalism," which holds that "colonial society diverged significantly from its parent culture." Instead, they have stressed the continuities between Europe and America and the "contribution of Old World cultures to New World society"; in fact, Fischer recalls the scholarship of Herbert Baxter Adams in arguing for a "modified 'germ thesis'" in his account of the perpetuation of British folkways in colonial America.[38] Britons in colonial America were still Britons. The traditional patriarchal forms and values of the Old World persisted in the New—in family life, society, and politics. Seventeenth- and eighteenth-century colonial America, it seems, was a kind of ancien régime after all. The established churches, weak as they may have been, still gave a statist tone to the culture. Social hierarchies and familial politics aped those of the mother country. The few dominated the many, and, as in Europe, ordinary people had little influence over the course of public life. Most commmon farmers in colonial America were content to live out their lives as their parents had; they seemed no more individualist or capitalist than their European counterparts.[39]

But more important in changing the historiography of colonial history than the reappreciation of discontinuity between the colonial and national eras has been the remarkable ways some historians of early America have enlarged their perspective—no longer focusing exclusively on the territory that became the United States but, as Bernard Bailyn has put it, seeing early modern worlds in motion from a satellite hovering somewhere over the Atlantic.[40] A century ago Herbert L. Osgood hoped eventually to see an American colonial history that "will be taken out of its isolation and will appear as a natural outgrowth of the history of Europe."[41] Historians of the past several decades have been well on the way not merely to fulfilling Osgood's hope but to surpassing it. The colonies are now seen as an outgrowth not just of Europe but of Africa as well. Historians have greatly broadened the boundaries of what constitutes early American history, almost to the point where they now seem limitless. For many historians early American history is no longer what it was for Bancroft and most historians of the 1890s, a means for understanding the origins of the United States; it has become an important and vital part of the pan-Atlantic world in the early modern era.[42] As nationhood has receded in importance, historians have become less interested in early America for its own sake and more for what it reveals about the great transformation from premodern to modern society.

American colonial history has not only become part of western European and African history, but it now seems to make sense only as it embraces the peoples of Hispanic America as well.[43] Some early American historians have called for entirely new conceptions of the colonial past, new conceptions that would "think of colonial history as a history of all of the Americas," and that would reintroduce the hemispheric perspective that Herbert E. Bolton tried and failed to make stick in the 1930s—a perspective that placed United States history in a comparative framework with Canada, Mexico, the Caribbean, and the countries of South America. These efforts to make the history of Santa Fe in 1776 just as important as the history of Boston in 1776 are not the idle chatter of a few multicultural-minded historians.[44] In fact, the Omohundro Institute of Early American History and Culture in Williamsburg, the center for early American studies in America and the publisher of the *William and Mary Quarterly*, has recently announced that it plans "to diversify its agenda." Without abandoning its traditional commitment to studying the British North American colonies, "Institute publications and programs are currently attempting to embrace a larger range of subjects, including especially the peoples of Hispanic America and West Africa."[45] Early American historians now have concerns other than the origins of the United States.

As historians have lost confidence that the United States has a collective identity with common origins, they have shifted their focus away from the nation as a whole and have zoomed in to the histories of groups or individuals within the larger community. Instead of writing about the nation or the British empire or even single colonies, many have concentrated on towns or counties or even obscure single families. Indeed, the most interior and private aspects of daily life have now become open to serious historical study—what the colonists ate, how they treated their children, how husbands and wives related to each other, how they managed their emotions. By trying ever harder to recapture the private spaces and personal lives of ordinary people, historians have written ever smaller and more intimate snatches of history, some of which, like Laurel Thatcher Ulrich's *A Midwife's Tale* and John Demos's *The Unredeemed Captive*, are truly marvelous to behold.

All these private and personal histories, however, were just aspects of a larger attempt at historical retrieval. In their earlier search for the origins of American identity, most historians of colonial America had tended to ignore the voices of a variety of peoples—slaves, artisans, women, and Indians—who did not appear to contribute to the traditional history of the exceptionalist nation. Since the 1960s all this has changed. By playing down America's collective identity and emphasizing its pluralism, the new social and cultural history of the past several decades has recovered many of these lost voices.

The shift of perspective from the sources of American nationhood to the larger early modern world has made the Indians especially visible.[46] Because of their preoccupation with the origins of America's peculiar national character, earlier historians had not been able to see the Native Americans with any clarity. Indeed, historians like Turner had scarcely acknowledged the existence of the Indian. For Turner the New World the Europeans came to in the seventeenth century was "virgin soil," an "unexploited wilderness" out of which American distinctiveness was born; it was "the fact of unoccupied territory in America that sets the evolution of American and European institutions in contrast."[47] As Louis Hartz pointed out long ago, this neglect of the Indian in early American historiography stemmed solely from the "interior perspectives" of historians like Turner. Since it was the fate of America "to destroy and exclude the Indian, life inside it has had a dwindling contact with him. How could he then be perceived? How could he be appreciated as a problem comparable to the rise of the 'common man' or the emergence of the trusts?" But, of course, Hartz said, once American historians get outside the narrow confines of the nation, "the very fact that the Indian was thus eliminated . . . becomes a matter of very great importance."[48]

Today historians who have sought to get outside the national history of the United States have a very different appreciation of the presence of the Indians.

During the past decade or so the numbers of books and articles on the native peoples of North America in the colonial period have multiplied dramatically. In the fifteen years of the *William and Mary Quarterly* between 1959 and 1973 only four articles on Indians appeared. But in the fourteen years between 1974 and 1988 there were twenty articles dealing with Native Americans. And since 1988 the number of contributions to what has come to be called "ethnohistory" has increased even faster. Indeed, as Ian Steele has recently said, the "field of ethno-history . . . is developing so quickly that any attempt at accessible synthesis is bound to be premature and incomplete."[49] Some of the best and brightest histori-ans in the United States have been turning to the Indians as a subject of research, and books on Indians in early America have begun winning prestigious prizes.[50]

Presumably these recent sensitive studies of the Indians in the colonial period have been a consequence, as Appleby has put it, of "the quickening of interest in non-Western cultures that came with the diminished credibility of the West's claims to be directing the path of human destiny."[51] The question now to be faced is whether such a "quickening of interest in non-Western cultures" by profes-sional historians will eventually weaken popular interest in early American his-tory. With colonial historians presently being urged to "avoid letting their field again become the prehistory of the United States," will citizens of that United States continue to be much interested in what these new colonial historians write?[52] There may be a limit to the degree to which the American people will put up with having a colonial history that pays no attention to the nation, "except," in John Higham's words, "as a villain in other people's stories."[53] Although few historians these days would write a history the way George Bancroft did, with, in Frank Craven's words, all "his willingness to let love of country illuminate the text," outright hostility to the country may not sit well with the American pub-lic.[54] Historians who see their role as simply being "a *critic* of the culture" whose principal task is "to illuminate conditions of the present by casting a harsh light on previous experience" may not be able to develop much of a popular following; most people do not seem very eager "to learn unpleasant lessons from their study of the past."[55] If the colonial era is to be simply an arena for criticizing American culture and is to be cut loose from the story of American nationhood or identity, will it continue to be meaningful to most Americans?[56] The old question of the relevance and irrelevance of the colonial past to American history seems once again on the table.

NOTES

1. Wesley Frank Craven, *The Legend of the Founding Fathers* (Ithaca, N.Y., 1956), 63: "Of these colonies," wrote George Chalmers in 1780, "it cannot be asserted, as it is of European nations, that their origin is uncertain or unknown: that their ancient history is fabulous and dark; or that their original institutions have come down the current of time, loaded wtih the disputations of the antiquary."

2. One textbook that collapsed time in this way was T. Harry Williams, Richard N. Current, and Frank Friedel, *A History of the United States* (New York, 1959), I, 95–96.

3. Adams, "Dissertation on the Feudal and Canon Law" (1765), in Gordon S. Wood, ed., *The Rising Glory of America, 1760–1820*, rev. ed. (Boston, 1990), 31.

4. Jack P. Greene, *The Intellectual Construction of America: Exceptionalism and Identity from 1492 to 1800* (Chapel Hill, 1993), 199.

5. For an illuminating account of the cultural politics of historical memory in the early republic, focusing on literary and historical accounts of Puritanism in colonial New England, see Philip Gould, *Covenant and Republic: Historical Romance and the Politics of Puritanism* (Cambridge, Eng., 1996).

6. Gould, *Covenant and Republic*, 17.

7. Gould, *Covenant and Republic*, 21.

8. Gould, *Covenant and Republic*, 29.

9. Craven, *Legend of the Founding Fathers*, 98.

10. Greene, *The Intellectual Construction of America*, 175; David D. Van Tassel, *Recording America's Past: An Interpretation of the Development of Historical Studies in America, 1607–1884* (Chicago, 1960), 69, 81.

11. George Bancroft, *History of the United States, from the Discovery of the American Continent* (Boston, 1853), I, vii.

12. Dorothy Ross, "Historical Consciousness in Nineteenth-Century America," *American Historical Review* 89 (1984): 915–19.

13. Bancroft, *History of the United States*, I, vii, 74.

14. Van Tassel, *Recording America's Past*, 117: Craven, *Legend of the Founding Fathers*, 133.

15. William Taylor, *Cavalier and Yankee: The Old South and American National Character* (New York, 1961, 1969).

16. Craven, *Legend of the Founding Fathers*, 158.

17. Craven, *Legend of the Founding Fathers*, 114–18.

18. Craven, *Legend of the Founding Fathers*, 158.

19. Craven, *Legend of the Founding Fathers*, 149–50, 157.

20. Celia Betsky, "Inside the Past: The Interior and the Colonial Revival in American Art and Literature, 1860–1914," and William B. Rhoads, "The Colonial Revival and the Americanization of Immigrants," in Alan Axelrod, ed., *The Colonial Revival in America* (New York, 1985), 242, 349.

21. John Higham, *History: Professional Scholarship in America* (Baltimore, 1983), 160–61; John Higham, "Herbert Baxter Adams and the Study of Local History," *American Historical Review* 89 (1984): 1225–39.

22. Jameson, quoted in Higham, "Herbert Baxter Adams," 1235.

23. Jameson, "*The American Historical Review*, 1895–1920," *American Historical Review* 26 (1920–21): 1.

24. Woodrow Wilson to J. H. Kennard, Jr., Nov. 18, 1884, quoted in Bernard Bailyn, *The Origins of American Politics* (New York, 1968), vii–viii.

25. Herbert L. Osgood, "The Study of American Colonial History," *Annual Report of the American Historical Association for the Year 1898* (Washington, D.C., 1899), 63–73; Charles M. Andrews, *The Colonial Background of the American Revolution: Four Essays in American Colonial History* (New Haven, 1924), 175, 178.

26. Andrews, quoted in Michael Kraus, *The Writng of American History* (Norman, Okla., 1953), 242.

27. Frederick Jackson Turner, "Western State-Making in the Revolutionary Era," *American Historical Review* 1 (1895–96): 70

28. Higham, *History*, 187.

29. Bridenbaugh,"The Neglected First Half of American History," *American Historical Review* 53 (1947–48): 506–17.

30. According to an index of over a thousand scholarly journals for the year 1980 compiled by the Institute for Scientific Information, the *William and Mary Quarterly* was judged to be the most frequently cited journal of historical scholarship in the world, during that one year at least. See *A News Letter from the Institute of Early American History & Culture* 73 (Mar. 1, 1983), 73.

31. For a summary of this 1950s scholarship see Bernard Bailyn, "Political Experience and Enlightenment Ideas in Eighteenth-Century America," *American Historical Review* 67 (1961–62), 339–51.

32. Carl Bridenbaugh, "The Great Mutation," *American Historical Review* 68 (1962–63): 315–31.

33. Philip Greven, "Historical Demography and Colonial America," *William and Mary Quarterly*, 3rd ser., 24 (1967): 438–54; David E. Stannard, *The Puritan Way of Death: A Study in Religion, Culture, and Social Change* (New York, 1977). Much of what follows draws on my article "A Century of Writing Early American History: Then and Now Compared; or How Henry Adams Got It Wrong," *American Historical Review* 100 (1995): 678–96.

34. Bernard Bailyn, *The Peopling of British North America: An Introduction* (New York, 1986), 6.

35. John Higham, "The Future of American History" *Journal of American History* 80 (1994): 1298.

36. Joyce Appleby, "A Different Kind of Independence: The Postwar Restructuring of the Historical Study of Early America," *William and Mary Quarterly*, 3rd ser., 50 (1993): 249; Higham, "Future of American History," 1298; Michael McGerr, "The Price of the 'New Transnational History,'" *American Historical Review* 96 (1991): 1066.

37. Mathew Mulcahy and Russell R. Menard, "Comment on 'Why the West Is Lost,'" *William and Mary Quarterly*, 3rd ser., 51 (1994): 741.

38. James Horn, *Adapting to a New World: English Society in the Seventeenth-Century Chesapeake* (Chapel Hill, 1994), 9, 10; David Hackett Fischer, *Albion's Seed: Four British Folkways in America* (New York, 1989), 4–5.

39. For a review of a number of these works see Gordon S. Wood, "Inventing American Capitalism," *The New York Review of Books*, vol. XLI, no. 11 (June 9, 1994), 44–49.

40. Bailyn, *Peopling of America*, 3.

41. Dixon Ryan Fox, *Herbert Levi Osgood: An American Scholar* (New York, 1924), 72.

42. Bernard Bailyn, "The Idea of Atlantic History," *Itinerario* 20 (1996): 1–27.

43. Bernard Bailyn, "The Challenge of Modern Historiography," *American Historical Review* 87 (1982): 2; A. Roger Ekirch, "Sometimes an Art, Never a Science, Always a Craft: A Conversation with Bernard Bailyn," *William and Mary Quarterly*, 3rd ser., 51 (1994): 657.

44. Mulcahy and Menard, "Comment on 'Why the West Is Lost,'" 743; Herbert E. Bolton, "The Epic of Greater America," *American Historical Review* 38 (1933): 448–74.

45. James A. Hijiya, "Why the West is Lost," *William and Mary Quarterly*, 3d ser., 51 (1994): 276–92; "'Why the West Is Lost': Comments and Response," forum in ibid., 717–54.

46. Appleby, "A Different Kind of Independence," 260.

47. Turner, "Western State-Making," 70–72.

48. Louis Hartz, *The Founding of New Societies: Studies in the History of the United States, Latin America, South Africa, Canada, and Australia* (New York, 1964), 94.

49. Ian K. Steele, *Warpaths: Invasions of North America* (New York, 1994), preface.

50. For an able summary of historiography about the Indians over the past hundred years see R. David Edmunds, "Native Americans, New Voices: American Indian History, 1895–1995," *American Historical Review* 100 (1995): 717–40.

51. Appleby, "A Different Kind of Independence," 259.

52. Mulcahy and Menard, "Comment on 'Why the West Is Lost,'" 743.

53. Higham, "The Future of American History," 1298.

54. Craven, *Legend of the Founding Fathers*, 100. In a 1994 op-ed piece Richard Rorty warned of the dangers for an academic left that, "in the name of 'the politics of difference,' . . . refuses to rejoice in the country it inhabits [and] repudiates the idea of a national identity, and the emotion of national pride." Such an academic left, said Rorty, "will become increasingly isolated and ineffective. An unpatriotic left has never achieved anything. A left that refuses to take pride in its country will have no impact on that country's politics, and will eventually become an object of contempt." Rorty, "The Unpatriotic Academy," *The New York Times*, Feb. 13, 1994. On this point see also Todd Gitlin, *The Twilight of Common Dreams: Why America Is Wracked by Culture Wars* (New York, 1995).

55. Daniel K. Richter, "Whose Indian History?" *William and Mary Quarterly*, 3rd ser., 50 (1993): 388.

56. Already, for example, historians of the Indians have begun lamenting that their professional new Indian scholarship, with its "oppositional perspective on the dominant culture," has not had much impact on the popular mind. Consequently, some of them have begun trying to stress the contributions of the Indians not only to the origins of American society and culture but also to the beginnings of American democracy and the formation of the Constitution. Richter, "Whose Indian History?" 380, 386, 388, 389. For the Indians' contributions to American democracy and the Constitution see Oren Lyons et al., eds., *Exiled in the Land of the Free: Democracy, Indian Nations, and the U.S. Constitution* (Santa Fe, 1992). For a debate on the issue see "Forum: The 'Iroquois Influence' Thesis—Pro and Con," *William and Mary Quarterly*, 3rd ser., 53 (1996): 587–636.

CHAPTER 8

Nineteenth-Century American History

GEORGE M. FREDRICKSON

IN THEIR SEARCH for the central theme of nineteenth-century American history, historians have nominated several candidates, some of which seem better qualified for the office than others. The traditional, self-congratulatory emphasis on "the rise of democracy" might serve for the first half of the century, but only if one forgets the fact that equal citizenship and political participation were strictly limited to white males. Since recent historians have tended to focus on the experiences of groups excluded from "the people" as defined by Jacksonian democrats—especially blacks, Indians, and women—the once-popular view of pre–Civil War American progress toward democratic perfection has few adherents among recent historians. For the post–Civil War era the democratization theme becomes even more problematic, despite the emancipation and extension of putative citizenship to African-Americans. By the end of the century, most historians would agree, new hierarchies of power and authority associated with corporate capitalism were threatening the democratic and egalitarian ethos that had developed earlier among the white male members of a society of yeomen farmers and small producers. Under such circumstances, the popular politics of mass meetings and high rates of voter participation was being replaced by a political system featuring appointed commissions, organized pressure groups, and lower rates of voter turnout.[1]

Implicit in much recent scholarship in social and labor history is a view of nineteenth-century development that comes close to turning the theme of democratic progress on its head. Its point of departure is a radical republican tradition originating with the left wing of the American Revolution and articulated in differing ways by thinkers like Thomas Paine and Thomas Jefferson. Its conception of equal rights and personal independence as essential to liberty inspired resistance on the part of artisans and yeomen farmers to the growth of commercialism, industrial wage labor, and the concentration of capital, a struggle that began with the workingmen's parties and agrarian radicals of the Jacksonian era and ended with the demise of the Knights of Labor and the Populist party in the 1890s. A grand synthesis of nineteenth-century American history along these lines would be challenging and provocative but might be open to the criticism that it idealizes a white male tradition that, for the most part, condoned the subordination of women, blacks, and Native Americans. Furthermore, its insistent and pessimistic antimodernism is likely to prove unacceptable to the many historians who continue to believe in the possibility of progressive reform within the framework of democratic capitalism.[2]

A candidate for central theme that assumes a similar pattern of change but is less ideologically charged (and pays close attention to winners as well as losers) comes from the historians of American society who emphasize broad patterns of socioeconomic change. For them the nineteenth century was preeminently the time of a great transformation from the distended society of families and communities dependent on agriculture, localized commerce, and artisan labor that existed in 1800 to the centralized, organized, and incorporated urban-industrial nation of the early twentieth century.[3]

Such changes can scarcely be denied, but to make virtually everything that happened a manifestation or reflection of deep societal transformation tends to foster a linear determinism that obscures the human agency, shifts in direction, and historical contingencies to which historians have become increasingly sensitive. It also deprives politics and government of the degree of autonomy that many historians, following recent trends in political science and political sociology, would like to assign to them. An exclusive preoccupation with this great transformation is likely to end historiographic discussion and debate rather than open it up, unless one asks how the juggernaut of socioeconomic development affected, or was effected by, specific groups, ideas, and events. Although it is obviously true in some sense, the "modernization" theme is too abstract and teleological to satisfy the majority of contemporary historians. It homogenizes too much experience that the United States shares with many other nations and does not encourage attention to what may be special or unique about the American past. One does not have to be an "American exceptionalist" in the full sense of considering the United States radically different from all other countries to relish America's peculiarities or at least its variations on the general themes of international history.

One way of differentiating American development from that of most other nations that industrialized and urbanized during the nineteenth century would be to follow in the footsteps of Frederick Jackson Turner by stressing the significance of the moving frontier. A westward movement that transformed the United States from an Atlantic seaboard republic into a continental one between 1815 and 1890 was clearly a major aspect of the nineteenth-century story. But recent historians have not assigned to the frontier the kind of fundamental importance given to it by Turnerians. Rather than spawning a new and unique American culture of democratic individualism, as Turner claimed, the frontier is now more commonly viewed as an arena in which forces and tendencies emanating from the settled East came into collision—for example sectional differences over the extension of slavery and conflicts between agrarians and commercial or industrial capitalists over the terms of trade in a market economy. The "new western history," emphasizing the Native American and Hispanic sides of the conflict over western land, makes the frontier the scene of unresolved racial and ethnic conflicts rather than the main source of consensual American values.[4]

The theme of nineteenth-century history that preoccupies the largest group of historians is the social, political, and ideological conflict that divided the nation and was resolved through sectional war and the subsequent reconstruction of the Union. The Civil War theme—broadly defined to include not only the war itself but also the story of slavery and the Old South, the sectional controversy over the expansion of slavery that led to secession from the Union, and the turbulent process of national reunification that took place after the war—has inspired more scholarship than any other nineteenth-century subject. One of its attractions is that it provides a persuasive argument for the uniqueness of American history that is not based on some claim to special virtue. Other nations experienced the trauma of economic and social modernization and saw the ebb and flow of democratic reform (some like Russia and Brazil even had moving frontiers), but none fought a devastating internal war over slavery. The apparent limitation of this emphasis is that it does not, at first glance, seem quite valid for the whole century but appears to lose its centrality in the 1870s.

This essay will focus mainly on how recent historians have dealt with the origins and impact of the Civil War, and it will argue that new work permits us to view the legacies and aftershocks of the war as lying at the root of many of the problems of the 1880s and '90s. It will also attempt to show the relevance of this historiography to much of the scholarship concerned more directly with the great transformation to modernity and advanced capitalism—even when that scholarship does not explicitly deal with the causes and consequences of the war.

Most historians of the United States would agree that the Civil War was the central event of the nineteenth century, if not of the nation's entire history. The period between 1789 or 1815 and the firing on Fort Sumter in 1861 is commonly referred to as the antebellum era, and the years between 1865 and the turn of the century are perhaps best designated as the post–Civil War period. The more common label for the century's last three decades—"the Gilded Age"—evokes certain tendencies of that era, but is perhaps less useful than one that calls attention to the shadow of the war. It was not, for example, until the 1890s that the race question that had to be faced when millions of African–Americans were emancipated from slavery was settled by the South's legalization of the new system of mandatory segregation, making a full reconciliation of the North and South possible. It was also in that decade that the bitter political struggle over the inflation or contraction of the currency, set in motion by the issuing of unredeemable "greenbacks" during the war, was resolved by the defeat of "free silver" in the election of 1896.

American historians have devoted massive and sustained attention to the Civil War. A debate on the causes of the war has been going on since Appomattox, and the issue plays a role in American historiography equivalent to that of the origins of the French Revolution in European historical studies. The war years themselves have received even greater attention if one can judge from the sheer number of books published, but much of that work has been narrowly conceived military history that bears little relationship to the central issues of nineteenth-century American historiography. The fixation on narratives of battles and campaigns has had the paradoxical effect of detaching the war from the mainstream of American history by plunging readers into a special world of intense experience and heroic action that has little apparent connection with the processes that affected people's lives and determined public policies over an extended period.[5]

Despite the tendency to an antiquarian form of narrative history in much of the writing about the war itself, a number of scholars have addressed the question of the war's impact on postwar America—most obviously in the burgeoning literature on Reconstruction. General works on the immediate postwar efforts to reunite the nation and determine the status of the ex-slaves often begin with what happened during the war itself and quite properly portray peacetime Reconstruction efforts as a continuation of wartime initiatives, especially the Emancipation Proclamation and the enlistment of black soldiers in the Union army. But the Reconstruction era is thought to have ended in 1877, and the question of the more enduring legacies of the war has been relatively neglected.

In fact there is a tendency to periodize American history in such a way as to create the impression that the war ceased to matter very much after the 1870s. When a publisher brings out a series of books covering all of American history, it is common practice to have a volume on the Civil War and Reconstruction, covering a period between the 1840s and the 1870s, followed by an offering on the late nineteenth and early twentieth centuries. The mid-nineteenth-century volume commonly reaches back into the early national and Jacksonian periods in search of the roots of the sectional conflict, but its successor is likely to ignore the consequences of the war entirely, implying that the last two or three decades of the nineteenth century were a prelude to the "Progressive period" of the early twentieth century rather than an extension of the postwar era. There is of course nothing sacred about the popular notion that history follows the calendar and that decades, centuries, or millennia have more than a conventional or heuristic significance. But it seems arbitrary and inconsistent to trace the war's origins back a half century or more and then ignore any legacies that may have lasted more than a decade.

The historiography of the war's causation has been the subject of innumerable essays and even one major book.[6] The way historians have conceived the war's impact has received less attention from historiographers, except to the extent that the results can be inferred from a conception of the causes. The possibility that the conflict had significant accidental or unintended consequences has not received the attention it deserves.

Recent treatments of the background, course, and aftermath of the Civil War have naturally been influenced by general trends in American historiography—new conceptions of what is important and what methods are needed to study it. Perhaps the most important of these is the vogue of social history or "history from the bottom up." A deemphasis on the ideas and actions of elites and a preoccupation with the "agency" of ordinary people and "subaltern" groups is reflected in studies of the struggles of African-American slaves for cultural and psychic survival under a harsh form of servitude and of the role they played in bringing about their own emancipation. Also receiving increased attention are the parts played by women and gender issues in the sectional crisis and its resolution, the experiences of common soldiers and home-front workers during the war, and the role of the freedpeople in the politics and socioeconomic adjustments of the Reconstruction era.[7]

These studies have enlarged our sense of who made history, but they have not obviated the need to study those who possessed power and were in a position, most of the time, to command the obedience of others. Although somewhat out of fashion among academic historians, many excellent studies of the ideas and actions of the men in command have appeared recently, and three of them have won Pulitzer prizes.[8] History from below has been a useful corrective to the traditional focus on elites, but it risks becoming a romantic evasion of historical reality if it is not accompanied by an acknowledgment of the power—exercised within limits that have to be determined by empirical investigation—that influential groups and prominent individuals have been able to exert over the lives and attitudes of those who have lacked the same access to physical resources, political leverage, and social prestige. It remains true that slaves by themselves did not overthrow slavery, although they did play a role in its demise. Common soldiers could not choose when and where to fight, although how they fought could determine the outcome of a battle. Women could not vote, run for office, or bear arms, but they could influence the behavior of the men who did. Freed slaves had some influence over politics and government in the South during Reconstruction, but in the end they lacked the power to block a white-supremacist counterrevolution.

A second trend that has affected the historiography of the sectional crisis and the Civil War has been the more subtle shift from a behaviorist approach to history to one that emphasizes the interpretation of culture. Two decades ago the cutting edge of historical scholarship on the nineteenth century seemed to come from quantitative work on social, economic, and political behavior. Some historians are still encoding data on voting patterns, legislative roll calls, social mobility, household composition, and the prices of land, labor, and commodities. But, as anyone who has directed doctoral dissertations in history departments in recent years can probably testify, this is not what interests most younger scholars. Quantitative history or "cliometrics" has become more than ever the preserve of economists, political scientists, and behavioral sociologists. Historians are now more likely to look to cultural anthropology or to the cultural studies movement in literary scholarship for interdisciplinary inspiration.[9]

The general trend toward looking at the past through the lenses of culture and language is evident in studies of slave folklore and religion, of political rhetoric (especially the legacy of Revolutionary-era "republicanism"), and in the discourse on the meaning of the war to be found in soldiers' letters home or in the journals and other private writings of civilians.[10] Objective conditions that can, as it were, be weighed and measured have become less important to many historians than the subjective states to be found in the "discourse" of historical actors. This trend has led to a deeper understanding of what people thought was at stake in the sectional quarrel and in the reunion process that followed, but it has also tended to obscure some of the structural factors that may have predisposed people to express themselves in the way that they did.

It is far from the case, however, that the new cultural history associated with the "linguistic turn" has eclipsed other paradigms in the historiography of the pre– and post–Civil War eras. The most influential scholars in the field continue to be those whose inspiration derives more from the Marxian or Gramscian tradition of class analysis and political economy than from nonmaterialist cultural theory (see especially the work of Eugene Genovese, Eric Foner, and Barbara Jeanne Fields). The most important work of these scholars has affirmed the reality of social class as an underlying determinant of cultural and ideological formations, including those associated with slavery and racial domination.[11]

Others have drawn on the Weberian tradition in sociological thought to make the argument that "race" played an autonomous role in the making of social dominance and in the construction of ideologies to defend or oppose it. Unlike idealist historians who make racism simply an enduring cultural trait of white Americans, the neo-Weberians view the essence of race as simultaneously structural and cultural; it is a form of what Weber called "ethnic status," and is fundamentally a hierarchical social relationship based on a differential assignment of honor and prestige to groups that differ in ancestry; only secondarily is it the specific set of racial stereotypes and images that is used to rationalize the subjugation of a particular subaltern group. The relationship between "race" and "class" is obviously a central and enduring problem for historians of the nineteenth-century South and its relationship to the rest of the nation.[12]

Strange as it may seem, the latest varieties of social and cultural history have not as yet had a decisive effect on how historians deal with the big question of what caused the Civil War. The reason for this might be that large questions of causation are alien to these specializations. Social history is at its best in dealing with small communities rather than whole nations, and those forms of cultural history that stress the interpretation of "texts" may dispense entirely with the study of causation, which normally requires attention to conditions or factors that are thought to have an existence independent of, and prior to, the recoverable discourses of historical actors.

An analysis of the preconditions and triggering events of an enormous convulsion like the American Civil War requires the talents of that increasingly rare breed—the historical generalist. It is not surprising therefore that the most valuable and authoritative discussions of the background of the war are still those that were written by distinguished members of the last great generation of eclectic general historians, men who came of age in the 1930s and '40s like David M. Potter and Kenneth M. Stampp.[13] Younger scholars who have rivaled them in the breadth and boldness of their discussions of the origins of the conflict are likely to be those, such as Eugene Genovese and Eric Foner, whose work is influenced by the Marxian tradition of class analysis, which of course generates its own special conception of general history.[14]

If there is one thing that the eclectic and neo-Marxian generalists have agreed upon, it is that slavery was at the root of the sectional conflict. In the words of

David Potter, "slavery really had a polarizing effect, for the North had no slave-holders—at least not of resident slaves—and the South had virtually no abolitionists. . . . slavery had an effect which no other sectional factor exercised in isolating North and South from each other."[15] This is not a discovery of modern historians and in fact merely repeats what has always been the most common—and commonsensical—explanation of the crisis leading to the Civil War. James Ford Rhodes, the premier late-nineteenth-century historian of the war period, put it succinctly: "The question [of causation] may be isolated by the incontrovertible statement that if the negro had never been brought to America, our Civil War could not have occurred."[16]

Potter's statement was historiographically significant because it signified his departure from the school of "revisionist" historians to which he himself had originally belonged. The revisionists, who were particularly influential in the 1930s and '40s, had viewed the war as an unnecessary conflict brought about by a combination of demagoguery, fanaticism, and political blundering. Slavery could not have been the real issue, they had maintained, because it was on its way to peaceful demise in 1860, and its sudden abolition was not worth the price in white lives that wartime emancipation had entailed.[17]

In the 1950s and '60s, historians and economists were finding the slave economy robust and unlikely to have collapsed under its own weight in the late nineteenth century. But a more significant reason for the decline of revisionism during the civil rights era was the racial insensitivity that it reflected. Historians of slavery as an institution were in the process of repudiating the previously ascendant view that the slave regime was a benign one that benefited blacks by "civilizing" them. If the regime was as brutal as Kenneth Stampp and Stanley Elkins claimed, and if blacks were not "natural children," inherently inferior to whites, the willingness of historians to countenance a few more decades of servitude as the price for avoiding civil war seemed downright immoral.[18]

But a modified form of revisionism survived in the work of those quantitative historians who analyzed political behavior and alleged that the northern voters and politicians who made the decisions that led to war did not do so because they shared the antislavery and antiracist convictions of modern liberal historians. Making slavery a "necessary cause" of the crisis did not of course explain why sectional division became unmanageable in the 1850s rather than sooner or later. Historians have generally agreed that the direct antecedent of secession and Civil War was the breakdown in the 1850s of the system of bisectional political parties that had developed in the 1830s. The new political historians claimed that the breakdown occurred, not so much because of ideological differences on the slavery issue, as because of the ethnoreligious tensions resulting from mass immigration. Whether or not the war was necessary to rid the nation of slavery, they argued, it could not be proved that differing attitudes toward slavery provoked the crisis that led to its abolition. In support of this hypothesis, they pointed to the widespread racism and indifference to black freedom that prevailed in the North and to the undeniable fact that the abolitionists were an unpopular minority until the exigencies of war provided a pragmatic justification for emancipation.[19]

A standard criticism of the neorevisionist "ethnocultural" explanation of political breakdown was that it had difficulty explaining why the collapse of the Whig party in the early-to-mid 1850s led to the rise of the Republicans and the sectionalization of politics over the issue of whether slavery should be allowed to spread to the federal territories. A more plausible outcome from this perspective would have been a realignment in which the antiimmigrant Know Nothing party would have survived as the alternative to the Democrats (who stood for a tolerant attitude toward non-English newcomers and the growing Catholic minority) instead of enjoying only an ephemeral success. Eric Foner's seminal study of Republican ideology, which appeared in 1970, described and analyzed the party's "free labor" ideology and its representation of the threat to the northern way of life represented by an expansionist "slave power," thus providing a plausible basis for making antislavery conviction, of a kind that was rooted less in pure idealism than in the class consciousness and perceived interests of a middle stratum of northern society, the key to northern sectionalism.[20]

More recently, William Gienapp has attempted with some success to synthesize elements of the ethnocultural explanation of party breakdown with Foner's ideological explanation of northern sectionalism by arguing that some of the same cultural biases that inspired nativism also helped to fuel the "free soil" movement and inspire vigorous resistance to "the slave power conspiracy."[21] Gienapp's work suggests that a weakness in Foner's interpretation of the rise of the Republicans is that it pays too little attention to the role of religion and culture in the worldview of the party's adherents.

Explaining why a sectionalist party emerged in the North in the late 1850s does not fully account for why the southern states seceded in response to the election of a Republican president in 1860, thereby dividing the Union and making Civil War likely if not inevitable. No recent historians of any stature have doubted that fears for the future of slavery were at the heart of southern concerns, but they have differed markedly on the question of precisely why the overwhelming majority of white southerners were so desperately committed to the defense of their "peculiar institution" that they were willing to go to war to defend it from any conceivable threat. In its essentials, the ongoing debate is between a "class" and a "race" interpretation of southern separatism. According to the neo-Marxian class interpretation put forth by Eugene Genovese and his followers, a premodern, precapitalist ruling class led the South into a war for its independence because it feared being dominated by the "bourgeois" elements that were coming to power in the North. This viewpoint makes the Civil War a bourgeois revolution in the European sense because it established the dominance of an emerging industrial capitalist class over an American equivalent of the landed aristocracies who resisted the rise of the bourgeoisie on the other side of the Atlantic.[22]

The critics of this interpretation—a prominent recent example is James Oakes—first of all deny that the South was genuinely precapitalist and thus deny that it departed categorically from the liberal and republican values that had inspired the American nation since its founding. The South's dominant ideology, according to Oakes, was less an attempt to repudiate everything that the North stood for than a desperate effort to reconcile slavery with its own persistent commitment to personal rights, economic individualism, and representative government.[23] The main device that permitted the coexistence of slavery with liberal and republican values was racism. If blacks were indeed subhuman there was no need to include them in the social contract and the rights-based polity that it sanctioned. Without denying that economic self-interest was a major source of proslavery commitment, this interpretation makes the fear of a loss of racial control and the status advantages that all white southerners—not just the minority that owned slaves—derived from black subordination the main element in the "crisis of fear" that simmered in the late 1850s and was brought to a boil by Lincoln's election.[24]

If Genovese's view of southern ideology complements Foner's class-based conception of the ideological sources of northern sectionalism, the alternative emphasis on race status and control has some affinity with the modified ethnocultural view of northern sectional politics put forth by Gienapp. A claim for the decisive influence of culture and ethnic or racial identities on many of the historical actors of this period does not preclude acknowledging that in other times and places ascriptive group consciousness may be overwhelmed by class consciousness deriving from economic inequality. For contingent historical reasons—the massive influx of immigrants in the 1840s and '50s and the antislavery movement's challenge to the social and economic subordination of four million blacks—Americans of the mid nineteenth century may have been more likely to embrace racial, ethnic, or religious identities than those that derived from their relationship to the market or means of production.

Explaining northern sectionalism and southern separatism does not quite account for the coming of the war. What remains somewhat mysterious is why the people of the North were willing to fight and die to preserve the Union. This final link in the chain of Civil War causation is just beginning to receive the attention that it deserves. Southern independence would have posed no obvious threat to the spread of the free labor system to the existing federal territories, and it should have put to rest any fears that the slave states would dominate the central government. One explanation that has been offered recently for the North's adamant Unionism is that it reflected a deep popular commitment to law and order under the Constitution and more specifically a fear of total national disintegration through further secessions if the southern states were allowed to depart in peace.[25] Recent studies of the correspondence of northern soldiers show that a large proportion of them had a strong commitment to Unionist ideology and a surprisingly sophisticated understanding of it. Like President Lincoln, many of them recognized that tolerating secession was incompatible with the survival of a democratic republic and that the emancipation of the slaves might prove essential to the preservation of the Union. At the root of this devotion to the northern cause, according to one historian, was a tendency to identify loyalty to the Union with the family obligations and values that were at the core of mid-nineteenth-century American culture.[26]

In an effort to account for the determination of those in power to preserve the Union at all costs, another recent historian has argued that a breakup of the Union was intolerable to northern elites because it would have threatened the alliance of western family farmers and eastern industrialists that formed the backbone of the Republican party and the new "political economy" that was emerging in the North. Without a shared enmity to the South, this coalition would allegedly have broken up.[27] Like most other explanations based on "political economy" this one is plausible but is difficult to substantiate—one would be hard-pressed to find the spokesmen for the economic interests in question calculating in this fashion. Their pronouncements on the crisis suggest that they believed, rightly or wrongly, that harmony between industry and commercially oriented yeoman agriculture was natural and inevitable.

If historians are generally agreed that slavery was at the root of the antebellum sectional crisis (if not on the question of whether sectional differences on the future of slavery provide a sufficient explanation for the war itself), they also agree that emancipation was a war measure that could not have occurred under any other conceivable circumstances at this stage of American history. No effort to belittle the direct impact of the Civil War can get around the fact that it altered the status of African-Americans in a fundamental way.

The other obvious and immediate effect of the war was that it put down secession and thus preserved and strengthened the federal government. It was now clearly established that the Union was not a voluntary compact among the states and that the authority of the central government was supreme within its sphere. But historians have disagreed on precisely how that sphere was now defined and on how radically the constitutional basis of the American nation had been altered. Some have emphasized the degree of autonomy still possessed by the states and the continued weaknesses of the federal government—its lack of "administrative capacities"—in comparison to most European national states of the nineteenth century.[28] Others have stressed the assumption of new federal functions and prerogatives during and immediately after the war.[29]

What needs more attention is the broader question of how much change of all kinds—political, social, economic, and cultural—can be attributed to the Civil War (beyond the elimination of chattel servitude and denial of the right of states to secede from the Union). How decisively and thoroughly did it alter American life in general? Was it really one of those great historical cataclysms that changes almost everything, or something less than that? Even when the issue is not explicitly addressed in these terms, much recent historical work on the postwar era provides at least a partial answer. But a review of this work reveals a striking lack of consensus and exposes an historiographical disagreement that badly needs analysis and clarification.

In the work of both Marxian and liberal practitioners of "political economy" one can often find a maximalist view of the effects of the war that follows logically from their analysis of its causes. The ancestry of this conception can be traced to the claims that Charles and Mary Beard made in the 1920s that the Civil War was "the second American revolution," because it signified the triumph of the industrial interests represented by the North over the agricultural interests championed by the South.[30] But Beard's successors have given much more weight to slavery than to agrarianism as a source of southern distinctiveness and have tended to jettison Beard's direct economic determinism in favor of an analysis that concedes some autonomy to class-based cultures and ideologies. Contemporary advocates of the maximalist position do, however, share the Beardian view that the war altered the nation's political economy in a decisive way. Instead of two competing regional ruling classes—one basing its power and deriving its worldview from a pre-modern form of labor exploitation and the other from the modernizing "free labor system"—there was now only one. The ascendancy of an industrial, commercial, and financial bourgeoisie deriving its wealth and influence from its control of wage labor constitutes, in the opinion of most maximalists, the lasting effect of the Civil War crisis.[31]

Significant disagreements have developed, however, on the question of whether the southern way of life was immediately and radically transformed by the war and emancipation. For the neo-Marxian followers of Eugene Genovese, antebellum precapitalism was rooted in the fact that labor was owned rather than hired. It therefore followed that emancipation constituted a fundamental shift from a slave-based form of production to an orthodox capitalist one, with all the cultural and ideological reversals that such a basic change entailed.[32] But other scholars influenced by Marxism have deemphasized slavery per se and have noted the survival of a plantation system based on variable forms of labor coercion well into the twentieth century. They have detected a revival or persistence of planter power in the postwar era, based on the quasislavery of sharecropping tenancy, that impeded the capitalistic modernization of the South, and to a lesser extent of the nation as a whole, for an extended period.[33]

The most distinguished and influential liberal historians of the postwar South have tended to second the argument of those in the Marxian tradition that war and emancipation transformed the region's political economy in a decisive way. In an impressive body of work spanning more than four decades, C. Vann Woodward has contended vigorously against "continuitarians" who deny basic change. He has consistently maintained that the antebellum planter aristocracy was displaced during the postwar years by an emerging middle class with bourgeois values alien to the culture of the Old South.[34] Gavin Wright, the foremost economic historian of the New South, has conceptualized the shift as the abrupt transformation from an economy dominated by "labor lords" to one responsive to the rather different interests of "land lords." Although he acknowleges that there was considerable overlap in the personnel of prewar and postwar elites, Wright argues that a new relationship to the means of production altered the economic and political behavior of the South's dominant class in fundamental ways.[35] The dominant current view among analysts of the South's political economy is that the war made it significantly different from what it had been before, but dissent from this position persists.[36] Whether the change that occurred should be regarded as truly revolutionary or as an example of the kind of reform and readjustment that puts old wine in new bottles remains debatable.

The argument of maximalists that the northern victory contributed to the hegemony of industrial capitalism in the political economy of the nation as a whole seems well grounded. Maximalists find evidence for a new order in the enactment, during and immediately after the war, of economic legislation designed to promote capitalist development, such as high protective tariffs, subsidization of transcontinental railroads and other internal improvements, and contraction of the currency to favor creditors over debtors. It was also reflected in an increased willingness to use coercive state power to preserve the kind of internal order and domestic tranquillity that capitalist enterprise seemed to require. The use of federal troops to protect Republican governments in the South came to an end in 1877, but in that same year they were used to put down a national railroad strike, an action based on the wartime precedent of using the army to suppress labor actions that allegedly impeded the military effort.[37]

A maximalist interpretation of the twists and turns of postwar politics cannot be as straightforward as it once was, because of the way that the Reconstruction era is now generally evaluated. For Charles A. Beard and earlier advocates of the "second American revolution" hypothesis, it was axiomatic that "Radical Reconstruction" was not about the rights of the freedpeople but was driven by the desire of northern capitalists to gain access to southern sources of wealth. But most contemporary historians of Reconstruction, including those who write from a political-economy perspective, are not as cynical as the Beardians were in evaluating the motives of the Radicals and are prepared to acknowledge that men like Thaddeus Stevens and Charles Sumner acted out of a kind of middle-class democratic idealism rather than at the behest of a hegemonic capitalist elite. If, however, the relatively brief period of federal activism on behalf of black rights (roughly 1867–72) is viewed as an afterglow of wartime zeal that increasingly lacked egalitarian conviction, or if the failure of Radical efforts to guarantee the civic equality of African-Americans is deemed virtually inevitable given the limited and inefficient means that the Republicans were willing or able to employ, it becomes possible to link the failure of the war-inspired attempt to reconstruct the South on the basis of black manhood suffrage to the decline of popular democratic politics that recent historians have detected toward the end of the century—and which to their way of thinking strengthened the position of dominant elites.[38] Requiring further study is the extent to which the chaos and failure of Reconstruction contributed to middle-class disenchantment with an electoral system based on universal manhood suffrage and nearly universal participation.

Virtually beyond challenge is the notion that the Republican party, once it harnessed or suppressed the radical-democratic impulse that to some extent expressed itself in congressional Reconstruction, became a party devoted primarily to the interests of the business community that was able to draw on its prestige as the Union-saving party to appeal to the patriotic and nationalistic sentiments of a majority of ordinary citizens in the northern states. Since the Republicans were nationally dominant in the entire period from 1865 to 1932, the identification with American nationalism that it derived from its role in the sectional crisis was, or so it could be argued, of central importance in the development of the corporate capitalist hegemony that allegedly characterizes twentieth-century America.

The contrary or minimalist view of the effects of the Civil War is more often expressed indirectly or implicitly than systematically expounded. The idea that the Civil War revolutionized the nation is implicitly criticized in the mass of scholarship dealing with the mid-to-late-nineteenth-century America that manages to discuss major trends in American life and thought with scarcely a mention of the Civil War.

Most works on the social, intellectual, and cultural history of the nineteenth century devote little or no attention to the war. If they are seeking "watersheds," or periods of a decade or so when the climate of opinion shifted decisively, they may find them, as John Higham has done, in the 1850s and the 1890s, rather than in the 1860s.[39] Those who have attempted to quantify various trends in social history have often found that their graphs seem little affected by anything that happened between 1861 and 1865. Cultural historians dealing with subjects like the changing role of women and gender in the public sphere, as Mary Ryan has done, may find that wartime activities reflected or exemplified new tendencies, but they attribute little direct influence to the war itself.[40] Economic historians have generally found that the war actually retarded industrialization and economic growth, although not in a way that had a lasting effect.[41]

Students of voting behavior have sometimes found little difference in the kind of cultural concerns expressed by the electorate in 1830s and '40s and in the 1880s and '90s. Historians and political scientists dealing with party systems have not found a significant "realignment" during the war or in the immediate postwar years (although they do recognize that one took place in the 1850s). They note that the Democratic party survived the war and remained nationally competitive for the next thirty years. In an analysis of the intense and evenly balanced partisan competition that characterized American politics between 1838 and 1893, Joel Silbey finds that the war had little effect on the basic pattern.[42] True Republican predominance was not achieved until the 1890s, when the GOP gained firm control of the Midwest for the first time. The combination of a solidly Republican Midwest and an even more solidly Democratic South brought an end to the era of close elections and huge voter turnouts.[43]

Some historians who have written directly about the war and its impact have also minimized its long-term significance. Morton Keller has argued, for example, that the war-inspired centralization of power and authority in the federal government did not survive the 1870s. In that decade, he contends, there was a partial reversion to the laissez-faire and localism that had characterized the prewar polity.[44] In national economic policy, the protective tariff survived the '70s but direct subsidization of capitalist enterprise, such as land grants to railroads, came to an end.

Historians of black-white relations can hardly deny that the freeing of the slaves made a difference in the situation of southern African-Americans, but they have also suggested that the "redemption" process that followed the brief Reconstruction episode caused a return, if not to slavery itself, at least to a status that in some ways was closer to servitude than to equal citizenship. Post-Reconstruction southern elites would never enjoy the kind of power over the federal government that their predecessors had exercised before the war, but a minimalist might stress the retarding effect that their reviving fortunes could still have on the modernizing and nationalizing projects of progressive northern elites.

Like most debates about change and continuity, the disagreement between the maximalists and the minimalists sometimes resembles a quarrel over whether a glass of water is half full or half empty. As is true of any cataclysmic event or apparent historical "watershed," some things change and others remain the same. An effort to strike a reasonable balance between radical transformationists and what C. Vann Woodward calls the "continuitarians" would be sensitive to change but careful not to overstate it. Wartime emancipation, for example, did not make blacks the political and social equals of whites, but it did shift the struggle for black liberation to a new plane. As both Kenneth Stampp and Eric Foner have pointed out—in major synthetic works on Reconstruction that were published nearly a quarter century apart—it was of lasting and vital significance that the Fourteenth and Fifteenth Amendments to the Constitution, like the Thirteenth abolishing slavery, were enacted during a brief window of opportunity offered by the fracture of the Union. Constitutional provisions for equal black citizenship made the twentieth-century civil rights struggle possible by giving African-Americans a claim to full democratic rights.[45] I would add that absent these amendments it is likely that separatist nationalism and emigrationism, rather than some form of integrationism or egalitarian ethnic pluralism, would have dominated black political thought and action.

The minimalists are correct to point out that many of the new powers and responsibilities assumed by the federal government during and immediately after the war were later surrendered or allowed to fall into disuse. But the reversion to localism and laissez-faire was not total, and an important precedent had been set for the assumption of extraordinary powers during a war or a national emergency that could be represented as the equivalent of a war. Because of the Civil War experience, it was probably easier than it might otherwise have been to enact conscription and suppress allegedly disloyal activities during World War I, and the precedent of both wars facilitated the enormous growth of governmental responsibilities by the Roosevelt administration during the Great Depression. Americans have remained culturally averse to an activist central state in what they considered to be normal times, but they have been remarkably receptive to appeals for a vast expansion of government responsibilities when their leaders could persuade them that national survival or well-being was at stake.

It can also be argued with some cogency that the war contributed significantly to the basic transformation of American culture that historians committed to evolutionary models of social change have viewed as the inevitable result of modernization. Had there been no war the great transition from the values that reflected the agrarian individualism of the early republic to a recognizably modern commitment to bureaucratic organization and technical efficiency—"rationalization" in the Weberian sense—would still have occurred sooner or later. But the war with its incentives for organized endeavor and the efficient use of resources probably accelerated the process. The notion that the Civil War was a catalyst for modernization was a major theme of Allan Nevins's magisterial *The War for the Union*, the last multivolume history of the war experience in all its dimensions and a work from which much can still be learned.[46]

But the modernization paradigm encompasses only part of the story of the war's cultural and institutional impact. Its total effect on the dominant trends toward a modernized American society was more ambiguous than this viewpoint readily permits us to acknowledge. Although it contributed in certain ways to the emergence of modernist modes of thought and action, in other ways the Civil War crisis may have served to deflect the nation from the pattern of development to which it may have been predisposed by the stage of socioeconomic and technological development that it had reached by the 1860s and '70s.

A distinguishing feature of postwar electoral behavior was the extent to which wartime loyalties determined voter allegiances. "Vote the way you shot," was perhaps the most effective appeal that politicians could make. As a result, the most prowar sections of the North remained overwhelmingly Republican, and the South, after suppressing the votes of black and white Unionist Republicans, became solidly Democratic. This persistence of sectional politics into the twentieth century impeded national alignments based on class or shared economic interests that might otherwise have occurred to a greater extent. It was one factor, according to Lawrence Goodwyn, that doomed the Populist insurgency of the 1890s.[47] The failure of the United States to generate a party system that expressed the rational, material concerns of national classes or interest groups was not due entirely to the Civil War—ethnoreligious loyalties and racial attitudes had strongly influenced political behavior before the conflict. But the persistence of sectionalism made politicians more likely than ever to appeal to voters' ascriptive identities rather than to ideologies deriving from class position and material circumstances.

The war may also have helped to make the United States different in its pattern of state formation from most other industrializing societies by producing an irregular and premature welfare state that had the effect of impeding twentieth-century efforts to establish a permanent system of old age pensions and social insurance. In work that historians have not paid enough attention to, historical sociologists Theda Skocpol and Ann Shola Orloff have argued that the relatively generous veterans' pensions, that by the 1890s actually made the United States a statistical world leader in providing support for elderly or disabled men and their widows and orphans, became a drag on subsequent efforts to introduce permanent social security systems. The fact that the war pensions served the interests of one political party and only one section of the country helped to convince reformers that the American political system, still heavily dependent on patronage and susceptible to corruption, could not be trusted to administer national programs for the security of its citizens in a fair and efficient way.[48]

Historian Stuart McConnell has exposed the regressive, antimodernizing ideology of the veterans' lobby in an important recent study of the Grand Army of the Republic.[49] The veterans, animated by a "millennialist republicanism," viewed their pensions as a just reward for the unique and nonrepeatable contributions they had made to saving the Union and perfecting the republic. This rationale not only precluded extending the system to noncombatants but even weakened the case for treating the veterans of future wars in a similarly generous fashion. Whether one emphasizes the response of political institutions, like Skocpol and Orloff, or follows McConnell in stressing the ideology that veterans had derived from their war experience, it seems clear that the impact of the soldiers' movement was to make it more difficult for the American state and political culture to confront some of the problems of an industrializing and urbanizing society.

The ongoing search for a nuanced middle ground between the minimalists and the maximalists on the question of how much difference the Civil War actually made is unlikely to come to any conclusions that will do violence to the popular perception that, next to the Revolution that brought the nation into being, the sectional crisis was the most significant and formative event in American history. The minimalist view that it was an anomalous interlude with little effect on the most significant processes at work in producing twentieth-century America remains unpersuasive. But equally dubious is the maximalist conception that the war made all the difference in the world and was in fact more important than the Revolution itself in determining the path of national development.

What is likely to emerge is the conclusion that the Civil War was not so much a second (and more decisive) American revolution as the completion of the first. It strengthened—but did not create—American nationalism. It moved African-Americans a step further toward equal citizenship, extending a process that began with gradual emancipation in the northern states during the post-Revolutionary era. It assisted the forces promoting capitalist development by shifting the balance of power from a primitive capitalism of ruthless accumulation and forced labor to a more progressive capitalism based on technological innovation and wage labor, although it would take almost a century for the South to overcome its legacy of social and economic backwardness. It encouraged new patterns of thought and culture but did not obliterate older ones.

Such a balance might be used to support the view, recently restated eloquently by James McPherson, that the war was indeed "the second American revolution."[50] But in many ways the effects of the war (if not the quantity of blood that it spilled) are more analogous to those of the major reforms or "revolutions from above" that strengthened or consolidated potentially powerful nation-states elsewhere in the world at about the same time—such as the tsar's abolition of serfdom in Russia, the Meiji Restoration in Japan, and the unification of Germany and Italy under Bismarck and Cavour—than to a radical overturning of the social and political order on the model of what happened in France in the 1790s, Russia in 1917, and China in the late 1940s. The war resulted in an amended and reinterpreted Constitution but not a totally new one. I doubt if one could find other cases that historians would generally agree to classify as socially and politically revolutionary that did not result, at the very least, in an unmistakably new and different charter of government. In 1850 the United States could have been described as a developing capitalist society with a representative, republican government and a racial qualification for full citizenship. The same general categorizations would have held true in 1900, although the meanings and functions of its capitalism, republicanism, and racism were not the same as they had been before the war. Significant change had certainly occurred, but I remain unconvinced that the transformation deserves to be called a revolution in any sense that would make it comparable to the events in world history that clearly deserve such a designation.

NOTES

1. Among the many recent works that find a regression from democratic values and practices during the late nineteenth century are Alan Trachtenberg, *The Incorporation of America: Culture and Society in the Gilded Age* (New York, 1982), and Michael McGerr, *The Decline of Popular Politics: The American North, 1865–1928* (New York, 1986). The new political system that was taking shape around the turn of the century is well portrayed in Richard L. McCormick, *From Realignment to Reform in New York State, 1893–1910* (Chapel Hill, 1981).

2. See such studies as Sean Wilentz, *Chants Democratic: New York and the Rise of the Working Class, 1788–1850* (New York, 1986); Alan Dawley, *Class and Community: The Industrial Revolution in Lynn* (Cambridge, Mass., 1976); Charles Sellers, *The Market Revolution: Jacksonian America, 1815–1846* (New York, 1991); Leon Fink, *Workingmen's Democracy: The Knights of Labor and American Politics* (Urbana, 1983). David Roediger takes note of the racial qualification in the tradition of artisan republicanism in his *Wages of Whiteness: Race and the Making of the American Working Class* (London, 1991).

3. This is the guiding paradigm of Robert H. Wiebe's influential synthesis *The Search for Order, 1877–1920* (New York, 1967) and, in a more restricted sense, of Alfred Chandler's definitive work, *The Visible Hand: The Managerial Revolution in American Business* (Cambridge, Mass., 1977).

4. On the current state of western and frontier history, see Patricia Nelson Limerick, *The Legacy of Conquest: The Unbroken Past of the American West* (New York, 1987), and "Turnerians All: The Dream of a Helpful History in an Intelligible World," *American Historical Review* 100 (1995): 697–716.

5. The military historian Albert Castel, reviewing Matthew Gallman, *The North Fights the Civil War: The Home Front* (Chicago, 1994), in *Reviews in American History* 22 (December 1994): 597, accuses Gallman of present-mindedness for even raising the question of the war's political and social consequences. Gallman argued that the war had relatively little immediate effect on society and politics. Castel agrees with him but criticizes the attention the book gave to the issue on the grounds that there could not conceivably have been "a radical transformation of the existing social and political order," since the North's war aim was to preserve the Union, not to change it. It is a curious concept of history that allows for no changes other than those that were envisioned at the outset by the instigators of actions or policies that clearly had unforeseen consequences.

6. Thomas J. Pressly, *Americans Interpret Their Civil War* (Princeton, 1954). An updating of this work would be valuable.

7. Among the most important works that provide a "bottom up" view of developments surrounding the Civil War are Eugene D. Genovese, *Roll, Jordan, Roll: The World the Slaves Made* (New York, 1974); Herbert G. Gutman, *The Black Family in Slavery and Freedom* (New York, 1976); Lawrence W. Levine, *Black Culture and Black Consciousness: Afro-American Folk Thought from Slavery to Freedom* (New York, 1977); John Blassingame, *The Slave Community: Plantation Life in the Old South*, rev. ed. (Oxford, 1979); Elizabeth Fox-Genovese, *Within the Plantation Household: Black and White Women of the Old South* (Chapel Hill, 1988); Deborah White, *Ar'n't I a Woman: Females Slaves in the Plantation South* (New York, 1985); Reid Mitchell, *The Vacant Chair: The Northern Soldier Leaves Home* (New York, 1993); Leon F. Litwack, *Been in the Storm So Long: The Aftermath of Slavery* (New York, 1979; and Iver Bernstein, *The New York City Draft Riots: Their Significance for American Society and Politics in the Age of the Civil War* (New York, 1989). Eric Foner's general history, *Reconstruction: America's Unfinished Revolution, 1863–1877* (New York, 1988), departs from earlier syntheses by paying more attention to grassroots struggles in the South than to national politics. An intriguing effort to interpret the postwar reunion process in terms of gender is Nina Silber, *The Romance of Reunion: Northerners and the South, 1865–1900* (Chapel Hill, 1993).

8. Three recent winners are James McPherson's *The Battle Cry of Freedom: The Civil War Era* (New York, 1988), which presents a good deal of "bottom up" material but not to the neglect of leadership and decision making; Mark E. Neely, Jr., *The Fate of Liberty: Abraham Lincoln and Civil Liberties* (New York, 1991), which is a conventional political narrative of high quality; and Garry Wills, *Lincoln at Gettysburg: The Words That Remade America* (New York, 1992). It is indicative of the gap between popular and academic conceptions of history that these well-written and deeply researched works have been more successful with the educated general public than among the professoriat.

9. For a sense of this trend as it affects historians generally, see Lynn Hunt, ed., *The New Cultural History* (Berkeley, 1989). Several of the works cited above as examples of "bottom up" history also make use of anthropological perspectives. The explicit use of postmodernist theory is still rare in Civil War historiography, but one can find some of it in work that adopts an interdisciplinary American Studies perspective, such as Anne C. Rose, *Victorian America and the Civil War* (Cambridge, Eng., 1992).

10. In addition to works cited above, such as Rose, *Victorian America*, Silber, *Romance of Reunion*, Levine, *Black Culture*, and Mitchell, *Vacant Chair*, see also Earl J. Hess's effort to study wartime rhetoric in terms of the discourse of "republicanism"—*Liberty, Virtue, and Progress: Northerners and Their War for the Union* (New York, 1988).

11. In addition to the works of Genovese and Foner, which are cited elsewhere, see Barbara Jeanne Fields, *Slavery and Freedom on the Middle Ground: Maryland in the Nineteenth Century* (New Haven, 1985). Class analysis became central to the study of nineteenth-century African-American communities in studies such as Thomas Holt, *Black over White: Negro Political Leadership in South Carolina during Reconstruction* (Urbana, 1977), and Nell Irvin Painter, *Exodusters: Black Migration to Kansas after Reconstruction* (New York, 1977).

12. For a further discussion of these issues and references to some of the relevant works, see George M. Fredrickson, *The Arrogance of Race: Historical Perspectives on Slavery, Racism, and Social Inequality* (Middletown, Conn., 1988). Among the historians who adopt an essentially Weberian approach to black-white relations in the South is William J. Harris. See his *Plain Folk and Gentry in a Slave Society: White Liberty and Black Slavery in Augusta's Hinterlands* (Middletown, Conn., 1985).

13. See especially David M. Potter, *The Impending Crisis of the South, 1848–1861* (New York, 1976), pp. 30–50; idem, "The Literature on the Background of the Civil War," in *The South and the Sectional Conflict* (Baton Rouge, 1968), pp. 87–150; and Kenneth M. Stampp, "The Irrepressible Conflict," in *The Imperiled Union: Essays on the Background of the Civil War* (New York, 1980), pp. 192–245.

14. Eugene Genovese has not actually written an essay on the causes of the Civil War, but his views can be inferred from his works on slavery and slaveholders, especially *The World the Slaveholders Made: Two Essays in Interpretation* (New York, 1969). For Foner's perspective, see his essays "The Causes of the American Civil War: Recent Interpretations and New Directions" and "Politics, Ideology, and the Origins of the Civil War," in *Politics and Ideology in the Age of the Civil War* (New York, 1980), pp. 15–53.

15. Potter, *Impending Crisis*, pp. 42–43.

16. Quoted in Stampp, *The Imperiled Union*, pp. 193.

17. The revisionist view was summed up in Avery Craven, *The Coming of the Civil War* (New York, 1942). Potter's earlier revisionism is evident in his *Lincoln and His Party in the Secession Crisis* (New Haven, 1942).

18. For differing interpretations of slavery that shared an implication that its persistence would have been morally untenable, see Kenneth M. Stampp, *The Peculiar Institution: Slavery in the Ante-Bellum South* (New York, 1956), and Stanley Elkins, *Slavery: A Problem in American Institutional and Intellectual Life* (Chicago, 1959).

19. Among the most important works in this tradition are Paul Kleppner, *The Third Electoral System: Parties, Voters, and Political Culture* (Chapel Hill, 1979); Michael Holt, *The Political Crisis of the 1850s* (New York, 1978); and Joel Silbey, *The Partisan Imperative: The Dynamics of American Politics before the Civil War* (New York, 1985).

20. Eric Foner, *Free Soil, Free Labor, Free Men: The Ideology of the Republican Party before the Civil War* (New York, 1970).

21. William E. Gienapp, *The Origins of the Republican Party, 1852–1856* (New York, 1987).

22. See various works of Eugene Genovese, especially *The World the Slaveholders Made* and *The Fruits of Merchant Capital: Slavery and Bourgeois Property in the Rise and Expansion of Capitalism*, coauthored by Elizabeth Fox-Genovese (New York, 1983).

23. James Oakes, *Slavery and Freedom: An Interpretation of the Old South* (New York, 1990), and *The Ruling Race: A History of American Slaveholders* (Knopf, 1982).

24. The best general statement of this argument is still Potter, *Impending Crisis*, chap. 17. For its application to one state, see also Steven A. Channing, *A Crisis of Fear: Secession in South Carolina* (New York, 1970).

25. Philip Shaw Paludan, *"A People's Contest": The Union and the Civil War, 1861–1865* (New York, 1988), chap. 1.

26. See James M. McPherson, *What They Fought For, 1861–1865* (Baton Rouge, 1994), on the role of ideology, and Mitchell, *Vacant Chair*, on the significance of familialism.

27. Richard Franklin Bensel, *Yankee Leviathan: The Origins of Central State Authority in America, 1859–1877* (Cambridge, Eng., 1990), p. 93.

28. See Harold Hyman, *A More Perfect Union: The Impact of the Civil War and Reconstruction on the Constitution* (New York, 1973), and Stephen Skowronek, *Building an American State: The Expansion of National Administrative Capacities, 1877–1920* (Cambridge, Eng., 1982), pp. 29–31 and passim.

29. For a strong statement of this position, see David Montgomery, *Beyond Equality: Labor and the Radical Republicans, 1862–1872* (New York, 1967), pp. 46–48.

30. See Charles A. and Mary R. Beard, *The Rise of American Civilization*, 2 vols. (New York, 1927), II, 53–54.

31. See the previously cited works by Genovese, Foner, Bensel, and Montgomery, among others.

32. Barbara Fields, in *Slavery and Freedom*, applies such a maximalist understanding of the changes induced by emancipation to the state of Maryland. James Roark examines the behavior and consciousness of the planter class from a roughly similar perspective in *Masters without Slaves: Southern Planters in the Civil War and Reconstruction* (New York, 1977).

33. Prime examples of scholarship that stresses planter or plantation persistence are Jay R. Mandle, *Not Slave, Not Free: The African American Economic Experience since the Civil War* (Durham, 1992), and Jonathan M. Wiener, *Social Origins of the New South: Alabama, 1865–1885* (Baton Rouge, 1978).

34. C. Vann Woodward set forth his basic interpretation in *Origins of the New South, 1877–1913* (Baton Rouge, 1951) and has reaffirmed it in *Looking Back: The Perils of Writing History* (Baton Rouge, 1986).

35. Gavin Wright, *Old South, New South: The Revolutions in the Southern Economy since the Civil War* (New York, 1986).

36. See, for example, Carl H. Moneyhon, *The Impact of the Civil War and Reconstruction in Arkansas: Persistence in the Midst of Ruin* (Baton Rouge, 1994).

37. See Leonard P. Curry, *Blueprint for Modern America: Non-Military Legislation of the Civil War Congress* (Nashville, 1968), and Grace Palladino, *Another Civil War: Labor, Capital, and the State in the Anthracite Regions of Pennsylvania, 1840–1868* (Urbana, 1990).

38. Michael McGerr describes the postwar tendency in *The Decline of Popular Politics* but makes no effort to trace the roots of the transformation of political culture to the war and Reconstruction.

39. John Higham, *From Boundlessness to Consolidation: The Transformation of American Culture, 1848–1860* (Ann Arbor, 1969), and "The Reorientation of American Culture in the 1890's," in *Writing American History: Essays on Modern Scholarship* (Bloomington, 1970), 73–102. An exception to the prevailing tendency to deemphasize the effect of the Civil War on intellectual history is George M. Fredrickson, *The Inner Civil War: Northern Intellectuals and the Crisis of the Union*, rev. ed. (Urbana, 1993; orig. pub. 1965).

40. See Mary Ryan, *Women in Public: Between Banners and Ballots, 1825–1880* (Baltimore, 1990).

41. Roger L. Ransom, an economic historian who has written a general study of the Civil War era, concludes that "the balance of scholarly opinion is that, taken on its broadest level, the direct economic impact of the war was to *retard* economic growth in the industrial sector, but probably to *stimulate* growth of agriculture outside the South. If we include the South, the net gain in agriculture was far less, and perhaps disappears altogether." He goes on, however, to acknowledge some important indirect effects. See *Conflict and Compromise: The Political Economy of Slavery, Emancipation, and the American Civil War* (Cambridge, Eng., 1989), p. 264 and passim.

42. See Joel H. Silbey, *A Respectable Minority: The Democratic Party in the Civil War Era, 1860–1868* (New York, 1977), and *The American Political Nation, 1838–1893* (Stanford, Calif., 1991).

43. See Richard J. Jensen, *The Winning of the Midwest: Social and Political Conflict, 1888–1896* (Chicago, 1971).

44. Morton Keller, *Affairs of State: Public Life in Late Nineteenth Century America* (Cambridge, Mass., 1977).

45. Kenneth M. Stampp, *The Era of Reconstruction, 1865–1877* (New York, 1965), pp. 214–15; and Foner, *Reconstruction*, pp. 611–12.

46. Allan Nevins, *The War for the Union*, 4 vols. (New York, 1959–71).

47. Lawrence Goodwyn, *Democratic Promise: The Populist Movement in America* (New York, 1976), pp. 4–24.

48. Theda Skocpol, *Protecting Soldiers and Mothers: The Political Origins of Social Policy in the United States* (Cambridge, Mass., 1992), pp. 102–51; Ann Shola Orloff, *The Politics of Pensions: A Comparative Analysis of Britain, Canada, and the United States* (Madison, 1993), pp. 230–39.

49. Stuart McConnell, *Glorious Contentment: The Grand Army of the Republic, 1865–1900* (Chapel Hill, 1992).

50. James M. McPherson, *Abraham Lincoln and the Second American Revolution* (New York, 1990).

CHAPTER 9

Americans and the Writing of Twentieth-Century United States History

JAMES T. PATTERSON

HISTORIANS of the United States have commented often—usually with asperity—about the enormous quantity of publications in many fields of research. Even the most industrious scholars, they complain, have time to read only small portions of the vast output that appears every year. That is surely the case concerning writing about twentieth-century United States history, a rich area indeed of historical research and publication. By my count, some 800 of the 1,400 articles identified in a recent comprehensive list compiled by the *The Journal of American History* are concerned with aspects of the United States since 1900.[1]

Most of these articles tend to be highly focused efforts that interest relatively few readers. Still, the numbers indicate that a great many scholars teach and write in the area of twentieth-century American history. Moreover, the field is undeniably popular among the reading public and among college and university students in the United States. Enrollments in widely offered courses dealing with recent American history—and in the twentieth-century segments of more specialized courses (such as diplomatic history, intellectual history, and urban history)—have long been large at universities in the United States. Student interest in American history from World War II to the very recent past seems especially intense.[2]

Given the popularity of twentieth-century American history, one might expect academic practitioners of it to feel bullish about the present and the future of the field. Many are indeed upbeat, pleased with both the quality of scholarship and with the range of research, which has explored subjects, especially in social and cultural history, that had often been slighted by earlier generations of historians. Other scholars, however, tend to be uneasy. They lament first of all that histories and biographies by popularizers are attracting wide readership while more analytical academic work gathers dust on the shelves. They worry also that they participate in a large, amorphous, and in some ways fractured field—one that some time ago lost faith in a primarily political narrative that had given coherence to research, publication, and university courses. History-writing about twentieth-century America, they add, is less a field than a thicket. This observation has much to commend it. Scholarship concerning the United States since 1900 reflects the rapid growth and specialization of the historical profession as well as the splintering of modern American society generally—a splintering that has encouraged a focus on ethnic distinctiveness, cultures of "resistance," and identity politics. Each group, it seems, has its own historian.

The irony of this situation is that as the United States has became more centralized by mass communications and political and economic forces, the vision that has emerged from many of our academically based studies of twentieth-century developments—especially from those that dwell on social and cultural change—is of a nation that stubbornly resists homogenization. Unsettled by these historiographical trends, some political, economic, and diplomatic historians have complained that scholars pay too little attention to the powerful forces—international as well as national—that affect all of us, and too much—maybe far too much—to the ways in which we are divided.

•

There is no doubting the appeal to the so-called general reading public of sweeping narratives and political biographies, many of them written by nonacademic historians, concerning the recent American past.[3] Among those that have sold well in the past decade are Stephen Ambrose's fast-paced account of the D-Day invasion, David Garrow's biography of Martin Luther King, Jr., Taylor Branch's epic treatment of the civil rights movement between 1954 and 1963, David McCullough's biography of Harry Truman, David Halberstam's history of the 1950s, Nicholas Lemann's narrative of African-American migration from Mississippi to Chicago (and back), and Doris Kearns Goodwin's book on the Roosevelts in the White House during World War II.[4] Three of these books—by Garrow, McCullough, and Goodwin—have won Pulitzer prizes. The personal lives of presidents, generals, and other high-level actors on the national scene seem to have an especially timeless appeal to the American public.[5]

Why so much interest in histories such as these? One is both obvious and long-standing: people tend to be fascinated by narratives of exciting happenings—especially in politics, battles, and statecraft—that have taken place within their own lifetimes. Readers seem to hope that such narratives will offer an "inside story" of events—and of personalities—that they remember but know only a part of. This fascination, while discernible among readers around the world, may be particularly strong in the United States, which has had an uncommonly brief history; for most Americans, there is no *longue durée* to explore. As Denis Brogan pointed out more than forty years ago in speculating on differences between English and American approaches to history, educated English people tend to have a "deep, reverential sense of unity with a remote past." Not so, he noted, in the United States. "The American is willing to look at the past, to display curiosity." But "the past with which he is really connected is so short that history is either purely antiquarian or genealogical, or is in spirit modern; how did we get this way in 1954?"[6]

Although Brogan was not critical of such attitudes, others have complained about the tendency of Americans to approach history from a utilitarian perspective. This may indeed be an especially strong tendency in the United States, whose forward-looking people have often held great expectations about the "relevance" of history to the present and the future. James Harvey Robinson and other "New Historians"—many of them caught up in the reform spirit of the Progressive era after 1900—had such notions in mind.[7] So did some of America's leading intellectuals at the time. "A knowledge of the past and of its heritage," John Dewey wrote in 1916, "is of great significance when it enters into the present, but not otherwise." He added, "the mistake of making the records and remains of the past the main material of education is that it cuts the vital connection of present and past, and tends to make the past a rival of the present and the present a more or less futile imitation of the past."[8] Taking Dewey literally, educationists tried to turn history into civics courses and civics courses into propaganda.[9] Other Americans of utilitarian temper, including an occasional policy maker, have imagined that "history" can provide "lessons" to help in steering the ship of state.[10] In these and others ways the presentist, utilitarian tenor of American life and thought may heighten the appeal of twentieth-century history in the United States, especially military, diplomatic, and political history of World War II and the more recent past.

Presentism, at any rate, is surely and perhaps inevitably a salient aspect of much writing about twentieth-century United States life. The recent past, after all, hardly features unfamiliar or exotic terrain, and it is difficult if not impossible for historians who explore it to approach it anthropologically—as an "other" world that is markedly different from the society in which they live. On the contrary, emotional contemporary issues, notably those that concern race, ethnicity, and gender, powerfully affect historians as they study the not-very-distant sources of present-day problems.[11]

The sheer quantity of source materials further explains the amount of writing about twentieth-century American history. To be sure, the proliferation of sources is hardly an unmixed blessing. Popular historians as well as scholars have been tempted to rely heavily on oral histories, both because such sources stand ready for use in the reconstruction of the recent American past and because they can help us to capture vividly the agency of ordinary people. Yet exploitation of personal recollections raises large questions of accuracy and verifiability. Moreover, the enormous amount of source material dealing with the recent past presents especially formidable problems of selectivity for the modern historian: many scholarly monographs dealing with twentieth-century United States history, as if despairing at the task of separating the wheat from the chaff, suffer from excessive detail. That is one large reason why they gather dust.[12] Finally, of course, many documents remain closed to researchers; this is a cause of special frustration among political and diplomatic historians.[13] Still, the abundance of source materials, which include not only letters, official documents, and an enormous array of newspapers and magazines, but also film, television, and recordings, has surely encouraged researchers, thereby attracting many people to write and teach in modern United States history.

For some in the general reading public, modern American history has probably had yet one further appeal: the story of the United States in the twentieth century—at least to the mid-1960s—has been a peculiarly happy one. The United States has been spared the invasions, bloodletting, and famines that have blighted the modern histories of so many other nations since 1914. It has never feared for its survival—or even for the stability of its major institutions. For all its racial and ethnic divisions, it has featured a degree of equality and freedom enjoyed by few other nations. Its people not only managed to preserve democratic institutions through the perilous years of the Great Depression but also assumed major roles in winning two world wars. Following World War II (the "Good War") the United States took unprecedentedly large steps toward establishing legal rights for African-Americans and other minorities. Surviving the excesses of McCarthyism, it witnessed substantial advances in the protection of civil liberties. The story of its economy from 1900 to 1970—the Great Depression excepted—was mainly one of fantastic progress.[14]

Given America's relatively happy modern history, it is hardly surprising that many popular books have dwelt on World War II, the 1940s and 1950s, and early 1960s—peak years of American power and progress. Historians who wrote at the time—an era of self-congratulatory feeling in the United States—tended to celebrate the stability of America's institutions, to extol its courageous role in the world wars and the Cold War, and to imagine that social "consensus" was blurring age-old divisions of race, class, ethnicity, and religion in the nation. By the early 1960s, many scholars—historians among them—cherished extraordinarily high expectations about the capacity of the nation to lead the "Free World" toward unprecedented levels of stability and happiness.[15]

Thereafter, a host of sobering events—the splintering of the civil rights movement, the rise of racial, class, and religious backlash, the war in Vietnam, the constitutional crisis of Watergate, the stagnation of the economy—induced historians (especially politically engaged academics) to offer much more jaundiced accounts of modern American life.[16] Still, it seems fair to say that many so-called general readers have resisted such critical approaches. Seeking more positive, patriotic accounts, they have found much to cherish as they read about recent American history, especially narratives that focus on the years between 1940 and 1965.

•

A look at the bulk of more academically based scholarship by historians about twentieth-century America provides a considerably less celebratory and more complex picture. Especially since the 1960s, the work of scholars in the field has tended to feature a seemingly bewildering outpouring of specialized histories, which in turn expose two major trends: the eclipse of state-centered political history and the explosion of writing in other subfields of the discipline. Both these trends reflect developments in the historical profession in general. They also reflect the ever sharper divisions of contemporary American society.

To be sure, there has long been a rough consensus among twentieth-century American historians on some matters. From the 1940s—when academic writing about the twentieth century began to flourish—to the present, most scholars and teachers specializing in recent American history have seemed to be relatively comfortable using the turn of the century as a periodizing point for the courses they teach and the texts that they assign to explore the years to follow.[17] This is because the decade between 1896 and 1905 has generally seemed pivotal in many ways. During these years the frightening depression of the mid-1890s came to an end; Populism, a vital agrarian movement and third party, collapsed; a "great merger movement" centralized the corporate world; the Republican party, especially strong in the urban-industrial Northeast and Midwest, rode to a dominance in national politics that it maintained until 1930; "muckrakers," exploiting a new mass-circulation journalism, energetically attacked malfeasance in American politics and business; intellectuals like William James, Thorstein Veblen, Charles Beard, and Dewey led a revolt against older formalisms; improved communications facilitated the rapid rise of national organizations, complex bureaucracies, and professional disciplines; lab-based science transformed teaching and research in medicine and other fields; a more hopeful "Progressive era" of social and political reform started to take shape; a modern style of politics, featuring direct primaries, declining partisanship, and the proliferation of powerful interest groups, asserted itself; a national administrative state began to spring into life; and the United States emerged as a major power on the international scene.[18] A few years later, many of the major characteristics of a mass consumer society— notably automobiles, motion pictures, advertising and public relations, and commercialized sports—were becoming central to the culture.

Since the 1950s the majority of scholars writing twentieth-century United States history have seemed fairly content also with another periodizing point: the era of World War II. It was in these years that earlier trends—the rise of industrial labor unions, the triumph of agribusiness, the emergence of a Democratic political coalition, above all the expansion of the state and of interest group politics— became more solidly established in American life.[19] Keynesian understandings of economic policy as well as a rights-based liberalism began slowly to evolve.[20] The years surrounding World War II also witnessed creation of the Manhattan Project and construction of the Pentagon, symbolizing the extraordinary power of military-industrial collaboration that persisted after 1945. And of course World War II, followed immediately by the rise of the Cold War, greatly expanded America's involvement with the rest of the world. Reflecting the domestic and international impact of the war, many courses and textbooks divide twentieth-century United States history somewhere around 1945.[21]

Otherwise, however, scholars working in twentieth-century United States history do not find much consensus about periodization or other major aspects of the era. Some, indeed, seem uncertain and even a little defensive about what they are doing. In general, the academic field of recent United States history, while huge in the quantity of writing produced, has not been one of the most celebrated research areas during the past twenty-five years. Other fields, notably research by "new" social historians specializing in the eighteenth and nineteenth centuries, have seemed more attractive to young scholars.[22]

There are many reasons for this uncertain state of mind among academic practitioners of modern American history. One is the extraordinary pace of change and the great complexity of American life since 1900—and especially since 1945. How is it possible to know what is important and what is not? A second is the relative lack of historical perspective available concerning the very recent past: as a rule, academic historians are uncomfortable trying to make sense of events close to their own lifetimes. In part for this reason, many appear willing to accept an informal "twenty-year rule" that leaves study of the most recent past to journalists, sociologists, and political scientists, even though these writers may lack a strong background in history. (What they often do claim to have are general theories and large data sets, resources about which historians are often ambivalent.)[23] Most academic historians, moreover, do not believe that events in the past provide "lessons" for the present or for policy makers. Rejecting utilitarian notions of history, they lament the present-mindedness of the general reading public and of undergraduate students. Not a few consider "modern history" (especially since 1945) to be something of an oxymoron.[24]

The main themes of scholarly writing about twentieth-century American history, moreover, tend to differ from those of earlier periods, therefore separating—in some ways isolating—academic historians of the period from other scholars. This separation stems in part from the aforementioned changes in American life one hundred years ago. Many historians of the eighteenth and nineteenth centuries, for instance, have dwelt on developments that seem less important in the twentieth-century world: the sources of the emergence of capitalism and market relationships, the role of the frontier and of westward expansion in the formation of American ideas and institutions, the rise and decline of sectionalism and states' rights, the ongoing struggle for democracy and republicanism, the Civil War and Reconstruction, the impact of industrialization and urbanization. While some of these subjects—notably industrialization and urbanization—play significant roles in writings about the twentieth century, they are less central in them. Instead, scholars of recent United States history have tended to focus on other stories—the rise of America to world power, the expansion of the state, the influence of interest groups, the role of modern science and medicine, the explosion of professionalism and bureaucratization, the rush to the suburbs, the triumph of consumerism, the growth and stalemate of the civil rights revolution, the travails of feminism, the manifold meanings of mass popular culture. In these and other ways, the substance of many histories dealing with our century seems to spring, as if lacking deep roots, from the soil of a new world that developed in the late 1890s. While sensitive scholars writing about the twentieth century are concerned with the same big questions that engage other historians, they often focus on different problems and turn to very different sources.[25]

Researchers interested in political trends, until the 1960s the most influential subfield of scholarship about modern American history, have been faced with especially large changes in historiographical emphases since that time. In the 1950s, Richard Hofstadter, among others, began drawing heavily on writings in social psychology to undercut a once dominant form of "progressive" political history that in turn had offered a narrative framework used by many social, economic, and intellectual historians. This framework had tended to perceive past politics as a dualistic struggle between the forces of good (progressives, New Dealers, and reformers) and the forces of evil (corporate leaders and conservatives).[26] Hofstadter, however, rejoined that many "reformers" (especially in the "Progressive" era before 1920) had been deeply concerned about their social status amid the sweep of industrialization, urbanization, and mass immigration. They looked backward—to protect older (mostly Protestant, middle-class) values and ways of life—not forward to a new and multicultural society. Spearheading crusades for prohibition and immigration restriction, they displayed a profoundly moralistic, conservative, and ethnocentric view of the world.[27]

Other historians in the late 1950s and 1960s criticized progressive versions of political and economic history from a somewhat different perspective, offering instead what became known as an "organizational synthesis" of twentieth-century America. Some of them drew heavily on theories of modernization that highlighed structural understandings of socioeconomic development. They also turned to sociology, especially to Weberian approaches stressing the rise of rational modes of decision making. Twentieth-century politics and social reform, these "organizational" historians insisted, have been highly complex, featuring shifting alliances of interest groups and ethnocultural rivalries. Significant local variations require careful research into specific communities. Scholars, these historians have emphasized, should pay less attention to progressive rhetoric and more to social structures, enduring ethnic and religious forces, and economic interests. A key development of modern American life, they have stressed, was the rise of large and powerful bureaucracies in the private sector, and a concomitant change in the nature of the political world—one that since 1900 has relied ever more heavily on "experts," regulatory agencies, and administrative resources.[28]

The organizational synthesis has for the most part been used by historians to describe economic and political change in America before 1945: much remains to be explored about large-scale bureaucracies, both public and private, in the postwar years. Moreover, it has not appealed to everyone. Heavy emphasis on bureaucratic structures—and more generally on the power of "modernization"— has seemed to some to be deterministic. Attention to large organizations has tended also to concentrate on the activities of elites, thereby (critics have argued) slighting the agency of ordinary people, the resistance of local groups to centralizing forces, and the role of dissenters on both the right and the left.[29] Still, the focus on significant structural changes, notably bureaucratization and economic centralization, has properly identified developments that are central to twentieth-century American life. Considerably more sophisticated than older dualistic approaches to political and economic history, the "organizational synthesis" has helped to replace an often episodic, personality-based study of politics and economic development with an analytical approach that emphasizes the role of underlying structural forces. It has largely replaced the overly simplistic progressive narrative of the recent past.

Many political (and other) historians since the early 1960s have taken especially deadly aim against another older belief—that there was a specially progressive *direction* to American development. Already weak by 1940, this vision, like the related notion that the United States had an "exceptional" history, lost strength amid the bitter political and cultural battles that ravaged American society in the 1960s. Few scholars any longer see linear—or cyclical—progression of "reform" in twentieth-century life. They reject a "liberal narrative" linking the Progressive era, the New Deal, and the New Frontier–Great Society of the 1960s.[30] Instead, most historians writing about the current century are struck by the degree of complexity and diversity in America and by the power of conservatism, racism, and backlash as well as of liberalism and progress.[31] There is today no clear consensus among academic historians about the direction or nature of American "reform" in the twentieth century.[32]

The rejection of "progressive" versions of twentieth-century political history has not led to a widespread embrace of Marxist approaches to the period. Why this is so refers us to a much wider question—why has Marxist theory had relatively little influence on the academy?[33] But it clearly reflects the weakness of radical ideas and institutions in American society since the 1940s. The Communist and Socialist parties have virtually disappeared. Organized labor, once a source of hope for American social democrats, has become yet another interest group—and a weak one at that. And class as a category of analysis in recent years, an era of powerful civil rights and feminist activity, has attracted less interest among historians than have race and gender.[34] Like social scientists generally, historians of twentieth-century America have tended to be leery of many (not all) Marxist ideas, especially as they relate to political trends, and to employ a more pluralistic approach to economic and social change in the United States.[35]

Still, there is no denying the critical, left-of-center stance of much academic history done since the mid-1960s about the recent American past. Radical and "New Left" approaches, while especially strong in the fields of labor and diplomatic history, have enjoyed a fair amount of broader appeal within the academy, mainly in the turbulent years of the 1960s and early 1970s.[36] A few works, indeed, claimed to discern significant conspiratorial activities by corporate leaders.[37] More commonly, historians sympathetic to the plight of the poor and the working classes have continued since the 1960s to highlight the particularly sharp inequality of American society, the sometimes impressive resistance of ordinary people to governmental and corporate centralization, and the persistence of republican-producerist ideas—in these respects, some of the main themes of social historians of earlier America have been carried forth into scholarship about the twentieth century.[38]

Cultural historians in recent years have offered especially sharp critiques of twentieth-century American life. While only a few of these have openly embraced the presuppositions of Marxism or of postmodernist ideas, some identify "structures of domination," "hegemonic" cultural forces, and paradigms and "discourses" that threaten to limit the agency of people.[39] Struck especially by the sweep of the consumer culture, they maintain that commercialization has run rampant in modern American life. Uniting many approaches of this sort are three important assumptions about twentieth-century American history: that consumerist capitalism has assumed special power—psychological as well as economic—since 1900; that it has deeply affected—and damaged—the quality of American civilization; and that it has given rise to much that is notably modern and postmodern about American culture.

The attractions of this approach—it is too much to call it a "school" or a synthesis—have helped to make research in the area of popular culture—film, the mass media, advertising—perhaps the most dynamic subfield of scholarship concerning twentieth-century United States history. The researchers engaged in this enterprise, many of them in American Studies departments of leading universities, argue energetically among themselves about the extent to which the consumer culture has affected the citizenry—some emphasizing the stubbornly maintained agency and individuality of ordinary people, others lamenting the hegemony of commercialization and commodification. Most scholars in this broad field of inquiry, however, tend to offer a view of twentieth-century United States history that comes from the left and that is highly critical of long-range trends.[40]

The growing appeal of cultural history reveals a larger historiographical trend since the 1960s—the tendency of younger scholars to distance themselves from a once dominant form of political history that had focused on the doings of federal government leaders and institutions. Coming of age amid the turmoil of dissent aroused by the civil rights movement, the Vietnam War, and Watergate, these younger scholars grew disenchanted with the state, which seemed to be a source of intrigue, corruption, and reaction. Much political and diplomatic history, they came to believe, was "old-fashioned"—the study of Elite and Powerful White Men. One manifestation of such disenchantment has been a turning away from research into two areas that had been very popular in the 1950s and early 1960s: the study of national politics in the Progressive and New Deal eras.[41] Instead, younger historians have focused on the private lives of ordinary people and on "webs of cultural discourse," thereby in some ways recalling the manifestos of the "New Historians" many years earlier.[42] Devoting special attention to the postwar era, they have often identified with critics of American life. They have sought especially to write about outsiders—activists in the civil rights movement, spokespersons for a New Left, feminists, ethnic militants—and more generally to revive "history from the bottom up."[43]

The growing interest of scholars of twentieth-century American life in history from the bottom up is of course part of a much larger story: the extraordinary explosion of social history that has shaken the profession in the past thirty years. This explosion, to be sure, has most significantly rattled other fields of American scholarship, especially those dealing with the eighteenth and nineteenth centuries. It has not done quite as much to transform writing about the twentieth century, where political and diplomatic history maintain some presence, albeit of a different sort from earlier years. The reason for this endurance is obvious: it is often impossible to leave the state—which has grown rapidly (especially since 1940)—out of the stories that we tell about the twentieth century. To do so, many scholars rightly insist, is to ignore the role of economic and political power—international as well as national—in the highly interconnected world of postwar America. The public irrevocably impinges on the private.[44]

Moreover, political scientists—and to a lesser extent, sociologists—have recently been reaching out to historians in order to revive the fortunes of national political history.[45] This is in part because of sharp divisions within these social sciences since the 1960s: many political scientists in particular have rejected what they consider to be the arid model-building, behaviorism, and ahistoricism within their discipline. In 1990 they formed a Section on Politics and History within the American Political Science Association. By late 1992 the section had more than five-hundred dues-paying members.[46] Some of these scholars have joined historians in writing for *Social Science History*, *Studies in American Political Development* (1986–), and the *Journal of Policy History* (1989–), which publish articles that attempt to bridge gaps between history and the social sciences.

A few of these political scientists and sociologists have attracted particular attention among political historians by arguing that the state has played an important autonomous role in modern American life.[47] Turning to the history of social policy to document their case, they have focused on the growing power of state bureaucracies and institutions.[48] Their work has surely not convinced all historians that the state has in itself been the dominant player in policy making— many tend instead to emphasize the primary role of extragovernment forces, especially lobbies and social activists.[49] Changes in policy, these critics say, depend more on pressure from the bottom up than from the top down. Moreover, significant theoretical issues continue to separate historians from social scientists: the notion still persists that history deals in "facts" and that social "science" excels in theory.[50] Still, it is clear that political scientists, sociologists, and political historians dealing with twentieth-century developments are talking with one another more today than was the case fifteen or twenty years ago.

If, finally, we define twentieth-century "political" history in a broader sense— as the study of social movements seeking to expand the rights of citizenship—we can see that it is alive and well. Research into the civil rights movement—with which many scholars have identified deeply—has especially flourished, as has work on the New Left and feminism.[51] While most of this writing has focused on the activists, not on the role of the state, some of it has necessarily concerned itself with the behavior of political institutions. For these reasons it is not entirely the case, as some political historians have tended to think, that social history is sweeping everything before it.[52] Rather, there is now some evidence of a trend toward greater integration of social history from the bottom up and political history from the top down. Exploring links between the public and the private seems to be high on the agenda of many young scholars today.

Notwithstanding these efforts toward bridging gaps, there is no doubt that the rise of social history, among other developments, has placed many political historians—those who focus on the role of federal government officials—on the defensive. This sort of political history has either attenuated, as in the case of "top-down" studies of policy and elections, or become separated from other forms of historical writing, as in the case of diplomatic history.[53] The relative marginalization of research and writing in these fields—once central to narratives about twentieth-century United States history—is an especially noteworthy historiographical development. The old adage "History is past politics, and politics present history" long ago lost its appeal among younger historians interested in America in the twentieth century.[54]

•

As the rise of social history indicates, a good deal of recent academic writing about twentieth-century America has highlighted the flaws of civilization in the United States. It has paid great attention to the development of perceived problems of our own times: the power of a "military-industrial complex," the hegemonic capacity of big business, the glaring limitations of the American welfare state, the persistence of racism, nativism, and sexism. Highly critical approaches such as these attest not only to the existence of real problems in the United States but also to the ways in which the post–World War II escalation of rights-consciousness in American culture—one of the the most compelling forces of our times—has expanded expectations about life. Americans are in many ways doing better, but nonetheless are feeling worse. Academic historians in the United States, most of them progressive in their politics, seem especially to reflect such feelings, and tend as a result to downplay the extraordinary technological, scientific, and political changes—many of them promoting freer, more comfortable lives for people—that have taken place in our lifetime.[55]

If American scholars were to do more to compare historical developments in the United States with those in other nations, they might arrive at somewhat less gloomy perspectives.[56] Seen in the comparative context of the catastrophes and brutalities that have afflicted many other parts of the world since 1914, the history of the United States in the twentieth century might seem a little less grim than it is often portrayed. "Progress," moreover, is not entirely a mirage or a myth in twentieth century America—witness the expansion of liberal public policies in such areas as civil rights and civil liberties. By and large, however, American historians who specialize in the twentieth century (as well as those who do not) have shied away from doing comparative studies, which involve formidable research agendas. Instead, they have tended to concentrate closely on trends in their own culture, paying little attention to major currents of European historiography.[57]

To end on such critical notes, however, is to obscure a final important trend: the increasing diversity of historical writing on twentieth-century American life. Many scholars who undertake this work, which ranges far beyond political and diplomatic history, do not identify themselves primarily as "twentieth-century American historians." Instead, they tend to write as specialists in topical areas, such as cultural, social, economic, urban, or intellectual history, and they are more likely to teach these specialties than to offer politically centered surveys of the United States in the twentieth century.

Their output, which can only be summarized here, is impressive both in quality and quantity—the more so, it seems, as time passes. In recent years historians have been giving more than passing attention to many of the most powerful forces of twentieth-century American life, notably the impact of technology, business, science, and medicine.[58] Educational history, though most often written by professors of education, attracts a few historians.[59] The study of twentieth-century intellectual and religious history has also maintained some appeal, especially since the 1980s, when it became obvious that religious commitments remained powerful in American society. Much of this research, moreover, makes a special effort to contextualize developments, relating them to important institutional and social trends.[60] Interest in regional and environmental history, also reflecting contemporary societal concerns, has also begun to thrive—often (but not always) among historians who are uncomfortable with the organizational synthesis. Many of these works, too, attempt to link social, intellectual, and political developments.[61] Labor history, while less central to scholarship on the late twentieth century than it is for earlier eras, continues to engage some scholars—a few of them focusing on the role of the state, others writing in the tradition of the new social history.[62] And legal history, while most often tackled by journalists, lawyers, and political scientists, remains an active subfield within the historical profession.[63]

Although the diversity of this scholarship has reflected the social fragmentation of our times, imaginative young historians continue to look for larger patterns. Lizabeth Cohen, for instance, has attempted with considerable success to bring cultural, labor, and (to a lesser extent) political history together in her book on Chicago industrial workers during the interwar period.[64] Steven Biel, exploring reactions to the sinking of the *Titanic*, has brought sophisticated cultural analysis to his subject.[65] Allan Brandt, among others, has looked at medical developments within the context of professionalization, cultural change, and political institutions: whiggish approaches to the history of science and medicine now seem very old-fashioned.[66] Carl Husemoller Nightingale has pulled together research into poverty, race relations, child-rearing patterns, and the consumer culture in order to offer a bold historical interpretation of postwar African-American life.[67] And James Goodman, another young scholar, has explored developments in race relations, gender conflict, political change, and the law to provide a study (postmodern in some of its narrative strategies) of the contentious issues surrounding the "Scottsboro boys" charged with rape in Alabama in 1931.[68]

Scholars looking at twentieth-century gender relations, one of the most rapidly growing academic fields, have come forth with a number of studies connecting women's, political, and social history, especially in work on social reform and social welfare. Indeed, the role that women have played in early and mid-twentieth-century politics—and more broadly in the supposedly masculine "public sphere"—has received great attention in the last few years, helping to revive historical interest in some aspects of reform activity during the Progressive era and the 1930s.[69] These and other historians make it clear that scholars are continuing to step beyond the boundaries of specialization and to look for ways to tell more integrated stories about the recent past.

It is doubtful, however, that academic historians of twentieth-century America will come to agreement about any single synthesis of the era (or, for that matter, of any era.) We live, after all, in an age which highlights relativistic and personal ways of looking at things and which makes us acutely aware of group conflicts— of class, race, region, religion, gender, and ethnicity. Much that we write about is therefore decentered—unavoidably so. Some popular histories, to be sure, will continue to tell more heroic stories, but scholars are unlikely to return to interpretations based on simple dualisms in life, to describe America as an "exceptional" land of progress, or to employ schemes of periodization that rely primarily on political epiphenomena, important though those often are. While Americans surely display distinctive values and styles of life, we are also a polyglot and contentious people. For these reasons we cannot resurrect such a thing as an "American character." Diversity and disagreement in historical scholarship about the United States in the twentieth century, as in modern life, seem destined to continue.[70]

Notes

1. "Recent Scholarship," *Journal of American History* 81 (September 1994): 847–917. According to my rough categorization, articles in intellectual/cultural history and in international relations are most numerous, followed by articles dealing with women's, African-American, and political history. For an annotated listing of 873 books and articles in United States history concerned with the years between 1920 to 1993, see American Historical Association, "United States History since 1920," *Guide to Historical Literature* (New York, 1995), 1459–1503.

2. Modern United States history also appears to be popular in parts of western Europe—both among researchers and students. See Willi Paul Adams, "On the Significance of Frontiers in Writing American History in Germany," *Journal of American History* 79 (September 1992): 463–71; Tony Badger, "Confessions of a British Americanist," ibid., 515–23; and Maurizio Vaudagna, "The American Historian in Continental Europe: An Italian Perspective," ibid., 532–42.

3. For comments on the place of nonacademic historical writing in comtemporary America, see Nicholas Lemann, "History Solo: Non-academic Historians," *American Historical Review* 100 (June 1995): 788–98.

4. Stephen Ambrose, *D-Day, June 6, 1944: The Climactic Battle of World War II* (New York, 1994); David Garrow, *Bearing the Cross: Martin Luther King, Jr., and the Southern Christian Leadership Conference* (New York, 1986); Taylor Branch, *Parting the Waters: America in the King Years, 1954–1963* (New York, 1988); David McCullough, *Truman* (New York, 1992); David Halberstam, *The Fifties* (New York, 1993); Nicholas Lemann, *The Promised Land: The Great Black Migration and How It Changed America* (New York, 1991); Doris

Kearns Goodwin, *No Ordinary Time: Franklin and Eleanor Roosevelt: The Home Front in World War II* (New York, 1994). Garrow is a political scientist. Branch, Lemann, Halberstam, McCullough, and Goodwin are independent writers.

5. Television series, too, have tapped this interest. Among the shows that have appeared in recent years are series dealing with the civil rights movement ("Eyes on the Prize"), the Great Depression, and the War on Poverty. Programs on national affairs—World War II, presidents (especially Franklin Roosevelt, John Kennedy, and Lyndon Johnson)—have also appeared.

6. "The Writing of History: An English Authority Compares British and American Viewpoints," *American Heritage* 6 (December 1954): 70–72. An exception to this generalization concerns the American Civil War, about which writings (especially on military matters) abound.

7. James Harvey Robinson, *The New History* (New York, 1912).

8. John Dewey, *Democracy and Education* (New York, 1916), 88.

9. Frances FitzGerald, *America Revised: History Schoolbooks in the Twentieth Century* (Boston, 1979), 174–79.

10. A recent example is Robert McNamara, *The Tragedy and Lessons of Vietnam* (New York, 1995). This quest for usable "lessons" has often been a futile effort. See Richard Neustadt and Ernest May, *Thinking in Time: The Uses of History for Decision Makers* (New York, 1986), for cogent examples.

11. See Alan Ehrenhalt, *The Lost City: The Forgotten Virtues of Community in America* (New York, 1995), for a lament about the loss of "community" in the United States since the 1950s.

12. Excessive detail is of course a problem of historical monographs in many fields, not just in recent American history.

13. Social historians also confront problems concerning sources. Manuscript census materials are generally closed to researchers for seventy years, thereby protecting privacy.

14. The contrast between this experience and the histories of other nations during the twentieth century (especially between 1914 and 1945) is highlighted in Eric Hobsbawm, *Age of Extremes: The Short Twentieth Century* (London, 1994). Also see James Patterson, *Grand Expectations: The United States, 1945–1974* (Oxford, 1996); and Michael Elliott, *The Day before Yesterday: Reconsidering America's Past, Rediscovering the Present* (New York, 1996).

15. For comments on these trends see John Higham, "The Cult of the American Consensus: Homogenizing Our History," *Commentary* 27 (February 1959): 93–100; Higham, "Beyond Consensus: The Historian as Moral Critic," *American Historical Review* 67 (April 1962): 609–25; Richard Pells, *The Liberal Mind in a Conservative Age: American Intellectuals in the 1940s and 1950s* (New York, 1985); David Ricci, *The Tragedy of Political Science: Politics, Scholarship, and Democracy* (New Haven, 1984); Robert Dahl, *A Preface to Democratic Theory* (Chicago, 1956); John Blum, *Liberty, Justice, Order: Essays on Past Politics* (New York, 1993), 4–6.

16. For trends in historiography after 1960 see John Higham, "Changing Paradigms: The Collapse of Consensus History," *Journal of American History* 76 (September 1989): 460–66; Higham, "The Future of American History," *Journal of American History* 80 (March 1994): 1289–1309; Michael McGerr, "The Price of the 'New Transnational History,'" *American Historical Review* 96 (October 1991): 1056–67; David Hollinger, "How Wide the Circle of the 'We'? American Intellectuals and the Problem of the Ethnos since World War II," *American Historical Review* 98 (April 1993): 317–37; Kenneth Cmiel, "History against Itself," *Journal of American History* 81 (December 1994): 1169–74; and Peter Novick, *That*

Noble Dream: The "Objectivity Question" and the American Historical Profession (New York, 1988), esp. 573–629.

17. For many European societies, 1914 is a more common break point than 1900.

18. Key sources concerning this era include Naomi Lamoreaux, *The Great Merger Movement in American Business, 1895–1904* (New York, 1985); Arthur Link and Richard McCormick, *Progressivism* (Arlington Heights, Ill., 1983); John Chambers, *The Tyranny of Change: America in the Progressive Era, 1900–1917* (New York, 1980); Richard McCormick, "The Discovery That Business Corrupts Politics: A Reappraisal of the Origins of Progressivism," *American Historical Review* 86 (April 1981): 247–74; Daniel Rodgers, "In Search of Progressivism," *Reviews in American History* 10 (December 1982): 113–32.

19. Brian Balogh, "Reorganizing the Organizational Synthesis: Federal-Professional Relations in Modern America," *Studies in American Political Development* 5 (spring 1991): 119–72, emphasizes the war years as the time when a strong "proministrative state" finally arose in America.

20. The best recent history of many of these developments is Alan Brinkley, *The End of Reform: New Deal Liberalism in Recession and War* (New York, 1995).

21. Some subfields of modern United States history, to be sure, employ other periodizing points. See Michael McGerr, "Political Style and Women's Power, 1830–1930," *Journal of American History* 77 (December 1990): 864–85, on cycles in feminism.

22. Alan Brinkley, "Writing the History of Contemporary America: Dilemmas and Challenges," *Daedalus* (winter 1984): 121–41. For overviews of various subfields of twentieth-century American history, see Richard McCormick, "Public Life in Industrial America, 1877–1917," Walter La Feber, "Liberty and Power: U.S. Diplomatic History, 1750–1945," Brinkley, "Prosperity, Depression, and War, 1920–1945," and William Chafe, "America since 1945," in Eric Foner, ed., *The New American History* (Philadelphia, 1990), 119–41, 271–90, 93–117, 143–60; and James Patterson, "United States History since 1920," in American Historical Association, *Guide to Historical Literature* (New York, 1995), 1453–57.

23. Among widely read books on post-World War II American politics and society—many of them used in history courses—are Thomas and Mary Edsall, *Chain Reaction: The Impact of Race, Rights, and Taxes on American Politics* (New York, 1992); E. J. Dionne, Jr., *Why Americans Hate Politics* (New York, 1991); Jonathan Rieder, *Canarsie: The Jews and Italians of Brooklyn against Liberalism* (Cambridge, 1985); Landon Jones, *Great Expectations: America and the Baby Boom Generation* (New York, 1980); J. Anthony Lukas, *Common Ground: A Turbulent Decade in the Lives of Three American Families* (New York, 1985); James Davison Hunter, *Culture Wars: The Struggle to Define America* (New York, 1991); Garry Wills, *The Kennedy Imprisonment: A Meditation on Power* (Boston, 1982); and Wills, *Nixon Agonistes: The Crisis of the Self-Made Man* (New York, 1970). The Edsalls, Dionne, Jones, and Lukas are journalists; Rieder and Hunter are sociologists.

24. Even so, it is probably true that scholarly openness to "contemporary history" is greater in the United States than in many other nations, especially those with self-perceived long histories. This is in part because of the aforementioned presentism of American culture and in part because graduate schools in many other nations continue to train relatively large numbers of young historians specializing in earlier periods. In these nations historians of the most recent eras thus tend to feel marginalized. See Maurizio Vaudagna, "American History at Home and Abroad," *Journal of American History* 81 (December 1994): 1157–68. "Contemporary" history also attracts considerable scholarly interest in Great Britain and in Germany.

25. For some areas of historical investigation, of course, the "turn of the century" has little if any meaning for periodization. These areas include the history of immigration and

ethnicity, of urbanization, of religious conflicts, and of technology. See John Bodnar, *The Transplanted: A History of Immigrants in Urban America* (Bloomington, Ind., 1985); and Samuel Hays, *City at the Point: Essays on the Social History of Pittsburgh* (Pittsburgh, 1989).

26. Several books in the prestigious New American Nation series, widely read by graduate students in the late 1950s and early 1960s, reflect this dualistic approach. Among them are George Mowry, *The Era of Theodore Roosevelt and the Birth of Modern America, 1900–1912* (New York, 1958); Arthur Link, *Woodrow Wilson and the Progressive Era, 1910–1917* (New York, 1954); and John Hicks, *Republican Ascendancy, 1921–1933* (New York, 1960). See especially Arthur Schlesinger, Jr., *The Age of Roosevelt*, 3 vols. (Boston, 1957–60).

27. Richard Hofstadter, *The American Political Tradition and the Men Who Made It* (New York, 1948); Hofstadter, *The Age of Reform: From Bryan to F.D.R.* (New York, 1955); and Hofstadter, *The Progressive Historians: Turner, Beard, Parrington* (New York, 1968). Also see Daniel Joseph Singal, "Beyond Consensus: Richard Hofstadter and American Historiography," *American Historical Review* 89 (October 1984): 976–1004.

28. Alfred Chandler, Jr., *The Visible Hand: The Managerial Revolution in American Business* (Cambridge, Mass., 1977); Samuel Hays, *The Response to Industrialism, 1885–1914* (Chicago, 1957); Robert Wiebe, *The Search for Order, 1877–1920* (New York, 1967); Louis Galambos, "The Emerging Organizational Synthesis in Modern American History," *Business History Review* 44 (autumn 1970): 279–90; Galambos, "Technology, Political Economy, and Professionalization: Central Themes of the Organizational Synthesis," *Business History Review* 57 (1983): 471 ff; Balogh, "Reorganizing the Organizational Synthesis." An early salvo fired at "old-fashioned" political history was Thomas Cochran, "The 'Presidential Synthesis' in American History," *American Historical Review* 53 (1948): 748–59. See also Lee Benson, *The Concept of Jacksonian Democracy: New York as a Test Case* (Princeton, 1961).

29. A criticism along these lines is Brinkley, "Writing the History of Contemporary America."

30. See three revealingly titled books: Steve Fraser and Gary Gerstle, eds., *The Rise and Fall of the New Deal Order, 1930–1980* (Princeton, 1989); Brinkley, *End of Reform*; and Allen Matusow, *The Unraveling of America: A History of Liberalism in the 1960s* (New York, 1984). See also David Burner, *Making Peace with the 60s* (Princeton, 1996), which focuses on the eclipse of liberalism in the 1960s.

31. A relevant exchange of views on aspects of this subject is Alan Brinkley, "The Problem of American Conservatism," *American Historical Review* 99 (April 1994): 409–29, and Leo Ribuffo, "Why Is There So Much Conservatism in the United States and Why Do So Few Historians Know Anything about It?" ibid., 438–49. See also Godfrey Hodgson, *The World Turned Right Side Up: A History of the Conservative Ascendancy in America* (Boston, 1996); and Michael Kazin, *The Populist Persuasion: An American History* (New York, 1995). Scholars looking at the American Red scare of the 1940s and 1950s have also emphasized the weakness of liberal ideas and institutions. For excellent syntheses see Richard Fried, *Nightmare in Red: The McCarthy Era in Perspective* (New York, 1990); and Stephen Whitfield, *The Culture of the Cold War* (Baltimore, 1991).

32. David Thelen, "The Practice of American History," *Journal of American History* 81 (December 1994): 933–68. Some historians, however, refuse to despair. See William O'Neill, *American High: The Years of Confidence, 1945–1960* (New York, 1986); and John Diggins, *The Proud Decades: America in War and Peace, 1941–1960* (New York, 1988), for more positive accounts of postwar United States history. My own view resembles theirs; see below.

33. Ian Tyrrell, *The Absent Marx: Class Analysis and Liberal History in Twentieth Century America* (Westport, Conn., 1986).

34. An important exception is Christian Appy, *Working-Class War: America's Combat Soldiers and Vietnam* (Chapel Hill, N.C., 1993).

35. See David Harvey, *The Urbanization of Capital: Studies in the History and Theory of Capitalist Urbanization* (Baltimore, 1985), for sophisticated use of Marxist ideas about capitalist accumulation.

36. See Gabriel Kolko, *The Triumph of Conservatism: A Reinterpretation of American History, 1900–1916* (New York, 1963); James Weinstein, *The Corporate Ideal in the Liberal State, 1900–1918* (Boston, 1968); Barton Bernstein, "The New Deal: The Conservative Achievements of Liberal Reform," in Bernstein, ed., *Towards a New Past* (New York, 1968); and Howard Zinn, ed., *New Deal Thought* (New York, 1966), xv–xxxvi. See also the work in diplomatic history of William Appleman Williams, such as *The Tragedy of American Diplomacy* (New York, 1959) and *The Contours of American History* (New York, 1961).

37. Notably Kolko, *Triumph of Conservatism*.

38. Examples—most of them books on American history before World War II—include David Montgomery, *The Fall of the House of Labor: The Workplace, the State, and American Labor Activism, 1865–1925* (New York, 1987); Alan Brinkley, *Voices of Protest: Huey Long, Father Coughlin, and the Great Depression* (New York, 1982); Jacquelyn Dowd Hall et al., *Like a Family: The Making of a Southern Cotton Mill World* (Chapel Hill, N.C., 1987); Gary Gerstle, *Working Class Americanism: The Politics of Labor in an Industrial City, 1914–1960* (New York, 1989); and James Grossman, *Land of Hope: Chicago, Black Southerners, and the Great Migration* (Chicago, 1989).

39. For an identification and critique of such emphases, see John Diggins, "Language and History," *Reviews in American History* 17 (March 1989): 1–9.

40. Two collections of essays edited by Richard Wightman Fox and T. J. Jackson Lears, *The Culture of Consumption: Critical Essays in American History, 1880–1960* (New York, 1983) and *The Power of Culture: Critical Essays in American History* (Chicago, 1993), offer useful starting points into this now large literature. See also Richard Butsch, *For Fun and Profit* (Philadelphia, 1989); William Leach, *Land of Desire: Merchants, Power, and the Rise of a New American Culture* (New York, 1993); Warren Susman, *Culture as History: The Transformation of American Society in the Twentieth Century* (New York, 1984); and Lawrence Levine, "The Folklore of Industrial Society: Popular Culture and Its Audiences," *American Historical Review* 97 (December 1992): 1369–99, and responses. Other studies include George Lipsitz, *Time Passages: Collective Memory and American Popular Culture* (Minneapolis, 1990); and James Baughman, *The Republic of Mass Culture: Journalism, Filmmaking, and Broadcasting in America since 1941* (Baltimore, 1992).

41. See Mark Leff, "Revisioning U.S. Political History," *American Historical Review* 100 (June 1995): 829–53. See also the thorough bibliography by Anthony Badger, *The New Deal: The Depression Years, 1933–1940* (New York, 1989). It indicates that most studies of politics and policies concerning the New Deal era were published before 1970 and that approaches to the subject have not changed much since then.

42. For a provocative lament about this trend, written from a radical perspective, see Tony Judt, "A Clown in Royal Purple: Social History and the Historians," *History Workshop* 7 (spring 1979): 66–94. For a complaint from the right, see Gertrude Himmelfarb, *The New History and the Old: Critical Essays and Reappraisals* (Cambridge, Mass., 1987); and Himmelfarb, "Some Reflections on the New History," *American Historical Review* 94 (June 1989): 661–70. Rejoinders to Himmelfarb are offered by Lawrence Levine, "The

Unpredictable Past: Reflections on Recent American Historiography," and Joan Wallach Scott, "History in Crisis? The Others' Side of the Story," ibid., 671–79, 680–92. For "webs of cultural discourse," see Fox and Lears, *Power of Culture*, 4.

43. See Gordon Craig, "Political History," *Daedalus* 100 (spring 1971): 323–38, for an early recognition of these trends. Manifestos supporting the virtues of social history long predated the 1960s. One of the most powerful came from Frederick Jackson Turner, "The Significance of History," *Wisconsin Journal of Education* 21 (October–November 1891): 230–34, 253–56. But the modern efflorescence of social history occurred after 1960.

44. Some labor historians have made a point of paying close attention to the state. See Nelson Lichtenstein, *Labor's War at Home: The CIO in World War II* (New York, 1982); Melvyn Dubofsky, *The State and Labor in Modern America* (Chapel Hill, N.C., 1994); and Robert Zieger, *The CIO, 1935–1955* (Chapel Hill, N.C., 1995).

45. For sociology see Andrew Abbott, "History and Sociology: The Lost Synthesis," *Social Science History* 15 (summer 1991), 201–38; and Dennis Wrong, "The Present Condition of American Sociology: A Review Article," *Comparative Studies in Society and History* 35 (January 1993): 183–96. For political science see Ira Katznelson, "The State to the Rescue? Political Science and History Reconnect," *Social Research* 59 (winter 1992): 719–37; and David Brian Robertson, "The Return to History and the New Institutionalism in American Political Science," *Social Science History* 17 (spring 1993): 1–36. Another relevant article, sounding a call for cooperation between historians and political scientists, is William Leuchtenburg, "The Pertinence of Political History: Reflections on the Significance of the State in America," *Journal of American History* 73 (December 1986): 585–600.

46. *Clio* (the newsletter of the section) 3 (fall & winter, 1992/1993): 10. The section also sponsored ten sessions at the September 1992 meeting of the American Political Science Association. By contrast, some historians of twentieth-century politics have felt marginalized at conventions of the Organization of American Historians. See William Leuchtenburg, "The Uses and Abuses of History," *History and Politics Newsletter* 2 (fall 1991): 6–8. This was the earlier title of *Clio*.

47. Eric Nordlinger, *On the Autonomy of the Democratic State* (Cambridge, Mass., 1981); Karen Orren and Stephen Skowronek, "Editors' Preface," *Studies in American Political Development* 1 (1986): 1; Skowronek, *Building a New American State: The Expansion of Administrative Capacities, 1877–1920* (New York, 1982); Theda Skocpol, "Bringing the State Back In: Strategies of Analysis in Current Research," in Peter Evans, Dietrich Rueschemeyer, and Skocpol, eds., *Bringing the State Back In* (New York, 1975), 9 ff.

48. A collection of essays in this field—most by historians—is Donald Critchlow and Ellis Hawley, eds., *Federal Social Policy: The Historical Dimension* (University Park, Pa., 1988). Key monographs include Hugh Davis Graham, *The Civil Rights Era: Origins and Development of National Policy, 1960–1972* (New York, 1990); and Theda Skocpol, *Protecting Soldiers and Mothers: The Political Origins of Social Policy in the United States* (Cambridge, Mass., 1992) (on old age and mothers' pensions from the 1870s into the 1920s).

49. See Samuel Hays, "Society and Politics: Politics and Society," *Journal of Interdisciplinary History* 15 (winter 1985), 481–99; and J. Morgan Kousser, "Restoring Politics to Political History," ibid., 12 (spring 1982), 569–95.

50. Abbott, "History and Sociology," 234.

51. In addition to the works by Garrow, Branch, and Lemann cited above, important historical studies of race relations and civil rights include John Dittmer, *Local People: The Struggle for Civil Rights in Mississippi* (Urbana, Ill., 1994); William Chafe, *Civilities and Civil Rights: Greensboro, North Carolina and the Black Struggle for Freedom* (New York, 1980); Steven Lawson, *Running for Freedom: Civil Rights and Black Politics in America since 1941*

(Philadelphia, 1991); Clayborne Carson, *In Struggle: SNCC and the Black Awakening of the 1960s* (Cambridge, Mass., 1981); Harvard Sitkoff, *The Struggle for Black Equality, 1954–1992* (New York, 1992); and Robert Weisbrot, *Freedom Bound: A History of America's Civil Rights Movement* (New York, 1990). Some of the many works on the left include James Miller, *"Democracy Is in the Streets": From Port Huron to the Siege of Chicago* (New York, 1987); Maurice Isserman, *If I Had a Hammer: The Death of the Old Left and the Birth of the New Left* (New York, 1987); and John Diggins, *The Rise and Fall of the American Left* (New York, 1992). On women and feminism, see William Chafe, *The Paradox of Change: American Women in the Twentieth Century* (New York, 1991); Sara Evans, *Personal Politics: The Roots of Women's Liberation in the Civil Rights Movement and the New Left* (New York, 1979); Nancy Cott, *The Grounding of Modern Feminism* (New Haven, 1987); and Ann Shola Orloff, "Gender in Early U.S. Social Policy," *Journal of Policy History* 3 (1991): 249–80.

52. For such a lament see Hugh Davis Graham, "The Stunted Career of Public History, A Critique and an Agenda," *The Public Historian* 15 (spring 1993): 15–37. Also "Roundtable: Responses to Hugh Davis Graham's 'The Stunted Career of Policy History: A Critique and an Agenda,'" ibid., 15 (fall 1993): 51–81.

53. Diplomatic historians, however, have responded to their marginalization within the profession by establishing strong institutions of their own, notably the Society for Historians of Foreign Relations, which had a membership of more than fifteen hundred in 1992, and sponsors an excellent journal, *Diplomatic History* (1977–). They have also forged links with students of international relations, most of them in the discipline of political science. See Michael Hunt, "The Long Crisis in U.S. Diplomatic History: Coming to Closure," *Diplomatic History* 16 (winter 1992): 115–40; "Writing the History of U.S. Foreign Relations: A Symposium," ibid., 14 (fall 1990): 553–605; and Jerald Combs, *American Diplomatic History: Two Centuries of Changing Interpretations* (Berkeley, 1983).

54. Thomas Bender, "'Venturesome and Cautious': American History in the 1990s," *American Historical Review* 81 (December 1994): 992–1003; Bender, "Wholes and Parts: The Need for Synthesis in American History," *Journal of American History* 73 (June 1986): 120–36.

55. Vaudagna, "American History at Home and Abroad," 1165–67, suggests that American historians (taking for granted their freedom and affluence) are more critical of their own recent history than are non-Americans working in the field.

56. A point made by Carl Degler, "In Pursuit of an American History," *American Historical Review* 92 (February 1987): 1–12; and Raymond Grew, "The Comparative Weakness of American History," *Journal of Interdisciplinary History* 16 (summer 1985): 87–101. See also George Fredrickson, "What Is the New History?" *Dissent* (summer 1991): 428–32.

57. Again there are exceptions to this generalization. Well-regarded comparative works include Fredrickson, *White Supremacy: A Comparative Study in American and South African History* (New York, 1981); Fredrickson, *Black Liberation: A Comparative History of Black Ideology* (New York, 1995); James Kloppenberg, *Uncertain Victory: Social Democracy and Progressivism in Europe and America, 1870–1920* (New York, 1986); Alfred Chandler, Jr., *Scale and Scope: The Dynamics of Industrial Capitalism* (Cambridge, Mass., 1990); and Susan Fainstein et al., eds., *Divided Cities: New York and London in the Contemporary World* (Cambridge, Mass., 1992).

58. For recent scholarship on developments in technology and industrial organization, see Alfred Chandler, Jr., "The Competitive Performance of U.S. Industrial Enterprises since the Second World War," *Business History Review* 68 (spring 1994): 1–72. For studies of business-political relations see Otis Graham, *Losing Time: The Industrial Policy Debate* (Cambridge, Mass., 1992); Kim McQuaid, *Uneasy Partners: Big Business in American Politics,*

1945–1990 (Baltimore, 1994); Elizabeth Fones-Wolf, *Selling Free Enterprise: The Business Assault on Labor and Liberalism, 1945–1960* (Urbana, 1994); and David Vogel, *Fluctuating Fortunes: The Political Power of Business in America* (New York, 1989). For works concerning science and industry, see David Noble, *Forces of Production: A Social History of Industrial Automation* (New York, 1984); Noble, *America by Design: Science, Technology, and the Rise of Corporate Capitalism* (New York, 1979); David Nye, *Electrifying America: Social Meanings of a New Technology, 1880–1940* (Cambridge, Mass., 1990); Stuart Leslie, *The Cold War and American Science: The Military-Industrial Complex at MIT and Stanford* (New York, 1993); and James Cortada, *Before the Computer: IBM, NCR, Burroughs, and Remington Rand, and the Industry They Created, 1986–1956* (Princeton, 1993). For developments in medicine and society, see Allan Brandt, *No Magic Bullet: A Social History of Venereal Disease in the United States since 1880* (New York, 1985); James Jones, *Bad Blood: The Tuskegee Syphilis Experiment* (New York, 1993); James Patterson, *The Dread Disease: Cancer and Modern American Culture* (Cambridge, Mass., 1987); Joan Brumberg, *Fasting Girls: The Emergence of Anorexia Nervosa as a Modern Disease* (Cambridge, Mass., 1988); David Rothman, *Strangers at the Bedside: A History of How Law and Ethics Transformed Medical Decision Making* (New York, 1991); and Robert Proctor, *Cancer Wars: How Politics Shapes What We Know and Don't Know about Cancer* (New York, 1995).

59. For example, Lynn Gordon, *Gender and Higher Education in the Progressive Era* (New Haven, 1990); Paula Fass, *Outside In: Minorities and the Transformation of American Education* (New York, 1989); Arthur Zilversmit, *Changing Schools: Progressive Educational Theory and Practice, 1930–1960* (Chicago, 1993); Roger Geiger, *To Advance Knowledge: The Growth of the American Research University* (New York, 1986); Geiger, *Research and Relevant Knowledge: American Research Universities since World War II* (New York, 1993); and Diane Ravitch, *The Troubled Crusade: American Education, 1945–1980* (New York, 1983).

60. See Paul Boyer, *When Time Shall Be No More: Prophecy Belief in Modern American Culture* (New York, 1992); George Marsden, *Fundamentalism and American Culture: The Shaping of Twentieth-Century Evangelicalism, 1870–1925* (New York, 1980); Leo Ribuffo, *The Old Christian Right: The Protestant Far Right from the Great Depression to the Cold War* (Philadelphia, 1983); Michael Lacey, ed., *Religion and Twentieth Century American Intellectual Life* (Washington, D.C., 1989); Ronald Numbers, *The Creationists: The Evolution of Scientific Creationism* (New York, 1992); Robert Wuthnow, *The Restructuring of American Religion: Society and Faith since World War II* (Princeton, 1988); and Philip Gleason, *Keeping the Faith: American Catholicism Past and Present* (South Bend, 1987). Major books in twentieth-century intellectual history include Richard Wightman Fox, *Reinhold Niebuhr: A Biography* (New York, 1986); Howard Brick, *Thorstein Veblen and His Critics, 1891–1963* (Princeton, 1992); Robert Westbrook, *John Dewey and American Democracy* (Ithaca, 1991); Dorothy Ross, *The Origins of Social Science* (New York, 1991); Michael Wreszin, *A Rebel in Defense of Tradition: The Life and Politics of Dwight Macdonald* (New York, 1994); and David Lewis, *W. E. B. DuBois: Biography of a Race, 1868–1919* (New York, 1993).

61. See William Cronon et al., eds., *Under an Open Sky: Rethinking America's Western Past* (New York, 1992); Samuel Hays, *Beauty, Health, and Permanence: Environmental Politics in the United States, 1955–1985* (New York, 1987); Hays, "The New Environmental West," *Journal of Policy History* 3 (1991): 223–48; Michael Lacey, ed., *Government and Environmental Politics: Essays on Historical Developments since World War Two* (Washington, D.C., 1989); Robert Dorman, *Revolt of the Provinces: The Regionalist Movement in America, 1920–1945* (Chapel Hill, N.C., 1993); Jon Teaford, *Cities of the Heartland: The Rise and Fall of the Industrial Midwest* (Bloomington, Ind., 1993); Carl Abbott, *The Metropolitan Frontier: Cities in the Modern American West* (Tucson, 1993); John Findlay, *Magic Lands: Western*

Cityscapes and American Culture after 1940 (Berkeley, 1990); Gerald Nash, *World War II and the West: Reshaping the Economy* (Lincoln, Neb., 1990); Donald Worster, *Rivers of Empire: Water, Aridity, and the Growth of the American West* (New York, 1986); and Bruce Schulman, *From Cotton Belt to Sunbelt: Federal Policy, Economic Development, and the Transformation of the South, 1938–1980* (New York, 1991).

62. In addition to works noted earlier—by Hall, Lichtenstein, Montgomery, Dubofsky, Gerstle, and others—see Steve Fraser, *Labor Will Rule: Sidney Hillman and the Rise of American Labor* (New York, 1991); Eileen Boris, *Home to Work: Motherhood and the Politics of Industrial Homework in the United States* (New York, 1994); and Richard Oestreicher, "Urban Working-Class Political Behavior and Theories of American Electoral Politics, 1870–1940," *Journal of American History* 74 (March 1988): 1257–86.

63. For example, Richard Kluger, *Simple Justice: The History of Brown v. Board of Education and Black America's Struggle for Equality* (New York, 1976); Mark Tushnet, *Making Civil Rights Law: Thurgood Marshall and the Supreme Court, 1936–1961* (New York, 1994); Laura Kalman, *Abe Fortas: A Biography* (New Haven, 1990); Stanley Kutler, *The American Inquisition: Justice and Injustice in the Cold War* (New York, 1982); Melvin Urofsky, *A Conflict of Rights: The Supreme Court and Affirmative Action* (New York, 1991); Richard Polenberg, *Fighting Faiths: The Abrams Case, the Supreme Court, and Free Speech* (New York, 1987); and William Leuchtenburg, *The Supreme Court Reborn: The Constitutional Revolution in the Age of Roosevelt* (New York, 1995). Kalman, Kutler, Urofsky, Polenberg, and Leuchtenburg are trained as historians.

64. Lizabeth Cohen, *Making a New Deal: Industrial Workers in Chicago, 1919–1939* (New York, 1990). See also Dana Frank, *Purchasing Power, Consumer Organizing, Gender, and the Seattle Labor Movement, 1919–1929* (New York, 1994).

65. Steven Biel, *Down with the Old Canoe: A Cultural History of the Titanic Disaster* (New York, 1996).

66. Brandt, *No Magic Bullet*. See also Proctor, *Cancer Wars*.

67. Nightingale, *On the Edge: A History of Poor Black Children and Their American Dreams* (New York, 1993).

68. James Goodman, *Stories of Scottsboro* (New York, 1994).

69. Paula Baker, *The Moral Frameworks of Public Life: Gender, Politics, and the State in Rural New York, 1870–1930* (New York, 1991); Linda Gordon, *Pitied but Not Entitled: Single Mothers and the History of Welfare, 1890–1935* (New York, 1994). See also Gordon, ed., *Women, the State, and Welfare* (Madison, Wis., 1990); Ellen Fitzpatrick, *Women Social Scientists and Progressive Reform* (New York, 1990); Robyn Muncy, *Creating a Female Dominion in American Reform, 1890–1935* (New York, 1991); Vivien Hart, *Bound by Our Constitution: Women, Workers, and the Minimum Wage* (Princeton, 1994); and Evans, Rueschemeyer, and Skocpol, eds., *Bringing the State Back In*. For efforts to build bridges between women's history and diplomatic history, see "Culture, Gender, and Foreign Policy: A Symposium," *Diplomatic History* 18 (winter 1994): 47–124, especially Emily Rosenberg, "'Foreign Affairs' after World War II: Connecting Sexual and International Politics," 59–70.

70. Hollinger, "How Wide the Circle of the 'We'?"

CHAPTER 10

Western Civilization

EUGEN WEBER

"THE RISE OF 'Western Civ' is one of the great success stories in the history of the historical profession in America," declares Gilbert Allardyce in a seminal essay designed not to praise "this wilted course" but to bury it. Yet the reasons Allardyce advances to explain why "the world has outgrown the old Western Civ idea"[1] could easily be turned round to explain the enduring use of it.

Like most chroniclers of Western Civ, Allardyce relates the birth of the course to the fin-de-siècle struggle between a "chaotic" elective system and those reacting against atomizing specialization and professionalism. A general education curriculum, some argued, should combat fragmentation and provide a common learning experience—above all exposure to that Western tradition that could equip citizens with the sense of a common identity, common past, and common purpose. American history had been about leaving the Old World behind. As the nineteenth century ended, as the twentieth century began, Americans started to rediscover the past that they had shed, no longer as restrictive but increasingly as inspiring or, at least, suggestive. More Americans traveled, more Americans traded abroad; more economic, social, political involvement in Europe meant more attention devoted to Europe. American culture was the offshoot of European culture. Growing interest in European culture brought growing interest in those origins that were the origins of American culture too, and in the sociopolitical evolution that was held to account for both.

There were good reasons for some kind of synthetic exposure that would provide young Americans with a sense of their past as part of a common Western experience, a common civilization that reflected and affirmed the forward march of liberty, democracy, and progress. But there was more to it.

Under the elective system, a professor of literature at Columbia declared, "an incomplete knowledge of enough courses leads to a degree."[2] But the same was true of the public and private schools whose graduates reached college. As Charles Homer Haskins reported to the American Historical Association in 1906, "the reason why we introduced this general education course on European history . . . is because students did not bring it to college with them."[3] Ninety years ago, just as today, at Haskins's Harvard as in most other schools, general education courses were remedial. They remained so. By the time of the First World War, "even those soldiers who are neither illiterate nor unable to command the English language showed to a distressing degree the inefficiency of our popular education."[4] All evidence testifies to an enduring problem. In recent years *New*

York Times surveys of college freshmen continue to reveal a dismal knowledge of history;[5] and some college teachers of history react by proposing history courses dedicated to the development of missing skills, like "a European survey course which stresses writing and reasoning skills."[6] And a bit of history too, no doubt.

This is the background against which Western Civ and proto–Western Civ courses were introduced. Part of a program of general education designed to counter the alleged shortcomings of the elective system, Western Civ and its predecessors were also part of a broader campaign to socialize, "civilize," and integrate immigrants and members of social groups entering college with little or no exposure to the general—dominant—culture. They were also a kind of civics: an education for democracy and for a more responsible awareness of the wider world, its background and its problems. They represented the affirmation of a national culture, rooted in the Mediterranean and the European past. This is what makes a college course like Western Civ so peculiarly American. Europeans prefer to teach and write national history. Americans do that too; but they conceive and present the national past as prolonged backward not into the British past alone but into a broader Western tradition, originating in the Fertile Crescent and in the Mediterranean of Greece and Rome, where the groundwork was laid for references and memories that resurface in the conflicts and creations of the Middle Ages, Renaissance, Reformation, Enlightenment, and so on.

French, British, Italian, German historians recognize similar sources. But French, British, Italian, German historians treat Europe and the wider world as context, whereas Americans treat Europe, and especially Western Europe, as text: as "roots." Western Civ provides the inescapable background of national history, to be followed in the past two hundred years by the international context within which our own national history evolves. Just how American this concept became can be seen from the fact that, whereas Winston Churchill never referred to Western Civilization in his great war and postwar speeches, preferring terms like "Western Democracies" or "Christian Civilization," Dean Acheson, in similar public circumstances, spoke of "that Western Civilization which we share with other nations bordering the North Atlantic."[7]

The shape that Western Civ would take was laid down in 1903, when Harvard's Outline of General History course was restructured to two hours of lecture and two section-hours taught by graduate assistants offering quizzes, map drills, perhaps a modicum of discussion. In 1904, Charles Homer Haskins (a medievalist) took over the course and introduced the use of original source material, and Western Civ never looked back. But it would be the First World War that turned General History into a survey of civilization past and present, designed to expose all young men to the history and culture of the warring nations and then, the war at an end, to turn students into "citizens who shall be safe for democracy."[8]

The War Issues or War Aims courses that some 540 colleges taught in 1917 and 1918 continued in 1919 and after as Peace Aims courses, offered by 300 or more of the original 540. This initial lecture-and-discussion prototype soon received a more academic label, like the Introduction to Contemporary Civilization in the West, or CC, that Columbia began to require of all freshmen in 1919.

CC was "concerned with the appearance and development of certain institutions and of certain problems which are the common possession of the peoples of Europe and the United States, and to a greater and greater degree of all the peoples of the world."[9] As the first course in social sciences to which Columbia students were exposed, it presented historical doings "not as isolated subject-matter but in their interrelations." And it emphasized, as the course syllabus declared, "the cross-influence of economics and politics, the interpretative and directive functions of philosophy, and the integration of art and religion with the social fabric, and the merging of all these in the historical totality of each period. . . ."[10]

While large survey courses at Harvard tended to feature "great men teaching about great men," the Columbia tradition broadcast a livelier and more socially conscious brand of history whose influence could be found as far as Stanford, where a course entitled Problems of Citizenship, instituted in 1920, was soon oriented toward history by Edward Eugene Robinson. In the early thirties Cit, as students called it, turned into a History of Western Civilization, dominated by a Columbia man, Max Savelle, and using the textbook of another Columbia man: Harry Elmer Barnes's *History of Western Civilization*.

We do well to remember that war only accelerated or facilitated trends already visible before its outbreak. John Erskine, professor of literature at Columbia, remembered how "in the prewar years . . . we all became aware of increasing tension in the world and responded to it with a general speeding up of our serious activities. We hatched so many schemes for improving education and saving mankind that we bewildered ourselves."[11] Erskine himself hatched one scheme with a great future. It turned about "the presentation of great authors and their works to young people," who "knew little or nothing . . . about the Bible, or Homer, or Vergil, or Dante, or the other giants . . . "; and it was about the best-sellers of ancient times: great books "that ha[ve] meaning and continue to ha[ve] meaning, for a variety of people over a long period of time."[12]

Unsuccessful at first, in 1920 Erskine at last persuaded the college faculty at Columbia to let him try out his Great Books course, in a class divided into discussion sections numbering between fifteen and thirty students, led by the like of Mortimer Adler, Mark Van Doren, Rexford Tugwell, Moses Hadas, and Clifton Fadiman. Continued at Columbia by teachers like Jacques Barzun and Lionel Trilling, carried to Chicago and elsewhere by Erskine's instructors and students, Great Books (or Great Books by any other name!) reflected the same spirit that gave rise to Western Civ. Jacques Barzun, who took CC in 1923 and later taught it for ten years, also took Honors (Erskine's Great Books course) between 1925 and 1927, before teaching it in turn. As he remembers in a letter of February 18, 1994:

> Mortimer Adler was one of the instructors of a section of "Honors" and when he joined Hutchins at Chicago he carried the idea with him. . . . From there, the pattern spread to the Loop—evening groups of Chicago business men reading *Antigone* and arguing about law and justice; and further still, to Aspen after its establishment as a

cultural center, where men and women of all professions spent two weeks in Executive Seminars based on the same scheme and the same type of readings. At one of these I had the pleasure of guiding the minds of Justice Hugo Black at one side of the table and, on the other, of Walter Reuther of the Auto Workers Union, through the mazes of Hobbes and Montesquieu and the *Federalist*.

Would that CC or Western Civ could claim as much! Still, the record is honorable. Printed syllabi for courses offered at Chicago and Columbia between the wars reflect real sophistication. At Chicago, where Ferdinand Schevill began in 1909 to teach a course called History of Civilization (meaning Europe), we learn that his lectures of 1920 sought to show the progressive development of culture and to provide "a synthesis of human activities and knowledge, to counter the development of specialized disciplines." In 1927, after Schevill retired, the General Humanities course took the name History of Civilization. As the "Syllabus" of the new course, recast and broadened by Arthur P. Scott, declared: "the course in the Humanities deals principally with the intellectual, emotional, and artistic values in life. It limits itself in the main to Western Civilization and its Mediterranean antecedents, without denying the interest and importance of other civilizations, notably those of Asia."[13] There as elsewhere, critical awareness of nationalism, imperialism, slavery, labor and industrial problems reflected the sensibilities of the interwar years—as indeed did the absence of women and minorities as specific topics of discussion. One has to avoid anachronism when viewing the work of other generations. But I remain impressed by their scope and by their perspective—as when imperialism, for example, described as conquest, rule, and exploitation of unwilling peoples, is identified not only in modern times but in the Ancient East "and more or less recurrent since."[14] It would seem that American historians were "social," "synthetic," "critical," and self-critical much sooner than we give them credit for.

Courses generate texts; texts mirror courses more often than they inspire them. The best way to follow the evolution of Western Civ is by looking at the textbooks it inspired, most (though not all) of which bear out Ralph Waldo Emerson's dictum that each age must write its own books. And here too, as in syllabi, my first impression is that, far from dumbing down an ill-prepared public, America's textbook writers reflected a lively intent to share very current notions, interests, and attitudes, more at the cutting edge of the profession than at its duller end. This was American too.

In 1893 already, the same year in which he published his essay on the Frontier, Frederick Jackson Turner insisted that "each age writes the history of the past anew, with reference to the conditions uppermost in its own time." Turner's age of economic successes and preoccupations looked to economics, where the age of Guizot and Ranke had looked to politics. But Americans knew that there was more to history than economics. In the country of the common man, all human and social activities attracted more and earlier attention than elsewhere. Teaching at the university of Michigan in the late 1850s and the early sixties, Andrew Dickson White (later the first president of Cornell) was stimulated by an atmosphere "in which history became less a matter of annals and more a record of the unfolding of humanity."[15] By the turn of the century, White was enlisting anthropology and comparative religion in the study of history, whilst at Columbia James Harvey Robinson insisted that all activities of man and all the "social" sciences that observed them were crucial adjuncts to a discipline more interested in conditions and institutions than in events.[16] That discipline was *The New History*, title of a collection of essays that Robinson published in 1912 but that he and others had practiced, as M. Jourdain practiced prose, for a good while before that.

New Historians echoed the *historikerstreit* unfolding in fin-de-siècle Germany around the work of Karl Lamprecht, with its insistence on what would later be called mentalités: plumbing collective consciousness; synthesizing cultural enterprises at a time when music and art, like politics and the economy, were treated as separate entities; trying to interpret how we got here from there (*wie ist es eigentlich geworden?*). Significantly, Lamprecht's most comprehensive statement of his belief in history as "primarily a socio-psychological science" would be delivered in the United States, where he was invited to speak at the St. Louis World's Fair of 1904.[17]

If German pronouncements loomed large, that may have been because they reinforced native tendencies. One always looks to others for ideas but, even more, for confirmation of one's own ideas. Leonard Krieger has referred to the "veritable flood of textbooks" appearing before 1914.[18] James Harvey Robinson may be regarded as a major contributor to this flow. Robinson had been trained at Harvard and in Germany, but neither seems to have marked him deeply. He taught at the university of Pennsylvania in the early nineties, then went to Barnard and Columbia, which he left only in 1919 to help found the New School for Social Research. Robinson's intellectual history course at Columbia was so famous that only the largest amphitheatre on campus could accommodate it. While not participating directly in the creation of Contemporary Civilization in 1919, he was regarded as one of the founders of a course with which many of his students were involved. He certainly personifies the New History, of which Krieger regards textbooks as a characteristic expression "appropriate to their philosophy of history as an instrument of social reform,"[19] and, one may add, propaganda. Robinson's contributions broadened their scope and effectiveness.

Late-nineteenth-century textbooks had been vehicles for learning by rote, in classes where lectures often repeated reading assignments and recitations repeated both. Furthermore texts, even sophisticated texts, were about politics. As Charles Seignobos, a learned and worldly man, insisted in the preface to his *Political History of Europe Since 1814* (New York, 1899), "I have avoided all social phenomena that have had no direct effect on political life: art, science, literature, religion, private manners, and customs." This self-denying sobriety was the very contrary of Robinson's view, in which history could no longer be past politics, or a string of past events: "Our so-called standard works on history deal at length with kings and popes, courtiers and statesmen, wars waged for territory or thrones, laws passed by princes and parliaments. But these matters form only a very small part of history. . . ." Old stuff now, but exciting in its day, as is Robinson's conclusion: "It is clear that our interests are changing and consequently the kind of questions we ask the past to answer [are changing too]."[20]

Old questions, old answers no longer suited new times that called for a history fit for the Common Man. That history, moreover, should no longer cling to inflexible centuries, to invented epochs like the Middle Ages or the Renaissance which Haskins had shown to be very dubious notions, even to generational categories, all of which were subject to time lags, overlappings, and significant variations in space. So, where official history still followed Thucydides, Robinson beat a path toward Herodotus. Conditions as well as events, transitional periods as well as crises, developments in the past, facets of the present, all these and more were grist to history's mill. All history was the business of history. To plumb such vast territories, the historian must use "the newer sciences of man": anthropology, archaeology historical and prehistorical, social and animal psychology, sociology, political economy, the comparative study of religions, but also the natural sciences which are not our rivals but our allies.[21] And, as a first step toward comprehensive history, Robinson, while still at the University of Pennsylvania, initiated a series of Translations and Reprints from the Original Sources of European History (University of Pennsylvania Press, 1894–99).

Then the textbooks started. In 1902, an *Introduction to the History of Western Europe* would be seconded by two volumes of *Readings in European History* (1904). From 1902 to 1924, the *Introduction* sold between 10,000 and 30,000 copies a year; the *Readings* sold about 83,000 copies in all: not a bad score. In 1907, together with his student, friend, and colleague Charles Beard, Robinson published *The Development of Modern Europe: An Introduction to the Study of Current History*, which, as the title indicates, subordinated past to present. The revised text of 1930 is especially attractive in the way it uses works of fiction as historical sources, and no less for the serious attention it shows to women: Mrs. Radcliffe, Jane Austen, George Eliot, the Brontë sisters of course; but also woman suffrage (six index entries), women's employment (two entries), women's rights (one entry). Not bad for its day.

A partial list of Robinson's students reads like an honor roll of interwar American historians of Europe, and of textbook writers too: Harry Elmer Barnes, Charles Beard, Carl Becker, Carlton Hayes, John H. Randall, Salwyn Schapiro, James Shotwell, Preserved Smith, Lynn Thorndyke; historians of the world like the brothers G. W. and J. B. Botsford; of civilization like Shotwell and Thorndyke; of the making of the modern mind like Randall and Preserved Smith; but above all narrators of European history, justified as "the seat of that continuous high civilization which we call 'western'—which has come to be the distinctive civilization of the American continents as well as of Europe."[22]

In the hands of good students the scope of history alters and expands. "Old landmarks drop out of sight," James Shotwell explained in the fourteenth edition of the *Encyclopedia Britannica*, "perspective changes. . . ." Hayes and Schapiro devoted more attention to the industrial revolution and to the problems it created. Written during the Great War and revised in 1926, Hayes's *Political and Social*

History of Modern Europe was followed in 1938 by a *Political and Cultural History of Modern Europe*. The shift from "social" to the more comprehensive "cultural" was significant. But more changed than nuances. The 1926 version offered maps but no illustrations; published as the thirties ended, its successor reveled in illustrations, many of them reproductions of Gilray, an eighteenth-century draftsman whose prejudices came close to those of the author. Perspective opened up. Robinson's *Ordeal of Civilization* began with the breakup of the Roman Empire and the rise of Christianity. Harry Elmer Barnes's *History of Western Civilization* (1935) begins with primitive societies, notes the agricultural revolution of the Neolithic Age, goes well beyond outdated versions of a heritage beginning only with the Greeks.

The 1930 edition of Columbia's *Introduction to Contemporary Civilization in the West* describes the postwar United States as "a scene of complacent well-being that verges upon smug self-satisfaction."[23] We know that this was changing even as the comment went to print. No one reflected this more vividly than Barnes, a reforming penologist, pacifist, and socialist. His *History of Western Civilization* and his *Intellectual and Cultural History of the Western World* (1937; revised 1941) make clear the author's belief that the mass slaughter of modern war challenged the doctrine of progress; that capitalism, nationalism, democracy, and religion were on their last legs; that militarism, crime, poverty, and "sexual misery" threatened an end to civilization.[24]

Robinson's apostolic succession appears at its most striking in the work of Carl Becker and of Becker's students: Geoffrey Bruun, Leo Gershoy, Louis Gottschalk and Robert Palmer, a doughty quartet of editors and writers. Becker wrote relatively little, and the texts that he wrote (though they made him independently comfortable)[25] were meant for high school use. His *Modern History* (1931) was subtitled *The Rise of a Democratic, Scientific and Industrialized Civilization*. Like *The Story of Civilization* (1940), it reflected Becker's secularism, pragmatism, relativism, gentle humor, and brilliant writing. Where Barnes's civilization lurches dangerously toward self-dug ditches, Becker's continues to advance thanks to the growth of scientific knowledge, the development of humane feelings, the persistence of democratic ideas, the spread of economic interdependence, the marriage of nationalism and liberalism. One would think that Cornell, where Becker taught, was beyond the reach of press or radio. It was not, however, beyond the reach of prejudice. This gentlest of men was denounced as a Communist in 1935 and again in 1940; but his publishers, Silver, Burdett & Co., successfully fought off both attacks. Their author's religious skepticism, on the other hand, created more serious problems. Becker had long believed that less religion and more manners would improve a lot of "good" people. When his treatment of indulgences offended Roman Catholics on school boards, notably in New York City, the offending passages had to be reworded.[26]

How subject were authors and publishers to ideological and political pressures? We can hazard a sketchy answer based on the correspondence between a successful author, Edward McNall Burns, and his editors at W. W. Norton.[27] The first edition of *Western Civilizations* was copyrighted in 1941, and, by the time of the second edition (1945), some forty colleges and universities (including Stanford, MIT, Vassar, Pomona, Emory, and Hunter) had adopted the book. But the author's views stirred criticism. As the publisher wrote in January 1942, "we must face the fact that your book will be hurt by your treatment of nationalism, war, and [by] the last hundred pages. Allen & Unwin were very keen on an English edition until they came to this last section." Despite other similar criticism of his Quaker pacifism, Burns held fast, and his publisher's files of the 1950s reveal frequent objections to the book's "propagandizing for pacifism." A letter of September 1956 quotes a Stanford critic: "Burns sticks his neck out on his little hobby horses: anti-religious feeling and pacifism." It was from the former that the real trouble came.

In November 1946, a priest in Newark, New Jersey, Father Toohey, while denouncing state education as atheistic, cited Burns's *Western Civilizations*, which "denies the divinity of Christ." The Convention of Holy Name Societies of Northern New Jersey adopted resolutions that denounced the United Nations and also, for good measure, Burns's text as "containing material offensive to all religious faiths." Responding to their pressure, the Colleges of New Jersey prohibited class use of the book after February 1947. Since Burns taught at Rutgers, this meant that he could not use his own book, any more than his students and colleagues could use it in other New Jersey establishments. Faced with a serious loss of sales, Norton's editors wrote to the New Jersey Committee of Education promising revisions "to meet in part at least" objections raised by "certain elements of the Roman Catholic Church" to remarks bearing on the divinity of Christ and the chastity of the clergy. Concurrently and more constructively, a Fordham historian was hired to go over the third edition, which he found "pervaded by atheistic naturalism and a crude Darwinism." The crucial suggestions of Professor Ross Hoffman's report must have borne fruit, since in 1950 New Jersey reauthorized use of Burns's text. Burns remained religiously suspect ("he must be a Jew"), but acceptable enough for more successful editions to continue to appear, as well as a companion text, *World Civilizations*, written with Philip L. Ralph.

We do well to remember that attempts to impose some kind of conformity are not new in the land, any more than attempts to challenge conformity. In 1835, Tocqueville could think of no other country where one found less independence of thought and freedom of discussion. That was American provincialism, and the restrictive side of its democracy. Provincialism waned, democracy grew more permissive, and censorship and self-censorship persisted; only terms and notions changed: in the days when one could be rude about Jews and blacks, one had to be careful what one said about Communists and Catholics. Some moral minority or majority has always been there, some intellectual and cultural hierarchies have always been menaced and asserted, some militants have always militated for their version of what is true and just, and always sparked opposition as militant and shrill. Yet authors and publishers of textbooks that are *also* commercial enterprises are likely to heed invitations and demands relevant to adoptions and sales. Euphemization of language, edulcoration of ideas, existed long before the wars of multiculturalism and of political correctness.

Burns's problems with critics of his religious views confirm my own impressions while teaching Western Civ from the McCarthy era of the early 1950s to the 1980s: religion proved a more sensitive subject than politics properly speaking. Becker's political liberalism had proved less troublesome than his secularist skepticism. Even so, and whatever the stumbling blocks, most textbooks I have seen, beginning with those of Robinson, reflect strongly held views. There is nothing bland about them, and they address readers as intelligent adults open to information and enlightenment. The author's personal orientation, whether Marxist with Barnes, pacifist with Burns, Catholic with Carlton Hayes, strikes me less as intrusive than as adding flavor and interest to urbane discourse.

This was going to change somewhat when more undergraduates were required to attend introductory surveys where they were told "to read on successive Mondays, Wednesdays, and Fridays, successive chapters in a prescribed textbook" destined to remain "the principal source of information for most students." That is what Carl Becker describes with resignation and some distaste in his editor's introduction to just such a book: Wallace Ferguson and Geoffrey Bruun's *Survey of European Civilization* (1936, 1939, 1942). The *Survey* was a true textbook as we have come to expect them—impersonal, detached, economical, not very memorable, but profitably enduring for Houghton Mifflin. After Becker's death, "editorship" would pass to William Langer and then to Leo Gershoy, a Becker student like Bruun. But, while the tone might change and differ from author to author, while coverage might begin with the Renaissance or Rome or Egypt or prehistoric times (many texts worked their way backward from one edition to another), one assumption remained constant.

As Ferguson and Bruun put it, Europe represented "the logical center and European history the logical axis for what is now almost a world civilization."[28] By their time, first the approach, then the experience of a second world war had made Western Civ steadily more relevant (universities like Iowa and Ohio introduced it in 1943, UCLA in 1950),[29] and the European origins of American history especially significant. Some of the great teachers of Western Civ were themselves exiled Europeans, like Ferdinand Schevill and Karl Weinberg in Chicago. It was one of these, George Mosse, who explained to the American Historical Association in 1948 that courses in modern European or United States history were no longer enough. Freshmen needed to understand the relation of Europe and America in order to appreciate America's share in the general Europeanization of the world: "the student thus, from the very start, obtains a new sense of proportion as far as the American development is concerned."[30]

So Western Civ remained steadfastly Eurocentric, but that was pretty much all that it *remained.* Cutting the cloth to fit the fashions that altered with the perceptions and problems of the moment, lectures and texts shed the confidence of the 1920s for the doubts and self-criticism of a less sanguine postwar. Change did not necessarily mean progress; progress did not illumine the history of social processes. As Burns wrote to his editor in March 1956, "we live in an age of chaos, not of order." What would he have written in 1986? Yet disorder made for choice or, at least, for variety. Great men, great ideas, great processes like urbanization, or the succession and leapfrog of ideas, all found their chroniclers and readers. Allardyce gives the impression that, after World War II, Western Civ shifted from facts to the interpretation of facts, from claims of objectivity to proclamations of relativity, from narrative to analysis.[31] But most of these novelties (or aspirations) could already be found between the wars, indeed in the New History that preceded the First World War. Some of the excellent suggestions for improving Western Civ advanced at a 1985 conference titled "What Americans Should Know" simply rehearsed approaches pioneered by Robinson: more primary documents, more comparative treatment, more contemporary references, more insistence that values are relative, more broad themes (how can Western Civ escape them?), and less parochialism—which was just what, each in his own way, Barnes, Becker, Carlton Hayes, and Mosse stood for.[32]

You can't blame historians for not reading old textbooks; it's all they can do to keep up with new ones. But we do keep reinventing the inventions of the past, even though our brio is less than that of our predecessors. And we do add new apprehensions. The experience of growth had inspired a confidence based on growth. The experience of conflict inspired interpretations based on conflict. Looming doldrums reinforced self-doubt. More recently, challenges to Western hegemony call for more attention to the challengers; challenges to a once unreflective domination evoke once subordinate groups that must be brought to notice. Cultural unity and integration are pressed out, cultural differences and disintegration march in; at least in theory. When, in 1982, participants in the American Historical Association discussion opened by Allardyce called for less parochialism, that was not in order to expose students to some transatlantic sophistication but rather, as Carolyn Lougee put it, "to formulate a vision of coherent diversity and cultural pluralism."[33] Easier said than done.

The history of history is—also—the history of history's taking notice of hitherto invisible or irrelevant groups: the people, the workers, the masses, most of whom began to get their due before and after the First World War. After the 1960s, new claimants for notice battered at the gates. Typically, in 1979, Abby Kleinbaum raised the question of women's history and the Western Civilization survey: the traditional survey ignored the majority—not just women but slaves and other groups that did not fit the popular stereotype of progress toward more freedom and more goods.[34] In fact, by 1979 that stereotype was far from popular, and a good few surveys hardly ignored either women or slaves. The index of my own *Modern History of Europe*, written in the late 1960s, published in 1971, sports nine entries dealing with women, including a five-page section about their emancipation; and twenty-nine entries dealing with slaves and slavery, rather more than what socialism gets. More representative, perhaps, the 1976 edition of Walbank, Taylor, and Bailkey's *Civilization Past and Present* includes a three-page "profile" on women in history and the wrongs they suffered. Its epilogue reflects a fraught, self-questioning mood, with two and one-half pages devoted to *1984*, three on the ecological crunch, two and one-half on the anguish of change (alienation, crime), and the remainder dwelling mostly on threats to the human condition.

The fact is that one can always find what one is looking for; and Abby Klein-baum was more right than wrong. A cursory survey reveals little or no attention paid to women in representative texts and readings of the 1950s and sixties, with one suggestive exception: Leon Bernard and Theodore Hodges's *Readings in European History* (Notre Dame, 1958). Edited by two Catholic historians, it includes a Christian martyr (Blandina), Joan of Arc, Francesca da Rimini chatting to Dante, a witch, and several crowned heads: Catherine of Aragon, Catherine the Great, Maria-Theresa. Saints, sinners, and great ladies: the Catholic church knows where its bread is buttered.

But things were going to change. Between 1956 and 1978, women's index entries in Robert Palmer and Joel Colton's classic text increased from nine to sixteen. Between 1959 and 1990, selections from women in my own *Western Tradition* rose from five to seventeen. Other things changed too. In 1929 as in 1907, Robinson and Beard's *Development of Modern Europe* contained maps but no illustrations. In 1942, Ferguson and Bruun's *Survey of European Civilization* offered black-and-white illustrations as well as maps. By 1957, Brinton, Christopher, and Wolf's *Modern Civilization* boasted illustrations almost as sophisticated as the text. Instructor's manuals were introduced to cater to the needs or to the sloth of those who decide what texts to adopt or who, the text once adopted, welcome help in teaching it.

Design increasingly complements substance, enhances it, sometimes replaces it. Swiftly revised editions, intended to counter the used-book market, accumulate creative gimmicks. Production values take over: art essays accompanying splendid color plates; complex cartographic essays like that by Michael Conzen in Chambers et al., *The Western Experience*; or "part-opening time-lines, a key topic list at the beginning of each chapter, thought-provoking questions with each of the more than 200 primary-source selections in the text, and chapter review questions" in Kagan, Ozment, and Turner's *Western Heritage*. Published in 1995 by D. C. Heath, Lynn Hunt, Thomas Martin, Barbara Rosenwein, Po-Chia Hsia, and Bonnie Smith's *Challenge of the West* comes equipped with *A Student's Guide to Reading Maps, Interpreting Documents, and Preparing for Exams*, and *Instructor's Guide* with annotated chapter outlines and lecture suggestions, a video-disc whose 2,100 images are bar coded, captioned, and indexed for classroom use, a *Computerized Testing Program* and *Test Item File* of over 4,000 questions, and a transparency set. All cater to shorter tolerance levels, abbreviated attention spans, and students who, Prentice Hall's marketing manager reports, "are simply not reading the material assigned to them, whether in the textbooks or from primary sources."[35]

That statement provides perspective about the plight of Western Civ as of other courses. Whatever we choose to call them, culture wars are as American as apple pie; curricular combat has always been a favorite academic sport; canons have evolved with perspective. If students don't read, does it matter that they don't read Toni Morrison rather than Pascal? Perhaps we should worry less about generations growing up ill indoctrinated and more about their growing up illiterate.

Newly fashionable notions, meanwhile, continue to be injected into revised editions like silicone, to amplify the original product and make it more appetizing. This too dates back to generations before illiteracy became a serious problem. Louis B. Snyder's *Making of Modern Man* (1967) already integrated documents with every chapter, added essays by "outstanding historians in the field," devoted serious attention to artistic and cultural activities as to psychological interpretations, included critical selections on imperialism. But its outstanding historians represented the grand old tradition (Becker, Salwyn Schapiro, Carlton Hayes), and the title itself would be unacceptable today. Wise production managers opt for less verbiage and more tricks. The 1976 edition of Wallbank's *Civilization* offered interchapter outlines, "profiles" of great men like Pascal or great topics like industrialism, color plates, maps, chronological charts, and a pronunciation key in the index providing the correct enunciation for all proper names of persons and places cited. Scott, Foresman were showing the way.

Production was not the only realm where authors were no longer left to work alone. Multiplicity of techniques called for multiplicity of skills in writing too. Generalists increasingly gave way to specialists working as a team, coordinated by production managers who were sometimes called editors. Collaborative world histories by many authors, like Lavisse and Rambaud's *Histoire générale* (1893–1901) or the *Cambridge Modern History* (1902–12) were nothing new. One-volume team enterprises bringing together two, three, or five authors were a new phenomenon. In the 1950s, joint authorship became a marketing ploy, before it established itself as the norm. William Langer lent his name and scholarship to a coproduction of Harper & Row with *American Heritage*, responsible for the illustrations. Prentice Hall sold Brinton, Christopher, and Wolf's excellent history "from Plato to Pareto" on the strength of a distinguished trio of names. Then confederates and auxiliaries began to show up.

In the late 1970s Houghton Mifflin offered *A History of Western Society* by John P. McKay, Bennett Hill, and John Buckler: social history was pulling ahead of intellectual history. More "relevant," more approachable, and just as well written as the Brinton book, McKay's acknowledgments list twenty-nine names of instructors "who have read and critiqued the manuscript through its development." By 1995 Hunt et al.'s *Challenge of the West* acknowledged by name 269 colleagues "who have contributed formal written reviews," 8 more who presumably gave aid and comfort, and 10 production staff collaborating in "the development of this textbook." A book is no longer written; it is developed.

It sounds like a cumbersome process; but the multiadvisor, multiauthor text drives out the single author generalist. In 1955, Stewart Easton of the City College of New York finished *The Heritage of the Past, from the Earliest Times to 1500*, and Richard Brace of Northwestern University completed *The Making of the Modern World, from the Renaissance to the Present*. Published by Holt, Rinehart in 1960, these were model textbooks, challenging and beautifully written, especially that of Easton. Holt, Rinehart prints them no more; they are no longer to be found. In 1973, D. C. Heath in search of new approaches published F. Roy Willis's *Western Civilization: An Urban Perspective*: three volumes keying civilization to the rise of the city and the process of urbanization. Twenty years later, Willis's urbane inter-lacing of cultural, political, and socioeconomic strands has been left to go out of print. It is not the publisher's fault: they print what sells, produce what courses will consume.

The vogue of World Civilization texts and courses is part of these adjustments to changed, or allegedly changing, demand. The Second World War spurred an interest in human rights extending beyond the Western Hemisphere. Colonial problems and decolonization, the self-assertion of colonial people and of blacks in America, the new scope of international relations publicized by penetrating media and by international bodies with a vested interest in global issues, the decline of Europe itself and the worldwide range of American interests, all sug-gested a new perspective. In the 1960s, just as UNESCO began to bring out its unwieldy *History of Mankind*, the Ford Foundation decided to encourage the study and teaching of history on a global scale. Supported by a Ford grant, Leften Stavrianos of Northwestern University, where the history department left fresh-men free to choose between introductory courses in Western Civ, World Civ, or American History, published his *World since 1500: A Global History* (1966). "Tra-ditional topics of European history," the preface declared, "are irrelevant for world history and must be discarded." In 1964, with a grant from the Carnegie Corporation, William McNeill of the University of Chicago began to write his *World History*, tried it out in an experimental course offered in 1964–65, and revised it by the end of 1966. Published in 1967 by the Oxford University Press, the book achieved a well-deserved *succès d'éstime*. On the market, as one pub-lisher put it, it proved a total bomb. Problems of compression, selection, interpre-tation, awesome enough in narrower fields, grew direr on a global scale; and the increasing abstraction that scale imposed went ill with the decreasing sophistica-tion of the student body. Besides, since World Civ grew out of Western Civ (whether as extension or as reaction), it was condemned to use its language and to reflect its values even when it rejected them.

More traditional texts sometimes did better, when they adjusted to the new trend. The preface to the 1976 edition of Wallbank's *Civilization* spoke of space-ship earth and the global village, and claimed that until 1942, when the first edition of the book appeared, "no college text had surveyed the history of civili-zation as the joint achievement of all humanity." Long before Ford or Carnegie broached such notions, Wallbank and Taylor apparently set out to "present a survey of global cultural history treating the story of humanity not as a unique European experience but as a global one." They did, indeed, devote significant space to overseas cultures, to *négritude*, to Indian and Latin American literatures. But the global village remained a cultural colony of Europe, whose "influence spread to virtually all parts of the non-European world," and whose colonial enterprise (that interwar texts vigorously denounced) was recognized as an "in-strument of cultural diffusion on a huge scale."

This is the great problem that world historians face: they flee Eurocentrism only to meet Europe in Samarra, where they are forced to recognize its leading role, especially "from about 1500 when the European Far West began to outstrip the other major civilizations of the world."[36] That is William McNeill, for whom the rise of the West to dominance over the globe constitutes the main theme of modern history. Why? Because "European inventiveness and ingenuity" contrasts with Chinese, Moslem, Hindu rejection of novelties.[37] Europe is ever transforming itself; others do not do so. Reluctant, retarded, or inert, non-Western dwellers in McNeill's world aspire to Westernization or are simply destined to it, "since power, wealth, and truth itself beckon men everywhere to pursue industrialization, democratization, and science—all of them stemming directly from the Western past."[38] Reasonable enough in the 1960s when they were formulated, such views ill fit the more demanding myths and aspirations of the 1990s. Though they may start out with exciting ideas, serious historians risk ending up politically incorrect when they write serious history.

That could be one of the reasons why the "stampede away from Western Civ" that John A. Scott observed in 1976[39] has slowed down since, and Western Civ texts today outsell World Civ by roughly two to one. What is true of texts is true of courses too. By 1985, most participants in the Michigan conference that led to the book *What Americans Should Know* "preferred a survey based on the history of Western Civilization."[40] Despite what may be the wave of the future, declared Richard Sullivan with an eye on a wave of the past, "I suspect that the Western Civilization survey will be part of the academic landscape for a while. . . . Along with the American survey course, the Western Civilization survey strikes me as the only fixed and firm anchor the historical profession has in the chaos of modern education."[41] Edward Fox said the same thing differently: "no young citizen of the United States can find his true historical identity outside the context of the European past . . . our modern world was created largely by Europe."[42]

These people do not want Western Civ to remain unaltered, they submit a wealth of suggestions for improving the old course, but once again most of their (excellent) suggestions are strongly reminiscent of Robinson's innovations or, at least, of their spirit. As Mr. Dooley observed: "I see grreat changes takin' place in my day, but no change at all ivry fifty years."

One of our day's great changes is the tendency of some teachers to reject texts for sources, and to abandon collections of readings crammed with many shortish passages for a few integral documents like Rousseau's *Social Contract*. There is plenty of room for debate on this (in the absence of text, what will furnish the context?), as there is in the proposed reforms of texts and syllabi criticized as too narrow, too blinkered, too exclusive or too contrived. But what William Bennett denounced in his 1992 book, *The De-valuing of America*, appears rather as a re-valuing, similar to reinterpretations that have never ceased since the inception of the course. Meanwhile, alternative courses designed to provide more self-esteem than learning compete with Western Civ but do not replace it.

Publishers so far have little reason to worry. Describing "The Decline and Rise of Western Civilization" in December 1982,[43] Karen Winkler reported the ninth edition of Burns's *Western Civilizations* selling more copies in 1980 than in any previous version, Wallbank's *Civilization* "selling better than ever," and other contenders proving "remarkably successful." From a national low of 200,000 or

300,000 students in the 1970s, Western Civ courses enrolled over 500,000 by the early 1980s. "Teachers are going back to the standard text. They are finding that students don't have the background in high school that allows them to follow the thematic approach."[44] Isn't that where we came in?

NOTES

1. Gilbert Allardyce, "Rise and Fall of the Western Civilization Course," *American Historical Review*, June 1982, pp. 695, 725.

2. John Erskine, *My Life as a Teacher* (Philadelphia, 1948), p. 26.

3. Annual Report of the American Historical Association for 1906 (Washington, D.C., 1907), p. 122, quoted in Allardyce, "Rise and Fall," p. 702.

4. Erskine, *My Life*, p. 154.

5. See *New York Times*, July 1, 1960, November 30, 1964, May 2, 1976, and, most recently, August 18, 1994.

6. Christine Naitove and Barbara Bartle in *AHA Perspectives*, June 1983, pp. 16–21.

7. Dean Acheson on the North Atlantic Pact in Eugen Weber, *The Western Tradition*, II (Lexington, 1995), p. 666.

8. Carol Gruber, *Mars and Minerva* (Baton Rouge, 1975). See also Committee of Seven, *The Study of History in Schools* (New York, 1899), p. 18: history meant to prepare students "for social adaptation and for forceful participation in civic activities."

9. Columbia University, *An Introduction to Contemporary Civilization in the West* (Columbia, 1930), assignment one.

10. Ibid., p. 4.

11. John Erskine, *The Memory of Certain Persons* (Philadelphia, 1947), p. 206.

12. Erskine, *My Life*, pp. 165–71.

13. See Richard Popp, ed., *Teaching Western Civ at Chicago* (Chicago, 1987), n.p.

14. Hayward Keniston, Ferdinand Schevill, and Arthur P. Scott, eds., *Introductory General Course in the Humanities: Syllabus* (Chicago, 1931 ff), pp. 338–39.

15. *Autobiography of Andrew Dickson White* (New York, 1905), p. 42.

16. A. D. White, *A History of the Warfare of Science with Theology in Christendom*, II (New York, 1903), pp. 393–96.

17. Karl Lamprecht, *What Is History?* (New York, 1905).

18. Krieger in John Higham, Leonard Krieger, and Felix Gilbert, *History* (New York, 1965), p. 258.

19. Krieger, ibid., p. 267. For Robinson, see Luther V. Hendricks, *James Harvey Robinson, Teacher of History* (New York, 1946), p. 106.

20. J. H. Robinson, *The New History* (New York, 1912), pp. 135–37.

21. "The New Allies of History," read to AHA in December 1910, reprinted in ibid., p. 83.

22. C. J. H. Hayes, *A Political and Cultural History of Modern Europe*, I (New York, 1936), p. vii. Interestingly, at practically the same time, the Introductory General Course in the Humanities at Chicago was described as essentially a course in "our ruling Western Civilization . . . our own Western Civilization . . . ," C. S. Boucher, *The Chicago College Plan* (Chicago, 1935), p. 44.

23. Columbia University, *Introduction to Contemporary Civilization*, p. 352.

24. Harry Elmer Barnes, *History of Western Civilization* (New York, 1935), p. viii; Barnes,

Intellectual and Cultural History of the Western World (New York, 1937; revised 1941), pp. 1116–17, 1214–15.

25. Burleigh Taylor Wilkins, *Carl Becker* (Cambridge, 1961), p. 152.

26. Ibid., pp. 172–73; Charlotte Watkins Smith, *Carl Becker: On History* (Ithaca, 1956), p. 11.

27. I am grateful to Don Lamm, president of W. W. Norton, and to the publishers for opening access to the Norton papers in the Department of Special Collections, Columbia University Library.

28. Wallace Ferguson and Geoffrey Bruun, *Survey of European Civilization*, I [to 1660] (Boston, 1936), preface.

29. At Harvard, Western Civilization first appears as a course title in 1946, with Crane Brinton's Introduction to the Social Inheritance of Western Civilization.

30. George Mosse, "Freshman History," *Social Studies*, March 1949, p. 3. First at Iowa, then at Wisconsin, Mosse was one of the legendary presenters of Western Civilization.

31. Allardyce, "Rise and Fall," p. 715.

32. Josef Konvitz, ed., *What Americans Should Know: Western Civilization or World History?* (Lansing, 1985).

33. Carolyn Lougee, "Comments" on Allardyce, in *American Historical Review*, June 1982, p. 729.

34. Abby Kleinbaum, "Women's History and the Western Civilization Survey," *History Teacher* (1979).

35. Alison Prendergast, marketing manager, history, for Prentice Hall, in a circular addressed to history teachers, designed to publicize the fifth edition of Kagan et al.'s *Western Heritage*.

36. William McNeill, *A World History* (New York, 1967), p. 416.

37. Ibid., p. 286.

38. Ibid., p. 437.

39. John A. Scott, "Invited Comment" on Beyond Western Civilization symposium, in *History Teacher*, August 1977, p. 538.

40. Konvitz, *What Americans Should Know*, p. 6. An original founder of the present Western Civilization course at Chicago, McNeill's attempts to replace Western Civ with World Civ there seem to have met scant success. Meanwhile at UCLA, where students can choose between the two courses, present enrollments in World Civilization courses tarry round one-fifth or one-sixth of those in Western Civ.

41. Ibid., p. 264.

42. Ibid., p. 205.

43. Karen Winkler, "Textbooks: The Decline and Rise of Western Civilization," *Chronicle of Higher Education*, December 1, 1982, pp. 23–24.

44. Ibid.

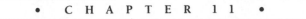
American Classical Historiography

RICHARD SALLER

THE HISTORIOGRAPHY of ancient Greece and Rome presents special problems in meeting the aim of this volume—that is, to explore the *distinctive* character of professional historical scholarship as it developed in the United States since the late nineteenth century. Classics as a field is especially transnational in character, based on a notion of a common European cultural heritage. Classical historians are expected to read publications written in French, German, or Italian, and a recent conference on the city-state in classical antiquity and medieval Italy pointedly eschewed translation of the conference papers into English for publication.[1] Through the twentieth century, there has been significant circulation of classical historians between the United States and Europe. Before World War I, many American classicists went to Germany for their doctoral research. Over the past twenty-five years, ancient historians educated in England have moved to the United States to occupy the majority of senior positions in classical history at major American research universities. This movement across national boundaries makes it difficult to isolate the distinctively American contribution.

To illustrate the difficulty, two of the towering figures in classical history in the twentieth century, M. I. Rostovtzeff and A. Momigliano, held appointments at American universities, but I cannot see how the intellectual formation of either man could be characterized as significantly American. Momigliano said of Rostovtzeff that he would not have written his great *Social and Economic History of the Roman Empire* (1926) if he had not left Russia in exile. That may be true in the sense that his exile to the United States was an important stimulus, but that is not to say that the work shows particularly American intellectual influences. The book was written soon after his arrival in the United States in 1920 and was marked by his Russian experience.[2] As for Momigliano, it has been suggested that he was more willing later in life to write about his Jewish heritage in an American milieu, but he was certainly writing about it before he took up the Whiting Visiting Professorship at the University of Chicago in 1974. As his colleague there, I would say that he did not convey the impression of intellectual assimilation to the United States.

To clarify the project and to keep it within manageable bounds, it seems sensible initially to define "distinctively American" rather narrowly by setting aside these problematic cases. In limiting my focus, I will admittedly pass over some of the most distinguished cosmopolitan scholarship in the field. To name only two major contemporary Roman historians at American institutions, I omit Peter Brown and Glen Bowersock on the grounds that, though they have made landmark contributions to late imperial history, I am unable to define qualities of their work that are *distinctively* American. My essay will trace the following themes: (I) the "native American" pragmatic thread of classical historiography; (II) the American rejection of, or disinterest in, Marxist approaches to classical history; and (III) classical historians' involvement in current American political controversies.

I. Chester Starr, one of the founders and first president of the American Association of Ancient Historians, recently reviewed the field of ancient history in the United States and pointed to what he believed to be distinctively American. American ancient historians are "far less inclined than their French or English peers to apply seriously concepts from anthropology or sociology; their analyses are much less theoretical than say Finley in *The Ancient Economy* or, better, *Politics in the Ancient World*. One might sum up the distinction by labeling American scholarship as pragmatic, a source of optimistic strength if also limiting the free play of imagination."[3] Setting aside M. I. Finley for the moment, I believe Starr is right to suggest that American classical historians' self-identity has been marked by a pragmatic, antitheoretical streak. The works of Tenney Frank and Lily Ross Taylor, the two most distinguished "native American" Roman historians of the earlier twentieth century, illustrate how this self-identity was manifested.

Tenney Frank is interesting for my purposes because he offers a direct comparison with Rostovtzeff. Frank (1876–1939; Ph.D., University of Chicago, 1903) published two major books in the second decade of the twentieth century: *Roman Imperialism* (1914) and *Economic History of Rome* (1920). Shortly after the latter appeared, it was put in the shade by Rostovtzeff's monumental *Social and Economic History of the Roman Empire* (1926). One year later Frank published a revised edition of his *Economic History*, which responded to Rostovtzeff's book. In the revision, we can see him defining his American understanding of Roman history against Rostovtzeff's understanding.

Frank took the view that American historians occupied a specially privileged position from which to understand the Roman republic. It was superior, in his mind, insofar as it was not distorted by oppressive European traditions with all their rigidities. The preface to his *Roman Imperialism* (1914), which argues the thesis that Roman expansion was a matter of defensive responses to others' aggression, makes this explicit: whereas "old-world political traditions have taught historians to accept territorial expansion as a matter of course," Frank as an American was able to discard that false premise and so more truly interpret Roman (and American) behavior.[4] Jerzy Linderski has elegantly demonstrated how "Tenney Frank's Rome was a mirror image of the America of McKinley and Theodore Roosevelt,"[5] but for Frank it was a matter of getting rid of the blinkers of Old World tradition. Frank's underlying assumptions of the unnatural distortions of the Old World are perhaps most starkly stated in his chapter on Egypt in the *Economic History of Rome*, where he notes the peculiarity of Egypt: "Nature long ago eliminated normal society in Egypt."[6] What did he mean by the disappearance of "normal society"? "The river imposed autocracy and servility as the price of existence. Individualism was out of place. . . ." By implication, he as an American was better able to appreciate the "natural"—that is, "individualistic"—than Europeans of his own day, who still lived within the "rigid class system of modern European states."[7]

It was Frank's view that Americans were especially well placed to understand the early Romans of the republic, because they were kindred spirits. The early Romans of Frank's *Economic History* were orderly, pragmatic agriculturalists, who from the beginning had a healthy respect for private property rights. (In fact, the "beginning" is wholly unattested by any evidence.) The respect for private property began after the Romans took land away from the early natives of Italy, but "it is not likely that the savages who were there before contested possession with any vigor. Peoples who use land chiefly as hunting ground do not risk enslavement or death in the defense of their lands."[8] In other words, the early Romans, like frontier Americans of Frank's own day, were justified in taking land from "savage" natives on the grounds that it was not fully utilized. Under Roman governance, Italy and the rest of the empire prospered through the second century after Christ under a policy of laissez-faire in accordance with natural individual liberty. "Economic and social laissez-faire has never been more consistently practiced [than under Augustus]. After all, it was probably the quickest road to success if he really cared for Romanization. Peace through the empire gave the opportunity for material development to those who desired it, and prosperity brought satisfaction and goodwill towards the government, which in turn invited closer relations and a natural assimilation of Roman customs."[9] In the Romans, then, Frank found the antecedents of American liberalism.[10]

As an American who naturally had a direct intuition of the truth about the Roman world, Frank had no need of conceptual sophistication. Instead of theory, Frank possessed American pragmatic common sense, as evidenced in his proverbs and his racism.[11] He explained the lack of commercial development in Rome in these terms: "Necessity, the mother of crafts as well as of arts, never forced [the Romans] into apprenticeship in those occupations that develop the love for artificial beauty and train the instincts for commercial enterprise."[12] The "instincts" were based on race, and changes of racial composition were the most basic cause of the major events of Roman history, including the fall of the empire. "The irresistible determination, the power of self-control, the stolid puritanism, as well as the hardness and self-sufficiency of the native old Roman were racial qualities, a part of the blood inheritance transmitted after the centuries of hard-handed struggle had weeded out the unfit."[13] As race accounted for Rome's success, so also it accounted for its decline. "It would be interesting to know how far the social transmutation we have tried to follow [i.e., the migration of slaves into Italy] accounts for the fundamental changes in the Empire. Was not absolutism inevitable when the Italian, who had so equally combined liberty with law, gave way to impulsive and passionate races that had never known self-government?"[14] Whereas Rostovtzeff narrated the decline of the Roman Empire in terms of class conflict (a revolt of the peasant class against the urban bourgeoisie), Frank told a story of the contamination of the hardy stock of Roman individualists. The contrast captures the difference between the Continental interpretation and the American.

Lily Ross Taylor, Frank's most distinguished student, took her Ph.D. at Bryn Mawr in 1912, and then after fifteen years at Vassar College returned to Bryn Mawr where she taught until her retirement in 1952. Her work shares certain characteristics with Frank's. Like him, she believed in the possibility of a kind of unmediated, direct understanding of Roman antiquity. Her colleague, T. R. S. Broughton, notes that her first visit to Rome in 1909 "aroused her lifelong love of Rome," and he remembers her saying that "my aim as a teacher is to make my students feel that they are walking the streets of Rome, and seeing and thinking what Romans saw and thought."[15] This is not an intellectual ambition that places value on finding an appropriate theory or developing an original method of analysis. With hindsight, we can see the anachronisms that point to the naiveté of the hope of direct experience motivated by a sentimental attachment to the classics.

Like Frank, Taylor had a limited appreciation of ancient Rome. As long as the Romans (like Americans) acted out their love of freedom during the republic, they were worth studying. But after the Romans degenerated into servility in the later decades of the empire, Taylor lost interest: "I have no interest in cataloguing the forms of flattery. . . . I abandoned the study of ruler cult when it was in danger of affecting my sanity."[16] In other words, she had no interest in understanding deep cultural differences, nor did she have any method for such an understanding. In her account of the development of emperor cult in *The Divinity of the Roman Emperor* (1931) she distinguished between the Italians, who had better sense than to worship a living man and so worshipped Augustus' Genius, and the eastern subjects of the Roman Empire, who had a long tradition of gullible servility. Recent research has shown that this distinction between west and east is bogus—a result of Taylor's reluctance to admit that the freedom-loving Romans so quickly accepted the deification of a living man.[17] Nevertheless, it has been the standard view for more than half a century.

Of Taylor's other books, the two on the voting assemblies of the Roman republic have been perhaps her most useful and enduring contributions, and were said by Broughton to illustrate her American pragmatic interest in how institutions work.[18] Her mostly widely read book, *Party Politics in the Age of Caesar* (1949), is not peculiarly American insofar as it follows Sir Ronald Syme's *Roman Revolution* (1939) in understanding Roman politics in terms of personal alliances of kinship and friendship among the aristocracy. In its focus on the political elite, Taylor's *Party Politics* is representative of the mainstream of American scholarship on Roman political history, illustrated more recently by Erich Gruen's *Roman Politics and the Criminal Courts, 149–78 B.C.* (1968) and *The Last Generation of the Roman Republic* (1974). A counterpoint may be found in Ramsay MacMullen's work, including *Enemies of the Roman Order* (1966) and *Roman Social Relations, 50 B.C. to A.D. 284* (1974), which extend the historical horizon to the lower classes, rural laborers, and social outcasts of the Roman Empire.

II. The rise of fascism in Europe provoked migrations that threatened to inject more sophisticated social theory into American classical historiography, in particular through the mediation of Moses Finley. It is of course ironic that Starr's exemplar of European theory in classical history is Moses Finley, who was born and educated in the United States (b. 1912; B.A., Syracuse University, 1927). Studying at Columbia University with W. L. Westermann in the 1930s, Finley came into contact with the Frankfurt school in exile. His reviews from the 1930s were published in the school's *Zeitschrift für Sozialforschung* and show the influence of Marxist and other sociological thought. World War II brought a long hiatus in Finley's publications. As his major works began to appear in the early 1950s, he was caught up in the McCarthy purges in American universities. Though no evidence was produced to prove that he belonged to the Communist party, he refused to testify before the Senate Subcommittee on Internal Security. As a result, he was fired from Rutgers University in 1952. Blackballed and unable to find another position for two years, Finley emigrated from the United States to England, where A. H. M. Jones secured a fellowship for him at Jesus College, Cambridge, in 1954. By this time, Finley was more Weberian than Marxist, but his past association with Marxists and his unwillingness to name names before congressional committees were sufficient grounds for de facto condemnation.[19]

Though Finley did not take a Marxist approach to classical history at the height of his career, he did insist that Marxism be taken seriously. With the loss of his voice, the politics of classical historiography in the United States took a different course from that in Europe. To simplify, the politics in European classical historiography was organized around the axis of Marxism and its critics.[20] In the Marxist historical-developmental scheme, of course, classical antiquity was characterized as dominated by the slave mode of production; consequently, the significance of slavery in antiquity became a central issue in the debate.[21] As late as the 1980s, fierce arguments over the explanatory value of the slave mode of production for the decline of the Roman Empire were going on in England and on the Continent. In England the focal point was G. E. M. de Ste Croix's *Class Struggle in the Ancient Greek World* (1981). On the Continent, the Gramsci Institute held a major conference on the slave mode of production in Pisa in 1979, which resulted in a three-volume publication entitled *Società Romana e Produzione Schiavistica* including papers by numerous Continental and British scholars, but no American classical historian.[22]

American classical historians generally absented themselves from the argument over Marxism and slavery. Finley's teacher at Columbia, W. L. Westermann, published in 1955 the major synthetic treatment in English of ancient slavery, *The Slave Systems of Greek and Roman Antiquity*, but the book takes a positivist approach that yields a collection of evidence, not organized by a Marxist or any other problematic (with the exception of the two chapters showing that

Stoicism and Christianity cannot take credit for the decline of slavery in the Roman Empire). Despite the importance of the subject, the book is disappointing for its lack of social or economic analysis.

Starr, a successor to Frank and Taylor in taking an "American pragmatic" approach to classical history, published an article in 1958 indicating why American classical historians did not take seriously the debate over the Marxist interpretation of slavery. In "An Overdose of Slavery," Starr urged "that one view ancient slavery without the blinkers of nineteenth-century humanitarianism or twentieth-century Marxist totalitarianism."[23] In a bare fifteen pages the article sets out to demolish some of the more extravagant claims of "British socialist historians" such as George Thomson and Benjamin Farrington, but it does not show an understanding of the issue of the location of slavery in the ancient social structure. Starr believed that he had undermined the Marxist interpretation with the assertion that the proportion of slaves in the classical Athenian population was "probably one third or one quarter *at most*" (that is, as large a proportion of the population as in the antebellum American South) and concluded that "one must seriously question modern attempts to derive *all* ancient immorality" from slavery.[24] No citation indicates what Marxist or humanitarian historian had claimed that slavery was responsible for *all* ancient immorality: Starr's simple conceptualization made his conclusion both obvious and useless. Not all European classical historians were persuaded that they suffered from "a bad overdose of slavery," and the controversy over the structural significance of slavery continued without much American contribution.[25] Lacking an obvious theoretical overlay, the books and articles of Ramsay MacMullen about the lower classes mentioned above did not directly participate in this debate.

III. In the United States contemporary political issues other than Marxism—especially problems of minority rights—have stimulated the most heated debates among classicists, which have received attention in the popular press.

In the 1960s and 1970s the war in Vietnam stood at the center of the political storms in the United States. The parallel between American intervention in Southeast Asia and Roman wars of expansion seemed apparent to some ancient historians: like Rome, the United States intervened far from its borders on the pretext of a local invitation, but in reality on account of its own amoral, material interests. In the wake of the Vietnam War were published two major studies of Roman imperialism by historians in the United States: W. V. Harris's *War and Imperialism in Republican Rome, 327–70 B.C.* (1979) and Erich Gruen's *The Hellenistic World and the Coming of Rome* (1984).[26] The debate over Roman motives for expansion was international, but the Vietnam War lent a special intensity to the arguments in these books and in classrooms around the country. An evaluation of a Roman history course written by an American student in the early 1970s bluntly protested that the professor should "get the Romans out of Vietnam."

Out of the civil rights movement has grown a variety of rights movements in American politics. The classicists' professional association, the American Philological Association, has provided a small stage for battles over women's rights, lesbian and gay rights, and multicultural studies. Among its other interest groups, the APA includes the Women's Classical Caucus and the Lesbian and Gay Caucus, which have occasionally struggled over the program and the venue of the annual meeting. The tension may be judged from the fact that several years ago the officers of the APA retained legal counsel to advise in their programmatic deliberations, and they acquired insurance for directors and officers to cover legal liability.

In the field of women's studies, Sarah Pomeroy's *Goddesses, Whores, Wives, and Slaves: Women in Classical Antiquity*, published in 1975, was a landmark for its historical synthesis of women's experience in Greco-Roman antiquity. The book, now translated into numerous languages, stressed the fundamental subordination of women. Pomeroy's was certainly not the first treatment of Greek or Roman women. A decade earlier J. P. V. D. Balsdon had written a book about Roman women in which he recognized the methodological problem of understanding women's experience through sources overwhelmingly dominated by male voices.[27] For Balsdon this meant that we hear more husbands' complaints about wives than wives' complaints about husbands, and he accepted the evidence of Roman imperial funerary inscriptions, which "record the uneventful happy marriages of thousands and thousands of ordinary men and women."[28] By contrast, Pomeroy (rightly) emphasized the inherently hierarchical nature of the (happy or unhappy) conjugal bond in Greek and Roman antiquity.

The reviews of *Goddesses, Whores, Wives, and Slaves* from the male academic establishment generally praised it for its range and grasp of the evidence, while noting that it was better regarding Greek women than Roman.[29] It is interesting that some of the most pointed criticism came not from male classicists but from a distinguished historian of American women, Anne Firor Scott. She identified in the book much the same fault that had been found in other works of classical social history written by Americans—that is, the lack of a clear analytical or theoretical framework or major historical questions: "There are an enormous number of 'facts' somewhat jumbled together. . . . There are indeed times when the author appears to believe that all facts are created equal."[30] This critique, I believe, represents an attitude widely held by American historians of later eras toward classical history, which they see as learned but out of touch with substantive and methodological interests of the discipline of history. Whatever the conceptual problems of Pomeroy's book, it has been important as a textbook, which (along with the Lefkowitz and Fant source collection, *Women's Life in Greece and Rome*) has enabled the curricular innovation of offering courses on women in the ancient world for thousands of American undergraduates.

Since publication of Pomeroy's book, women's studies have assumed a far greater importance in the classical field. Some of the work is particularly informed by feminist theory, but that influence is more evident in literary studies (for example, H. Foley, ed., *Reflections of Women in Antiquity*) than among works by those trained as Greco-Roman historians. For instance, the book on Roman marriage by the Oxford-trained historian Susan Treggiari of Stanford University presents a magisterial survey of the evidence, but without any particular theoretical inclination. In fact, it barely notices the controversy aroused by Foucault's *History of Sexuality*, though its conclusions have a direct bearing on that controversy.[31]

The impact of feminism on the mainstream of American classical historiography has been limited. I do not believe that any classical historian at one of the top five research universities in the United States today would describe herself or himself as motivated primarily by feminist theory. (There are very few women at all in such positions.) Nevertheless, in contemporary *literary* studies the efforts to understand the construction of gender categories are having an impact on the work of social historians. At the most recent meeting of the APA, the Women's Classical Caucus sponsored a panel entitled Women and Slaves in Classical Studies. The papers on gender and social categories in Greek epic and tragedy and Roman comedy were written by young scholars trained in literary criticism, but could just as well have been labeled "cultural history." Because the standard sources for classical history are so heavily literary, the field is especially susceptible to the blurring of the line between sociocultural history and literary criticism. In my view, that blurring can be beneficial in furthering our understanding of Greco-Roman culture, but it can also lead to a lack of the rigor regarding chronology and evidence that has traditionally been valued in the historian's work.

The history of women in antiquity has been only one site of a feminist debate of much wider historical dimensions, and I do not believe that classical historiography has had a leading or distinctive role in the argument. By contrast, the classical world has had a special place in the contest over lesbian and gay rights. Foucault's radical historicization of sexual morality in *The History of Sexuality* started from the Greco-Roman experience and has had a deep influence on classical scholars. Sir Kenneth Dover had already shown in *Greek Homosexuality* (1976) that classical Greek attitudes differed markedly from later Christian condemnation. The Yale medieval historian John Boswell then advanced the more sweeping claim in *Christianity, Social Tolerance and Homosexuality* (1980) that antipathy toward homosexual behavior in western European history began only in the thirteenth century of the Christian era. It followed that the existence of a prior era before repression opened the possibility of a return to a more tolerant, happier time, because attitudes toward homosexual relations are no more than arbitrary cultural constructs. Furthermore, repression of homosexuality was the historical exception rather than the rule. As a review of Boswell's book in the popular press noted, "to characterize this analysis as revolutionary—in its implications for historical studies, for Christianity, for the current debate over sexual mores—is to state the obvious."[32]

Ramsay MacMullen, a Roman social historian also at Yale, quickly responded with a critique arguing that pre-Christian, Roman mores expressed strong disapproval of homosexual behavior, active and passive. Though homosexual behavior certainly existed, MacMullen argued, it was regarded with suspicion as a Greek import.[33] Later, in a major article and a book David Cohen, a Greek historian at Berkeley, demonstrated that even in classical Greece the moral valuation of homosexual relations was contested, as some Greeks claimed that some homoerotic behavior represented an act of hubris against the passive member of the relationship.[34]

Cohen's article in *Past & Present* led to a scholarly debate in that journal, but a far larger uproar arose several years later from the Colorado case known as *Romer v. Evans*. In 1992 the voters of Colorado approved an amendment to the state constitution forbidding special protection against discrimination on the basis of sexual orientation. The amendment was challenged as unconstitutional in the courts. Both sides in the case appealed to classical antiquity in the dispute over whether homosexuals constituted a traditionally "suspect class," and whether disapproval of homosexuality stemmed historically from "one narrow strand of a single religious tradition."[35] If the latter is true, then it could be argued that the Colorado amendment represented an enforcement of a particular religious sect's morality. John Boswell and Martha Nussbaum were summoned as expert witnesses to testify for the plaintiffs that the disapproval was based on "a sectarian Catholic argument" and that before Christianity same-sex relationships were not regarded as "indecent or immoral" or "shameful." Ramsay MacMullen was asked by the defense to submit an affidavit to refute these claims and showed that Boswell and Nussbaum mispresented classical authors in order to substantiate their point and to suppress the truth. MacMullen concluded his affidavit with a strong accusation that it would be reasonable to infer that we find in Boswell's testimony "a sort of high treason in research, . . . deliberate deceit—the intent to fool people."[36] Only on this occasion have I received from a colleague a legal affidavit circulated as an offprint.

If the charges and countercharges have provided fuel for the bitter battles over political correctness and intellectual integrity, it is not obvious that they produced any substantial conclusions relevant to the Colorado case: Judge Bayless's decision noted (wearily?) "that the plaintiffs filled the witness stand with doctors, psychiatrists, genetic explorers, historians, philosophers, and political scientists," but he apparently found no compelling relevance of classical antiquity to the legal issues at hand.[37] The contentious Colorado case allowed classical scholars to claim a share of the public spotlight with the assertion that ancient practices and values are relevant to contemporary issues: unfortunately, the outcome has raised more questions about academic integrity than it has resolved about the history of sexual mores.[38]

The debate has reemerged with its bitter edge in the press in recent months with the publication of Boswell's final book, *Same-Sex Unions in Premodern Europe* (1994). A similar pattern of exchange is evident, with charges of quoting out of context and countercharges of lack of linguistic expertise.[39] Classical history will remain a specially charged field for debate of these issues, owing to the importance attached to pre-Christian moral values as a baseline from which to judge the peculiarity of Catholic doctrine condemning homosexual behavior in a nation that attempts to maintain a separation between church and state.

The politics of gender studies in classical history has another dimension in the conflict between the feminists and the gay-lesbian group. The latter's claim of originality in historicizing gender categories has drawn an angry response from some feminist classicists like Amy Richlin, who believes that feminist scholarship has gone unnoticed or uncredited by gay classicists, as well as by their traditional male colleagues. Neglect of women's experience is rooted in Foucault's lack of interest in the *History of Sexuality*: even as he argued that symmetry in the marital bond developed during the Roman Empire, his focus was overwhelmingly on the subjective experience of self-fashioning males.[40] This has been a bitter pill for some feminists to swallow, as Richlin points out, since "feminists, historians of sexuality, and theorists should be natural allies; certainly they are lumped together by the right."[41]

A third area in which classical historiography has entered contemporary political controversy is the debate over the privileged position of European culture in a multicultural American nation. The complexities of the debate defy brief summary, but the reception of Martin Bernal's *Black Athena* among classical historians deserves comment. An expert in Chinese politics, Bernal set out to challenge the authoritative position of classical Greece as the foundation of European civilization by arguing that "Greek culture had arisen as the result of colonization, around 1500 B.C., by Egyptians and Phoenicians who had civilized the native inhabitants."[42] Bernal claims that the Greeks themselves believed this to be true, and that the contemporary understanding of Greek culture as primarily Indo-European is a figment of "Northern European racism of the nineteenth century."[43] As for the consequences of this position, "if I am right in urging the overthrow of the Aryan Model and its replacement by the Revised Ancient one, it will be necessary not only to rethink the fundamental bases of 'Western Civilization' but also to recognize the penetration of racism and 'continental chauvinism' into all our historiography, or philosophy of writing history."[44]

Despite its confrontational posture, *Black Athena* was initially received favorably by some senior classicists, who were persuaded by Bernal's intellectual history of the construction of the "Aryan Model."[45] However, his treatment of the ancient linguistic and archeological evidence, especially in the second volume, has been read with increasing skepticism by classicists and Near Eastern specialists alike. On closer inspection, it has been pointed out, classical scholarship had already been moving toward a recognition of Near Eastern influences on Aegean civilization. Three decades before publication of *Black Athena*, Moses Finley had already placed the Mycenaean palaces of the late Bronze Age at the periphery of the world of redistributive temple economies of the Near East.[46] Bernal's specific claim of second-millennium colonization of Greece by the Egyptians has generally been resisted by specialists as unsubstantiated by archaeology. Nor have scholars been willing to follow Bernal in placing greater confidence in the ancient legends reported by Herodotus than in the continuity of the material remains. More fundamentally, archaeologists and anthropologists find Bernal's unidirectional diffusionist theory outdated: they are willing to accept the idea of cultural exchange in the eastern Mediterranean of the second millennium, but not to assume that the influence moved in only one direction. Bernal is trapped in the same illusory search for proprietary origins as those he criticized.[47]

The discussion of Black Athena has been international, but with a special political edge in the United States, where it has become part of the debate over Afrocentrism and Western Civilization.[48] In becoming a lightning rod in the battle over multiculturalism, the argument over Black Athena regarding cultural influences in the eastern Mediterranean has been polarized, distorted, and confused. Behind the resistance to his rewriting of history, Bernal sees European racism and cultural arrogance; critics of Bernal respond that he, like earlier Afrocentrists, is trying to avoid the common critical standards of scholarly debate (for example, in his selective acceptance of the historical veracity of Greek myths and legends).[49]

The three political rights movements—feminism, the gay/lesbian activism, Afrocentrism—have inspired new histories that have challenged the standard narrative of America's European cultural heritage in different ways. Feminist classical historiography has pressed for expanding the circle of historically significant actors to include women. Though this inclusion does not necessarily challenge the privileged place of Europe in Americans' historical consciousness, it is at least indirectly subversive insofar as it denies the traditional criteria of historical significance that emphasized power as embodied in (male) politics and war. Through this shift of focus feminist historiography may also directly challenge the traditional historical valuations in the American historical curriculum: for instance, should Western Civilization courses celebrate Athenian democracy, if that democracy excluded and oppressed women (and slaves)? In contrast, the lesbian and gay classicists seem happy to privilege and celebrate classical Greco-Roman antiquity as an era (they claim) before the tyranny of sexual inhibitions imposed by the Christian Church. The Afrocentrists have aimed to deflate the pretensions of classical Europe, and then to claim credit for European culture embodied in classical Greece. Against these politically inspired movements, a political opposition has formed in the National Association of Scholars under the banner of the protection of scholarly standards. Its members have been part of the wider political debate about standards for the history curriculum in American high schools, but both the association and its opponents have had relatively little impact on the scholarship of professional circles of both established and younger classical historians.

Established classical historians in the United States have in the past decade produced important books about the nature of Greek democracy.[50] These works have participated in an international discussion about how democratic ancient Athens was and how its political institutions worked. The intense interest in democracy flows in part from the contemporary concerns of political theory about the participation of individuals in electoral processes.[51] Although the interest in the Athenian experience with democracy certainly cannot be claimed to be distinctively American, it is worth pointing out that it represents a change from the interest of the American founding fathers in the classical world. The Federalists among them generally condemned ancient Athens as an example of corruption; even among "the more democratically inclined" anti-Federalists, "the handful of references . . . to classical Athens were either negative or neutral."[52] For the Federalists, republican Rome was more relevant as a political model of mixed government that limited the power of the masses.[53] Today, the electoral assemblies and the senate of republican Rome seem too different from contemporary American institutions to make them interesting as models for discussion.[54] In an age of mass media, the lack of mediation between politician and voter in Athenian democracy makes it appear more relevant. In any case, this shift in interest of political theory from Roman republicanism to Athenian democracy, like so many other aspects of classical historiography, has been transnational, not peculiarly American.

The truly powerful resistance to the challenge posed by the new women's, gay and lesbian, and Afrocentric histories comes not from the National Association of Scholars but from the inertia of "native American" classical historiography as displayed in the new generation of practitioners. A survey of titles of dissertations completed at major American research universities since 1990 suggests that the recent entrants into the profession are by and large traditional in their choice of subjects. If traditional is defined as conventional political or military history or historiography, then the traditional dissertations in classical history have outnumbered the nontraditional by two to one. In 1994 from the University of California at Berkeley, the University of Pennsylvania, and Harvard—three of the most respected and most active graduate institutions in classical history—came dissertations with the following titles: "Agathokles of Syracuse and the Greek West: The Coinage," "The Family of Konon and Timotheos," "The Political Biography of Gaius Gracchus," "Evidence of Interpolation in the Text of Thucydides," "The Rhodian Navy," and "Early Greek Democracies outside Athens."[55] These titles would not have been out of place at any time since the nineteenth century. Ramsay MacMullen may well be right that the resistance to broadening the subject of classical history is rooted in the philological training required in the doctoral programs, which concentrate on translating texts by elite male authors rather than exploring alternative methods to approach new problems.[56] I would add from my own experience that many of the students applying for graduate study in classical history seem to be self-selected for interests in traditional political and military history, which are often hard to change. The minority of less traditional dissertations today display an interest in rhetoric, symbolism, and ideology. The standard training in classical literature in American doctoral programs may serve classical historians well in developing these approaches.

American classical historiography has to be understood within the context of a transnational field of study, one in which the senior positions at American universities are held by foreign-born or foreign-trained scholars. As a result, much of the classical history written in the United States is indistinguishable from European or British scholarship, and I have not tried to review that corpus. Rather, I have attempted to delineate the identity adopted by American classical historians in contrast to their European counterparts, and to show how that identity fit with more general notions of American exceptionalism among intellectuals in the early twentieth century. I have suggested how American classical historiography has been shaped recently by the more general political context. Since the Second World War Marxism has not been a strong force in the United States, and has not formed an urgent part of the intellectual agenda of American classical historians. Instead, political rights movements have provoked new histories. Those histories of women, gays and lesbians, and Africans in antiquity have not been peculiar to the United States, but the American political context has given them a controversial intensity and a special visibility in the American press, which is otherwise generally indifferent to classical scholarship.

NOTES

1. Anthony Molho, Kurt Raaflaub, and Julia Emlen, eds., *City States in Classical Antiquity and Medieval Italy* (Ann Arbor, 1991).

2. Arnaldo Momigliano, *Studies in Historiography* (New York, 1966), 92. Brent D. Shaw, "Under Russian Eyes," *Journal of Roman Studies* 82 (1992): 216–28, discusses the Russian and German intellectual influences on Rostovtzeff but does not mention the possibility of an American intellectual influence. As William Calder notes, Rostovtzeff's teaching at Yale produced students skilled in papyrology but none with his breadth of historical vision or methodological innovation ("Classical Scholarship in the United States: An Introductory Essay," in W. Briggs, Jr., ed., *Biographical Dictionary of North American Classicists* [Westport, Conn., 1994], xxxi).

3. Chester Starr, "Ancient History in the Twentieth Century," *Classical World* 84 (1991): 184.

4. Tenney Frank, *Roman Imperialism* (New York, 1914), vii.

5. Jerzy Linderski, "Si vis pacem, para bellum: Concepts of Defensive Imperialism," in W. Harris, ed., *The Imperialism of Mid-Republican Rome*, Papers and Monographs of the American Academy in Rome (Rome, 1984), vol. 29, p. 147.

6. Tenney Frank, *Economic History of Rome*, 2d ed. (Baltimore, 1927), 380.

7. Ibid., 334.

8. Ibid., 2.

9. Ibid., 406.

10. Frank fits the broader pattern of liberal reaction of American exceptionalism to the historicist and structural intellectual currents of Europe described by Dorothy Ross, *The Origins of American Social Science* (New York, 1991), 346.

11. The wide acceptance of the explanatory power of race in American social sciences of this period is documented by Ross, *Origins of American Social Science*, 322 and passim.

12. Frank, *Economic History*, 67.

13. Ibid., 124.

14. Ibid., 217.

15. T. R. S. Broughton, "Lily Ross Taylor," in Ward W. Briggs, Jr., and William M. Calder III, eds., *Classical Scholarship: A Biographical Encyclopedia* (New York, 1990), 454.

16. Ibid.

17. Ittai Gradel, "Mamia's Dedication: Emperor and Genius. The Imperial Cult in Italy and the Genius Coloniae in Pompeii," *Analecta Romana Instituti Danici* 20 (1994): 45.

18. Broughton, "Lily Ross Taylor," regarding *The Voting Districts of the Roman Republic: The Thirty-Five Urban and Rural Tribes*, Papers and Monographs of the American Academy in Rome, vol. 20 (Rome, 1960), and *Roman Voting Assemblies from the Hannibalic War to the Dictatorship of Caesar* (Ann Arbor, 1966). At the conference Professor Emilio Gabba similarly characterized G. W. Botsford's earlier *The Roman Assemblies from the Origin to the End of the Republic* (New York, 1909).

19. See the editors' introduction to M. I. Finley, *Economy and Society in Ancient Greece*, ed. Brent D. Shaw and Richard P. Saller (New York, 1981), ix–xxvi.

20. For the powerful effect of Marxism on French intellectual life in postwar France, see Tony Judt, *Past Imperfect: French Intellectuals, 1944–1956* (Berkeley, 1992).

21. M. I. Finley, *Ancient Slavery and Modern Ideology* (New York, 1980), chap. 1. Much European classical historiography was directed toward technical questions without overt political tendencies.

22. A. Giardina and A. Schiavone, eds., *Società Romana e Produzione Schiavistica* (Rome-Bari, 1981), with the review article by D. Rathbone, "The Slave Mode of Production in Italy," *Journal of Roman Studies* 73 (1983): 160–68.

23. C. Starr, "An Overdose of Slavery," *Journal of Economic History* 18 (1958): 31.

24. Ibid., 22, my italics; ibid., 31, his italics.

25. A notable exception is Michael Jameson's "Agriculture and Slavery in Classical Athens," *Classical Journal* 72 (1977–78): 122–45.

26. Both books were published after the American withdrawal of troops from Vietnam in 1975, but both were started during the war. Ernst Badian's *Roman Imperialism in the Late Republic* (Ithaca, 1968) was written before his immigration to the United States and took an overtly anti-Marxist position in a more general debate about imperialism by colonial powers.

27. J. P. V. D. Balsdon, *Roman Women* (London, 1962), 212–14.

28. Ibid., 206–7.

29. E. Badian, "The Lives of Ancient Women," *New York Review of Books*, Oct. 30, 1975, 28–31.

30. Anne Firor Scott, review of *Godesses, Whores, Wives, and Slaves*, in *History—Review of New Books* 4 (1975): 36.

31. Susan Treggiari, *Roman Marriage: Iusti Coniuges from the Time of Cicero to the Time of Ulpian* (Oxford, 1991).

32. M. B. Duberman, *New Republic*, Oct. 18, 1980, 33.

33. Ramsay MacMullen, "Roman Attitudes to Greek Love," *Historia* 31 (1982): 484–502.

34. David Cohen, *Law, Sexuality, and Society: The Enforcement of Morals in Classical Athens* (Cambridge, 1991), 182–83.

35. M. Nussbaum, affidavit 21 Oct. 1993 in *Romer v Evans*, para. 67, 18.

36. R. MacMullen, affidavit Oct. 1993 in *Romer v Evans*, para. 26.

37. *Romer v Evans*, 63 Empl. Prac. Dec. (CCH) 42,719 at 77,938 (Colo. Dist. Ct. Dec. 14, 1993). The philosophical witnesses were summoned by the plaintiffs to show that homosexuals are a traditionally "suspect class"—a claim which Judge Bayless denied.

38. In the aftermath of the initial legal hearings, both Nussbaum and her chief opponent, John Finnis of Oxford, have published long arguments and counterarguments in law journals, and have spoken on campuses across the country (Martha C. Nussbaum,

"Platonic Love and Colorado law: The Relevance of Ancient Greek Norms to Modern Sexual Controversies," *Virginia Law Review* 80 [1994]: 1515–1651; John M. Finnis, "Law, Morality, and 'Sexual Orientation,'" *Notre Dame Law Review* 69 [1994]: 1049–78). The results have been in some respects humorous and in other respects distressing. As an appendix to her 136-page article in the *Virginia Law Review*, Nussbaum tried to specify the qualifications for "expert witnesses" on classical subjects, including a sight-reading examination in Greek and Latin to be graded by Sir Hugh Lloyd-Jones or someone of comparable standing. More discreditable were Nussbaum's tactics to impugn the qualifications of certain scholars rather than to grapple with the substance of their arguments. For example, rather than address the arguments of Cohen's *Law, Sexuality, and Society*, Nussbaum (affidavit 21 Oct. 1993 in *Romer v. Evans*, para. 30) summarily dismissed Cohen because "he is not a classicist, . . . has never been employed by a department of Classics," but is a professor of rhetoric who is dependent on translations of ancient texts. In reality, Cohen has a Ph.D. in classics from the University of Cambridge, has a joint appointment in the Departments of Classics and Rhetoric at the University of California, Berkeley, and uses Greek texts in his book. The only element of truth in Nussbaum's dismissal is that Cohen is not a member of the American Philological Association, which is open to anyone ready to pay the membership fee. Among the other ironies of this testimony is the fact that Nussbaum herself no longer holds an appointment in a department of classics—a fact which presumably does not disqualify her from giving expert opinions in classical philosophy.

39. Brent Shaw's review in *New Republic*, July 18 and 25, 1994, 33–41, with reply by Ralph Hexter and counterreply by Brent Shaw in *New Republic*, Oct. 3, 1994, 39 ff.

40. David Cohen and Richard Saller, "Foucault on Sexuality in Greco-Roman Antiquity," in J. Goldstein, ed., *Foucault and the Writing of History* (Oxford, 1994), 35–60.

41. Amy Richlin, "Zeus and Metis: Foucault, Feminism, Classics," *Helios* 18 (1991): 177.

42. Martin Bernal, *Black Athena: The Afroasiatic Roots of Classical Civilization* (New Brunswick, 1987), 1.

43. Ibid., xv.

44. Ibid., 2.

45. G. Bowersock, review of *Black Athena, Journal of Interdisciplinary History* 19 (1989): 490–91; M. Vickers, review of *Black Athena* in *Antiquity* 61 (1987): 480.

46. Finley, *Economy and Society in Ancient Greece*, chap. 12; more recently, Walter Burkert, *The Orientalizing Revolution: Near Eastern Influence on Greek Culture in the Early Archaic Age*, trans. Walter Burkert and Margaret E. Pinder (Cambridge, Mass., 1992; German ed. orig. pub. 1984).

47. M. Shanks, review of *Black Athena* in *History Today* 42 (1992): 56.

48. S. Burstein, *Classical Philology* 88 (1993): 157–62, provides a balanced and knowledgeable account of the debate. Carol Thomas, *Myth Becomes History: Pre-Classical Greece* (Claremont, Ca., 1993), 54.

49. M. Lefkowitz, "Not out of Africa," *New Republic*, Feb. 10, 1992, 29–36.

50. For instance, Martin Ostwald, *From Popular Sovereignty to the Sovereignty of Law: Law, Society, and Politics in Fifth-Century Athens* (Berkeley, 1986), and Josiah Ober, *Mass and Elite in Democratic Athens: Rhetoric, Ideology, and the Power of the People* (Princeton, 1989).

51. M. I. Finley, *Democracy Ancient and Modern* (New Brunswick, 1973).

52. Jennifer Tolbert Roberts, *Athens on Trial: The Antidemocratic Tradition in Western Thought* (Princeton, 1994), 185.

53. Carl J. Richard, *The Founders and the Classics: Greece, Rome, and the American Enlightenment* (Cambridge, Mass., 1994), 53–84 and esp. 131.

54. The exception is the recent book of Paul A. Rahe, *Republics Ancient and Modern: Classical Republicanism and the American Revolution* (Chapel Hill, 1992).

55. *American Philological Association Newsletter*, June and Aug. 1994.

56. Ramsay MacMullen, "History in Classics," in P. Culham and L. Edmunds, eds., *Classics: A Discipline and Profession in Crisis?* (Lanham, Md., 1989).

CHAPTER 12

In the Mirror's Eye

THE WRITING OF MEDIEVAL HISTORY
IN AMERICA

GABRIELLE M. SPIEGEL

THE TITLE of my essay—"In the Mirror's Eye"—derives both from the name of the most prominent journal dedicated to medieval studies in North America, the journal *Speculum*, edited and produced by the Medieval Academy of America, and from the image that adorns its cover. As E. K. Rand, the first editor, explained in the journal's inaugural issue, the choice of name was guided by the sense that

> *Speculum*, this mirror to which we find it appropriate to give a Latin name, suggests the multitudinous mirrors in which people of the Middle Ages liked to gaze at themselves and other folk—mirrors of history and doctrine and morals, mirrors of princes and lovers and fools. We intend no conscious follies, but we recognize satire, humor and the joy of life as part of our aim. Art and beauty and poetry are a portion of our medieval heritage. Our contribution to the knowledge of those times must be scholarly, first of all, but scholarship must be arrayed, so far as possible, in a pleasing form.[1]

For Rand and his cofounders of the academy and what they aspired to make its leading journal, medieval studies in America were thus consciously directed at overcoming the prejudices and ideological contamination that the very term "medieval" had acquired over the centuries, connoting a dark, backward, superstitious, "Gothic" age, what Karl Marx once called humankind's "zoology," or animal history. Instead, the image that the *speculum* of medievalism in America should display was, whatever its ultimate shape, above all, as Rand's prefatory remarks indicate, to be comely, a portrait of the attractive state of the profession it served. To represent this goal, the founders placed on the front cover a picture of a hand holding up an empty mirror, devoid of any image, to the viewer/reader's gaze. As icon of both the journal and the studies it hoped to promote, *Speculum*'s barren mirror thus invited the medievalist to cast his or her own image upon its vacant specular face. To do so, however, required a willed investment of the self (in effect, a narcissistic self-involvement) in order to generate those images by and through which to contemplate the meaning of the past.

In the choice of name and iconographic gloss, the founders of the Medieval Academy unconsciously underlined what was and remains the determinative condition of possibility for the study of medieval history in America: absence. For like all countries formed by western European settlement since 1492, America lacks a medieval past. Any attempt to argue the importance and relevance of medieval history, therefore, must first overcome (or repress) its evident "otherness," its utter alterity and lack of connection to any visible, shared national or cultural "American" past.

The "alterity" of the Middle Ages, of course, is hardly unique to the American consciousness of the era. Indeed, as Lee Patterson has repeatedly insisted, the Middle Ages has from the beginning served postmedieval Western historical consciousness as one of the primary sites of otherness by which it has constituted itself.[2] As constructed by Renaissance humanists, the Middle Ages comprised the West's shadowy "other," against which the Renaissance and modernity itself was defined, a modernity delineated above all by its difference from the premodern Middle Ages. As Patterson conveniently sums it up: "humanism, nationalism, the proliferation of competing value systems, the secure grasp of a historical consciousness, the idea of the individual, aesthetic production as an end in itself, the conception of the natural world as a site of colonial exploitation and scientific investigation, the secularization of politics and the idea of the state—all of these characteristics and many others are thought both to set the Renaissance apart from the Middle Ages and to align it definitively with the modern world."[3] From this perspective, the Middle Ages is precisely that, a millennium of middleness, a space of empty waiting and virtual death until the reawakening of the West to its proper nature and purpose in the period of the Renaissance.

For Europeans, the Middle Ages, if not modern, is at least "there," evident in the monuments erected during those years and the traditions that stand presumptively at the origin of the modern European national states. It is, in fact, one of the peculiarities of medieval study everywhere that it constantly hovers between the dual consciousness of the Middle Ages as a place and time of nonorigin (that is, the dark, deathly period constructed in and by the Renaissance) and that of origin (the origin of the modern state). Caught in this double bind of nonorigin and origin, lack and plenitude, the Middle Ages, Kathleen Biddick has argued, can be "everywhere, both medieval and modern, and nowhere, sublime and redemptive."[4] It is, in part, this alterity—this "otherness—of the Middle Ages that has given medievalists their sense of professional legitimacy, since the very strangeness and "difference" signified by the distant past suggests a special virtue required for its study. In America, however, the paradox of presence and absence common to medieval studies generally is incommensurably more acute; and precisely to the degree that the Middle Ages constituted an "absent other" in America, just so did the first American scholars insist, in a highly overdetermined fashion, on its place in a continuous stream of history stretching from the Teutonic past to the American present.[5] To overcome absence and otherness, the original students of the medieval past in America construed alterity rather as identity. Given this, it is hardly surprising that the study of medieval history in the United States has from the beginning been marked by inherent paradoxes.

To begin with, although medieval civilization represented the triumphal past of "Catholicism" and "Gothic culture," a world organized according to the dictates of a deeply traditionalistic outlook on life and social customs, in North America its first historians tended to be Protestant, enlightened, and revolutionary founders. Thomas Jefferson and other early American revolutionaries were immersed in myths of Anglo-Saxon democracy, whose laws and chronicles, they believed, foreshadowed their ambitions for democracy. So indebted did Jefferson feel to Anglo-Saxon culture and what he took to be its legacy of Germanic liberties that he planned to put two Anglo-Saxon heroes, Hengist and Horsa—invited by Vortigern into Britain, according to Bede's *History of the English Church and People*, to aid in the defense of the country against enemies to the north—on the great seal of the new republic, whose obverse side would bear an image of the pillar of fire that led the Chosen People into the Promised Land (Exodus 13:21–22). According to John Adams, to whom he had communicated his wishes, Jefferson saw Hengist and Horsa as representing "the form of government we have assumed,"[6] thereby tracing American democratic institutions to their origins in the social practices of the pre-Christian Germanic peoples.[7] Jefferson cannot have read his Bede very carefully, though, since the latter made it clear that, although Hengist and Horsa had arrived in the guise of England's protectors, "nevertheless, their real intention was to subdue it," which, having done, Hengist become the founder of a *royal* line.[8] More striking still was the coupling with the Old Testament pillar of fire, signifying not guidance or protection but an emblem of conquest, a vivid illustration of the young country's territorial ambitions.[9] The underlying contradictions that marked such use of medieval figurations of American destinies would remain a characteristic feature of the American search for identity and origins in an absent and displaced medieval past.

To be sure, Henry Adams ushered in a new era by embracing with emotional intensity what were in some sense—at least from the perspective of Enlightenment thinkers—medieval history's most offensive aspects, but his passionate, slightly irrational celebration of the medieval past was not to be incorporated even into his own teaching of medieval history at Harvard. Adams illustrates a split in the approach to medievalism that was to continue for some time. In his writing he used the Middle Ages and what he saw as its vital, collective, organic culture as an exemplary counterpoint to the "anomic, dehumanized industrializing world that he himself inhabited."[10] His *Mont-Saint-Michel and Chartres*, a work F. N. Robinson characterized as "that sensitive, poetic tribute of a skeptically minded, sometimes disillusioned modern to the spirit of the Middle Ages,"[11] turned to the Middle Ages as warrant for medievalism's antimodern agenda. In this, Adams participated in a burgeoning Romantic idealization of the Middle Ages that in America was largely the preserve of Catholic apologists who, like Adams, sought in the medieval world an idealized vision of an alternative social model against which the defects of the modern world could be judged.[12] In a famous chapter of *The Education*, Adams contrasted the spirit of the Virgin, to whom so much of the artistic and intellectual products of the High Middle Ages were dedicated, to that of the modern dynamo, image of the materialistic, dehumanizing greed and technology of the modern age.[13] For Adams, what was attractive about the Middle Ages was precisely its alterity; it was, he observed, "the most foreign of worlds to the American soul."[14] The New World, Adams believed, had not inherited medieval institutions, patterns of social organization, or religious beliefs; the study of medieval history, therefore, could offer no great truths or lessons for the guidance of American life.[15] Its utility, by implication, lay merely in the escape that it provided from the increasingly harsh realities of the modern world, a realm of fantasized otherness in which to locate the antimodernist self.

Thus, in 1871, when Harvard president Charles W. Eliot invited the young Adams to teach the Middle Ages at Harvard, Adams could think of little to offer his students but the dry facts of political and legal history, learned during his two years of advanced historical training in Germany, where he had been taught to read documents in the new, philologically oriented, manner of the German seminar. For seven years, as lecturer in History 2 (forerunner of the modern Western Civilization course), Adams taught the stuff of history with all the discipline and purposeless of antiquarian research.[16] Adams's legacy to the study of medieval history in America was thus a double and divided one: his writings articulated a conservative strain in American medievalism which would serve as a refuge for those wishing to retreat into a world of preclass, preindustrial society.[17] His teaching, on the other hand, inaugurated what was to become, under the leadership of Charles Homer Haskins, an almost exclusive concern with the political and institutional development of the monarchical states of northern Europe, in particular England and France, that persisted virtually down to the present time.

If Adams was the first to teach medieval history professionally in America, Haskins was America's first true professional medieval historian.[18] Moreover, if Adams represents American medievalism's antimodernist agenda, Haskins was the first and most powerful figure in promoting its modernist agenda. And like his Enlightenment forebears, to whom as a progressive Democrat he was heir, Haskins was to do this by resolutely stressing the continuity of the American present with past medieval institutions.

Haskins came from an affluent Protestant family in Pennsylvania. A child prodigy, he learned Latin and Greek from his father before he was seven, and at the age of fifteen he entered a local college, from which he transferred to Johns Hopkins in his second year, graduating from Hopkins with a B.A. in 1887 and a Ph.D. in American history from Herbert Baxter Adams (in 1890) by the time he was twenty. From Hopkins, Haskins went to Wisconsin to teach American history but after a few years determined to become a medievalist, and so, as required for aspiring medievalists at the turn of the century, he decamped for Europe, entering France's prestigious Ecole des Chartes, designed to train the country's archivists and (in that period) historians in the scientific investigation of medieval documents that goes by the name of diplomatics. After a half dozen years spent in study at the Ecole des Chartes and travel to various archives in England, France, and Sicily, Haskins accepted a professorship at Harvard in 1910. At Harvard he subsequently became dean of the Graduate School of Arts and Sciences, which delayed his major publications until the last half of his academic career, roughly the period from 1918 to 1929. In 1928, three years before the stroke that would incapacitate him, he found his successor in Joseph Reese Strayer, a graduate of Princeton who came to study with him at Harvard before returning to Princeton to teach for the remainder of his career. Between them, Haskins and Strayer were to direct and dominate the practice of medieval history in North America from the 1920s down through the late eighties.[19]

Haskins's formation at Hopkins was to have an enduring impact on his career and ideas. The Department of History had graduated Woodrow Wilson but a few years earlier, and throughout his life Haskins would prove an ardent Wilsonian progressive (i.e. Democratic liberal), sharing with Wilson a deep faith in progress, rational reform, and the benefits of government, beliefs that significantly shaped his historical practice. Not content to implement his views in the classroom, Haskins accompanied Wilson to the Paris Peace Conference in 1919 and 1920 as one of three principal advisers. With Robert Lord, he helped to create Czechoslovakia and Yugoslavia, states carved out from the Austro-Hungarian Empire.[20] On returning to Cambridge, he assumed the directorship of the American Council of Learned Societies, from which position he helped to found and finance the Medieval Academy of America in 1925 and its new journal, *Speculum*,[21] both intended to signal the coming of age of American medieval studies by rivaling in seriousness, exacting standards of scholarship, and formal (not to say deliberate) dullness the great academies of European learning, on which these American institutions were consciously modeled.

Medievalism's modernist agenda that Haskins sought to implant on American soil in its broadest sense took the form of an alliance between positivism, Idealism, naturalism, and objectivity, many of whose components derived, ultimately, from the German scientific historiography of the late nineteenth century, but which Haskins was to cast in a distinctly American, early-twentieth-century, progessivist mold.[22] To do so, however, Haskins had first to cover the absence of a medieval past in America, to guarantee the relevance of medievalism to precisely the vision of continuity and progress that informed his activities both as a professional historian and as an adviser to President Wilson. Few American historians have argued the relevance of medieval history to Americans as eloquently or with as profound conviction as Haskins. While recognizing, as he said, that "American history is our first business," it was not, he believed, "our sole business," and in any case, the two were ultimately part of the same story. European history, Haskins argued in a 1923 essay, "European History and American Scholarship," published in the *American Historical Review*, is "of profound importance to Americans. We may at times appear more mindful of Europe's material indebtedness to us than of our spiritual indebtedness to Europe; we may in our pharisaic moods express thanks that we are not even as these sinners of another hemisphere; but such moments cannot set us loose from the world's history. Whether we look at Europe genetically as the course of our civilization, or pragmatically as a large part of the world in which we live, we cannot ignore the vital connections between Europe and America, their histories ultimately but one."[23] And of all the available European pasts, Haskins signaled America's natural affinity with that of England, for, he declared, "English history is in a sense early American history."[24]

This insistence on continuity and relevance was institutionalized subsequently in the founding of the Medieval Academy and *Speculum* in 1925, whose embracing purpose was to promote American study of the Middle Ages in all its varieties and subdisciplines in order to help Americans, wrote George R. Coffman in the official report of the foundation, "to comprehend our medieval ancestors." Help was needed, he confessed, given the obscure and complex nature of medieval civilization, and it would require the "cooperation and the creative energy of students of art, archeology, folk-lore, government, law, literature, medicine, philosophy, theology and all other branches" of knowledge to elucidate.[25] Thus, from its inception, the professional study of the Middle Ages in America disclosed a durable structure of paradox in American medievalism—the sense of the absolute remove of the medieval past, its strange, difficult, occult nature, combined with an equally absolute sense of filiation with it.

Haskins was not unaware of this paradox and in his books and essays sought to resolve it in directions that would promote the modernist agenda for which his appropriation of the medieval past stood. His enduring tribute to the modernity of the medieval past was his work *The Renaissance of the Twelfth Century*, published in 1927, in which he contested the master narrative of Western civilization according to which the modern world began in the Renaissance. But, Haskins insisted,

> the continuity of history rejects such sharp and violent contrasts between successive periods, and . . . modern research shows us the Middle Ages less dark and less static, the Renaissance less bright and less sudden than was once supposed. The Middle Ages exhibit life and color and change, much eager search after knowledge and beauty, much creative accomplishment in art, in literature, in institutions. The Italian Renaissance was preceded by similar, if less wide-reaching movements; indeed it came out of the Middle Ages so gradually that historians are not agreed when it began, and so would go so far as to abolish the name, and perhaps even the fact, of a renaissance in the Quattrocento.[26]

Thus, instead of viewing the Middle Ages as Western civilization's premodernity, Haskins pushed the beginnings of modernism back to the twelfth century, thereby strengthening at one and the same time the continuity of the Middle Ages with the present and the centrality of its study as the seedbed or parent civilization of the modern West. Although little read today except for its genuine contributions to the history of science,[27] Haskins's argument in *The Renaissance of the Twelfth Century* for the modernity of the Middle Ages began that "revolt of the medievalists"[28] which sought a new legitimacy for the medievalist's professional identity against the charges of obscurantism, irrelevance, and technical virtuosity that continually haunted the practice of medievalism in America in the face of its clear lack of connection with national identity.

Making a virtue out of necessity, Haskins argued that America's lack of direct connection with the Middle Ages cultivated detachment on the part of its scholars—"one of America's great advantages as regards many aspects of European history . . . enabling the historian to trace [the history of European civilization] without those national prejudices from which his European confreres cannot wholly emancipate themselves,"[29] he claimed—thus reinforcing the scientific character of scholarship done in the German, positivist mold. In that sense, the very alterity of the Middle Ages abetted the entrenchment of positivism as *the* scientific form of scholarly method in American medieval historiography, whose counterpart in literary study was an equally fervent espousal of philology, both part and parcel of the specific kind of "source criticism" or *Quellengeschichte* that American scholarship generally learned during its early period of tutelage in the German seminar.[30]

Translated into the realm of historical practice, Haskins's positivist objectivity and German-style historicism took the form of a search for the rational basis of the political and administrative development of monarchical institutions in Europe, especially those of the Anglo-Normans and French. Like Wilson an admirer of the British constitution and political achievement, Haskins focused his attention on the Normans, whose governmental genius he believed had reconstituted the British political system after the Norman conquest of 1066, bringing to the disordered and backward Anglo-Saxon realm the peculiarly systematized and centralized form of feudalism that the Normans had first developed in France. The fruits of this research had begun to appear in articles after Haskins started teaching at Harvard, but his magisterial work *Norman Institutions* was not published until 1918, thus favoring a more widely based reorientation in American medievalism away from the study of German/Anglo-Saxon history after World War I.[31] Hence one effect of Haskins's concentration on Norman institutions was to maintain the traditional orientation of American scholars toward British history but at the same time subtly to redefine what was best in Britain as "French" (or Anglo-Norman), thus permitting American scholarship to evade any possible stigma attached to German history as a result of the war, a move more than validated (and strongly reinforced) by the outcome of World War II.[32]

In Haskins, the influence of Wilsonianism can be seen in his focus on the inherent rationality of the Norman brand of feudal organization, with it tendency to centralize, hence place power in the hands of a court elite, at the expense of an anarchic baronage, and its establishment of political and judicial order to bring peace and stability to the realms under Norman sway, in Sicily as well as England.[33] The lesson that medieval monarchies thus bequeathed to the American present was the power of government to effect unity and consensus out of fragmentation and discord. And no one was to sound this lesson more clearly than Haskins's premier student, Joseph Reese Strayer.

Strayer shared with his mentor a dedication to the investigation of what he called "the medieval origins of the modern state,"[34] in particular by studying the growth of royal bureaucracies, governmental powers, and the legal and constitutional principles by which medieval kings were able to secure not only the ability to rule through force but also the affection and loyalty of their subjects. As in the case of Haskins, the focus on monarchy was more or less accidental, and Strayer's real concern was for the elements that promoted governmental stability and effectiveness and allowed the state to protect its subjects.[35]

Strayer's Harvard dissertation for Haskins, published as *The Administration of Normandy under Saint Louis*,[36] continued his mentor's focus on the Normans, but in a Normandy reintegrated into the French realm as a result of its reconquest by Louis's grandfather, Philip Augustus, in 1204. Once again, the questions Strayer posed were Haskins's questions concerning the impact of a specifically Norman style of government, now upon the French monarchy. In particular, he wondered if Norman customary law had tempered the activities of the Roman lawyers of the French crown in the thirteenth century, while teaching them how to develop their own systems of administration and taxation.[37] Behind this question stood the desire to reinterpret French monarchical institutions in such as a way as to make them compatible with American democratic principles, to divest the French monarchy (at least in the Middle Ages), that is, of the charge of absolutism, a form of political governance that Strayer found personally distasteful and historically irrational and ineffective, since he fervently believed that despotic regimes were naturally weak by virtue of their inability to win their subjects' adherence.

Strayer's attempt, in effect, to "Americanize" royal history in the Middle Ages proceeded along three lines. The first, which owed most to Haskins's influence, was to argue for the innovative, ameliorative impact of the centralizing monarchies in twelfth- and thirteenth-century England and France, whose actions brought order out of chaos and national unity out of feudal fragmentation. Government, as such, was a "good" thing, securing for its subjects the necessary peace and stability that enabled them to prosper. Moreover, and most important, medieval kings like Henry II of England and Philip the Fair of France achieved these results not through violence but by instituting a legal system able to deliver cheaper and more effective forms of justice to their subjects. Royal centralization, therefore, far from tending to absolutism, was the first step in the implementation of Western constitutionalism, a rational system for the adjudication of national issues and a style of government beneficial to subjects of the king. Strayer devoted a lifetime to demonstrating that this, *not absolutism*, represented the true achievement of medieval monarchies. The result of this work was his famous article, "Philip the Fair—a 'Constitutional King,'" published in the *American Historical Review* in 1956, in which Strayer argued, against the grain of previous scholarship, that Philip the Fair, far from representing a capricious, tyrannical king who used a rising class of lawyers brandishing the principles of Roman law to argue for the status of the king as beyond the reach of law (*rex legibus solutus est*), was instead a "constitutional" king, who used legal principles to ensure the welfare and security of his realm to the benefit of his subjects.[38] After being criticized for this view by scholars,[39] Strayer later, in his monumental work, *The Reign of Philip the Fair* (1980), modulated his position to emphasize instead the efficiency and efficacy of Philip's government, in lieu of the somewhat anachronistic claims concerning royal "constitutionalism" in the 1956 article, but his underlying point remained the same: strong and legitimate govenment was a positive force in society and in the history of western European state-building.

Strayer was aware, of course, that in France the monarchy ultimately took an absolutist turn, for which he offered a basically "geographical" explanation. In a series of interesting essays,[40] Strayer argued that the reason that England become a true constitutional monarchy, with effective parliamentary government, was due to its restricted size and early centralization. Because the realm was small and highly organized by English monarchs, who drew upon their subjects' services in the administration of law, it fostered unity among the barons, who, when the monarchy turned capricious under King John, were able to band together to oppose royal power and, ultimately, to institutionalize that opposition in the creation of Parliament. France, in contrast, was too large and too late in developing habits of centralized consultation for this to occur. Because the king was so long weak, the barons had little motive to unite against him, and once the monarchy became powerful, as it did beginning with Philip the Fair, it was too late for the barons to develop those habits of cooperation and concerted action that in England combined to produce a parliamentary form of government. Instead, French kings, when they needed to consult their subjects over questions of taxation, tended to do so by individual region rather than in a unified assembly, promoting fragmentation and particularization among the nobility, which worked ultimately to the monarchy's advantage. For this reason, the Estates-General in France never developed in the same way as Parliament in England, and France took an absolutist turn that would, to be sure, call forth its corresponding opposition in the French Revolution (thus confirming Strayer's deeply held belief that absolutist regimes never finally succeed). The effect of this "geographical" argument was to exculpate the king of any charge of tyranny, since it represented a historical constraint that medieval monarchs simply did not have the resources to overcome. The "moral" upshot of this argument was to preserve the "virtue" of the French king as a legitimate and lawful ruler, who held true to the principles of rational, just government, even if in the end he was betrayed perforce by the recalcitrant conditions of the realm he governed.

The "virtuous" character of medieval monarchy—an analogue, no doubt, of the American virtue that both Haskins and Strayer sought to extol and promote—can best be seen in the second of Strayer's main lines of research, a series of articles dedicated to demonstrating the ideological means by which royal government in the Middle Ages was able to procure and maintain the loyalty and affection of the governed, affirming along the way Strayer's conviction that no government could rule by violence alone. In articles like "Defense of the Realm and Royal Power in France," and "France: The Holy Land, the Chosen People and the Most Christian King,"[41] Strayer argued powerfully that French kings had succeeded in winning the devotion of their subjects by successfully articulating the legitimate basis of their rule and, especially under Saint Louis, by presenting themselves as rulers worthy of affection and obedience, producing a cult of kingship in France that was centered on the person of the ruler. It was this ideological legitimacy, a mystique of monarchy that encouraged "Frenchmen" to look to the king as the focal point of an emergent sense of national identity, and not the deployment of powers of coercion, that fundamentally explained the success of the French medieval monarchy. So effective were the administrative systems put in place by medieval governments, and so secure the loyalty of their subjects, that the emerging national states of Europe, Strayer argued in his presidential address to the American Historical Association in 1971,[42] were able to withstand the crises of the fourteenth century, in sharp contrast to the Roman Empire, doomed to succumb to the vagaries of the fourth century precisely because it lacked the bureaucratic mechanisms and affective legitimacy that medieval kings had successfully brought into being.

The precondition for these developments, and the third vector of Strayer's research, was what he termed the "laicization" of society in the thirteenth century.[43] By this term Strayer meant something close to Weber's "disenchantment" of the world, a tendency to place faith in human rather than divine figures, and the human figures who became the repository of that faith were, of course, kings. In claiming that the thirteenth-century medieval world was increasingly secular in outlook and sentiment, Strayer challenged the core image of that "greatest of centuries" (the title of Catholic historian James J. Walsh's book on the period) and the conviction that what made medieval monarchs powerful were the sacral (not the judicial) powers that they exercised.

Beginning in the 1930s and continuing on until the 1980s, Strayer's long career of teaching and research on the writing of medieval history characterizes a dominant (though by no means exclusive) orientation of American scholars of his era, a group that includes Charles McIlwain and Charles Taylor at Harvard, Sidney Packard at Smith College, Carl Stephenson and Brian Tierney at Cornell, and Sidney Painter and John W. Baldwin at Johns Hopkins, Bryce Lyon at Brown University, Thomas Bisson at Berkeley and Harvard, as well as C. Warren Hollister at the University of California at Santa Barbara, Gavin Langmuir at Stanford, and Robert Brentano at Berkeley, to name only a handful, all of whom were centrally concerned with questions of legal/constitutional and institutional history in relation to issues of both feudalism and state formation. Over the course of half a century these men trained generations of students whom they sent out throughout the country, populating centers of medieval study from the East to the West Coast. If one includes Haskins, between them they span virtually the entire length of professional medievalism in America, shaping it with their notions of scientific methodology, rationality, and progressive ideology. A parallel consequence of their dominance, Norman Cantor has argued, was to leave medieval studies in America firmly in the hands of "a small, enclosed world of determined, middle-class WASPs, ruling unchallenged (before the German-Jewish emigration of the late thirties) on the history of Roman Catholic Europe."[44] And it was precisely a sea change in the recruitment of medievalists in the sixties and seventies that was to change the face of American medievalism almost beyond the point of recognition. This new generation, entering graduate school in the sixties and the profession in the midseventies, completely reoriented the study of medieval history in America, creating a new landscape of concerns that could hardly have been anticipated. In this, medieval history was scarcely alone. The changes it experienced were part of a much broader movement which, from the perspective of the nineties, can be seen as the importation and adaptation of postmodernism[45] into the heart of American scholarship in all fields.

In some ways, medieval studies might have been thought to be ideally placed to exploit the historicist strain in postmodern thought, since it had always insisted on *difference* ("alterity") as the privileged category defining the relationship of the Middle Ages to the modern world of scholarship. Given that a dominant impulse in postmodern criticism is precisely the attempt to "think" difference, that is, as Eric Santner explains it, "to integrate an awareness of multiple forms of otherness, to identify . . . across a wide range of unstable and heterogeneous regionalisms, local knowledges and practices,"[46] medievalists were in principle predisposed to the hermeneutic posture that postmodernism demanded of its practitioners. Moreover, the vaunted complexity of medieval documents, the necessity for highly technical approaches to them, implied that meaning in medieval texts was *not* naturally accessible and that such texts were, by nature, opaque, at least to the modern reader. In that sense, philology—the principal technical apparatus in the medievalist's arsenal of interpretation—might have seemed compatible with the emerging sense of the opacity of all writing (of writing as *différance*, in Derrida's sense) and with the turn to textuality as the matrix and condition of possibility for all forms of knowledge. Similarly, the sense of marginality, and the quest for it, that haunts the postmodern should be equally congenial to the medievalist, whose object of study lies outside the master narrative of Western modernity and whose own relationship to the profession is often considered to be, if not marginal itself, at least of marginal utility in a national environment committed to innovation and relevance.

And yet, American medievalists—and among them, historians in particular—have been slower than almost any group in the academy to take up the challenge of postmodernism. In part this was due to the highly overdetermined nature of the discourse of continuity and progress that had marked the American relation to its patently absent past virtually from the time of Jefferson on, and which had subtended the modernist agenda of the profession in its very formation. In part, and somewhat paradoxically, it was also due to the conservatism of some who joined the profession, for whom the Middle Ages retained its appeal as an alternative model of social being, belief, and intellectual elitism. (Medieval history was, after all, hard to do, demanding a mastery of languages that few Americans naturally commanded.) And in part, it may also be due to the sensed implication that the very disarray of modernism that *post*modernism by definition portends threatens to deprive the Middle Ages of whatever *negative* interest it once had as the refuge of the unenlightened, irrational, and "other."[47] In all these ways, the arrival of postmodernism must have seemed to undermine the unstated but nonetheless powerful investments of the self that medievalists brought to their work and in which they mirrored their professional identities. It was, therefore, not until the seventies, at the earliest, that there began to appear those currents of thought in medieval historical scholarship in America that can be linked to the influence of postmodernism.

In my view,[48] there were three dominant trends in historical work in the late seventies and eighties that made themselves felt in the domain of medieval historiography and that, in sum, constituted a virtual "revolution" in the American (and, in the Haskins-Strayer sense, "Americanizing") writing of history. The first constituted a rejection of the positivist certainties and foundationalism of the "old" historicism—together with its implicit, universalizing humanism—in favor of a "new" historicism that took its lead from the creation of "discourse" studies written under the sign of Foucault (at least initially) and which resulted in a social "constructionist" approach to the past that would issue, ultimately, in the practice of "cultural history."[49] Another way of characterizing this shift is as a transformation in the idea of history from a narration of, in the old Rankean formulation, *wie est eigentlich gewesen*, to history as representation, a recognition that the investigation of the past occurs only through the mediatory and mediating texts that it bequeaths and that, therefore, what is "recovered" is not so much the "truth" of the past as the images of itself that it produced, images conditioned, indeed determined, by its ambient, and historically determinate, discourses.

Second, and closely allied to this shift, was the so-called linguistic turn, or what might, in its most general sense, be termed a transformation in the understanding of documents as texts rather than sources. For medievalists, this shift, conducted under the impact of both symbolic anthropology of the Geertzian sort and semiotics (and, in part, Derridean deconstruction, though Derrida's influence was felt primarily in the field of criticism, rather than history), contested the positivist and philological center of all medieval studies, and is perceived by the older generation of medievalists in America as a threat to the very enterprise of medievalism in America. This because, in treating documents as texts rather than sources, it suggests the instability and opacity of all and any knowledge of the past, while at the same time (perhaps more importantly?) attacking the very foundations on which medievalists had constructed their professional legitimacy, involved as it had always been with mastery of highly technical (rather opaque) fields such as paleography, diplomatics, codicology, etc., not to mention all those "dead" languages. Together, these two movements are creating a "new medievalism" (in the title of a recent collection of essays) that is, in Eugene Vance's words, "a science not of things and deeds but of discourses; an art not of facts but of encodings of facts."[50]

The third (chronologically earliest) transformation came about as a result of the emergence of American feminist historiography and, ultimately, gender studies, whose impact was to shift attention away from precisely the "public" sphere that had engaged the work of American medievalists in the Haskins-Strayer tradition to the private, domestic, and, increasingly, carnal (that is, bodily) spheres. Although initially feminist historiography concerned itself with demonstrating the presence of women in the Middle Ages, making them "visible" as actors upon the historical (if not public) stage—a strategy of *inclusion*, of reading women into the then dominant historical discourse—it quickly developed into a much broader interrogation of the very basis of a practice that claimed "truth" while omitting from its purview fully half the population, a result of which was to demonstrate the ways in which patriarchy itself (especially in its highly misogynist, medieval variant) relied upon a gendered view of nature and power for its success.[51] From there it was but a short step to an exclusive concern with women themselves, a concern that has been especially prominent in the field of medieval spirituality[52] and literary study,[53] where the search for authentic women's "voices" is producing highly paradoxical uses of poststructuralist interpretations of the extant texts.

While these changes have characterized American historiography in general from the seventies on,[54] in the field of medieval history, what might, for the sake of symmetry, be here called medievalism's postmodernist agenda required a prior, and double, analytical move: first, a "demodernization" of medievalism's modernist project that had stood at the core of virtually all medieval disciplines since the late nineteenth century and had endowed American medievalists especially with a professional purpose and identity; second, a (postmodern) "defamiliarization" of the resulting—demodernized—cultural artifacts, an analytical gesture that at the moment appears to entail a certain "demonizing" of the Middle Ages, the corollary of which is what Paul Freedman has called "the return of the grotesque in medieval historiography."[55] What is taking place, therefore, is not so much the product of the unearthing of new texts (although, inevitably, it has led to the discovery of them) as a massive interpretive shift in the meaning of the Middle Ages that has emerged as a consequence of a complete refocusing away from the normal to the contested, from an optimistic and "progressive" decoding of the past to a reappropriation of its otherness,[56] an alterity now construed not merely as the boundary demarcating the premodern from the modern but as a radical form of "otherness" that almost defies comprehension.

The three directions of change I have indicated might all be seen as aligning themselves beneath the Foucauldian banner: *inquiéter tous les positivismes*—to disrupt all forms of positivism. I am not trying to suggest that Foucault has been the determinative influence on the development of American medievalism's postmodern agenda. Indeed, if one takes literary studies and their impact on historians into account, equal, if not greater, weight must be given to semiotics and deconstruction. But since Foucault committed himself to working through the implications of postmodernism within history, it has to some extent been easiest for medieval historians to absorb the principles of postmodernism via his writings.

Foucault's work has been especially influential within the domain of historicism, where he has argued that, in a postmodern age, the problem of history "is no longer one of tradition, of tracing a line, but one of division, of limits; it is no longer one of lasting foundations, but of transformations that serve as new foundations";[57] which is to say that history is a form of archaeology. To take Foucault's notion of archaeology seriously, therefore, meant abandoning the master narrative of continuity and progress that had informed historical practice at least since the nineteenth century (indeed, earlier) in favor of a fractured, discontinuous, and ruptured sense of the past. As a practical matter, it has promoted a concentration on small microhistories which are no longer assumed to reside within a larger, lineal network of continuous relationships. If genealogy once meant for historians the tracing of direct lines of descent from past to present, under the sign of Foucault it now stands for all that is contingent, invasive, aleatory in history, the constant irruptions and disruptions, misalliances and failures that mark familial relations over time.

At the same time, the implications of a Foucauldian notion of discourse make a belief in objectivity, positivism's ethical twin, virtually untenable, since no thought (or thinker) can escape the knowledge-power systems of its own historical, archaeologically disjunct, era, thus problematizing in fundamental ways the transactions between past and present required for genuine historical understanding, creating a seemingly unbridgeable hermeneutic gap. Within the domain of textuality, Foucault's archaeological metaphor points to the treatment of documents as "monuments," that is, as "mute," as that which no longer "speak" to us clearly and directly from the past but must be submitted to an intrinsic analysis (like the silent stones of the archaeological site) before they can be made to yield up their secrets.[58]

Within women's history, Foucault's constructivist view of discourse, when applied to issues of sexuality, has powerfully abetted the feminist view that sexual categories that were once thought to be natural, universal, and given, the very bedrock of identity and being, are instead historically produced under determinate, discursive conditions and in the service of specific material (patriarchal) interests and power relations. Thus gender differences have themselves been revealed as part of a master narrative that, in unmasking, feminist historiography seeks to dethrone. While few medievalists have followed feminists like Judith Butler in affirming a wholly performative notion of gender, the very instability, lability, and obscurity of medieval notions of sexuality have lent themselves readily to this kind of treatment.[59] In particular, Caroline Bynum's work on late medieval spirituality has disclosed the centrality of the body and bodily practices to a form of asceticism that is peculiarly female, both in its recourse to food as a central symbol of transcendence (in particular, through consumption of the Eucharist) and in its highly penitential, self-punishing mode of bodily deprivation (fasting, self-flagellation, etc.).[60]

And finally, Foucault's attack on the normalizing mechanisms of modern epistemological regimes has promoted a sensitivity to ways in which knowledge-power systems marginalize and exclude—silence, in effect—some while valorizing others, and has led medieval historians to take a fresh look at the operations of the church and its systematic theology in the High Middle Ages as well as to seek out those elements of medieval society that both contest and thus seem to escape their power. The result of this view of the "normalizing" tendencies of all discursive formations and the desire to undermine their efficacy has been, within medieval history, a complete reinterpretation of the thirteenth century as witness to what has been called "the rise of a persecuting society."[61] Thus, the "greatest of centuries" is no longer seen as the center of a modern, rational, progressive movement but as a Foucauldian panopticon of discipline and colonization, seeking out in order to tame and punish all those perceived as dissenting from the church's regime. This has encouraged, as its obverse, new interest in heretical groups,[62] in Jews and in Jewish-Christian relations,[63] in children, in popular culture, in gays and other marginalized groups.[64] Subjects once themselves marginalized are inching toward the center of concern: Pope Joan, the inquisition, visionary hysteria, the *droit de seigneur*, and the like. If the latest meetings of the Medieval Academy are to be trusted, multiculturalism, postcolonialism, "orientalism," and "sodometries" are soon to follow.

What is particularly striking about medieval work done in this vein, moreover, is the degree to which it focuses not only on the marginal but on the grotesque. Thus Bynum trains her eye on extraordinary acts of asceticism among the women she treats, who drank seeping pus from wounds, fasted to the point of starvation, and submitted to horrifying acts of self-deprivation all in the name of spiritual transcendence. Jewish historians have recently returned to the study of the massacres of 1096, with their images of piles of dead and mutilated bodies.[65] Even within the most traditional domain of feudal studies, there is a growing emphasis on violence as the engine that drives the feudal machine.[66] Indeed, the latest work on the Normans, Eleanor Searle's *Predatory Kinship and the Creation of Norman Power*, stresses the violent, ritualized nature of their exercise of power, in sharp contrast to Haskins's view of the rational, systematic nature of Norman feudalism. Thus violence, conflict, and marginality are producing similar effects in many fields of research: the "defamiliarizing of what previously seemed canonical, progressive, and modern in favor of the ironic[67] and fantastic."[68]

If one inquires into the reasons for the emergence of these new currents in the practice of medieval history in America, the answer, it seems to me, lies not so much in the impact of postmodernism per se but in the reasons for the American receptiveness to postmodernism's agenda. And to understand these reasons it is necessary to return to the social recruitment of American medievalists in the sixties and seventies. In addition to the entrance of women and blacks into the American academy for the first time, there was also a new wave of participation among classes and what, for lack of a better word, can be called ethnic groups, among them Jews, all of whom entered the university in newly massive numbers in the early sixties, thus constituting a clientele whose interests needed to be addressed and a pool from among which future professionals could, and would, be recruited. Hence, John Van Engen, in seeking to understand the motivations that have prompted Americans to take up the study of the Middle Ages, in whatever aspect, in light of its absolute remove in space as well as time from their personal and/or familial experience, has pointed to the ambivalence with which these "new" groups of Americans have approached the study of European, and specifically medieval, history. Even for those with cultural roots in Europe, Van Engen believes, most came from among peasants, the unfree, or dispossessed, retaining, therefore, "little personal stake in the old European order." Moreover, Van Engen insists, "the sting of that removal was real . . . the heirs to those immigrants have never been able to decide whether they should spitefully keep their distance, avoiding the old corruption, or return to Europe with pent-up intensity, reclaiming or making space for all that was once denied them. The study of the European Middle Ages remains for Americans a continuing dialectic between connection and disjunction, the tug of social and cultural features still influential among us and the shimmer of something totally and yet perceptibly other."[69] Surely this, together with the influence on American scholarship of the German-Jewish refugees and their children, provides one of the profound reasons for the current disorientation, or to put it more positively, reorientation, in the study of the Middle Ages. For ours is the first generation of those immigrants, both from among the dispossessed of the "old European order" and the refugees from Hitler's Europe, to enter the American academy in large numbers, bringing with it all the ambivalence toward and desire for mastery over that world we have all, in some deep way, lost.

Given this, it is hardly surprising that the most powerful sense of the Middle Ages current in the academy is what goes under the name of its "alterity," for that hermeneutic alterity offers the best means of escaping from the model of total (and totalitarian) identification which was the chief mode of studying the Middle Ages in the past. In that sense, as Robert Stein recently suggested to me, "in its resistance to totalitarian identifications, the position of loss may well be an advantageous position from which genuine scholarship can proceed." Alterity, from this perspective, is the name we give to the recognition that the past inevitably escapes us, that words, names, signs, functions—our fragile instruments of research and scholarship—are at best only momentarily empowered to capture the reality of the past, the knowledge of which as a lived, experienced, understood repository of life is always slipping away, if indeed it was ever knowable to begin with.

What has changed in the postmodern understanding of medieval alterity, and serves sharply to distinguish it from the earlier modern construction of it, is the simultaneity of our desire for history and the recognition of its irreparable loss, a recognition that paradoxically nourishes the very desire it can never satisfy. This desire has, therefore, an elegiac component, in which it is transformed into a kind of mourning for the unpossessed (or lost) "other." In postmodern historiography, I would argue, the tension between our sense of the past's erasure through the annihilation of memory and our desire for history harbors a longing for presence, a presence we simultaneously acknowledge as always already absent, and thus like the past itself, an unattainable object of desire. Thus what I call the desire for history not only represents the desire to recuperate the past or the other but also marks the inaccessibility of that absent other, an irony that seems to me to be the very figure of history in the late twentieth century.

Our desire for the past is, thus, borne alongside our recognition of its loss, a loss we no longer can, or care, to mask beneath the modernist guise of continuity and progress. If postmodernism has seemed to this generation a viable, indeed crucial, theoretical context out of which to work, this is so, I believe, because postmodernism invites us to mourn, as Eric Santner has written, "the shattered fantasy of the (always already) lost organic society that has haunted the Western imagination."[70] The "alterity" of the Middle Ages, it would appear, is our own estrangement from that fantasy writ large. On the cover of *Speculum*, there is no longer a mirror.

NOTES

1. The author would like to thank the members of the San Marino conference and Professor John W. Baldwin for their helpful criticism of this paper as well as to acknowledge a special debt to Dorothy Ross, who has been consistently willing to instruct a neophyte in American history and the development of social science methodology in the subtleties of the subject. I never fail to learn from her, whether through reading or conversation. "Editor's Preface," *Speculum* 1 (1926): 4.

2. Lee Patterson, introduction, "Critical Historicism and Medieval Studies," in Lee Patterson, ed., *Literary Practice and Social Change in Britain, 1380–1530* (Berkeley, 1990), p. 2. See also his *Negotiating the Past: The Historical Understanding of Medieval Literature* (Madison, 1987) and "On the Margin: Postmodernism, Ironic History and Medieval Studies," *Speculum* 65 (1990): 87–108.

3. Patterson, "Critical Historicism and Medieval Studies," p. 2.

4. Kathleen Biddick, "Bede's Blush: Postcards from Bali, Bombay, Palo Alto," in John Van Engen, ed., *The Past and Future of Medieval Studies*, Notre Dame Conferences in Medieval Studies, IV (Notre Dame, 1994), p. 16.

5. On the "Teutonic germ" theory of institutional history, which claimed that the seed of American democracy had been created in the Black Forest, taken to Anglo-Saxon England, and thence across the ocean to America, see W. Stull Holt, "The Idea of Scientific History in America," *Journal of the History of Ideas* 1 (1940): 352–62; Dorothy Ross, "On the Misunderstanding of Ranke and the Origins of the Historical Profession in America," *Syracuse Scholar* 9 (1988): 31–41; idem, *The Origins of American Social Science* (Cambridge, Eng., 1992); idem, "Historical Consciousness in Nineteenth-Century America," *American Historical Review* 89 (1984): 909–28. A particularly egregious example of historical work done in this vein is Herbert Baxter Adams, "The Germanic Origins of New England Towns," *Johns Hopkins University Studies in Historical and Political Science* 1 (1883): 5–38. For the "rhapsodic racialism" that ran through the intellectual agenda of Baxter Adams's seminary at Johns Hopkins University see Marvin Gettleman, ed., *The Johns Hopkins University Seminary of History and Politics: The Records of an American Educational Institutions, 1877–1912*, 5 vols. (New York and London, 1987–90). Although especially dominant in the work of Baxter Adams and his students, the Teutonic germ theory was equally prevalent in many writings of medievalists around the turn of the century and is a central premise of the research and writing done in Henry Adams's seminar on Anglo-Saxon legal institutions during his seven years of teaching at Harvard. The work of the seminar was subsequently published as *Essays in Anglo-Saxon Law*, ed. Henry Adams (Boston, 1876), to which Adams himself contributed an article, "The Anglo-Saxon Courts of Law." Unlike Baxter Adams, however, Henry Adams's espousal of the theory was tepid at best, and not of long duration, though it does inform his work on the hundred courts that resulted from his Harvard research seminar.

6. Cited in Allen J. Frantzen, *Desire for Origins: New Language, Old English and Teaching the Tradition* (New Brunswick, 1990), p. 16. Another design formulated by a committee composed of Benjamin Franklin, John Adams, and Thomas Jefferson—also rejected—

derived from a drawing by Pierre-Eugène du Simitière (a Swiss painter living in Philadelphia) and consisted of a shield divided into six sections, on which the arms of England, Scotland, Ireland, France, Germany, Belgium, and Holland were painted. Above the shield would be the "Eye of Providence in a radiant Triangle"; below the motto *E Pluribus Unum*. As Jay Fliegelman indicates, "what is fascinating about the design is that in its first official appearance, the *E Pluribus Unum* motto refers as much to the process whereby America derived from the six 'countries from which these States have been peopled' as it does to America as a union of States." Hence the insistence on continuity with the European past, despite the more radical implications of the Revolution itself, was to be inscribed in America's emblematic self-representation. On this see Jay Fliegelman, *Declaring Independence: Jefferson, Natural Language and the Culture of Performance* (Stanford, 1993), p. 161.

7. Peter W. Williams, "The Varieties of American Medievalism," *Studies in Medievalism* 1, no. 11 (spring 1982): 8.

8. Bede, *A History of the English Church and People*, trans. Leo Sherley-Price, revised by R. E. Latham (New York, 1977), pp. 55–56.

9. Frantzen, *Desire for Origins*, p. 16.

10. Williams, "The Varieties of American Medievalism," p. 10.

11. F. N. Robinson, "Anniversary Reflections," Presidential Address delivered at the Twenty-Fifth Annual Meeting of the Medieval Academy, *Speculum*, 25 (1950): 494.

12. Philip Gleason, "American Catholics and the Mythic Middle Ages," in *Keeping the Faith American Catholicism Past and Present* (Notre Dame, 1987), p. 20. Unfortunately, space does not allow me to pursue the development of Catholic medievalism in North America, which, at least in its initial stages (before the Neo-Thomist revival) was conducted largely outside the mainstream of the academy. Gleason's article offers a sensitive and comprehensive discussion. See also John Van Engen, "The Christian Middle Ages as an Historiographical Problem," *American Historical Review* 91 (1986): 519–52. On the Romantic components of late-nineteenth-century medievalism as they affected both popular culture and historical writing see the excellent article by Robin Fleming, "Picturesque History and the Medieval in Nineteenth-Century America," *American Historical Review* 100 (1995): 1061–94. For an extremely insightful treatment of medievalism's antimodernist agenda see T. J. Jackson Lears, *No Place of Grace: Antimodernism and the Transformation of American Culture, 1890–1920* (reprint, Chicago and London, 1994).

13. William J. Courtenay, "The Virgin and the Dynamo: The Growth of Medieval Studies in North America 1870–1930," in Francis G. Gentry and Christopher Kleinhenz, eds., *Medieval Studies in North America Past, Present and Future* (Kalamazoo, Mich., 1982), p. 21, note 8.

14. Cited in ibid., p. 10.

15. Ibid., p. 5.

16. The judgment of his teaching offered by Courtenay, ibid., p. 6.

17. See Patrick Geary, "Visions of Medieval Studies in North America," in John Van Engen, ed., *The Past and Future of Medieval Studies* (Notre Dame and London, 1994), pp. 51–52. Alternatively, however, Susan Mosher Stuard has argued that Adams was the first to focus on the "social balance" between the sexes, particularly in the family, as an important element in Europe's dynamic pattern of growth, a phenomenon disrupted by the processes of state building. In that sense, Adams was among the first medievalists to introduce a concern with the family, women, and gender as a counterpart to the history of state, a view with a potentially subversive edge for American historiography. See her "A New Dimension? North American Scholars Contribute Their Perspective," in Susan Mosher Stuard, ed., *Women in Medieval History and Historiography* (Philadelphia, 1987), p. 84. But

Stuard acknowledges that Adams failed to incorporate these concerns, like his concerns with cultural history, into his teaching, which was restricted to precisely the history of political reigns, wars, and administrative milestones whose centrality his writings might have contested. Adams is, however, an extremely complex figure, whose work does not fall easily into categories, being at once informed by some highly modernist tendencies (see, for example, the recent essay by Dorothy Ross, "Modernist Science in the Land of the New/ Old," in Dorothy Ross, ed., *Modernist Impulses in the Human Sciences 1870–1930* [Baltimore, 1994], pp. 171–89), evident most especially in Adams's lifelong interest in science, as well as the better known antimodernist aspects of *Chartres* and the last three chapters of *The Education*. The bibliography on Adams is enormous, but a good starting place is J. C. Levenson, *The Mind and Art of Henry Adams* (Boston, 1957), together with the standard multivolume biography by Ernest Samuels, *The Young Henry Adams* (Cambridge, Mass., 1948); *Henry Adams: The Middle Years* (Cambridge, Mass., 1958); *Henry Adams: The Major Phase* (Cambridge, Mass., 1964).

18. Certainly, the most important writer of medieval history before Haskins was Henry Charles Lea (1825–1909), author of such works—to name only a few—as *Superstition and Force: Essays on the Wager of Law, the Wager of Battle, the Ordeal, Torture*, 4th ed. (Philadelphia, 1892); *A History of the Inquisition in Spain*, 4 vols. (New York, 1906–7); *History of Sacerdotal Celibacy*, 4th ed. (London, 1932) and *Materials toward a History of Witchcraft*, ed. Arthur C. Howland, 3 vols. (Philadelphia, 1939); *Torture* (Philadelphia, 1973). Lea, however, was not a professor but a publisher. Indeed, the first generation of American medievalists tended to be gentlemen scholars, whose private wealth funded their amateur historical scholarship. It is a tribute to Lea's industry and intelligence that he could produce such important work on such a massive scale while still functioning as a publisher in Philadelphia. Another important medieval scholar of the late nineteenth century, author of a widely circulated book, *Thirteenth, Greatest of Centuries* (New York, 1912), was James J. Walsh, a medical doctor who had trained under Rudolph Virchow in Germany. Although Walsh was an important contributor to the tradition of popular medievalism, the impact of his work lay largely outside academia. On Walsh see Gleason, "American Catholics and the Mythic Middle Ages," pp. 19 ff.

19. For details of Haskins's and Strayer's lives and early careers see Norman Cantor, *Inventing the Middle Ages: The Lives, Works, and Ideas of the Great Medievalists of the Twentieth Century* (New York, 1991), chap. 7, "American Pie, Charles Homer Haskins and Joseph Reese Strayer," passim. On Haskins see also Sally Vaughn, "Charles Homer Haskins (1870–1937)," in *Medieval Scholarship Biographical Studies on the Formation of a Discipline*, vol. 1, *History*, ed. Helen Damico and Joseph B. Zavadil (New York and London, 1995), pp. 169–84.

20. Ibid., p. 252.

21. On Haskins's role in the formation of the Medieval Academy and *Speculum*, a role rather more restricted than Cantor intimates, see George R. Coffman, "The Medieval Academy of America: Historical Background and Prospect," *Speculum* 1 (1926): 5–18.

22. On Germany's influence on American historiography, due to the training that so many of the first generation of professional historians received there, see Jurgen Herbst, *The German Historical School in American Scholarship: A Study in the Transfer of Culture* (Ithaca, 1965).

23. Charles Homer Haskins, "European History and American Scholarship," *American Historical Review* 28 (1923): 215.

24. Ibid., p. 18. Behind the profound passion of this statement lies, to be sure, an equally profound anxiety over just how marginal and irrelevant medieval history must

seem to most Americans. In 1971, Strayer openly articulated the threat underlying the American practice of medieval history, warning a new generation of students to whom he addressed his remarks that, without concerted effort, they were in danger of being "shoved into the back corner along with Sanskrit, Assyriology and other subjects" (i.e., all the *dead* languages, betraying the threat of nonbeing that always haunts the medievalist's imaginary). For, Strayer reminded his young audience, "We should never forget our greatest danger: we began as antiquarians and we could end as antiquarians" ("The Future of Medieval History," *Medievalia et Humanistica*, n.s. II [1971]: 179). The insistence on continuity and relevance marked the American appropriation of the medieval past for decades. In his presidential address on "Humanistic Studies and Science" on the occasion of the fifth annual meeting of the Medieval Academy, John Matthews Manly sounded its plea once again, imploring that "the infinitely various and fascinating period we roughly call the Middle Ages must not be neglected. It lies close to us. In it arose many of our most important institutions. Our social life, our customs—our ideals, our superstitions and fears and hopes—came to us directly from this period; and no present-day analysis can give a complete account of our civilization unless it is supplemented by a profound study of the forces and forms of life, good and evil, which we have inherited from it" (*Speculum* 5 [1930]: 250). As late as 1963, S. Harrison Thomson, surveying the field, echoed Haskins's sentiment by declaring that "The Middle Ages are early American history and they should be so presented." See S. Harrison Thomson, "The Growth of a Discipline: Medieval Studies in America," in Katherine Fischer Drew and Floyd Seyward Lear, eds., *Perspectives in Medieval History* (Chicago, 1963), p. 17.

25. Coffman, "The Medieval Academy of America, p. 17.

26. Charles Homer Haskins, *The Renaissance of the Twelfth Century* (reprint, New York, 1964), pp. vii–viii.

27. Haskins's appreciation of the importance of science to medievalism's modernist agenda was implemented in his important research on medieval science (see his *Studies in the History of Mediaeval Science* [Cambridge, Mass., 1924]). This aspect of Haskins's influence was continued and amplified by Lynn White's investigations into the history of technology, beginning in the 1950s, the effects of which were, in John Van Engen's helpful phrasing, "to rewrite medieval culture to approximate American dynamism." See his "An Afterword on Medieval Studies; or, the Future of Abelard and Heloise," in Van Engen, ed., *The Past and Future of Medieval Studies*, p. 414.

28. The term was popularized by Wallace K. Ferguson, *The Renaissance in Historical Thought: Five Centuries of Interpretation* (Boston, 1948).

29. Haskins, "European History and American Scholarship," p. 224; 226.

30. Space does not allow for a full discussion of the impact of German positivism and philology on Medieval Studies in America, but its perduring effects would be difficult to overestimate. For a discussion of this from various points of view see, among others, Frantzen, *Desire for Origins*, passim; Patterson, *Negotiating the Past*, passim; idem, "Critical Historicism and Medieval Studies"; and especially the wide range of essays in the collective volume edited by R. Howard Bloch and Stephen G. Nichols under the title *Medievalism and the Modernist Temper* (Baltimore, 1996). The author would like to thank the editors for allowing her to read the book in manuscript. Especially useful essays in that volume are David Hult, "Gaston Paris and the Invention of Courtly Love," and Stephen G. Nichols, "Modernism and the Politics of Medieval Studies." On the alliance of philology with French and German national movements see also R. Howard Bloch, "Naturalism, Nationalism, Medievalism," *Romanic Review* 76 (Nov. 1985): 341–60, and Hans Ulrich Gumbrecht, "Un Soufle d'Allemagne ayant passé: Friedrich Diez, Gaston Paris and the Genesis of National

Philologies," *Romance Philology* 40 (Oct. 1986): 1–37. It is interesting that American medievalists' allegiance to positivism survived World War I intact, despite the well-known "crisis of historicism" in Germany in the immediate postwar years, echoed in America primarily in the work of Charles Beard and Carl Becker. Indeed, Peter Novick has demonstrated that, among American historians, medievalists were most resistant to the currents of relativism that surfaced after World War I. Whereas Carl Becker and Charles Beard used the occasion of their presidential addresses in 1931 and 1933 respectively to articulate their relativist doctrines—Becker in his "Everyman His Own Historian," *American Historical Review* 37 (1932): 221–36; Beard in "Written History as an Act of Faith," *American Historical Review* 39 (1934): 219–31—Charles McIlwain devoted his presidential address of 1936 to attacking Beard's of three years earlier, in order to uphold the premises of scientific objectivity against his colleagues' relativism. See his "The Historian's Part in a Changing World," *American Historical Review* 42 (1937): 207–24. Medievalists were not alone in defending the "noble dream" of objectivity, but they were universally on its side in the debate that erupted. On this see Peter Novick, *That Noble Dream: The "Objectivity Question" and the American Historical Profession* (Cambridge, Eng., 1988), esp. chap. 9. Also useful is John Higham, *History Professional Scholarship in America* (Baltimore and London, 1965).

31. According to William J. Courtenay, the most striking effect of the war on Americans was to redirect both attention and training away from Germany to France, Belgium, and England ("The Virgin and the Dynamo," p. 14ff). One consequence of this shift was to inaugurate a small but powerful following in America of the Belgian historian Henri Pirenne, among whose most famous students were Carl Stephenson, James Bruce Ross, and Bryce Lyon. Another was the virtual extinction of German history as a field in North America, a phenomenon that remains true down to the present day. On this latter phenomenon see Patrick J. Geary, "Medieval Germany in America," *Annual Lectures 1990* (Washington, D.C.: The German Historical Institute, 1991); Edward J. Peters, "More Trouble with Henry: The Historiography of Medieval Germany in the Angloliterate World, 1888–1995," *Central European History* 28 (1995): 47–72; and aspects of Giles Constable, "The Many Middle Ages Medieval Studies in Europe as Seen from America," in Jacqueline Hamesse, ed., *Bilan et Perspectives des Etudes Médiévales en Europe* (Louvain–la Neuve, 1995), pp. 1–22.

32. Here, again, Charles McIlwain provides the most interesting example. In contrast to his firm maintenance of scientific historiography and objectivity in his 1936 presidential attack on Beard's relativism, already before the end of World War II McIlwain found himself responding to political events via a revision of his earlier understandings of Roman law. Thus, in an article entitled "Medieval Institutions in the Modern World" (*Speculum* 16 [1941]: 275–83), McIlwain allowed present events in Germany to reorient completely his notion of the place of Roman law in Western constitutionalism, arguing that "if we find the outcome of the Germanic origin of our institutions in the barbarous tribal orgy and the fantastic tribal history of the Germany of today, we may well begin to wonder if we have not been overdoing our own notions both of the continuing importance of our Germanic origins and of the accuracy, or at least the adequacy of the von Maurers of yesterday or of the von Gierkes of today." In place of his insistence in his presidential address that objectivity was not only possible but incumbent upon the historian, and that it could be maintained in the face of the sort of presentist concerns that both Beard and Becker stressed, McIlwain now confessed that "for myself it has been the tribal excesses of present-day Germany which, as much as anything else, have led me to question the group theory of von Gierke's *Genossenschaftsrecht* either as an explanation of medieval life or as a principle of practical politics" (pp. 279–80). Moreover, McIlwain opined, the Nazi repudiation of Roman law suggested that medievalists had greatly overemphasized the despotic character

of that great legal corpus and had, conversely, greatly underrated the "importance of Roman constitutionalism in the early development of our own" (p. 278). This domestication and democratization of what had earlier been seen as the absolutist tendencies of Roman law, begun in an American context by McIlwain, was to gain powerful allies from the German émigré community of medievalists, among them Stephen Kuttner, Walter Ullmann (in England), and especially Ernst Kantorowicz, whose students included Robert Benson and Ralph Giesey. See also the essays of Gaines Post, collected in his *Studies in Medieval Legal Thought* (Princeton, 1964). A parallel group of works has emanated, as the anonymous reader of this volume for Princeton University Press helpfully pointed out, from Brian Tierney and his students, who devoted themselves to "the study of the relationship between medieval constitutionalism and the origins of the modern liberal state." McIlwain's 1941 article is notable for its prescient awareness of the impact that the war would have on American scholarship.

33. Norman Cantor has persuasively argued that Haskins's achievement as a medieval historian lay in applying the basic tenets of Wilsonian progressivism to the study of medieval history, leading him to insist on the beneficial consequences of centralized power in the hands of an educated and professional elite, whether medieval or modern. See *Inventing the Middle Ages*, p. 249.

34. As in the title of his book, Joseph Reese Strayer, *On the Medieval Origins of the Modern State* (Princeton, 1970).

35. See Cantor, *Inventing the Middle Ages*, p. 260.

36. Published by The Medieval Academy of America (Cambridge, Mass.), in 1932.

37. Cantor, *Inventing the Middle Ages*, p. 258.

38. Joseph Reese Strayer, "Philip the Fair—a 'Constitutional King,'" *American Historical Review* 62 (1956): 18–32.

39. In particular by Bryce Lyon, "What Made a Medieval King Constitutional," in *Essays in Medieval History Presented to Bertie Wilkinson* (Toronto, 1969). I am indebted to Professor John W. Baldwin for this reference.

40. See Joseph Reese Strayer, *Studies in Early French Taxation* (Cambridge, Mass., 1939), passim.

41. The first was published in *Studi in onore di Gino Luzzatto*, 1 (Milan, 1949), pp. 289–96; reprinted in John Benton and Thomas Bisson, eds., *Medieval Statecraft and the Perspectives of History: Essays by Joseph Reese Strayer* (Princeton, 1971), pp. 12–27; the latter in Theodore K. Rabb and Jerrold E. Siegel, eds., *Action and Conviction in Early Modern Europe: Essays in Memory of E. R. Harbison* (Princeton, 1969), pp. 3–19, reprinted in Benton and Bisson, eds., *Medieval Statecraft and the Perspectives of History*, pp. 300–314.

42. Joseph Reese Strayer, "The Fourth and the Fourteenth Centuries," *American Historical Review* 77 (1972): 1–14.

43. Joseph Reese Strayer, "The Laicization of French and English Society in the Thirteenth Century," *Speculum* 15 (1940): 76–86, reprinted in Benton and Bisson, eds., *Medieval Statecraft and the Perspectives of History*, pp. 251–65.

44. Cantor, *Inventing the Middle Ages*, p. 254.

45. The term *postmodernism* first gained renown with the publication of Jean François Lyotard's *La condition postmoderne: rapport sur le savoir* (Paris, 1979) in 1979 but probably was not widespread in American historiography until the translation of Lyotard's book in 1984. On this, see William D. Paden, "Scholars at a Perilous Ford," in William D. Paden, ed., *The Future of the Middle Ages Medieval Literature in the 1990s* (Gainesville, 1994), p. 8.

46. Eric L. Santner, *Stranded Objects: Mourning, Memory, and Film in Postwar Germany* (Ithaca, 1990), p. 51.

47. On the negative appeal of the Middle Ages see Paden. "Scholars at a Perilous Ford," p. 21.

48. For a fuller discussion of much of what follows see my "History, Historicism and the Social Logic of the Text in the Middle Ages," *Speculum* 65 (1990): 59–86, and my response to the debate on "History and Postmodernism" it generated in *Past and Present* 135 (1992): 194–208.

49. To some extent, this kind of work might be thought to derive from Marc Bloch's emphasis on mentalité, an initially neglected aspect of the "Annales paradigm," but there has been very little work in specifically medieval history (in contrast to early modern history) in America that takes its primary impetus from the Annales school. Not only does there not exist an identifiable American school dedicated to the study of medieval mentalités, neither can the profound changes represented by the rise of discursively oriented work really be traced back to the Annales, however compatible the Annalist emphasis on mentalité might at first seem to be with it. In truth, they employ quite different views of language, hence of the nature of medieval textuality and the uses to which it can, and should, be put.

50. Eugene Vance, "Semiotics and Power: Relics, Icons and the *Voyage de Charlemagne à Jérusalem et à Constantinople*," in Marina S. Brownlee, Kevin Brownlee, and Stephen G. Nichols, eds., *The New Medievalism* (Baltimore, 1991), p. 227.

51. The earliest work in medieval women's history, such as that of Jo Ann McNamara and Suzanne Wemple, focused on the ways that historical scholarship had occluded women's historical presence and sought to restore them to view. See, for example, the 1981 book by Suzanne Wemple, *Women in Frankish Society: Marriage and the Cloister, 500 to 900* (Philadelphia, 1981), and McNamara's essay in her edition of papers from the Fifth Berkshire Conference on the History of Women, *Women and the Structure of Society: Selected Research from the Fifth Berkshire Conference on the History of Women* (Durham, N.C., 1982), and as well the collected works of this "Columbia school" of women's history in *Women of the Medieval World: Essays in Honor of John H. Mundy* (Oxford, 1985). The basic impulse of this early work was to make women visible upon the historical stage, but as Wemple's and McNamara's own developments indicate, an exclusive focus on women soon became normative. See, for example, McNamara's later books, *Sisters in Arms: Catholic Nuns through Two Millennia* (Cambridge, Mass., 1996) and *Sainted Women of the Dark Ages* (Durham, N.C., 1992). Interestingly, McNamara's feminism has now carried her into a study of masculinity as well, in her recent work *Medieval Masculinities: Regarding Men in the Middle Ages* (Minneapolis, 1994). For an overview of these developments in the field of medieval history see Susan Mosher Stuard, "A New Dimension? North American Scholars Contribute their Perspective," in Stuard, ed., *Women in Medieval History*, pp. 81–99. See also the recent special volume of *Speculum* 68 (1993) dedicated to women's history, now published as Nancy Partner, ed., *Studying Medieval Women, Sex, Gender, Feminism* (Cambridge, Mass., 1993). Feminist scholarship on medieval women is now far too extensive to cite comprehensively, but an example of this sort of work is Penny Shine Gold, *The Lady and the Virgin: Image, Attitude and Experience in Twelfth-Century France* (Chicago, 1985).

52. Here the work of Caroline Bynum has been decisive, especially her *Holy Feast and Holy Fast: The Religious Significance of Food to Medieval Women* (Berkeley, 1987) as well as her most recent works, *Fragmentation and Redemption: Essays on Gender and the Human Body in Medieval Religion* (New York, 1991) and *The Resurrection of the Body in Western Christianity, 200–1336* (New York, 1995).

53. See, for example, the collective article by E. Jane Burns, Roberta Krueger, and Helen

Solterer, "Feminism and the Discipline of Old French Studies," in Bloch and Nichols, *Medievalism and the Modernist Temper*, passim.

54. An extremely useful survey of these changes is Michael Kammen's "The Historian's Vocation and the State of the Discipline in the United States," in Michael Kammen, ed., *The Past before Us: Contemporary Historical Writing in the United States* (Ithaca, 1980), pp. 19–46; see also the essay on medieval historiography by Karl Morrison, "Fragmentation and Unity in American Medievalism," in ibid., pp. 49–77.

55. Paul Freedman, "The Return of the Grotesque in Medieval Historiography," in Carlos Barros, ed., *Historia A Debate: Medieval* (Santiago de Compostella, 1995): 9–19.

56. Ibid., p. 16.

57. Michel Foucault, *The Archeology of Knowledge* (New York, 1972), p. 5

58. On the significance of treating texts as "monuments" rather than "documents" see Frantzen, *The Desire for Origins*, which seeks to apply these principles to the study of Anglo-Saxon literature.

59. Very recent examples of work done in this vein are Joan Cadden, *The Meaning of Sex Differences in the Middle Ages* (Cambridge, Eng., 1994); John W. Baldwin, *The Language of Sex: Five Voices from Northern France around 1200* (Chicago, 1994); E. Jane Burns, *Bodytalk: When Women Speak in Old French Literature* (Philadelphia, 1993). There is a huge literature on medieval sexuality, beginning with the work of Vern L. Bullough, *Sexual Practices and the Medieval Church* (Buffalo, 1982), and James Brundage, *Law, Sex, and Christian Society in Medieval Europe* (Chicago, 1987).

60. See the works of Caroline W. Bynum cited in note 52.

61. R. I. Moore, *The Formation of a Persecuting Society: Power and Deviance in Western Europe, 950–1250* (Oxford, 1987); and idem, *The Origins of European Dissent* (New York, 1985); idem, *The Birth of Popular Heresy* (New York, 1976). John E. Boswell, "Jews, Bicycle Riders and Gay People: The Determination of Social Consensus and Its Impact on Minorities," *Yale Journal of Law and the Humanities* 1 (1989): 205–28. See also the series of works by Jeffrey Russell, *Dissent and Order in the Middle Ages: The Search for Legitimate Order* (New York, 1992); idem, *Lucifer: The Devil in the Middle Ages* (Ithaca, 1984); idem, *Religious Dissent in the Middle Ages* (New York, 1971). For a general bibliography see Carl Berkout, *Medieval Heresies: A Bibliography, 1960–1979* (Toronto, 1981). Also relevant is the work of Edward J. Peters, *Heresy and Authority in Medieval Europe* (Philadelphia, 1988); idem, *Inquisition* (New York, 1988); idem, *Torture* (New York, 1985); idem, *The Magician, the Witch and the Law* (Philadelphia, 1978); idem, with Alan Kors, *Witchcraft in Europe* (Philadelphia, 1972).

62. Norman Cohn, *Europe's Inner Demons: An Enquiry Inspired by the Great Witch-Hunt* (New York, 1975).

63. See William Chester Jordan, *The French Monarchy and the Jews: From Philip Augustus to the Last Capetians* (Philadelphia, 1989), and his *Women and Credit in Pre-industrial and Developing Societies* (Philadelphia, 1993) , which in part concerns financial transactions (loans) between women and Jews.

64. The work of the late John Boswell is critical here, especially his two books, *Christianity, Social Tolerance and Homosexuality: Gay People in Western Europe from the Beginning of the Christian Era to the Fourteenth Century* (Chicago, 1980) and *Same-Sex Unions in Premodern Europe* (New York, 1994).

65. See the work of Robert Chazan, *European Jewry and the First Crusade* (Berkeley, 1987); idem, *Daggers of Faith: Thirteenth-Century Christian Missionizing and Jewish Response* (Berkeley, 1989); idem, "The Representation of Events in the Middle Ages," *History and*

Theory 27 (1988): 40–55; and of Ivan Marcus, "History, Story and Collective Memory: Narrativity in Early Ashkenazic Culture," *Prooftexts* 10 (1990).

66. See Eleanor Searle, *Predatory Kinship and the Creation of Norman Power* (Berkeley, 1988); and Thomas N. Bisson, "The 'Feudal Revolution,'" *Past and Present* 142 (1994): 6–42.

67. Thus Lee Patterson has specifically advocated the adoption of an ironic mode of history as that best adapted to a postmodernist treatment of the medieval past. See his "On the Margin," passim.

68. Freedman, "The Return of the Grotesque," p. 9.

69. Van Engen, "An Afterword on Medieval Studies," p. 414.

70. Santner, *Stranded Objects*, p. 7.

The Italian Renaissance, Made in the USA

ANTHONY MOLHO

I

The Renaissance Today. The Renaissance in Italy was the firstborn son of modern Europe. So wrote Jacob Burckhardt in 1860. Eighty years later, in Wallace K. Ferguson's influential book-length essay *The Renaissance* (1940), the "firstborn son" became "the most intractable problem child of historiography." Contrast this sentiment to the lament expressed by William Bouwsma, one of America's most distinguished historians of the Renaissance. In his presidential address to the American Historical Association in 1978, Bouwsma, gazing at a historiographical spectacle which struck him for its desolation, quipped that "the venerable Renaissance label has become little more than an administrative convenience, a kind of blanket under which we huddle together."[1] So, the edifying image of the firstborn son of the late 1860s had, by the late 1970s, been transformed into the dispiriting spectacle of a band of scholars who, for no apparently good intellectual reasons, found themselves huddling under an ill-fitting blanket. *Sic transit. . . .*

We have witnessed in these years a sea change in the work of American historians of late medieval and early modern Italy. Nearly two decades ago, one of the pioneer American feminist historians of the Renaissance posed the question forthrightly: "Did women have a Renaissance?" she asked. Her answer was that they did not, and it seemed that the very use of the term Renaissance was being challenged, for if it could not be applied to (indeed, if it distorted) the experience of women, then, obviously, one would have to rethink its meaning and utility.[2] Such questioning is by no means confined to the work of feminist historians. There is a view widely shared among North American historians that recent research, in the words of Samuel Cohn, "raises problems for the old Burckhardtian formulation and its more recent proponents. It questions a simple transition from medieval to modern, [and] notions of individualism."[3] Anthony Grafton, soon after launching his studies on the history of humanism, realized that "standard histories of classical scholarship arranged the field into a neatly teleological system of ages. . . . The neatness of this classification revealed its spuriousness at once." As a result of this reflection, he set out to accomplish no less a task than to "challenge the orthodox history of Western culture," most crucially the standard chronology of the humanist movement and, by implication, of the Renaissance itself.[4] Perhaps even more fundamentally, with the abandonment of the classical humanistic curriculum, the sense that our world continues to be linked to the world of the Renaissance has met as serious a challenge as it is possible to imagine.[5]

The current American efforts to redefine the Renaissance do not merely bespeak the existence of a heated scholarly *querelle*, nor does this discussion cast light only on an agitated academic controversy. Since the nineteenth century, the Renaissance has held a place of special honor within the larger American view of European history. This view was deeply rooted in the tastes of a wider public, who had often grown attached to the culture of Italy in the Renaissance. For the past nearly two centuries, one of the axioms of historical wisdom in America has been the nexus between the Renaissance and modernity. Americans have always thought of themselves as being modern, their culture standing for change and innovation. For this reason, they have identified in the Renaissance a historical moment which was especially akin—in its tastes, values, and seemingly endless willingness to challenge the moral priorities of the past—to their own society and ideology. The success of Renaissance studies in North American universities—a much greater success than one finds in any postwar European academic tradition—is inexplicable unless one remembers this long-standing, nonscholarly interest. The filial metaphor, coined by Burckhardt and given its psychologizing twist by Ferguson and other North American scholars, conveyed a sense of the cultural kinship which intellectuals, scholars, and members of the wider public imagined between their country's culture and that of the Italian Renaissance. Against this background, briefly surveyed in the following section, the extent and profundity of this present change in attitude toward the Renaissance becomes clear.

II

The Italian Renaissance in Nineteenth-Century America. The Italian Renaissance reached the shores of the New World around the middle of the eighteenth century. Within a hundred years—before the American historical profession was institutionalized, historical curricula were worked out, or a well defined scholarly tradition of studying the Renaissance became established in America—the existence of the Renaissance as a key moment in European history had become well ensconced in the consciousness of the American educated public. It is important to keep in mind this preprofessional life of the Renaissance in America. Without it, the American study of the Renaissance as a professional field of historiography might well have had a different history. Suffice it to remember the general neglect among American professional historians in this century's first six or so decades of the histories of Holland, of the Ottoman, Habsburg, and Iberian Empires, or, with the exception of the religious reformation, of medieval and early modern Germany, or of the Italian South. One then realizes that individual moments of the European past were recognized, legitimated, and inserted in the historical genealogy of North America on the basis of indigenous, *American*, cultural preferences. By the end of the nineteenth century, the Italian Renaissance was ensconced in America's distinguished and honored ancestry.

In most important respects, there were no differences between American and European images of the Renaissance; both were fashioned in the late eighteenth and early nineteenth centuries, when the Renaissance emerged in the historical consciousness of scholars and intellectuals as a key moment—for some, *the* key moment—in the history of European civilization. This enthusiasm was shared in England, France, the Germanies, and, no less so than elsewhere, in America. J. B. Bullen's recent book traces the invention of the Renaissance myth, from Gibbon and Voltaire in the late eighteenth century to Hugo, Ruskin, and Pater through the nineteenth.[6] Bullen shows that this myth consisted of various parts. But its key component, the element which elicited unreserved enthusiasm and conviction among its proponents, was the thought that aesthetic refinement had reached its apogee at the time of the Italian Renaissance. In J. A. Symonds's embarrassingly exuberant formulation, the Renaissance was "the most marvelous period the world has ever known."[7] And it was marvelous precisely because giants such Michelangelo, and Leonardo, had yearned toward a level of beauty that rarely if ever had been imagined before or after them.

This breathless enthusiasm was shared by many American writers, artists, and travelers, who in diaries, letters, and books, and often in rapturous tones, described their impressions of Italy, and of its artistically unexcelled accomplishments. American painters and sculptors had, of course, been to Italy in the eighteenth century as well, and helped introduce the culture of the Renaissance to their patrons and clients.[8] But it was only with the beginning of the new century that the number of travelers increased, and a tradition—an American tradition—of describing and praising the culture of Italy, and of the Renaissance in particular, began developing.[9] The resilience of this tradition is striking, for it has survived, its vigor undiminished, over the past nearly two centuries.

Throughout the nineteenth century, there persisted a keen American sensibility to, and a profound admiration for, the aesthetic refinement of Renaissance culture. At the turn of the century, the American painter Washington Allston, who lived in Rome from 1804 to 1808, mused that the period we call the Italian Renaissance had been "the Golden Age." And he continued, striking a theme to be echoed time and again by American travelers to Italy: "I cannot well conceive how any imaginative man can return from Rome and Florence without having felt that there are other truths besides such as are begotten through the senses."[10] Italy, especially the Renaissance, helped men [sic!] discover art, refinement, and beauty. At just about the same time, Washington Irving repeated the same sentiment: "Men discover taste and fancy in Italy," he confided to his diary.[11] Half a century later, Mrs. Nathaniel Hawthorne unabashedly shared this romantic sentiment: "My beautiful Florence! The flower of cities, the most highly cultivated of communities, the very rose of civilization."[12]

Time and again, through the century, the artistic achievements of the Renaissance were used as points of reference in fostering and measuring native artistic traditions, as the Renaissance was by now deeply embedded in the consciousness of the cultured public in the USA. By the 1830s, Dante had become one of the favorite poets of the Boston Brahmins. Angelina La Piana calculated that *The North American Review* from the year of its foundation in 1815 to 1850, and the *American Quarterly Review* (1827–37) published more essays, articles, and notes on Italian literature, art, and history than on those of France, Germany, or any other European country except England.[13] By the 1890s, perhaps in coincidence with Columbus's fourth centenary, this penchant reached a remarkable intensity. Repeatedly on major occasions, American artists could not refrain from linking their aspirations to the exalted achievements of Italian Renaissance artists. Thus, for example, in 1893, while discussing plans for the World's Fair, the American sculptor Augustus Saint Gaudens, casting his attention on the American artists gathered in Chicago, blurted out to his friends: "Do you realize that this is the greatest meeting of artists since the fifteenth century?"[14] In the next year, when the American Academy was founded in Rome, it was "the Rome of the Renaissance, with its roots in antiquity" that was claimed as inspiration for this new American institution. And when in 1914 the academy's twentieth anniversary was celebrated by the American art critic Royal Cortissoz, the hope was expressed that the academy would "subject [American artists] to the ennobling pressure of classical and Renaissance influences."[15] A genealogy of this American sentiment can be traced down to our very days, through the distinguished careers of such nonacademic writers as Charles Eliot Norton, William Roscoe Thayer, Bernard Berenson, Eugene Schuyler, Mary McCarthy, Sidney Alexander, Iris Origo, Eve Borsook, and several more.

The career and writings of James Jackson Jarves offer a limpid expression of this American sentiment, of the notion that, however different nineteenth-century America might have been from the Italian states of the fifteenth and sixteenth centuries, the two cultures were bound by recognizable moral and ideological affinities. In truth, more than a few American travelers to Italy in the second and third quarters of the nineteenth century had ventured the thought that American and Italian Renaissance societies had somehow been placed on parallel tracks, that the former was, *in nuce*, what the latter had been, and that lessons of the Italian past could profitably be applied to a materialistic and crass society in the USA. "These old merchants," mused James Fenimore Cooper, referring to Florence's merchant princes of the fourteenth and fifteenth centuries, "men who truly ennobled commerce and not commerce them, have left behind them more durable remains of their ascendancy than can be seen almost any other place."[16] But it was Connecticut-born Jarves—traveler, art collector, and aesthete—who expressed this sentiment more forthrightly and enthusiastically than any of his compatriots.

In an essay suggestively entitled "A Lesson for Merchant Princes," Jarves presented his impressions of Giovanni Rucellai, the mid-fifteenth-century Florentine patrician merchant. In his panegyric, Jarves marveled at the long list of "great names of Florentine history . . . painters, sculptors, poets, writers, philosophers, and statesmen." What was the cause of such success? "When a city has acquired a solidarity of fame like that of Florence, it is instructive to trace its causes to their deepest roots. . . . In Florence the root of roots was trade. Its real builders were not its great architects, artists, and barons, but its traders." And with that thought, he turned his attention to Giovanni Rucellai, and to his world. "Here we see the ideal Florentine, the complete type of enterprising, sagacious, 'level-headed' citizen, respectable, successful, and esteemed in every relation of life, pious without bigotry, acquisitive without stinginess, thrifty and yet munificent, every action closely calculated in its consequences, scholarly, moral, hospitable, and self-controlled, one of the veritable makers of Florence; not so absorbed in the narrow horizon of self or 'set,' as not to take a broad view of the interests of his city, and to give and labor zealously to promote them. . . ." But why must one expatiate at such lengths on the virtues of so extraordinary a man? Because of the similarities between fifteenth-century Florence and nineteenth-century America, which render Florentine history "particularly interesting to Americans, whose social distinctions, if not their political, and whose riches on which these are founded are made in the same manner as were the Florentines. We are traveling the same road, socially, mercantilely, and artistically, if not yet politically." And so, "if we are to build on American soil cities like Florence, world renowned for art and science even more than for commerce and luxury, we must breed merchant princes cultured like Rucellai, and deeply imbued with his maxims, that it is pleasanter and more honorable to spend money for wise purposes than to make it."[17] Here was not simply a program of study suggested for scholars and erudites. This was an American *Bildung* worthy of the best citizens and of their country.

There is something else worth noting about Jarves's influence. His call for an American, patrician *Bildung* gave voice to one of two (largely contrasting) American attitudes toward modernity. As will be seen below, many American writers and historians attracted to the study of the Renaissance were convinced that there existed a vital link between the Renaissance and modernity. For them, modernity represented a positive set of values, and the Renaissance was important precisely because it contributed to their affirmation. For Jarves and his followers, modernity also was an issue. But modernity conveyed valences which were not always positive, or attractive. In fact, for many—scholars and laypeople—modernity was dangerous; it had to be resisted, alternatives to it invented. Thus, from the beginning, the Renaissance in America was closely hitched to a vocal and influential antimodernist movement. The tension between Jarves's call for the American adoption of Renaissance values—seen as an antidote to the ills of modernity—and the celebration of modernity in the work of many American historians of the Renaissance economy and politics surfaced with particular force late in the late twentieth century. This is a point to which we shall return below.

To be sure, not all Americans shared Jarves's sentiment. A long succession of American writers from John Adams and James Madison expressed their criticism, even their disgust, at what they took to be the corrupting spectacle of late medieval Italian politics. Venice, celebrated in seventeenth- and eighteenth-century English political thought as the paragon of republicanism, was overwhelmingly seen by Americans, in the picturesque expressions of George Stillman Hillard, as a place where "there was long and unbroken calm. . . . it was the repose of death, like a mummy in a sarcophagus," a city "sealed by the arctic frost of despotism."[18] Others, in a tradition which extends from Hawthorne through Mark Twain to Henry James himself were more inclined to see the Renaissance as an expression of an oppressive, arbitrary, and tyrannical aristocratic rule. "Who is this Renaissance?" exclaimed Mark Twain, "Where did he come from? Who gave him permission to cram the republic with his execrable daubs?"[19] But even in their denunciations, these writers made it clear that the Renaissance would occupy an important place in the American reflection on America's European past.

A glance at the history of historical instruction in the nineteenth century helps to place this discussion in better perspective. If the experience of Brown University were not unique, it would seem that well before the establishment of the historical profession, and the invention of the concept of Western Civilization, the public's predilections had ensured that the Renaissance would become an integral part of courses on the history of civilization. Lecturing to his students in the autumn of 1860, William Gammell, Brown's first professor of history, imputed to the Renaissance characteristics which his New England students would have had little difficulty in appreciating: "The great preparation for the Reformation," he said, according to the notes kept by one of his students, Charles D. Cady, "is undoubtedly to be found in the revival of ancient learning. . . . This habit of enquiry which was thus created, the new and startling truths which were thus communicated and above all the general culture and intelligence which were diffused must give rise to new views and enterprises. The ignorance, the brute force, the feudal insubordination of the middle age were passing away, and the new intellectual activity immediately directed itself to the questions of religion, for these had long occupied the largest share of the thoughts and interests of men."[20] Twenty years later, when J. L. Diman was teaching the course, and one of his prize pupils was Charles Evans Hughes, future chief justice of the U.S. Supreme Court, the Renaissance was conceived as the key, pivotal moment in the unfolding of that historical process which culminated in the creation of the United States. The "Italian Renaissance," which in the architecture of Diman's course occupied the first substantial segment of the second semester, "implied not only revival of letters, but whole transition from medieval to modern times. It was period of a new birth, and hence revolutionary. Certain conditions were required for this change, partly social, and partly political, which were first brought together in Italy."[21] There followed suggestions for further reading, diligently noted by Hughes in his notebook: Sismondi on the Italian republics, Roscoe on Lorenzo de' Medici, and, perhaps most remarkably, Burckhardt, available in English translation for less than a year.

One additional point is worth emphasizing about the experience of mid-nineteenth-century Brown students. Their encounter with the Renaissance was made in courses whose specific object was to illuminate the historical traditions of the United States. Gammell began his course with the sixteenth century and brought it up to the 1830s, examining in the process the secular and parliamentary traditions which, in his view, defined his country's character. Diman's course, although more elaborate and longer, was informed by the same spirit. Following a set of lectures on the "nature of the study of history," whose object was to establish the scientific basis of historical study ("the Anatomy, Physiology, the Physiognomy of History"), Diman devoted most of the first semester to medieval Europe ("the formative period of European civilization"), opened the second semester with a lengthy analysis of the Renaissance, and slowly brought the subject to the nineteenth century, the course's last three topics devoted to an examination of "modern political theories," the "constitutional history of the United States," and, finally, the "U.S. Constitution."[22] In short, the Renaissance—as an essential moment in the birth of modernity and as a concept which encapsulated values fundamental to the definition of the USA—was examined within the context of a theory of modern democracy and citizenship which Brown's professors presented to their students.

Under these circumstances, it is not surprising to discover that even as profoundly conservative and Protestant a scholarly community as was the late nineteenth- and early twentieth-century historical establishment in America would acknowledge the contribution of a Mediterranean, Catholic society to the country's cultural ancestry. In the very opening article of the *American Historical Review*, William M. Sloane presented a clear programmatic statement of the newly created historical association's aims and of its journal's scope. "We are," he explained, "Europeans of ancient stock, and a change of skies did not involve a new physical birth for our society. Doubtless, environment modified our development, but the well ordered, serious life which we brought with us from England, Scotland, Ireland, Holland, Germany, and France we have preserved and developed, at least as well as those who stayed at home."[23] Sloane's scheme allowed little room for the study of any part of Italian history. And yet, from the very beginning, the Renaissance was incorporated in the concept of Western Civilization. Alongside England, Scotland, Ireland, and the other northern European regions from where had sprung the genuine and hardy English-American culture, one found also a fragment of Italian history, that portion to which was attached the label of the Renaissance. The rest of Italian history—the long centuries preceding and following, Italy's "forgotten centuries," as Eric Cochrane would dub them—were not worthy of redemption. The Renaissance was. And it was, no doubt, because of both its rootedness in the culture of the nonacademic reading public and its allegedly rationalistic, individualistic, and antireligious ideas, in short because of the ideology of modernity which was imputed to it.

By the turn of the new century, the Renaissance occupied a strategic role in the configuration of courses on the history of Western Civilization. An examination of college textbooks written in the first decades of the twentieth century shows that they largely followed the topical sequence of Diman's courses at Brown, and no doubt of comparable courses elsewhere. The canon of historical knowledge dictated that the Renaissance be given the honor of inaugurating the modern era, and this for very much the same reason that Diman had adduced in his course. In short, the Burckhardtian vision had been embraced by American historians, even if, in contrast to Burckhardt, they overwhelmingly took a positive and optimistic view of modernity. But quite beyond and preceding this Burckhardtian, modernizing vision, American historians were also deeply influenced, already during the central decades of the nineteenth and well into the first decades of the twentieth century, by the favorable, sympathetic assessment of the Renaissance prevalent in the nonacademic culture.

While the nonacademic interest in the Renaissance was as strong as ever in the first few decades of the century, little scholarly work on the Renaissance, or for that matter on any aspect of Italian history, was carried out in America. This contrasts sharply both with the increasingly systematic work of American medievalists and with the very first American scholarly work on the history of art history, and Neo-Latin philology, a good deal of which was concentrated on Renaissance subjects.[24] When, in the late 1920s, Chester P. Higby of the University of Wisconsin undertook a survey of 250 American specialists in the history of "modern" (that is, of postmedieval) Europe, he discovered that not a single one of his respondents identified Italian history as a principal field of study. More significantly, while 72 had spent time working in British libraries and archives, and another 32 in the Bibliothèque Nationale and the Archives Nationales, none had visited Italian libraries and archives.[25] In the United States through the 1920s and beyond, the Renaissance remained, above all, a phenomenon with greater appeal to the nonacademic public than to the newly professionalized scholarly, academic community. To nonacademics, the period underscored Jarves's lesson: it evoked feelings about artistic creativity, represented a sense of the high potential inherent in human history, and expressed a strong voluntarist—a modern—penchant with which educated and affluent Americans in the late nineteenth and early twentieth centuries were eager to identify themselves. For professional historians, on the other hand, the Renaissance illustrated more general and theoretical views of the development of European (and, by extension, human) history, in schemes which were profoundly indebted to idealist philosophical traditions, but rarely and then only minimally informed by the study of sources.[26]

Abroad in America. All this changed in the 1930s, when, as a result of the flight to North America of a large number of European, mostly German, scholars, the Renaissance became an intensely cultivated field of historical scholarship. Two questions are worth posing about the epic of the German, mostly Jewish scholars who transformed the American study of the Renaissance. To begin with, how to account for the apparent ease with which a host of them made a successful transition to an unknown and not always hospitable academic environment? To be sure, one tends to remember only the successes, and, in the great saga of the "intellectual migration," it is easy to understand that there were more stories that ended unhappily than those with relatively happy endings. But anyone familiar with the recent history of Renaissance studies in America cannot fail to be struck by the number of German scholars who, within a short time of their arrival to America, established the intellectual agendas followed in this country for about half a century starting in the late 1930s: Hans Baron, Felix Gilbert, Paul Oskar Kristeller, Theodor Mommsen, Erwin Panofsky, and in the thematic margins of the field, but with great influence on it, Hojo Holborn, Ernst Kantorowicz, Helene Wieruszowski, Richard Krautheimer. Secondly, why should it be that, of all fields in humanistic studies, with the possible exception of postunification German history, the Renaissance should have profited most by the presence of new, Continental ideas and methods of study? In trying to suggest answers to these questions, three points are worth keeping in mind: historical method, ideological orientation, and the state of Renaissance studies in Germany and the United States.

German scholars who took refuge in America, and who, in great number, tended to be in their thirties and in the formative stages of their careers,[27] found themselves in close agreement with their American hosts as to historical method. Many of them had either studied with Friedrich Meinecke (Baron, Gilbert, Holborn) or had come under his close influence (Mommsen and Wieruszowski), and had shared their master's insistence upon enlarging the scope of historical research beyond the traditional fields of institutional, political, and military history. In a search for a better and deeper understanding of the past, Meinecke taught his students to focus their attention on ideas, society, and, more widely, culture. If Burckhardt's, Dilthey's, Droysen's, and Lamprecht's influence among the émigré historians was pronounced, in their own recollections it was Meinecke's lesson which stood out.[28] In her moving preface to her collected essays published in 1971, Wieruszowski evoked Meinecke's method of "research leading to understanding" (*forschend zu verstehen*) in the field of the history of ideas,[29] while in his autobiography Gilbert recalled how Meinecke "had shaken up German historical scholarship by emphasizing the relations among intellectual movements, political thought, and political action."[30]

American historians who had come under the influence of the New History could easily share their new colleagues' views. Since the early years of the century, the advocates of the New History had urged historians to enlarge their horizons by writing not only about politics and institutions but also society, economics, and ideas, and to move the focus of research closer to the histories of common people. Turner himself likened the framework of a nation to the anatomy of a body: "Behind institutions, behind constitutional forms, lie the vital forces that call these organs into life and shape them to meet changing conditions."[31] If the metaphors used by German and American historians were different, their aims largely overlapped, and it was thus possible to engage in a meaningful dialogue on an issue which was central to the interests of both groups. The need to do what we call "interdisciplinary" history was fully and urgently felt by both German and American historians in the 1920s and 1930s. In the words of Ernst Schulin, as a result of the work of the German émigré historians, "political, intellectual, and social developments in Europe were presented as a mutually controlling interplay of interests, in the same way that American New History had done with America's domestic history."[32]

The two groups' overlapping political and ideological orientations served to solidify this sense of community. It is obvious—but then perhaps only in retrospect—that many of the European exiles to the United States would embrace a left-wing identity. They had, after all, paid an intolerable personal price for the policies of a rightist, nationalistic, and antirational regime. Even if Kantorowicz's early professional history, and Hans Rothfels's entire career, show that there was nothing inherently left-wing about these scholars' ideological position, by the late 1920s those who studied with Meinecke tended to line up among the defenders of parliamentary and democratic rule, a choice which, in the context of politics in the late Weimar republic, placed them firmly on the left.[33] And it was predominantly those young scholars, whether or not they were Jewish, who fled Germany after 1933. American New Historians, if not on the left as the term was understood in Europe, were progressives, as Brinton pointed out in 1939, under the spell of such figures as H. G. Wells and G. B. Shaw. They believed that an active government policy could ameliorate social conditions, and that the application of rational planning would redound to the benefit of all.[34] A strong distaste on the part of most American New Historians toward the Nazi regime, and a conviction that the United States should oppose it, further united German émigrés and their American hosts in a common ideological orientation.

This common ideological orientation was further reinforced by a striking similarity in German and American views about the aim of historical study. For German scholars since the early nineteenth century, especially for Jews intent on assimilating themselves in German society, the study of the past was inseparable from the notion of *Bildung*, the idea that education must serve to improve and strengthen an individual's character, and by so doing reinforce the bourgeois order. There was a powerfully moral and social dimension to education.[35] So it was with American historians, for whom much time and energy from the 1890s to the 1940s was devoted to discussing their social and civic responsibilities. If it was not quite the idea of *Bildung* which was at the heart of this discussion, the notion of citizenship, and of the inculcation of proper values on the myriad newcomers who had flocked to America before World War I, was central to the American discussion. For German historians the preservation of a middle-class social order was vital to the entire educational enterprise. For many American historians the central issue was how to steer the American citizenry clear of radical social change, at the very moment when the rise of communism and fascism coincided with the challenge faced by the need to acculturate to the values of the American establishment the millions of recently arrived immigrants from eastern and southern Europe. "Unless we are alert to the necessity for constant adjustment," mused Conyers Read, "we create a condition of maladjustment which is the inevitable forerunner of Revolution, whether that Revolution take the Russian or the Italian form. . . . I believe that the study of history has an important social function to perform of just this sort."[36] Beyond the specific use of history in the civic education of the citizenry, there was the broader but no less crucial need to reflect on the meaning of the humanities and its placement in the educational mission of the universities. For many German historians, as Carl Landauer recently reflected in his fine study of Panofsky, this was a conscious "strategy of escape," and one which fitted nicely in the "rising [American] cultural ideology that linked the humanities and the classical tradition to a definition of humanity."[37]

Thus, despite the obvious and seemingly profound differences between the two historical traditions, and the far from negligible differences in the social and institutional contexts within which the two groups of historians had been trained, questions of method and of ideological orientation helped to fashion a community of interests. Then, there is the further question of understanding the enormous, in some ways unexpected, success of Renaissance studies in America following the arrival of the German scholars. Whatever the explanation for this phenomenon, it is important to remember the dimensions of this success. Few subdisciplines of the historical profession grew so rapidly following World War II, and acquired as enviable a reputation as did Renaissance history. For about twenty years following the mid-1950s, Renaissance history was a great success story, if one is to measure success by the number of interesting and much admired works produced in it and by the number of intellectually ambitious young historians who were attracted to the field. There is little question that this turnabout was the result of the German émigrés' influence on the profession. So, once again, we return to the question: Why should the German scholars have had such influence on American historiography on the Renaissance?

An initial answer might consist of several parts. On the American side there was the persistence of a general interest in the Renaissance; the existence of a simple, powerful, and seemingly convincing general view about the development of European history since the Middle Ages; and the absence of an indigenous scholarly tradition, and of anything like a clear research agenda on the Renaissance. The principal overarching concept available to American historians of Europe was the concept of Western Civilization, which they used to impose order and discipline on the myriad facts of European history. The simultaneous existence of the general paradigm, the placement of the Renaissance in a strategic position within this paradigm as the inaugurator of the modern era, and the lack of a solid scholarly tradition offered German scholars the possibility of influencing the course of Renaissance historiography in the United States.

For their part, these German scholars brought to bear their superb technical tradition—outstanding training in philology and the ancillary historical sciences—and their long familiarity with problems and sources of medieval Italian history. But even more important was the broad context of German Renaissance studies since at least the middle of the nineteenth century. This context was to provide the platform which enabled them to undertake a useful and productive dialogue with American historians. The one important characteristic of the German tradition of Renaissance studies was what might be defined as its absence of specialism. Burckhardt himself was anything but a specialist. His studies on the Renaissance were framed within a broad context of his interests in the emergence of modern European *Kultur*, and the consequent defeat of an older set of values which had its roots in the triumph of Christianity in the age of Constantine. The study of the Renaissance was significant for the very reason that it cast light on this broader historical process. So it was with all the great German historians and philosophers who, in the late nineteenth and early twentieth centuries, wrote on the Renaissance, and for whom the Renaisssance had marked one of the vital turning points of European history. For Dilthey, the Renaissance was an important chapter in the human struggle toward intellectual freedom, the beginnings of modern religious, political, and historical thought. For Troeltsch, the Renaissance represented a reaction against Christian asceticism; for Cassirer, it witnessed the beginnings of the modern scientific view of the world; for Goetz, it signified the advance of the bourgeoisie, and all the consequences of this phenomenon. In short, they invariably examined the Renaissance within the broader context of modern European civilization. None of these scholars could be defined as a historian of the Renaissance. They studied the Renaissance because of its essential contributions to the formation of modern Europe.

So did the younger German historians who were forced to transplant themselves to the United States in the 1930s. For almost none of them was the Renaissance only a field of specialist study. It offered, for all of them, a point of observation from which to examine the making of modern Europe and its culture. As Riccardo Fubini very properly observed, Hans Baron was engaged not simply in an analysis of Florentine humanism, however complex and ambitious his project, but rather in "a search for the origins of the positive values of modern European civilization—in the tradition of Burckhardt and Dilthey."[38] When Gilbert, following his studies of modern diplomatic documents, and of Droysen's historical thought, turned his attention to the Italian Renaissance, it was, as he recalled in his autobiography, to study "the origin of the idea of balance of power."[39] For Mommsen, the starting point of observation was the medieval empire, and it was from there that he moved his attention to the history of Florence (a project which he abandoned shortly after arriving in the States, putting two of his prize American pupils, Gene Brucker and Bill Bowsky, to work on it); for Wieruczowski, the larger issue was the history of education, and the dissemination of classical studies, already in the generation preceding Dante; for Panofsky, one of the cardinal issues was to determine what imprint the fifteenth-century Renaissance left on the "cultural activities in the rest of Europe";[40] for Kantorowicz, as Carl Landauer recently argued, what was at issue was the description of a cosmopolitan ideal from Frederick II's age in the thirteenth century all the way to his own generation.[41] The one notable exception was Paul Kristeller, whose scholarly interests, all the while embedded in an expansive vision of the history of European philosophy, were explicitly focused on the Renaissance. But the majority of the German exiles took their philosophical cues from broad and general questions easily recognizable by historians used to thinking about the course of Western Civilization.

An apparent similarity in conceptual language between Germans and Americans made it possible for the former to appreciate the capacious and pliable category of Western Civilization, and for the latter to accommodate within it the specific and rigorous researches carried out by their newly arrived guests. It is a truly remarkable fact that within months (not years) of their arrival, these German refugees, for most of whom this was the very first experience in the USA and English was still a foreign language, felt welcome enough in their new surroundings to present often elaborate and ambitious projects about the future direction of Renaissance studies in America. The 1943 issue of *The Journal of the History of Ideas*, with its intense discussion on the Renaissance (and Panofsky's powerful response in the *Kenyon Review* of the next year), came in the wake of other such ambitious proposals.[42] Perhaps the most notable of these was Kristeller's lengthy and dense article, jointly written with John Herman Randall, Jr., in which Kristeller presented a program of research which he and his students would faithfully follow for the next half century:

> The crying need for the further study of Renaissance philosophies is not general lectures, nor handbooks based on the conventional generalizations . . . but first, an effort toward making the actual texts available to scholars, and secondly more interpretive studies based on actual reading and understanding of those texts. . . . It seems likely that if we approach our texts with any one of the common interpretations of the Renaissance, we shall end by discarding it. . . . The closer we can get to the problems of the Renaissance itself, and the farther we can get away from viewing them in terms of problems of later incidence, the more likely we are to arrive at a genuine understanding.[43]

This general programmatic statement was followed by a very specific one, in which Kristeller alone submitted a long list of philosophers—from Achilles Tatius to Zosimus—each accompanied by the name of an American scholar who had agreed to undertake a close study of his texts.[44] If Kristeller was perhaps the best organized, and in a sense the most entrepreneurial, of his fellow émigrés, the rest were equally anxious to point their American hosts and colleagues in directions in which to continue their researches. Landauer's insight into Panofsky could usefully be extended to the entire group of German exiles. These scholars "had special reasons to use their cultural studies as a strategy of escape." And, following not one but a series of deracinations for nearly all of them, one should add, of survival.

Under this kind of stimulus, and within the context of an academic culture which made it possible for American and German scholars to communicate in the conviction that they understood each other, it is not at all surprising that Renaissance historiography in America flourished. It did so because for a few decades it possessed three strengths essential for success: wide popular appeal, a large paradigm of historical study which assigned to the Renaissance a precise and important role, and the formidable scholarly infrastructure provided by the German scholars. It took only a few years following the war—time enough to train the first crop of young American scholars—for a remarkable change to become evident. A cohort of strikingly able young people were now entering the field, often belonging to social classes and ethnic groups without ready access to university instruction in the preceding generations. Many of them were not directly trained by the refugees, for the simple reason that few of the German scholars had been able to find positions in universities with graduate programs: Baron, after a series of heartrending disappointments in search of an academic position, ended up as a bibliographer at the Newberry Library; Gilbert taught at Bryn Mawr, where there was a tiny graduate program; Kantorowicz, following several years at Berkeley, resigned in protest at the requirement of a loyalty oath, and moved to the Institute for Advanced Study; Olschki, although he settled in Berkeley, was unable to find a regular, tenured position; Wieruczowski spent years holding an underpaid position in a private girls' school before relocating to the City University of New York. Only Mommsen, Kristeller (at Columbia's Philosophy Department, from where his influence radiated to graduate students in history), and Panofsky (and he, of course, in the field of art history, but eagerly read by historians) secured positions in first-rate universities, where, almost from the start, their seminars became great centers of scholarly activity. But even schools such as Harvard and the University of Pennsylvania, with no German historians on their faculties, soon attracted young Americans eager to study the Italian Renaissance.

A development on the margins of Renaissance historiography points to the importance of these new academic discussions. In the 1930s, inspired by European sociologists and economists such as Gustave Schmollar and Alfons Dopsch, a group of American historians, mostly at the University of Wisconsin, began to study the origins of capitalism, especially in the practices of medieval European communes. They, too, were in search of the roots of modernity, but the Renaissance did not occupy much of a place in their thinking. For them, the key contributions to the development of capitalistic institutions had been made by the merchants of the twelfth and thirteenth centuries. In fact, when in 1941 F. Nussbaum undertook a survey of "the economic history of the Renaissance," he could hardly contain his dislike of much recent discussion. The very opening sentence of his essay was that "the general development of historiography with an economic intention has made less place than almost any other specialization for the conceptual pattern for which we use the symbol 'Renaissance.' . . . The utility of the concept 'Renaissance' has been increasingly questioned even in the fields in which it originated . . . it may be said that economic history does not know the Renaissance."[45] Robert Lopez, one of the most brilliant exiled historians, forced to abandon his Italian professorship in 1938 because of the Fascist racial laws, shortly after arriving in America obtained a Ph.D. in medieval history at the University of Wisconsin. Initially, he was not himself particularly sympathetic to the concept of the Renaissance. Yet it took only a few years in American universities before he would adjust his focus to accommodate current scholarly interests. He started in 1952 with his well-known talk at the Metropolitan Museum of Art, in which he begrudgingly accepted the notion of the Renaissance, adding that in economic terms it had coincided with a period of sharp economic decline. By the end of the 1960s, he delivered his characteristically brilliant lectures at the University of Virginia on "The Three Ages of the Italian Renaissance."[46] Lopez's experience, as well as in many respects that of Raymond de Roover (Belgian by birth and initial training, but American in the development of his scholarly interests), and of Frederick Lane, suggest that in the decade or two following the end of

World War II even economic historians, ever skeptical about the grand schemes and claims of Renaissance historians, had to take into account and, in some respects, accept the current generalizations about the Renaissance.

An Academic Triumph. Indeed, starting in the late 1930s, Renaissance historiography had begun to prosper. Young American historians—Wallace Ferguson, Myron Gilmore, Garrett Mattingly, Charles Trinkaus—just launching their professional careers were attracted to the field, even if often their initial training had not been in Renaissance subjects. In 1940, the American Council of Learned Societies sponsored the creation of the Committee on Renaissance Studies, a forum in which Renaissance scholars could now pursue common interests. Eight years later, the committee started its own journal.[47] By the 1950s, the pace of publication on various aspects of Renaissance history began to accelerate, and by the early 1960s a number of important and influential books were making their appearance. Post–World War II American historical scholarship on the Renaissance can fairly be divided into two periods, the first ending in the mid-to-late 1970s and the second covering more or less the last decade and a half.

For the first three or so decades following the conclusion of the last war, American Renaissance historiography was above all defined by two traits: the study of the history of ideas, and the discovery and systematic explorations of the State Archives in Florence. All Americans who entered the field during those years fastened onto the idea that the Renaissance—whether in the realm of thought or in the political and economic institutions fashioned during the period from the fourteenth to the sixteenth centuries—had made an essential contribution to the fashioning of modernity. It was natural that the influence of such mentors as Baron, Gilbert, and Kristeller would attract a number of Americans to the study of the history of ideas, a field which had, in any case, its own American tradition (but not in the field of the Renaissance). Two profoundly influential books appeared in 1955, which marked the field for many years: Hans Baron's *The Crisis of the Early Italian Renaissance* and Paul O. Kristeller's *Renaissance Thought: The Classic, Scholastic, and Humanist Strains.* Inspired by them, a small army of American historians entered the arena of the history of ideas in the Renaissance, drawn to the *disputa* about the nature of humanism. It would be difficult to capture a specifically American tone to this discussion. While he was still at the University of Berlin, Baron had been called upon to defend his method, and one has the sense that this controversy crossed the Atlantic and comfortably nestled itself in the American academe without very much changing its character, and with the Germanic accents of the debate remaining largely unchanged since the early decades of the century.[48] The terms of the discussion on humanism would not become redefined until much later. In the 1980s and 1990s, in a series of suggestive studies, Anthony Grafton, trained at the University of Chicago by Eric Cochrane and Noel Swerdlow, sought to locate the innovative aspects of humanistic culture not in the traditional links between humanism, rhetoric, and political theory but in humanism's relations with contemporary science.[49]

The American discovery (or, as a not entirely sympathetic critic quipped in the 1960s, the colonization) of the Florentine Archivio di Stato was altogether a different story, a notable and very successful American story. Under the inspiration above all of Theodor Mommsen (who himself in the early 1930s had assisted Robert Davidsohn, the doyen of German Florentinists), young American historians made the trek eastward and began their own archival campaigns. The ease with which Americans could now travel to Europe, and the comfortable lives they could lead there, no doubt encouraged their devotion to the pursuit of archival projects. The results became apparent early in the 1960s, with the publication of two superb books by Gene Brucker and Lauro Martines. They are the first books on Florentine history written by native American scholars and are based on first-hand, systematic archival explorations. The importance of their publication was not lost to outside observers. The anonymous reviewer for the *Times Literary Supplement*, in a front-page and lengthy essay, noted the fact that such important books "come from across the Atlantic." The reviewer then remarked that in America there existed "a thriving industry in Renaissance history" but that, until then, that industry had produced "primarily articles, lectures, and unpublished theses."[50] These publications, he seemed to say, signaled the coming of age of American historiography on the Renaissance. These two books were soon followed by a host of others: Marvin Becker's on fourteenth- and early fifteenth-century Florence, Donald Weinstein's on Savonarola, Richard Goldthwaite's on the history of the Florentine family, Martines's second book on the Florentine jurists, Brucker's synthetic history of Florence. And, on the margins of the history of Renaissance Florence, four other books, themselves notable contributions to the study of late medieval and early modern Italian history: William Bowsky's on the emperor Henry VII's Italian policy, one of the great themes of nineteenth- and early twentieth-century German historiography, "the conflict of Empire and city-state"; Eric Cochrane's book on the Tuscan academies in the age of the Enlightenment; and David Herlihy's pathbreaking studies of Pisa (actually published in 1958) and of Pistoia. In addition, all through these years, the transplanted German scholars continued publishing their own works. One need only remember Kantorowicz's magisterial *King's Two Bodies* (1957), de Roover's superb book of the Medici bank (1963), Gilbert's major study on the context of Machiavelli and Guicciardini's thought (1965), the second edition of Baron's *Crisis* (1966) and his collection of essays (1968), the steady stream of Panofsky's and Kristeller's essays, and Wieruszowski's collected papers to get a sense of the intensity and depth of publications on the Renaissance in that decade.

Notwithstanding the controversies which surrounded some of these books, one can identify in them a number of common elements—of style, approach, and assumptions about the past. To begin with, one cannot help but be struck by the degree to which American and Italian historiographies on medieval and early modern Italy moved along parallel and rarely intersecting tracks. While it is true that American historians read with some interest the work of Eugenio Garin (and fastened onto those parts of Garin's opus which overlapped Baron's studies of humanism), one cannot really say that Morandi, Sestan, even Cantimori, and

Spini, who towered over historical studies at the University of Florence in the 1950s and 1960s, exerted more than passing influence over the new generations of American historians of the Renaissance. And, vice versa, one will vainly look before the 1970s for any noticeable influence exerted by the pioneering works of Marvin Becker, William Bowsky, Gene Brucker, and Lauro Martines upon Italian historians. The drastically changed situation of the last two decades, the intense and continuous exchanges among younger Italian and American historians, should not obscure the fact that, in the very years when American Renaissance historians were establishing their enviable scholarly record, they and their Italian colleagues were animated by largely different questions.

This contrast also extended to the subject matter to which American and Italian historians were drawn in the immediate postwar decades. Italian historians of the Middle Ages, under the spell of Antonio Gramsci, were turning their almost undivided attention to the study of the countryside, and to the emergence of ties of dependence between city and country which, it was evident to them, lasted until well into the twentieth century. American historians, with the possible exception of David Herlihy, did not appear interested in that sort of question. They moved along a different track, intent on capturing what happened inside the city walls, most especially Florence's walls. There was ample and deeply felt conviction among them for this focus: Florence was the repository of values which had molded our own modern intellectual formation. It was in the crucible of Florentine culture that the great contrasts between medieval and Renaissance (i.e., modern) values had taken place: medieval asceticism as against modern worldliness; a corporately as against a bureaucratically organized state; forms of recognizably modern socialization which went beyond the medieval family; capitalistic structures and mentalities; and, most importantly, new, modern psychological forms of perception, from Giotto and Dante in the early fourteenth century to Machiavelli and Michelangelo in the early sixteenth.

The persistent urban, and Florentine, focus cannot be separated from what, for lack of a better word, can be described as this historiography's ideological texture. Much of the Western Civ orientation, in the interwar years but even more pronouncedly in the decades following World War II, was shaped by the persistent concern with extolling the United States's moral superiority over its totalitarian enemies. It was not rare to assume in those years that a sort of intellectual mobilization was the aim of the Western Civ courses, a goal to be reached by inculcating students with a sense of their country's privileged role and special responsibilities in the world. Conyers Read uttered perhaps the best known, if also the most embarrassingly extreme, of these views in his presidential address to the American Historical Association (1949), when he urged American historians to resist the claims of totalitarian governments: "Total war, whether hot or cold, enlists everyone and calls upon everyone to assume his part. The historian is no freer from his obligation than the physicist. . . . This sounds like the advocacy of one form of social control as against another. In short, it is."[51] Mosse, himself one of the distinguished German exiles to the United States, advanced a similar argument when he suggested that courses in the history of Western Civ would make American students less vulnerable to communist propaganda.[52] William McNeill, one of the most prolific and influential post–World War II historians, in an essay significantly entitled "History for Citizens," summed up the prevailing view. The fundamental idea of courses on the history of Western Civilization, he wrote, was that "humanity had fumbled through the centuries towards truth and freedom as expressed in modern science and democracy, American style."[53]

The interests of many American historians of the Renaissance were inscribed within this broader ideological context. The insistence with which fourteenth- and fifteenth-century republican thought and forms of government were cast in the role of American democracy's ideological and political progenitors was very often accompanied by either a neglect or outright condemnation of *signorial* regimes, imagined as Renaissance equivalents of twentieth-century dictatorships, relics of a retrograde, antimodern past. Hans Baron's description of Florence's wars against Milan all too unhesitatingly evoked images of more recent confrontations between democratic and totalitarian regimes. And this predilection was echoed, often no more explicitly than in the insistence with which American historians returned to the study Florence's history. On occasion, the link was made even more explicitly. Significantly, Frederick Lane devoted his presidential address to the American Historical Association not to a theme drawn from his lifelong studies of Venice's economic history but to the republican tradition of Italy's city-states in the Renaissance.[54] Some Italian historians, themselves caught in the rigid mental categories of the 1950s and 1960s, were surely exaggerating to suggest that, somehow, the exaltation of republicanism was an ideological instrument of the Cold War.[55] But they were not off the mark to point out that the work of Renaissance historians in North America was not free of ideological overtones. Interestingly, the first American monograph on the history of late medieval Milan did not appear until the early 1990s.[56] It took decades for American historians to bridge the psychological distance which separated their historiographic traditions from *signorial* courts (i.e., from what they took to be totalitarian regimes). The only other book written by an American on a *signorial* regime, and published in the early 1970s, sought to cast the Este family as a set of benevolent rulers, who drew on their people's consensus to govern them.[57] If Florence was imagined as a city-state that was ruled by a republican regime which by its very nature generated consensus, a *signoria* also had to be domesticated to the prevalent values of mid-twentieth-century American ideology.

In addition to the archival and empiricist penchant of this work and to its ideological texture, another trait also seems to unite much postwar scholarship on the Renaissance. The *TLS* reviewer of Brucker's and Martines's books had pointed out that, more than their European colleagues, American historians often sought inspiration and methodological guidance in the social sciences. For Renaissance historians, Florence, thanks to the extraordinary riches of its archives, could serve as a test case for the working out of social processes, especially the modernization of its political culture. The study of the Renaissance had always encouraged a degree of interdisciplinariness, with historians of art, literature, and politics learning and borrowing ideas from each other. The American contribution to this tradition was to add to this dialogue questions generated by sociologists, political scientists, economists, and, in later years, anthropologists.

It would be tempting to stop our analysis here, to recount admiringly many Americans' pioneering archival forays in Florence and Siena, their almost passionate commitment to an Italy they discovered in the years immediately following the conclusion of the last world war, and their contributions to the study of medieval and Renaissance Italian political history, a field largely neglected by their contemporary Italian colleagues. Behind this self-satisfied facade, however, lurks a series of smaller stories, of tensions and fissures in the dominant view of postwar Renaissance historiography. These stories are also worth noting. Perhaps most important is the very mixed academic success of many émigré German scholars. Their intellectual triumph is unquestioned. But while American scholars proved eager to absorb and apply the scholarly lessons of their German colleagues, American institutions of higher learning did not always prove as accommodating to the new immigrants as one might have thought. Hans Baron's career odyssey is the most striking of these failed academic transitions. Kantorowicz's anti-McCarthy stand at Berkeley and his resignation from that university, Mommsen's suicide, Wieruczowski's years of teaching in an extremely modest school position, and the stories of a large number of less well-known scholars offer a modest if real counterpoint to the often self-satisfied tones used to recount the story of the "intellectual migration." Even Paul Kristeller, as successful and well-integrated a German scholar as any of his fellow immigrants, responded to recent changes in American culture with a vehemence and bitterness which suggest, at the very least, that his understanding of and integration into his adopted country were more complex than one might have thought in the 1950s and 1960s.[58]

Two figures stand apart from this panorama. They help to further complicate the story of the immediate postwar trends of American Renaissance scholarship. Some striking parallels mark Eric Cochrane's and David Herlihy's careers. In addition to their Californian origins, and to their adherence to Catholicism, which offered to both a deeply felt spiritual anchoring, both received their graduate training at Yale, where they came under the influence of Robert Lopez, and both died young, when they were at the apex of their careers. Most strikingly for purposes of this analysis, both, in their initial scholarly explorations, studied periods of time which were outside the canonical definition of the Renaissance. In a real sense, neither was, nor considered himself to be, a specialist of Renaissance history. But the force of their ideas was certainly felt by Renaissance historians.

Following initial explorations of Byzantine and medieval Russian history, Herlihy settled on a study of Tuscan economic and social history from the ninth to the thirteenth centuries. His first publications, culminating in his pathbreaking book on Pistoia, proved the possibilities inherent in an intelligently rigorous application of serial analysis to medieval documents. Quite beyond the substance of his scholarly contributions, which in their time were striking for their originality, his work is a testament to his pioneering role of mediation, which he pursued almost single-handedly through the 1970s, between medieval history and the more statistically oriented social sciences. For a long time, he was the only American medievalist who not only applied to his studies such social scientific methods, but whose own work was used by social scientists themselves—above all demographers but also economic geographers and sociologists—interested in extending their inquiries to premodern societies.[59] If the chronological precocity of his initial research interests excluded Herlihy from the field of Renaissance studies, Cochrane self-consciously set himself apart from the field of Renaissance scholars by initially concentrating his attention on the history of ideas in eighteenth-century Tuscany. Picking his cues from Italian historians, above all Delio Cantimori, who devoted their lives to the study of the often subterranean reformist traditions in Italy from the sixteenth to the twentieth centuries, Cochrane, contrary to every other American historian of Italy until the late 1970s, stressed the importance of the period bounded by the Renaissance and the Risorgimento to an understanding of the history of Italy and of Western Civilization. But beyond his contribution to enlarging the chronological horizons of American *italianisti*, Cochrane performed an unsurpassed role in mediating relations between Italian and American historians. In review essays of recently published Italian works, in translations of Italian historians' essays, in the erudite commentary with which he interlaced his articles' and books' footnotes, and in his often acid assessment of American historians' resistance to recognizing the importance of Italian scholarship, he was indefatigable in his determination to introduce to an Anglophone audience a corpus of historical scholarship largely unknown outside Italy.

By the end of their sadly abbreviated careers, Herlihy and Cochrane had greatly enlarged the chronological and thematic ranges of their researches. Had American Renaissance historians been somewhat less certain of the importance of the period they were studying, they might well have noticed that the chronological framework of Cochrane's and Herlihy's work, and its conceptual implications, provided a different perspective from which to examine the history of Italy from the mid fourteenth to the mid sixteenth centuries. As it was, these implications were not drawn, and the usual, if somewhat superficial but not mistaken, assessment of these two remarkable historians' work was that it represented a sign of the vitality of American scholarship on the Renaissance.

In the 1970s, this intense American concentration on the history of Florence began to be dissipated. In a certain sense, competition became too intense; too many Americans (not to speak of the English, Australians, French, and the Italians themselves) were crowding each other in the reading room of the Florentine archives, anxious to come up with just the right documents to answer a big and interesting question. While the supply of unexplored documents had hardly been exhausted, the questions asked about Florence were becoming predictable and narrow. Already by the end of the 1960s, some scholars began casting their attention in other directions—outside Florence, and beyond the range of questions of institutional, political, and intellectual history. Venice was first to have attracted attention. Frederick Lane's presence at Hopkins had maintained a constant if low-level American interest in Venetian history, if for no other reason but Lane's systematic explorations, already in the 1930s, of the Venetian archives.[60] A turn was signaled in 1968, when William Bouwsma applied Hans Baron's approach to the history of late sixteenth-century Venetian political ideas.[61] Then, through the 1970s and 1980s, a number of young American historians, inspired by Felix Gilbert's decision to shift his scholarly attention to Venice, began exploring the archives and libraries of the Serenissima, with articles and books predictably trailing their Venetian sojourns.[62] Soon, the geographical range of American historical scholarship was greatly enlarged: Rome, Ferrara, Siena, Pescia, Lucca, Vicenza, Perugia, Genoa, Milan, the Friuli, Naples, and Sicily all found their American historians. Initially, the example to emulate was the 1960s historiography of Florence. Brucker's model studies of Florentine politics and his cautious excursions into the emergence of political ideologies, Martines's exemplary investigations of the social worlds of groups of intellectuals, and Becker's penetrating analyses of the nexus between institutional change and the conception of the state continued to inspire younger scholars. Interestingly, among them, with very few exceptions, comparative studies were few and far between. A form of *campanilismo* marks, even to our day, American historiography on the Renaissance, with each historian wedded to a city, or at best a region, intently and faithfully exploring its history. But for nearly all American scholars of the Renaissance, their work's fundamental, underlying assumption was the vital nexus between the Renaissance and modernity.

The Renaissance: Modern or Not? The past twenty years have wrought a striking change in the scholarly and intellectual contexts within which the Italian Renaissance is studied in America. The legacy of the first, pioneering years is far from exhausted, and a number of scholars who entered the profession in the 1960s and early 1970s continue to study topics which first emerged in the discussions of the preceding years. But more often than not, today, younger historians are quicker to point to the conceptual distance between their work and that of the German-American historians. Neither the concept of *Bildung* nor that of Western Civilization nor, more significantly, a teleological orientation toward our day's presumed modernity offers a common platform between younger scholars and their scholarly ancestors.

Ironically, some of the older scholars, by urging their students to consider the Renaissance as a period apart from the modern age, may have inadvertently contributed to bringing about a state of affairs which, in later years, they came to deplore. In 1941, Paul Kristeller argued that "the closer we can get to the problems of the Renaissance itself, and the farther we can get away from viewing them in terms of problems of later incidence, the more likely we are to arrive at a genuine understanding."[63] A number of exiled historians would have been hard-pressed to endorse such a call. A teleological orientation—however differently each might have defined the modernity of this telos—was an integral part of the intellectual baggage they carried across the Atlantic. Their work is defined by a tension between the need to examine Renaissance culture in its own terms and in a temporally extended, centuries-long context reaching the modernity of their age. For them, the notion that a historical epoch such as the Renaissance could be isolated from the present and dealt with only in its own terms would have been unacceptable. None would deny the need to avoid anachronism. But all would argue that one could do that while linking present to past.

Kristeller's call, however, did not go unheeded. Among those who echoed his views with some insistence was Charles Trinkaus, who, in a survey of "the content and the motivation of [English language] Renaissance historiography in the last decade," complained that "a major distortion in Renaissance historiography continues to be the contemporary effort to locate the beginnings of rationalism and political liberalism in that period." He continued that "retrospective historiography, looking for paradigms and seedbeds of admired contemporary developments, or even of deplorable ones had become an obstacle to authentic understanding of the Renaissance."[64] Kristeller's and Trinkaus's calls proved attractive, especially since, starting in the late 1960s, they coincided with the introduction in American historical discourse of French historiography and of cultural anthropology.

So it was that, starting in the late 1970s, Renaissance historians showed a seemingly endless fascination for questions and approaches suggested by the work of Clifford Geertz, Victor Turner, and Mary Douglas. The desire to provide "thick descriptions" of past cultures, and the determination to penetrate a distant and alien reality ("the world we have lost," "the past is a foreign country") have produced the desired effect, with the Renaissance appearing as an often fascinating culture, perhaps only slightly less exotic than the Balinese and Berber societies described in Geertz's much admired essays. It is hard to find in these works traces of the basic article of faith which sustained many older scholars' researches: the link between the Renaissance and modernity. Indeed, in many, the severing of this link—the separation of the Renaissance from the modern world—is forcefully asserted. Thus, it seemed that Kristeller and Trinkaus had their way, with the Renaissance cut off from modernity. But in this manner the Renaissance lost its privileged position in the hierarchy of subjects worthy of study, for if its contribution to the making of modernity is questioned, why study the Renaissance? One senses that this question, insistently asked by younger historians, was not exactly what Kristeller and Trinkaus had in mind in their own antiteleological strictures.

This change—from the teleological paradigm of Western Civilization to a kaleidoscopic one of cultural anthropology—and the conceptual, not to say psychological, severing of the Renaissance from the present could come about only as a result of a combination of circumstances, some inherent to the profession itself but most bespeaking changes in the wider culture. The huge enlargement and consequent democratization of the profession, the consequences of the Vietnam War, social changes in the academy, especially the entrance into the historical profession of women and of members of ethnic groups often grossly underrepresented in the past, and the attraction of new epistemological paradigms have all contributed to challenging the past view of the Renaissance as an essential stepping-stone toward the emergence of the centralized state, capitalism, and the bourgeois ethic. Furthermore, if we have entered a postmodern era, and if the present was not "modern" (in the sense that Burckhardt, Goetz, Ferguson, or Baron had understood modernity) what of the Renaissance? What of its links to and moral affinities with the present? This was an easier question to ask than to answer. A great deal of intellectual fumbling about ensued the realization that the previous paradigm did not hold. And it is this fumbling about that has generated much intellectual tension and many new ideas.

The most notable recent development is the search for new analytical categories with which to discuss the Renaissance. As a result, there has been a notable expansion in the range of themes studied by American historians of the Renaissance. This expansion did not result merely in an enlargement of scholarly horizons. Its consequences were more far-reaching, for the society and culture depicted in these newer works might often be unrecognizable to readers nurtured on traditional images of the Renaissance. In a series of studies on ritual behavior published from the midseventies to the mideighties, Richard Trexler and Edward Muir signaled their determination to extend their attention to realms of behavior which, in the past, had largely gone unexplored.[65] Trexler and Muir cast their hypotheses against ongoing social scientific discussions on the nature of urban communities and of collective behavior. For all the novelty of their findings, one should perhaps note that, in their works, as often in the works of other similarly inspired historians, the historical specificity of the Renaissance, as an epoch which in the past historiographic tradition had made a well-defined contribution to the formation of a European ethos, was papered over. Florence and Venice emerged in their works as large and complex urban societies, whose ritual and social practices could be documented with a wealth of evidence not available for other, comparable cities. The same concern with the language and concepts refined by social scientists is evident in the substantial body of recent American studies on the history of political patronage.[66] From ritual behavior and patronage, attention was soon extended to individuals and groups whose histories had gone largely unnoticed in the past: workers, peasants, people or groups persecuted by the law, homosexuals, and, increasingly in the past decade or so, women in all the manifestations of their social and cultural lives. The ideological thrust of a good deal of this work is often evident in the determination to document practices which undermine an older image of the Renaissance as a productive, entrepreneurial, bourgeois, republican society, a crucible of the industrious modernity which Americans so often in the past prided themselves in having constructed. The social and intellectual symmetries of much older work have been often purposefully overturned, to be replaced by images of tension, of oppression and exploitation, of emargination and domination.[67]

This historiography's intense concentration on the behavior of individuals and groups has had an important consequence: a sharp lessening of interest in the history of institutions and in philology. Institutional history had always been one of the strengths of American studies on the Renaissance. In the postwar years, Becker, Bowsky, Brucker, de Roover, Goldthwaite, Lane, Martines, Weinstein, and others continued an older American tradition, which for nearly half a century following the 1920s had enriched the study of medieval and early modern European history. Yet it is hard to think of more than one or two young American historians who in the past decade and a half have been interested in such studies.[68] Philology, on the other hand, was never an especially strong interest of American scholars. In contrast to their Italian colleagues, only a minuscule number of American historians ever undertook the work required for the preparation of critical editions of texts. Now, with attention more focused on behavior, philology seems to be almost a superfluous extra.

One could argue that the preceding reflections apply to other fields of historical study; that the questioning of the Western Civ paradigm and the influence of cultural anthropology are felt equally by students of Antiquity, the Middle Ages, and the Reformation, and not only them; that the nexus which previous generations of historians had imagined between past and present has been frayed in many other fields of historical inquiry. Yet the crisis of American Renaissance historiography may be more profound and more deeply felt, for it has penetrated closer to the field's vital historiographic and ideological core. The preceding considerations offer a context for the crisis of Renaissance historiography. But in itself this context may be insufficient for grasping the specific nature of the self-questioning and the repeated and insistent calls for refashioning or outrightly rejecting assumptions, conclusions, and aims on which a century-and-a-half-old historiographic tradition had sustained itself. The following brief considerations may point to the specificity of the malaise expressed by Bouwsma in his presidential address and echoed by many younger historians.

Above all, the study of the Renaissance in America has been conditioned by two contrasting evaluations of modernity. Was modernity a great advance of moral and cultural values, to be prized by citizens and praised by historians? In that case, the Renaissance would be celebrated for having made an essential contribution to the forging of this modernity. Or was modernity a repository of pernicious forces, to be combatted by reference to the transcendent values of the Renaissance? If so, then the Renaissance would be praised for offering an alternative to modernity, for allowing historians and their readers to imagine a refuge from the degrading conditions of contemporary society. For a goodly number of historians (especially, but not only, historians of art) this antimodernist penchant offered a strong scholarly impulse.

Already from the early decades of the nineteenth century, it was thought that the especial expression of Renaissance culture was its artistic and aesthetic manifestation. There was a deeply Hegelian coloring to this view, the notion that "the genius of mankind expresses itself more completely and more characteristically in art than in religion."[69] Hegel's intuition gained widespread currency through the nineteenth century, influencing, as Gombrich pointed out, even scholars such as Burckhardt, who tried to distance themselves from Hegel's metaphysics.

The conviction that art was at once the most genuine expression of a culture's highest values and that it offered a privileged point of observation for studying that culture informed the views and animated the enthusiasms of endless numbers of students of the Renaissance. Until the turn of our century, this notion was reinforced by the obvious idea that prevalent aesthetic standards could trace their ancestry to the canons of representing reality established by Masaccio and Brunelleschi. But could Burckhardt's filial metaphor fit into the modernity of early twentieth-century artistic expression, once Cézanne and Picasso launched their revolution?

Yet Jarves's visionary call to his fellow patricians to contribute to their country's civility by grafting the values of the Renaissance onto American society began being implemented almost in perfect coincidence with the revolutionary artistic experiments at the turn of the twentieth century. There was no better way to heed the call than to surround oneself with material objects of the Renaissance. Starting in the 1890s, America's patrician homes and museums, generously supported by merchant princes, were filled with European works of art, especially with Renaissance works of art. Bernard Berenson's activities on behalf of his American clients have been well documented. His enterprise, as well as that of other art historians, dealers, and their patrons who eagerly snapped up the merchandise being offered, underscores the link between American upper-class, nonacademic culture and the Renaissance, incarnated in the Pieros, Titians, Leonardos, and other "minor" masters emigrating to the USA, at the very time when millions of southern Italians were also leaving their homes for the promise of the New World.

The enthusiasm of American patrons and of their advisers for the "masterpieces" of the Renaissance bespeaks a profoundly conservative aesthetic sensibility with which many Americans who studied the Renaissance, consciously or unconsciously, associated themselves. Bernard Berenson's contempt for contemporary art—"unart," he is alleged to have called it[70]—may have been extreme but does not seem to have been uncharacteristic. Even Ernst Gombrich, an infinitely more subtle and balanced thinker than Berenson, in a recent interview expressed his lifelong distaste for the ideological underpinnings of modern art.[71] In the work of the great Renaissance art historians who have marked the history of their discipline in the United States—from the Princeton art historians of the 1910s and the 1920s to Panofsky, Millard Meiss, and many more—one will vainly look for more than a casual (not to say begrudging) treatment of contemporary art. It is therefore difficult to escape the conclusion Meyer Schapiro presented in his study of the Armory Show that, in American society (but, of course, not only there), contemporary art was seen not simply in aesthetic terms; it possessed a powerful ideological charge. It imposed upon observers "a definite choice." One was for or against it.[72] Those who were against it often opted for the art of the Renaissance as an aesthetic—but only aesthetic?—counterweight to contemporary trends they found distasteful, even threatening. Given Berenson's extraordinary legacy in the advancement of post–World War II American Renaissance studies, it does not seem unreasonable to suggest that the early twentieth-century orientation left a visible, if not always readily acknowledged, sedimentation in the scholarly work of American historians.

In almost perfect coincidence with the insistence with which several historians began reflecting upon this antimodernist slant, a group of mostly younger scholars proceeded on what can only be described as a systematic attempt to undermine, if not demolish, many of the old paradigm's conceptual infrastructures. It is in this context that one can begin to understand the recent determination to explore and understand the histories of people—not only women but artisans, laborers, peasants, and others, not members of their societies' elites—who not even by the most daring stretch of the imagination could be thought to have shared the experience imputed to the Renaissance. There is an often tacit assumption, from well before Burckhardt to Baron and beyond, that whatever else it might have been, at the very least, Renaissance culture was a phenomenon that concerned the social and intellectual elites of Italian urban societies. Whether one studied patronage, literary or artistic creativity, political machinations, the age's entrepreneurial spirit, or "individualism," there was little question that the object of inquiry was the elites. A book written by an English historian, but read mostly by American undergraduates and their teachers, contained an appendix in which were listed all members of the Italian Renaissance's "creative elite."[73] These were the real heroes—the makers—of the Renaissance. To the degree to which other groups partook of the Renaissance, they did so by embracing and sharing the ethos developed by their elites. It takes little effort to imagine that, notwithstanding the failure of Marxist historiography to leave much of an imprint on the work of American Renaissance historians, young scholars who came into their intellectual maturity following the 1960s would be uncomfortable with their spiritual parents' and grandparents' assumptions. The older paradigm could still hold so long as the focus of observation was the social and mental world of a city's politically dominant classes, or groups of artisans who participated in the production of objects much prized by their contemporaries or by art historians. But when the focus of research shifted to the "liminal" groups, the connection between the Renaissance and these research projects was not easy to establish. It followed that, often, the specificity of many social analyses led to the conviction that there was no comfortable fit between one's research and the phenomenon of the Renaissance. And, conversely, the sense that the Renaissance was unconnected to study projects favored by social historians led to a more intense search for specific manifestations of social life, for more than one historian assumed that the importance of a narrowly conceived project could be established by its concreteness and precision.

Finally, this sense may have been exacerbated by the renewed perception that republicanism—for many American scholars, the first and last defense of their scholarly endeavors on the Renaissance—was not equivalent to democracy, that republican institutions were often instruments of oligarchic control. Leonardo Bruni's privileged role in the fashioning of a "modern," republican ideology could not easily be sustained once historians who studied the Renaissance began paying close attention to the ideological and political contributions of twelfth- and thirteenth-century glossators and jurists.[74] And it became more than amply clear that the emergence of impersonal, "modern" government owed as much, perhaps, to thirteenth- or late fifteenth- and sixteenth-century monarchical government as it did to fifteenth-century Florence. Once again, the question of the Renaissance's alleged modernity was key.

III

Afterthoughts. One of the principal claims made in this essay is that the long and resilient history of the Renaissance in the United States can be understood because of the tradition of interest, dating at least to the beginning of the nineteenth century, which the broader culture showed for the Renaissance. This nonacademic interest survives to this day; perhaps it is even greater than ever before. Future historians of late twentieth-century American "popular" culture will no doubt ponder the curious sedimentation and persistence of ideas about the Renaissance in postmodern, technologically oriented America. Renaissance fairs, festivals, and banquets are in fashion these days, with thousands upon thousands of visitors each year frequenting these strange spectacles where exotic, contrived, and historically improbable recreations of imaginary events and rituals are reenacted, with the label of the Renaissance nonchalantly attached to them. Were it not for the stubborn persistence of the Renaissance label, one might, in fact, be justified in ignoring these rituals, signs of the Renaissance's long American life. Even if one discounts these exercises in "creative anachronism," the general public remains curious in good stories of condottieri, artists and their patrons, explorers and entrepreneurs, heroes who are made to express the proverbial "spirit" of the Renaissance age.

For Renaissance scholars, things are very different. By the early 1990s, the link which generations of their predecessors had imagined between the Renaissance and modernity was greatly weakened. American historians of the Renaissance—as was the case with American historians of other periods and places—had become highly professional scholars, specialists of their subject matter, intent, above all, on discussing their ideas with other specialists. The large historical panorama against which past discussions on the Renaissance had been cast, a panorama whose essential quality was the modernization of Western culture, had become profoundly transformed. Complex epistemological and methodological issues had now taken the place of previous assumptions about teleology and modernity. Fragmentation and erudition, not the search for an age's spirit, define current studies on the Renaissance. In this general situation, with historians of the Renaissance pursuing their largely scholarly agendas, one may ask: What of the future of Renaissance historiography in America?[75] Will American scholars be able to imagine a concept comparable to that of modernity, in all its positive and negative valences, with which to root American culture in a past as distant as that of late medieval and early modern Italy?

NOTES

I wish to thank Giovanni Ciappelli, Diogo Curto, and Andrea Zorzi for their help.

1. William J. Bouwsma, "The Renaissance and the Drama of Western History," *American Historical Review* 84 (1979), 1–15: 3.

2. Joan Kelly, "Did Women Have a Renaissance," in *Becoming Visible: Women in European History*, ed. Renate Bridenthal and Claudia Koonz (Boston, 1977), 139–64.

3. Samuel Cohn, Jr., "Burial in the Early Renaissance: Six Cities in Central Italy," in *Riti e Rituali nelle società medievali*, a cura di Jacques Chiffoleau, Lauro Martines, e Agostino Paravicini Bagliani (Spoleto, 1994), 39–57: 39–40.

4. Anthony Grafton, *Defenders of the Text: The Traditions of Scholarship in an Age of Science* (Cambridge, Mass., 1991), 3–4, 11.

5. Paul Grendler, *Schooling in Renaissance Italy: Literacy and Learning, 1300–1600* (Baltimore and London, 1989), chap. 14.

6. J. B. Bullen, *The Myth of the Renaissance in Nineteenth-Century Writing* (Oxford, 1994).

7. Cited in ibid., 252.

8. For an excellent overview see Theodore E. Stebbins, Jr., *The Lure of Italy: American Artists and the Italian Experience, 1760–1914* (Boston and New York, 1992).

9. Paul R. Baker, *The Fortunate Pilgrims: Americans in Italy, 1800–1860* (Cambridge, 1964), 19–28.

10. Quoted in William L. Vance, *America's Rome* (New Haven and London, 1989), vol. 1, p. 106.

11. Quoted in Van Wyck Brooks, *The Dream of Arcadia: American Writers in Italy, 1760–1915* (New York, 1958), 13.

12. Mrs. Nathaniel Hawthorne, *Notes in England and Italy* (New York, 1875), 372.

13. Angelina La Piana, *Dante's American Pilgrimage: A Historical Survey of Dante Studies in the United States* (Torino, 1948), 2–13. Angelina La Piana, *La Cultura Americana e l'Italia* (Torino, 1938), 169–70, lists the titles of articles published in these journals.

14. Lucia Valentine and Alan Valentine, *The American Academy in Rome, 1894–1969* (Charlottesville, 1973), 2.

15. The references to the American Academy come from William L. Vance, *America's Rome* (New Haven and London, 1989), vol. 1, pp. 281–82, vol. 2, pp. 272, 274.

16. [James Fenimore Cooper], *Gleanings in Europe: Italy, by an American* (Philadelphia, 1838), vol. 1, p. 32.

17. James Jackson Jarves, *Italian Rambles: Studies of Life and Manners in New and Old Italy* (New York, 1883), chap. 15, quotations on pp. 361–63, 378–79.

18. George Stillman Hillard, *Six Months in Italy* (Boston, 1863), 82. The book records impressions of a trip in 1847.

19. Quoted by Richard H. Brodhead in his introduction to Nathaniel Hawthorne, *The Marble Faun* (New York, 1990), xxviii.

20. Charles D. Cady, manuscript notebook, "Lectures on the History of Civilization," Professor Gammell (Brown University Archives, 1860–61).

21. Charles Evans Hughes, manuscript notebook, "Lectures on the History of Civilization," Professor Diman (Brown University Archives, 1879–80).

22. One should note that Diman must have been anything but a marginal figure in the community of American historians of his day. In 1876, he was offered the position of professor of history at the Johns Hopkins University, and it is only after he declined it that Herbert Baxter Adams was called to fill that post. W. Stull Holt, *Historical Scholarship in the*

United States, 1876–1901: As Revealed in the Correspondence of Herbert B. Adams (Baltimore, 1938), 13.

23. William M. Sloane, "History and Democracy," *American Historical Review* 1 (1895), 1–23: 5, 9–10, 15, 16.

24. For an early assessment of the development of medieval historiography in the United States, see C. W. David, "American Historiography of the Middle Ages, 1884–1934," *Speculum* 10 (1935), and, also, the somewhat envious comments of one of the American founders of the Renaissance Society of America, L. Bradner, "The Renaissance," *Medievalia et Humanistica* 5 (1948), 62–72, esp. 62; for art history, see the comments of Erwin Panofsky, "The History of Art," in *The Cultural Migration: The European Scholar in America* (Philadelphia, 1953), 86–88; for Neo-Latin philology, James Hankins, "Neolatin Philology in North America During the Twentieth Century," in *La Filologia Medievale e Umanistica Greca e Latina nel Secolo XX* (Rome, 1993).

25. Chester P. Higby, "The Present Status of Modern European History in the United States," *Journal of Modern History* 1 (1929), 3–8.

26. One possible exception was Ferdinand Schevill of the University of Chicago. Schevill's major and most original work was devoted to the medieval history of Siena, which, however, as William Bowsky points out in his presentation of the modern reprint edition, was neither as original nor as deeply steeped in the sources as Schevill himself claimed. See Ferdinand Schevill, *Siena: The History of a Medieval Commune* (New York, 1909; reprint, 1964, with an introduction, viii–xxxviii, by William Bowsky).

27. Baron was born in 1900, Holborn in 1902, Gilbert, Kristeller, and Mommsen in 1905; of our group, Panofsky and Kantorowicz had been born in the preceding decade, in 1892 and 1895, respectively.

28. In his brilliant article on Hans Baron, Riccardo Fubini, "Renaissance Historian: The Career of Hans Baron," *Journal of Modern History* 64 (1992), 541–74: 550–52, no doubt is correct to argue that Meinecke's influence on Baron was altogether tenuous and that, in the formation of his ideas, Baron had been more profoundly influenced by Ernst Troeltsch (some of whose papers Baron edited following Troeltsch's premature death) and Walter Goetz, "my teacher and friend," to whom Baron dedicated the first edition of his magnum opus. Yet Baron had studied with Meinecke, and in developing his method, especially his lifelong conviction that ideas be understood in the context of political and institutional developments, Baron shared and sought to apply Meinecke's view.

29. Helene Wieruszowski, *Politics and Culture in Medieval Spain and Italy* (Rome, 1971), x.

30. Felix Gilbert, *A European Past: Memoirs, 1905–1945* (New York, 1988), 69.

31. Cited in Peter Novick, *That Noble Dream: The "Objectivity Question" and the American Historical Profession* (Cambridge, 1988), 89. For a near eyewitness account of the aims of the New History, see Crane Brinton, "The 'New History' and 'Past Everything,'" *The American Scholar* 31, 8 (1939), 144–57: 150–51; and for a more recent, authoritative account, John Higham, *History: Professional Scholarship in America* (Baltimore, 1986), 104–15. For some contrasts but also similarities between the two historical professions, see also Georg G. Iggers, "The Image of Ranke in American and German Historical Thought," *History and Theory* 2 (1962), 17–40: 17–18.

32. Ernst Schulin, "German and American Historiography in the Nineteenth and Twentieth Centuries," in Hartmut Lehmann and James J. Sheehan, eds., *An Uninterrupted Past: German-Speaking Refugee Historians in the United States after 1933* (Cambridge, 1991), 27.

33. For general considerations, see George L. Mosse, *German Jews beyond Judaism* (Bloomington, 1985), a short but extremely penetrating book, esp. 42–55. More specific

analysis in Wolfgang J. Mommsen, "German Historiography during the Weimar Republic and the Emigre Historians," in Lehmann and Sheehan, eds., *An Uninterrupted Past*, 52–54.

34. Brinton, "The 'New History,'" 151.

35. The best treatment known to me is Mosse, *German Jews*; I have also profited from reading Louis Dumont, *Homo Aequalis II: L'idéologie allemande, France-Allemagne et retour* (Paris, 1991).

36. Quoted in Novick, *That Noble Dream*, 192. Much of chap. 7 of Novick's excellent book deals with this discussion.

37. Carl Landauer, "Erwin Panofsky and the Renascence of the Renaissance," *Renaissance Quarterly* 47 (1994), 255–81: 255, 267. Marvin Trachtenberg, "Richard Krautheimer's 'Flirtation' with Renaissance Architecture" (unpublished paper, 1995). I am grateful to Professor Trachtenberg for having allowed me to read his moving and perceptive eulogy of Richard Krautheimer.

38. Fubini, "Renaissance Historian," 542.

39. Gilbert, *A European Past*, 42.

40. Erwin Panofsky, *Renaissance and Renascences in Western Art* (London, 1970), 42.

41. Carl Landauer, "Ernst Kantorowicz and the Sacralization of the Past," *Central European History* 27 (1995), 1–25.

42. "Symposium on the Renaissance," *Journal of the History of Ideas* 4 (1943), 21–49; Erwin Panofsky, "Renaissance and Renascences," *Kenyon Review* 6 (1944), 201–28.

43. Paul Oskar Kristeller and Herman Randall, "The Study of the Philosophies of the Renaissance," *Journal of the History of Ideas* 2 (1941), 449–96: 485, 496.

44. [Paul O. Kristeller], "Medieval & Renaissance Latin Translations and Commentaries," *Renaissance News* 2 (1949), 37–40.

45. F. Nussbaum, "The Economic History of Renaissance Europe: Problems and Solutions during the Past Generation," *Journal of Modern History* 3 (1941), 527–45: 527.

46. *Il Medioevo* (1987) contains a complete bibliography of Lopez's writings. The titles of his works enable one to trace Lopez's movement to accommodate in his own studies the concept of the Renaissance.

47. The early history of the Committee on Renaissance Studies (later renamed the Renaissance Society of America) can be followed in the first issues of *Renaissance News*.

48. Few discussions on any Renaissance subject attracted as much attention and generated as much controversy as did Baron's interpretation of Florentine humanism. The reader can begin to reconstruct the outlines of these discussions in three recent contributions: Fubini, "Renaissance Historian," a sympathetically critical and balanced assessment; James Hankins, "The 'Baron Thesis' after Forty Years, and Some Recent Studies of Leonardo Bruni," *Journal of the History of Ideas* 56 (1995), 309–38, which updates old charges and criticisms against Baron; and Ronald Witt's, John M. Najemy's, Craig Callendorf's, and Werner Gundersheimer's contributions in "AHR Forum," *American Historical Review* 101 (1996), 107–44.

49. The most recent and judicious assessment of Grafton's work is found in Marcia L. Colish's review of Grafton's intellectual biography of Joseph Scaliger, in *Società e Storia*, no. 69 (1995), 651–57.

50. "Florentine Formulas," *The Times Literary Supplement*, no. 3,232 (1964), 97–98.

51. Conyers Read, "The Social Responsibilities of the Historian," *The American Historical Review* 55 (1950), 275–85: 283–84.

52. Cited in Novick, *That Noble Dream*, 312.

53. Quoted in ibid., 313.

54. Frederick Lane, "At the Roots of Republicanism," *American Historical Review* 71 (1966).

55. Renzo Pecchioli, "'Umanesimo Civile' e interpretazione 'civile' dell' umanesimo," *Studi Storici* 13 (1972), 3–33. For a retrospective, somewhat acerb reflection on this controversy, see J. G. A Pocock, "Between Gog and Magog: The Republican Thesis and the *Ideologia Americana*," *Journal of the History of Ideas* 48 (1987), 325–46.

56. Gregory Lubkin, *A Renaissance Court: Milan under Galeazzo Maria Sforza* (Berkeley and Los Angeles, 1994).

57. Werner Gundersheimer, *Ferrara: The Style of a Renaissance Despotism* (Princeton, 1973).

58. Paul Oskar Kristeller and Margaret L. King, "Iter Kristellerianum: The European Journey (1905–1939)," *Renaissance Quarterly* 47 (1994), 907–29, should be juxtaposed to Paul Oskar Kristeller, *A Life of Learning* (New York, 1990).

59. Regrettably, there are no comprehensive studies of Cochrane's career and work. Two excellent overviews, by Julius Kirshner and Anthony Grafton, published in a memorial pamphlet issued by the Department of History of the University of Chicago, could offer a starting point for a systematic analysis: *Eric W. Cochrane: May 13, 1928–November 29, 1985* (Department of History, University of Chicago, 1986); for Herlihy, see the contributions by Anthony Molho, Christiane Klapisch-Zuber, Elena Fasano, and Samuel Cohn in *Archivio Storico Italiano* 152 (1994), 173–221; and Anthony Molho, introduction to David Herlihy, *Women, Family, and Society in Medieval Europe: Historical Essays, 1978–1991* (Providence, 1995), ix–xx.

60. Edward Muir, "The Italian Renaissance in America," *American Historical Review* 100 (1995), 1095–1118; the reference to Lane is on p. 1106.

61. William Bouwsma, *Venice and the Defense of Republican Liberty: Renaissance Values in the Age of Counter Reformation* (Berkeley, 1968).

62. James S. Grubb, "When Myths Lose Power: Four Decades of Venetian Historiography," *Journal of Modern History* 58 (1986), 43–94.

63. Kristeller and Randall, "The Study of the Philosophies of the Renaissance."

64. In fairness to Trinkaus, one should add that he also considered it important for historians to critically examine the self-fashioning myths advanced during the period of the Renaissance itself. Charles Trinkaus, "Humanism, Religion, Society: Concepts and Motivations of Some Recent Studies," *Renaissance Quarterly* 29 (1976), 676–713: 676–77.

65. Richard Trexler, *Public Life in Renaissance Florence* (New York, 1980); Edward Muir, *Civic Ritual in Renaissance Venice* (Princeton, 1981).

66. For an example, Ronald F. E. Weissman, *Ritual Brotherhood in Renaissance Florence* (New York, 1982), preface and chap. 1.

67. Edward Muir, *Mad Blood Stirring: Vendetta & Factions in Friuli during the Renaissance* (Baltimore and London, 1993), xxx: "Instead of the usual absorption with the institutions and culture of the large city-states, this book ponders the extrainstitutional, marginally literate, rural, feudal, and provincial, what might be called the other side of Renaissance Italy, the things the intellectuals and their patrons in the cities tried to forget or surmount."

68. The most notable contribution in this area is John Najemy's superlative, if curiously uninfluential, study of Florentine electoral politics. John M. Najemy, *Corporatism and Consensus in Florentine Electoral Politics, 1280–1400* (Chapel Hill, 1982). One could perhaps suggest that Julius Kirshner and his students (above all Thomas Kuehn and Osvaldo Cavallar), in their focus on the history of the law, have made an effort to approach, from a different and original perspective, questions of institutional history largely neglected by

other historians. A list of some of Kirshner's articles can be found in the bibliography of Thomas Kuehn, *Law, Family, & Women: Toward a Legal Anthropology of Renaissance Italy* (Chicago, 1991), a work important in its own right. Osvaldo Cavallar, *Francesco Guicciardini giurista: I ricordi degli onorari* (Firenze, 1991); Osvaldo Cavallar, Susanne Degenring, and Julius Kirshner, *A Grammar of Signs: Bartolo da Sassoferrato's Tract on Insignia and Coats of Arms* (Berkeley, 1994).

69. Quoted in E. H. Gombrich, *In Search of Cultural History* (Oxford, 1969), 13.

70. Meryle Secrest, *Being Bernard Berenson: A Biography* (New York, 1979), 9, 370.

71. Didier Eribon and E. H. Gombrich, *Il linguaggio delle immagini* (Torino, 1994), 99.

72. Meyer Schapiro, "The Introduction of Modern Art in America: The Armory Show," in his *Modern Art* (New York, 1978), 138.

73. Peter Burke, *Culture and Society in Renaissance Italy, 1420–1540* (London, 1972).

74. Quentin Skinner, *The Origins of Modern Political Thought* (Cambridge, 1978); James Hankins, "Humanism and the Origin of Modern Political Thought," in *The Cambridge Companion to Renaissance Humanism*, ed. Jill Kraye (Cambridge, 1995), 118–41.

75. This is a question recently also asked by Randolph Starn. "Who's Afraid of the Renaissance?" in *The Past and the Future of Medieval Studies*, ed. John Van Engen (South Bend, Ind., and London, 1994), 137–38, 141.

CHAPTER 14

Between Whig Traditions and New Histories: American Historical Writing about Reformation and Early Modern Europe

PHILIP BENEDICT

IN ITS DEPICTION of professorial paladins of many nationalities jetting from conference to conference across oceans and time zones, David Lodge's academic novel *Small World* neatly captures one of the essential features of the contemporary world of scholarship—the dramatically increased pace of international scholarly cross-fertilization and migration. Perhaps no field of American historical writing has felt the effects of this more than the study of European history from 1500 to 1789. This period has been the focus of much of the most innovative work of the major European movements of "new history" in the past generations: the Annales school, the group of English historians around *Past and Present*, and the Italian microhistorians around *Quaderni Storici*. In the years since the second great expansion of the American historical profession began amid the postwar educational boom of the late fifties and sixties, the growth of support for international research, cheap transatlantic airfares, several consecutive decades of a strong dollar, and the multiplication of international conferences and exchanges all combined to increase commitment to archival research and to transform the ambitions and horizons of American scholars in this field. So many have produced archive-based monographs of a depth and sophistication comparable to those written in Europe that the prominent specialist in French history who advised his colleagues in 1958 that Americans could not compete in this domain and that they should concentrate instead on synthesizing European archival work graciously acknowledged in 1991 that he had been proved wrong.[1] Meanwhile, the relative wealth and openness of the American university system has drawn to the United States so many prominent European early modernists—Heiko Oberman, Lawrence Stone, Carlo Ginzburg, J. H. Elliott, Simon Schama, to name just a few—that it is hard even to know where to draw the boundaries of "American" scholarship.[2] A few native scholars have assumed a position among the most influential historians anywhere in the world. Many others are now interlocutors in international discussions on an equal standing with their counterparts in the various countries of Europe. The problems to which early modern historians working in the United States address themselves, as well as the methods they employ, are as much those of the different European historiographic traditions with which they interact as those they share with domestic colleagues in other fields.

For all this increased internationalization of recruitment and perspectives, long-established curricular and organizational patterns nonetheless continue to lend a distinctive configuration to American research on this period of European history. Despite a growing tendency for all who work in this field to conceive of themselves as "early modernists," American specialists in the history of this era subdivide themselves into several distinct, if occasionally overlapping, communities of discourse. For those concerned with the European continent, teaching responsibilities divide specialists in the early part of the period from specialists in its later centuries, with the study of the Reformation defining the central focus of the initial period—a vestige of the long-standing emphasis within the American teaching curriculum on "Ren-Ref." By contrast, the period of continental European history from 1600 to 1789 has always lacked a clear identity or scholarly organizations similar to those which exist for the sixteenth century. English history from the sixteenth through the eighteenth centuries has meanwhile always constituted a field separate unto itself, one whose self-definition around the dubious dichotomization between Britain and Europe imparts to it an unusually high degree of insularity in its preoccupations with its particular debates and methods. Far smaller groups of early modernists also devote their attention to the history of science and—rare indeed—to Jewish history, each of which again is conventionally defined as constituting a separate field.

Despite the recent adoption of new methods and new problems under the influence of innovative historiographic currents both domestic and European, certain long-standing preoccupations still attract the attention of most people working on the seventeenth and eighteenth centuries. Political history, broadly understood, retains pride of place. Intellectual history, especially the genealogy of secular rationalism, also remains an enduring concern. Continuity may also be observed in the fact that the advance of specialization and the sheer increase in the work devoted to the period has brought no perceptible alteration of the long-standing concentration on the history of just a few countries within Europe, especially England and France. The growth of aspirations to produce archivally based studies of a quality comparable to the best European research and the advance of topical and national specialization have led fewer American historians to attempt the interpretive syntheses on a European scale that David Pinkney considered the finest products of the previous generation. With some distance, however, it can be seen that most American research about this period continues to be related to certain grand themes that have long defined its significance in the minds of American historians. Supplemented by some new big stories introduced in the past generation, these themes continue to structure most classroom instruction about this period and to suggest many of the topics deemed worthy of research. In this respect, these fields contrast sharply with the current situation in Renaissance history, as described by Anthony Molho in chapter 13.

The Deep Structures

Thirty years ago, Leonard Krieger accurately highlighted two particularly important influences on the shape of American historical scholarship about Europe. The first was what he called the "predominance of the undergraduate teaching function" in American academic life. American history professors are responsible for teaching large chronological or thematic swatches of the European past. The experience of having to create, year after year, convincing, integrated accounts of this subject for previously uninitiated undergraduates draws them toward a relatively high level of generalization, attracts their attention to certain possible objects of study, and obscures others. The second influence was the understandable attraction the first American historians of this era had for those aspects of the European past that seemed either to anticipate elements of American history, culture, and political traditions, or to define the distinctive features of American history by revealing what it was not. John Lothrop Motley's brave little Holland fighting the first great war of independence and John William Draper's and Andrew Dickson White's centuries-old "warfare between science and religion" exemplify the former.[3] William H. Prescott's imperial Spain condemned to decline because of its intolerant Catholicism and tyrannical government and Henry Charles Lea's Catholic Church of the Inquisition, auricular confession, clerical celibacy, and other blendings of superstition and force illustrate the latter.

The great liberal historians of nineteenth-century Europe also shaped the connection that educated Americans established with the European past. The required surveys of postclassical history that were a standard part of the curriculum at many colleges by the middle of the nineteenth century assigned works such as Guizot's *History of Civilization* (a staple) and Hallam and Stubbs on English constitutional history.[4] Within this context, the vision that nineteenth-century liberal historiography presented of the Reformation as a central episode in the emancipation of the human mind commended this subject for particular attention. For the seventeenth and eighteenth centuries, the central tradition of Whig historiography stressed the juxtaposition of English and French constitutional developments.[5]

The conservative evolutionism of America's first generation of professional historians reinforced concern with such topics. As autonomous departments of history took shape between 1885 and 1910 and the first wave of professional expansion produced a varied menu of specialized courses, a substantial fraction—often more than half—of the menu was devoted to medieval and early modern Europe. Each college curriculum developed in its own manner, but the recurring staples of instruction for the period from 1300 through 1815 were those aspects of the European past considered to have either a clear genetic connection to American political and religious institutions and traditions, to illuminate by contrast the character of the American Revolution, or to be of larger significance in the great saga of gradual human emancipation: the Renaissance and Reformation, English history, and the French Revolution. Continental European history from roughly 1600 until that point in the later eighteenth century when the courses on the French Revolution picked up their story was covered on a far more selective and aleatory basis. Certain courses made particularly clear the genetic connections that were seen between the elements of the early modern past that the curriculum emphasized and American history; this is seen most graphically in the course that Herbert Darling Foster taught at Dartmouth for many years: The Puritan State in Geneva, England, and Massachusetts Bay.[6]

The configuration of instruction about late medieval and early modern European history has changed only modestly since the early twentieth century. To be sure, as history departments grew, so did the number and range of courses about this period. Expansion was greatest between the late 1950s and 1970 and chiefly involved greater investment in the previously neglected seventeenth and eighteenth centuries. Courses on the intellectual and the economic history of the era were also introduced early in the century in certain universities; the scientific revolution became a staple offering with the rise of the history of science; and recently many departments have begun to offer courses on women's history in this period. Still, in the absence of strong student demand or an evident national or political interest to be served by curricular expansion in this area, the initial heavy investment in the medieval and early modern European past has faded, as growth in course offerings about these centuries has lagged far behind that in American, more recent European, or non-Western history. Course offerings on the years 1600–1789 still diverge significantly from university to university, and for significant stretches of the postwar period, prestigious institutions were content to teach no courses at all on continental Europe between the Reformation and the onset of the French Revolution. Meanwhile, the pairing of the Renaissance and Reformation proved a hardy perennial, allowing instructors to ring a variety of changes on either the contrast between the secularizing, rationalist aspects of the Renaissance and the biblicism of the Reformation or the continuities between the humanist recovery of letters and the Protestant recovery of the gospel. Today the pairing carries less conviction for most specialists, and The Age of the Renaissance and The Age of the Reformation are most often taught as separate courses. But few who teach courses on the fifteenth or sixteenth century have dared to abandon the advertising power that these labels retain.

One result of these patterns was a long-standing tendency for early modernists in America to concentrate much of their attention on the history of the sixteenth century. The chronological distribution of articles in the most prestigious American and foreign journals shows that through the 1960s American scholars published more about the sixteenth century than about either of the subsequent two (see Table 1). This has now changed, but comparison with the situation in many European countries (e.g., France) might still suggest an unusually high level of concern with the sixteenth century.

The focus on the Renaissance and Reformation has also bred a covey of professional institutions, with their attendant scholarly journals: the American Society for Reformation Research (incorporated in 1947), the Renaissance Society of

TABLE 1

Chronological Focus of Articles Devoted to the Period 1500–1789 by American Scholars in Four Major Historical Journals, 1900–1990

	1900–10	1930–40	1960–70	1980–90
16th century	10 (40%)	18 (37%)	22 (40%)	21 (20%)
17th century	8 (32%)	17 (35%)	18 (33%)	32 (30%)
18th century	7 (28%)	14 (29%)	15 (27%)	53 (50%)

Note: Based on a survey of articles by scholars affiliated with North American universities appearing in *The American Historical Review* (AHR), *The Journal of Modern History* (JMH), *Annales* (An.), and *The Historical Journal* (HJ). Articles have been classified with reference to their chief century of focus. Those covering a sweep of several centuries have been omitted.

America (founded in 1954), and the Sixteenth Century Studies Council (established in 1972). No comparable institutions have developed for the seventeenth century or for early modern European history as a whole, while the Society for Eighteenth-Century Studies (founded in 1969), although attracting the participation of some historians, is more strongly dominated by scholars of literature and art. Historians working on the later centuries find their chief professional peer groups in the many associations devoted to the history of individual European countries or topical specializations, such as the Society for French Historical Studies, the Council for British Studies, or the Social Science History Association.

REFORMATION HISTORY

The construction in America of the distinct field of Reformation history and its precocious institutionalization in the history curriculum did not result from just the prominence that nineteenth-century liberal historiography accorded the rise of Protestantism in its saga of the advance of liberty. The centrality of the period for the historical self-definition of so many Protestant churches also commended the subject to the attention of the Protestant-dominated academic culture of the late nineteenth and early twentieth century. To this day, a powerful impetus attracting scholars to this subject remains the concern of Christian believers to explore the roots of their diverse traditions. Important work continues to be carried out not simply in the history departments of research universities but also within divinity schools, departments of religion, and small denominational colleges. The distinctive configuration of American religious life has consequently left a clear impress on this branch of American historiography. Its governing concerns and assumptions have changed substantially since the day when Protestantism's special contribution to the making of the modern world was axiomatic. The past generation has brought particularly dramatic transformations. Yet the field remains a point of encounter between agnostics and those attached to a specific religious vision or heritage. Considerable creative tension between different outlooks, methods, and foci of concern has resulted.

In the early years of the American historical profession, relations were strained between the more secular-minded Reformation historians and those who approached the subject with strong religious sensibilities. Thanks largely to the efforts of the energetic Philip Schaff (1819–93), the great pioneer of church history in America, ecclesiastical historians formed their own learned society in 1888, the American Society of Church History. The society decided in 1896 to merge with the American Historical Association, resolving that "Church history is only a part of general history." But ten years later its members reestablished the organization, for they felt marginalized within the AHA and had trouble getting their papers published in the larger association, whose officials feared that printing excessively narrow research about the history of Christian doctrine or institutions might violate the separation of church and state and endanger the association's government support.[7] In the meantime, an aggressively secular historiography, committed to rescuing the subject from what were perceived to be the blinkered perspectives of the church historians, developed among the ranks of the "New Historians." James Harvey Robinson proclaimed in 1903 that the field stood on the brink of a new understanding of the Reformation that would highlight its social, political, intellectual, economic, and institutional changes. His students investigated early Protestant social welfare policy and pioneered the application of Freudian analysis to Martin Luther's biography.[8] The substantial attention that the New Historians devoted to the history of science also gave them a heightened sense of the distance between the Reformation era and the contemporary world. It was in these circles and this generation that American historians assimilated for the first time the concept of the scientific revolution, with its identification of the critical turning point in European thought between the late sixteenth and the eighteenth centuries.[9] The synthetic *Age of the Reformation* (1920) by Robinson's leading student, Preserved Smith, set the Reformation amid a far broader range of economic, political, and intellectual contexts than comparable earlier works. The book was also notably devoid of pronouncements about the superiority of the Protestant nations over the Catholic and of statements about the importance of the Reformation in "the permanence and progress of civilization" such as those found fifty years earlier even in the work of George Park Fischer, one of the early ecclesiastical historians who most eagerly embraced the ideal of value-neutral scholarship.[10]

Between the 1930s and the 1960s, the tension that had previously characterized the relations between secular and church-minded historians largely dissipated. Broad currents within the historical profession attenuated the emphasis that the New Historians had accorded economic forces and enhanced appreciation for the autonomous force of ideas. The discovery of Luther's early lectures promoted within Protestant theological circles a vision of the young reformer as a great existential hero of faith, and this vision stimulated renewed appreciation of the potential relevance of Reformation thought for contemporary society. Until ongoing examination of the critical early texts led the majority of experts to shift in the 1960s and 1970s toward a later dating of Luther's critical "tower experience," this vision also pictured a reformer who had achieved his critical theological insights before the press of events forced him reluctantly into opposition to Rome. All this lent powerful support to the view that the Reformation was in origin a theological revolution, incomprehensible without a good understanding of the history of Christian doctrine.[11]

Until the 1960s, American Reformation scholarship focused overwhelmingly on the Protestant side of the story. Most elite research universities remained tied to a liberal Protestant outlook well into the twentieth century, with few Catholics or Jews on the faculty until the postwar years. Catholic higher education was self-enclosed and parochial; the limited amount of historical scholarship carried out within its confines centered overwhelmingly on the Middle Ages, which were seen as the great age of Catholic faith and learning, or the Catholic contribution in American history. When John Dolan surveyed "Church History in England and America in the Nineteenth and Twentieth Centuries" for the 1965 Catholic *Handbook of Church History*, the discussion of American research required less than a page and did not cite a single work on the era of the Counter-Reformation.[12]

Within the history of Protestantism, a broad variety of subjects attracted the attention of American scholars, a consequence of the exceptional range of Protestant denominations found on American soil. Schaff's work surveyed all the major churches to emerge from the magisterial Reformation and can be seen as the attempt of a pioneer Protestant ecumenicist to understand and appreciate the origins and points of difference between the many different creeds he encountered as an immigrant from Germany to America. Other historians of theology would follow the trail that Schaff had blazed from Germany to America, notably Wilhelm Pauck in 1925. Until the Nazi era, the continuing prestige of German theological learning also lured many American church historians to Germany for part of their education. In consequence, the center of gravity of American Reformation scholarship increasingly became the politics of the Reformation in Germany and the thought of Martin Luther—a situation reinforced after 1945 by the agreement of the American Society of Reformation Research to publish the *Archiv für Reformationsgeschichte* jointly with the German Verein für Reformationsgeschichte. Yet a country with as strong a Calvinist heritage as the United States could hardly ignore the Reformed tradition. In the first part of the twentieth century, important studies were devoted to Zwingli and Zurich, to Calvin and Geneva, and to the French Wars of Religion.[13] In the generation of Perry Miller, William Haller, and M. M. Knappen, Americans distinguished themselves in the study of Old English as well as New England Puritanism.[14] Above all, the presence on American soil of many churches that traced their descent to the "left wing of the Reformation," as well as the constitutionally mandated separation of church from state that has led American scholars to view separatist groups positively as precursors in the struggle for religious liberty, produced unusual concern with the "radical Reformation."

As the most exacting critics, such as Pauck, have observed, it was only in this field of study that American researchers prior to the 1960s made truly substantial contributions to international Reformation scholarship. Several holders of the most prominent chairs in ecclesiastical history during the interwar and immediate postwar decades devoted much of their original research to exploring the sectarians and dissenters of the sixteenth and seventeenth centuries, notably Yale's Roland Bainton and Harvard's George Huntston Williams.[15] But nobody was more influential than the Mennonite Harold S. Bender (1897–1964), whose efforts to accumulate the materials for, and to promote research about, Anabaptist history made Goshen College in Indiana an internationally reputed center for the study of the subject. In his major publications, Bender depicted Anabaptism as springing from a single source in Zurich, where a small band of people dared to carry the Reformation principle of *sola scriptura* to its full, logical, pacifist consequences, from which the magisterial reformers shrank back out of fear and calculation. It was a depiction that offered an inspiring, historically based sense of identity for America's Mennonites, who had just created the institutions of higher learning long characteristic of other Protestant denominations and were struggling to come to grips with the wider world of modern historical knowledge and Biblical scholarship that this implied. At the same time, Bender's work posed a sharp challenge to the historical self-understanding of the mainline Protestant confessions and a powerful stimulus for further research.[16] The expansion in knowledge about the radical Reformation promoted so energetically by Bender and others rescued the views of a wide range of groups and individuals formerly dismissed as fanatics by earlier church historiography. It also helped to reveal the full richness and variety of the reform programs generated amid the ferment of the early Reformation and drew attention to the political and social dynamics that promoted the institutionalization of certain visions of church reform and the marginalization of others. In so doing, it effected one of the central transformations of twentieth-century Reformation historiography.[17]

From the late 1960s onward, the field began to change dramatically. These years also saw one of the most internationally influential of all American historians emerge from within it: Natalie Zemon Davis.

Two central trends within historical scholarship in the past generation have been the expansion of historians' vision to encompass far more securely than previously the entire population of the place and period under study, and the shift within this expanded field of vision from an emphasis on the material conditions of life to an emphasis on culture. It does not seem entirely fortuitous that the scholar recognized as the most sophisticated and influential American trailblazer in the exploration of the culture of ordinary men and women should have emerged from Reformation history, where so much emphasis had already come to be placed on the need to respect the force and integrity of theological systems. But the personal intellectual trajectory that led Davis through the field was anything but ordinary. A secular Jew, she was drawn to the study of "Ren-Ref" as a student in the late 1940s at Smith College by an inspiring undergraduate teacher, Leona Gabel; by the still powerful belief that the origins of the modern world were to be found in the period; and by the intellectual excitement then being generated in the field by such figures as Hans Baron and Paul Kristeller.[18] Her engagement with radical politics and Marxism led her first to study the materialist philosophers of sixteenth-century Italy, then, for her Ph.D., the Protestant printing workers of sixteenth-century Lyon. To study the latter was to engage with the work of Henri Hauser, the great French pioneer of labor history whose 1899 interpretation of the early Protestant movement as the cause of journeymen alienated by the advance of capitalism and the closure of access to master status was still the most forceful social interpretation of the Reformation. Davis's archival research into the identity of Lyon's Protestants revealed that the guild masters and journeymen did not line up on opposite sides of the religious question, and indeed that no clear divisions of economic interest could predict who joined the Reformed Church and who remained Catholic. Her work did show, however, that such features of social experience as literacy, migration, and individual craft traditions and identities appeared to correlate with religious choice.

From 1952 to 1959, Davis was refused a passport by the State Department because of allegations of Communism against her and her husband, who was blacklisted and jailed for invoking the First Amendment before the House Un-American Activities Committee. During these years she had to set aside archival research in Europe in favor of reading about matters relevant to her subject in American rare book rooms. When her most important articles began to appear from the mid-1960s onward, they deployed an exceptional range of source materials, both archival and printed, in the service of a history that recognized the force of social groupings in shaping the experience and life choices of their members, but revealed the social order as a far more complex set of age, sex, and professional groupings than simple Marxist models of class analysis allowed. At the same time, her work insisted upon the no less significant power of religious symbols and ideologies in shaping collective behavior and rejected the attempt to reduce these to the expression of putatively deeper economic or social interests. In subsequent articles and books, Davis displayed an ever generous receptivity to new intellectual influences: successively, French folklore studies; English Marxist work on collective action; renascent women's history; the cultural anthropology of the seventies; Italian microhistory; and literary theory. With time, the socioeconomic focus of her early work gave way to a sociocultural history in which the cultural element became ever more autonomous. But the varied intellectual influences that she absorbed were always brought into dialogue with extensive archival and library research carried out with great methodological imagination, giving her work a rootedness in the sources and a technical virtuosity that specialists could not fail to appreciate. By the later years of her career, her influence had come to be felt far beyond the confines of American Reformation scholarship. As of 1993, books of hers had been translated into nine languages. One of most successful recent American manifestos for a "new" history, Lynn Hunt's 1989 *New Cultural History*, invoked her as a patron saint alongside Clifford Geertz, Michel Foucault, and E. P. Thompson.[19]

Within American Reformation history, Davis's work of the 1960s and 1970s joined with a variety of imported influences to generate a move toward what quickly began to be labeled the social history of the Reformation. Bernd Moeller's *Imperial Cities and the Reformation* (1962; English translation 1972) pushed historians to see the German Reformation as an "urban event." The simultaneous appearance in 1971 of Keith Thomas's *Religion and the Decline of Magic* and Jean Delumeau's *Catholicism between Luther and Voltaire* (English translation 1977) proved still more important. Each at once articulated a bold new interpretation of the course of religious change over a long Reformation era and illustrated new methods that could be used to recover the religious practice of ordinary believers—in Thomas's case, the wide reading through an anthropological lens of a range of printed sources and court records; in Delumeau's case, the methods of serial and quantitative history of the Annales school and the religious sociology of Gabriel Le Bras.[20] John Bossy's neo-Durkheimian work soon added still another, often stimulatingly contradictory, perspective of like ambition and subject matter.[21] Together, these works defined nothing less than a vast new research program for the field. In addition to recovering the theology of the reformers in all its original richness and accounting for the political history of the Reformation, Reformation history would now involve charting the long-term shifts in the character of parish-level religious practice throughout Europe from the fifteenth through the eighteenth centuries.

Coming at a time when so many other currents within American historiography and life were also promoting "history from below," the social history of the Reformation proved hard to resist. Although many scholars, especially within divinity schools, held firm to older methods and preoccupations, such leading historians of theology as Heiko Oberman and Steven Ozment proclaimed themselves converts and altered the focus of their work. Students from thoroughly secular backgrounds perceived in the field the fascination of studying worldviews scarcely less alien to them than those of the Hopi or the Azande, but of undeniable centrality for European history. Their entry into the field altered the sociology of its recruitment and weakened the influence of filiopietistic and confessional impulses. Change was most dramatic in the study of the French Reformation, where Davis's work inspired a spate of other studies of early Protestantism and religious violence, and in the study of the Counter-Reformation, which suddenly became one of the most active areas of American scholarship. This latter subject attracted both non-Catholics inspired by Delumeau and Bossy to examine the impact of the Counter-Reformation on local religious life, and Catholics formed in the more cosmopolitan intellectual outlook of Catholic universities after 1960 and eager to reexamine their post-Tridentine heritage in the wake of Vatican II.[22]

Within the Germanocentric Protestant core of the field, anthropological sensitivities or the techniques of serial history advanced more slowly. Those in this area continued to orient themselves to the debates and preoccupations of German Reformation scholars, who largely ignored the methods of French religious history and shunned folklore studies because of the political associations they had assumed during the Nazi period. Processes of long-term religious change that historians working in the Franco-Anglo-American historiographic triangle described through quantitative appraisals of shifting tendencies or the exegesis of contrasting religious styles were consequently cast by American historians of the

German Reformation as questions of whether the Reformation was "good for women" or a "success or failure." The predictable debates that ensued rarely transcended the simple terms in which they were originally framed.[23]

American historians of the German Reformation nonetheless contributed important elements to the examination of the appeal and dynamics of the early evangelical movement. This has been perhaps the central focus and greatest achievement of the past generation of German Reformation scholarship. At the same time these historians have begun to engage with more recent German theses about the dynamics of "confessionalization."[24] Sixties-inflected fascination with popular movements and the dynamics of radicalism also combined with the tradition of study founded by Bender to make the historiography of Anabaptism a continuing locus of important discoveries. The last generation's work has made evident the confessional character of Bender's vision of the subject, set the different traditions of Anabaptism more firmly within the reform aspirations and millenarian dreams of the late middle ages and early evangelical movement, and laid bare the political dynamics that changed groups that originally aspired to transform all society into sects comprised of only those willing to undergo adult baptism.[25] At the same time, the impressive tradition of scholarship on late medieval theology and its connections with the Reformation that was gathering steam under the impetus of Heiko Oberman and his students in the 1960s has lost momentum.

Many Reformation specialists now stand in a very different personal relation to their subject than did their predecessors. Over the past thirty years, international Reformation scholarship has seen the advance of a widely shared, largely ecumenically inspired concern among historians of all denominations to study and appreciate traditions other than their own. Together with the discovery of many aspects of post-Reformation Catholic piety that promoted greater literacy, more systematic habits of self-discipline, and tighter codes of morality among the laity, this has led to an emphasis on the parallel consequences of the "two Reformations" and to the rejection of long-entrenched views that supposed a privileged link between Protestantism and modernity—a modest contribution of Reformation scholarship to the weakening salience of confessional difference in contemporary America. With the continuing advance of secularization and more than a generation of work in socioeconomic history built around the preindustrial/industrial dichotomy, most current Reformation scholars also now have an even stronger sense than did Preserved Smith and his peers that the age of the Reformation was less the origin of the modern world than a "world we have lost."[26] Yet the motives drawing historians to study the subject remain varied. Confessional agendas have not entirely disappeared, and certain historians continue to find in their subject matter values that they see as a possible source of continuing inspiration—witness Steven Ozment's sympathetic evocation of the loving patriarchalism that he finds in the writings about the family of the Protestant reformers, or the closing sentences of Elizabeth Gleason's recent biography of Gasparo Contarini: "Contarini can be a wonderful partner in a dialogue with modern interlocutors who care about questions of political and religious order, of liberty and authority. His thought still invites them to meditate on unresolved issues and on thinkable alternatives to the course of events in church and state, then and now."[27]

Whether moved by a sense of the anthropological otherness of sixteenth-century Christianity or of its potential relevance for modern life and belief, most contemporary American historians of the Reformation nonetheless seem to share a confidence in the vitality of their field. "There is no field of historical study today that is more alive with change and fresh ideas that that of Reformation Europe," Ozment began his 1982 *Reformation Europe: A Guide to Research.*[28] A powerful and coherent new research program concerning the story of parish-level religious practice has recently expanded the agenda of questions and the repertoire of methods, while each year brings new monographs that help flesh out the emerging story. The recovery of the full complexity of the early evangelical movement and the concern to root out the many confessional agendas that once controlled so much Reformation historiography have led to major shifts in the interpretation of central elements in the established narrative of Protestantism's growth and institutionalization. If fewer contemporary Reformation historians see their subject as one of the birthpoints of modernity, most still see it as confidently as ever as one of the central transformations within preindustrial Europe, with broad implications not simply for the history of European ecclesiastical institutions, theology, and high politics but also for local religious life, literacy, family and gender relations, and social discipline. In this, the situation of Reformation history contrasts markedly with that of its erstwhile alter ego, Renaissance history. The Reformation, far more than the Renaissance, was a movement of ideas that swept up large elements of the European population and ushered in changes with broad implications for many aspects of religious, political, and social life. Reformation history could consequently absorb the historiographic movement of the past generation toward a more broadly inclusive history and retain the sense of connection with the narrative that initially gave the field its significance within the American history curriculum. Renaissance history could not.

The Rest of the Field

American scholarship about aspects of early modern European history other than the Reformation has always been characterized by far less thematic and institutional coherence. With some distance, however, it is possible to discern considerable continuity in the central preoccupations of American historians studying this era from the middle of the nineteenth century through the 1960s. The absorption of the new influences associated with the Annales school and the historians around *Past and Present* then expanded the scope of the field. The advance of research within long-established sectors modified the content of some of the older stories told about the period. Yet the majority of specialists continue to focus their research on the political and institutional history of England and

France. This continuity bespeaks the surprising durability of many old structures and assumptions.

The theme that long dominated American interest in the seventeenth and eighteenth centuries was that of the variegated evolution of European governmental forms and practices over this period, with the contrast between the gradual growth of constitutional government in England and the rise and fall of absolutism in France forming the heart of the story. For the better part of the century, whether approached with primary emphasis on the political and biographical dimension (as in the work of Conyers Read and John B. Wolf), on the institutional dimension (as in the work of Wallace Notestein), or on the dimension of political theory (as in the work of Charles McIlwain, William Farr Church, and Caroline Robbins), important American scholarship about these centuries centered around the rise of Parliament and the theorization of liberty in England and the rise and fall of absolutism in France.[29] Not only did this story provide a critical element in the genealogy of American politics and institutions; the many twentieth-century threats to the survival of representative government gave it continued topicality from the era of fascism's rise through the Cold War. The ideological polarization of World War II and the Cold War also bred a sense of kinship with the diplomatic and political intrigues of that earlier era of ideological polarization, the late sixteenth century, inspiring Garrett Mattingly's best-selling 1959 classic of narrative history, *The Armada*, and research by his students into the role of Geneva and Spain in destabilizing French domestic affairs.[30]

Another important current of American historiography about this period dedicated itself to intellectual history. White, Draper, and the Englishman W. E. H. Lecky first shaped certain of the themes that American historians of this subject would explore. James Harvey Robinson launched its fortunes within the curriculum with his course The Intellectual History of Western Europe at Columbia in 1904. From Lynn Thorndike's eight-volume *History of Magic and Experimental Science* (1923–58), Carl Becker's *The Heavenly City of the Eighteenth-Century Philosophers* (1932), and A. O. Lovejoy's *The Great Chain of Being* (1936) through Richard Popkin's *The History of Scepticism from Erasmus to Descartes* (1963) and Peter Gay's *The Enlightenment: An Interpretation* (1967), a series of eminent early modernists attempted to trace the complex mixture of continuity and innovation that marked the history of early modern thought. With the development of the history of science (the History of Science Society was founded in 1924, but the great growth of the field came after World War II, as anxieties about the frightening power of modern technology and the need to bridge the gulf between C. P. Snow's "two cultures" fueled massive support), a substantial body of specialists in that field added their contribution to the story.[31]

Perhaps the most novel addition to the menu of scholarly concerns in the first part of the twentieth century was the rise of economic history. Although located uneasily between departments of economics and of history and slow to develop an autonomous professional society, the subject was widely taught by the first decades of the century, thanks largely to the influence of Harvard's well-connected Edwin Gay, professor of economic history from 1906 to 1936 with time out for service as dean of the Business School, government war service, and the editorship of the *New York Post*. Entry into economics departments dominated by the ahistorical and theoretico-deductive predilections of the neoclassical school was gained largely by accepting a de facto division of labor. Premodern economic behavior was construed to differ fundamentally from modern in being shaped as much by values and institutions as by rational economic calculation. It was hence deemed suitable for inductive, historical investigation, while the contemporary economy was left to neoclassical modelbuilding. Gay was also concerned to promote the accumulation of long-term statistical series about such matters as prices and wages that might aid in the formulation of economic policy. Such concerns and assumptions attracted attention to the early modern centuries and inspired work centered on institutional structures, economic doctrines, and long-term movements of wages and prices, notably Abbott Payson Usher's still admired 1913 study of the French grain trade, Julius Klein's work on the Mesta, Earl J. Hamilton on American treasure and the price revolution, and Charles Woolsey Cole on French mercantilism.[32]

Some measure of the extent to which these long-standing patterns of interest have been modified in the past generation may be obtained from a quantitative breakdown of the articles about this period that American-based historians have published since the early part of the century in four leading professional journals. The exercise has its pitfalls, for the advance of specialization has bred a proliferation of journals devoted to geographic or topical subfields, with the result that even those journals that have sought to maintain a catholicity of subject matter and approach have become more narrowly typecast. In the past decades, American scholars have also published more in the most prestigious foreign journals, a mark of the growing internationalization of scholarship and the increased respect abroad for American research. To minimize the distortions introduced by these trends, four journals of a broad, relatively nonspecialized character, two American and two European, have been sampled at regular intervals: *The American Historical Review*, *The Journal of Modern History*, *Annales*, and *The Historical Journal*. The sample may still underestimate the expansion of the discipline into new subject areas.

Table 2, which presents the geographic foci of American production, shows how overwhelmingly early modern "European" history in the United States has always been, and remains to this day, the history of certain larger European nations, particularly England and France. Spain and the Netherlands captured the attention of Prescott and Motley in the nineteenth century, and from R. B. Merriman through Richard Kagan and Simon Schama, academic historians working in the United States have continued to write important books about these countries. Yet their histories have never received a level of attention commensurate to their evident importance in this period; when Kagan wished to begin his study of Spanish history in the late 1960s, he had to go to England for his doctoral training. Still more striking is the virtual absence of work on the smaller countries of Europe, despite the presence on American soil of so many immigrants from Scandinavia, Portugal, and eastern Europe. If anything, as table 2 shows, the

TABLE 2

Geographical Distribution of Articles by American Historians on European History, 1500–1789, in Four Major Historical Journals

	1900–10		1930–40				1960–70					1980–90				
	AHR	Total	AHR	JMH	An.	Total	AHR	JMH	An.	HJ	Total	AHR	JMH	An.	HJ	Total
Britain	13	(46%)	11	19		30 (45%)	13	6		7	26 (43%)	5	9	3	31	48 (36%)
France	5	(18%)	4	10		14 (21%)	6	2	1	2	11 (18%)	10	16	13	3	42 (32%)
Germany & Austria	5	(18%)		3		3 (5%)		3			3 (5%)	2	8		1	11 (8%)
Spain				1	1	2 (3%)	1	1		2	4 (7%)	4	1	1		6 (5%)
Italy	2	(7%)	1	1		2 (3%)	2	1	1		4 (7%)		5			5 (4%)
The Netherlands				1		1 (2%)										
Belgium								1			1 (2%)			1		1 (1%)
Switzerland	1	(4%)												2		2 (2%)
Russia				1		1 (2%)	1	1			2 (3%)				1	1 (1%)
Scandinavia				2		2 (3%)										
Andorra				1		1 (2%)										
Armenia				1		1 (2%)										
Ottoman Empire			1			1 (2%)	1				1 (2%)					
Yugoslavia								1			1 (2%)					
"Central Europe"												1				1 (1%)
General European	2	(7%)	1	7		8 (12%)	4	2		1	7 (12%)	8	3	3		14 (12%)
Total	28		18	47	1	66	28	18	2	12	60	30	42	23	36	131

Note: See table 1 for journal titles.

concentration on a select subset of European nations has only grown in the past decades, even though the concomitant increase in the number of actively publishing specialists in the field might have been expected to spawn expansion into neglected geographic areas. The rather dramatic expansion that table 2 reveals in the volume of research devoted to French history in the past decade is probably explained by the particular attractiveness of French history during the period of peak prominence for the Annales school from the late 1960s into the early 1980s, as well as by the simple fact that French was for long the foreign language most studied in American high schools by students with intellectual aspirations. With native French research productivity waning over the same decades, due to a long dearth of new faculty positions and the redirection of energy by established historians toward satisfying the intense appetite for history of the larger French-reading public, by the 1980s a considerable amount of the most important archival investigation of French history was being written across the Atlantic.[33] If the percentage of work devoted to England declined in the same decade, English history has nonetheless succeeded remarkably in maintaining itself down to the present as a distinct specialization whose representation is still required within most major history departments. For no other country is the disproportion between the amount of work devoted to this subject and the country's demographic or power-political weight within early modern Europe more evident. These patterns reveal the continued and largely unthinking continuation of the Whig pairing of England and France as central to the story of early modern Europe, the tendency of specialists to replicate their specializations through their students, the reluctance of departments to hire candidates working outside the largest and most familiar national specializations, and the persistent conviction that the study of early modern England offers essential background for the study of early America.

As table 3 shows, important changes may be discerned in the questions and themes to which American historians of this restricted range of European countries have addressed themselves. Particularly noteworthy is the shift in recent years toward social and cultural history. Within the broad sphere of political and administrative history, the attention of American scholars has also moved away from the study of high politics and diplomacy toward the study of crowd and local politics and of political culture.

Much of the shift must be linked to the reception of the new historiographic currents represented by Past and Present and the Annales. Without slighting the work of such native pioneers as Franklin Ford or Robert Forster, it is probably fair to date the arrival in force of these influences to the years between 1963, when Lawrence Stone was hired at Princeton, and 1972, when Fernand Braudel's The Mediterranean appeared in English translation to broad acclaim. In this period, departments such as Princeton's and Michigan's established regular faculty exchanges with the Parisian Ecole Pratique des Hautes Etudes. The same historian who distanced himself condescendingly from recent Annales work in 1968 was translating essays from the journal by 1974.[34] The growing numbers of those drawn to French history in this period by the lure of a "history from below" with

TABLE 3

Topical Distribution of Articles by American Historians on European History, 1500–1789, in Four Major Historical Journals

	1900–10	1930–40				1960–70					1980–90				
	AHR	AHR	JMH	An.	Total	AHR	JMH	An.	HJ	Total	AHR	JMH	An.	HJ	Total
High politics, political biography	7 (30%)	3	11		14 (24%)	5	5		1	11 (20%)		3		3	6 (4%)
Institutions, administration, law	2 (9%)	3	4		7 (12%)	3	3		4	10 (18%)	2	15	1	8	26 (19%)
Intl. relations, diplomacy, military	3 (13%)	3	5		8 (14%)	1	2		1	4 (7%)		3	1		4 (3%)
Crowd and local politics											1	6	1	9	17 (12%)
Political thought, political culture	1 (4%)	1	6		7 (12%)	3			2	5 (9%)	2	6	4	10	22 (16%)
State and society						3	1			4 (7%)	2		2		4 (3%)
Church and religion	5 (22%)	1	2		3 (5%)		2		3	5 (9%)	4	2	1		7 (5%)
Intellectual hist., hist. of science		1	6		7 (12%)	3		1		4 (7%)	3	8	1	2	14 (10%)
Cultural hist.		1	1		2 (4%)						5	8	3	1	17 (12%)
Hist. of art, music, literature													2		2 (1%)
Economic hist., historical geography	2 (9%)	2	5	1	8 (14%)	3	2	1		6 (11%)	3	1	2		6 (4%)
Maritime empires	1 (4%)	1			1 (2%)	1				1 (2%)	1	1			2 (1%)
Social and demographic hist.						1	1			2 (4%)					
Hist. of technology			1		1 (2%)	2	1			3 (5%)	5		6		11 (8%)
Source criticism	2 (9%)														

Note: See table 1 for journal titles.

a particularly sophisticated Continental methodological flair were especially likely to produce works of social and cultural history themselves, and this has been the national specialization where such works have been the most abundant.[35] American scholars also played a vital role in introducing newer currents in social history to national historiographies whose own intellectual and political traditions largely sealed them off from such viewpoints, notably Germany and Spain.[36] In English history, by contrast, American scholars have been far less drawn to the newer areas of social or cultural history. Here the noteworthy trends have been the increasing tendency for leading positions in the United States to be filled with specialists imported from Britain's Thatcher-shocked universities, and perhaps a greater attachment of American-based historians of England to the traditional interpretation of that country's seventeenth-century political upheavals as landmarks in the struggle for constitutional rights. Whig traditions die hard here.

Of course, the reception of the new historiographic trends represented by *Past and Present* and the *Annales* did not occur in a vacuum. Contemporary concerns about problems of economic growth in underdeveloped societies, the hopes and fears about revolution both at home and abroad, the need felt both by many students with some experience of radical politics to understand why transformation proved harder to achieve than had initially been thought and by those who remained on the sidelines of campus activism to convince themselves of the futility of such efforts, and the powerful streak of romantic identification with the dispossessed—all facilitated the assimilation of a historiography focused on economic and demographic cycles in rural societies, the social origin of revolution and the motivation of crowd action, the lives of the poor, and society's deep, change-resistant structures. As always, the process of reception involved selective assimilation and creative appropriation. Steeped in the history of politics and reluctant to accept the full Braudelian vision of people trapped within economic and geographic structures beyond their control, many American social historians sought to avoid too sharp a divorce from *histoire événementielle*. The economic models derived from classical French political economy that informed so much *Annales* historiography appeared alien and were rarely absorbed. Lastly, a major pole of concern for American social historians would always be the crises, transformations, and catlike survival of aristocratic power throughout the early modern centuries. Indeed, J. H. Hexter highlighted the importance of studying the continuities and transformations of aristocratic power as early as 1950, and the study of the nobility became the first American bridgehead into social history, even before the larger arrival of *Annales* influences in the United States. The evident connection of this subject with the grand narratives of political development and state building, with their long-standing foregrounding of the presumed contest for power between crowns and aristocracies, accounts for the precocious interest in this topic.[37]

As new political concerns, notably feminism and identity politics, came to the fore later in the seventies and eighties, still other new subjects and new intellectual influences commanded increasing attention among all American historians.

Here, the study of early modern Europe may have been less affected than other specializations. Table 3 subsumes articles that deal primarily with women or gender roles under the broader methodological categories of social or cultural history, but a classification scheme that put articles on these topics in a separate category would also—unsurprisingly—reveal growth in recent years. The 5 percent figure that such articles would obtain in the 1980s probably falls short of the figures that might be obtained for many other time periods and parts of the world. The impulse to recover the experience of women has manifested itself among American early modernists as among American historians working in other fields, but the quest to discover the origins and persistence of patriarchy first directed the attention of women's historians less to these early modern centuries, which were marked by only modest changes in women's status and few organized struggles for women's rights, than to more distant or more recent eras.[38] Michel Foucault's dramatic rise to the top of the citation charts in the 1980s—he topped the *Social Sciences Citation Index* between 1985 and 1990, after placing third between 1980 and 1985 behind Clifford Geertz and Claude Levi-Strauss[39]—was also accompanied by increased influence in many corners of the historical profession. While several important recent books by historians that cut through this period, most notably Thomas Laqueur's *Making Sex: Body and Gender from the Greeks to Freud* (1990), show a strong Foucaultian influence, such tendencies again appear relatively muted among early modern historians. This might initially seem surprising, since so much of Foucault's earlier work focused heavily on this period, but that in fact probably explains much of this situation. The great surge of interest in Foucault's writings across the historical profession came with his power/knowledge essays (translated 1980), whose radical critique of disciplinary structures of knowledge meshed perfectly with feminist and multiculturalist politics of group assertion, and with his subsequent work on the history of sexuality, which energized the emerging field of gay and lesbian history. Well prior to that time, however, early modernists had been assaying his writings about the history of madness and the structures of Western thought and subjecting them to sharp empirical criticism. Also contributing to the relative weakness of Foucaultian influence in this field was the relative scarcity of interdisciplinary networks linking historians to literary scholars, New Historicist literary study having been Foucault's chief point of entry into the American academy.[40]

Table 3 reveals the recent shift toward social and cultural history, but it also suggests considerable continuity in the broadest thematic preoccupations of American early modernists. If a small but important subset of American early modernists always devoted themselves to economic history, the same continues to be true today. Reinvigorated by new methods for reconstructing local economies on a quantitative basis, their monographic research has focused primarily on the actual performance of individual industries, merchant communities, or regional economies, rather than on institutional structures or economic doctrines. But their contribution within the international community of economic historians to the past generation's enormous growth of detailed local knowledge about the preindustrial European economy has been far less important than the broader models they have articulated to characterize the major changes in the structure of the European economy in what is now seen as the long, slow run-up to the technological breakthroughs of the late eighteenth century. Franklin Mendels's model of "proto-industrialization," Immanuel Wallerstein's "world systems," Robert Brenner's neo-Marxist interpretation of capitalist agriculture, and Jan de Vries's complex vision of multiple reorganizations within the internal structure of the European economy have largely set the terms of international debate and research about the long-term course of economic change over these centuries.[41] Here, American historians have continued to play the role that David Pinkney assigned them in 1958: generating broad synthetic interpretations based upon the combination of archival research and secondary reading.

In an age when the study of Latin continues to wane in America, the high level of skill in the classical languages required by the daunting erudition of so many sixteenth- and seventeenth-century thinkers has created severe barriers to entry to the field of early modern intellectual history. Nevertheless, another small but internationally respected band of holdouts has continued to cultivate this garden. Inspiration and reinforcements have often come from the ample ranks of the historians of science.[42] At the heart of most of this work, one can still see the long-standing preoccupation with tracing the elaboration across these centuries of various forms of critical rationalism—now done, however, in a far less celebratory mode, and with an intense concern to avoid anachronism. Some prominent historians of science have carried sociologizing programs to the point where the central ambition of their work has become to show that the triumph of central elements of the new science depended fundamentally on networks of power or cultural values—not simply, or even primarily, their superior explanatory power or evidentiary basis. Their work in turn has sparked withering criticism. The debates bursting out over these issues form part of the larger contemporary battles surrounding the cultural authority of science and show how significant the historical interpretation of this era remains for the larger assessment of Western thought.[43]

Above all, it remains the case that the majority of all research devoted by American historians to the seventeenth and eighteenth centuries still concerns political and institutional history. True, fewer American scholars have recently felt the attractions of royal or ministerial biography, high politics, and international diplomacy. Instead, their attention has shifted toward exploring the links between politics and administration on the one hand, and society or culture on the other. The macrosociological tradition of Barrington Moore, Charles Tilly, and Perry Anderson, the work of Roland Mousnier and his pupils in France on the social origins and recruitment of Old Regime administrative corporations, and the no less influential studies by Hans Rosenberg and Francis Carsten of the interaction of princes, parliaments, and protobureaucracies within the Holy Roman Empire have all in their different ways directed much American attention to the actual workings of the different component parts of early modern government and administration, to the recruitment of their personnel, and to the broader relationship between state and society.[44] The reinvigoration of the history of political thought by the theoretical writings of Quentin Skinner and J. G. A. Pocock, as well as the broader linguistic turn within American historical writing, has stimulated considerable exploration of "political culture."[45] Meanwhile, the tradition of Ernst Kantorowicz's brilliant analyses of political ceremonial was maintained across two scholarly generations by Ralph Giesey and his pupils, who between 1960 and 1986 produced an important series of studies of the ritual practices of the French monarchy that constitute perhaps the most distinctive American school within this field.[46] In different ways, all these newer concerns can be seen as partaking of the larger rejection of the classical emphasis on the actions of political leaders in favor of the examination of deeper structures, recurring patterns of behavior and thought, and collective agency that are so much a part of broader trends within the past generation's historiography. The driving force behind this research has nonetheless remained that perduring concern of American historians of this era: the effort to lay bare the character and chronology of the movement toward either the loosening or the tightening of the restraints on autocratic power in the major states of western Europe.

Many particulars of the early modern political landscape now look different than they did a generation ago. The insights and analytical vocabulary of Marx, Weber, and Otto Hintze have become part of the working apparatus of American scholars. The theme of the growth of the state occupies ample room within the broad narrative of political development alongside the older stories of the rise and fall of different countries in the international arena and the evolution of their internal constitutional arrangements—evidence of increased appreciation that the sheer power of modern governments is one of the most basic phenomena of the contemporary world whose history demands illumination. Interpretations that emphasized the link between the growth of monarchy and the rise of the bourgeoisie have given way to an appreciation of the continuing influence of a transformed nobility, the importance of warfare in promoting institutional innovation, and the coexistence of bureaucratic and patrimonial forms of administration within early modern government. Above all, the now abundant evidence of the force of representative assemblies in many parts of Europe across the early modern period, of the limitations on the power of even so paradigmatic an "absolute monarch" as Louis XIV, and of the fact that the various currents of thought advocating mixed constitutions or republicanism in the "age of the democratic revolutions" were of many national pedigrees and often considerable antiquity has called into question the old Whig themes of the distinctiveness of English constitutional evolution and its exceptional importance for the larger study of European liberty.

These lessons have been obscured at times by the division of those who specialize in the history of early modern government and politics among so many national and chronological subspecialties. The tendency toward fragmentation has reached the point where even those concerned with adjacent centuries of the same national history can lose touch with one another. Many historians of eighteenth-century French political culture, for instance, currently organize their work around the breakdown of a political culture that they depict as monolithically and self-consciously absolutist under Louis XIV, while their counterparts specializing in seventeenth-century French government emphasize the many compromises the Sun King was forced to make with powerful groups within the kingdom and the absence of any systematic absolutist project.[47] Together with the neglect of so many parts of the European political map, this advancing specialization has impeded the establishment of convincing continentwide syntheses of the evolution of government and political thought over the course of this period. Those who have done the best job of seeing the forest for the trees have often been social scientists coming to the field from the outside, such as Nannerl Keohane and Brian M. Downing.[48] Downing has recently demonstrated that considerable order can be brought to the political and institutional history of Europe in this period by writing it around the theme of why certain regions were able to check more successfully than others the powerful tendencies toward autocracy created by the great growth in the size of the continent's armies. The collective history patronized by the new European Science Foundation on the origins of the modern state in Europe demonstrates that constructing a genuinely continentwide political and institutional history is very much the order of the day in a Europe caught between movements toward greater integration and toward resurgent regionalism and nationalism, but American historians had little role in or influence on this project.[49] It remains to be seen whether or not U.S. historians, to whom it once came naturally to think about European history as a whole, will be able to overcome current tendencies toward national specialization and capture more attention in continuing discussions of this topic.

With the exception of the well-structured area of Reformation history, the situation of those American early modernists investigating the era's political, constitutional, and administrative history—divided among themselves into congeries of specialists on different periods and countries, yet perhaps stumbling together toward a more coherent history of European state formation—is in many ways emblematic of the larger field of early modern European history in America. In the past generation, American Europeanists have largely renounced the function of offering in their writings broad, synthetic interpretations of European history, embracing instead an increasingly zealous commitment to detailed archival research in dialogue with the historians native to the countries about which they write. In tandem with the broader tendencies promoting the advance of specialization within modern academia, this has led to ever greater fragmentation around national and thematic subcommunities, each with its own local debates. Some American specialists may even feel that it has levitated them into a curious liminal space, midway between two or more national cultures. And yet, most American research still clusters around what have always been the great stories of this period: the economic developments that prepared the ground for Europe's escape from the constraints of a preindustrial economy; the elaboration of different modes of secular rationality and their complex relationships with the continued survival of organized religion; and the survival of traditions of representative government and a reign of law in the face of powerful impulses making for increased autocracy and state power. Work in the newer areas of social, cultural, or women's history often clusters around other, sometimes much debated, grand narratives: the emergence of modern family arrangements, the advance of social discipline, and the reconfigurations of social and sexual hierarchies. For one powerful force continues to counteract the tendencies toward fragmentation and uprooting: the undergraduate teaching function. In the classroom, American historians of early modern Europe still need to generate broad narratives capable of illuminating the central developments of these centuries in a manner that captures the attention of successive generations of students. So long as their narratives can accommodate the swing toward a more socially inclusive, structural history of the sort that has become the common feature of all the most important new currents of history of the past generation—as the central narratives of the Reformation and early modern period have proven capable of doing—the classroom experience continues to nudge American research toward problems that in some way or another are suggested by these narratives, and that contribute to their further refinement.

NOTES

This paper profited greatly from the discussions, formal and informal, at Providence and San Marino in connection with the conference entitled The State of Historical Writing in North America. Also helpful was a lively discussion at Harvard's Workshop in Early Modern British and European History. I would further like to thank Francisco Bethencourt, Diogo Curto, Jonathan Dewald, and Brad Gregory for their observations on earlier drafts of this essay, many of which I have incorporated into this version.

1. David H. Pinkney, "The Dilemma of the American Historian of Modern France," *French Historical Studies* 1 (1958): 11–25; "Time to Bury the Pinkney Thesis?" *French Historical Studies* 17 (1991): 219–23.

2. For the purposes of this paper, I shall define as American scholarship all work produced by individuals while holding positions at American universities, but I shall accord greater weight to those who received their higher education in the United States. Imperialistically but not, I believe, unjustifiably, I also include American-educated scholars teaching in Canadian universities.

3. Leonard Krieger, "European History in America," in John Higham et al., *History: The Development of Historical Studies in the United States* (Englewood Cliffs, N.J., 1965), pp. 235, 238–54.

4. *Catalogue of the Officers and Students of Dartmouth College for the Academical Year 1850–51*, p. 24; *Catalogue of Dartmouth College 1857–1858*, p. 30; *Catalogue of Dartmouth College 1863–1864*, p. 30; *Register of the University of California 1870–1871*, p. 56; *Register of the University of California 1874–1875*, p. 46; *Catalogue of the Officers and Students in Yale College 1872–1873*, p. 53.

5. Successive lectures in the course that J. Lewis Diman taught at Brown University in 1880–81 took students from "The Italian Renaissance" and "The European State System" through "The Reformation"; "Civil Wars in France, Wars in the Netherlands and the Thirty Years War"; "The Rise of Monarchy in France," "Limited Monarchy in England," "The European Colonial System," "The Balance of Power," and "Modern Political Theories," before culminating with "The Constitutional History of the United States." Brown

University Archives, Student Lecture Notes, Ms 1M-2, lecture notes of Charles Evans Hughes on modern history 1880–81.

6. These observations about the growth of the history curriculum are based upon an examination of the course catalogues of five institutions: Brown, California, Chicago, Dartmouth, and Yale. I have also found useful Richard Hofstadter, "The Department of History," in R. Gordon Hoxie et al., *A History of the Faculty of Political Science, Columbia University*, The Bicentennial History of Columbia University (New York, 1955), pp. 207–49. Beyond the rapid establishment of courses on the Renaissance and Reformation, English history, and the French Revolution, these reveal for the first decades of the twentieth century an occasional continentwide survey of the seventeenth and eighteenth century with a title such as "The Political and Military History of Europe from 1618 to 1763" or "Europe by Treaty from 1648 to 1789," as well as some nation-specific courses devoted to France, Spain (a curricular fixture at California from 1909–10 onward, but otherwise rare), and (surprisingly frequently) Prussia. The number of courses on the rise of Prussia testifies both to the important links between American and German historical scholarship in this period and to a broader fascination with the growth of a powerful new nation in the heart of Europe.

7. Henry Warner Bowden, *Church History in the Age of Science: Historiographical Patterns in the United States 1876–1918* (Chapel Hill, 1971), pp. 58–68, 239–45. That the assistant secretary at the Smithsonian who oversaw the operation of congressionally funded periodicals was Jewish furthered the disaffection of at least one prominent ecclesiastical historian, Samuel Macauley Jackson, who led the secession of the church historians. In submitting for publication the paper of one colleague, he added that if it were rejected (as it subsequently was) "it will be incumbent upon me to announce to my clerical friends whom I ask to write papers for the Association that their papers will not be published because a Jew says they must not be!"

8. James Harvey Robinson, "The Study of the Lutheran Revolt," *American Historical Review* 8 (1903): 205–16; Jacob Salwyn Schapiro, *Social Reform and the Reformation* (New York, 1909); Preserved Smith, "Luther's Early Development in the Light of Psychoanalysis," *American Journal of Psychology* 24 (1913): 360–77; Hartmut Lehmann, *Martin Luther in the American Imagination* (Munich: W. Fink, 1988), pp. 211n, 227; Henry Warner Bowden, *Church History in an Age of Uncertainty: Historiographical Patterns in the United States, 1906–1990* (Carbondale, Ill., 1991), p. 3.

9. I. Bernard Cohen, *Revolution in Science* (Cambridge, Mass., 1985), pp. 391–96; H. Floris Cohen, *The Scientific Revolution: A Historiographical Inquiry* (Chicago, 1994).

10. Preserved Smith, *The Age of the Reformation* (New York, 1920); George Park Fischer, *The Reformation* (New York, 1873).

11. Higham, *History*, chap. 5; Sydney Ahlstrom, "Continental Influences on American Christian Thought since World War I," *Church History* 27 (1958): 256–72; James M. Stayer, "The Eclipse of Young Man Luther: An Outsider's Perspective on Luther Studies," *Canadian Journal of History* 19 (1984): 167–82.

12. The character and preoccupations of much Catholic historical writing in America can be inferred by surveying the early decades of the *Catholic Historical Review.* See also Hubert Jedin and John Dolan, eds., *Handbook of Church History* (New York, 1965); and, for the broader context, George M. Marsden, *The Soul of the American University: From Protestant Establishment to Established Nonbelief* (Oxford, 1994); Peter Novick, *That Noble Dream: The "Objectivity Question" and the American Historical Profession* (Cambridge, 1988), pp. 69n, 172–74, 364–66; Philip Gleason, "American Catholic Higher Education, 1940–1990:

The Ideological Context," in George M. Marsden and Bradley J. Longfield, eds., *The Secularization of the Academy* (Oxford, 1992), pp. 234–58.

13. Samuel M. Jackson, *Huldreich Zwingli* (New York, 1901); Williston Walker, *John Calvin, the Organizer of Reformed Protestantism* (New York, 1906); James Westfall Thompson, *The Wars of Religion in France 1559–1576* (Chicago, 1909).

14. William Haller, *The Rise of Puritanism* (New York, 1958); M. M. Knappen, *Tudor Puritanism: A Chapter in the History of Idealism* (Chicago, 1939).

15. Roland Bainton, *David Joris, Wiedertäufer und Kämpfer fur Toleranz im 16. Jahrhundert* (Leipzig, 1937); idem, *Hunted Heretic: The Life and Death of Michael Servetus, 1511–1553* (Boston, 1953); George Huntston Williams, *The Radical Reformation* (Philadelphia, 1962).

16. Bender's most important publications were "The Anabaptist Vision," *Church History* 13 (1944): 3–24; and *Conrad Grebel, 1498–1526: The Founder of the Swiss Brethren* (Goshen, 1950). For his life, work, and context: *The Mennonite Quarterly Review* 38 (1964), "Harold S. Bender Memorial Number"; James C. Juhnke, *Vision, Doctrine, War: Mennonite Identity and Organization in America 1890–1930* (Scottdale, 1989), esp. pp. 277–82.

17. A. G. Dickens and John M. Tonkin, *The Reformation in Historical Thought* (Oxford, 1985), chap. 9, "Rediscovered Dimensions: The Reformation Radicals."

18. Personal communication from Natalie Zemon Davis, March 10, 1995. Many valuable biographical details about Davis may also be found in MARHO, The Radical Historians Organization, *Visions of History* (New York, 1984), pp. 100–122; and now *A Life of Learning: Natalie Zemon Davis: Charles Homer Haskins Lecture for 1997*, American Council of Learned Societies Occasional Paper 39.

19. The evolution of Davis's interests can be followed most clearly through these works: "A Trade Union in Sixteenth-Century France," *Economic History Review* 19 (1966): 48–69; *Society and Culture in Early Modern France* (Stanford, 1975); "The Sacred and the Body Social in Sixteenth-Century Lyon," *Past & Present* 90 (1981): 40–70; *The Return of Martin Guerre* (Cambridge, Mass., 1983); *Fiction in the Archives: Pardon Tales and Their Tellers in Sixteenth-Century France* (Stanford, 1987). Longer analyses and appreciations of the central themes of her work may be found in Barbara B. Diefendorf and Carla Hesse, "Introduction: Culture and Identity," in Diefendorf and Hesse, eds., *Culture and Identity in Early Modern Europe (1500–1800): Essays in Honor of Natalie Zemon Davis* (Ann Arbor, 1993), which includes a full bibliography of her publications; and Suzanne Desan, "Crowds, Community, and Ritual in the Work of E. P. Thompson and Natalie Davis," in Lynn Hunt, ed., *New Cultural History* (Berkeley, 1989).

20. Keith Thomas, *Religion and the Decline of Magic* (New York, 1971); Jean Delumeau, *Le Catholicisme entre Luther et Voltaire* (Paris, 1971). Delumeau's work was translated into English, with an important foreword by John Bossy, in 1977.

21. John Bossy, "The Counter-Reformation and the People of Catholic Europe," *Past & Present* 47 (1970): 51–70; "The Social History of Confession in the Age of the Reformation," *Transactions of the Royal Historical Society*, 5th ser., 25 (1975): 21–38; "Essai de sociographie de la messe, 1200–1700," *Annales: E.S.C.* 36 (1981): 44–70; *Christianity in the West 1400–1700* (Oxford, 1985).

22. For just some of the most important illustrations of these tendencies, see Philip Benedict, *Rouen during the Wars of Religion* (Cambridge, 1981); Philip T. Hoffman, *Church and Community in the Diocese of Lyon, 1500–1789* (New Haven, 1984); Ronald Po-Chia Hsia, *Society and Religion in Münster, 1535–1618* (New Haven, 1984); Barbara B. Diefendorf, *Beneath the Cross: Catholics and Huguenots in Sixteenth-Century Paris* (Oxford, 1991);

Marc R. Forster, *The Counter-Reformation in the Villages: Religion and Reformation in the Bishopric of Speyer, 1560–1720* (Ithaca, 1992); Sara T. Nalle, *God in La Mancha: Religious Reform and the People of Cuenca, 1500–1650* (Baltimore, 1992); Philip M. Soergel, *Wondrous in His Saints: Counter-Reformation Propaganda in Bavaria* (Berkeley, 1993); John W. O'Malley, *The First Jesuits* (Cambridge, Mass., 1993); Elizabeth G. Gleason, *Gasparo Contarini: Venice, Rome and Reform* (Berkeley, 1993).

23. As historians working in this field are beginning to recognize. See Bruce Tolley, *Pastors and Parishioners in Würtemberg during the Late Reformation 1581–1621* (Stanford, 1995), p. 86; and the review of this book by Gerald Strauss, *American Historical Review* 101 (1996): 1231. For the contrast between the different patterns of analysis, cf. Natalie Z. Davis, "City Women and Religious Change," in Davis, *Society and Culture*, and Steven Ozment, *When Fathers Ruled: Family Life in Reformation Europe* (Cambridge, Mass., 1983); Bernard Vogler, *Vie religieuse en pays rhénan dans la seconde moitié du XVIe siècle (1556–1619)* (Lille: Service de Reproduction des Thèses, 1974), and Gerald Strauss, "Success and Failure in the German Reformation," *Past & Present* 67 (1975): 30–63; James M. Kittelson, "Successes and Failures in the German Reformation: The Report from Strasbourg," *Archiv für Reformationsgeschichte* 73 (1982): 153–75; Geoffrey Parker, "Success and Failure during the First Century of the Reformation," *Past & Present* 136 (1992): 43–82.

24. Steven Ozment, *The Reformation in the Cities* (New Haven, 1975); Paul A. Russell, *Lay Theology in the Reformation: Popular Pamphleteers in Southwest Germany, 1521–1525* (Cambridge, 1985); Carlos M. Eire, *War against the Idols: The Reformation of Worship from Erasmus to Calvin* (Cambridge, 1986); Mark U. Edwards, Jr., *Printing, Propaganda and Martin Luther* (Berkeley, 1994); Ronald Po-Chia Hsia, *Social Discipline in the Reformation* (London, 1989); Paula Sutter Fichtner, *Protestantism and Primogeniture in Early Modern Germany* (New Haven, 1989).

25. The reinterpretation of Anabaptism in the past generation has involved European and North American scholars alike. See in particular James M. Stayer, *Anabaptists and the Sword* (Lawrence, Kans., 1972); K. Deppermann, W. O. Packull, and Stayer, "From Monogenesis to Polygenesis: The Historical Discussion of Anabaptist Origins," *Mennonite Quarterly Review* 49 (1975): 83–121; Hans-Jürgen Goertz, ed., *Umstrittenes Täufertum 1515–1975: Neue Forschungen* (Göttingen, 1975); Deppermann, *Melchior Hoffman* (Göttingen, 1979); Stayer, *The German Peasants' War and Anabaptist Community of Goods* (Montreal, 1991); Claus-P. Clasen, *Anabaptism: A Social History, 1525–1618* (Ithaca, 1972).

26. For a clear expression of this view, see Thomas A. Brady, Jr., Heiko A. Oberman, and James D. Tracy, "Introduction: Renaissance and Reformation, Late Middle Ages and Early Modern Era," in *Handbook of European History 1400–1600: Late Middle Ages, Renaissance and Reformation* (Leiden, 1994), I, xiii–xvi.

27. Ozment, *When Fathers Ruled*; Elizabeth Gleason, *Contarini*, p. 301.

28. Steven Ozment, ed., *Reformation Europe: A Guide to Research* (St. Louis, 1982), p. 1.

29. Ample bibliographic indications may be found in Krieger, "European History in America."

30. Robert M. Kingdon, *Geneva and the Coming of the Wars of Religion in France, 1555–1563* (Geneva, 1955); DeLamar Jensen, *Diplomacy and Dogmatism: Bernardino de Mendoza and the French Catholic League* (Cambridge, Mass., 1964).

31. On the development of the history of science, see Arnold Thackray, "History of Science," in Paul T. Durbin, ed., *A Guide to the Culture of Science, Technology and Medicine* (New York, 1980), pp. 12–19; Arnold Thackray and Robert K. Merton, "On Discipline Building: The Paradoxes of George Sarton," *Isis* 63 (1972): 473–95.

32. Usher, Klein, and Hamilton were all students of Gay's. Abbott Payson Usher, *The*

History of the Grain Trade in France, 1400–1710 (Cambridge, Mass., 1913); Julius Klein, *The Mesta: A Study in Spanish Economic History, 1273–1836* (Cambridge, Mass., 1920); Earl J. Hamilton, *American Treasure and the Price Revolution in Spain, 1501–1650* (Cambridge, Mass., 1934); Charles Woolsey Cole, *Colbert and a Century of French Mercantilism* (New York, 1939). For the development of economic history, see Arthur H. Cole, "Economic History in the United States: Formative Years of a Discipline," *Journal of Economic History* 28 (1968): 556–89; Steven A. Sass, *Entrepreneurial Historians and History: Leadership and Rationality in American Economic Historiography 1940–1960* (New York, 1982), chap. 1; *Dictionary of American Biography*, supplement four, 1946–50 (New York, 1974), s.v. "Edwin Francis Gay."

33. Jeremy D. Popkin, "'Made in U.S.A.': les historiens français d'outre-Atlantique et leur histoire," *Revue d'Histoire Moderne et Contemporaine* 40 (1993): 317–18, provides a revealing discussion of the motivations that drew many Americans into French history in these years. For evidence of the shifting balance of research activity, see Roland Mousnier's review of Barbara B. Diefendorf, *Paris City Councillors in the Sixteenth Century*, in *Revue Historique* 271 (1984): 174; Pinkney, "Time to Bury the Pinkney Thesis?" 222–23.

34. Cf. Orest Ranum, *Paris in the Age of Absolutism: An Essay* (New York, 1968), pp. 297–98; Robert Forster and Orest Ranum, eds., *Biology of Man in History: Selections from the Annales Economies, Sociétés, Civilisations* (Baltimore, 1975).

35. A small sampling of important recent American works on the social history of Old Regime France that indicates the range of topics examined: Robert Forster, *The House of Saulx-Tavanes: Versailles and Burgundy 1700–1830* (Baltimore, 1971); Kathryn Norberg, *Rich and Poor in Grenoble 1600–1814* (Berkeley, 1985); Steven Laurence Kaplan, *Provisioning Paris: Merchants and Millers in the Grain and Flour Trade during the Eighteenth Century* (Ithaca, 1984); Cissie Fairchilds, *Domestic Enemies: Servants and Their Masters in Old Regime France* (Baltimore, 1984); Robert Darnton, *The Great Cat Massacre and Other Episodes in French Cultural History* (New York, 1984).

36. Witness the pioneering stature within the respective national historiographies of works such as David W. Sabean, *Power in the Blood: Popular Culture and Village Discourse in Early Modern Germany* (Cambridge, 1984), and idem, *Property, Production and Family in Neckarhausen, 1700–1870* (Cambridge, 1990); Christopher R. Friedrichs, *Urban Society in an Age of War: Nördlingen, 1580–1720* (Princeton, 1979); Richard L. Kagan, *Students and Society in Early Modern Spain* (Baltimore, 1974), and idem, *Lawsuits and Litigants in Castile 1500–1700* (Chapel Hill, 1981); James S. Amelang, *Honored Citizens of Barcelona: Patrician Culture and Class Relations, 1490–1714* (Princeton, 1986).

37. J. H. Hexter, "The Education of the Aristocracy in the Renaissance," *Journal of Modern History* 22 (1950): 1–20, idem, "A New Framework for Social History," *Journal of Economic History* 15 (1955), and idem, "'Factors in Modern History,'" all collected in idem, *Reappraisals in History* (Evanston, 1961); Franklin L. Ford, *Robe and Sword: The Regrouping of the French Aristocracy after Louis XIV* (Cambridge, Mass., 1953); Robert Forster, *The Nobility of Toulouse in the Eighteenth Century: A Social and Economic Study* (Baltimore, 1960). The history of the early modern French nobility has subsequently been one of the subjects most extensively examined by American social historians of this period, most impressively by Jonathan Dewald, *The Formation of a Provincial Nobility: The Magistrates of the Parlement of Rouen 1499–1610* (Princeton, 1980); idem, *Pont-St-Pierre 1398–1789: Lordship, Community, and Capitalism in Early Modern France* (Berkeley, 1987); idem, *Aristocratic Experience and the Origins of Modern Culture: France, 1570–1715* (Berkeley, 1993).

38. Important books by American historians on women's history in this period include Carolyn C. Lougee, *Le Paradis des Femmes: Women, Salons, and Social Stratification in Seven-*

teenth-Century France (Princeton, 1976); Merry E. Wiesner, *Women and Gender in Early Modern Europe* (Cambridge, 1993).

39. Mark A. Schneider, *Culture and Enchantment* (Chicago, 1993), p. 188n.

40. Prominent expressions of the reserved reception accorded Foucault by American early modern historians include H. C. Erik Midelfort, "Madness and Civilization in Early Modern Europe: A Reappraisal of Michel Foucault," in Barbara C. Malament, ed., *After the Reformation: Essays in Honor of J. H. Hexter* (Philadelphia, 1980), pp. 247–66; George Huppert, "*Divinatio et eruditio*: Thoughts on Foucault," *History and Theory* 13 (1974): 191–207. On the broader issue of the reception of Foucault, see Schneider, *Culture and Enchantment*, p. 188; Allan Megill, "The Reception of Foucault by Historians," *Journal of the History of Ideas* 48 (1987): 117–41; Jan Goldstein, ed., *Foucault and the Writing of History* (Oxford, 1994); and Joan Wallach Scott, *Gender and the Politics of History* (New York, 1988), esp. pp. 1–11, a central text.

41. Franklin Mendels, "Proto-industrialization: The First Phase of the Industrialization Process," *Journal of Economic History* 32 (1972): 241–61; Myron P. Gutmann, *Toward the Modern Economy: Early Industry in Europe, 1500–1800* (New York, 1988), pp. 245–46, for a listing of the most important titles within the vast literature spawned by Mendels's article; Immanuel Wallerstein, *The Modern World System*, 4 vols. to date (New York, 1974–); Patrick O'Brien, "European Economic Development: The Contribution of the Periphery," *Economic History Review*, 2nd ser., 35 (1982): 1–18; Robert Brenner, "Agrarian Class Structure and Economic Development in Pre-industrial Europe," *Past & Present* 70 (1976): 30–74; T. H. Aston and C. H. E. Philpin, eds., *The Brenner Debate: Agrarian Class Structure and Economic Development in Pre-industrial Europe* (Cambridge, 1985); Jan de Vries, *The Economy of Europe in an Age of Crisis, 1600–1750* (Cambridge, 1976); idem, *European Urbanization 1500–1800* (Cambridge, Mass., 1984); idem, "The Industrial Revolution and the Industrious Revolution," *Journal of Economic History* 54 (1994): 249–70.

42. For some important recent work in this field, Anthony Grafton, *Joseph Scaliger*, 2 vols. (Oxford, 1983–93); idem, *New Worlds, Ancient Texts* (Cambridge, Mass., 1992); Grafton and Lisa Jardine, *From Humanism to the Humanities* (Cambridge, Mass., 1986); Margaret C. Jacob, *The Radical Enlightenment* (London, 1981); idem, *Living the Enlightenment* (Oxford, 1991); Alan C. Kors, *Atheism in France 1650–1729* (Princeton, 1990). The intense examination of actual scholarly and pedagogic practice that Grafton has used to revitalize the history of humanist education and classical scholarship derives from the history of the exact sciences via Grafton's Chicago teacher Noel Swerdlow. Jacob is a historian of science by training.

43. Steven Shapin and Simon Shaffer, *Leviathan and the Air-Pump* (Princeton, 1985); Shapin, *A Social History of Truth* (Chicago, 1994); Mordechai Feingold, "Essay Review: When Facts Matter," *Isis* 87 (1996): 131–39; letters to the editor by Shapin and Feingold, ibid., 681–87; Mario Biagioli, *Galileo, Courtier: The Practice of Science in the Culture of Absolutism* (Chicago, 1993); Michael H. Shank, "Essay Review: Galileo's Day in Court," *Journal for the History of Astronomy* 25 (1994): 236–43; Biagioli, "Playing with the Evidence," *Early Science and Medicine* 1 (1996): 70–105; Shank, "How Shall We Practice History? The Case of Mario Biagioli's *Galileo, Courtier*," ibid., 106–50.

44. Particularly important studies of this sort include James A. Vann, *The Making of a State: Württemberg 1593–1793* (Ithaca, 1985); William Beik, *Absolutism and Society in Seventeenth-Century France: State Power and Provincial Aristocracy in Languedoc* (Cambridge, 1985); John Brewer, *The Sinews of Power: War, Money and the English State, 1688–1783* (New York, 1989).

45. Important examples in different registers: J. G. A. Pocock, *The Machiavellian Mo-*

ment: *Florentine Political Thought and the Atlantic Republican Tradition* (Princeton, 1975); Dale Van Kley, *The Damiens Affair and the Unraveling of the Ancien Regime, 1750–1770* (Princeton, 1984); Marc Raeff, *The Well Ordered Police State: Social and Institutional Change through Law in the Germanies and Russia, 1600–1800* (New Haven, 1983); Sarah Maza, *Private Lives and Public Affairs: The Causes Célèbres of Prerevolutionary France* (Berkeley, 1993).

46. Ralph Giesey, *The Royal Funeral Ceremony in Renaissance France* (Geneva, 1960); idem, *Cérémonial et puissance souveraine: France, XVe-XVIIe siècles*, Cahier des Annales 41 (Paris, 1987); Sarah Hanley, *The Lit de Justice of the Kings of France* (Princeton, 1983); Richard A. Jackson, *Vive le Roi! A History of the French Coronation from Charles V to Charles X* (Chapel Hill, 1984); Lawrence M. Bryant, *The King and the City in the Parisian Royal Entry Ceremony* (Geneva, 1986). This school has been especially warmly received in France since the mid-1980s, when François Furet initiated a move toward a more philosophical history of politics.

47. Cf. Daniel Gordon, *Citizens without Sovereignty: Equality and Sociability in French Thought, 1670–1789* (Princeton, 1994), pp. 3–5, 40; William Beik, "Louis XIV and the Cities," in James L. McClain, John M. Merriman, and Ugawa Kaoru, eds., *Edo and Paris: Urban Life and the State in the Early Modern Era* (Ithaca, 1994), pp. 68–85.

48. Nannerl Keohane, *Philosophy and the State in France: The Renaissance to the Enlightenment* (Princeton, 1980); Brian M. Downing, *The Military Revolution and Political Change: Origins of Democracy and Autocracy in Early Modern Europe* (Princeton, 1993).

49. At the time this volume went to press, the following volumes of this project had appeared: Richard Bonney, ed., *Economic Systems and State Finance* (Oxford, 1995); Janet Coleman, ed., *The Individual in Political Theory and Practice* (Oxford, 1996); Wolfgang Reinhard, ed., *Power Elites and State Building* (Oxford, 1996); Peter Blickle, ed., *Resistance, Representation, and Community* (Oxford, 1997); Antonio Padoa-Schioppa, ed., *Legislation and Justice* (Oxford, 1997). The comparison between this project and the most important recent American undertaking of the sort, the volumes in the Rise of Modern Freedom series produced under the auspices of Washington University's Center for the History of Freedom, illustrates once again the continuing force of Whig traditions in America.

CHAPTER 15

Prescott's Paradigm

AMERICAN HISTORICAL
SCHOLARSHIP AND THE
DECLINE OF SPAIN

RICHARD L. KAGAN

I BELIEVE the Spanish subject will be more *new* than the Italian, more *interesting* to
the majority of readers, more *useful* to me by opening another & more practical
department of study, & *not* more *laborious*, in relation to the authorities to be con-
sulted, and *not* more *difficult* to be discussed, with the lights already afforded me by
judicious treatises on the most intricate parts of the subject, and with the allowance
of the introductory year for my novitiate in a new walk of letters. The advantages of
the Spanish topic, on the whole, overbalance the inconvenience of the requisite preliminary year.

For these reasons, I subscribe to the history of Ferdinand and Isabel.[1]

With these words, entered into a memorandum on 19 January 1826, William
Hickling Prescott—a wealthy New Englander with a taste for letters—inaugurated the writing of Spanish history in the United States. Equally importantly,
Prescott's decision to investigate the achievements of the Catholic Monarchs,
Ferdinand and Isabel, represented a milestone within American historical scholarship itself. While Americans in the early nineteenth century read European
history—primarily as interpreted by Edward Gibbon, David Hume, William Robertson, and Voltaire—no American scholar had yet dared, as Prescott proposed,
to utilize original documents in order to write something *new* about the history
of any nation other than the United States. Not until the end of the nineteenth
century did other American historians, medievalists mostly, duplicate the kind of
original synthesis envisioned by Prescott in 1826 and subsequently realized in his
History of the Reign of Ferdinand and Isabel, published on Christmas Day 1837, a
work still well worth reading today.

As a historian Prescott (1796–1859) was not particularly innovative, either in
terms of method, philosophy, or technique. Influenced primarily by Gibbon
(whom he found nonetheless "circumloquacious" and disliked because of his
"egotism" and "skepticism") and by Abbé Mably (whose rules of history he admired), Prescott sought to write history that was "romantic" yet also "useful,"
studded with what he called "general reflections" of a philosophical bent.

Whether in his history of Ferdinand and Isabel or his later books on the conquests of Mexico (1843) and Peru (1847), Prescott attempted to incorporate insights gleaned from documents, contemporary chronicles, and other sources into what he described as "a continuous closely connected narrative" centering on "political intrigue."[2] Yet Prescott also wanted his books to be "very interesting" and accessible to a wide audience. In terms of his aims and method, therefore, Prescott resembled his contemporaries: George Bancroft, Francis Parkman, and other historians of the "romantic" school. Nevertheless, Prescott emerged, in America at least, as the Lycurgus of Spanish history and as the scholar who shaped both the character and direction of historical research in Spanish studies for well over a century. This essay examines the specific nature of Prescott's contribution and, more importantly, the extent to which his ideas about the juxtaposition of Spanish decadence and American progress—summarily referred to here as "Prescott's paradigm"—still exert influence over Spanish historical scholarship, particularly of the early modern era, in the United States.

PRESCOTT'S PARADIGM

To begin with, it is interesting that an individual of Prescott's background—Boston, Unitarian, money, Harvard— even contemplated a subject dealing with Spanish history.[3] No American had ever done so before, not even Thomas Jefferson, who otherwise collected Spanish books and encouraged study of "the language, manners, and situation" of both Spain and Portugal.[4] In general, early nineteenth-century America's impression of Spain was colored by the Black Legend, first popularized by Dutch and English Protestant writers in the sixteenth century. One variant of this legend, traceable to Bartolomé de las Casas's condemnation of Spanish atrocities in the New World, described Spaniards as barbaric bigots with an insatiable lust for gold. Another variant of the legend, rooted in the early seventeenth-century treatises of Spanish *arbitristas* ("economic projectors"), among them writers such as Pedro Fernández de Navarrete, portrayed Spanish society as one sunk in the depths of decline: a nation that wasted the silver it had mined in the Indies on monasteries and religious wars without bothering to invest it productively in commerce.[5]

To a large extent young America's antipathy toward Spain owed much to the British—to the Scottish historian John Campbell (1708–75), who painted a rather negative portrait of "Old Spain" in his *Concise History of the Spanish America* (1741) as well as in other works,[6] to Adam Smith, whose *Wealth of Nations* (1776) highlighted Spain's failure to develop economically, and to William Robertson (1721–93), whose *History of America* (first ed., 1777) commented at length about the Spanish indifference to agriculture and commerce and the extent to which "the enormous and expensive fabric of their ecclesiastical establishment . . . greatly retarded the progress of population and industry."[7] American authors repeated these observations, adding several of their own. Jedidiah Morse's *Ameri-*

can Universal Geography (first ed., Boston, 1793), a popular schooltext, taught several generations of young Americans that Spaniards (and Portuguese) were not only "bigotted Catholics" subject to "despotic monarchy" but lazy, indolent people prone to "the practice of every vice."[8] Other textbooks depicted Spaniards as "a poor, lazy, idle, dirty, ignorant race of almost semi-savages,"[9] and literary journals of the period regularly published essays critical of both Spain and its people. Typical were the derogatory remarks about Spanish intellectual achievement included in the essay "Trait of Spanish Character" that appeared in the *North American Review* in 1817: "as a nation, the Spaniards are at present a full century behind every other nation of Europe in the arts of life, the refinements of society, and enlightened views of civil polity; and almost a millennium, in modes of education, and intellectual culture. It may be questioned whether they have taken a step in the right road of learning since the days of the Cid."[10]

Beginning in the 1820s, writers of the romantic school helped temper this negative image. Washington Irving (1783–1859) and Henry Wadsworth Longfellow (1807–82), although critical of Spain and its institutions, were favorably disposed to the Spaniards and their culture. For these writers, who fastened on the more traditional aspects of Spain's rural economy, the country was "picturesque" because it was both exotic and backward—a quintessential Other, still medieval, still subject to Moorish and other "Oriental" influences. On a visit to Madrid and Seville in 1828, for example, Longfellow remarked "There is so little change in the Spanish character, that you find everything as it is said to have been two hundred years ago."[11] Irving, on the other hand, who had been invited to Spain in 1826 in order to translate certain Columbus documents that had recently come to light, offered an Orientalist interpretation of the Spanish character. With reference to Madrid's inhabitants, he observed that "these people preserve the Arab look and manner." Irving's first glimpse of Andalucía elicited an equally fanciful comment: "country like a historic map—full of history and romance, where the Moors and Christians have fought."[12]

Young Prescott's view of Spain must have been somewhat similar. Although he never visited the country, Prescott regarded it as one whose people had suffered from the evil effects of both monarchical absolutism and Roman Catholicism. This also was his view of Portugal. In 1815, only twenty and just out of Harvard, Prescott stopped off in the Azores en route to London in order to seek treatment for an ailment that had deprived him of much of his sight. A brief visit sparked the following comment: "Whatever opinion I had formed of the Portuguese, I could have no idea of the debasement which our capacities may suffer when crampt by arbitrary government and Papal superstition."[13]

Under the circumstances, it seems somewhat odd that Prescott, who was determined to follow a literary career, opted to write about Spain. He entertained other alternatives: a "history of the revolution of Ancient Rome which converted the republic into the Empire"; a "biographical sketch of eminent geniuses, with criticisms on their productions and on the character of their ages"; a study of Italian literature during the Renaissance. By December 1825, however, only a year or so after he started reading Spanish history and literature, the Spain of Ferdinand and Isabel attracted him more and more: "I shall probably select [Spain], as less difficult than [Rome], & as more novel and entertaining than [the biographies]."[14] In addition, Spain offered a connection with America's origins, a linkage that was already apparent to Irving and that led to his highly romanticized but enormously successful biography of Christopher Columbus, first published in 1828. Prescott, more of a historian than Irving, also understood that Spain afforded numerous opportunities for philosophical reflection. He summarized the many advantages—as well as the possibilities—of such an inquiry in a memo to himself in early January 1826. These included "a retrospective picture of the constitutions of Castile & Aragon; of the Moorish dynasty—the causes of its decay & dissolution? Then I have the Inquisition, with its bloody persecutions,—the conquest of Granada a brilliant passage,—the exploits of the 'Great Captain' in Italy, a proper character for romance as well as history,—the discovery of a new world, my own country—the new policy of the monarch towards the overgrown aristocracy &c &c." [15]

Here, in short, were all the elements an "entertaining" and "interesting" narrative required: battles against Moors, the exploits of courageous captains, the discovery of continents and oceans. Prescott was clearly, as David Levin has argued, a romantic.[16] Yet as the above list suggests, Prescott knew his Livy, his Tacitus and Polybius as well, and in keeping with the work of Gibbon, Abbé Raynal, Robertson, and other "philosophical" historians, he sought to determine the forces that destined certain societies for greatness, others to decadence and decay. With respect to his Spanish project, he noted these concerns in a short memo of 1828: "How many of the seeds of the subsequent decay of this great empire are to be fairly imparted to the constitutions of Ferdinand and Isabel? Could not a skilful contrast show that they are mainly imputable to the defective policy of the succeeding monarchs?" (that is, the Habsburgs).[17]

What is not immediately apparent in these notes, but what was evidently paramount in Prescott's mind, was the comparison between the relative fortunes of America and Spain. Toying with the prospect of writing a history of America, Prescott recurrently reflected upon the factors that were helping to make America great. So, when he decided in January 1826 to write about the Spain of Ferdinand and Isabel, he was also writing about the young United States. In both countries, Prescott detected the enlightened leadership, the sound government, national will, and the dynamism necessary for monumental achievement. Prescott was undoubtedly thinking of the United States when, in a review of Irving's *Conquest of Granada*, he used the following language to describe late-fifteenth-century Spain: "It was the season of hope and youthful enterprise, when the nation seemed to be renewing its ancient energies, and to prepare like a giant to run its course."[18]

For all his pro-Spanish sympathies, Prescott could not escape the Protestant prejudices of his age. He believed that Spain had two deep-seated weaknesses from which America was exempt. One was Catholicism, cruelly manifested in the

Inquisition that his avowed heroes, the Catholic Monarchs, had helped to create.[19] His memo book reads: "The reign of Ferdinand and Isabel will thus form an epoch lying between the anarchy of the proceeding period and the despotism & extravagant schemes of the succeeding, during which epoch the nation attained its highest degree of real prosperity; although the seeds of its most degrading vice, religious bigotry, were then implanted. ([W]ere they not before?)."[20] Spain's other fatal flaw was royal absolutism, the inherent defects of which were manifested less by the Catholic Monarchs than by their Habsburg successors, most notably, Philip II (1556–98), whose biography Prescott published in 1855. For Prescott, a staunch proponent of liberty, the "tranquility that naturally flows from a free and well-conducted government," and the "spirit of independence" embodied in the United States, Philip II was evil incarnate: "[he] ruled . . . with an authority more absolute than that possessed by any European prince since the day of the Ceasars." Prescott, moreover, faulted Philip for having "nurtured schemes of mad ambition" that undermined the dynamism and energy Ferdinand and Isabel brought to Spain, forcing the nation into "a state of paralytic torpor" that contributed, directly and inevitably, to its economic and political decline. Even more reprehensible was Philip's narrow brand of Catholicism, a religion that "admitted no compromise" and led the monarch to embrace persecution and its handmaiden, the Inquisition, as his principal weapon.[21] Firm in his belief that progress required liberty in the guise of democratic institutions, freedom of worship and of expression, and laissez-faire economics, Prescott blamed Philip for having denied Spain the opportunity to join the modern world.

For Prescott, then, an unhealthy combination of political despotism and religious bigotry set Spain and America on two fundamentally different paths. America, as a republic, enjoyed the energy, enthusiasm, and the "bold commercial spirit" that liberty engendered—the qualities nations required for lasting success. In Prescott's view, medieval Spain had exhibited most of these qualities in the guise of "free institutions," "liberal and equitable forms of government," "independence of character," "lofty enthusiasm," and "patriotism." However, in the course of the sixteenth century the Habsburg monarchy, aided by the Inquisition, conspired to crush Spain's ancient "liberties," creating a huge gulf between America and the nation that had helped to discover it. In the United States, liberty ensured both individual enterprise and national prosperity. In Spain its absence created economic backwardness, intellectual stagnation, political weakness, and moral decay, each compounded by the sloth and corruption that the riches of empire brought in its wake.[22] In the Middle Ages, Spaniards were energetic, hardworking, their future still bright. But by the end of the sixteenth century all this had changed, and Prescott offered a particularly gloomy assessment of the country's future near the end of Philip II:

> folded under the dark wing of the Inquisition, Spain was shut out from the light which in the sixteenth century broke over the rest of Europe, stimulating nations to greater enterprise in every department of knowledge. The genius of the people was rebuked, and their spirit quenched, under the malign influence of an eye that never

slumbered, of an unseen arm ever raised to strike. How could there be freedom of thought, where there was no freedom of utterance? Or freedom of utterance, where it was dangerous to say too little as to say too much. Freedom cannot go along with fear. Every way the Spanish mind was in fetters.[23]

•

What I call "Prescott's paradigm" is an understanding of Spain as America's antithesis. Most of the elements contained in this paradigm—anti-Catholicism, criticism of absolutism, support for commerce and individual liberty—were to be found in the work of many Enlightenment writers, but Prescott bundled them into a single package that offered a means of approaching Spanish history through the lens of that of U.S. history. Just as Prescott cherished the notion of "American exceptionalism," the idea that his own country possessed an unique history that destined it for greatness, Spain was equally exceptional but seen from the inverted perspective of a nation separated from the European, that is, Protestant, mainstream and consequently bereft of the progress and prosperity that flowed in its wake. Earlier New England writers, Cotton Mather and Samuel Sewall among them, had also espoused a negative view of Spain, but Prescott was the first to adopt a truly comparative perspective, setting the trajectory of the two nations side by side. Medieval Spain provided Prescott—and presumably other Americans who shared his whiggish political views—with an example of a society in which individual liberties had been productively channeled into nation building, a heroic enterprise that offered ready comparison with America's colonial era, and for Prescott at least, one that may also have served as a refuge from the dangerous populist tendencies Jacksonian democracy had unleashed.[24] But Spain's principal attraction was that its history, especially in the Habsburg era— the period Prescott regarded as its nadir—represented everything that his America was not. America was the future—republican, enterprising, rational; while Spain—monarchical, indolent, fanatic—represented the past. As it developed, however, Prescott's paradigm was less a clear analytical model of analysis than a series of assumptions and presuppositions about the inherent backwardness of Spanish culture, the progressiveness and superiority of that of the United States. Yet this particular formulation, especially when combined with pervasive belief in national character engendered by the rise of nineteenth-century nationalism, exerted a powerful influence on the way succeeding generations of U.S. scholars thought and wrote about Spain.[25]

NINETEENTH-CENTURY AMERICAN HISPANISM

Prescott's juxtaposition between America (the new) and Spain (the old) undoubtedly counted among the many reasons why *Ferdinand and Isabel* sold so well. Prescott himself could hardly believe the book's success, and at one point, shortly after the publication of his *Conquest of Mexico* in 1843, he candidly admitted to a Spanish friend that "My countrymen . . . seem to me more in love with Spanish history than the Spanish themselves."[26] The old adage that opposites attract may also explain why other nineteenth-century American scholars found themselves drawn to Spain. Romanticism provided an additional lure. George Ticknor (1791–1871), Harvard's first professor of modern languages, visited Spain in May 1818, only to find it woefully backward—"Imagine a country so deserted and desolate, and with so little travelling and communication, as to have no taverns"—and lacking in both "cultivation and refinement," an absence he attributed to "the long, *long*, oppression of tyranny and inquisition." On the other hand, Ticknor found the common people both natural and graceful. Even their "resting positions," he wrote, were "picturesque."[27] Harvard's third professor of modern languages, James Russell Lowell, held an equally romantic view of Spain and its people. Writing in 1878, he admitted to a friend that "you can't imagine how far I am away from the world here—I mean the modern world. Spain is as primitive in some ways as the books of Moses and as oriental." As for the people, Lowell echoed Irving when he wrote that "they are still orientals to a degree one has to live among them to believe . . . they don't care about the same things that we are fools to believe in [ledgers]. . . ." This opinion led Lowell to conclude that hardworking Americans preferred the economic benefits associated with the "mill-pond" while Spaniards preferred the peaceful pleasures derived from the "brook."[28]

Lowell's letters from Spain never mentioned those aspects of Spanish society—railroads, industry, commerce—that smacked of modernity. The Spain he and other American scholars wanted to see was the Spain of the Middle Ages, the sole era in which, as Prescott described it, Spaniards enjoyed the benefits of liberty. Medievalism of this sort pervaded most nineteenth-century American scholarship about Spain, initially manifesting itself in Ticknor's *History of Spanish Literature* (1849).[29] Ticknor's was the first critical survey of a European literature ever written by an American scholar.[30] It was also replete with Prescottian language, freely employing such romanticized terms as "enthusiasm," "spirit and activity," "vigor and promise" to describe the temper of Spain's Middle Ages. For Ticknor, such qualities made for great literature, and he probably had Sir Walter Scott in mind when he presented the popular ballads and chronicles of the period as Spain's greatest literary accomplishments, its true Golden Age. And Ticknor, like Prescott before him, saw Spain's early cultural florescence as doomed to decay. In his words, "that generous and manly spirit which is the breadth of intellectual life of any people was stifled and restrained"—by the corrosive forces of courtly life, by corrupt and despotic government, by the Inquisition. From his perspective, glimmers of Spain's "old spirit" briefly survived in early seventeenth-century theater, but even the stage soon succumbed to the forces that crushed Spain's "heroic temperament." The work of Miguel de Cervantes Saavedra, Francisco Quevedo y Villegas, and Pedro Calderón de la Barca notwithstanding, Ticknor's seventeenth century was more iron than gold, an era in which "life . . . was evidently passing out of the whole Spanish character."[31]

William H. Prescott died in 1867, but his paradigm lived on. It lay at the core of John Lothrop Motley's *The Rise of the Dutch Republic* (1856), an immensely popular work that presented the Spain of Philip II as the enemy of democracy, the nation opposed to the (liberal) forces shaping the modern world. Motley (1814–77), another wealthy Bostonian, was close to Prescott and was both helped and influenced by his older friend. He also shared Prescott's presuppositions. Motley vilified aristocrats ("extravagant and dissipated"), elevated both commoners and commerce ("the mother of freedom") to lofty rank, and presented Spaniards as the personification of religious intolerance and hate. Motley thus found it relatively easy to describe the principal shortcomings of his villain, Philip II:

> He [Philip] was entirely a Spaniard. The Burgundian and Austrian elements of his blood seem to have evaporated, and his veins were filled alone with the ancient ardour, which in heroic centuries had animated the Gothic champions of Spain. The fierce enthusiasm for the Cross, which in the long internal warfare against the Crescent had been the romantic and distinguishing feature of the national character, had degenerated into bigotry. That which had been a nation's glory now made the monarch's shame. . . . Philip was to be the latest and most perfect incarnation of all this traditional enthusiasm, this perpetual hate.[32]

Philip's foil, and the hero of Motley's narrative, was the Dutch leader, William of Orange, an individual whose "political genius," "eloquence," and patriotism practically made him an American, a figure comparable to George Washington.[33] It follows that the United Provinces appeared in the pages of Motley's history as a miniature United States. Just as Washington had led his people in their struggle for freedom against England, William led the Dutch in their battle for liberty— and thus the future—against the forces of the past embodied in the Spaniard and epitomized in the person of Philip II.

If Motley's *Rise of the Dutch Republic* strengthened the negative Spanish stereotype inherent in Prescott's paradigm, the next and indeed last generation of America's gentlemen-historians inscribed it in stone. Their ideas about Spanish backwardness and decadence came to the fore in various books and essays published at the moment of the Spanish-American War of 1898, a short but decisive conflict that simultaneously ended Spain's imperial era while initiating that of the United States. Many of these publications presented Spain's defeat as inevitable, the foreordained outcome of three centuries of decline and decay.[34] The most nuanced and, in a way, most Prescottian explanation for Spain's defeat came from Henry Charles Lea (1825–1909), the Philadelphia businessman turned church historian who developed a special interest in the corrosive effects of "clericalism" upon humanity. Already known for his scholarly *History of the Inquisition of the Middle Ages* (1887–88), Lea became interested in Spanish history largely to determine what he described as "the profound modification wrought in the Spanish character by the Inquisition."[35] He published a preliminary book on the subject in 1890 and in 1898 was preparing what later became his monumental *History of the Inquisition of Spain* (4 vols., New York, 1906–7) when he was asked by the editor of *The Atlantic Monthly* to offer his interpretation of Spain's defeat. Lea seized the opportunity to convey to a wide audience his ideas concerning the detrimental effects of the Inquisition on Spanish society.[36]

Lea's essay, "The Decadence of Spain," published in July 1898, began on a distinctly triumphal note, attributing Spain's defeat to a national character distinguished by a "blind and impenetrable pride" and a "spirit of conservatism which rejected all innovation in a world of incessant change." Spaniards, he wrote, were incapable of adapting to "modern industrialism." Nor could Lea resist the opportunity to criticize the Catholic Church. Whatever the defects in Spain's "national trait," "clericalism" served only to make them worse, as it ignited a "ferocious spirit of intolerance" that rendered the Spaniards "unfit" for self-government, led to the expulsion of the Jews, helped to create the Spanish Inquisition, and eventually "benumbed the intellectual development of the people." Lea, moreover, knew exactly where such misfortunes would lead. "While the rest of the civilized world was bounding forward in a career of progress, while science and the useful arts were daily adding to the conquests of man over the forces of nature, and rival nations were growing in wealth and power, the Inquisition condemned Spain to stagnation." Finally, to add yet another familiar scapegoat to the story of Spanish decadence and defeat, Lea concluded with a ringing attack on Habsburg absolutism and the extent to which "ineffective governance" prevented the nation from developing the "liberal institutions" necessary to lead it into the modern world. "There was," he wrote, "no national political life, no training in citizenship, no forces to counterbalance the follies and prejudices of the king and his favorites."[37]

At the dawn of the twentieth century, therefore, political events seemingly confirmed Prescott's contention that Spain and America inhabited different worlds. Most scholars accepted this premise; so did the popular press. Even Archer M. Huntington (1870–1955), founder of the Hispanic Society of America in New York (1908), benefactor of the Hispanic Division of the Library of Congress, and a connoisseur otherwise interested in promoting Spanish art and culture, accepted "Spain" and "modernity" as antithetical concepts. Like Irving, Huntington's Spain was romanticized. "In Spain," he wrote, "fanaticism is natural, chivalry a necessity."[38] Yet Huntington resembled Prescott to the extent that he took seriously the general trajectory of Spanish history, especially the reasons for what he perceived as the nation's failure to modernize along Western lines. Prescott's influence, for example, may be detected in the list of the ingredients Huntington concocted to explain Spanish decadence: "Pride, a weak monarch, a dissolute court, religious intolerance, all these are admirable starting points from which to prove a nation's decline." To this master recipe Huntington added one, albeit vital, ingredient: "Spain lacks the trading spirit . . . the great primitive developing agency," the very absence of which condemned Spain to centuries of isolation and decay.[39] To escape this era, Huntington, like Prescott and Ticknor before him, took refuge in Spain's Middle Ages, especially in that of El Cid, a heroic figure whose *Poema* he endeavored to translate. It follows that the art of medieval Spain figured as the centerpiece of the museum Huntington outfitted in

New York. For similar reasons, the first American historians of Spanish art—
Charles Caffin, Georgiana Goddard King, A. Kingsley Porter, Chandler Post, and
John Kenneth Conant—also displayed a distinct preference for the Middle Ages.
An exception was Charles B. Curtis, who in 1883 had published a detailed catalogue of paintings by Diego de Velázquez y Sylva and Bartolomé Esteban Murillo.
But Curtis viewed Spain's seventeenth century in wholly romantic terms, claiming that upon first visiting Madrid "I found myself carried in a day to the middle
of the seventeenth century. I discovered a country that had preserved almost
unchanged their habits, customs, and traditions of a long-buried age."[40] In comparison, Chandler Post, Harvard's hardheaded historian of Spanish art, attributed
Spain's artistic achievements in the seventeenth century to that "rare artist"
(probably Velázquez) with a "rugged, weird, and titanic spirit," one able to free
himself from the grave Spanish temperament and the strictures of the Catholic
Church.[41]

THE PARADIGM AND THE PROFESSORS

The professionalization of American history, starting in the 1890s, did relatively
little to challenge the basic presuppositions about Spanish culture and politics
that Prescott and his immediate followers set forth. Admittedly, the university-
based historians endeavored to strip away some of the more romantic and overtly
anti-Catholic components of Prescott's ideas about Spain, but the topic of Spanish decline, coupled with the notion that the Spanish character was somehow
defective, or at least incompatible with modernity, remained paramount, so
much so that it left little room for alternate approaches to the Spanish past.

Foremost among the first generation of professional scholars dealing with
Spain was the great Harvard historian Roger B. Merriman (1876–1945). Together
with Charles Homer Haskins, his medievalist colleague, Merriman in 1903–4
introduced Harvard's history curriculum to the study of *Kulturgeschichte*, a reform
that allowed for the discussion of historical issues and problems only tangentially
related to what had previously been the focus of European history at Harvard: the
origins of American institutions. One of the first undergraduates to benefit from
this reform was Samuel Eliot Morison, who, in 1908, long before he developed
an interest in Columbus, wrote an essay, "The Expedition of Cádiz, 1596," which
analyzed the Earl of Essex's daring raid on the Spanish port city. The topic, for an
American historian at least, was original, and clearly one that reflected Merriman's influence. However, the young Morison simply repeated entrenched
stereotypes when he concluded that "the demoralization of Spain's society, culture and art was both the cause and effect of Spain's military defeat."[42]

Spanish decline was also implicit in Merriman's work. His four-volume *Rise of
the Spanish Empire in the Old World and the New* (1918–34) began as a series of
lectures in 1903, and when the first volume appeared, Merriman dedicated it,
pointedly, to Prescott. Merriman, however, dealt with decline by ignoring it, ad-
mitting at the outset that his narrative would end with Philip II and leave "decline

and fall" to others. It was a pleasure, he wrote, "to emphasize the other side of the coin." Accordingly, Merriman devoted his study to a detailed analysis of the internal structures that contributed to Castile's imperial expansion. Yet decline hovered over the book like a rain cloud, and even Merriman, despite his initial promise, felt compelled to discuss the topic at the end of his final volume. There, he offered a sophisticated, multicausal analysis that attributed Spanish decline to a series of cultural and political factors, among them the monarchy's refusal to exchange the old idea of imperial preponderance for "national individuality" and what he called "the transfer of energy and genius from conquest and war to literature and art."[43] Significantly, Merriman's list of factors did not include any reference to Lea's "clericalism" nor reference to any particular flaw in the Spanish national character.

But Merriman was ahead of his times. Other American historians who wrote about Spain stayed well within the familiar confines of Prescott's paradigm. The inaugural 1893 issue of the *Journal of Political Economy*, for example, contained an article by Bernard Moses, an economic historian from the University of California, that attributed Spanish decline to such factors as indolence, idleness, and the nation's excess of churches.[44] Similarly, Sarah Simons's essay "Social Decadence," published in the 1901 issue of the *Annals of the American Academy of Political and Social Science*, utilized Spain (along with traditional China) as the model of what she defined as "a society which is not capable of maintaining a former level of excellence in social products." Simons, more sociologist than historian, was not herself a hispanist, but she had no qualms about blaming the church for Spain's deterioration from "an active, enterprising, independent people to the inert, servile race we know today." As she explained it, "The mind of the Spaniard did not want to improve; they were satisfied with their inheritance; they were and still are unable to doubt; and this is the fault of the church."[45]

Simons's anti-Spanish bias was palpable, but her reading of Spain and its people differed only in degree from that of other professional scholars, including some of the first North American historians to specialize in the history of Latin America. References to the "dead hand" of the church and the "vanity" of the Spanish people figure prominently in Clarence H. Haring's important *Trade and Navigation between Spain and the Indies in the Time of the Hapsburgs* (1918). That same year, the first issue of the *Hispanic American Historical Review* appeared with an article titled "The Institutional Background of Spanish American History." Its author, Charles H. Cunningham, attributed Spanish decline to "the individual inefficiency of the Spaniard from a mercantile point of view."[46]

Prescott's paradigm carried equal weight for the first economic historians to write about Spain, most of whom did little more than to quantify what they already understood: Spain's seventeenth-century decline. Julius Klein's classic account of the Mesta (1920), the Spanish sheepherders' guild, was a case history of the evils of state intervention in economic affairs. Klein, who studied with Merriman at Harvard, was interested in the economic foundations of newly organized states and studied the Mesta in order to measure the role of a specific raw material—in this case, wool—in nation building. Klein offered a clear, documented exposition of the Mesta's history, yet his assumptions about the relationship between economic and political phenomena, especially his notion that state intervention in the economy was incompatible with free trade, had a Prescottian ring. Klein was certain, for example, that royal support for the Mesta sparked Spanish regionalism, undermined the "unifying spirit" the nation had possessed during the fifteenth century, and thus contributed to "the general decay of the country" in later times. Like Prescott, moreover, Klein pointedly portrayed the seventeenth century as one of "dismal depression and sordid melancholy" in order to draw attention to the adverse effects arising from the "autocratic government" of Philip II and the "feeble incompetence of his successors."[47]

The ideas embodied in Prescott's paradigm were equally important for the work of Earl J. Hamilton, arguably one of the most influential economic historians of the 1930s and a scholar whose research on Spanish prices of the sixteenth and seventeenth century is still useful today. Hamilton originally conceived his *American Treasure and the Price Revolution in Spain 1501–1650* (1934) as an effort to analyze the transformative powers of precious metals, a problem which drew him to the question of whether the influx of silver bullion from the Americas had created greater upheavals in Spain than in other parts of Europe. By the time of publication, however, Hamilton added a new issue: the extent to which bullion contributed to "Spanish economic decadence" and whether this decadence was "provincial or national in character." Hamilton, meticulous in his scholarship, pointed out that most "liberal" historians exaggerated Spanish decadence in order "to place absolutism, the Inquisition, the persecution of minorities, and the Moorish expulsions in the worst light." As he saw it, the Germans and French had grossly and purposefully overestimated the extent of Spain's seventeenth-century decline in order to glorify their own countrys' achievements.[48] Hamilton was right, and in this respect he ranks as one of the first scholars to examine Spain's history comparatively and to examine the presuppositions underlying its "decline." Nevertheless, his book suggests that he was also determined to marshal the statistical evidence necessary to prove what he described—unproblematically—as Spain's "economic decadence." In a subsequent article, "The Decline of Spain" (1938), Hamilton repeated his assertion that economic causes were the primary reasons for Spain's political decline; yet his conception of decline remained equally unproblematic, and the list of factors he presented to account had a definite Prescottian ring: "the dead hand of the church," a deterioration in the character of the Spanish monarchs, poor administration, and so forth.[49]

Spain Is Different

In the decades immediately following the Spanish Civil War, Prescott's paradigm enjoyed continued vitality. If anything, General Franco's victory in 1939 gave it renewed life by reaffirming existing ideas about the endemic backwardness of Spanish culture and political life. Hemingway's *For Whom the Bell Tolls* (1940) had romanticized ordinary Spaniards by depicting them as heroes struggling for political freedom, but the prevailing image of Franco's Spain was that of nation openly hostile to the democratic values that the United States and its allies fought to defend in World War II. John B. Crow, whose *Spain: The Root and the Flower* (1963) was widely read in classes on Spanish literature and civilization, neatly summarized American postwar attitudes toward Spain with a pithy quotation borrowed from the English author J. B. Trend: "What was lost in the [civil] war was not merely a government, but a whole modern culture."[50]

In this era, American colleges and universities were investing heavily in "Western Civilization," "area studies" (especially on Latin America), as well as the specialized study of individual national histories, particularly those of nations determined either to be of strategic importance for the United States or those considered to have made significant contributions to the emergence of Western democratic institutions and ideas. Prescott's paradigm, however, recently invigorated by the antipathy of most American scholars toward Franco, effectively curtailed America's investment in Spanish history. One early indicator of this indifference was Harvard's failure to appoint a scholar in Spanish history to succeed Merriman, who had died in 1945. Another was the Prescottian portrayal of Spain's "gloomy fanaticism" and "lack of vitality" in books published in William L. Langer's influential series The Rise of Modern Europe, the first volumes of which appeared in 1951.[51] During this era, when Spain was practically a pariah, shunned by most of the Western democracies, one of the few American scholars who seriously engaged its history was John E. Longhurst (University of New Mexico). But Longhurst's books on the Inquisition's persecution of Spanish Erasmians and Lutherans, partially inspired by McCarthyism, reinforced old notions about the ingrained repressiveness of Spanish society.[52]

So pervasive were these ideas that, by the 1960s, the American historical establishment decided virtually to ignore Spain, employing the persistence of Spanish fascism together with Spaniards' own explanations of their nation's alleged "difference" as convenient excuses. With few notable exceptions—the University of California at Berkeley, UCLA, and the University of Virginia, where Julian Bishko taught the history of Spain's Middle Ages—instruction in Spanish history (as opposed to Spanish literature and civilization) languished, creating a situation which not only limited opportunities for students to enter the field but assured the survival of Prescottian stereotypes.[53]

Meanwhile, the scholarly contributions of that handful of Americans who continued to work in the area did little, if anything, to alter the paradigm Prescott had set into place. What little original scholarship there was either focused on the twentieth century, highlighting the Spanish Civil War and the nation's failure to develop stable democratic institutions, or the eighteenth century and the somewhat abortive experiment of the Spanish Bourbons with Enlightenment.[54] Research on the sixteenth and seventeenth centuries remained equally sparse, restricted to either diplomatic history or traditional Black Legend themes, such as the Inquisition's persecution of Protestants. Of particular influence was Garrett Mattingly's best-selling study, *The Armada* (1959), which—echoing Prescott—

presented Elizabethan England as the champion of freedom, a latter-day David destined to triumph over the tyrannical Goliath: Philip II of Spain.[55]

Much American scholarship on Spanish topics during the postwar era fell under the influence of Spanish philosophy, especially that of Miguel de Unamuno (1846–1936) and José Ortega y Gasset (1883–1955), both of whom, like Prescott before them, isolated Spain by portraying it as a nation whose history did not bear comparison with that of other European states. Spanish literary scholars in the United States were especially susceptible to this particular variant of Spanish exceptionalism, particularly followers of the brilliant Spanish émigré Américo Castro (1885–1976), whose books taught that Spaniards were constitutionally different from other Europeans owing to their particular admixture of Christian, Jewish, and Moorish blood and the particular set of ethnic and religious problems this heritage had engendered. Castro also cultivated a particular interest in Spain's *converso* population, and under his influence, persecution of this minority of former Jews served as a powerful reminder of Spanish religious intolerance and hate. *Conversos* consequently attracted inordinate attention as the historians and literary scholars who studied them not only diminished the extent to which they successfully assimilated into Spanish society but also exaggerated the negative effects that resulted from their persecution by the Spanish Inquisition.[56] Ideally, the study of the challenges confronting the *conversos* might have been connected with those of Europe's other ethnic and religious minorities, yet what was described as the "*converso* problem" was customarily presented as solely a Spanish problem and therefore yet another reason why Spain was inherently unique.

The first break from this particular pattern occurred late in the 1960s as a number of scholars, united in their doubts about the utility of national character as a causal factor in Spanish history, employed other means to examine the nation's past. Influenced by the emergent Annales school of history, these scholars—and I include myself among them—through detailed archival investigation and methods borrowed from the social sciences, endeavored to create a Spain that was at once more vital and more varied than the Prescottian paradigm allowed. Nevertheless, the topics selected, many of which still touched on issues connected to Spain's intellectual stagnation or economic decline, did little to alter the prevailing image of Spain as a country whose contribution to Western history did not merit serious scholarly investigation.[57]

A PARADIGMATIC SHIFT?

At present, signs of a shift in the paradigm Prescott formulated are somewhat mixed. On the one hand, there are some positive signs, including increases in the number of scholars associated with Spanish history and the continuing availability of financial support for both publication and research on topics relating directly to Spain.[58] On the other, academic positions in Spanish history are still relatively few, although there is the likelihood of more as North America's

Hispanic population looks beyond their more immediate linkages with Spanish America to the culture and history of Spain itself. Whatever the future, the field is starting to attract new adherents from increasingly diverse educational and ethnic backgrounds, which augurs well for a more pluralistic and, ultimately, a less Prescottian approach to the study of the Spanish past.

One current approach may be characterized as a shift away from Spanish exceptionalism and its concomitant emphasis upon decline as an intrinsically "Spanish" phenomenon. Such an approach began with Hamilton, but it was Merriman's *Six Contemporaneous Revolutions* (1937) that offered the first comparative analysis of the political history of seventeenth-century Spain, largely in an effort to determine the extent to which the revolts which rocked Europe's monarchies in the 1640s belonged to an international movement, possibly even a conspiracy. At the time, Merriman was interested in drawing parallels between these revolts and the spread of European fascism, but over the decades his study had the effect of reattaching Spanish history to European history. This particular movement gained momentum in the 1960s, owing primarily to the work of the influential English scholar John H. Elliott, who, having rejecting the notion that an immutable national character rendered the Spanish incapable of innovation and change, interpreted the erosion of Habsburg power in the 1640s as part of the "general crisis of the seventeenth century."[59] Elliott's comparative approach to Spanish history won wide acceptance in France and England—and, somewhat more slowly—in Spain itself. It also attracted adherents in the United States, itself a sign of movement in the Prescottian paradigm as well as a signal of a fundamental change in the way American scholars think and write about Spain.

One thing is certain: old orientations and presuppositions are definitely under attack. In Spanish art history, for example, the medievalism of the early part of the century is giving way to emphasis on the art of more modern periods, including that of the era generally associated with Spanish decline. This change in focus is accompanied by a willingness to reexamine some of the fundamental premises associated with Spanish seventeenth-century art. Early in the century, Chandler Post argued for Spanish artistic exceptionalism. No country, he believed, was "less responsive to foreign influences than Spain."[60] Yet recent work on a wide range of topics—individual artists, architecture, palace decoration, artistic genres such as still life—suggests that Spain was anything but isolated from the main currents of European art.[61] Jonathan Brown, moreover, has written extensively about the art patronage and collecting of Philip IV (1621–65), emphasizing the extent to which this monarch's preference for painting not only created the largest—and most envied—art collection in seventeenth-century Europe but also served to make painting, as opposed to sculpture and tapestries, the most respected of all the arts.[62] In this perspective, paintings that Prescott might have used as evidence for the decadence of Spain's monarchs are being refigured as markers of the nation's cultural vitality and intellectual interchange, two qualities which it supposedly lacked.

Also seen is a willingness to challenge the old teleology of Spanish economic backwardness and decline. David Ringrose, for example, has recently achieved this by disaggregating the Spanish economy into various "urban networks" and reevaluating its performance (upward) in the eighteenth and nineteenth century through the use of data that previously escaped attention. His findings are by no means definitive, but they do suggest that the Spanish economy was far more modern—and changing—than earlier historians of the Spanish economy, Hamilton included, would have ever allowed.[63]

The old teleology is also suffering at the hands of scholars less interested in the ups and downs of the Spanish empire than in exploring the internal character of Spanish society and culture.[64] The monolithic "Spain" that Prescott and other historians presented is currently being dismantled as scholars examine it micro-historically, divide it into regions, examine peripheries rather than centers, and peer into the minutiae of everyday life.[65] Furthermore, Prescott's stereotype of the Spaniard as the cruel conquistador and the indolent priest is gradually giving to way to a more varied picture of individuals of vastly different stripes—a Catalan artisan coping with the rigors of plague, a young Castilian girl who dreamed of a better life, university-educated clergymen struggling to educate their parishioners in the rudiments of the faith, Basque shipbuilders diligently attempting to make a profit in difficult times, olive-growing nobles determined to introduce commercial agriculture into southern Spain, and courtiers who, together with other European office-seekers, made the promotion of their family and their friends a primary concern.[66] Even more pronounced is the growing tendency to temper Prescott's image of omnipotent Habsburg absolutism with that of a monarchy whose power was circumscribed by numerous constitutional and juridical checks.[67]

Today's historians of Spain can therefore be likened to iconoclasts, bent on breaking the old images that had formed the Spain envisioned by their forebears and, in some cases, their own teachers as well. One young historian, partly on the basis of new evidence gleaned from the Spanish state archives in Simancas, is currently suggesting that Juana I (1479–1555)—the "mad" queen from whom the feeblemindedness of the later Habsburgs allegedly derived—may not have been nearly as deranged as formerly assumed.[68] Similarly, recent work on Pedro Ciruelo, a humanist attached to the University of Alcalá de Henares, is challenging the traditional notion that the Inquisition and state censorship successfully crushed all that was innovative and vital in sixteenth-century Spanish thought.[69] Meanwhile, another scholar—a Canadian in this instance—is at this moment transforming the bullfight—once emblematic of Spanish cruelty, and for the romantics, of the Spanish picturesque—into a symbol of Spanish commercial enterprise as he documents the way in which nineteenth-century promoters of the corrida transformed what had been a popular festival into a commercialized, professionalized, mass-market spectator phenomenon.[70] But perhaps the most significant shift in Prescott's paradigm involves the study of the role of religion in Spanish history. Of particular interest here is the work of scholars who have used the trial records of the Inquisition not, as Lea would have done, to emphasize the institution's cruelty but rather as a vast historical database containing materials that can be used to explore a culture far more complex and far more heterodox than previously imagined.[71] In addition, what Prescott, Lea, Hamilton, and others derided as the fanaticism and superstition of Spanish Catholicism is being converted into a vital, constituent force that drew its energy from village society and provided the peasantry ways of managing the difficulties of everyday life.[72]

Yet, for all of these signs of a shift in the paradigm, old perceptions die hard. Inherited notions of Spanish exceptionalism, for example, help to explain why so many historians in the United States still write and teach European history as if the continent, as Alexandre Dumas suggested, actually stopped at the Pyrenees. Habits of a similar sort may also be responsible for the tendency of American scholars who actually write Spanish history to employ what John Elliott has described as an "excessively 'internalist' approach" to their subject.[73] Too frequently, it seems, Spain remains something of an aberration, a nation inherently different from the rest of Europe albeit a Europe that is generally (and erroneously) equated with either England or France. With respect to absolutism, for example, a recent study rightly highlighted the political fragmentation that resulted in Castile from the Habsburgs' "sale of towns," but did so without reference either to central Europe or even to neighboring Portugal, where the local, institutional, and corporate checks on Leviathan were just as important as those in Castile.[74] This "excessively 'internalist' approach" describes other questions equally well—discrimination toward women and religious minorities, ethnic and linguistic differences, regional rivalries—all of which are still conceived as if rooted to what Prescott would have called Spain's national "spirit," what Lea described as its national "trait," or what is now called *españolismo*, Spanishness.[75] Otherwise, it is difficult to understand why a new and fascinating study of Spanish funeral customs would attribute, if obliquely, Spain's economic decline in the seventeenth century to the excessive investment in postmortem masses arising from the Spaniards' alleged, and supposedly ongoing, collective obsession with death.[76]

The personal stakes involved in Spain's presentation in exceptional terms are none too clear. Yet, for many historians, and possibly many other Americans as well, Spain remains a nation whose leaders only recently declared it hostile to the political and religious pluralism championed by the United States. Spain remains something of an Other, a nation synonymous with the ominous figure of Tomás de Torquemada (as in Mel Brooks's 1981 film, *The History of the World, Part I*) and connected, inextricably perhaps, to Columbus, to Cortés, and the other conquistadores now credited with the extermination of the civilizations as well as the ecology of the New World, as in Kirkpatrick Sale's *The Conquest of Paradise* (1991) and other publications occasioned by the quincentenary of 1992. In fact, it turns out that many of the books and celebrations associated with this anniversary did little more than to spark a revival of Black Legend themes, thus making it even easier for Americans, even those with little of the anticlericalism evinced by Prescott and Lea, to distance themselves from both Spain and it history. In part, this distancing can be attributed to lack of mass emigration from Spain to the United States, in part to Americans' inability to associate Spain with anything

except the pathetic figure of Don Quixote tilting at windmills or the more picturesque elements of its culture: bullfighting, castles, flamenco dancers, and
gypsies.[77] Racism, too, plays a role here, as few Americans truly understand the
difference between Spaniards—known traditionally in Latin America as *gachu-
pines* or *peninsulares*—and the Latinos in search of citizenship in the United
States. It is no accident, therefore, that a best-selling Spanish olive oil in the
United States is marketed under the assumed Italian name of Pompeian. Put
simply, a gap still separates the two societies, reinforcing (mutual) misunderstanding and increasing the temptation on the part of all Americans to view Spaniards through a Prescottian lens.

Yet something has definitely changed since Prescott first published *Ferdinand
and Isabel* over 150 years ago. In the nineteenth century, this country's historians
regarded Spain as their opposite. They looked back to its seventeenth century as
the exemplum of everything America was not: backward, enervated, a society in
decline. Few scholars understood—or cared to understand—that "decline" was
a relative rather than an absolute concept. Even fewer compared Spanish accomplishments, economic and otherwise, to those of nations other than Great Britain,
France, Germany, or the United States. Fortunately, such rigid thinking is increasingly a thing of the past, and the changeover is accompanied by the understanding that imperial power is rarely long-lasting. Increasingly popular, therefore, is the view that Spain's American empire—with a life span of more than
three centuries—needs to be examined in terms of the factors that contributed to
its longevity instead of those that contributed to its decay. Even so, the image
of Spanish decline remains tempting, and even in our own day, in the guise of
Paul Kennedy's best-selling *The Rise and Fall of the Great Powers* (1987), seventeenth-century Spain, though still at arm's length, has acquired new meaning.
Prescott's Protestant bias is absent; so too are references to Spaniards' instinctive
abhorrence for trade. What remains is the portrait of a mismanaged kingdom
top-heavy with military expenditures, and through this image Kennedy literally
transforms a society that Prescott conceived as America's antithesis into a specter
of what an overextended America might soon become.[78]

VIVA PRESCOTT!

A final anecdote, trivial perhaps, will serve to illustrate that the topic of Spanish
decline retains much of the popularity Prescott described in 1843. About a year
ago, during a routine medical exam, my physician, upon learning about my interest in Spain's history, asked me for a quick summary of what I considered the
reasons for the nation's decline as a great power. The question, he avowed, was
one he had long considered, but never resolved to his satisfaction. As a historian,
I tried to explain decline as a relative phenomenon, briefly alluding to Kennedy's
book, the seventeenth century's general crisis; I even asked him to consider carefully what he meant by the term decline itself. The exam was soon over, my shirt
buttoned up, but my measured response to the query was clearly inadequate. My

doctor's view of Spain is surely different from Prescott's; yet, without saying so directly, what he wanted was an answer with at least one of the elements that Prescott would have assigned to Spanish decline: the rise of the Inquisition, the expulsion of the Jews, the defeat of the Spanish Armada, the leadership qualities of the Habsburg monarchs, possibly even Spanishness itself. Generalizations are risky, but the incident does seem to suggest that Spanish history possesses a popular appeal far greater than most universities and colleges are likely to admit. More important, it serves as a reminder that America's identity may still depend on national histories that are both conceived and constructed as antithetical to its own.

Notes

Except for some corrections and minor revisions, this essay is identical to the version published in *The American Historical Review* 101 (April 1996): 423–46.

1. *The Literary Memoranda of William Hickling Prescott*, ed. C. Harvey Gardiner, 2 vols. (Norman, 1961), 1:68.

2. *Literary Memoranda of Prescott* 1:51, 66, 97. These memoranda are invaluable for understanding Prescott's methodology.

3. For his biography, see George Ticknor, *The Life of William Hickling Prescott* (Boston, 1864); Stanley T. Williams, *The Spanish Background of American Literature* (New Haven, 1955), 2:78–121, and, most recently, C. Harvey Gardiner, *William Hickling Prescott: A Biography* (Austin, 1969). Also useful is the *Hispanic American Historical Review* 100 (1959), which contains a brief biography ("William Hickling Prescott: The Man and His Work") by R. A. Humphreys and other articles celebrating Prescott's achievement.

4. Thomas Jefferson to John Rutledge, Paris, July 18, 1788, cited in Edward Dumbauld, *Thomas Jefferson, American Tourist* (Norman, 1946), 148. Jefferson's Spanish books are catalogued in *Thomas Jefferson's Library: A Catalog with the Entries in His Own Order*, ed. James Gilreath and Douglas L. Wilson (Washington, D.C., 1969). For the teaching of Spanish in the colonial era, see J. R. Spell, "Spanish Teaching in the United States," *Hispania* 10 (1927): 141–59, and Edith F. Helman, "Early Interest in Spanish in New England (1815–1835)," *Hispania* 29 (1946): 326–51.

5. The phrase "Black Legend" was coinded by the Spanish scholar Julián Juderías in *La leyenda negra: Estudios acerca del concepto de España en el extranjero* (Madrid, 1914). The most recent survey of Black Legend history is Ricardo García Carcel, *La leyenda negra: historia y opinion* (Madrid, 1992). English titles on the subject include Charles Gibson, *The Black Legend: Anti-Spanish Attitudes in the Old World and the New* (New York, 1971); William S. Maltby, *The Black Legend in England: The Development of Anti-Spanish Sentiment, 1558–1660* (Durham, N.C., 1971); and Philip W. Powell, *Tree of Hate: Propaganda and Prejudices Affecting the United States Relations with the Hispanic World* (New York, 1971). For the *arbitristas*, see J. H. Elliott, "Self-Perception and Decline in Early Seventeenth-Century Spain," in his *Spain and Its World, 1500–1700* (New Haven and London, 1989), 241–61.

6. John Campbell also wrote about Spain in *The Present State of Europe* (London, 1753), 304–56, as well as in volumes 20–22 of *The Modern Part of the Universal History*, 44 vols. (London, 1759–66), which Prescott read in 1827–28; *Literary Memoranda of Prescott*, 1: 88, 94.

7. William Robertson, *History of America*, 7th ed. (London, 1776), book 8, p. 245.

Prescott, who first read this book in 1827, noted that "*Robertson's* extensive subject is necessarily defficient in connection," but he praised the author for his "sagacious reflections," "clear & vigorous diction," and for his "interesting, philosophical, and elegant narrative." *Literary Memoranda of Prescott*, 1:82–83.

8. Jedidiah Morse, *The American Universal Geography*, 3rd ed., 2 vols. (Boston, 1796), 2:394, and 6th ed., 2 vols. (Boston, 1816), 2:349. See also the entries for Spain in Morse's *Geography Made Easy*, 5th ed. (Boston, 1796).

9. Quoted in Sister Marie Leonore Fell, *The Foundations of Nativism in American Textbooks, 1783–1860* (Washington, D.C., 1941), 37. See also Francis Fitzgerald, *America Revisited: History Schoolbooks in the Twentieth Century* (Boston, 1972), 49.

10. "Trait of Spanish Character," *North American Review* 5 (1817): 30.

11. *The Letters of Henry Wadsworth Longfellow*, ed. Andrew Hilen, 6 vols. (Cambridge, Mass., 1966), 1:222. In 1833, Longfellow, who taught literature at Bowdoin College, published an essay, "Spanish Language and Literature," in the *North American Review* 36 (1836), 316–334. Longfellow was subsequently Professor of Modern Languages at Harvard from 1834 to 1855. For his interests in Spanish literature, see Iris L. Whitman, *Longfellow and Spain* (New York, 1917), and Williams, *Spanish Background*, 2:152–79. For the various meanings attached to the term "Oriental," see Edward Said, *Orientalism* (New York, 1978).

12. *The Complete Works of Washington Irving*, ed. Wayne R. Kime and Andrew B. Meyers (Boston, 1984), vol. 4, *Journals and Notebooks*, 140. Irving had been invited to Madrid by Alexander Hill Everett, the American consul, to translate the first volume of Manuel Fernández de Navarrete, *Colección de los viajes y descubrimientos que hicieron por mar los españoles desde el fin del siglo XV*, 5 vols. (Madrid, 1825–37).

13. *The Papers of William Hickling Prescott*, ed. C. Harvey Gardiner (Urbana, 1964), 8.

14. *Literary Memoranda of Prescott*, 1:65.

15. *Literary Memoranda of Prescott*, 1:66.

16. David Levin, *History, a Romantic Art: Bancroft, Prescott, Motley, Parkman* (Stanford, 1959).

17. *Literary Memoranda of Prescott*, 1:97.

18. William H. Prescott, *Biographical and Critical Miscellanies* (New York, 1845), 118. His review of Irving first appeared in 1829. Prescott resented Irving's intrusion into a subject he regarded as his own, once confiding to a friend that Irving "helped himself to two of the biggest and fattest slices" in the Catholic Monarchs' reign. See *The Correspondence of William Hickling Prescott 1833–1847*, ed. Roger Wolcott (Boston, 1925), 204, Prescott to Jarold Sparks, February 1, 1841.

19. Prescott's view of the Inquisition was undoubtedly influenced by José Antonio Llorente, *A Critical History of the Inquisition of Spain* (London, 1823). The book, originally published in French, *Histoire critique de l'inquistion d'espagne* (Paris, 1817–18), was first mentioned by Prescott in 1826. See *Literary Memoranda of Prescott*, 1:74, 96.

20. *Literary Memoranda of Prescott*, 1:140.

21. William H. Prescott, *History of the Reign of Philip II of Spain*, 3 vols. (Boston, 1855), 1:3, 145, 554. Many of Great Britain's nineteenth-century hispanists held similar views of Spain, the Inquisition in particular. See, for example, Richard Ford, *A Hand-Book for Travellers in Spain and Readers at Home* (1845), ed. Ian Robertson, ed., 3 vols. (Carbondale, 1966), 1:418–21. The history of British hispanism, along with the American, remains to be written, although the latter may be approached through Williams, *Spanish Background*.

22. Prescott's negative view of empire, derived in part from Adam Smith, helps to explain his determined opposition to the Mexican War and the annexation of Texas. See, for example, *Correspondence of Prescott*, 627, Prescott to George Sumner, April 1, 1847, where

he refers critically to "our mad ambition for conquest." See also the letter to Sumner cited below in footnote 24.

23. Prescott, *History of the Reign of Philip II,* 2:446.

24. For Prescott's political views, see Gardiner, *William Hickling Prescott,* 95, 166–68. That history offered Prescott a refuge from domestic politics became patently clear in 1846, when in the midst of writing *History of the Conquest of Peru* and with specific reference to the Mexican War, Prescott wrote the following to George Sumner: "I am sick of our domestic troubles . . . I take refuge from them in Peruvian hills, where the devildoms I read of—black enough—have at least no reference to ourselves." *Correspondence of Prescott,* 597, May 15, 1846.

25. For the myth of national character, with particular reference to Spain, see Julio Caro Baroja, *El mito del caracter nacional* (Madrid, 1970).

26. *Correspondence of Prescott,* 428, Prescott to Pascual de Gayangos, December 21, 1843. The book, first translated into Spanish in 1846, also enjoyed commercial success in Spain. However, the book's reception there, its influence on subsequent Spanish historiography, and its particular appeal among Spanish *liberales* sympathetic to Prescott's anticlericalism and hostility to absolutism awaits detailed study.

27. George Ticknor, *Life, Letters and Journals of George Ticknor* (Boston, 1876), 198–99.

28. *Letters of James Russell Lowell,* ed. Charles Eliot Norton (New York, 1893), 2:235, Lowell to Thomas Hughs, November 17, 1879; 2: 241, Lowell to W. D. Howells, May 2, 1879. Lowell was professor of modern languages at Harvard from 1855 until 1877, when he was named minister to Spain. For his life, see Martin Duberman, *James Russell Lowell* (Cambridge, Mass., 1966). Lowell's friend Henry Adams regarded Spain as equally out-of-date after he visited the country in 1879. See *The Letters of Henry Adams,* ed. J. C. Levenson, 6 vols. (Cambridge, 1982), 2:379–83. Francis Parkman had a similar reaction during his visit in 1887. See *Letters of Francis Parkman,* ed. Wilbur R. Jacobs, 2 vols. (Norman, 1960), 2:200.

29. On nineteenth-century medievalism in the United States, see T. J. Jackson Lears, *No Place of Grace: Anti-modernism and the Transformation of American Culture, 1889–1920* (New York, 1981), 141–81; John Fraser, *America and the Patterns of Chivalry* (Cambridge, 1982); and Robin Fleming, "Picturesque History and the Medieval in Nineteenth-Century America," *American Historical Review* 100 (October 1995): 1061–94.

30. Ticknor's literary achievement is summarized in Williams, *Spanish Background,* 46–77. See also Thomas R. Hart Jr., "George Ticknor's *History of Spanish Literature:* The New England Background," *Proceedings of the Modern Language Association,* March (1954): 76–88. Note that the first comprehensive survey of French literature by American scholars was William A. Nitze and E. Preston Duncan, *A History of French Literature* (New York, 1922).

31. George Ticknor, *History of Spanish Literature,* 3rd ed. (Boston, 1866), 413, 417, 433. In comparison, Frederick Boutewerk's *History of Spanish Literature,* published initially (in German) between 1805 and 1817 (first English edition, 3 vols., London, 1847), noted that Spain's literary "spirit" survived until 1665, when it finally succumbed to a "vicious system of government" (3:254).

32. John Lothrop Motley, *Rise of the Dutch Republic,* Everyman edition (London, 1906), vol. 1, part I, chap. 2, p. 132.

33. Motley, *Rise of the Dutch Republic,* vol. 2, part 6, chap. 7, pp. 449, 454.

34. This literature is best approached through Williams, *Spanish Background,* 1:113–17, and Powell, *Tree of Hate,* 122–25.

35. Lea to W. E. H. Lecky, April 9, 1888, quoted in E. S. Bradley, *Henry Charles Lea* (Philadelphia, 1931), 328.

36. Lea by this date had also published several scholarly articles on Spanish history, including "The First Castilian Inquisitor," which appeared in the premier issue of the *American Historical Review:* 1 (1896): 46–50.

37. Henry Charles Lea, "The Decadence of Spain," *Atlantic Monthly* 82 (1898): 36–46. Lea's subsequent book on the Inquisition reaffirmed his belief in the negative effects of the Holy Office upon Spanish society. See *A History of the Inquisition of Spain,* 4 vols. (New York, 1906–07), esp. 4:438, 472–513. For Lea's scholarship in general, see Bradley, *Henry Charles Lea;* Williams, *Spanish Background,* 1:153–57, and Edwards Peters, "Henry Charles Lea and the 'Abode of Monsters,'" in Angel Alcalá, ed., *The Spanish Inquisition and the Inquisitorial Mind* (Barcelona, 1984; Boulder, 1987), 577–608.

38. Archer M. Huntington, *Note-book on Northern Spain* (New York, 1898), 2.

39. Huntington, *Note-book on Northern Spain,* 2, 7.

40. Charles B. Curtis, *Velázquez and Murillo: A Descriptive and Historical Catalogue . . .* (New York and London, 1883), 1.

41. Chandler Rathfon Post, *A History of Spanish Painting,* 14 vols. in 20 (Cambridge, 1930–66), 1:10. This work was preceded by E. W. Washburn, *The Spanish Masters* (New York, 1884); Charles H. Caffin, *The Story of Spanish Painting* (New York, 1910); Georgiana Goddard King, *Way of St. James* (New York, 1920); John Kenneth Conant, *The Cathedral of Santiago de Compostela* (Cambridge, 1926); and A. Kingsley Porter, *Spanish Romanesque Sculpture* (Florence, 1928).

42. Cited in Gregory M. Pfitzer, *Samuel Eliot Morison's Historical World* (Boston, 1991), 24.

43. Roger B. Merriman, *The Rise of the Spanish Empire in the Old World and the New* (New York, 1918–34), 4:678.

44. Bernard Moses, "The Economic Condition of Spain in the Sixteenth Century," *Journal of Political Economy* 1 (1893): 513–94.

45. Sarah E. Simons, " Social Decadence," *Annals of the Academy of Political and Social Science* 18 (1901): 251–79.

46. Clarence H. Haring, *Trade and Navigation between Spain and the Indies in the Time of Hapsburgs* (Cambridge, 1918), 131, 179; and Charles H. Cunningham, "The Institutional Background of Spanish Economic History," *Hispanic American Historical Review* 1 (1918): 24. More balanced assessments of Spain's colonial achievement came from Yale professor Edward G. Bourne, *Spain in America* (New York, 1906), and the University of California's (Berkeley) Herbert E. Bolton, "The Mission in Spanish-American Colonies," *American Historical Review* 23 (1917): 42–61. Bolton's article, a western historian's response to the Turner thesis on the role of the frontier in American history, actually referred to "Spain's frontiering genius." Although the image of Spain in twentieth-century U.S. scholarship on colonial Latin America requires detailed study, in general it appears that historians of Latin America have resisted use of the paradigm outlined in this essay.

47. Julius Klein, *The Mesta: A Study in Spanish Economic History, 1273–1836* (Cambridge, 1920), 244, 352. Klein, in a later publication, repeated his contention that the reign of Ferdinand and Isabel marked the beginning of a "long and sordid chronicle of decay and of royal exploitation." See his "Medieval Spanish Guilds," in *Facts and Factors in Economic History* (New York, 1932), 187. Klein by this date was an assistant secretary in the U.S. Department of Commerce.

48. Earl J. Hamilton, *American Treasure and the Price Revolution in Spain, 1501–1650* (Cambridge, Mass., 1934), 303.

49. Earl J. Hamilton, "The Decline of Spain," *Economic History Review* 8 (1938): 168–79.

50. John Crow, *Spain: The Root and the Flower* (New York, 1963; reprint ed., Berkeley,

1985), 340. Crow, a specialist in Spanish literature, had been educated in pre-Franco Spain.

51. Cited here is Carl J. Friedrich, *The Age of the Baroque, 1610–1660* (New York, 1952), 226, and John B. Wolf, *The Emergence of the Great Powers, 1685–1715* (New York, 1951), 123.

52. The first of John E. Longhurst's books were *Erasmus and the Spanish Inquisition: The Case of Juan de Valdés* (Albuquerque, 1950), and *Luther and the Spanish Inquisition: The Case of Diego de Uceda, 1528–1529* (Albuquerque, 1953).

53. My own experiences reinforce the point. In 1964, when I first considered studying the history of Habsburg Spain, opportunities to do so in the United States were extremely limited, as few research universities had specialists in Spanish history. Notable exceptions were Joan Connelly Ullman (University of Washington) and Stanley Payne (UCLA; he moved to Wisconsin in 1968), both of whom worked primarily in the twentieth century. Early modernists associated directly with Spain were Richard Herr (University of California, Berkeley), author of *The Eighteenth-Century Revolution in Spain* (Princeton, 1958), Charles H. Carter (Tulane University), a diplomatic historian whose *The Secret Diplomacy of the Habsburgs, 1598–1625* (New York, 1964) had only just appeared, and Ruth Pike, then assistant professor at Hunter College and still writing her *Enterprise and Adventure: The Genoese in Seville and the Opening of the New World* (Ithaca, 1966). In order to pursue my graduate studies, I found my way to Cambridge University in England, where I completed my doctoral dissertation in 1968 under the direction of John H. Elliott.

54. Noteworthy U.S. contributions to twentieth-century Spanish history included Stanley G. Payne, *Falange: A History of Spanish Fascism* (Stanford, 1961), as well as his *Politics and the Military in Modern Spain* (Stanford, 1967); Gabriel Jackson, *The Spanish Republic and the Civil War, 1931–1939* (Princeton, 1965); and Joan Connelly Ullman, *The Tragic Week: A Study of Anti-clericalism in Spain, 1875–1912* (Cambridge, Mass., 1967). Interest in the eighteenth century increased following the 1958 publication of Richard Herr's important book, *Eighteenth-Century Revolution in Spain*.

55. Garrett Mattingly, *The Armada* (Boston, 1959), 401. Note that in his other books, notably *Renaissance Diplomacy* (London, 1955), Mattingly lauded the many innovations introduced during the Spain of Ferdinand and Isabel. The first major postwar publication on medieval Spain by a U.S. scholar was Robert I. Burns, S. J., *The Crusader Kingdom of Valencia: Reconstruction on a Thirteenth-Century Frontier*, 2 vols. (Cambridge, Mass., 1967).

56. Many of Castro's ideas about Spanish culture may be found in his influential study, *The Structure of Spanish History*, trans. Edmund King (Princeton, 1954), a book which elicited considerable criticism. See especially Eugenio Asensio, *La España imaginada de Américo Castro* (Barcelona, 1976).

57. Representative titles include Ruth Pike's book on the role of the Genoese in the Atlantic economy (see above, n. 53) and its companion piece, *Aristocrats and Traders: Sevillian Society in the Sixteenth Century* (Ithaca, 1972); David R. Ringrose, *Transportation and Economic Stagnation in Spain 1750–1850* (Durham, 1970); and my own *Students and Society in Early Modern Spain* (Baltimore, 1974).

58. The Society for Spanish and Portuguese History, which held its first annual meeting in 1969, currently possesses over 400 members, of whom approximately 300 are from the United States. Such a figure is dwarfed by that of the French Historical Society, with a membership of almost 2,000. As for funding, the Program for Cultural Cooperation between the Spanish Ministry of Culture and U.S. universities, which was founded in 1983 at a base in Minneapolis, offers inducements for the study of Spanish history in the form of publication subsidies and grants for travel and research. For a decade the program

worked in conjunction with the U.S.-Spanish Joint Committee for Cultural and Educational Exchange, an agency connected with the Council for the International Exchange of Scholars, but the Joint Committee is now defunct.

59. Of crucial importance was Elliott's essay, "The Decline of Spain," *Past and Present* 20 (1961): 52–75, now reprinted in his *Spain and Its World*, 217–240.

60. Post, *History of Spanish Painting*, 1:23.

61. Representative titles include Jonathan Brown, *Images and Ideas in Seventeenth-Century Spanish Art* (Princeton, 1978), and his *Velázquez: Painter and Courtier* (New Haven and London, 1986); Jonathan Brown and John H. Elliott, *A Palace for a King: The Buen Retiro and the Court of Philip IV* (New Haven and London, 1980); William B. Jordan and Peter Cherry, *Spanish Still Life from Velázquez to Goya* (London, 1995); and Cathy Wilkinson-Zerner, *Juan de Herrera: Architect to Philip II of Spain* (New Haven and London, 1993).

62. Jonathan Brown, *Kings and Connoisseurs: Collecting Art in Seventeenth Century Europe* (Princeton, 1995).

63. David R. Ringrose, *Patterns, Events, and Preconceptions: Revisiting the Structures of Spanish History, 1700–1900* (Cambridge, 1995). David Sven Reher employed a similar methodology in his *Town and Country in Pre-industrial Spain: Cuenca 1550–1870* (Cambridge, 1992).

64. Representative titles include Ida Altman, *Emigrants and Society: Extremadura and America in the Sixteenth Century* (Berkeley, 1989); Jodi Bilinkoff, *The Avila of Santa Teresa: Religious Reform in a Sixteenth-Century City* (Ithaca, 1989); Carla Rahn Phillips, *Ciudad Real, 1500–1700: Growth, Crisis and Readjustment in the Spanish Economy* (Cambridge, Mass., 1979); and David Vassberg, *Land and Society in Golden Age Castile* (Cambridge, 1983).

65. The Catalan periphery has proved especially attractive in view of the many differences between this part of the peninsula and Castile, the region that Prescott and indeed most historians have identified with Spain. Catalonia is the focus of James S. Amelang, *Honored Citizens of Barcelona: Patrician Culture and Class Relations, 1490–1714* (Princeton, 1986); and Peter Sahlins, *Boundaries: The Making of France and Spain in the Pyrenees* (Berkeley, 1989).

66. I allude here to James S. Amelang, *A Journal of the Plague Year: The Diary of the Barcelona Tanner Miquel Parets, 1651* (New York, 1991); Richard L. Kagan, *Lucrecia's Dreams: Politics and Prophecy in Sixteenth-Century Spain* (Berkeley, 1990); Sara T. Nalle, *God in La Mancha: Religious Reform and the People of Cuenca, 1500–1650* (Baltimore, 1992); Carla Rahn Phillips, *Six Galleons for the King of Spain: Imperial Defense in the Early Seventeenth Century* (Baltimore, 1986); and James Boyden, *The Courtier and the King: Ruy Gómez de Silva, Philip II and the Court of Spain* (Berkeley, 1995).

67. Helen Nader, *Liberty in Absolutist Spain: The Habsburg Sale of Towns, 1516–1700* (Baltimore, 1991), examines the checks limiting the exercise of monarchical power in Castile. I expect that the formulation of the Habsburg monarchy as more limited than absolute will soon establish itself as a new orthodoxy.

68. Bethany Aram, "Joanna 'the Mad's' Signature: Linking Individual and Corporate Bodies," unpublished paper. Ms. Aram, whose senior thesis at Yale dealt with Juana, is presently a graduate student in history at Johns Hopkins.

69. See Lu Ann Homza, "Religious Humanism, Pastoral Reform, and the Pentateuch: Pedro Ciruelo's Journey from Grace to Law," Ph.D. dissertation, University of Chicago, 1992.

70. Adrian Shubert, *At Five in the Afternoon* (Oxford University Press, forthcoming).

71. Among a recent avalanche of revisionist works on the Inquisition, notable studies

by American authors include Stephen Haliczer, *Inquisition and Society in the Kingdom of Valencia* (Berkeley, 1990), and E. William Monter, *Frontiers of Heresy: The Spanish Inquisition from the Basque Lands to Sicily* (Cambridge, 1990).

72. See William A. Christian, Jr., *Local Religion in Sixteenth-Century Spain* (Princeton, 1981), and its companion study, *Apparitions in Late Medieval and Renaissance Spain* (Princeton, 1981). Both employ an anthropological approach to Spanish Catholicism, emphasizing its local character and functional importance.

73. Elliott, *Spain and Its World*, 69.

74. I refer to Nader, *Liberty in Absolutist Spain* (see above, n. 67), which, its lack of a comparative focus notwithstanding, remains an important and provocative book. James Amelang has offered similar criticism of this and other recent books (primarily by American authors) on various aspects of early modern Spain; see *Journal of Modern History* 65 (June 1993): 357–74.

75. Crow, *Spain*, 9.

76. Such ideas are expressed in the introduction and conclusion of Carlos Eire, *From Madrid to Purgatory: The Art and Craft of Dying in Sixteenth-Century Spain* (Cambridge, 1995).

77. These stereotypes may be found in James Michener's *Iberia* (New York, 1968), but they are by no means unique to the United States. Encouraged in part to foment tourism in the 1960s by the Spanish Ministry of Tourism, they can also be found in Bartolomé Bennassar, *L'homme espagnol* (Paris, 1975); English trans., *The Spanish Character: Attitudes and Mentalities from the Sixteenth to the Nineteenth Century* (Berkeley, 1979).

78. For Kennedy's discussion of Spanish decline, see Paul Kennedy, *The Rise and Fall of the Great Powers* (New York, 1987), 31–55.

CHAPTER 16

The American Historiography of the French Revolution

KEITH MICHAEL BAKER AND
JOSEPH ZIZEK

IN SEPTEMBER 1792, the expatriate American Joel Barlow—lawyer, pamphleteer, merchant, and sometime poet—proffered words of advice to the members of the newly assembled National Convention. Excoriating the defunct Constitution of 1791 and the conduct of earlier assemblies, Barlow argued that the survival of the nascent republic was critical precisely because the Revolution stood for the cause of "human nature at large." The current epoch of crisis and possibility was, he insisted, "perhaps the most interesting portion of the most important period that Europe has hitherto seen."[1]

Barlow's rhetoric of historical prodigy does not, by any modern disciplinary standard, entitle us to call him the first American historian of the French Revolution—although a career which ranged from Yale class poet to death in a Napoleonic baggage train surely deserves our indulgence. Barlow's assessment of the Revolution's unique interest, however, was echoed by equally fascinated contemporaries such as Thomas Jefferson, Gouverneur Morris, and Thomas Paine. Subsequent generations of American historians have found the Revolution to be no less consuming: even a cursory assessment of publications, teaching, and graduate training bears out the truism that, over the decades, American scholars have devoted substantial attention to it.[2]

Yet to ask whether there exists (or has existed) a distinctively *American*[3] historiography of the French Revolution is to pose a more difficult question. Does the concept of an American historiography have any analytic use in this regard? Has American scholarship on the French Revolution expressed distinctive methodological, thematic, or political orientations?

This post-bicentennial moment may be the best time to ask such questions. The dominant development of the past few decades of revolutionary historiography has been the demise of the classic "social interpretation" and the rise of "revisionism."[4] This historiographical transformation has owed much to the mutually profitable interaction of Anglo-American and French scholarship, and the bicentennial itself has indisputably affirmed that research in the field is today an international endeavor.[5]

Yet if it is fair to say that today's scholarship is dominated by revisionist currents, that domination is hardly unproblematic. Apart from the challenge of defining revisionism in a meaningful way, there remains the delicate task of advancing a positive synthesis in a field exhilaratingly open to new departures. Of more particular relevance to the present essay, revisionism has so far failed in its attempts to counteract the selective foreshortening of the professional gaze.[6] A conscious effort is still required to make late nineteenth- or early twentieth-century scholarship reappear on our academic radar. This presentism has weighed particularly heavily on American historians; apart from rare exceptions—the names of Donald Greer and Crane Brinton spring immediately to mind—it is unusual to see American writing on the Revolution more than a few decades old cited in today's research.

It scarcely needs to be emphasized that American historians have long faced interpretive difficulties stemming from the unique place of the Revolution in modern French culture. Some of these difficulties are on the order of anthropological generality: writing the history of another country invites reflection on the possibilities and constraints which come with observational perspective and ethnographic distance. Observation suffers if the observer becomes too close to, or remote from, the natives. Apart from such generalities, there are also culturally specific issues to consider. It is hard to imagine any American historian of this century crafting an essay entitled "The French Revolution Is Over."[7] Where the American historian might see in this phrase a declaration of chronological obviousness, the French scholar envisions a historically resonant web of national identities and political investments.

For better or worse, American historians have not observed the French Revolution through the same political or cultural prism as their French colleagues. This is not to say, though, that American research on the topic has been free of personal investment. Our political and intellectual concerns have usually taken other forms: the French Revolution as a privileged site of methodological contestation, as a domain for the investigation of human agency and historical change, as an originary instance of political modernity, as an illustration of the contradictions of modern universalism (particularly in the domain of gender politics), or as a contrast—implicit or overt—to the American experience.

Such differences make this a propitious time to reexamine the contours of American historiography on the French Revolution. The present essay makes no claim to comprehensive coverage, nor does it offer a detailed analysis of the current state of scholarship in the field. Rather, it seeks to place the distinctive features of American scholarship in historical perspective, thereby to make certain lines of interpretation more visible in retrospect. Over several decades, American historians have displayed a striking interest in political interpretations of the Revolution and an abiding discomfort with socioeconomic ones. Beyond expressing skepticism toward economic and class-based readings of the Revolution, American scholars have frequently shown dramatic willingness to investigate the Revolution's political character. Yet their interest in political phenomena has been characteristically pragmatic, located in the close analysis of activity and intention rather than in the reading of systemic trajectories. For such reasons, many classic American lines of interpretation retain their vitality in the present climate of scholarly revision and have much to say about the origins and force of the revisionist departure.

•

In 1919, Professor Fred Morrow Fling of the University of Nebraska—at the time, one of the primary centers of North American research on the French Revolution—offered French readers a cogent survey of American scholarship on the Revolution and the Napoleonic period. Although promising work was beginning to emerge from America's expanding universities, Fling conceded that the American contribution to scholarship was still depressingly modest. "Up to the present," he noted mordantly, "no complete and scientific study of the French Revolution has been written by an American scholar." This made for both insecurity and hope. If American research on the period was "truth to tell, nothing much," the very sketchiness of the contribution was to be expected: "It's the first step. We need to be patient and work. And America will work!"[8]

America had actually been working for some time. It is generally agreed that the closing decades of the nineteenth century witnessed the firm disciplinary establishment of historical study in the United States. A generation of leading American scholars, many of them trained in German universities, transformed the study of history by adapting European standards and practices (such as the seminar) to new research and teaching environments.[9]

Yet the American experience was part of an international trend. French historical study was also transformed and professionalized during the closing decades of the nineteenth century, and the consequences for study of the French Revolution were profound. It was the first "period" to have its history officially institutionalized when, in 1891, Alphonse Aulard assumed the Sorbonne's newly created Chair in the History of the French Revolution.[10] On positivist and republican grounds, Aulard and his disciples attempted to make study of the Revolution scientific: one key aspect of their effort involved the intensified collection and systematic publication of documents dealing with the history of the Revolution. Effectively, the Sorbonne's powerful combination of institutional continuity and scientific erudition made the Chair in the History of the Revolution the preeminent focus for decades of scholarship.[11] Until well after the Second World War, this chair's successive occupants—scholars such as Philippe Sagnac, Georges Lefèbvre, Marcel Reinhard, and Albert Soboul (not to mention Albert Mathiez, who was denied the chair)—largely defined the contours of French Revolution scholarship not just in France but throughout much of the world.

In contrast, American scholarship on the Revolution has never been shaped by a domestic, institutionalized school of interpretation. Nor have American scholars experienced the kinds of institutional and personal rivalries which have dramatically marked the historiography in France. Some of the reasons are obvious. In comparison to France and Europe, the growth of university education and research in the United States was and has remained highly decentralized. The

initial stages of American historical interest in Europe were comparatively con-
flict-free, largely because the issue of national identity was posed only indirectly:
European history was contentious only in those instances—such as the case of
"Germanic institutions"—where it affected the interpretation of American constitutional history.

Accordingly, despite disciplinary transformations, the turn-of-the-century
boundaries of American research on the French Revolution were decidedly modest. Before 1900 it is difficult, for example, to point to an original American
contribution to the study of the Old Regime or the Revolution though the earliest
American attempt at a scholarly account may date to 1859.[12] Many historians
were familiar with the range of nineteenth-century European scholarship on the
Revolution, but turn-of-the-century American scholars seldom ventured beyond
providing judicious assessments of that literature or offering synthetic contributions to it.[13]

The topical range and scholarly value of those synthetic contributions were
highly uneven. When American historians initially turned to the Old Regime,
their attention seems to have fallen primarily on issues of religious oppression
(the Huguenots were a favorite topic), but they understandably displayed a dread
fascination with absolute monarchs and their presumably tyrannical ministers.[14]
When they turned to the Revolution, by contrast, many American scholars seem
to have made a serious effort to grapple with authoritative European interpretations. In 1901, for example, the University of Chicago's Shailer Mathews published a popular survey of the Revolution which drew upon work by Heinrich
von Sybel, Albert Sorel, Alphonse Aulard, and H. M. Stephens. Mathews highlighted the emergence of a "revolutionary spirit" and a liberal public opinion
among the French, arguing that the Revolution was not a degenerate collapse but
a vital achievement.[15] Other widely disseminated surveys examined the Revolution's causes and the political commitments it exacted: much of this literature
strikingly depicted the Revolution in a positive light, as a reaction against the
constraints which a despotic French government and an inegalitarian social order
placed on a nation increasingly desirous of liberty.[16]

To the extent that the French Revolution could be rendered as a struggle for
liberty or equality, it had obvious resonance for Americans. Yet the problem of
understanding the French Revolution's radical qualities was also particularly
acute, perhaps because it was here that the French and American Revolutions
seemed most dramatically different. From the outset, American historians ex-
pended considerable effort on assessing the relationship between the two revolutions, a project frequently carried out in terms of American "opinion" of, or constitutional "influence" upon, the dramatic events across the Atlantic.[17]

Yet at the turn of the century, American historians also engaged the issue of
revolutionary radicalism by turning to the close investigation of French political
mobilization and social conflict. In studies of Parisian municipal politics, for example, H. E. Bourne pointed to the creation of a mechanism of political action—
the sections—with unanticipated and long-ranging consequences; in effect, he
argued, the Jacobin triumph in 1792 emerged from the structures erected by the

"bourgeois" moderates of 1789.[18] Other historians conducted biographical investigations of the link between Old Regime experiences and revolutionary activity after 1789. Nebraska's Fred Fling, for example, examined Mirabeau's critical contribution to revolutionary legislation and oratory, but insisted that his opposition to a "despotic" Old Regime was not inconsistent with his later defense of monarchy during the Revolution.[19]

Fling subsequently engaged a coterie of students at Nebraska in a broad reappraisal of the motivations and significance of events ranging from the Tennis Court Oath to the uprising of 20 June 1792. The tenor of this work was often explicitly political: some studies emphasized the divisiveness of episodes such as the verification of credentials for the Estates-General; some argued that the intelligibility of moments such as the Tennis Court Oath depended on the "historical setting" of the struggle against royal despotism; some echoed Aulard or Mathiez in claiming that certain upheavals (20 June 1792, for example) had to be understood not as outbursts of popular irrationality but as the rational (yet spontaneous) interventions of a Parisian citizenry exercising astute political judgment.[20]

Turn-of-the-century American historians seem quite comfortably to have adapted their understanding of revolutionary radicalism to a political narrative. Frequently, however, the guiding model of politics was neither the Aulardian dialectic of circumstance and necessity nor the Mathiezian focus on socio-economic forces. Instead, some Americans pointed to the actual mechanics by which political moderation had been tragically abandoned. Andrew Dickson White, the University of Michigan historian who later became Cornell University's founding president, offered in 1876 a searing portrait of the political, social, and moral repercussions of the Revolution's fiscal measures; the disastrous resort to "fiat money," White insisted, both illustrated the unalterable "social physics" of specie and served as a cautionary lesson for Americans as they pondered their own currency situation.[21] Few historians mined the Revolution in such utilitarian fashion, but even when it was examined on its own terms it offered no less striking instances of immoderation. From the perspective of political history, C. H. Lincoln offered an analysis of the *cahiers des doléances* which stressed the presence of a "compromise spirit" within noble and clerical *cahiers*. Lincoln argued that "differences of wealth and conditions between the nobility and the Third Estate have often been exaggerated," and that the Revolution's "terrible character" resulted from political failures in its assemblies: "there must have been somewhere a great lack of organizing ability, a dearth of the spirit of what we term practical politics, to allow such forces of moderation to have been wasted and a small minority of the dissatisfied sections to carry with them an Assembly the majority of which was composed of well-meaning delegates anxious to avail themselves of some practical way out of the difficulties which surrounded them."[22] Similarly, a noted Columbia University historian argued, the Revolution's religious policy showed how moderation had been shattered on the shoals of class envy, monarchical distrust, and confessional hatreds.[23] Though it generally remained unspoken, the implied contrast with the American Revolution was clear.

Although these early historians were grappling with important issues, their research was frequently derivative of major French interpretations. Too often they were forced to rely upon a familiar and narrow base of available sources: personal memoirs, newspapers, accessible manuscripts, published archival documents, and collections such as the *Archives parlementaires* (about which leading French scholars harbored serious reservations). Prior to World War One, extensive archival explorations by Americans seem to have been exceedingly rare; few scholars ventured into the Archives Nationales—that preferred terrain of the French historian—and even fewer made forays into departmental and local archives. Yet some leading American scholars clearly expressed an awareness that greater archival expertise was necessary.[24]

Perhaps as a consequence, the pressing problem faced by American historians at the turn of the century—and well into the interwar decades—stemmed from the difficulty of establishing the independent status of American research on the French Revolution and, more generally, on European history. As Harvard's famous medievalist, Charles Homer Haskins, argued in a presidential address to the American Historical Association, the real question was whether Americans were willing to have European history come to them "second-hand," or whether they would participate as equals in the venture of research and scholarship. "The question," Haskins insisted, "concerns the future of American scholarship, its dignity, its independence, its creative power."[25]

•

For the nascent American historical profession, one powerful answer to the problem of establishing intellectual independence from European scholarship came from the proponents of the "New History," the intellectually diverse movement championed by figures such as Frederick Jackson Turner, Charles Beard, James Harvey Robinson, and, later, Carl Becker. In 1906, Robinson was one of the first to suggest that study of the French Revolution was in substantial need of renewal and that American scholars might contribute to that project. Surveying recent French work on the Revolution, he bemoaned the limits of a narrow focus on high politics, called for research into the local history of the Revolution, and offered a stinging critique of the tendency to fixate on Old Regime scandals or on the dramatic events of 1789. By indulging their "disproportionate fondness for political and military affairs," Robinson insisted, scholars neglected a fuller, more socially useful history. To understand the Revolution's place "among the great transformations of history," in his view, it was imperative to "bring the history of France from 1789 to 1800 into organic relation not only with the Ancien Régime but with the developments throughout Western Europe in the half-century immediately preceding the assembling of the Estates-General." This could only be accomplished, Robinson argued, if historians adopted a methodological perspective which could capture the Revolution "in its most fundamental aspects as a *reformation*, social, political, and economic."[26]

A call to place the Revolution in its broadest possible context clearly invited methodological eclecticism. But Robinson's claim that the French Revolution was also a moment of profound historical transformation additionally implied a need to reassess assumptions about the modern world. Although it had occurred half a world away, the French Revolution remained important for Americans because understanding the nature of "historical continuity" and comprehending the "meaning of any great period of human development" were critical to self-knowledge, to "our great contemporaneous task of human betterment."[27]

That task became even more vital with the advent of World War One, which marked a turning point for the self-understanding of the American historical profession. The experience of total war graphically illustrated ties to the Continent and heightened interest in European issues, but also faced historians with the uneasy prospect of political mobilization and (after 1917) propagandistic duties. For some, the war posed the problem of the civic utility of European history in the starkest terms; a noted Columbia University historian thus pressed the Revolution into propagandistic service, noting that it proffered critical lessons of liberty and patriotism when "now, as then, civilization hangs upon the arbitration of the sword."[28]

Less stridently, the preeminent institutional and pedagogical expression of heightened interest in European history seems to have been the rise of the "Western Civilization" course.[29] Many concurrent developments, however, were of specific benefit to French Revolution studies. The interwar years brought the publication of a broader array of translated primary sources, as well as the appearance of brief syntheses on European and French Revolutionary history specially designed for college and university instruction.[30]

Yet adapting study of the French Revolution to American contexts was more difficult than merely exalting its symbolic value or placing it within the context of a common European heritage. Some of the developments within French scholarship served as a powerful deterrent to foreign scholars interested in the Revolution. The intense exploitation of archives by French scholars, for example, frequently produced studies whose exhaustiveness and length were difficult for foreign scholars to emulate.[31] If French academic specialization highlighted the difficulty of legitimating independent American research on the Revolution, so too did the willingness of leading French historians to engage in personal polemics which Americans generally found distasteful. As the University of Chicago's Louis Gottschalk explained in 1932, it was precisely the absence of a "major American study of the French Revolution" which made the influence of masters such as Albert Mathiez so striking, even as Mathiez's own fiery polemicism left American historians reluctant to embrace his arguments unreservedly.[32]

The New History, by contrast, offered American historians a long-term avenue of historiographical exploration which avoided both hostile distancing and passive alignment. The late 1920s and early 1930s brought forth a generation of American historians—Louis Gottschalk, Crane Brinton, Donald Greer, and Leo Gershoy—whose careers were marked by methodological experimentation as well as specialization in the history of the French Revolution. While these scholars were vitally interested in the nature of the revolutionary dynamic, their leading works also focused attention on the contextual and biographical variability of revolutionary radicalism, the seeming incommensurability of social origins and extremism (particularly during the Terror), and the need to reappraise the presumed economic or social determinations of revolutionary behavior.

Louis Gottschalk's influential 1927 study of Jean-Paul Marat revealed the limits to Mathiezian influence. In a study self-consciously "partial to the materialistic interpretation of history," Gottschalk humanized Marat and suggested that his social and political radicalism, despite its extreme manifestations, was largely a response to revolutionary circumstances. Far from being a socially marginal, embittered criminal under the Old Regime, Marat was a moderately respectable and comfortable scientist. Similarly, although he was acquainted with the Enlightenment's "radical" ideas, and became increasingly obsessed with a sense of professional ill-treatment, Marat was no precocious extremist. In 1789 he did not conceive of the Revolution "as a popular movement"; in his institutional sympathies he long remained a monarchist; and even in 1793 his social philosophy was nothing more systematic than a "vague, uncrystallized longing for social justice." Gottschalk argued that Marat's influence owed less to his ideas of popular sovereignty or social justice than to his exemplary self-identification as the Revolution's fervent defender.[33]

Gottschalk's work belonged to a small flood of Old Regime and Revolutionary biographies which American scholars offered through the interwar period. Many of these biographies strikingly employed the interpretive frameworks of contemporary political history—albeit frequently informed by New Historical currents—to frame (or predetermine) the investigation of individual careers. Malesherbes, Condorcet, and Turgot became the reformist forefathers of political and economic liberalism, the abbé Sieyès and Robespierre appeared as protonationalist politicians, while leading Jacobins (Saint-Just, Robespierre) and their eventual opponents (Brissot) were made to embody the Enlightenment's optimism, idealism, fanaticism, and impracticality.[34]

The practice of political biography was but one approach to plumbing the meaning and evolution of revolutionary activity. The question of radicalism was posed very differently by the young Harvard historian Crane Brinton in *The Jacobins: An Essay in the New History* (1930). Brinton's subtitle clarified his methodological allegiances, and the work—innovative in both scale and focus of research—marked a real departure for his American colleagues.[35] Today, we would be tempted to characterize his approach as a study in "political culture."

Brinton used the copious evidence of Jacobin activity in the clubs scattered across France to construct a collective profile of radicalism. He insisted that the available evidence showed that the Jacobins, far from being disgruntled *déracinés*, were reasonably prosperous and moderately successful members of an (albeit diverse) Old Regime bourgeoisie. The intractable problem of their *political* behavior, especially in the years 1793–94, could not, in Brinton's view, be derived from their socioeconomic experience. It had to be sought in the rituals, ceremonies, and collective practices which transformed their belief in republican unity, patriotism, and mundane moral virtues into something approaching religious fanaticism.[36]

Brinton's work posed a fundamental question for American historians of the day, since, much as is the case with current scholarship, the Terror had been for some time a particular focus of attention. At the turn of the century, both Henry Morse Stephens and James Harvey Robinson had attempted to revise approaches to the Terror, eschewing hyperbolic exaggeration in favor of dispassionate analysis of its circumstances.[37] By the 1920s, however, some American historians had adopted a Mathiezian line, arguing that the Terror was indeed a "class war" which necessarily struck down the Revolution's enemies.[38]

Brinton, however, posed the question differently. If the social experience of Jacobins could explain neither their collective behavior nor their ideological postures, "the heart of our problem, then, is this: how did the Jacobins come to produce, at least to accede to, the Terror?" Brinton offered an answer in the cult-like and religious aspects of Jacobinism, in its puritanical attempt to close the gap between what men were and what they could be. He insisted that "the economic interpretation of history is not the whole explanation" and that political comportment and "religious feelings" had to be significant factors in any analysis of the Terror.[39]

The interpretation of the Terror in political rather than social terms was deepened by one of Brinton's first Ph.D. students, Donald Greer. In a statistically grounded "social anatomy," Greer analyzed the Terror as a French rather than simply a Parisian phenomenon. In place of a class war he depicted a regime of retribution that steadily attacked and suppressed political opposition to the Republic, took most of its victims in regions of civil war, and exhibited an "astoundingly diverse" social incidence. He additionally argued that the Terror was rarely exercised as an instrument of economic policy: the majority of its victims were nonnobles, although the proportion of aristocratic victims increased markedly in later stages.[40]

Greer's analysis has been justly influential. He largely undermined the justificatory defense of "circumstances" and, in this respect, his work has provided substantial support for modern revisionist perspectives on the Terror.[41] In the early 1930s, however, Greer and Brinton were perhaps the most forceful exponents of methodological and argumentive points of interpretation which sharply differentiated American scholars from their French contemporaries. They both relied on quantification but made it serve very different ends. In Greer's view, a statistical analysis offered the only possibility for dispassionate, nonpolemical examination of the Terror. For Brinton, the statistical analysis of Jacobin culture was couched as a quasiscientific exercise in predictive possibility—or "retrospective sociology"—comparable to meteorological forecasting.[42]

Yet more important, Brinton and Greer hinted at the lingering American dissatisfaction with economic explanations. Both insisted that "monistic" interpretations of the Terror were unworkable, and that it was intelligible only as the ultimate product of complex causality. Brinton, for example, did not deny the importance of social conflict or the radicalizing circumstance of war; he simply refused to accept that such factors could explain the quasireligious nature of the Terror's utopian coercion.[43]

The tendency to view the radicalism of the Revolution as a form of extreme religious sensibility was hardly idiosyncratic, nor was Brinton the only American historian to use the notion of religion in an anthropological rather than a political or confessional sense.[44] Such approaches were symptomatic of a common methodological shorthand according to which "religion" was a master concept describing belief and activity structures oriented to wholehearted commitment, unrealistic aspirations, and unrelenting rigor of application.[45] Yet the analogical resort to religious sensibility was also characteristic of a long-term orientation among American historians: unlike their French colleagues, American scholars were dramatically willing to investigate the Revolution's political expressions in their own right.

Political interests were frequently handled in rather innovative ways. As early as 1912, E. F. Henderson had examined the important role of revolutionary pictorial symbolism, textual allegory and satirical art, arguing that it both expressed "the spirit of the time" and was consciously intended to influence "public opinion."[46] By the 1930s, American scholars were showing sustained interest in the political dimensions of revolutionary pamphleteering, oratory, and rhetoric. As might be expected, the issue of nationalism was then a critical focus for political interpretation.

Columbia's Carlton J. Hayes focused the attention of an entire school of historians on the critical role of revolutionary nationalism, its diverse sources, and its modern legacies.[47] In retrospect, much of this work now appears vitiated by a tendency to read twentieth-century nationalism into eighteenth-century contexts.[48] Yet in the research of Beatrice Hyslop this initial interest in nationalism produced two highly important studies, which for several decades served American—and French—historians as an essential introduction to the *cahiers des doléances* of 1789.[49]

Revolutionary politics also received substantial attention in the 1930s. Mitchell Garrett, for example, examined the pamphleteering clashes of the early Revolution as an exercise in the popular deployment of competing political theories; while the "privileged classes" relied on traditional constitutional positions, he argued, the Third Estate groped improvisationally for a politics, and the monarchy adopted a policy of "divide and rule."[50] Similarly, H. T. Parker examined the role of classical Antiquity within the Revolution, eventually concluding that classical examples and precedents had only an ambiguous and uncertain political impact. Partly because eighteenth-century education could supply only a distorted view of the classics, he contended, the revolutionaries drew no consistent politico-moral model from Antiquity; disputing contradictory examples and amorphous goals, they were nevertheless able to draw psychological reinforcement from heroic exemplars.[51] With J. G. A. Pocock's studies of classical republicanism in mind, American historians are today beginning to revisit this topic.

In retrospect, many of the American explorations of revolutionary politics in the 1930s now seem less significant in their findings than in their belief that political activity, national identity, and moral imperatives were worthy of independent examination. It is clear, however, that the study of the conjunction of revolutionary moralism, patriotism, and politics did produce at least one classic study: R. R. Palmer's collective biography of the Committee of Public Safety, *Twelve Who Ruled* (1941).[52] Palmer debunked the myth that the committee was an instrument of Robespierreian dictatorship and depicted the Terror as a circumstantial creation born of the Revolution's own, self-inflicted disunity. What is today striking about the work is not simply that it linked the Terror decisively to the imperatives of a desperate war effort, thereby replicating the Aulardian defense of "circumstances," but that it equally stressed the cardinal importance of Robespierre's "political morality"—a theme virtually ignored by leading French historians.[53] Palmer's work offered an additional subtext fully understandable in 1941. Highlighting the tension between the ideals of democracy, the practical requirements of wartime patriotism, and the possibility of dictatorial government, he stressed the extreme difficulty of negotiating "the narrow way" to modern democracy.[54]

Through the 1930s—for obvious reasons—American historians found systemic questions about democracy and dictatorship most compelling. A short-lived but influential school of "natural historians" of revolution (most of whom were sociologists or journalists) briefly made comparative analysis a familiar mode of investigating such issues. American historians were largely introduced to such methods by Crane Brinton, who became perhaps the most influential interwar proponent of a sociologically inflected, comparative study of revolution. Brinton's most controversial work remains *The Anatomy of Revolution* (1938). In that study, he extended the major lines of interpretation sketched in *The Jacobins*—insufficiency of economic determinism and the "religious" quality of the Terror—to the analysis of four distinct episodes: the seventeenth-century Puritan Revolution in England, the eighteenth-century American and French Revolutions, and the Russian Revolution of 1917. As the title of the work suggests, the organizing metaphor was clinical. Brinton attempted to describe revolutions as social pathologies (using "fever" analogies) while insisting that clinical "detachment" was still possible.[55]

Focusing on the proximate causes of revolutionary upheaval and its differing phases once unleashed, Brinton identified a series of "uniformities"—the financial and military weakness of the state, the political organization of opposition, the transfer of intellectuals' allegiances, the necessary escalation of revolutionary extremism, and the inevitability of both a "Terror" and a "Thermidor"—which marked each nation's revolutionary experience. But, echoing Tocqueville, he also took explicit aim at economic determinism, arguing that in each revolutionary episode the economic crises at work were matters of state fiscality, not reflections of the general prosperity of the societies in question.[56]

Perhaps because *Anatomy of Revolution* concentrated on the trajectory of revolutionary radicalization—from the prerevolutionary "transfer of allegiance of the intellectuals" to the revolutionary triumph of "extremists" over "moderates"— Brinton ascribed considerable importance to ideas and political mobilizations.

Yet he sidestepped (as sterile and ultimately insoluble) the question of whether ideas "caused" revolutions, preferring, in characteristically epigrammatic fashion, simply to note a striking uniformity of prerevolutionary situations: "no ideas, no revolution."[57]

Brinton's work also raised critical questions about the relationship between revolutionary upheaval and civil society. His argument for the inevitability of Thermidorean denouements rested on the claim that, after the cauldron of Revolution, simple "human nature" yearned for a return to normality. This typological analysis of revolutionary process owed a considerable debt to the Chicago school of sociology, and particularly to the now forgotten work of Lyford Edwards.[58] Perhaps because of such influences, what seems today to be the striking characteristic of Brinton's anatomical investigation is the restricted and ahistorical nature of his comparisons. In most cases, he was interested in discerning uniformities rather than explaining divergences; Brinton's revolutions literally seem to be events thrown up for dispassionate observation, discussed and compared without regard to chronology or historical context. Accordingly, the work embodied a certain degree of conceptual naiveté: as the usage of terms such as Terror and Thermidor implies, Brinton's model of revolutionary process was based on the French case, while his schema of extremist ascent—stressing an avant-garde of the hard and pure—seems strikingly Leninist.[59]

Perhaps because of its almost militantly ahistorical approach, Anatomy of Revolution has had little direct or lasting influence on the historiography of the French Revolution.[60] Yet this lack of influence also reflects a deeper disciplinary shift. American historians have largely abandoned the comparative study of the French Revolution: with rare exceptions, its modern practitioners tend instead to be sociologists and political scientists.[61] The causes of this abandonment can be traced partly to the general devaluation of macrosociological interests during the 1960s and early 1970s, when the "New Social History" turned historians toward the exhaustive, highly empathetic examination of nonelite communities; but the comparative enterprise has also been regarded unfavorably because it necessarily relies on secondary sources, and thus remains extremely vulnerable to "paradigm shifts" in interpretation.

The general reluctance of American historians to cast the French Revolution into comparative perspective has left a gap. Perhaps because it represents an implicit challenge to the politics of national uniqueness, French historians have never been enamored of comparative investigations of the Revolution, leaving foreign scholars to bear responsibility for raising those questions best visible in a comparative light. In this context, the American turn away from comparative history seems unfortunate because the example of historiographical revision in other fields—early modern Britain, for example—has raised important questions which French revolutionary historiography has been somewhat slow to take up.[62] As Patrice Higonnet's Sister Republics: The Origins of French and American Republicanism (1988) has shown, the comparative enterprise offers the potential for a substantial reevaluation of the place of individualism and universalism in determining the different trajectories of revolution in America and France.[63] Work such as this suggests that careful comparisons of particular national cases would be immensely fruitful at this point.

•

It is striking that the first major instance of collaboration between leading American and French scholars, partial though it was, derived precisely from attempts to distill cross-national commonalities while reflecting on the constitutive features of democracy. Beginning in the mid-1950s, Jacques Godechot and R. R. Palmer began to sketch the contours of the "Atlantic Revolution" thesis, a line of argument which would raise the ire of the institutionalized French school of interpretation. Working independently and in concert, these two scholars advanced arguments which partially dethroned the French Revolution from its position of historical specificity and made it an aspect of a larger process. Yet the contrasting arguments each made within the context of this collaboration suggest the differences that remained in approaches to the French Revolution from the two sides of the Atlantic.

Godechot contextualized the Revolution against a series of demographic and social changes affecting the Atlantic world as a whole, changes which effectively created the widespread socioeconomic grievances that were the raw material of revolutionary upheaval.[64] Palmer's reading was more explicitly political. Focusing broadly on European nations—ranging from Russia and Poland to England— as well as their Atlantic colonies, Palmer argued that, beginning in about 1760, the old European order was progressively shaken by a series of internal conflicts whose fundamental dynamic was democratic.[65]

The immediate crises, Palmer argued, stemmed from the fiscal and constitutional struggles which pitted eighteenth-century monarchies, desperately searching for new sources of income, against their own "constituted bodies"— assemblies, parliaments, law courts, and so on. Such constituted bodies were the decisive locales which maintained privilege, hereditary right, and aristocratic self-governance, and which effectively militated against monarchical fiscal independence. That European and American struggle of elites was critical, Palmer argued, because it gradually opened a political space into which entered disparate coalitions of groups and individuals opposed to the principles of hereditary rule, inherited privilege, and enclosed elites. Insofar as Palmer noted commonalities across different national experiences, those commonalities were relentlessly political: if Enlightenment ideas were influential, it was because they fit an already created context of political contestation; if the American Revolution was important and radical, it was because it represented the stunning example of a society capable of autoconstitution according to the principles of popular sovereignty. From this perspective, Palmer saw the general frustration of democratic aspirations through most of the period as symptomatic: "if these events prove anything," Palmer suggested, "it is perhaps that no purely middle-class or 'bourgeois' revolution could succeed."[66]

Palmer's enterprise represented an effort not so much of comparative history as of sequential, multiple history. Although he occasionally extracted broad comparative points, the work largely focused on the specifics and peculiarities of each national experience. Yet his study, like Brinton's *Anatomy of Revolution*, posed controversial questions about the similarities and differences between the American and French Revolutions.[67] Brinton's comparative approach had posed social-systemic issues of stability; Palmer's probed the meaning and significance of revolutionary legacies. Yet each helped establish a line of interpretation that asked whether episodes of revolutionary transformation—and necessarily violent ones—were not a condition of possibility for Western democracy.[68]

Not surprisingly, given the Cold War background, the claim for an eighteenth-century "Democratic" or "Atlantic Revolution" was greeted with considerable skepticism (not to say hostility) by French scholars.[69] Nor has the thesis had any lasting influence on current English-language historiography; to most observers, the debate now seems rather passé.[70] It is fair to say, however, that many of Palmer's conclusions and insights hold up well in the climate of political reinterpretation associated with revisionism. It remains highly profitable to revisit his pragmatic readings of constitutionalism and revolution, the effects of "ideological war," and the nature and genesis of the Terror. And the more we learn about the political culture of the prerevolutionary period, the clearer it becomes that France was indeed part of an Atlantic political culture through which ideas about the nature of liberty and despotism in a modern commercial society circulated rapidly.

In retrospect, it seems clear that the partial collaboration between R. R. Palmer and Jacques Godechot marked a turning point in the relationship between American and French historians of the Revolution. Until the Second World War, American specialists in the field had been concerned to establish their own professional autonomy vis-à-vis French scholars. They achieved a distinctive research tradition that was fully cognizant of historiographical developments in France but developed at a certain distance from them. After the war, however, American researchers began increasingly to compete with their French counterparts, quite literally on their own ground. In the late 1950s and early 1960s, for the first time, it became generally possible for graduate students (as opposed to those already holding the Ph.D.) to make research trips of substantial length; the appearance of Fulbright and other specialized research grants, and the advent of inexpensive air travel, made in-country research an expected part of the predoctoral itinerary.[71] American historians of France began to enter the archives in appreciable numbers.

When this generation of scholars was conducting its research, the dominant reading of the Revolution was surely Georges Lefèbvre's. His "social interpretation" was most familiar to American scholars through the classic synthesis, *1789*, ably translated into English by R. R. Palmer as *The Coming of the French Revolution* (1947). In that work, Lefèbvre disaggregated the Revolution into separate but complementary movements—aristocratic, bourgeois, urban artisanal, and peasant—whose coherence came from originary forces (resentment of feudal constraints, capitalist expansion, bourgeois leadership) as well as ultimate trajectories (the founding of egalitarianism, the liberation of capitalism). The virtue of Lefèbvre's synthesis, of course, was that it simultaneously explained both the Revolution and the social and economic conditions of the Old Regime.

Accordingly, when American scholars of the Revolution began to enter the French archives in substantial numbers in the late 1950s, they did so largely with the goal of a more fully researched social history in mind. Some North American scholars inspired by Lefèbvre (and by British historians such as Richard Cobb) initially came to the support of the socioeconomic interpretation. George Rudé's influential study, *The Crowd in the French Revolution* (1959), stressed the "traditional" rationality and middling social composition of Parisian crowds. With few exceptions, he argued, the crowds which participated in the Revolution's critical *journées* were composed of *menu-peuple* and artisans rather than proletarians; although they acted on immediate economic concerns—subsistence rather than workplace issues—Rudé insisted that Parisian crowds were gradually politicized by the Revolution's "bourgeois" leaders.[72] One of R. R. Palmer's doctoral students, Jeffry Kaplow, likewise examined the variations of bourgeois ascent in Elbeuf (Normandy) during the eighteenth century, modifying Lefèbvre's analysis to emphasize the interplay between urban social structures, textile manufacturing interests, industrial workers, and local politics. If Elbeuf's upper bourgeoisie had not made the Revolution, Kaplow noted, it had certainly been an opportunistic beneficiary.[73]

Yet few American historians writing in the late 1950s and early 1960s found the study of social history on Lefèbvre's terms—from below, with a Marxian slant—to be unproblematic. Lefèbvre's work itself was well respected, but the same could not be said of the politically charged study of urban radicalism. North American reactions to Rudé's work, and to Albert Soboul's pioneering analysis of the Parisian *sans-culottes*, often focused unfavorably on the Marxian or Communist perspectives of such studies. As R. R. Palmer noted dryly in 1960, "these books are part of the cold war" (with characteristic candor he added, "so is their present reviewer").[74]

The Cold War may have served as an essential backdrop to the undermining of the social interpretation, but the first fundamental challenge to that interpretation came partly on methodological grounds. Beginning in 1954, the University of London's Alfred Cobban systematically denied that the Revolution had been made by a rising commercial bourgeoisie striking out against the stultifying constraints of an outmoded feudal society; instead, he argued, the Revolution was less a movement for capitalism than a reaction against it. The core of his challenge was a methodological critique of the distorting effect of sociological theory: the long-dominant Marxian approach oversimplified the complexity of eighteenth-century society, subsuming a multiplicity of social conflicts under the misleading dichotomy between "feudal" and "bourgeois." To understand the conflicts of the Revolution, Cobban argued, it was necessary to view them in their own terms rather than through the anachronistic lens of Marxian sociology or Leninist political analysis.[75] The struggle between Girondins and Jacobins, for example, could not be reduced to a competition between social classes, nor could it be explained anachronistically as a conflict between political parties. One of Cobban's earliest North American students, Michael Sydenham, made this abundantly clear in an influential study of the Girondins published in 1961.[76]

It was to be two or three decades before the social interpretation of the French Revolution was to collapse in the face of such arguments. American research during the intervening years had much to do with the outcome. But given the degree to which Cold War politics made the study of popular movements suspect to non-Marxists, it should not be surprising that much of the fundamental research done by American scholars in the 1960s focused initially on French elites. Robert Forster's local study of the Toulousan nobility, for example, helped debunk the stereotype of an atavistic, backward-looking aristocracy. Forster made a persuasive case that the nobility of Toulouse was readily involved in varied kinds of rationally organized business enterprise, yet it regulated such involvement according to a mentality that was rentier rather than capitalist. In effect, his Toulousan nobility eschewed both aristocratic profligacy and capitalist avarice, managing familial resources rationally in the maintenance of social position.[77]

Forster carefully noted that his findings were not easily extended beyond the region in question, but other American studies were making the point that economic position and social interests were not necessarily congruent. Elinor Barber's now forgotten sociological examination of the eighteenth-century "bourgeoisie" stressed the extent to which this group embraced rather than criticized the "anti-egalitarian presuppositions of French society." She concluded that far from disdaining the nobility, the bourgeoisie sought assiduously to enter it, even defending the exclusionary principles that made nobility desirable. As a result, the bourgeoisie helped produce the very crisis of social mobility that toppled the world of privilege.[78]

If the study of social classes offered such seemingly counterintuitive findings, what of the broad socioeconomic environment in which those classes existed? In an enormously influential series of articles in the early and mid-1960s, George V. Taylor articulated the claim that eighteenth-century French capitalism itself was highly differentiated, that it was—well, hardly capitalist. Far from being primarily commercial and risk-oriented, Taylor argued, the dominant forms of capitalist enterprise in the eighteenth century were proprietary and aristocratic, and substantial sections of the nobility and "middle class" were united rather than divided by their economic interests.[79]

Such findings made the interpretation of eighteenth-century capitalism considerably more complicated. As various socioeconomic explanations for the revolutionary outbreak were challenged, so, too, was the assumption that "bourgeois" radicals assumed political leadership in 1788 and 1789. Perhaps the most direct American challenge to the social explanation came from Elizabeth Eisenstein, whose rereading of Georges Lefèbvre's classic synthesis critically evaluated the question, "who started the French Revolution?" In Eisenstein's view, Lefèbvre's work begged profound questions of revolutionary mobilization, wrongly presuming the intervention of a conscious, active bourgeoisie. She noted that the actual cohort of revolutionaries whose actions were central to popular mobilization—groups such as the Society of Thirty—comprised a flexible, minority coalition made up primarily of liberal nobles, but also included the most atypical part of the Third Estate.[80]

Eisenstein's critique, delicately framed as a specific commentary on Lefèbvre's text, nevertheless suggested that the problem of immediate revolutionary origins had been misconstrued; repudiating the claim that the Revolution was a creation of the bourgeoisie, she offered evidence of the heterogeneous class character of the Society of Thirty which acted as the fulcrum between origins and realization. Critical of this implicit collapsing of analysis, Eisenstein indicted the temptation to read the Revolution according to any "grand design"—the rise of the bourgeoisie, the philosophic plot, the force of circumstances—since such readings necessarily confused participants' intelligible goals with unanticipated consequences which were visible only in historical retrospect. To assess the Revolution's beginnings fairly, Eisenstein insisted, it was necessary to illuminate the discrete actions of individuals as they worked toward a conscious political goal, for "a static framework derived from a structural analysis is incapable of containing this sort of dynamic group action."[81]

The broad reappraisal initiated by Cobban and advanced by the arguments of Taylor and Eisenstein did much to weaken an explanatory framework which depended upon the postulates of capitalist expansion and bourgeois ascent. These postulates were further undermined by an influential study of state fiscality offered by John Bosher from York University in Toronto. He emphasized the professional reformism of royal and revolutionary governments, arguing that the final decades of the eighteenth century witnessed a profound evolution away from private, capitalistic state finance toward a bureaucratic, professional model of public fiscality. If this change was finally achieved by the Revolution, it was nevertheless initiated by royal administrators (notably Necker and Brienne); neither the structure of the Old Regime's state finance nor the Revolution's "invention of an administrative weapon for social and political domination" were explicable according to the social interpretation.[82]

Subsequent research into the nature of eighteenth-century privilege and its social institutions destroyed the conceptual unity of another key part of the classic synthesis: the "aristocratic reaction." Until the early 1970s, historians ranging from Lefèbvre to Palmer largely accepted the claim that a widespread aristocratic resurgence—directed against both the royal government and a rising middle class—was critical to explaining the Revolution's origins. Even American historians who advocated the study of the Old Regime in and of itself, such as Franklin Ford, tended to stress the social and ideological factors which prepared an eighteenth-century aristocratic resurgence in defense of privilege.[83]

The very concept of an aristocratic reaction, however, was powerfully challenged by American historians in the early 1970s. In a groundbreaking study, David Bien argued that it was misleading to interpret measures such as the French army's Ségur ordinance of 1781, which restricted entry to the officer corps to those who could prove four quarterings of nobility, as evidence for the social reaction of a besieged nobility. Bien convincingly argued that the army's officer corps was, in its social composition, similar to the other privileged institutions of French society—the parlements, the lower courts, the royal administration—in that it was securely dominated by a hereditary aristocracy: across the eighteenth century, the proportion of officers with "bourgeois" social origins was minuscule and largely static. Rather than an offensive against a nonexistent climbing bourgeoisie, the Ségur regulation and analogous measures were more plausibly evidence of disputes within the nobility itself. In the army's case, Bien suggested, the appearance of social restriction served meritocratic rather than privileged ends. The Ségur regulation was primarily an attempt to professionalize the officer corps by excluding nobles of relatively recent origin—whose comportment was seen as the antithesis of military professionalism—and making officer ranks more accessible to the scions of families traditionally devoted to military service.[84]

While such institutional research did much to bring out the internal divisions of the eighteenth-century French nobility, the relevant social historiography swiftly evolved in the direction of a revisionist consensus. The combined findings of American, British, and French historians led to the elaboration of a model of social conflict based not on the clash between an elite and a nonelite but on disputes internal to what was—in terms of shared culture—a single elite.[85] Yet the emerging consensus revealed some characteristic differences between American and French scholarship. In the 1960s and 1970s, for example, French historians were frequently dismissive of American interest in the twin problems of social mobility and social stratification; the French frequently regarded these problems as a product of naively empirical social science and a reflection of America's own cherished myths of upward mobility.[86] As for terminological disputes, R. R. Palmer found it necessary, while explaining the Taylor-Eisenstein controversies to a French readership, to emphasize that "bourgeoisie" was a concept linguistically and sociologically foreign to American culture and historiography.[87]

Despite such misunderstandings, American scholars played their part in dismantling an explanatory framework which depended on socioeconomic lines of fracture. The cumulative result of such research was to highlight the impossibility of assigning a leading revolutionary role to a particular social constituency or defining the Revolution as the culmination of a unitary socioeconomic process. In effect, the massive accumulation of empirical evidence which came with the turn to social history played a decisive role in disaggregating the "social interpretation": the evidence was often contradictory, but its sheer diversity made any consistent social determination of revolutionary origins or process highly untenable. A critical mass of socially focused history was thus the precondition for an effective challenge to the socioeconomic reading of the Revolution's origins.

To be successful ultimately, this challenge had to come from within France. It did so when François Furet, responding to dogmatic criticisms leveled by Soboul, Claude Mazauric, and their followers against a general history of the Revolution he had written with Denis Richet, denounced what he called the "Revolutionary Catechism." In a justly influential analysis, Furet displaced attention from the question of social determinations to the nature of the "Revolution as mode" and the "semiotic" constitution of a new form of political legitimacy. But the return to the political passed by way of the social: in demonstrating that the socioeconomic interpretation of the Revolution had simply collapsed under the weight of contradictory findings that could never yield a coherent explanation, Furet drew generously on American (and British) scholarship.

So it should be no surprise that Furet's interpretation of the French Revolution found its most open reception in the United States. In France, the new interpretation met opposition from the Sorbonne on methodological, doctrinal, and institutional grounds; in England, it encountered the skepticism of an empirical social history tradition little inclined to explore the dizzying logic of "semiotic circuits." In the United States, conversely, historians were highly receptive to Furet's suggestion that the pressing task facing historians of the Revolution was to "rediscover the analysis of the political as such."[88]

For American scholars, Furet's work opened the way for a new approach to the study of the French Revolution (and its origins) in terms of a conception of "political culture." Among others, historians of the Old Regime such as Keith Michael Baker and Dale Van Kley began fundamentally to reappraise the nature and implications of the crises of political contestation that marked the system of absolutism in its final decades, while scholars of the Revolution such as Lynn Hunt entered into a highly productive dialogue with the new interpretation. By 1987, when the first of the international conferences exploring the new approach to the political culture of the French Revolution was held in Chicago, American scholars had done much to investigate the field of intellectual possibilities which it offered.[89] Yet if American historians were receptive to Furet's new interpretation, one of the reasons was that they had for some time been working, on their own terms, to recover the political.

•

Even as the social interpretation was establishing its brief postwar hegemony, American students of the eighteenth century were frequently reiterating the belief that a narrowly construed social history was butting up against its explanatory limits. Well before the revisionism of the 1960s, some American historians had even called for a political or socio-political reinterpretation of the waning years of the Old Regime and the origins of the Revolution.[90] Much American scholarship—notably R. R. Palmer's "Democratic Revolution" thesis—expressed a dramatic willingness to investigate the political in a broad sense, comprising not just the narrative of political struggle but also the ideas and ideologies which actuated confrontation.

Yet the willingness to investigate the political also reflected the presence within American historiography of a disciplinary tradition—intellectual history—which had no French equivalent.[91] On methodological and interpretive grounds, for example, French and American historians had long differed on the extent to which politics could be understood as autonomous. For much of this century, French historians—under the dual impulsions of the "social interpretation" and the Annales school—were generally indifferent to the claim that ideas or ideologies should be taken seriously in an examination of the Old Regime and the revolution origins.[92] In America, by contrast, a strong tradition of intellectual history had been established for several decades by the 1970s, in large part through the contributions of scholars forced to emigrate from Germany in the 1930s. Threatened by the hegemonic claims made on behalf of social history in the 1960s and early 1970s, historians working in this tradition had begun to formulate a counterresponse in one of two ways: either by offering a project for a "social history of ideas" which would place emphasis on such issues as diffusion, readership, and the organization of the book trade, or by taking the "linguistic turn" in a direction that would open all discursive claims in the social world to the purview of intellectual historians.[93]

The ambition to write a "social history of ideas," initially advanced by Peter Gay as a corrective to ideal or abstract readings of the Enlightenment, was reformulated by Robert Darnton along lines influenced, on the one hand, by the Annales school and, on the other, by the work of Daniel Mornet. In effect, Darnton set out to rewrite Mornet's *Les Origines intellectuelles de la Révolution française* (1933), the pioneering work which had first attempted to measure which books were most widely circulated in eighteenth-century France, and how a prerevolutionary mentality had developed. Yet this attempt to revisit Mornet equally revived a question from which American scholars had, by the 1960s, increasingly distanced themselves: the link between the Enlightenment and the Revolution.[94]

Like Mornet, Darnton sought to explore the communication networks which helped delegitimize the monarchy and make revolutionary radicalism possible. His early work, for example, stressed the extent to which the Enlightenment became part of the established order of eighteenth-century society. In an influential analysis of the "Grub Street" literati, he argued that the Enlightenment's radical charge was not to be found in a pacified and domesticated world inhabited by the philosophes but at the social margins: in an intellectual netherworld populated by literary hacks excluded from the academic positions and royal emoluments which the philosophes now dominated. The resentment of these "gutter Rousseaus" fueled not only their avid participation in the world of illicit and libelous publication but also their advocacy of "scientific" fads—such as Mesmerism—which could serve as vehicles for bitter if amorphous radicalism.[95]

In subsequent work, Darnton has continued to look at ways in which the official culture of the Old Regime was at once penetrated from within by the "High" Enlightenment and undermined from without by the "low life" of radical, often pornographic literature. His study of the publishing history of the *Encyclopédie*, in addition to showing the cutthroat commercial practices of the publishers and purveyors of that work, also mapped the social geography of its diffusion through the administrative and cultural centers of the Old Regime into the world of small-town notables and country gentlemen, suggesting the way in which an ideology of progressive change suffused the traditional order.[96] By contrast, his more recent study of "forbidden books" shows not an Ancien Régime open to the possibility of transformation by the Enlightenment, but one pilloried by clandestine writers as arbitrary and corrupt, vile and degenerate in its public life and private morals, and above all despotic. Among his forbidden best-sellers, Darnton finds the philosophical, pornographic works he had expected, but he also finds works that we would now describe as political journalism: polemical interventions in the great political struggles of the 1760s and 1770s and beyond, muckraking attacks on political figures, court gossip now laid out for a new public. He finds, in short, the essential issue of "despotism."[97]

In this manner, taking the indirect route of textual diffusion, Darnton has rejoined other American historians who have been seeking by more direct means to recover the importance of a topic neglected by both Tocqueville and Mornet: the political and constitutional conflicts that dominated French public life from midcentury onward. It has been clear for some time that much libelous literature, initially presumed to be evidence of the social resentments of "Grub Street" hacks proliferating at the margins of the Old Regime, emerged from the center of the political regime: it originated from within or was commissioned by the court aristocracy, effectively taking court politics "public."[98] But it has also become clear that the world of legitimate, sanctioned journalism had its potentially subversive qualities, visible in the frondeur journalism studied by Nina Gelbart but also, as Jeremy Popkin has argued, in the coverage of French affairs in influential foreign newspapers such as the *Gazette de Leyde*, tolerated in France and used as much as possible by both monarchical and antimonarchical protagonists in continuing constitutional struggles.[99] Viewed in these terms, the distance between the center and the margins of French political culture seems steadily to shrink, and the distinction between the two becomes blurred.

With such phenomena in mind, American historians have increasingly argued that French politics "broke out of the absolutist mold" in the latter part of the eighteenth century, thereby creating a politics of contestation that eventually made the French Revolution thinkable. In a series of articles, Keith Michael Baker has explored the political culture of the Old Regime along lines complementary to Furet's reinterpretation of the Revolution but also influenced by the work of Cambridge historians of political thought and by Foucauldian discourse theory.[100] Working from the direction of intellectual history and the history of political ideas, he has insisted that the analysis of eighteenth-century political culture entails examination of how contemporaries articulated, negotiated, contested, and adjudicated varied discursive and symbolic claims about the nature of political community. Baker has deployed the "linguistic turn" in the service of a fundamental reappraisal of two notionally independent but practically interconnected problems: the Old Regime's "language of politics" and the French Revolution's "ideological origins."[101] His aim has been to explore the manner in which the language of a revolutionary politics was created under conditions of possibility produced from within the Old Regime.

Several general claims run through Baker's essays. The first is that the political culture of absolutism had already been transformed, in the decades preceding the Revolution, by a series of political crises that were simultaneously moments of intense invention, moments in which actors and institutions sought to improvise new claims to legitimacy and articulate new titles to political participation. The second is that, in the course of this transformation, a new kind of politics emerged in which the nature and grounds of French collective identity were increasingly placed in question, and in which the authority of an abstract "public opinion" progressively replaced that of the monarchy as the ultimate court of appeal. The third is that this same process led to the conceptual disaggregation of the traditional attributes of monarchical rule into a new discursive triad consisting of a constitutionalist discourse of "justice," an administrative discourse of "reason," and a political discourse of "will." From the competition among these contending discourses, Baker has argued, and by actors elaborating and improvising upon them, a new revolutionary language was invented.[102]

It is important to note that the discursive approach has come in for its share of criticism. In methodological terms, it has been castigated for its neglect of "the social" and its seemingly headlong rush toward deconstructive disaster.[103] On empirical grounds, the claim for a linguistically constituted space providing the conditions of possibility for revolutionary "invention" has been challenged by quasi-Namierite analyses which stress the insular interests of eighteenth-century parlementary and court politics; similarly, the argument that 1789 already presented a fundamental and decisive array of political choices has been challenged by research which suggests that revolutionary radicalism unfolded relatively slowly and uncertainly.[104]

Without treating such criticisms in a cavalier fashion, it is nevertheless possible to suggest that they understate the value of the linguistic turn and overlook its power to illuminate the unanticipated consequences of otherwise ordinary political contestation. It now seems clear that the monarchy's difficulties largely stemmed from struggles over *meaning*, struggles to resolve political claims made on the basis of shared cultural inheritances, grounded in common conceptual frameworks, and declared in polyvalent political languages. One implication of this approach is to move beyond a posing of the question of the ideological origins of the French Revolution in terms of a simple dualism: Enlightenment/ Revolution. The idiom of the Enlightenment was but one of several languages in play at the end of the Old Regime: classical republicanism, physiocracy, parlementary juridicalism, and Jansenism were also among the political vocabularies available to political actors and their publics in the prerevolutionary period.

The importance of Jansenism in this regard has been demonstrated, above all, by Dale Van Kley. He has convincingly shown that during much of the eighteenth century—but particularly from midcentury onward—Jansenism fueled the divisive political conflicts in which the monarchy was pitted against its own sovereign courts, and particularly against the Parlement of Paris. In the aftermath of royal endorsement of the controversial papal bull *Unigenitus*, religious issues and jurisdictional concerns were indissociably linked by a small but highly organized coterie of Jansenist magistrates and barristers, whose bitter opposition to the monarchy's religious policy eventually assumed decisive political importance. Van Kley argues that through episodes such as the midcentury "denial of sacraments" controversy and the expulsion of the Jesuit order, the edifice of "sacral absolutism" was undermined—not by Enlightenment rationality but by Jansenism transformed into a program of constitutional resistance.[105]

Thanks largely to Van Kley's work, it is now impossible to ignore the fundamental contribution made by Jansenist ideologues to eighteenth-century parlementary constitutionalism. Despite the gradual fading away of Jansenist organization after the triumphs of the 1760s, there is a tenuous but nonetheless discernible genealogy—continuities both ideological and personal—linking the struggle against *Unigenitus* in the early decades of the eighteenth century to the "patriot" opposition to the Maupeou coup in the 1770s and to the parlementary obstruction of monarchical initiatives in 1787 and 1788. Yet if Van Kley's work has helped to renew interest in the critical importance of politico-religious disputation in the eighteenth century, it has done so in a substantially different manner than have studies of monarchical "desacralization" or popular "dechristianization." In contrast to such sociologically inflected approaches, Van Kley has focused attention upon a mutating political theology. Understood in terms of theory, Jansenism developed a language of contractual obligation and conciliar sovereignty which readily lent itself to the politico-moral condemnation of royal "despotism," as to the articulation of a patriotic concept of national sovereignty. Understood as practice, Jansenism (through the institutional agency of *parlementaires* and barristers) found increasingly sophisticated ways to disseminate and circulate its ideological claims, holding the monarchy's acts up to public scrutiny so effectively that successive administrations were compelled to enter the same arena of publicity.[106]

Jansenism functioned effectively as a solvent of absolutism precisely because its parlementary defenders deployed terms, precedents, and idioms which the French monarchy and episcopacy could not fully disavow without undermining their own legitimacy.[107] Even though Van Kley and many other historians have conducted their research independently of the linguistic turn—often, however, moving into close engagement with it—they have contributed to erecting an interpretive framework which explains political struggles and their consequences according to a political rather than a social dynamic. In this respect, American historians have done much to build upon the pioneering work of Jean Egret, who launched an initial challenge to the thesis that parlementary resistance was actuated by aristocratic self-interest, arguing instead for the importance of constitutionalism and nominally disinterested patriotism. American research has persuasively deepened the case for political rather than social determinations by stressing the consequences of discursive struggles over legitimacy and jurisdiction, and by mapping the extent to which parlementary confrontations bridged the gap between the Old Regime's "traditional" politics, the acute crises of 1787–88, and the Revolutionary refusal to view historical continuity as a claim to political legitimacy.[108]

Pioneering American research into the actual operation of privilege within the Old Regime's institutional history has further complicated any simple equation of social background and political practice. David Bien and Gail Bossenga, for example, have offered compelling answers to the question that has emerged as central to recent debates over the French Revolution: how revolutionary principles and practices could have been created within the institutional milieu of the Old Regime. In reconsidering the relationship between corporate society and the growth of the administrative monarchy, Bien and Bossenga have offered a "neo-Tocquevillian" rereading of the vital relationship between corporate society, privilege, and monarchical government. As the private credit of officeholders became increasingly central to the monarchy's fiscal stability, and in the face of heavier taxes imposed in the desperate search for new revenues, the very same corporate bodies which served the monarchy's fiscal needs increasingly embraced a rhetoric of accountability, citizenship, and civic equality that had extraordinary implications. In effect, the political imperatives of monarchical fiscality helped make the world of privilege a laboratory for the creation of "egalitarianism" and structured political participation.[109]

From very diverse perspectives, then, current American research on the Old Regime has underlined the difficulty of reducing its forms of conflict and contestation to the mere play of interests. Whether or not historians accept the linguistic turn, one of its fundamental insights seems inescapable: "interests" and "intentions" are not immutable referents but constituted as possible moves within a political game. In reorienting attention to the creativity of the political, the linguistic turn has attuned historians to the difficulty of reducing the play of discursivity to the concreteness of social referents, political intentions, or objective realities. Claims must be articulated and outcomes justified; in the process meanings are invariably placed at risk, loosed into a world of cultural negotiations and unanticipated consequences.[110] This suggests that in the broad reappraisal of Old Regime political contestation, the primary value of the linguistic turn lies not in its ability to provide firm causal explanations but in its power to map fields of ideological possibility, to sketch the event horizons of revolutionary political culture.

This has been made abundantly clear even in the most interesting and suggestive effort so far made to reintroduce "the social" into the revolutionary equation: William Sewell's *Rhetoric of Bourgeois Revolution: The abbé Sieyès and* What Is the Third Estate? (1994). Having done much himself, in an important earlier study of the language of labor in France from 1750 to 1850,[111] to reveal the conceptual and symbolic aspects of social action, Sewell has recently offered a cogent critique of the "mistaken tendency" (of Furet and Baker) "to eliminate social considerations from revolutionary history and from the study of revolutionary texts." But his own investigation of Sieyès's famous pamphlet, undertaken to "demonstrate the unavoidable presence of the social in the text," nevertheless works (despite his disclaimers) largely in a discursive fashion: instead of the social he finds the social imaginary.[112] Sewell shows Sieyès creating a language he is subsequently powerless to control.

•

At the same time that some American historians were conducting a reappraisal of political practice under the Old Regime, others were turning to the independent examination of the Revolution's political dynamic. A few American scholars had by the early 1970s embraced the radical implications of treating the Revolution as a contingent political event; George V. Taylor, for example, somewhat controversially suggested that the Enlightenment/Revolution conundrum was irrelevant because the Revolution was not the result of radical ideologies but the event which produced them.[113] More commonly, however, American historians interested in the Revolution as an event focused on the residual problems which social historians had left them and to which homegrown revisionism increasingly pointed: politicization and revolutionary participation.

Much of the pioneering research of the 1960s into revolutionary crowds—whether examining urban artisans, rural laborers, or peasants—underlined the problematic relationship between social life and political consciousness.[114] The same research trends that weakened the social interpretation led many historians to explore (directly or indirectly) the factors which led varied social groups to participate in or withdraw from revolutionary activity. Examinations of specific occupational groups and their political activity reiterated that socioeconomic position was a highly unreliable indicator of subsequent revolutionary commitment; while such studies effectively fragmented the "social history of politics" at the local level, they also began to point to the way in which individuals and communities set their sails to the new winds of revolutionary politics.[115]

In this vein, American scholars—particularly those working in provincial archives—made important contributions to the study of rural communities, market relations, and urban networks. Their research increasingly indicated that adherence or resistance to the Revolution was mediated by situationally discrete factors: geographical peculiarities, corporate relations, urban structures, religious patterns, local variations in the spread of market relations. This was particularly true in the study of the countryside and the urban hinterland, where North American historians advanced sophisticated, multicausal analyses indicating the dramatic extent of popular counterrevolution. Pathbreaking studies of the Vendée and Brittany conducted by Charles Tilly, Donald Sutherland, and T. J. A. Le Goff showed that individual and communal allegiances varied dramatically according to patterns of social structure, urbanization, cultivation, land tenure, market development, and military conscription.[116]

In conjunction with the pioneering work of French scholars such as Paul Bois, American research helped transcend the powerful tendency within French republican historiography to explain the counterrevolution in terms of religious fanaticism or rural backwardness. While the Vendée remains—to this day—a highly polemical topic for French scholars, it is possible to discern a new receptivity to the notion, advanced by Timothy Tackett, that western France was the arena in which not merely a socioeconomic but a cultural "confrontation of worlds" took place.[117]

Through the 1970s and early 1980s, the issue of popular politicization also received direct attention as historians investigated the presumptive mechanisms by which ideologies were transmitted (newspapers) and political activism inculcated (popular societies). Jack Censer's exploration of radical newspapers in the Revolution's early years, for example, pointed to the role of Cordelier propagandists motivated by a belief in popular sovereignty and mindful of the cleavage between "people" and "aristocrats."[118] In concurrent investigations of revolutionary associations such as the Cercle Social and the Jacobin clubs, American researchers stressed the centrality of political journalism to such groups, yet simultaneously debunked the notion that provincial Jacobins marched in lockstep with the Parisian mother society or that Jacobin "democratic republicanism" died in 1794.[119] In the aggregate, such studies tended to emphasize that radical opinion existed on a spectrum and that it often defied simple correlation with sociological factors or critical events.

While American historians thus displayed a durable and independent interest in the problem of politicization, it would be accurate to say that Furet changed the paradigm according to which the politics of the Revolution was construed. As American scholars were drawn into closer engagement with French revisionism, they increasingly turned their attention to the analysis of revolutionary politics in systemic rather than factional terms. In 1984, rethinking her approach to the Revolution's "social history of politics" in the light of arguments advanced by Furet and Mona Ozouf, Lynn Hunt published *Politics, Culture, and Class in the French Revolution*. She essentially approached Furet's "semiotic circuit" from an anthropological perspective, focusing on the gestures, rituals, and enunciations which were constitutive of political culture. Hunt analyzed the symbolic practices—changes in language, ritual, clothing, and visual representation—which reconfigured the new community, uneasily stabilized a culture that had unmoored itself from the past, and provided the elements of self-definition for a "new political class." In her analysis, the political culture of the Revolution embodied an ever shifting "mythic present" in which foundational anxieties as well as democratic possibilities were negotiated in the search for a politics of transparency.[120]

Hunt's influential study became the principal example of the "New Cultural History" brought to bear on the phenomenon of the French Revolution.[121] Much subsequent research has extended the Furetian insight regarding the "creativity" of revolutionary political culture: far from being reducible to social conflicts or epiphenomenal to them, cultural struggles have been revealed to be a critical domain in which revolutionary identity was constructed and in which the goals and objectives of revolutionary politics were defined.

As Carla Hesse has shown, for example, the Revolution created a dynamic print culture which drew upon the contradictions inherent to Old Regime notions of authorship, literary property, and public enlightenment; revolutionaries accordingly found it difficult to reconcile the "Rights of Genius" with a free literary market and the national and public requirements of a cultural *patrimoine*.[122] Others have explored the inherent contradictions of revolutionary political culture and the difficulty of drawing boundaries in those domains—politics, religion, education, art, literature, architecture—where creation and destruction, conservation and rejection, proceeded hand in hand.[123] One of the striking aspects of work open to the influence of the New Cultural History is its interdisciplinary scope: in exploring the shaping of revolutionary culture, for example, historians have increasingly engaged in dialogue with formerly neglected fields such as literature and art history.[124]

Exploring the complexity of this cultural revolution from other perspectives has also yielded some of the central achievements of American historiography in recent years. Timothy Tackett, for example, has influentially examined religious culture and community under the Old Regime and during the Revolution, showing that communities and individuals were increasingly faced with a nearly infinite array of choices for or against commitment. In many regions, as Tackett has shown, conflicts over the loyalty oath to the Civil Constitution of the Clergy were not simply a matter of revolutionary politics but crises deeply grounded in the local community; in effect, to be for or against the Revolution often meant choosing between the expansion of a new kind of community or the defense of a traditional one.[125] As Suzanne Desan has similarly argued, revolutionary political culture and Catholicism could exist in a symbiotic relationship: the Revolution provided frameworks and justifications for public involvement which an active laity could use to remodel communal religious identity.[126]

More generally, American historians have turned to the fascinating issue of how the Revolution offered, in effect, several templates for political activity and identity. David Jordan, for example, was one of the first historians to explore the implications of a Furetian interpretation in the context of an individual biography, examining Robespierre's revolutionary career and the ideological, personal, and political factors behind his successful embodiment of the Revolution. In creating the "totally political self" that was the Incorruptible, Jordan argues, Robespierre succeeded not simply in identifying with the Revolution but in being identified with it to an unmatched degree—an identification that was both the source of his dramatic influence and the motivation for his political goals.[127]

American historians have also explored how the institutions of the Revolution, and the administrative and political practices they fostered, contributed to refashioning collective identities. Isser Woloch has argued that, in reconfiguring electoral politics, military service, legal culture, education, and other domains, the Revolution created a "new civic order" which would exert lasting influence on French life.[128] Even the more specific case of geographical and urban reorganizations, as Ted Margadant has shown, provides a way of reading what used to be called the "municipal revolution" in a broader context. The Revolution's projects of urban reorganization and judicial reform offered towns and cities an arena in which to compete amongst themselves for authority, power, and resources; yet, in fundamental ways, it seems that the Old Regime's municipal legacies did much to shape the new "politics of parochialism" and the revolutionary dynamic of intercity competition.[129]

•

Despite much collegial collaboration and shared inspiration, American researchers have also adopted some distinctive approaches which, for better or worse, are rarely shared by French scholars. The emergence of an eighteenth-century "public sphere" is one theoretically informed domain of research to which American historians have proved considerably more receptive than their French colleagues (here again, perhaps, the critical difference lies in the American proclivity toward intellectual history). But American scholars have generally modified the framework first advanced by Jürgen Habermas in order to liberate the notion of the public sphere from the social determinations which Habermas had given it.[130] Keith Michael Baker has supplied one formulation, suggesting that the Old Regime's political crises incessantly invited "appeal beyond the traditional forms of absolutist politics." As such appeals were routinely made by both the monarchy and its opponents, he has argued, the notion of "public opinion" came to represent an abstract, depoliticized tribunal of political legitimacy, a court before which the entire Old Regime could eventually be indicted. After midcentury, a public politics—a politics of contestation couched in terms of appeals to "public opinion"—became a "structural" feature of French political culture.[131]

American studies of the professional world of the law have yielded clear examples of the manner in which the claims of individuals or groups could be refashioned by deploying the intellectual possibilities offered by the notion of "public opinion." Darlene Levy, in a pioneering work, did much to make sense of the enigmatic figure of Simon-Nicolas-Henri Linguet in these terms.[132] More recently, David Bell has depicted the process by which several "distinct moments of political crisis"—most notably the Maupeou coup—successively destroyed the informal but self-regulating institutions of the Paris bar. When finally freed from the restraints of legal tradition, the foot soldiers of eighteenth-century law— barristers shaped by Jansenist struggles, patriotic self-images, and public pleading—invoked a new world of politics, transforming themselves into the "tribunes" of the public.[133] The celebrated court cases in which this new political dynamic was played out have been skillfully depicted by Sarah Maza.[134] Overall, it now seems clear that such mutations in the world of the law had the effect of destabilizing the monarchy's political sovereignty over the long term.

While American investigations have largely confirmed the salience of "publicity" in late eighteenth-century political culture, several historians have attempted to shift attention toward the more ambiguous effects of different forms of association. For it has become increasingly evident that many of the Old Regime's institutional practices seem to have been governed by logics—egalitarian exchange, democratic sociability, or individual autonomy—which either placed them in implicit conflict with monarchical political culture or created apolitical zones of coexistence with it.

The analysis of Old Regime sociability at a conceptual level strikingly reveals such tensions. Daniel Gordon has suggested that sociability, as it was conceptually elaborated in the eighteenth century, fabricated an apolitical domain—an "idealized space called société"—which insulated individuals from the rigidities of absolutist political culture. But it simultaneously offered a model of self-governing citizenship predicated on the cultivation of sociable, public consensus.[135] Dena Goodman, by contrast, has argued for a reconceptualization of the Enlightenment in terms of new forms of sociability cultivated in a distinctive cultural institution: the salon. By encouraging sociable conversation and epistolary exchange, she argues, the salonnière crafted a domain of collective enlightenment and polite reciprocity. Yet this form of sociability, regulated by women, could not be preserved in the face of masculine rebellion and bitter literary polemics—it was eventually replaced by male forms of association that often mutated into revolutionary clubs. Goodman's work thus suggests that, in its operation as well as its consequences, the Enlightenment's salon culture must be read as a mode of political sociability.[136]

The question of whether sociable interchange was structurally antithetical to the monarchy's political culture has increasingly (as in Goodman's work, for example) pointed to the importance of gender relations in understanding the Old Regime's political sociability. While French revisionism has (until very recently) been reluctant to ascribe fundamental importance to gender relations, American scholars have assiduously and innovatively examined the nature of gender politics from the Old Regime to the Revolution.[137]

Gender considerations have, for example, entered the debate over the Habermasian public sphere and the nature of Old Regime culture. In an influential study, the philosopher Joan Landes argued that Habermas's claim for the emergence of a public sphere was vitiated by its neglect of gender; in constituting a new public sphere, she insisted, the Revolution elaborated a critical dichotomy— between "public" men and "private" women—latent in republican ideology. In the new world of public sovereignty the Revolution gave political meaning to presumed natural differences between the sexes. In effect, masculine gender bias grounded the structure of nineteenth-century "bourgeois" and democratic society.[138]

Landes's work has been severely criticized in recent scholarship on both analytical and historical grounds.[139] However, recent studies by other American historians have more subtly articulated the role of gender in constituting the collective "imaginary" of the prerevolutionary and revolutionary periods. Sarah Maza, for example, has stressed the importance of the eighteenth century's most ubiquitous form of uncensorable sociopolitical melodrama: the legal *mémoire*. Particularly from the 1770s onward, legal briefs played upon the theatricality of "literary-political themes," linking diatribes against aristocratic predation with concerns of personal morality, casting both into a searching examination of "the nature of the prevailing political system." Lawyers and their audiences effectively elaborated a large domain of public discussion and sociomoral critique; as Maza has noted, the interrelation of gender, social vocabulary, and publicity raises interesting questions about the possibility of transmuting political languages into social ones.[140]

Lynn Hunt has similarly argued that gender-sensitive analyses are critical in explaining the forms and trajectories of the political culture of the Revolution. Although her approach in *Politics, Culture, and Class in the French Revolution* was predicated on the enabling effects of an ideology of historical rupture, Hunt's more recent analysis of the Revolution's "Family Romance" has attempted instead to trace particular Old Regime legacies into revolutionary political culture. By focusing on the long-term disenchantment of paternal kingship, the cultural effacement of the father, and the validation of political fraternity, she has sought to illuminate the shifting and contradictory modes by which the "family model of politics" could be imagined. Gender relations, in this perspective, become the fundamental site where contemporaries fought out (whether consciously or unconsciously) the issues of charismatic authority, individual identity, and communal sacrality. Hunt's stimulating, provocative, and highly adventurous argument has generated a substantial debate about historians' approaches to the interpretation of literature and iconography.[141]

One of the most intriguing developments in the analysis of gender relations in the Revolution is the current reevaluation of the issues of "rights" and "universalism." Recent years have seen efforts both to historicize and to universalize the theory and practice of rights. On the one hand, the Revolution's language of rights has been profoundly contextualized, seen as an outgrowth of the distinctive nature of French monarchical culture and the contingent requirements of a declaratory document in 1789.[142] On the other hand, it has been reappraised (as against earlier feminist readings) as founding a universalistic logic whose significance surpasses the particularism of any national experience, as well as the limits placed upon its most immediate implementations. As Lynn Hunt has recently noted, there are considerable stakes involved in depicting the Revolution as a moment either of rights creation or of rights foreclosure.[143]

•

Writing in the early 1960s, John McManners, a well-known British historian of the Old Regime and Revolution, remarked that the historiography of the Revolution was finally becoming less polemical. Viewed over the long term, it seemed, scholarship in this field had moved beyond ad hominem attacks to become a full-fledged "intellectual industry," in which foreign historians—Americans in particular—increasingly played an important role. "French intervention in the War of American independence," McManners wrote, "is being repaid in historiographical coin."[144]

In retrospect, it appears ironic that McManners cited the waning of polemical engagements on the eve of the bitter controversies touched off by revisionism. Yet in singling out the American contribution his instincts were sound. Revisionists would draw upon that historiographical repayment, and proponents of the social interpretation would see it as confirmation of America's ingratitude (to say nothing of Albion's perfidy), but neither school could ignore the new "historiographical coin" of American mintage. If American scholarship has contributed to the search for a new interpretation of the Revolution, it also did much to make that search necessary.

This fact is perhaps the clearest possible sign that the Revolution's historiographical economy has truly become global. Viewed from the post-bicentennial vantage, it is no longer clear that there is today a distinctive American historiography of the French Revolution. Certainly, the research enterprise continues to reveal that American and French scholars think rather differently about a variety of issues—ranging from linguistic and collective practices to gender and the public sphere. But the fundamental interpretive alignments are no longer dictated by national schools or linguistic boundaries; instead, they are increasingly defined according to methodological approaches and historical genres—without respect to national boundaries. Study of the Revolution is now, more than ever, a collective and cosmopolitan enterprise which unites similar schools and divides dissimilar ones.

NOTES

1. Joel Barlow, *A Letter to the National Convention of France, on the Defects of the Constitution of 1791, and the Extent of the Amendments Which Ought to be Applied* (London, 1792), reprinted in *The Works of Joel Barlow*, ed. W. K. Bottorff and A. L. Ford, 2 vols. (Gainesville, Fla., 1970), 1:24–25.

2. Analyses of exclusively American writing on the French Revolution are very rare, but a recent example is Lynn Hunt, "Forgetting and Remembering: The French Revolution Then and Now," *American Historical Review* [hereafter AHR] 100 (1995): 1119–35. Important reviews of American scholarship in the general field of French history include R. R. Palmer, "A Century of French History in America," *French Historical Studies* [hereafter FHS] 14 (1985): 160–75; David Pinkney, "The Dilemma of the American Historian of Modern France," *FHS* 1 (1958): 11–25; idem, "The Dilemma of the American Historian of Modern France Reconsidered," *FHS* 9 (1975): 170–81; and idem, "Time to Bury the Pinkney Thesis?" *FHS* 17 (1991): 219–23. See also Jeremy Popkin, "Made in U.S.A.": Les historiens français d'Outre-Atlantique et leur histoire," *Revue d'histoire moderne et contemporaine* 40 (1993): 303–20.

3. Our use of the term "American" in what follows is intentionally flexible: we take it to denote those historians—irrespective of nationality—who have spent a substantial part of their careers in the United States. The close professional and institutional connections between the U.S. and Canadian historical professions lead us to include Canadian scholars within the rubric. Obviously, if the definition of American were to depend merely on the accidents of residency and citizenship, it would have little merit. We hope to show, however, that a looser definition has both analytic purchase and interpretive utility.

4. Excellent accounts of this historiographical evolution include William Doyle, *Origins of the French Revolution* (Oxford, 1988), and T. C. W. Blanning, *The French Revolution: Aristocrats versus Bourgeois?* (Atlantic Highlands, N.J., 1987). The "Jacobin" perspective is presented in Michel Vovelle, *Combats pour la Révolution française* (Paris, 1993).

5. Recent French surveys which show reliance upon American research include Jacques Solé, *Questions of the French Revolution: A Historical Overview*, trans. Shelley Temchin (New York, 1989), and Roger Chartier, *The Cultural Origins of the French Revolution*, trans. Lydia G. Cochrane (Durham and London, 1991). The leading French revisionist, François Furet, has consistently acknowledged a debt to English-language scholarship; see the forum "François Furet's Interpretation of the French Revolution," *FHS* 16 (1990): esp. 792, 799–800.

6. The call for a fuller appreciation of the classic early efforts to understand the Revolution is made in François Furet and Mona Ozouf, eds., *A Critical Dictionary of the French Revolution*, trans. Arthur Goldhammer (Cambridge, Mass., 1989), xvi.

7. The famous phrase belongs to François Furet, *Penser la Révolution française* (Paris, 1978), translated as *Interpreting the French Revolution*, trans. Elborg Forster (Cambridge, 1981).

8. Fred Morrow Fling, "La Révolution française et la période Napoléonienne," *Revue de synthèse historique* 29 (1919): 263, 269.

9. For an excellent introduction to the nature of this disciplinary transformation, see Peter Novick, *That Noble Dream: The "Objectivity Question" and the American Historical Profession* (Cambridge, 1988).

10. See William R. Keylor, *Academy and Community: The Foundation of the French Historical Profession* (Cambridge, Mass., 1975), 68–69, 102–3. See also Felix Gilbert, "European and American Historiography," in John Higham et al., *History* (Englewood Cliffs, N.J., 1965), 332.

11. For a critical perspective, see François Furet, "The Academic History of the Revolution," in Furet and Ozouf, eds., *Critical Dictionary*, 881–99.

12. In that year, John Abbott, an instructor at Bowdoin College, offered a history of the Revolution which utilized contemporary memoirs and journals, and also engaged scholarship by Tocqueville and Michelet. His interpretation was also providential, alluding to lessons that the American republic might draw from the French experience. See John S. C. Abbott, *The French Revolution of 1789 as Viewed in the Light of Republican Institutions* (New York, 1859), v–vii. Abbott also wrote several popular biographies dealing with revolutionary themes. See Abbott, *History of Madame Roland, with Engravings* (New York, [1850]); idem, *History of Maria* [sic] *Antoinette* (New York, 1868); idem, *The History of Napoleon Bonaparte*, 4 vols. (New York, [1883]). It is generally agreed, however, that the most important pre-1900 American work on European and French Revolutionary themes belonged to an instructor at the Navy War College, Captain Alfred Thayer Mahan, author of *The Influence of Sea Power on History, 1600–1783* (Boston, 1890) and *The Influence of Sea Power on the French Revolution and Empire* (New York, 1892). See Palmer, "Century of French History," 164–65, 167; and Fling, "La Révolution française et la période Napoléonienne," 264.

13. See Charles Kendall Adams, *A Manual of Historical Literature, Comprising Brief Descriptions of the Most Important Histories in English, French, and German, Together with Practical Suggestions as to Methods and Courses of Historical Study, for the Use of Students, General Readers, and Collectors of Books* (New York and London, 1889), 352–62, 398, 400, 403. According to R. R. Palmer, Adams listed approximately 150 works in French history, only 7 of which were by Americans; see Palmer, "Century of French History," 162 n. 2.

14. Early American works on the Old Regime and Revolution include J. B. Perkins, *France under the Regency with a Review of the Administration of Louis XIV* (Boston and New York, 1892); idem, *France under Mazarin, with a Review of the Administration of Richelieu*, 2 vols. (New York and London, 1886); idem, *France under Louis XV* (Boston and New York, 1897); and idem, *The French Parliaments* (Washington, D.C., 1903). R. R. Palmer judged the first scholarly American book on modern French history to be Charles Kendall Adams, *Democracy and Monarchy in France* (New York, 1874). See Palmer, "Century of French History," 162–63.

15. Shailer Mathews, *The French Revolution* (London and Bombay, 1901). Mathews's survey was reprinted fifteen times between 1901 and 1923.

16. The centennial of 1789 inspired works such as Hermann Lieb, *The Foes of the French Revolution* (Chicago, New York, and San Francisco, 1889). Revolutionary origins were examined from a somewhat Tocquevillian perspective by E. J. Lowell, *The Eve of the French Revolution* (Boston and New York, 1892). See also Richard Heath Dabney, *The Causes of the*

French Revolution, 2nd ed. (New York, 1889); R. M. Johnston, The French Revolution: A Short History (New York, 1909); and Perkins, France under Louis XV, 2:474 ff.

17. Some of the earliest American monographs examined the issue of Anglo-American reactions to the Revolution. See Charles Downer Hazen, Contemporary American Opinion of the French Revolution (Baltimore, 1897), and W. T. Laprade, England and the French Revolution of 1789–1797 (Baltimore, 1909). Horace Mann Conaway examined constitutional influences in "The First French Republic: A Study of the Origin and the Contents of the Declaration of the Rights of Man, of the Constitution, and of the Adoption of the Republican Form of Government in 1792" (Ph.D. dissertation, Columbia University, 1902); see also Henry Bourne, "American Constitutional Precedents in the French National Assembly," AHR 8 (1903): 466–86. From the perspective of foreign policy, see Clyde Augustus Duniway, "French Influence on the Adoption of the Federal Constitution," AHR 9 (1904): 304–9. Such turn-of-the-century discussions were often much influenced by the work of Georg Jellinek, professor of law at Heidelberg University. Jellinek argued that the spirit of modern liberty—as enunciated in the eighteenth-century declarations of rights—owed much to the demand for religious toleration and freedom of conscience. See Jellinek, The Declaration of the Rights of Man and of Citizens: A Contribution to Modern Constitutional History, trans. M. Ferrand (New York, 1901).

18. Henry E. Bourne, "Improvising a Government in Paris in July, 1789," AHR 10 (1905): 280–308, and idem, "Municipal Politics in Paris in 1789," AHR 11 (1906): 263–86. See also the valuable discussion in Hunt, "Forgetting and Remembering," 1123.

19. Fred Morrow Fling, "Mirabeau, a Victim of the Lettres de Cachet," AHR 3 (1897): 19–30; idem, "The Youth of Mirabeau," AHR 8 (1903): 657–82; and idem, Mirabeau and the French Constitution in the Years 1789 and 1790 (Ithaca, 1891). See also R. M. Johnston, "Mirabeau's Secret Mission to Berlin," AHR 6 (1901): 235–53.

20. See Fling, "The Oath of the Tennis Court," The University Studies of the University of Nebraska [hereafter US] 2 (October 1899): 1–10. Among other studies, see Julia Crewitt Stoddard, "The Causes of the Insurrection of the 5th and 6th of October, 1789," US 4 (October 1904): 267–327; Charles Kuhlmann, "On the Conflict of Parties in the Jacobin Club (November 1789–July 17, 1791)," US 5 (July 1905): 229–50; Mae Darling, "The Opening of the States General of 1789 and the First Phase of the Struggle between the Orders," US 14 (July 1914): 203–87; Ethel Lee Howie, "The Counter Revolution of June-July 1789: The Role of the Assembly from June 30 to July 11," US 15 (July–October 1915): 283–419; and Jeanette Needham, "The Meeting of the Estates-General, 1789: The Union of the Three Orders, June 24 to June 27," US 17 (April–July 1917): 115–317. The sole Ph.D. dissertation to emerge from the Nebraska studies before World War One stressed that 20 June 1792 "was not . . . a wild outbreak of unreasoning popular fury, but a demonstration of the political intelligence of the residents of the faubourgs of Paris." See Laura B. Pfeiffer, "The Uprising of June 20, 1792," US 12 (July 1912): 328.

21. Andrew Dickson White, Fiat Money Inflation in France (1876; San Francisco, 1980), 19–24, 56–59.

22. C. H. Lincoln, "The Cahiers of 1789 as an Evidence of a Compromise Spirit," AHR 2 (1897): 227–28. See also Hunt, "Forgetting and Remembering," 1122. Lincoln's brief (4 page) study was based entirely on cahiers reprinted in the Archives parlementaires. A similarly elegiac reading of the Revolution's politics was offered by Lowell, Eve of the French Revolution, 388.

23. William Milligan Sloane, The French Revolution and Religious Reform: An Account of Ecclesiastical Legislation and Its Influence on Affairs in France from 1789 to 1804 (New York, 1901), 81, 97.

24. See H. E. Bourne, "A Decade of Studies in the French Revolution," *Journal of Modern History* [hereafter *JMH*] 1 (1929): 250–79. A survey directed by Chester Higby in 1929 confirmed the narrow institutional concentration of American research within France: results are noted in William McNeill, "A Birthday Note," *JMH* 51 (1979): 2.

25. See Charles Homer Haskins, "European History and American Scholarship," *AHR* 28 (1923): 215, 223.

26. James Harvey Robinson, "Recent Tendencies in the Study of the French Revolution," *AHR* 11 (1906): 538, 545–47. For objections to Robinson's paper by Henry Morse Stephens and Fred Fling, see the December 1905 discussion recorded in *AHR* 11 (1906): 506–7. See also Robinson, *The New History: Essays Illustrating the Modern Historical Outlook* (1912; New York, 1922), 201–2; and Novick, *That Noble Dream*, 104–6, 150–56.

27. Robinson, *New History*, 14–15, 17–21.

28. See Charles Downer Hazen, *The French Revolution and Napoleon* (New York, 1917), 192–203, 227–28, 277.

29. See Gilbert Allardyce, "The Rise and Fall of the Western Civilization Course," *AHR* 87 (1982): 695–725, and the ensuing commentary, 726–43. See also Lloyd Kramer, Donald Reid, and William L. Barney, eds., *Learning History in America: Schools, Cultures, and Politics* (Minneapolis and London, 1994).

30. Influential interwar surveys of the Revolution included Louis Gottschalk, *The Era of the French Revolution* (Boston, 1929); Leo Gershoy, *The French Revolution, 1789–1799* (New York, 1932); and Crane Brinton's contribution to the famous "Langer Series," *A Decade of Revolution, 1789–1799* (New York and London, 1934).

31. Keylor, *Academy and Community*, 102–3.

32. Louis Gottschalk, "L'influence d'Albert Mathiez sur les études historiques aux États-Unis," *Annales historiques de la Révolution française* [hereafter *AHRF*] 9 (1932): 224–29; Brinton, *Decade of Revolution*, 301. Robinson had earlier remarked distastefully on French polemics: see "Recent Tendencies in the Study of the French Revolution," 531, and *The New History*, 197–98.

33. Louis Gottschalk, *Jean Paul Marat: A Study in Radicalism* (1927; Chicago, 1967), xi, 14–31, 103–5, 172–78. For Mathiez's generally favorable review, see *AHRF* 4 (1927): 599–602. Gottschalk continued his biographical exploration of revolutionary activism with the more congenial figure of Lafayette, whose career also illustrated the importance of prosaic and circumstantial factors in defining individual responses to revolutionary situations. See especially Gottschalk, *Lafayette Comes to America* (Chicago, 1935), and *Lafayette between the American and the French Revolutions, 1783–1789* (Chicago, 1950). A partial synopsis is presented in Gottschalk, *The Place of the American Revolution in the Causal Pattern of the French Revolution* (Easton, Pa., 1948).

34. Such biographical studies included Robert Perry Shepherd, *Turgot and the Six Edicts* (New York, 1903); John M. S. Allison, *Lamoignon de Malesherbes, Defender and Reformer of the French Monarchy, 1721–1794* (New Haven, 1938); J. Salwyn Schapiro, *Condorcet and the Rise of Liberalism* (New York, 1934); Glyndon van Deusen, *Sieyès: His Life and His Nationalism* (New York, 1932); James Michael Eagan, *Maximilien Robespierre: Nationalist Dictator* (New York, 1938); Geoffrey Bruun, *Saint-Just: Apostle of the Terror* (Boston and New York, 1932); Eugene Newton Curtis, *Saint-Just: Colleague of Robespierre* (Morningside Heights, N.Y., 1935); and Elloise Ellery, *Brissot de Warville: A Study in the History of the French Revolution* (Cambridge, Mass., 1915). One American historian's biographies were extensively translated into French, perhaps because they dealt rather sympathetically with Robespierre and Saint-Just as leaders of the "fourth estate" (the proletariat, not the print-media). See Ralph Korngold, *Saint-Just*, trans. Albert Lehman (Paris, 1937); idem, *Robes-*

pierre, le premier dictateur moderne (Paris, n.d.); and idem, *Robespierre and the Fourth Estate* (New York, 1941).

35. Palmer, "Century of French History," 170–71. Brinton was one of the first American historians to conduct substantial research in provincial depositories. American studies of departmental politics later included John B. Sirich, *The Revolutionary Committees in the Departments of France, 1793–1794* (Cambridge, Mass., 1943), and Richard M. Brace, *Bordeaux and the Gironde, 1789–1794* (Ithaca, 1947).

36. Crane Brinton, *The Jacobins: An Essay in the New History* (1930; New York, 1961), 66, 235–39.

37. For an argument on the relatively limited impact of the Terror, see H. M. Stephens, *A History of the French Revolution*, 2 vols. (New York, 1891), 2:321–61, 414; see also Robinson, *New History*, 201. An array of current approaches is presented in Keith Michael Baker, ed., *The Terror*, vol. 4 of *The French Revolution and the Creation of Modern Political Culture* (Oxford, 1994).

38. Wilfred B. Kerr, *The Reign of Terror, 1793–1794: The Experiment of the Democratic Republic, and the Rise of the Bourgeoisie* (Toronto, 1927), 27–28, 439–40, 461. Kerr was trained in Britain and Canada but taught at the University of Buffalo.

39. Brinton, *Jacobins*, 232, 235. Extending this criticism, Brinton later argued that "the men who made the Terror were not thinking in terms of economics"; see Brinton, *Decade of Revolution*, 137.

40. Donald Greer, *The Incidence of the Terror during the French Revolution: A Statistical Interpretation* (Cambridge, Mass., 1935), 1, 18, 39, 85, 96–97, 107–9, 117–20, and tabulated data on 135–66.

41. Influential revisionist evaluations of the Terror's temporality include Furet, *Interpreting the French Revolution*, 11–12, 61–72, 125–31, and Mona Ozouf, "War and Terror in French Revolutionary Discourse," reprinted in T. C. W. Blanning, ed., *The Rise and Fall of the French Revolution* (Chicago, 1996), 266–84. It is now forgotten, however, that Greer was echoing a commonplace observation among American historians. For examples, see Kerr, *Reign of Terror*, 458, and Brinton, *Decade of Revolution*, 295–97.

42. Greer, *Incidence of the Terror*, 3; Brinton, *Jacobins*, 1–3.

43. Brinton, *Decade of Revolution*, 161–63; Greer, *Incidence of the Terror*, 127.

44. As late as 1949, Cornwell Rogers could conclude from a detailed study of pamphlet literature, songs, and "public opinion" that the revolutionary sentiment of 1789 was, in its regenerative hopes, "essentially a religious spirit." See Cornwell B. Rogers, *The Spirit of Revolution in 1789: A Study of Public Opinion as Revealed in Political Songs and Other Popular Literature at the Beginning of the French Revolution* (Princeton, 1949), 258–64.

45. Before the widespread use of the concept of "ideology" in the 1950s and 1960s, American historians frequently relied on expansive notions of "religious" sensibility. For one controversial application, see Carl Becker, *The Heavenly City of the Eighteenth-Century Philosophers* (1932; New Haven, 1963), 159. For an influential critique of such religious analogies, see Peter Gay, *The Party of Humanity: Essays in the French Enlightenment* (New York, 1971), 162–81, 188–210.

46. E. F. Henderson, *Symbol and Satire in the French Revolution* (New York and London, 1912), vi.

47. On the importance of nationalism and "racial" sensibilities in the context of the Old Regime and the Revolution, see Carlton J. Hayes, *The Historical Evolution of Modern Nationalism* (New York, 1931); Jacques Barzun, *The French Race: Theories of Its Origins and Their Social and Political Implications prior to the Revolution* (New York, 1932); van Deusen, *Sieyès*; Leo Gershoy, "Barère, Champion of Nationalism in the French Revolution," *Political Science*

Quarterly 42 (1927): 419–30; and Boyd C. Shafer, "Bourgeois Nationalism in the Pamphlets on the Eve of the French Revolution," *JMH* 10 (1938): 31–50.

48. An exception to this charge is R. R. Palmer's fine essay, "The National Idea in France before the Revolution," *Journal of the History of Ideas* 1 (1940): 95–111.

49. Beatrice F. Hyslop, *French Nationalism in 1789 according to the General Cahiers* (New York, 1934), and idem, *A Guide to the General Cahiers of 1789, with the Texts of Unedited Cahiers* (New York, 1936).

50. Mitchell B. Garrett, *The Estates General of 1789: The Problems of Composition and Organization* (New York and London, 1935).

51. Harold T. Parker, *The Cult of Antiquity and the French Revolutionaries* (Chicago, 1937).

52. Palmer, *Twelve Who Ruled: The Year of the Terror in the French Revolution* (Princeton, 1941). Palmer's work has recently been termed the best book on the Terror in any language. Given the impossibility of archival research in 1941, it was based entirely on printed sources and stands as an example of how the inheritance of turn-of-the-century documentary publication assisted Americans. For an excellent discussion of these points, see Isser Woloch, "On the Latent Illiberalism of the French Revolution," *AHR* 95 (1990): 1452–70.

53. Palmer noted that Aulard entirely neglected Robespierre's speech of 5 February 1794 ("On Political Morality") while Mathiez gave it five sentences; see Palmer, *Twelve Who Ruled*, 56–60, 64, 272–75.

54. Palmer, *Twelve Who Ruled*, 277–79, 385–87.

55. Crane Brinton, *The Anatomy of Revolution* (New York, 1938), 13–14, 25–26. Brinton's work must be understood as part of a broader effort among American social scientists to revisit the question of revolutionary process in a prognostic—and presumably preventive—fashion. This school of "natural historians" of revolution included Brooks Adams, *The Theory of Social Revolutions* (New York, 1913); Lyford P. Edwards, *The Natural History of Revolutions* (1927; Chicago, 1965); George Sawyer Pettee, *The Process of Revolution* (New York, 1938); and George Soule, *The Coming American Revolution* (New York, 1934).

56. Brinton, *Anatomy of Revolution*, 47, 64, 71, 75–78.

57. Brinton argued that the significant element was never the *content* of ideas but their *expression*. Mere contestation was less critical than the emergence of an "intelligentsia" willing publicly to debate and criticize. See Brinton, *Anatomy of Revolution*, 63.

58. Brinton's causal framework and pattern of revolutionary process were largely borrowed from Edwards's work. This debt is assessed in Morris Janowitz's foreword to Edwards, *Natural History of Revolutions*, ix–xiii.

59. The sensibility of the work, however, was distinctly American, as proved by the numerous baseball metaphors scattered through the first edition but deleted in the 1965 revision. Brinton dryly noted that baseball could even help define the character of extremist leadership: "No good revolutionary leader would ever bunt." Brinton, *Anatomy of Revolution*, 242.

60. Although *Anatomy of Revolution* was reprinted several times—most recently in 1965, in an edition revised to take into account debates over "totalitarianism"—the work today commands little attention. Even historical sociologists accord it only glancing if not condescending mention; see Theda Skocpol, *States and Social Revolutions* (Cambridge, 1979), 38.

61. Important comparative works by sociologists and political scientists include Barrington Moore, Jr., *Social Origins of Dictatorship and Democracy: Lord and Peasant in the Making of the Modern World* (Boston, 1966); Skocpol, *States and Social Revolutions*; Reinhard Bendix, *Kings and Peoples: Power and the Mandate to Rule* (Berkeley, 1978); and Jack Gold-

stone, *Revolution and Rebellion in the Early Modern World* (Berkeley, 1991). For an important methodological exchange, see William H. Sewell, Jr., "Ideologies and Social Revolutions: Reflections on the French Case," *JMH* 57 (1985): 57–85 and Theda Skocpol, "Cultural Idioms and Political Ideologies in the Revolutionary Reconstruction of State Power: A Rejoinder to Sewell," *JMH* 57 (1985): 86–96.

62. The sprawling debate on Tudor-Stuart revisionism has raised fundamental points of critique—the absence of class conflict, the importance of intraelite disputes, the mobilizing force of religious questions, the role of military defeat in delegitimizing the existing regime—which surely have relevance in the French context. A useful survey of recent Tudor-Stuart revisionism is Thomas Cogswell, "Coping with Revisionism in Early Stuart History," *JMH* 62 (1990): 538–51.

63. Patrice Higonnet, *Sister Republics: The Origins of French and American Republicanism* (Cambridge, 1988).

64. Causal factors are summarized in Jacques Godechot, *France and the Atlantic Revolution of the Eighteenth Century, 1770–1799*, trans. Herbert H. Rowen (New York, 1965), 7–26.

65. R. R. Palmer, *The Age of the Democratic Revolution*, 2 vols. (Princeton, 1959–64).

66. Palmer, *Democratic Revolution*, 1:85–99, 133, 213–14, 368.

67. Palmer conceded the unique importance of the French Revolution (and especially its radicalization by the war) but nevertheless insisted that the American Revolution had been much more "revolutionary"—that is to say, radical—than usually conceded. See Palmer, *Democratic Revolution*, 1:185–90, 232–35. Brinton had earlier suggested that the American Revolution had its own violent and "terroristic aspects" but was on the whole an "incomplete" revolution spared by utopianism. See Brinton, *Anatomy of Revolution*, 34. In the 1960s, the comparison between the American and French cases was influentially taken up by some philosophers, most notably Hannah Arendt, *On Revolution* (New York, 1963). Currently, the "radical" character of the American Revolution is a vigorous subject of debate among historians: see Gordon Wood, *The Radicalism of the American Revolution* (New York, 1991), and the vigorous forum in *The William and Mary Quarterly* 51 (1994): 679–716.

68. Brinton, *Anatomy of Revolution*, 243 ff, 284–85. The link between violent revolution and democracy was also central to Moore, *Social Origins of Dictatorship and Democracy*.

69. Jacques Godechot's own reservations are expressed in *Un Jury pour la Révolution* (Paris, 1974), 358–59. A judicious overview of the "Atlantic Revolution" controversy is Olivier Bétourné and Aglaia I. Hartig, *Penser l'histoire de la Révolution: Deux siècles de passion française* (Paris, 1989), 117–23.

70. For example, the debate is barely mentioned in Doyle, *Origins of the French Revolution*, 40.

71. On the importance of the Fulbright-Hays Act of 1961, see Richard T. Arndt and David Lee Rubin, *The Fulbright Difference, 1948–1992* (New Brunswick, N.J., 1993).

72. George Rudé, *The Crowd in the French Revolution* (Oxford, 1959), 178–79, 196, 200, 225. Rudé, though educated in England and Australia, spent most of his academic career teaching in Canada.

73. Jeffry Kaplow, *Elbeuf in the Revolutionary Period: History and Social Structure* (Baltimore, 1964). In 1965, Kaplow helped familiarize North American audiences with the newest generation of French work; see Kaplow, ed., *New Perspectives on the French Revolution: Readings in Historical Sociology* (New York and London, 1965).

74. R. R. Palmer, "Popular Democracy in the French Revolution," *FHS* 1 (1960): 445–69. See also Novick, *That Noble Dream*, 281–319.

75. Alfred Cobban, *The Social Interpretation of the French Revolution* (Cambridge, 1964), 16–22, 79–80, 130–31, 162, 172.

76. M. J. Sydenham, *The Girondins* (London, 1961).

77. Robert Forster, *The Nobility of Toulouse in the Eighteenth Century: A Social and Economic Study* (Baltimore, 1960).

78. Elinor Barber, *The Bourgeoisie in 18th Century France* (Princeton, 1955), 139–44.

79. George V. Taylor, "Types of Capitalism in Eighteenth-Century France," *English Historical Review* 79 (1964): 478–97, and idem, "Non-Capitalist Wealth and the Origins of the French Revolution," *AHR* 72 (1967): 469–96. Even the Paris Bourse, Taylor noted, was more characteristic of "court capitalism" than any form of industrial revolution. Taylor, "The Paris Bourse on the Eve of the French Revolution," *AHR* 67 (1972): 951–77.

80. Eisenstein also pointed to the difficulty of equating literacy—so vital to the agitation of 1788—with "status, occupation, economic class, [or] style of life." See Elizabeth Eisenstein, "Who Intervened in 1788? A Commentary on *The Coming of the French Revolution*," *AHR* 71 (1965–66): 77–103.

81. Eisenstein, "Who Intervened in 1788?" 101–3.

82. J. F. Bosher, *French Finances, 1770–1795: From Business to Bureaucracy* (Cambridge, 1970), 312–13. A polemical defense of Necker and his reform program was mounted by another American historian, R. D. Harris, in *Necker: Reform Statesman of the Ancien Régime* (Berkeley, 1979), and idem, *Necker and the Revolution of 1789* (Lanham, 1986).

83. Franklin L. Ford, *Robe and Sword: The Regrouping of the French Aristocracy after Louis XIV* (1953; New York, 1965).

84. David Bien, "La Réaction aristocratique avant 1789: l'exemple de l'armée," *Annales E.S.C.* 29 (1974): 23–48, 505–34.

85. The signposts include Denis Richet, "Autour des origines idéologiques lointaines de la Révolution francaise: Elites et despotisme," *Annales E.S.C.* 24 (1969): 1–23; Colin Lucas, "Nobles, Bourgeois, and the Origins of the French Revolution," *Past and Present* 60 (1973), reprinted in Douglas Johnson, ed., *French Society and the Revolution* (Cambridge, 1976), 88–131; and Guy Chaussinand-Nogaret, *The French Nobility in the Eighteenth Century: From Feudalism to Enlightenment*, trans. William Doyle (Cambridge, 1985).

86. For French historians, Louis Dumont's work on caste and social hierarchy was a more sophisticated touchstone of reference. See Richet, "Autour des origines idéologiques lointaines de la Révolution," 1–4.

87. R. R. Palmer, "Polémique Américaine sur le rôle de la bourgeoisie dans la Révolution française," *AHRF* 29 (1967): 369–80.

88. Furet, *Penser la Révolution française*, 52.

89. See *The French Revolution and the Creation of Modern Political Culture*, vol. 1, *The Political Culture of the Old Regime*, ed. Keith Michael Baker (Oxford and New York, 1987); vol. 2, *The Political Culture of the French Revolution*, ed. Colin Lucas (Oxford and New York, 1988); vol. 3, *The Transformation of Political Culture, 1789–1848*, ed. François Furet and Mona Ozouf (Oxford and New York, 1989). During these years, too, the *Journal of Modern History*, edited by Keith Michael Baker, John Boyer, and Julius Kirshner, became a particularly important vehicle for the publication of the new research in this field. For a selection of articles, see Blanning, ed., *Rise and Fall of the French Revolution*.

90. See, for example, Louis Gottschalk, "Philippe Sagnac and the Causes of the French Revolution," *JMH* 20 (1948): 145–46.

91. Roger Chartier has noted that "in France, *histoire des idées* hardly exists, either as a notion or as a discipline." Chartier, "Intellectual History or Sociocultural History? The

French Trajectories," in Dominick LaCapra and Steven L. Kaplan, eds., *Modern European Intellectual History: Reappraisals & New Perspectives* (Ithaca, 1982), 13–14, 21.

92. Both the "social interpretation" and the Annales school—the two dominant orientations of twentieth-century French historical scholarship—deprecated the importance of a history focused on political ideologies or political conflict, which were regarded as epiphenomenal to deep socioeconomic structures or else as the transient froth of *l'histoire événementielle*. For such reasons, much of this century's outstanding French-language work on eighteenth-century thought and the origins of the Revolution has come from nonhistorians, among them Paul Hazard, Daniel Mornet, and Elie Carcassonne.

93. Many aspects of this effort to redefine intellectual history may be seen in LaCapra and Kaplan, eds., *Modern European Intellectual History*.

94. The leading synthesis of the 1960s omitted discussion of the Enlightenment/Revolution problem, regarding it as a distraction from the intrinsic interest of the Enlightenment. See Peter Gay, *The Enlightenment: An Interpretation*, 2 vols. (New York, 1966–69).

95. Robert Darnton, "The High Enlightenment and the Low-Life of Literature," in idem, *The Literary Underground of the Old Regime* (Cambridge, 1982), 1–40. See also Darnton, *Mesmerism and the End of the Enlightenment in France* (1968; New York, 1970), 104 ff, 161–67.

96. Robert Darnton, *The Business of Enlightenment: A Publishing History of the Encyclopédie, 1775–1800* (Cambridge, Mass., 1979).

97. Robert Darnton, *The Forbidden Bestsellers of Pre-Revolutionary France* (New York, 1995), esp. 169–246. Darnton had highlighted the importance of "Grub Street" condemnations of "despotism" in much of his earlier work—including his Oxford D.Phil. thesis—but such diatribes were consistently read as apolitical or even nihilistic. He originally saw the critique of despotism to be less a function of political consciousness than of social loathing, or of the acute (even paranoid) belief among pamphleteers and "Grub Street" literati that their individual genius had been stifled by persecution.

98. See Jeremy Popkin,"Pamphlet Journalism at the End of the Old Regime," *Eighteenth Century Studies* 22 (1989): 351–67, and, for a somewhat different perspective, Elizabeth Eisenstein, *Grub Street Abroad: Aspects of the French Cosmopolitan Press from the Age of Louis XIV to the French Revolution* (Oxford, 1992).

99. Nina Rattner Gelbart, *Feminine and Opposition Journalism in Old Regime France: Le Journal des Dames* (Berkeley, 1987); Jack Censer and Jeremy Popkin, eds., *Press and Politics in Pre-Revolutionary France* (Berkeley, 1987); Popkin, *News and Politics in the Age of Revolution: Jean Luzac's Gazette de Leyde* (Ithaca, N.Y., 1989); idem, "The Prerevolutionary Origins of Political Journalism," in Baker, ed., *Political Culture of the Old Regime*, 203–23; and Censer, *The French Press in the Age of Enlightenment* (London, 1994).

100. Drawing upon speech-act theory, Quentin Skinner and J. G. A. Pocock influentially redefined the study of political theory in terms of "idioms" and historically specific dialogic contexts—an approach which broke down the artificial and retrospective boundary between the *pièce de circonstance* and the canonical work of theory. For important sketches, see Pocock, "Languages and Their Implications: The Transformation of the Study of Political Thought," in *Politics, Language and Time: Essays on Political Thought and History* (1971; Chicago, 1989), 3–41, and idem, "The Concept of a Language and the *métier d'historien*: Some Considerations on Practice," in Anthony Pagden, ed., *The Languages of Political Theory in Early-Modern Europe* (Cambridge, 1987), 19–38.

101. Such problems are notionally independent because the varied political idioms which circulated within eighteenth-century monarchical culture took on meaning against

their own, specific contexts. Yet such problems are also practically interconnected because they imply the possibility of a nonteleological interpretation of the relationship between Old Regime and Revolution.

102. These are among the arguments presented in Keith Michael Baker, *Inventing the French Revolution: Essays on French Political Culture in the Eighteenth Century* (Cambridge, 1990).

103. See Dorinda Outram, "'Mere Words': Enlightenment, Revolution, and Damage Control," *JMH* 63 (1991): 327–40, and William H. Sewell, Jr., *A Rhetoric of Bourgeois Revolution: The Abbé Sieyes and* What Is the Third Estate? (Durham, 1994), 29 ff. Roger Chartier has outlined a practice-based critique of the linguistic turn in Chartier, *Cultural Origins of the French Revolution*, 18–19. For a judicious survey of recent debates see John Toews, "Intellectual History after the Linguistic Turn: The Autonomy of Meaning and the Irreducibility of Experience," *AHR* 92 (1987): 879–907.

104. David Bell offers a searching evaluation of recent works in eighteenth-century political history in "How (and How Not) to Write *Histoire Evénementielle*: Recent Books on Eighteenth-Century French Politics," *FHS* 19 (1996): 1169–89. For a challenge to the radical importance of 1789, see Timothy Tackett, "Nobles and the Third Estate in the Revolutionary Dynamic of the National Assembly, 1789–1790," *AHR* 94 (1989): 271–301, and the fuller argument sketched in idem, *Becoming a Revolutionary: The Deputies of the French National Assembly and the Emergence of a Revolutionary Culture* (Princeton, 1996).

105. Dale Van Kley, *The Jansenists and the Expulsion of the Jesuits, 1757–1765* (New Haven, 1975), and idem, *The Damiens Affair and the Unraveling of the Ancien Regime, 1750–1770* (Princeton, 1984). In a classic study, R. R. Palmer (Van Kley's dissertation adviser) suggested that the expulsion of the Jesuits was one of the few triumphs which could be ascribed to a Jansenist-*parlementaire* coalition: see Palmer, *Catholics and Unbelievers in Eighteenth-Century France* (1947; Princeton, 1967), 25. For different politically inflected examinations of monarchical "desacralization," see Michael Walzer, ed., *Regicide and Revolution: Speeches at the Trial of Louis XVI*, rev. ed. (New York, 1993), and Jeffrey W. Merrick, *The Desacralization of the French Monarchy in the Eighteenth Century* (Baton Rouge, La., 1990).

106. See Dale Van Kley, "Church, State, and the Ideological Origins of the French Revolution: the Debate over the General Assembly of the Gallican Clergy in 1765," *JMH* 51 (1979): 629–66; idem, "The Religious Origins of the Patriot and Ministerial Parties in Pre-Revolutionary France: Controversy over the Chancellor's Constitutional *coup*, 1771–1775," *Historical Reflections/Réflexions historiques* 18 (1992): 17–64; and idem, "The Estates-General as Ecumenical Council: The Constitutionalism of Corporate Consensus and the Parlement's Ruling of 25 September 1788," *JMH* 61 (1989): 2–52. Many of these arguments have now been incorporated in Van Kley, *The Religious Origins of the French Revolution: From Calvin to the Civil Constitution of the Clergy* (New Haven, 1996). On somewhat different grounds, the ideological legacies of the Maupeou coup have been emphasized by Durand Echeverria, *The Maupeou Revolution: A Study in the History of Libertarianism, France, 1770–1774* (Baton Rouge and London, 1985).

107. Van Kley, *Religious Origins*, 211.

108. See, for example, Dale Van Kley, "The Jansenist Constitutional Legacy in the French Prerevolution 1750–1789," in Baker, ed., *Political Culture of the Old Regime*, 169–201, and idem., "New Wine in Old Wineskins: Continuity and Rupture in the Pamphlet Debate of the French Prerevolution," *FHS* 17 (1991): 447–65. See also Vivian Gruder, "A Mutation in Elite Political Culture: The French Notables and the Defense of Property and Participation, 1787," *JMH* 56 (1984): 598–634, and idem, "The Bourbon Monarchy: Re-

forms and Propaganda at the End of the Old Regime," in Baker, ed., *Political Culture of the Old Regime*, 347–74. See also Bailey Stone, *The French Parlements and the Crisis of the Old Regime* (Chapel Hill, N.C., 1986).

109. Gail Bossenga, *The Politics of Privilege: Old Regime and Revolution in Lille* (Cambridge, 1991), and David Bien, "Offices, Corps, and a System of State Credit: The Uses of Privilege under the Ancien Régime," in Baker, ed., *Political Culture of the Old Regime*, 89–114.

110. Baker, *Inventing the French Revolution*, 6–7. See also Marshall Sahlins, *Islands of History* (Chicago, 1985).

111. William H. Sewell, Jr., *Work and Revolution in France: The Language of Labor from the Old Regime to 1848* (Cambridge, 1980).

112. Sewell, *A Rhetoric of Bourgeois Revolution*, 29, 38.

113. George V. Taylor, "Revolutionary and Nonrevolutionary Content in the *Cahiers* of 1789: An Interim Report," *FHS* 7 (1972): 479–502.

114. Disparities could be reconciled with Marxian theory (as with Rudé and Soboul) or used to identify the *sans-culottes* as mere "accidents" (as with Richard Cobb), but the general problem remained: how did artisans, peasants, and other social groups come to participate in political activity on the "national" scale inaugurated by the Revolution?

115. Philip Dawson, *Provincial Magistrates and Revolutionary Politics in France, 1789–1795* (Cambridge, Mass., 1972), and Lenard Berlanstein, *The Barristers of Toulouse in the Eighteenth Century (1740–1793)* (Baltimore, 1975). For an attempt to write the "social history of politics" in the provinces see Lynn Hunt, *Revolution and Urban Politics in Provincial France: Troyes and Reims, 1786–1790* (Stanford, 1978).

116. Charles Tilly, *The Vendée: A Sociological Analysis of the Counterrevolution of 1793* (Cambridge, Mass., 1964). For overviews, see Harvey Mitchell, "The Vendée and Counterrevolution: A Review Essay," *FHS* 5 (1967–68): 405–29, and idem, "Resistance to the Revolution in Western France," *Past and Present* 63 (1974): 94–131. See also James N. Hood, "Patterns of Popular Protest in the French Revolution: The Conceptual Contribution of the Gard," *JMH* 48 (1976), and John Markoff, "Peasant Grievances and Peasant Insurrection: France in 1789," *JMH* 62 (1990): 445–76. Significant studies by British-trained historians who work in North America include Donald Sutherland, *The Chouans: The Social Origins of Popular Counter-revolution in Upper Brittany, 1770–1796* (Oxford, 1982); T. J. A. Le Goff, *Vannes and Its Region: A Study of Town and Country in Eighteenth-Century France* (Oxford, 1981); and Sutherland and Le Goff, "The Revolution and the Rural Community in Eighteenth-Century Brittany," *Past and Present* 62 (1974): 96–119.

117. See Timothy Tackett, "The West in France in 1789: The Religious Factor in the Origins of the Counterrevolution," *JMH* 54 (December 1982); republished in Blanning, ed., *Rise and Fall of the French Revolution*, 352. A useful synopsis of French controversies over the issue of "genocide" in the Vendée is Steven Laurence Kaplan, *Farewell, Revolution: The Historians' Feud, France, 1789/1989* (Ithaca, 1994), 37 ff.

118. Yet, Censer noted, radical opinion seemed less dependent upon political events than upon cultural milieux: what was needed was "a social history of ideas in the Revolution itself with emphasis on the ideological formation of the would-be opinion makers of the decade." See Jack Richard Censer, *Prelude to Power: The Parisian Radical Press, 1789–1791* (Baltimore and London, 1976), 112. A more "cultural" approach is offered in Jeremy Popkin, *Revolutionary News: The Press in France, 1789–1799* (Durham, N.C., 1991), while the role of an antagonistic press is examined in idem, *The Right-Wing Press in France, 1792–1800* (Chapel Hill, N.C., 1980).

119. See Gary Kates, *The Cercle Social, the Girondins, and the French Revolution* (Princeton, 1985); Michael Kennedy, *The Jacobin Clubs of Marseilles, 1790–1794* (Ithaca, 1973); idem, *The Jacobin Clubs in the French Revolution: The Early Years* (Princeton, 1982); idem, *The Jacobin Clubs in the French Revolution: The Middle Years* (Princeton, 1988); and Isser Woloch, *Jacobin Legacy: The Democratic Movement under the Directory* (Princeton, 1970).

120. Lynn Hunt, *Politics, Culture, and Class in the French Revolution* (Berkeley, 1984), 9–15, 214 ff.

121. Defining the "New Cultural History" remains a difficult enterprise, but for characteristic approaches see Lynn Hunt, ed., *The New Cultural History* (Berkeley, 1989).

122. Carla Hesse, *Publishing and Cultural Politics in Revolutionary Paris, 1789–1810* (Berkeley, 1991). See also the relevant essays in Robert Darnton and Daniel Roche, eds., *Revolution in Print: The Press in France, 1775–1800* (Berkeley, 1989).

123. See, for example, Emmet Kennedy, *A Cultural History of the French Revolution* (New Haven, 1989), and James Leith, *Space and Revolution: Projects for Monuments, Squares and Public Buildings in France, 1789–1799* (Montreal, 1991). See also Lynn Hunt, "The French Revolution in Culture: New Approaches and Perspectives," *Eighteenth Century Studies* 22 (1989): 293–301.

124. One particularly influential work among historians, for example, is Thomas E. Crow, *Painters and Public Life in Eighteenth-Century Paris* (New Haven, 1985). For an early study of the art of the Old Regime and the Revolution from the perspective of political mobilization, see James Leith, *The Idea of Art as Propaganda in France, 1750–1799: A Study in the History of Ideas* (Toronto, 1965).

125. See Timothy Tackett, *Priest and Parish in Eighteenth-Century France: A Social and Political Study of the Curés in a Diocese of Dauphiné, 1750–1791* (Princeton, 1977), and idem, *Religion, Revolution and Regional Culture in Eighteenth-Century France: The Ecclesiastical Oath of 1791* (Princeton, 1985).

126. Suzanne Desan, *Reclaiming the Sacred: Lay Religion and Popular Politics in Revolutionary France* (Ithaca, 1990).

127. David P. Jordan, *The Revolutionary Career of Maximilien Robespierre* (New York, 1985). An earlier North American study of Robespierre, compatible with the social interpretation but also sensitive to political and personal contingency factors, was George Rudé, *Robespierre: Portrait of a Revolutionary Democrat* (London, 1975). American literary scholars have equally approached the issue of revolutionary political language and identity construction from perspectives of interest to historians; see, for example, Carol Blum, *Rousseau and the Republic of Virtue: The Language of Politics in the French Revolution* (Ithaca, N.Y., 1986), and Bernadette Fort, ed., *Fictions of the French Revolution* (Evanston, Ill., 1991).

128. Isser Woloch, *The New Regime: Transformations of the French Civic Order, 1789–1820* (New York, 1994). Conversely, the potential applicability of Foucauldian insights to the issue of governmentality in the Revolution has been suggested by Keith Michael Baker, "A Foucauldian French Revolution?" in Jan Goldstein, ed., *Foucault and the Writing of History* (Oxford, 1994), 187–205.

129. Ted W. Margadant, *Urban Rivalries in the French Revolution* (Princeton, 1992). In its interests and emphases, much of this recent American research into the Revolution's institutional repercussions has been cross-pollinated by a particularly vibrant strain of French scholarship in political geography and urban history. See, for example, Bernard Lepetit, *Les Villes dans la France Moderne* (Paris, 1988), and Marie-Vic Ozouf Marignier, *La Représentation du territoire française à la fin du 18e siècle* (Paris, 1989).

130. See Keith Michael Baker, "Defining the Public Sphere in Eighteenth-Century

France: Variations on a Theme by Habermas," in Craig Calhoun, ed., *Habermas and the Public Sphere* (Cambridge, Mass., 1992), 181–211. See also Anthony J. La Vopa, "Conceiving a Public: Ideas and Society in Eighteenth-Century Europe," *JMH* 64 (1992): 79–116.

131. Baker, "Public Opinion as Political Invention," in *Inventing the French Revolution*, 167–99. For a broad but conceptually oriented investigation of the notion of "public opinion" in French political life, see J. A. W. Gunn, *Queen of the World: Opinion in the Public Life of France from the Renaissance to the Revolution*, vol. 328 of *Studies in Voltaire and the Eighteenth Century* (Oxford, 1995).

132. Darlene Gay Levy, *The Ideas and Careers of Simon-Nicolas-Henri Linguet: A Study in Eighteenth-Century French Politics* (Urbana, Ill., 1980). On one of Linguet's important collaborators, see Frances Acomb, *Mallet Du Pan (1749–1800): A Career in Political Journalism* (Durham, N.C., 1973).

133. David A. Bell, *Lawyers and Citizens: The Making of a Political Elite in Old Regime France* (New York and Oxford, 1994).

134. Sarah Maza, "Le Tribunal de la nation: Les Mémoires judiciaires et l'opinion publique à la fin de l'ancien régime," *Annales* 42 (1987): 73–90.

135. Daniel Gordon, *Citizens without Sovereignty: Equality and Sociability in French Thought, 1670–1789* (Princeton, 1994), esp. 242–43. A case for the "civic" radicalism of Freemasonry has been advanced by Margaret Jacob, *Living the Enlightenment: Freemasonry and Politics in Eighteenth-Century Europe* (New York and Oxford, 1991).

136. See Dena Goodman, *The Republic of Letters: A Cultural History of the French Enlightenment* (Ithaca, 1994).

137. Karen Offen has noted that "women" was not one of the categories profiled in Furet and Ozouf, eds., *Critical Dictionary*. Yet the bicentennial did see substantial French work on gender, some of it examined in Offen, "The New Sexual Politics of French Revolutionary Historiography," *FHS* 16 (1990): 909–22. Perhaps out of aversion to American "feminism," many leading French scholars prefer models of gender complementarity (rather than contestation), which they find more congenial to French culture. Some of these differences have been revealed in the debate over Mona Ozouf, *Les Mots des femmes: essai sur la singularité française* (Paris, 1995), and Joan Wallach Scott, *Only Paradoxes to Offer: French Feminists and the Rights of Man* (Cambridge, Mass., 1996).

138. Joan Landes, *Women and the Public Sphere in the Age of the French Revolution* (Ithaca, 1988).

139. See Baker, "Defining the Public Sphere in Eighteenth-Century France," in Calhoun, ed., *Habermas and the Public Sphere*, 198–207; Dena Goodman, "Public Sphere and Private Life: Towards a Synthesis of Recent Historiographical Approaches to the Old Regime," *History and Theory* 31 (1992): 1–20; and Daniel Gordon, "Philosophy, Sociology, and Gender in the Enlightenment Conception of Public Opinion," *FHS* 17 (1992): 882–911.

140. Sarah Maza, *Private Lives and Public Affairs: The Causes Célèbres of Prerevolutionary France* (Berkeley, 1993), esp. 313–22.

141. Lynn Hunt, *The Family Romance of the French Revolution* (Berkeley, 1992). The stimulating debate opened by Hunt's work is visible in the forum in *FHS* 19 (1995): 261–98 (contributions by Madelyn Gutwirth, Colin Jones, and a response by Hunt). See also Philip Stewart, "This Is Not a Book Review: On Historical Uses of Literature," *JMH* 66 (1994): 521–38, and Hunt, "The Objects of History: A Reply to Philip Stewart," *JMH* 66 (1994): 539–46.

142. See the essays in Dale Van Kley, ed., *The French Idea of Freedom: The Old Regime and the Declaration of the Rights of Man of 1789* (Stanford, 1994).

143. See the Introduction to Lynn Hunt, ed., *The French Revolution and Human Rights: A Brief Documentary History* (Boston and New York, 1996), and Hunt, "Forgetting and Remembering," 1133.

144. John McManners, "The Historiography of the French Revolution," in A. Goodwin, ed., *The New Cambridge Modern History,* vol. 8, *The American and French Revolutions, 1763–93* (Cambridge, 1965), 650.

CHAPTER 17

Modern Europe in American Historical Writing

VOLKER BERGHAHN AND CHARLES MAIER

INTRODUCTORY CONSIDERATIONS

Any effort to summarize the contribution of North American scholars to the history of twentieth-century Europe encounters some grave obstacles from the start. Questions of specificity, of coherence, and of quality must be confronted at the outset.

Questions of *specificity* because at their best American historians of Europe aspire to overcome whatever differentiates their approach from the historians they admire who are themselves European. Can they, therefore, constitute an identifiable school or group? It is difficult to establish any claim for a specific American national contribution to recent European history. The effort seems all the more a challenge because America's historians of Europe themselves set little store today in making a case for their own specific contribution. They tend to discount the lingering paradigm of American exceptionalism that has shaped much of the United States writing on American society.[1] Not that they are not willing to explore important differences between the formation of American and European societies, such as the absence of a "feudal legacy" in North America or the impact of vast expanses of free land, the important political roles of parties and courts, the long legacy of African-American slavery, or the myths and realities of upward mobility, just to cite some of the major tropes of the "exceptionalist" paradigm. As discussed below, the unique factors of American development seemed particularly important during the era when the collapse of democracy abroad made it important to understand its domestic strengths and its European vulnerabilities. Nonetheless, this agenda has since faded in urgency. America's Europeanists grant the differences between their own country and those they study. Nonetheless, they tend to believe that every society has its own exceptionalism and treads its own *Sonderweg*. Why then presuppose that Americans write a characteristic history of Europe?

Questions of *coherence* arise because the American historiography of modern Europe is a sprawling field. Since the nineteenth century and following the rise of national and nationalist writing, European history has fragmented into nation-state components. The specialization of historical writing that has followed has affected the scholarship on the American side of the ocean as well as in Europe itself. If up to the 1930s and certainly before 1914 American historians still wrote in a more comprehensive European mode, the expansion of higher education after World War II promoted the hiring of more specialized British, German, French, Russian, or other national-field experts. Fragmentation was exacerbated by the advent, especially since the 1960s, of new genres and approaches to historiography.[2] On the one hand, this meant that the United States universities devoted a truly extraordinary collective effort to the history of societies abroad. The commitment to teaching and research on European subjects has amounted to perhaps one-quarter of faculty time and positions; libraries have invested heavily; Ph.D.s in European subjects continue to emerge. At a time when medical and legal costs claim ever larger shares of the national output, when public budgets are under pressure, this remains a remarkable commitment.

Nonetheless, such a broad sustained effort had to lead to a certain diffuseness. For as long as political and diplomatic historians dominated the field, Europe continued to be viewed as a larger whole.[3] Once social historians and historians of popular culture, of minorities, or of gender became active, Europe as such became a less privileged locus. The new historians explored social practices that were often highly localized, and often were exemplified outside as well as inside Europe. The class struggle, the *charivari*, the differentiation of male and female labor might be exemplified within Europe, but were not usually analyzed as European per se.

The questions of *quality* tend to arise more from prejudice than objective fact. Just as the articles in the first part of this volume reveal the widespread assumption among American historians of the United States that with few exceptions the contribution of European scholars to the exploration of North American history has been marginal, or at least minimal in impact, so have many historians in Europe tended to take American research on their own national histories less seriously. Perhaps the French were most ethnocentric about foreign contributions, but similar judgments could be heard if more indirectly in Britain, Italy, and Germany.[4] And indeed the American historian of Europe did face handicaps: a briefer access to the archives, a remoteness from the sustained cut and thrust of historical debate, the need to catch up, if one might at all, on the cultural legacy the native European acquired in early education. Nonetheless, the American was no worse off confronting the dense texture of French or German cultural background than a historian from Italy or Britain, and he or she could often bring the advantage of training in a broad range of social sciences or other comparative disciplines.

This article in fact presupposes that American historians of Europe remained attuned to the methodological and disciplinary debates and advances that were taking place among Europe's own historians. Even though Peter Novick's main concern in *That Noble Dream* is with the "objectivity question" in American historiography, his study provides ample evidence that the philosophical and methodological preoccupations of historians in Europe as well as European social, political, and economic thought left a distinct mark on research and debates on the American side of the Atlantic.[5] The migration of ideas may have been particularly massive during the 1930s, but in effect it never stopped since it began in the second half of the nineteenth century, when American historians began to constitute themselves as a profession. What this article hopes to establish is that the relationship was not just one of absorbing European concepts and that the historiographical product made by North Americans was not irrelevant to the work being done in Europe itself.

In fact the *questions préalables* about coherence and quality are best answered together. The American contribution has been the most stimulating at those moments it has engaged the large problems of European history as such. The important and fruitful work on the American side of the ocean has addressed the major trends of European development: it achieves distinction by tackling significant issues. We believe that there have been about a half dozen such issues where American scholarship has left a clear mark on research and analysis. Over the course of the twentieth century they have included the classic agenda of international history, including the origins of the First World War; the structure of the interwar settlement, both within countries and between them; the history of the Cold War and the breakdown of liberal democracy; and the rise of Fascism, Nazism, and totalitarianism.

THE AFTERMATH OF WORLD WAR I

While these methodological problems have complicated our search in this article for themes that have been holding the quilt of European nation-state historiography together, there is little doubt that such themes exist and, more importantly for our purposes, that American historians of modern Europe have, throughout the decades, made a tangible contribution to defining them. If we focus on the period since 1918, it is not because no significant history of Europe was being written before World War I; on the contrary, as Leonard Krieger has shown, there was "a veritable flood of textbooks on world history, European history, and the national histories of the European nations" at this time; but the impact of American research is more difficult to trace and fathom for this period than it is for the years after 1918.[6]

If World War I crystallized "the political community between America and Europe and made the study of diplomacy a primary vehicle for locating the American role in human history," this development lured some of the best American historians into the European field.[7] The 1920s saw the publication of a large number of studies and the founding, in 1929, of the *Journal of Modern History* as a forum for scholarship on Europe since the Middle Ages. It is against this background, but also amid the growing isolationist atmosphere in the United States, that Charles H. Haskins crafted his presidential address for the 1921 convention of the American Historical Association (AHA), in St. Louis.[8] "European history," he argued, "is of profound importance to Americans. We may at times appear more mindful of Europe's material indebtedness to us than of our spiritual indebtedness to Europe. . . . Whether we look at Europe genetically as a source of our civilization, or pragmatically as a large part of the world in which we live, we cannot ignore the vital connections between Europe and America, their histories ultimately being one." But how, he asked, will "European history . . . [in fact exist] with us?" Haskins partly answered his question by discussing various books that he believed demonstrated that American historians could hold their own vis-à-vis European work and even act as "interpreter[s] between nations." For there were "common elements in European civilization" that the American scholar could "be the first to discern" and whose history he could "trace without national prejudices from which his European confrères cannot wholly emancipate themselves." His address culminated in the postulate that Europe and America were "now in the same boat along with the still older Orient" and that the "historians' world is one."

No doubt many of Haskins's colleagues would have agreed with his claim to greater detachment when looking at European, and particularly very recent European, history. But this detachment often took a highly critical form, and behind it lurked a political and ideological value judgment that was diametrically opposed to Haskins's Wilsonian Atlanticism. The issue over which all this came to a head was, of course, the debate in the 1920s on the "war guilt" question and the responsibility for the outbreak of World War I. This debate quickly and sharply divided the profession.[9] On the one side were well-known scholars like Carlton Hayes, Charles Hazen, Roland Usher, Raymond Turner, Charles Seymour, and others who held Germany primarily responsible for unleashing a catastrophic conflict, with the most sustained and powerful argument making this point ultimately coming from Bernadotte E. Schmitt. On the other side emerged Sidney Fay, who was the first to publish several articles in the *American Historical Review (AHR)* challenging the notion of German war guilt. He was joined by Elmer Barnes, probably the most acerbic and radical scholar in the "revisionist" camp. To Fay 1914 had essentially been an accident, while Barnes went much further by charging Serbia, France, and Russia with the main responsibility.

Although the fierce debate that continued for more than a decade was not without ironies, it is important to remember that, unlike the "Cold War revisionists" to be discussed below, the "World War I revisionists" were not Young Turks but respected figures at major institutions, among them Charles Beard, Carl Becker, William Langer, and Arthur Schlesinger. Nor were they a small band; the revisionists had sympathizers in many history departments. What is important in terms of our topic is that the debate not only compared the "war guilt" of individual European countries but also took aim at Europe as a whole. For what the "revisionists" tried to demonstrate was the rottenness of *European* colonialism and nationalism, power politics and militarism. As the analysis of book reviews in the *AHR* for this period shows, militarism and the imbalance between military and civilian authority in pre-1914 Continental Europe were frequent themes which, it was believed, had decisively contributed to pushing the world into a catastrophic war. With Wilsonian internationalism defeated at the Paris Peace Conference by seemingly cynical European politicians and generals, had not the

Old Europe been victorious once more? The implications of this position were paradoxical. The "revisionists" treated Europe as a continent, but only to draw isolationist conclusions from it: the American entry on the Allied side had been a mistake; it was time to let postwar Europe stew in its own juice and to avoid involvement in European politics. But if American intervention really proved unavoidable, it should be on the German side in order to renegotiate reparations and to rescind of the "war guilt" charge which had been based on prejudice, ignorance, and hatred.

The American debate on Europe's responsibility for World War I not only had isolationist implications for the United States but also influenced European research into the subject. The "antirevisionists" obviously offered welcome support to French and British historians who similarly had no doubt about who had unleashed the war. The work of Fay and Barnes, by contrast, was grist to the mill of German historians and of the German government, which had established several generously funded agencies charged with refuting German "war guilt."[10] Could anything have been more helpful to the German public relations campaign abroad than the books by "objective" American historians teaching at major schools in the United States? At the same time, in an effort to combat domestic criticism of German policy before 1914, Fay's and Barnes's books were quickly translated into German. The German embassy in Washington presented Barnes with all forty volumes of *Die grosse Politik der europäischen Kabinette*, the edition of German documents relating to pre-1914 international diplomacy that was later found to be flawed by deliberate omissions of important documents. Barnes was also invited in Germany to spread his revisionist gospel in lectures.

The emergence of fascism and the unquestionable responsibility of the Axis powers for the wars of aggression, exploitation, and extermination that began in 1939 inevitably discredited the revisionist position. And yet echoes of it can be found in the arguments that American historians used thirty years later during the controversy unleashed by the Hamburg University historian Fritz Fischer.[11]

INTERNATIONAL HISTORY RENEWED

One of the main peculiarities of this debate over the responsibility for World War I was that, while the work on both totalitarianism and fascism (to be discussed below) drew on social science theory and indeed promoted interdisciplinary cooperation, the Fischer controversy of the 1960s, at least initially, returned to the traditional territory of an exclusively diplomatic and political historiography. Following the very hostile reception in the Federal Republic of Fritz Fischer's work on German annexationism in World War I and on the unleashing of the war by the Kaiser and his advisers (seen as a deliberate attempt to establish Germany as a world power),[12] his colleagues across the Atlantic felt much sympathy for Fischer. It also helped that Fay and Barnes had been virtually forgotten. Since World War II, Bernadotte Schmitt's hypotheses had predominated in American classroom instruction, and few American historians of Europe had any doubt that Berlin and Vienna were primarily responsible for pushing Europe over the brink in 1914.

However, while Fischer combated his conservative and disbelieving colleagues back home by pulling new and ever more compromising documents from his pocket and by haggling with them, in Rankean fashion, over the precise meaning of particular words in diplomatic dispatches, American historians of Europe moved into the history of mentalities. Fritz Stern, among the first to be allowed to consult the notorious Riezler diaries, presented a study of the agonized and agonizing Reich Chancellor Theobald von Bethmann Hollweg. Konrad Jarausch's biography of Bethmann similarly tried to worm its way into the mind of a "reforming conservative" faced with insoluble domestic and international problems.[13]

It is in the context of such approaches that skepticism of Fischer's more radical hypotheses spread. American and British historians began to insist that the decision-making processes of other powers be subjected to the same scrutiny as those of Germany. The net effect of all the ensuing research has been to modify Fischer's work. Thanks in no small part to the work of American historians of Europe, it is now more generally accepted that the Kaiser and his advisers did not push for a world war ever since 1912, as Fischer had argued in his second book; that they first pursued a more limited strategy in July 1914, trying to achieve a localized victory for Austria-Hungary in the Balkans; and that they took a catastrophic *Flucht nach vorn* only at the end of July when it became clear that the original design was going awry. The net result of this work has, to be sure, not been a return to Barnes's radical revisionism of the 1920s. But as the dust of the Fischer debate settled in the 1970s, the picture became more differentiated and sober. Indeed, Sidney Fay, if he were still alive, would probably recognize some of his points in the more recent American writing on the July crisis of 1914.[14] No less intriguingly, research on Europe between the wars has undergone a similar evolution, and again American historians played an important role.

The Fischer debate of the 1960s—but certainly not just the echoes of that German controversy—helped to prompt among American historians a renewed interest in modern European international history, no longer just in the origins of World War I but in the whole era from 1900 to 1945. Several different impulses were at work. The first derived from a new focus on the domestic sources of foreign policy, especially expansionist policies. In Germany Fischer's general argument was a claim for the so-called *Primat der Innenpolitik*: the role of political elites in fomenting a nationalist and aggressive foreign policy to reinforce a domestic leadership that was being challenged by democratic participation and the growth of an industrial working class.[15] Historians in the United States were pressing the same claims independently. Hans Gatzke, an émigré from Germany, had indeed largely prefigured Fischer's arguments (though without the explosive archival documentation) in his book, which attributed German annexationism in the West to the domestic preoccupations of German conservatives.[16] Historians in the United States, as in Germany, went back to reread Eckart Kehr, who, after all, had depended upon the early sponsorship of Charles Beard to pursue research in Washington.[17]

Via Beard, Kehr's emphasis on the primacy of domestic policy had an impact on William Appleman Williams, whose work in turn exerted a major influence on Lloyd Gardner, Gabriel Kolko, and other United States historians critical of America's world role.[18] The "revisionist" charge that Washington was primarily responsible for the Cold War proved easily as divisive in the United States as the Kehr-Fischer history of the responsibilities for German expansionism before and during the First World War. For the American historians working on Europe, the "primacy of domestic policy" was a less politically explosive historiographical paradigm.[19]

As a stimulus to European international history in the 1960s, the methodological approach of Arno J. Mayer was probably more innovative than Fischer's. Mayer's books generalized the primacy of domestic policy to all the major European powers and the United States. First in his 1959 study, *Political Origins of the New Diplomacy*, later retitled *Wilson versus Lenin*, and then in his 1967 sequel on the Paris Peace Conference, Mayer envisaged a confrontation between forces of order, exploiting traditional nationalism, and forces of movement, split into Wilsonian and Leninist camps.[20] The paradigm was methodologically exciting, uniting as it did domestic and diplomatic histories, and it exerted an undoubted ideological appeal in the 1960s and 1970s. It seemed to free historians from a servitude to diplomatic documents and sent them as well to parliamentary debates, public speeches, newspapers, and other records of political opinion.

Yet at the same time, access to new archival material prompted another major renewal of international history, above all of the interwar era, the sources for which significantly expanded by the 1970s. Until the 1960s, historians concerned with Europe's interwar turmoil tended to rely on the published series of *Documents on German Foreign Policy* and *Documents on British Foreign Policy*.[21] Perhaps most notable among the early efforts was the collection of essays focusing on particular statesmen of the interwar states, *The Diplomats*, organized by Gordon Craig and Felix Gilbert.[22] The availability of the papers of Gustav Stresemann, foreign minister from 1924 to 1929, allowed reexamination of German diplomacy in the 1920s and prompted early studies of Stresemann (such as Hans Gatzke's) that tended to "discover" the continuing revisionist aspirations of a statesman who had earlier been celebrated for his moderation.[23] But there were new sources to exploit as well: Gerald Feldman's 1966 book on the role of German industry and labor during the First World War opened up the revealing archives of Ruhr firms and interest groups, not to explain economic but political outcomes.[24]

The new 1970s interest in issues of political economy reflected a more general social science preoccupation as young scholars contemplated the economic difficulties of their own decade and compared contemporary stagflation with interwar crises. In addition, the welcome if belated access to French archival holdings for the 1920s, public and private, prompted a reevaluation of interwar stabilization and its vulnerability. The new archival documentation allowed a greater sympathy for the dilemmas of French policy at Versailles and a colder look at the continuing efforts of Weimar diplomacy to recover great-power status. Doctoral students turned their attention from the overt crises of the 1930s to the less explored issues of the previous decade in what an early contributor, Jon Jacobson, dubbed the new international history. Several research interests intersected in the new work. The reassessment of French policy and the new concentration on political economy came together in the contributions of Charles Maier, Stephen Schuker, Marc Trachtenberg, Sally Marks, and Carol Fink, among others.[25] All these historians criticized the received wisdom of French intransigence at Versailles and after, which Keynes's brilliantly written tract, *Economic Consequences of the Peace*, had originally implanted among most readers.[26] Carol Fink examined the issues of the Genoa economic conference of 1922. Stephen Schuker's major work focused on what he assessed as the fundamental sacrifice of French advantages earlier achieved by the 1918 victory. In a broad examination of archives in France, Germany, Britain, Belgium, and the United States, and informed by sophisticated economic theory, he examined the failure of the Ruhr occupation and the new limits on French policy set by the Dawes Plan negotiations. Charles Maier's *Recasting Bourgeois Europe* came to these issues within the context of examining domestic stabilization strategies in France, Germany, and Italy, and argued that an emerging "corporatist" settlement adumbrated a new and far-reaching (if ultimately short-lived) safeguarding of elite interests in Europe. All these contributions were characterized by an insistence on the importance of issues of public finance, international economics, and the role of economic interest groups. American scholars, it is fair to say, were as active as their European counterparts in exploiting the newly accessed documents in Germany, France, and elsewhere. Coming with a transatlantic perspective, they sometimes proved more avid to use multiarchival approaches than Europeans who plunged preeminently into their own national archives or tended to undertake business and economic investigations that went well beyond traditional diplomatic history.

THE COLD WAR

When American historians turned from the diplomacy of the interwar period to that of the Cold War, they revealed some of the same moral preoccupations that they had shown with the 1920s. But now historians in the United States were caught up very directly in this story. They were not merely telling it about others; their political leaders were central actors along with the leadership of the Soviet Union. Not only that, the history they narrated was their own national epic, the assumption of the mantle of world power. At first there was little questioning of the beneficence of this process: it was a necessary and unselfish response to Stalinist aggressiveness in postwar Europe. Despite an occasional demurral (Denna Fleming's early "revisionist" account of 1961 based largely on published sources),[27] the accepted version of the early 1960s was epitomized by Herbert

Feis's coverage of wartime diplomacy, *Roosevelt, Churchill, and Stalin*, which lent a ponderous gravitas to the conventional wisdom.[28] In 1964, however, Gar Alperowitz opened a fierce controversy with his claim, based in part on Stimson's diaries, that the Truman administration had used nuclear weapons against the Japanese primarily to overawe the Russians, who were newly perceived as the emerging postwar threat to American interests.[29] This disturbing claim did not bear on European history directly, but it opened a major wave of revisionism especially as the fissuring of American politics in the late 1960s—most crucially around the issue of the commitment in Vietnam—helped popularize a neo-Marxian literature on the apparent political consequences of American capitalism. Gabriel Kolko's *The Politics of War* and its sequel, written with Joyce Kolko, examined the division of Europe and Asia. Kolko, followed by numerous other interpreters, claimed that American capitalism's need to have universal access to world markets and thus oppose the postwar advance of socialism made a confrontation with the Soviet Union inevitable.

A decade or more of vigorous debate (often imprecisely joined on both sides), the subsequent ebbing of sympathy for third-world guerrillas, and, by 1980, the new disillusion with Soviet missile upgrading or policies in Afghanistan helped produce a climate in which more traditional views regained plausibility. The result was, to cite John Gaddis's term, a "postrevisionist synthesis" that might tolerantly grant some credit to dissenting historians for raising interesting issues but finally agreed, sometimes with considerable self-satisfaction, about the wisdom of America's policies of deterrence and containment.[30] The breakdown of the communist regimes at the end of the 1980s, the continuing revelations about Stalinist ambitions from Soviet archives (which the Cold War International History Project, lodged at the Woodrow Wilson Center for Scholars, publicizes for a wide readership),[31] the feeling that nuclear deterrence had proved to be quite robust and perhaps the most stable way to navigate the fierce geostrategic and ideological rivalry of the Cold War—all have undercut revisionist approaches. In fact, throughout the debate American historians who took part in it tended to be less concerned about events in Europe per se than their own country's policy and strategic debates. Eventually, however, John Gaddis, Melvyn Leffler, Michael Hogan, and others became interested in the American impact on postwar European society, just as American researchers trained as Europeanists, such as Richard Kuisel and Victoria de Grazia, turned to this subject. It did not take long for the latter, then, to make a link with cultural history, leading in the 1980s and 1990s to innovative research among American historians of Europe on "Americanization" and the rise of a "Fordist" consumer culture across the Atlantic as well as to a lively argument about European resistance to it and the attendant waves of anti-Americanism.[32]

In retrospect it is surprising that it took so long for the fact of nuclear stalemate to exert an impact on history writing. But by the 1980s, international history was clearly responding to the questions of deterrence and crisis that the stepped-up arms race of the early part of that decade stimulated. One result was to encourage renewed examination of the origins of World War I; 1914 provided an obvious source for fruitful analogies, although historians contributed with more diffi-dence than political scientists.[33] American historians sought to develop formal methods of analogizing or constructing "controlled case studies," of which the July crisis of 1914 always represented the most gripping and challenging. Conse-quently across half a century or more we can establish a historiographical pro-gression: an early effort to explain the international catastrophe that was based upon the quickly published documentation and that got caught up in the great debate about "war guilt"; later the impact of Fischer and the new availability of archives; and most recently a return to the compelling issue of origins but with eminently analytical rather than political or moral interests. The issue of crises was also stimulated by America's reflection on the Cuban missile crisis of 1962 after twenty-five years.

Indeed, comprehensive accounts of the major themes in international history after 1945, it is clear in retrospect, could no longer be captured by the term European history. Rather, the relations between Europe and its former depen-dencies—the drama of decolonization (preeminently related for Britain by Wil-liam Roger Lewis)[34]—and the overriding issues of atomic diplomacy, which en-gaged the United States and Soviet Russia, constituted the subject matter of world history. Diplomatic history might have been overwhelmingly European when William Langer wrote in the 1930s, but any major analysis of international affairs in the last fifty years had to find new frameworks of analysis. Where, then, was European history to be found?

NAZISM, TOTALITARIANISM, AND THE FINAL SOLUTION

For almost half the twentieth century—but only half the century—Europe served as a laboratory of political pathology. For those historians not primarily inter-ested in international relations, European history involved preeminently the story of democratic collapse. Most researchers in the United States who were concerned with this theme focused on German developments.[35] They seemed, rightly so, most consequential. The collapse of democracy and the abandonment of liberalism certainly was the major historical theme for American historians during the decades after 1945.

Why this preoccupation? One reason, naturally enough, was the inherent im-portance of the theme. After all, the rejection of nineteenth-century bourgeois liberalism *was* the biggest European story of the first half of the century. Then, too, some of the leading historians were themselves exiles from authoritarian regimes—above all from National Socialism.[36] Another was the sense of Ameri-can exceptionalism cited above. However, not all historians of Europe accepted the belief that the United States enjoyed a privileged trajectory of historical devel-opment. In fact, it was "Americanists," that is, analysts of United States culture and politics, who celebrated American exceptionalism. By contrast, New York intellectuals, many of them second-generation Jewish immigrants, and Protestant chroniclers of New England refused to extol American uniqueness.[37]

Again, there were "boundary" problems. Historians were hardly alone in investigating these issues; from the 1930s on, political scientists and sociologists contributed to the scholarship. Indeed, in reviewing a half century of American historical contributions to the study of twentieth-century authoritarian regimes, one can hardly single out United States historians as preeminent. The great theoretical studies came from other disciplinary vantage points: from Franz Neumann, Robert Brady, Rudolf Heberle, later Hannah Arendt and Barrington Moore.[38] The most probing historical accounts or institutional analyses also tended to come from scholars abroad—and when not, from the afflicted countries themselves over the course of three, four, or five decades.[39]

Although they also produced important monographic work with a strong empirical base,[40] American historians and social scientists were in the forefront of trying to develop the typology of totalitarianism as a category for historical understanding. Among the various attempts at conceptualizing totalitarianism, that by Carl J. Friedrich and Zbigniew Brzezinski was probably the most influential.[41] They devised six criteria which, they argued, could be applied equally to Nazi Germany and Soviet Russia. In May 1948, Arthur Hill, the chair of the National Security Resources Board, came up with a fifteen-point list of similarities between "Nazi-Fascist" and communist systems.[42] Other analysts who thought less of a taxonomical approach and were more philosophically inclined interpreted totalitarianism as an outgrowth of twentieth-century mass society and technology. These scholars—and Arendt in particular—highlighted the atomization of industrialized and urbanized societies and the loneliness of the individual in the face of large anonymous bureaucracies. They also stressed the irrationalism of the masses, who, disoriented and torn from their traditional moorings, were deemed to have become easy prey to ruthless charismatic leaders.[43] If there was rationality in totalitarian regimes, it was a "rationality without reason" (C. W. Mills) that destroyed individuality and turned men and women into soulless automatons.

This world of modern tyrants, faceless bureaucrats, camps, and relentless popular mobilization through cunning propaganda—all of which George Orwell or Arthur Koestler had fictionalized in their successful novels—stood, of course, in stark contrast to a world of democracy, civil liberties, and the rule of law that represented the West. During World War II, when Stalinist Russia was an ally and the Axis powers were the enemy, the totalitarian comparison receded into the background. But it reemerged with full force after 1945, when it became the central paradigm for explaining what was at stake in the escalating East-West conflict. For American historical writing on Europe this ideological development had important consequences, in that it counteracted persistent isolationist tendencies from the interwar period and reinforced wartime notions of an Atlantic community.

C. J. H. Hayes's address as AHA president at the 1945 annual convention put the new imperatives neatly into a nutshell.[44] Starting off with the great impact that Frederick Jackson Turner's frontier thesis had had on American historiography, Hayes pleaded for a broadening of the frontier conception, implying that it was now global and marked by the Iron Curtain. Hayes thought it unfortunate that this broader vision was shared by relatively few specialists in American history. He criticized the narrow training of graduate students and the imbalance between the production of Ph.D.s in American and European history, adding: "The present trend, if unchecked, can only confirm the popular myths that the 'American way of life' is something entirely indigenous, something wholly new and something vastly superior to any other nation's." He thought it "astonishing and paradoxical" that at a time when the United States was leaving its military and economic isolationism behind "we should keep alive and actually intensify an intellectual isolationism." In earlier days, he continued, "we used to know that we were Europeans as well as Americans." The task was therefore to remember and mobilize the unifying force of Europeanism. Americans, he said, were not only "co-heirs" of the Atlantic community but should also be its "co-developers." Discussing the ingredients of this Atlantic world (the Greco-Roman and Judeo-Christian traditions, individualism, limitation of state power, social responsibility, and a sense of mission), he exhorted his colleagues finally to help strengthen America's ties within this community.

The Atlantic community that was the theme of Hayes's address was also the larger context in which the concept of totalitarianism was to be seen. Totalitarianism became an all-pervasive term that informed American historical research on Europe and cropped up in the most remote and unexpected places, such as Hans Rosenberg's study of eighteenth-century Prussia.[45] Nor would it seem too far-fetched to assert that the larger context of the Cold War similarly informed the idea of an Atlantic revolution that Robert Palmer discovered taking place in that same century.[46]

But then, by the late 1950s, criticism of the totalitarianism paradigm began to mount. The assumption that Nazism and Stalinism were "basically alike" was thought to be too mechanistic and crude, riding roughshod over the very different societal blueprints that Nazis and Soviets had proclaimed. This led to the question of whether the relationship between the two regimes was better understood in dialectical terms; whether the Bolshevik revolution of 1917 had produced a fascist counterrevolution. It was Ernst Nolte who first began to ask this question systematically and to reorient research toward an internal comparison of the various fascist movements that had mushroomed throughout Europe in the interwar period. Was this not an "epoch of fascism" rather than of totalitarianism?[47]

If the ensuing debate on European fascism had originated in Europe with Nolte and others, it was quickly picked up by American historians. More important, they shunted it off the philosophical and phenomenological track that Nolte had built and moved it in a socioeconomic and sociopolitical direction. American sociologists, such as Seymour Lipset and Talcott Parsons, helped to shape the emergent framework of analysis,[48] while the Berkeley historian Wolfgang Sauer pleaded for a coexistence of the term fascism with the notion of totalitarianism rather than "a replacement of one interpretation by another."[49] A particularly concise sociopolitical argument by an American historian of Europe can be found in Henry Turner's essay "Fascism and Modernization," which discussed the antirevolutionary character of various fascist movements and associated fascism's emergence with the question of relative backwardness.[50] To Turner and others, fascism was not an outgrowth of advanced industrial countries, as Marxists and also the adherents of the totalitarianism paradigm had maintained. Fascist solutions were, in this view, adopted by countries that were lagging behind in the process of modernization; it was the more modern societies of western Europe and the United States that were able to avoid them.

Whatever differences of opinion developed among American historians of Europe during the debate on fascism, its significance lies in the fact that Europe (and certainly its Continental parts) was once again studied as an entity. Fascism was seen as a transnational phenomenon. What was of interest were not only intra-European national differences but also the similarities that had produced fascist mentalities and movements, and modernization theory seemed to offer the key.

THE HOLOCAUST DEBATE

In the American scholarly context, research on totalitarianism has probably become overshadowed by the particular theme of the Holocaust. The murder of the European Jews tended to receive initial scholarly scrutiny as a consequence of German anti-Semitism and the seizure of power by the National Socialists. Sometimes it appeared as a particularly targeted form of totalitarian terror. Only by the 1960s did it emerge as perhaps the paradigmatic example of Europe's twentieth-century horrors—its lurid spectacle throwing many of the earlier concerns with the war or general terror into shadow. American scholars, again many of them immigrants, played a major role in making the Holocaust into a vast and historically compelling field for research. When Raul Hilberg constructed the first exhaustive chronicle of the Final Solution, his work encountered indifference and even hostility.[51] Contemporary developments, however, had a decisive impact on the historiographical agenda: Hannah Arendt's brilliant if sharply contested essay on the Eichmann trial, a growing thematization of the Holocaust in the American Jewish community, the television series of 1977—all responded to a growing fascination.[52] American historians, joining Canadian, British, Israeli, and German historians, researched the history of the Jewish destruction to explore the degree of control of the National Socialist regime, to reexamine the painful question of the Jewish Councils' role in administration of the ghettos slated for extermination, and to consider United States or British policy toward refugees.[53] Most recently the policies of neutral countries like Switzerland and Sweden have also come under scrutiny.

Holocaust studies has been established as a field of scholarship in many universities, and the officially sponsored U.S. Holocaust Museum conducts a major program of scholarship. American historians continue to participate in an international debate over the sources of genocidal policy. Did it originate in the central ideological program of the leading Nazis and was it therefore traceable to certain statements and orders (the position Tim Mason had defined as intentionalism), or did it arise from an escalation of violence that emerged from the dynamic of the Nazi movement, or the bureaucratic momentum of the party-state (a view Mason called functionalist)?[54] What was the relationship to the progress of the Second World War? Were the war in the East and the murder of the Jews results in some respects of the European elites' frustrated preoccupation with extirpating Bolshevism, as Arno Mayer claimed;[55] or did the Holocaust spring from the particular logic of specifically German anti-Semitism, as Daniel Goldhagen insisted?[56] These were issues that American scholars played a major role in debating, often with strong conflicts among themselves. In one case at least it fell to an American and a Canadian historian virtually to reconstitute a historical field for the national community they researched: that is Robert Paxton and Michael Marrus, who compelled the French to reexamine the role of Vichy's collaboration and participation in the deportation of the country's Jews.[57]

There was a general consensus that the Holocaust in its negative way was a sort of moral nadir of twentieth-century history. It has become the paradigmatically cruel and "unexplainably" evil event that the historical repertory offers. The Soviet purges run a close second—dearer to the concerns of anticommunists perhaps. Historians of Stalinism could claim that the Soviet body count was higher than Hitler's. In any case, Auschwitz, the Gulag, and occasionally Hiroshima became morally freighted terms that demanded research, but by their very sacral solemnity could also inhibit investigation. The fact that in terms of moral trajectory these dreadful culminations arrived fifty years before the century ended has fundamentally influenced historiographical production.

A generation ago, the class conflicts of the twentieth century—the destruction of the German trade unions and Social Democratic Party, the Spanish Civil War, even the British General Strike of 1926, and so on—provided an epic resource at least for historians on the left. They retained the aura of epic events because they were highly morally charged; they were normative reference points. But with the attrition of a Marxist Left in the 1980s, these subjects lost their compelling nature. The difficulty with such morally charged historical themes is, of course, that they can make other historical subjects seem trivial and noncompelling. German history, naturally enough, was written for a long time in the shadow of 1933–45, and subsequent German development—its continuities with pre-1933 history— was usually treated as an appendix. American university curricula reinforced this tendency because they tended for many decades after the Second World War to confirm the caesura of 1945 as an end point of European history. The mass media also helped to shape the overriding preoccupation with the scarifying events of 1933–45.

AFTER AUSCHWITZ

But of course history has continued since 1945. That has left scholars of the contemporary or most recent era a choice. While some have continued to study pre-1945 European history, others have gone on to stress postwar developments as if, in effect, they comprised a second twentieth century. They have also gone beyond Cold War politics and taken up such themes as the creation of sustained postwar prosperity and consumerism, the nature of the multiple crises of the 1970s and after (economic slowdown, interest group conflict, social movements, terrorism), and the impact of wartime resistance and collaboration on the recurring ideological contests in Europe. The renewed institutional activity in the European Union since the mid 1980s on has reawakened interest in the construction of Europe, and of course the events of 1989 have compelled us to reexamine the divisions in our enterprise between Western and Eastern Europe.

Other historians, however, have endeavored to explore developments that bridge the pre-and post-1945 epochs. Precisely because of the public preoccupation with National Socialism and its consequences, one of the most significant recent endeavors for academic historians in the United States in the 1990s has been to develop concepts for interpreting a longer developmental trajectory of twentieth-century history that can both take account of the moral centrality of Nazi outrages but "historicize" them as well. What historiographical strategies have emerged that allow integration of the first and second halves of the century?

One major approach has been to elaborate the categories of cultural "modernism"—a historical approach that has allowed interpretation of Weimar Germany not just as an antechamber to the Third Reich but as an early experiment in radical modernism, that is, as a sort of democratic "theater" for a mass public.[58] Historians have joined intellectual forces with students of German culture and literature in this interpretive venture. Other researchers have explored developments in political economy—the impact of the assembly line and "Fordism"—to discern the continuities of mass society from about 1910, across the interwar period, into the 1960s.[59] The subhistories of advertising, the department store, scientific management, of automobile and aviation development have also provided toeholds for a scaling of a long twentieth century that did not simply culminate in 1945. Innovative works concerning the history of gender, even when focused on the prewar or postwar period, also opened up longer-term perspectives. Each of these approaches has helped historians to rethink longer traits of a twentieth-century history. But once again, the twentieth-century experience that emerges tends to link all industrial societies within a common cycle of modernism and social engineering; and American historians have worked as fully integrated contributors to a broad international research community.[60]

In Search of European History

If, as we have indicated at the beginning, the gradual internationalization of European historiography has continued, what then is left of European history as such from the American shore of the Atlantic? This question has become all the more topical after it was raised in a 1996 article by AHA president Caroline Walker Bynum in *Perspectives*, the monthly newsletter of the AHA.[61] Unlike her predecessors Haskins and Hayes, who had appealed to their colleagues after World War I and World War II not to ignore Europe, Bynum wondered whether she was a member of the "last Eurocentric generation." This, she added, did not mean that she would give up teaching and researching the Middle Ages, her specialty; however, she did believe that "my generation's agenda is over and done with. We must learn from the next generation, and to that generation the agenda is—and must be—the world." However, there were ambiguities in her "call for globalization," and they came out even more strongly in what John Gillis had to say on the subject a mere two months later.[62]

Gillis's article was based on a somewhat unsystematic survey of more than "two dozen seasoned scholars" and found, on the one hand, that "European history may well have reached its apogee in this country" and that it was no longer "*the* surrogate for world history." On the other hand, Gillis pointed "to the proliferation of nationally oriented journals and organizations with frequent regional meetings." He also stressed that "European history is now being practiced under a number of rubrics—gender, social, cultural, family, labor, comparative, and economic history—that have their own meetings, journals, and constituencies. Taken together, there is probably more activity in the European field today than any one scholar can ever comprehend, much less participate in."

Much of this 1990s activity focuses on the modern period and twentieth-century Europe in particular, presumably not least because—whatever may be said about globalization—it still raises some of the biggest and most daunting problems that the profession continues to grapple with. Whether one adopts or modifies or rejects the perspective of a "short" twentieth century, from 1914 to 1989, as suggested by Eric Hobsbawm, the impending conclusion of the calendar's century, along with the collapse of the Communist regimes—a fixture no one really expected to disappear so suddenly—has rekindled an interest in periodization;[63] we realize that we need to place the postwar era (the era of divided Europe) in the context of a whole century. Having lived through what is clearly the end of an epoch in 1989–91, we are also compelled to ask what this latest caesura may imply about the earlier ruptures of 1914–19 or 1941–45. One facile answer to periodization that post-1991 commentators have frequently advanced in op-ed and similar essays—namely that the end of communism has merely reopened the ethnic conflicts of 1914—is surely incomplete. New efforts at periodization will have to get beyond just political ruptures of 1914–19 or 1945, to consider long-term social and cultural transitions, such as the transition from steel to silicon, the impact of computer technology, and the changing relations of Europe to what we used to call the third world.

Faced with this historical flux (which for many reasons we would date from the late 1960s) twentieth-century Europeanists are reacting in much the same way other European (and American) historians are reacting. First, they are caught up in an intensely self-reflective phase in which the mental processing of past events becomes as much of a historical subject as the events themselves. The history of memory has thus become a "growth industry" for many twentieth-century historians, and at least one new journal, Saul Friedlander's *History and Memory* (an American-Israeli collaborative product), reflects the trend. The topic has become all the more gripping since the century's events led to several spectacular blockages or repressions of individual and collective memory, whose opening up (the historians' version of "transference") evokes tremendous catharsis. The testimonies of Holocaust survivors, the uneasy coming to terms with collaboration and resistance, and the contests over public monuments are primary texts for this reflexive history. Of course, the trend is international; both historical practitioners and historical subject matter encompass Europe and Latin America as well as the United States and Canada.

Similar transnational work has been done by European historians—and in this case from all over the globe—on the cultural impact and memory of World War I. Starting with Paul Fussell's pioneering book on the "Great War," this work has been highly innovative and interdisciplinary and promises to yield further important results.[64] And, like the research on World War II, it has, if anything, promoted a "Europeanization of European history" that Gillis has alluded to—or rather, in terms of the evolution of the profession traced in this article, a "re-Europeanization."

Second, of course, twentieth-century historians are caught up in the postmodern problem of agency (which Dorothy Ross addresses),[65] the fading of which must complicate all our stories. And if all agents tend to melt into air, the fading away of one particular agent has hit historians especially hard: that is, many have been bereft by the collapse of the myth of the virtuous Left, or the disappearance of a Left *tout court*. The point is that twentieth-century historians are having to explore or investigate beyond epic and catastrophe to reflexivity and diffuseness.

There is no inherent reason to believe, however, that these self-reflexive trends will last longer than any other cycle of historiographical focus. Indeed, other major thematic issues have claimed major attention, and will continue to do so. One is the distinction between private and public. Reexamination of private and public domains (theorized for American as well as European historians most notably by Jürgen Habermas)[66] has become a major theme in all recent historical writing. Although the issues of public and private spheres have played a key interpretive role for historians of gender and of eighteenth- and nineteenth-century bourgeois society, the theme takes on a special importance as well for historians of twentieth-century Europe. It allows the post-1945 period to make a claim for our attention that is as compelling as the pre-1945 era.

A second major theme, already long adumbrated, that will inform a contemporary historiography involves the further dissolving of Europe. Europe is no longer a privileged subject. Is it even a coherent one? On the one hand, historians will work to set Europe in a world historical context: the economic, demographic, and intellectual trends at the end of the century virtually ensure this outcome. Thus Europe will be studied against the non-European: Christianity against Islam; the native-born against the migrant. On the other hand, Europe exemplifies or shares trends with the world of advanced industrial and postindustrial economies: it is a locus for transformations that take place also in Japan and North America and elsewhere. These two great fin-de-siècle tendencies may indeed be in conflict; if so we shall witness not the clash of regional civilizations (to cite Samuel Huntington's prognosis) but the dialectic struggle between global postindustrial values and stubborn allegiances to province or land or faith that try to revalorize sites of local meaning.[67] History remains a struggle for boundaries, no longer particular national frontiers, but just the possibility of bounded territory as a matrix of allegiance. All the more reason for the continued centrality of history as a discipline, since, along with anthropology, it remains the social science (or quasi social science) most respectful of local knowledge and real places.

As historians, convinced of our own disciplinary contribution, we are prepared to explain why history must remain a privileged analytical tool. No one who has written a chapter in this volume will contest that the historian's armamentarium of documentation, causal narration (issues of *why* as well as *what*, answered by chains of sequential development), and contextualization (the relation of part to whole) are essential for understanding. And the contemporary historian remains committed to the claim that these tools are just as essential for nonclosed developments still under way. This does not mean that thoughtful journalists and historically minded political scientists cannot practice this enterprise. History is an eminently trespassable field.

Is there, then, at the end of the twentieth century no European history as such? We would suggest, in conclusion, that Europe has served as an important heuristic site precisely for historians working outside of Europe and most particularly across the Atlantic. (Asian historians will, however, probably find America equally instructive in the same way.) Europe is a place to see developments occurring that might be obscured at home. The United States has been easily identified with the very forces and processes of restless transformation, whereas Europe has been assigned the role (exaggerated and semimythic to be sure) of exemplifying persistence. Europe offers the clearest view of the dialectic conflict outlined above between a restless deterritorialization and the claims of the local, the provincial, the national and the regional. Just as Herzen in 1849 claimed that western Europe was the preeminent battleground between liberalism and reaction, one might claim that Europe today—eastern as well as western—is the major arena for the contest over territorially based identity. It would be foolish to renounce the explanatory resources of European sites and European history because they tend to erode before the advance of multiethnic societies and so-called globalization. Indeed, the more assaulted, the more revealing they shall be. American historians will return to or remain in Europe precisely to understand the great contests provoked by more universal historical changes. These changes may again lead historians to emphasize anew the roles of technology, demography, and political economy, which have tended in recent years to seem less compelling than interpretative approaches focusing on culture and ethnicity. The debate on the appropriate economic role of the state or the capacity of the market has already produced a European-American dialogue to which historians of the welfare state shall have a significant contribution to make. Of course, they will find European colleagues engaged in the same work, but we believe that American scholars will play a role of equal importance; for the task of historical explanation, interpretation, and representation will depend as much on comparative analysis as immersion in the local scene.

NOTES

1. See chapter 1 by Daniel Rodgers in this volume.

2. See, e.g., G. G. Iggers, *New Directions in European History* (Middletown, Conn., 1975).

3. To be sure, British history remained an idiosyncratic exception before 1950: it was often cultivated, not as a component of Europe, but as part of a joint Anglo-American narrative of liberal institutions and free people—a view that culminated with the common struggle in World War II and then began to pass into a genteel antiquarianism or eventually to find intellectual asylum in U.S. colonial history.

4. This may now be changing as more and more European scholars are anxious to have their works translated into English, the language that has increasingly become the means of global communication, not least due to the Internet.

5. P. Novick, *That Noble Dream: The "Objectivity Question" and the American Historical Profession* (Cambridge, 1988).

6. L. Krieger, "European History in America," in J. Higham, *History* (Englewood Cliffs, N.J., 1965), p. 258. Krieger's analysis still provides an excellent critical introduction to American historical writing on Europe in this early period. See also W. H. McNeill, "Modern European History," in M. Kammen, ed., *The Past before Us: Contemporary Historical Writing in the United States* (Ithaca, 1980), pp. 95–112.

7. Ibid., p. 270.

8. C. H. Haskins, "European History and American Scholarship," in *American Historical Review* 28, no. 2 (1923): 215, 226.

9. For details on this debate see, e.g., Novick, *Noble Dream*, pp. 206 ff.; J. W. Langdon, *July 1914. The Long Debate, 1918–1990* (Oxford, 1991), pp. 18 ff.

10. See, e.g., W. Jäger, *Historische Forschung und politische Kultur* (Göttingen, 1984), pp. 44 ff; K. Wilson, ed., *Forging the Collective Memory* (Oxford, 1996).

11. See F. Fischer, *Germany's War Aims in the First World War* (New York, 1967). See also Langdon, *July 1914*, pp. 66 ff.; J. A. Moses, *The Politics of Illusion* (New York, 1975).

12. Fischer radicalized his hypotheses in his second major book on the subject: *War of Illusions* (New York, 1973).

13. F. Stern, *Bethmann Hollweg und der Krieg: Die Grenzen der Verantwortung* (Tübingen, 1968); K. H. Jarausch, *The Enigmatic Chancellor* (New Haven, 1973).

14. See, e.g., J. Remak, ed., *The First World War* (New York, 1971); S. R. Williamson, Jr., *Austria-Hungary and the Coming of the First World War* (New York, 1990).

15. See F. Fischer, *From Kaiserreich to Third Reich* (New York, 1986).

16. H. Gatzke, *Germany's Drive to the West* (Baltimore, 1950).

17. E. Kehr, *Der Primat der Innenpolitik* (Frankfurt, 1970). On Kehr's influence in the U.S., ibid.

18. W. A. Williams, *The Tragedy of American Diplomacy* (New York, 1959); L. C. Gardner, *Economic Aspects of New Deal Diplomacy* (Madison, 1964), and idem, *Architects of Illusion* (Chicago, 1972); G. Kolko, *The Politics of War: The World and United States Foreign Policy, 1943–1945* (New York, 1968); also G. and J. Kolko, *The Limits of Power: The World and United States Foreign Policy, 1945–1954* (New York, 1972); and for a recent work in the same tradition, J. McCormick, *America's Half Century: United States Foreign Policy in the Cold War* (Baltimore, 1989).

19. For critiques of the "revisionist" version of the Cold War, see A. Schlesinger, Jr., "Origins of the Cold War," *Foreign Affairs* 46 (October 1967): 22–52; C. S. Maier, "Revisionism and the Interpretation of Cold War Origins," *Perspectives in American History* 4

(1970): 313–47; R. Tucker, *The Radical Left and American Foreign Policy* (Baltimore, 1971); J. L. Gaddis, *The United States and the Origins of the Cold War* (New York, 1972); V. Mastny, *Russia's Road to the Cold War: Diplomacy, Warfare, and the Politics of Communism, 1941–1945* (New York, 1979).

20. A. J. Mayer, *Political Origins of the New Diplomacy, 1917–1918* (New Haven, 1959), reissued as *Wilson versus Lenin*, and idem, *Politics and Diplomacy of Peacemaking: Containment and Counterrevolution at Versailles, 1918–1919* (New York, 1967).

21. The major collections of promptly published interwar documents included R. Sontag, J. W. Wheeler-Bennett, M. Baumont, et al., eds., *Documents on German Foreign Policy, 1918–1945* (Washington and London, 1949–), and E. L. Woodward, R. Butler, J. P. T. Bury, D. Dakin, and M. E. Lambert, eds., *Documents on British Foreign Policy, 1919–1939* (London, 1946). French records for the 1930s appeared much later, and material for the 1920s remained unpublished. See Ministère des Affaires Etrangères, *Documents Diplomatiques Francais (1932–39)* (Paris, 1963–).

22. Gordon Craig and Felix Gilbert, *The Diplomats* (New York, 1953).

23. H. Gatzke, *Stresemann and the Rearmament of Germany* (Baltimore, 1954).

24. G. D. Feldman, *Army, Industry and Labor in Germany* (Princeton, 1966).

25. J. Jacobson, *Locarno Diplomacy: Germany and the West, 1925–1929* (Princeton, 1972); C. S. Maier, *Recasting Bourgeois Europe: Stabilization in France, Germany, and Italy in the Decade after World War I* (Princeton, 1975); S. Marks, *The Illusion of Peace: International Relations in Europe, 1918–1933* (New York, 1976); W. A. McDougall, *France's Rhineland Diplomacy, 1914–1924* (Princeton, 1978); S. A. Schuker, *The End of French Predominance in Europe: The Financial Crisis of 1924 and the Adoption of the Dawes Plan* (Chapel Hill, N.C., 1976); M. Trachtenberg, *Reparation in World Politics: France and European Economic Diplomacy, 1916–1923* (New York, 1980).

26. J. M. Keynes, *The Economic Consequences of the Peace Treaty* (London, 1919).

27. Denna F. Fleming, *The Cold War and its Origins, 1917–1960*, 2 vols. (Garden City, N.Y., 1955).

28. H. Feis, *Roosevelt-Churchill-Stalin: The War They Waged and the Peace They Sought* (Princeton, 1957).

29. G. Alperowitz, *Atomic Diplomacy: Hiroshima and Postdam* (New York, 1965). Alperowitz's reading was vigorously contested. His critics argued that bureaucratic momentum and continuing fear of the huge casualties that the scheduled invasions of the Japanese home islands would cost fully explained the use of the bomb. Nonetheless, the question he reopened—why the United States resorted to such a weapon of mass destruction at a moment when the Japanese seemed slated for defeat—has continued to stimulate heated debate, most recently focused on the fiftieth anniversary exhibit of the Hiroshima raid that the Smithsonian Institution canceled after heavy pressure from veterans' organizations and members of Congress.

30. J. L. Gaddis, "The Emerging Post-revisionist Synthesis on the Origins of the Cold War," *Diplomatic History* 7 (summer 1983): pp. 171–90.

31. *The Cold War International History Project Bulletin* has appeared periodically since spring 1992.

32. J. L. Gaddis, *The Long Peace: Inquiries into the History of the Cold War* (New York and Oxford, 1987); M. P. Leffler, *A Preponderance of Power: National Security, the Truman Administration, and the Cold War* (Stanford, 1992); M. Hogan, *The Marshall Plan: America, Britain, and the Reconstruction of Western Europe, 1947–1952* (Cambridge and New York, 1987); R. F. Kuisel, *Seducing the French: The Dilemma of Americanization* (Berkeley and Los Angeles, 1993); also I. M. Wall, *The United States and the Making of Postwar France, 1945–*

1954 (Cambridge and New York, 1954); and C. S. Maier, "The Politics of Productivity: Foundations of American International Economic Policy after World War II," *International Organization* 31 (autumn 1977): 607–33; also Maier, "The Making of 'Pax Americana': Formative Moments of United States Ascendancy," in D. Ahmann, A. M. Birke, and M. Howard, eds., *The Quest for Stability: Problems of West European Security, 1918–1957* (Oxford, 1993), pp. 389–434. See also below, notes 59 and 60.

33. The influential journal *International Security* devoted a seventieth anniversary issue to the lessons of the 1914 crisis, later published as S. Miller, ed., *Military Strategy and the Origins of the First World War* (Princeton, 1985), and including among other contributions S. Van Evera, "The Cult of the Offensive and the Origins of the First World War," in vol. 9, no. 1 (summer 1984); see also M. Trachtenberg, "The Coming of the First World War, a Reassessment," *International Security* 15, no. 3 (winter 1990–91), and reprinted in Trachtenberg, *History and Strategy* (Princeton, 1991).

34. William Roger Louis, *The British Empire in the Middle East, 1945–1951: Arab Nationalism, the United States, and Postwar Imperialism* (Oxford, 1984).

35. See V. R. Berghahn, "Deutschlandbilder 1945–1965: Angloamerikanische Historiker und moderne deutsche Geschichte," in E. Schulin, ed., *Deutsche Geschichtswissenschaft nach dem Zweiten Weltkrieg, 1945–1965* (Munich, 1989), pp. 239–72.

36. Ibid.

37. Ibid.

38. F. Neumann, *Behemoth* (London, 1942); R. Brady, *The Spirit and Structure of German Fascism* (New York, 1937); H. Arendt, *The Origins of Totalitarianism* (London, 1951); B. Moore, Jr., *Social Origins of Dictatorship and Democracy* (Boston, 1967).

39. K. D. Bracher, *The German Dictatorship* (New York, 1970); M. Broszat, *The Hitler State* (New York, 1981); H. Mommsen, *Der Nationalsozialismus und die deutsche Gesellschaft* (Reinbek, 1991); A. Tasca, *Nascita e avvento del fascismo* (Florence, 1950); R. de Felice, *Il fascismo* (Bari, 1970); idem, *Mussolini* (Turin, 1965); A. Aquarone, *Il dopoguerra in Italia e l'avvento del fascismo* (Naples, 1967); H. Finer, *Mussolini's Italy* (New York, 1935); T. Mason, *Social Policy in the Third Reich* (Oxford, 1993); I. Kershaw, *The Hitler Myth* (Oxford, 1987).

40. See, e.g., the works by W. S. Allen, H. A. Turner, P. Hayes, and M. Kater. Only D. Abraham may be said to have had strong conceptual ambitions, but he got himself into trouble because of his use of sources. D. Abraham, *The Collapse of the Weimar Republic* (New York, 1984, 1989); on the controversy surrounding his book see the special issue of *Central European History* 17 (1984).

41. C. J. Friedrich and Z. Brzezinski, *Totalitarian Dictatorship and Autocracy* (New York, 1956). For a full and up-to-date discussion of the evolution of this debate see A. Gleason, *Totalitarianism* (Oxford, 1995).

42. Gleason, *Totalitarianism*, pp. 80–81.

43. See Arendt, *Origins*, passim.

44. C. J. H. Hayes, "The American Frontier—Frontier of What?" *American Historical Review* 51, no. 2 (1946): 199–216.

45. H. Rosenberg, *Bureaucracy, Aristocracy and Autocracy* (Boston, 1966), pp. 1f.

46. R. Palmer, *The Age of the Democratic Revolution*, 2 vols. (Princeton, 1959–64), and above, notes 18 and 19.

47. E. Nolte, *The Three Faces of Fascism* (New York, 1965). Title of the German original, more poignantly: *Der Faschismus in seiner Epoche* (Munich, 1965).

48. S. Lipset, *The Politics of Unreason* (New York, 1970); T. Parsons, *Political Man* (Baltimore, 1981).

49. W. Sauer, "National Socialism: Totalitarianism or Fascism?" in H. A. Turner, Jr., *Reappraisals of Fascism* (New York, 1975), p. 95.

50. Ibid., pp. 117–39.

51. R. Hilberg, *The Destruction of European Jewry* (New York, 1985).

52. H. Arendt, *Eichmann in Jerusalem* (New York, 1961).

53. See, e.g., I. Trunk, *Judenrat* (New York, 1977), and many works on Jewish resistance inside and outside the ghettos.

54. For the best summary of the various approaches and debates see I. Kershaw, *The Nazi Dictatorship* (London, 1985).

55. A. J. Mayer, *Why Did the Heavens Not Darken?* (New York, 1988).

56. D. J. Goldhagen, *Hitler's Willing Executioners* (New York, 1996).

57. R. Paxton and M. Marrus, *Vichy France and the Jews* (New York, 1981).

58. See especially D. K. Peukert, *The Weimar Republic: The Crisis of Classical Modernity* (New York, 1992).

59. See, e.g., F. Costigliola, *Awkward Dominion* (Ithaca, 1984); M. Nolan, *Visions of Modernity* (New York, 1995); see also C. S. Maier, "Between Taylorism and Technocracy: European Ideologies and the Vision of Industrial Productivity in the 1920s," *Journal of Contemporary History* 5, no. 2 (April 1970): 27–61; A. Rabinbach, *The Human Motor: Energy, Fatigue, and the Origins of Modernity* (New York, 1990).

60. For just a few of the diverse recent works which bring together the themes of modernity, mass culture, the social organization of labor and consumption, and the structuring of gender in the twentieth century, see Victoria De Grazia, *The Culture of Consent: Mass Organization of Leisure in Fascist Italy* (Cambridge and New York, 1981); also idem, *How Fascism Ruled Women* (Italy, 1922–45; Berkeley and Los Angeles, 1992); H. Chapman, *State Capitalism and Working-Class Radicalism in the French Aircraft Industry* (Berkeley and Los Angeles, 1991); P. Fritzsche, *A Nation of Fliers: German Aviation and the Popular Imagination* (Cambridge, Mass., 1992); S. Pedersen, *Family, Dependence, and the Origins of the Welfare State: Britain and France, 1914–1945* (Cambridge and New York, 1993); R. G. Moeller, *Protecting Motherhood: Women and the Family in the Politics of Postwar West Germany* (Berkeley and Los Angeles, 1993); R. Pommerin, ed., *The American Impact on Postwar Germany* (Oxford, 1995); H. Fehrenbach, *Cinema in Democratizing Germany* (Chapel Hill, N.C., 1995).

61. C. Walker Bynum, "The Last Eurocentric Generation," *Perspectives* 34, no. 2 (February 1996): 3–4.

62. J. R. Gillis, "The Future of European History," ibid., no. 4 (April 1996): 1–6.

63. E. Hobsbawm, *The Age of Extremes* (New York, 1994).

64. P. Fussell, *The Great War and Modern Memory* (Oxford, 1975). See also, e.g., M. Eksteins, *Rites of Spring* (New York, 1989); G. M. Mosse, *Fallen Soldiers* (New York, 1990); J. W. Winter, *Sites of Memory, Sites of Mourning* (Cambridge, 1995).

65. See chapter 4 by Dorothy Ross in this volume.

66. J. Habermas, *Communication and the Evolution of Society* (Boston, 1979); idem, *The Structural Transformation of the Public Sphere* (Cambridge, Mass., 1989).

67. See, e.g., B. Barber, *Jihad vs. McWorld* (New York, 1995).

CHAPTER 18

Clio in Tauris

AMERICAN HISTORIOGRAPHY ON RUSSIA

MARTIN MALIA

Oh old world! so long as you have not yet perished,

. . . .

Halt, perplexed, like Oedipus,
Before the Sphinx with its ancient riddle!

Russia is a Sphinx. Rejoicing and grieving,

. . . .

She stares, stares, stares, at you,
With hatred and with love.

For the last time—awake, old world!
To the brotherly feast of labor and peace,

. . . .

You are summoned by a barbarian lyre!

Aleksandr Blok, *The Scythians*, 1918.

IN THE SAME WAY that Russia under Communism was not "just another European country" but a world set provocatively apart, so American, and in general all Western, historiography about Russia in this century could not be the "normal" investigation of yet another European national story. After 1917, in the remote and mysterious new Soviet world—the land of the barbaric yet vital Scythians as the visionary poet, Aleksandr Blok, warned the "old world" of Europe—our familiar, classical Clio had to speak under constraints quite unknown in the established historiographies of the West. American and Western historiography on Russia was thus as firmly set apart in modern scholarship as was its subject matter in modern culture and politics.

This apartness had two aspects. The first was the ideological pretension of Soviet Communism to represent the "end of prehistory," as Marx put it, and the dawn of mankind's real history under Socialism triumphant. Nor was it possible to ignore or dismiss this pretension as some temporary revolutionary exaggeration. This was in part because of the existence of militant Communist parties around the world, and in part because of the power of the Soviet state; but it was due above all to the lure of the socialist ideal as the fullness of human equality, an ideal universal in its appeal because it was indeed an inescapable deduction from the premises of modern democracy. The familiar reasoning behind this deduction was that men could not be genuinely free so long as they were divided by differences of wealth, which are also differences of power; so the solution was socialism defined as the "abolition of private property," in the operative phrase of the Communist Manifesto, which meant also the suppression of profit and the market. Socialism, therefore, in its strong sense (as distinguished from the half-way house of social democracy, which keeps both the market and private property), meant full noncapitalism, and the transcendence of the entire previous human condition.

Thus the Soviet "utopia in power"[1] fed on the outside world's guilt at its own inadequacies, in conjunction with hope for a better future for which the new Russia might be a model. At the same time, however, the millenarian Soviet pretension frightened as many people as it attracted, for the Leninist "dictatorship of the proletariat" quickly hardened into totalitarianism at home, while after 1945 the Soviet superpower appeared to aspire to world hegemony abroad. And so, whether as a hope or as a menace, the Communist specter became an actor in the domestic politics of all other nations, and everyone had to take a position, whether explicit or implicit, about how to come to terms with it.

To be sure, a similar international polarizing influence may be claimed for Fascism and Nazism in the interwar period. Mussolini and Hitler had a few pocket imitators, and there indeed existed a diplomatic and military Axis after 1937 that no one could ignore or dismiss. But, except for some prominent ideological Western fellow travelers in the thirties and a few bands of skinheads today, this was an international magnetism of repulsion, not attraction, and it lasted only some twenty years, not seventy-four. The real international impact of such broad "fascism," rather, has been the reflex of "antifascism" in the Western democracies, a phenomenon assiduously exploited by the Communists from the mid 1930s onward to mobilize the liberal left and center by their side.[2] It is indeed a remarkable comment on the political culture of our century that fifty years after the disappearance of the last credible fascist regimes, "antifascism" should still be a mobilizing force in modern life. But perhaps this is not so remarkable after all; for the perennial antifascist reflex is emotionally the obverse of the egalitarian and fraternal hope expressed by the communist ideal, though hardly by Communist practice.

And so the red specter remained a universal presence without rival in our "short twentieth century" (as the standard expression now has it); and no American or Western historian could write about Communist Russia in wholly neutral or "value-free" fashion. Some measure of partisanship was unavoidable, and to pretend otherwise was either naiveté or hypocrisy. The real question is the manner and degree of inevitable partisanship in grappling with Soviet Russia. Since this issue is central to understanding any historical writing about both Communist Russia and its roots in the Old Regime, it is necessary to say a preliminary word about the assumptions in this article regarding objectivity and commitment in history.

In this regard, two pitfalls are to be avoided: radical positivism and nihilistic relativism. First, the social sciences are not the natural sciences, despite the misguided ambition of many social scientists to remake their disciplines on the prestigious model of the latter. This positivistic enterprise cannot work, if only because we are always part of the historical and social processes that we observe. Our contemporary values thus always enter into our historical judgments, and in this sense no historical writing can be absolutely "objective." On the other hand, this fact does not justify a certain postmodern absolute relativism that reduces the historical process to a series of equivalent "texts," without any corresponding objective "reality." Without entering into the now involved metaphysics of discourse, the position taken here will be that of the commonsense middle way, namely, that we can indeed know the past, albeit always imperfectly, and subject to the limitation that our perception of the past is always, in some measure, governed by our political and ethical concerns in the present.*

For it should be self-evident that the Soviet system was all too real, as was the challenge it represented to everything that was not itself. Historians working in societies that claim to be democratic, therefore, were constrained to some measure of partisanship, whether overt or covert, regarding Soviet Russia, a partisanship governed by their assessment of their own societies' record in realizing democratic values. And since the Communist pretension was so absolute, the normal space for suspended judgment or equivocation in assessing it was correspondingly diminished. To illustrate: it is possible for democratic American historians to write fairly dispassionately about the achievements of the Third French Republic or the succession of English Reform Bills, because these were never advertised as absolute or universal in their import, whereas the Soviets' millenarian "building of socialism" through Stalin's Five-Year Plans (capped by his purge trials) leaves little space between apologia and condemnation. Thus the first particularity of Western writing on Soviet Russia is not only that it could hardly be value-free, but that it was downright passion-prone.

The second aspect of the apartness of American historiography on Russia is of a professional rather than a political nature. For other European countries, the main burden of the historiography is borne by native scholars working within well-established national traditions and with privileged access to the sources. In this situation, American historians play largely a supporting or supplementary role, their work contributing to the national debate, often in very innovative fashion, but never supplanting that tradition. Thus John Baldwin's *The Government of Philip Augustus* is at the same time a major contribution in its own right

---

* Thus, the present overview of Russian history does not pretend to Olympian objectivity. Although the author's colors will become clear in the telling, it is best to state at the outset that his personal experience spans the whole of the crucial period of Russian studies in America, after 1945, and that he finds the efforts of social history "revisionism" since 1970, though often valuable in detail, to be misleading in the aggregate.

and a development of the insights and methods of the Annales school, as is Robert Darnton's *The Business of Enlightenment* for the French eighteenth century, and so on to Robert Paxton's pathbreaking, though more "*événementiel*," study of Vichy France.[3] Similarly, Americans have expanded on, or argued against, the Bielefeld school's thesis of a German *Sonderweg*, just as they have been an integral part of the British debates on whether the mid-seventeenth-century English turmoil was a revolution or simply a "crisis of parliaments"—that is, when major British historians, such as Lawrence Stone or Conrad Russell, were not actually practicing in the United States.

In the case of Russia, however, the native tradition for the past seventy-odd years was such that American and Western historians were given very little to work with, and so had to play an inordinately prominent, indeed primary, role in conceptualizing their field. The reason for this is, of course, that after 1930 there was a single, state-imposed interpretation of "the history of the USSR" (not just Russia) from the earliest times to the "building of socialism" in the 1930s, a subject presented teleologically as if all the peoples of the former Soviet Union were destined from the beginning to form a single, and socialist, state. Even in the 1920s, though there was not yet a Party line for all historical problems, the hegemony of the school of Mikhail Pokrovskii imposed on most historical writing a crudely reductionist, class-struggle interpretation, a perspective combined under Stalin with the new emphasis on the building of the Soviet Socialist state.

And this Soviet Marxist perspective was singularly ill-adapted to the particularities of Russia's actual development. Marx's scheme of history is a set of putatively universal generalizations from the standard Western European periodization of ancient, medieval, and modern history, a progression recast in socioeconomic terms to yield the succession of slaveholding, feudal, and capitalist societies. Imported into Russia, this scheme produces a not very credible slaveholding society in Kievian Rus to around 1100, an unmanageably long feudalism from Kiev to the emancipation of the serfs in 1861, and then a truncated capitalism from that date to 1917, a schematization that does violence to most of the real problems of Russia's *Sonderweg* in European history. Moreover, this socioeconomic periodization makes no sense when applied to Russia's "superstructure," which was uniformly autocratic during most of both "feudalism" and "capitalism," that is, from the sixteenth century to 1905. As if this conceptual straitjacket were not enough to stifle thought, another major impediment to a normal historiographical development in Soviet Russia was that under Stalin the archives for the modern period were largely closed, while from his death to perestroika they were only selectively open for Soviet scholars, and even more selectively for foreigners.

•

The conjunction of the ideological challenge of Soviet Communism with the conceptual deficiencies of its official historiography meant that American historians analyzing the Soviet Russian "enigma," as Churchill (unwittingly echoing Blok) famously described it, had to construct their discipline largely out of their own resources. This was all the more true since Russian studies everywhere in the West was a young discipline, but especially so in the English-speaking countries. In France and Germany reasonably well-developed Russian studies had emerged in the forty years before the First World War, a development due in part to French need of Russia against Germany on the one hand and to German fear of Russia on the other. Thus we have Anatole Leroy-Beaulieu and Alfred Rambaud in France and Otto Hoetzsch and Theodor Schiemann in Germany.[4] England was less precocious, producing the figure of Sir Bernard Pares only on the eve of the First World War. And all these European figures had direct contact with Russia and with Russian historians. America did not contribute significantly to Russian studies until after 1945. Once it began, however, the sheer size of the American academic plant, in conjunction with American leadership in opposing the post-war Soviet Union, soon made the United States the center of what would hence-forth be a steadily expanding Western scholarly endeavor. In other words, American historical writing about Russia developed massively just when the Soviet pretension appeared most challenging to the West, and at a time when direct contact with Russia and with Russian historians was impossible.

American historians of Russia reacted to the peculiarities of their situation in different ways for the prerevolutionary and the Soviet periods. Leaving the latter for subsequent consideration, we must note first that for prerevolutionary Russia they could, and largely did, ignore the Marxist conceptual grid of Soviet scholar-ship, and address instead the often rich empirical work produced by Soviet histo-rians, both for its insights on precise institutional, social, or other problems as well as for the archival material it contained and that was not otherwise available. In this respect, however, certain periods and problems of prerevolutionary his-tory were more favored than others. A rough rule of thumb is that the farther back one goes in time from 1917, the better Soviet scholarship becomes. Kiev was best of all—for example, as treated in the various works of B. D. Grekov on the medieval peasantry;[5] old Muscovy was next best (although the tsardom's role in creating a centralized state had generally to be praised); but from Peter the Great onward quality declined steadily as an increasingly rigid canon was developed for every significant problem, and for every major figure. By the time one reached the nineteenth century, anything to do with workers, peasants, or the revolutionary movement, especially if Lenin had once written a word on the subject, was tagged, either positively or negatively, with its obligatory cliché; thus the "gentry revolutionary" Aleksandr Herzen and the "revolutionary democrat" Nikolai Chernyshevskii had to be praised, whereas Mikhail Bakunin and the pro-peasant populists (*narodniki*) had to be condemned. And by the time Lenin himself emerged on the scene in the 1890s, we enter fully the domain of sacred history. From this date onward Russian history became the forward march of the revolu-tionary workers and peasants, always however under the leadership and direc-tion of the Leninist Party, to the Great October Revolution and the subsequent building of socialism.

Such an historiographical agenda, obviously, could be used only sparingly by American scholars. Since few of them worked in medieval or pre-Petrine Russia, the best part of Soviet historiography remained underutilized. American interest in Russia was focused primarily on the nineteenth and early twentieth centuries, where the Soviet canon was most rigid and sterile. This situation produced a mixed effect. On the one hand, the Soviets' agenda of topics, and the source materials they chose to publish, made the "history of the social movement" (*istoriia obshchestvennogo dvizheniia*: a term which includes everything from public opinion to reformist pressure to revolutionary activity) the central thread of modern Russian history—as indeed the events of the century before 1917 also easily suggest. On the other hand, the relentless Soviet reduction of politics and culture to a social base, and the slighting of the state and reform for the masses and revolution, gave to Russia's nineteenth century a more radical cast than it had at the time, and so fostered a kind of red whiggism leading the country "*zakonomerno,*" or "logically," to October 1917—a view that could easily rub off on Westerners working in the field.

Fortunately, however, Westerners had another resource on which to build, and that is the very rich historiographical tradition of imperial Russia. And it must be emphasized how rich and creative that tradition was, something all the more necessary since it is very little known abroad. Briefly put, Russian historical writing first came to maturity in the 1840s and 1850s with the "state school" of historiography, whose most prominent representative was Sergei Soloviev. Influenced by both Hegelianism and the German historical school of law of Friedrich Karl von Savigny, this school presented Russian history as a process of nation building through the "binding" of all social classes to state service and then their progressive "unbinding" to form a modern, law-based society. Its political implications were that the imperatives of constructing and safeguarding the Russian imperial state were such as to permit only gradual, state-initiated modernization from above, as in the Great Reforms of Alexander II, which were unfolding as Soloviev was producing the twenty-nine volumes of his *History of Russia from the Earliest Times.*

And this "unbinding" reached its culmination with the abolition of serfdom in 1861. The conditions thereby were created for the emergence of what may be called a populist or *narodnik* historiography, whose most prominent representative was Vasilii Kliuchevskii. Shifting the focus from the state to the people, Kliuchevskii presented Russian history as the colonization of a hostile environment by the peasants and their subsequent subjection to boyar and gentry lords, themes developed in a series of major works from the 1870s to the early twentieth century and of which his *A History of Russia* is the best known in the West. With this extensive corpus of writings and his numerous pupils, Kliuchevskii in effect created the modern field of agrarian social and economic history, thus putting Russia ahead of the European norm at a time when Western history was overwhelmingly political, institutional, military, and diplomatic.

Indeed, the school of Kliuchevskii soon became a major stimulus to the development of economic and social history in the West. One of his pupils, Paul Vinogradoff (later professor at Oxford and knighted), inspired the great English medievalist Frederick Maitland to produce his *Domesday Book and Beyond*, thus moving English historiography beyond preoccupation with the development of the constitution to the concrete life of society. At the same time, N. I. Kareev and I. V. Luchitskii initiated the study of the Old Regime French peasantry, thereby again inaugurating a shift from politics to society and preparing the way for Georges Lefèbvre's recasting of the history of the French Revolution. Finally, in the early twentieth century another pupil of Kliuchevskii, Michael Rostovtseff, created almost single-handed the field of the economic and social history of the ancient world. Indeed, Russian populist historiography had as much to do with launching European social and economic history as did Marxism, whose major influence did not come until after the First World War.[6]

But the main achievements of the Old Regime Russian historical school lay, of course, in Russian history itself. To mention only two names, there is first Sergei Platonov, whose comprehensive *Lectures on Russian History* is available in French translation as *Histoire de Russie* and whose major study of medieval Russia is available in English as *Time of Troubles: A Historical Study of the Internal Crisis and Social Struggle in 16th and 17th Century Muscovy;* there is perhaps no better example of the fusion of political and social history in any European language. On the same level is Paul Miliukov, whose works on the reforms of Peter the Great and the history of Russian culture were pathbreaking in their day and remain major accomplishments even now, a contribution which may be sampled, along with that of other pre-1917 liberal historians, in his three-volume *Histoire de Russie.*[7]

Although other names could be cited, the point is that late imperial Russian historiography ranked with the best that turn-of-the-century Western Europe, from Maitland to Lavisse to Meinecke, had to offer. At the same time, however, it should be noted that, as with Soviet historiography, the best of this tradition is concerned with the centuries from Kiev to Catherine the Great. After that period, quality begins to decline, as we move toward the then delicate subjects of modern reform and the progress of the "social movement." Moreover, until the Revolution of 1905, Russia had censorship: such basic documents as Vissarion Belinskii's incendiary "Letter to Gogol" of 1847 or the works of Herzen or Chernyshevskii could not be published in Russia, and anything to do with sovereigns from Catherine the Great onward had to be treated with the utmost tact. The short period of modern freedom from 1905 to 1917 was not enough to overcome these handicaps, and for all practical purposes Old Regime Russian academic historiography stops with the end of the reign of Alexander II in 1881.[8]

•

It is with these materials that, after 1945, fledgling American historians of Russia had to begin to construct their field. Since Soviet historiography was of little help, the novices' principal resource was living contact with émigré Russian historians professionally trained under the Old Regime—most notably George Vernadsky, the son of the last pre-Soviet rector of Moscow University, at Yale, and Michael Karpovich, the nephew of the eminent Petersburg historian Aleksandr Presniakov, at Harvard. Both were aided in the work of transmitting prerevolutionary culture by such other émigrés as the outstanding linguist and literary scholar

Roman Jakobson, or the economist Alexander Gerschenkron, and in a more informal way by Menshevik and Socialist-Revolutionary (SR) exiles in New York. For the development of Russian history as an academic discipline, however, the most important of these living contacts was Karpovich, whose seminars of 1947 and 1948, totaling some twenty individuals, produced most of the first generation of American historians of Russia, who then trained the next generation, which is now producing its own students.[9]

The intellectual importance of this vicarious contact with Old Regime Russian historiography was not the transmission of a subject matter, since most American historians of Russia worked on the nineteenth and twentieth centuries, not on the earlier periods perferred by the Russian school. What was transmitted, rather, was an attitude toward Russian history for *any* period, an attitude of mixed intellectual sobriety and cultural sympathy toward a subject that could all too easily appear either barbaric or exotic, whether as the eternal Oriental despotism believed in by much of American public opinion, the hopeful utopia advocated by John Reed and Trotsky's *History of the Russian Revolution*, or the fount of deep spirituality offered by Nikolai Berdiaev. Instead, the differences between Russia and the West were presented, as they appear in most of Russia's grand historiography, as "differences of degree, not of kind," as Karpovich liked to put the matter.

The result of this contact between Old Regime Russian culture and the postwar American mega–graduate school was twenty years of research and publications on Russian politics, institutions, and thought, with a special emphasis on the "social movement," for the eighteenth and nineteenth centuries. Until around 1970, Soviet history was largely left to the political scientists, the economists, and an occasional sociologist. One reason the first generation of American historians of Russia focused on late imperial political and intellectual history was that until almost 1960 research in Russia was impossible, and even after that date research on the Soviet period was inordinately difficult. But an even more important reason was that in the two decades after the Second World War, political and institutional history was largely what people still did, in all historical fields. Economic history, of course, was also practiced, but it was never considered the key to, or the "base" of, all the rest.

It is easy now to forget how revolutionary it appeared in the late 1930s when such figures as Crane Brinton advocated injecting sociology into history, and tried his hand at the task himself by using Vilfredo Pareto to establish an "anatomy" of modern revolutions.[10] Just as easy is it to forget how bold and daring Arthur Lovejoy's launching of the "history of ideas" appeared in the same period, or when G. M. Trevelyan took to practicing "social history," defined as "history with the politics left out." Indeed, it is only in the late 1930s that American sociology assumed mature form in the work of Talcott Parsons, and that history itself was "sociologized" on a large scale by the Annales school of Marc Bloch and Lucien Fèbvre. And it was only after the Second World War that separate faculties of social sciences emerged first in American, then in European, universities, thus promoting those disciplines to the rank of one the three great provinces of

human learning, alongside the humanities and the natural sciences. But the results of this escalation of sophistication took time to spread throughout the various fields of history, and in the meanwhile politics and high culture enjoyed
pride of place, as they had from Herodotus and Thucydides to Ranke and
Meinecke.

And this was just as well for the fortunes of Russian history in America, for
what that field needed in its postwar *Grundzeit* was a reliable sketch of the main
lines of political and high cultural development from Peter the Great to the end
of the Old Regime. By and large, this task was accomplished in about twenty
years through a series of significant studies in the political, administrative, and
intellectual history of those two centuries. In this development, intellectual history perhaps played a proportionately larger role than in American studies of
other European countries because of the centrality in Russian life of the "social
movement," from Aleksandr Radishchev and the Decembrists to the Great Reforms of Alexander II, to the Kadet (liberal), SR (neopopulist), and Marxist parties
of the beginning of the twentieth century.[11]

The premise of most of this literature was that Russia after Peter had become
a European Old Regime, simpler, poorer, and more brutal than those of the West,
but a variant of European absolutism nonetheless. And the central problem of
interpretation this literature addressed, often explicitly and almost always implicitly, was: could the Russian "social movement," and the nation's constant oscilla-
tion between reform, reaction, and the threat of revolution, a process which culminated a first time in the "constitutional experiment" of 1905–17—could this
process, if it had not been interrupted by the brutal intervention of the First
World War, have brought Russia to a fully European modernity in constitutional
democracy? Or in other words, could Russia have avoided Bolshevism? These
questions, of course, were not, and could not have been, answered conclusively;
but a solid structure of research and debate was established within which the
field could continue to develop. Just as important, this effort produced a body of
literature to which thoughtful and independent Russian historians, chafing under
the Soviet ideological grid, have often looked as a space of freedom in which their
own cultural tradition was able to grow in exile.

Then, as time passed, the gap between Western and Soviet historical writing
on Russia, well-nigh absolute until Stalin's death, slowly began to narrow; for
after 1960 Western graduate students were able to do research in the Soviet
Union, and with this came direct contact with Soviet reality and with the diversity of Soviet scholarship behind the facade of obligatory obeisance to the "classics of Marxism-Leninism." Schematically put, on the one hand, there were the
"orthodox," such as P. V. Volobuev, who, though empirically scrupulous, remained within the conceptual canon as defined by those "classics" and who eventually formed working relations with certain American social historians.[12] On the
other hand, there were those who might be called positivists, whose credo was to
stay away from politics and ideology, from all broad generalizations and interpretations, and to stick scrupulously to the facts as these are revealed by the archives.
Here the great name is P. A. Zaionchkovskii, whose corpus of writings ranges

from the Emancipation of 1861 to the end of the century, and whose message (for he was not just a positivist) was that the Russian Old Regime was in fact making progress in solving its problems. Finally, for pre-Petrine Russian history there was the radically innovative figure of A. A. Zimin, who moved beyond the Soviet canon to alter significantly our understanding of old Muscovy.[13] These figures, and other, nonorthodox Soviet historians had a highly beneficial influence on visiting American scholars.

•

Prolonging the Old Regime Russian tradition abroad, however, could not remain central to the Western discipline indefinitely, nor was the help of the nonorthodox wing of Soviet historiography enough to counteract fully the ideological grid of the dominant Soviet tradition. The only solution therefore was to develop Russian history in America by adapting new Western methodologies and strategies of research to Russian problems and data. And it so happened that the postwar decades witnessed a revolution of sophistication and a diversification of subfields in Western historiography unprecedented since nineteenth-century positivism had tried to make history "scientific."

Broadly speaking, this development may be characterized as a turn away from politics and high culture to social history, though not in any sense that Trevelyan—or even the populist Kliuchevskii—would have recognized. The social history involved was primarily the history of what once would have been called the lower classes, but which were now viewed as the exploited, the oppressed, the dominated, the victims, or in general the excluded of the political establishment chronicled by Clio's classic modern votaries: the Rankes, the Lavisses, the Macaulays—or the Solovievs—of their respective traditions. This social history of the lower orders, moreover, was to be analyzed with the full panoply of the methods, models, and approaches of the now proliferating social sciences.

Obviously, this great endeavor, no more than earlier history, could hardly be "value-free" in any literal sense of that term, an exercise in understanding for understanding's sake in the way that Galileo and Newton reputedly worked. Although the best of this effort was motivated by a desire to expand our horizons of historical understanding, in particular with the Annales school's social, demographic, and anthropologized explorations of the *longue durée* of Western European history, many of the successive waves of the new social and "cultural" history, particularly as we move into the *courte durée* of modernity, also had the civic agenda of promoting "human emancipation" from the inequalities, servitudes, and exclusions of the past. Indeed this was inevitable in a society committed to democratic values, and in view of the fact that we cannot really separate our roles of observer and observed in the historical process.

Thus, as the postwar American equilibrium gave way to the activist sixties, the academic historical agenda moved progressively from class to race to gender; and this trio had its negative counterparts in those systems of oppression that were capitalism, racism, and patriarchy. Similarly, on a theoretical level the role of primary "demystifier" of these oppressive systems devolved from the prophet of the proletariat, Marx, onto the Frankfurt school's critics of Enlightenment (i.e., bourgeois) culture, to the critic of humanist (i.e., bourgeois) discourse, Michel Foucault, and, latterly, to the critic of culture as (bourgeois) class-capital, Pierre Bourdieu.

This intellectual transformation of the advanced countries could not fail to have a decisive impact on the historiographical fortunes of backward Russia. To be sure, the older tradition of political history, emphasizing the totalitarian nature of the Soviet regime, continued to produce important works, notably Robert Conquest's pathbreaking study of the purges of the 1930s, *The Great Terror*, and Richard Pipes's various books interpreting Soviet totalitarianism as an updated form of inveterate Russian "patrimonialism," in which the ruler is proprietor of the land and its inhabitants (a polity more usually called "Oriental despotism").[14] But this political approach no longer represented the "cutting edge" of the discipline; for after 1970, American historians of Russia shifted their focus from the state and its opponents among the intelligentsia to workers, to women, and to the popular culture of the masses, or *narod*.

These new approaches, when applied to the last century or so of the Old Regime, on the whole produced enriching results. The working class (putatively slated to come to power in October 1917) received priority attention, particularly with respect to its embarassingly recent origins in the peasantry; this latter class was also, though much less frequently, investigated in its own right; and this subject in turn raised the matter of the political role of the peasant army in 1905 and in the First World War.[15] At the same time, women's history first emerged as a subdiscipline, as did popular "culture," by which is meant the mores and mentalités of the relatively uncultivated, thus making it in fact another form of social history.[16] In short, the turn to social-cum-cultural history had the same effect for Russia that it did for other modern European nations: it fleshed out beneficially the existing political, administrative, and "high" cultural tableau. Still, it is difficult to see that it shed much new light on what remained the central issue of Russian history after the 1860s, namely, how the crisis of the Old Regime would work out.

•

Quite different were the consequences of this turn to social history for the analysis of Soviet Russia. This period at last began to be examined by historians around 1970, that is, just at the moment of the social-history breakthrough. But the techniques of American social history, particularly labor history, changed their meaning when applied to the Communist story; for seeking the key to history in its social dimension finally brought Western historians into interaction with the class-struggle and reductionist ideological grid of Soviet scholarship. A perhaps unintended result of this interaction was that Western methodological sophistication and empirical scrupulosity wound up serving to tell the Communist story more effectively and plausibly than the Soviets themselves ever did.

This outcome was facilitated by the fact that for the Soviet period American historiography was far less a national enterprise than for the Old Regime. Indeed, long before the Americans got started, Isaac Deutscher and E. H. Carr in England had staked out the Soviet field on a monumental scale, the former with a lyrical

Trotskyite vision of the Revolution betrayed-but-not-destroyed, and the latter with a blandly stated, factually meticulous exposition of the unavoidable travails of building socialism in a backward country, a perspective which in fact amounted to a justification of Stalin's Five-Year Plans.[17] So preponderant was this philo-Sovietism in Britain that the chief dissenter, Leonard Schapiro, confronted with Carr's obstruction at home, was able to get his first book published only in the Cold War United States.[18] Carr's enterprise was continued after his death by Robert Davies of the University of Birmingham, an institution which would later welcome two of the leaders of the next generation of Soviet historians in America, Moshe Lewin, who arrived from a wartime background in Russia and academic training in Paris, and Sheila Fitzpatrick, who came from Australia to do her doctorate in the shadow of Carr's monumental opus.

It was in this international context that American historians entered the Soviet field. They started with the revolutionary year 1917, then (after somewhat slighting the coercive War Communism of 1918–21) moved on to the quasimarket New Economic Policy, or NEP, of the twenties, and finally, in the 1980s, began to explore the troubling Stalinist thirties. The political scientists, economists, and sociologists were not driven from the field, but for the first time the historians came to dominate its activities; what actually emerged from this interaction was a symbiosis of the disciplines, as we might expect in the now mature American social-science culture. Although for the period after 1939 the historians once again largely left the Soviet story to their social-science colleagues, this is of secondary importance in understanding their role in Soviet history overall; for the twenties and thirties were the formative period of the Soviet system such as it would endure, in its basic structures, until 1991. And for this formative period, especially for the years 1917–33, the historians made a very impressive contribution on an empirical level, outclassing most other social scientists and going well beyond the Soviet historians. Thus the main factual outlines of the early years of the Soviet regime are now far clearer than they were before the turn to social history.

The great issue with which this social-science, or "revisionist," history was concerned was the displacement of the "totalitarian model" with "modernization" theory, often interlaced with Marxism, as the key to understanding Soviet society. And this "paradigm shift" was also a debate—sometimes articulated explicitly, almost always assumed implicitly—about the Soviet system's capacity to reform itself, after the excesses of Stalinism, in a more democratic direction. As such, the Sovietological problematic was a kind of updated replay of the historical profession's earlier concerns with the capacity of the Russian Old Regime to transform itself short of revolution.

Concretely, the "totalitarian model" held that the ideological Party-state molded an "atomized" society coercively from above, and the "modernization model" argued that socioeconomic forces had first generated from below the Bolshevik revolution and then confronted it with all the problems of backwardness that would thereafter plague its course. The totalitarian model, which until the mid-1960s dominated Russian studies in America (though hardly, as we have seen, in Europe), was objectionable to the "revisionists" on two grounds. First, it was abstract and a priori, reducing the complexity of the Soviet experience to a one-way process of the control of society by a monolithic Communist Party. Second, this model was considered to be, in fact, a means of mobilizing Western opinion to fight a dangerous and unfair Cold War against the Soviet Union. On both scholarly and civic grounds, therefore, this model had to be combated by a vigorous dose of what was presented as a value-free, positivistic concern with the facts, and nothing but the facts.

Now, both of these accusations are half-true—which is also to say that they are half-false as well. The original totalitarian model, as developed while Stalin was still in power by such figures as Hannah Arendt, Zbigniew Brzezinski, and Merle Fainsod, indeed turned out, under the softer rule of his successors, to be incapable of detailed empirical elaboration to depict a society totally controlled from above by Party power. This does not mean, however, that totalitarianism did not retain its validity as an ideal type, or norm, or Platonic form, to which the system constantly tended, though always imperfectly; and it is in this sense that the East European dissidents took up the term just as it was becoming taboo in Western Sovietological circles. As for the Cold War, the label "totalitarianism" did in fact play a role in designating the adversary; yet we should not forget that the contest itself was no mere product of Western malevolence, or of some failure of communication, but a very real conflict between two genuinely incompatible worldviews and social systems. Though after 1945 the stakes of this contest were no longer world proletarian revolution, they were, schematically put, the expulsion of American power from Eurasia and Soviet hegemony over its neutralized components. What has already emerged from the Soviet archives makes it amply clear that the international policies of the Communist regime were pretty much what Western "cold warriors" took them to be.[19]

Given this agonistic context, American revisionist history of Communist Russia could only be a mixed scholarly-political enterprise, both an empirical effort to flesh out the Soviet record and an ideological effort to "de-demonize" the Soviet adversary. And both efforts entailed showing that the Soviet system was not an unchanging and monolithic regime but an evolving and diversified society, as Russia's slow and halting de-Stalinization after 1953 seemed to indicate. In short, what the revisionist challenge to the totalitarian model was ultimately about was the defense of the Soviet system's capacity to reform itself democratically without ceasing to be socialist.

The first step of the revisionist enterprise was to rehabilitate the October Revolution, which the totalitarian school considered a "coup d'état," as a genuine proletarian revolution. This rehabilitation had still another purpose, which was to challenge Soviet orthodoxy by showing that the Party was less a leader than a follower, and thus to take 1917 back from Lenin and return it to the workers, a Menshevik position more palatable to Western democratic taste than the official Bolshevik one. This rehabilitation was putatively achieved by a meticulous investigation of strike actions and worker pressure on the Party leadership interpreted as indices of class "polarization"—an enterprise which, indeed, showed mounting worker radicalism in 1917. This empirical effort, however, simply begs the conceptual question of whether the progression from "bourgeois" to "proletarian" revolution is a meaningful way of organizing Russian (or any other) history; and this of course is the real question.[20]

Now it is indisputable that in Russia in 1917 there was a great social revolution (social breakdown would be a more accurate term) in the midst of which the Bolshevik Party seized power; and it is also indisputable that the discourse of "proletarian revolution" was that of the Bolshevik leaders, and that at the time this discourse had significant appeal among the workers and in the army. But in view of the equally indisputable fact that the most palpable result of this revolution was the creation of a Party-state which monopolized power for seventy-four years, it is now simply quaint to maintain that October brought the "proletariat" to power, or that the Party dictatorship was in any meaningful sense a "workers' state." Such a view is essentially a product of Marxist metahistory. Its basic premise is qualified acceptance of the Bolshevik substitution of the Party dictatorship for the real proletariat, as this premise was refined by the sociological sophistication of the New York Mensheviks—a conflation that was further strengthened by the populist bent of the new Western social history, as well as by such Western Marxist concepts as E. P. Thompson's "moral economy of the working class." And the resulting social metaphysics had an implicit long-range ideological purpose: to give working-class legitimacy to the Soviet enterprise overall, and thus to situate it, for all its defects, in a grand logic of History leading to Socialism.

With the October base secure, then came the problem of the "defects," which meant above all Stalin: Was his rule an aberration from, or a fulfillment of, the Leninist promise? And on this great issue the revisionists divided. A majority, most notably Moshe Lewin and the political scientist Stephen Cohen, held to the aberration thesis, which, synoptically put, runs as follows. The West's failure to take up the torch of October left the Bolsheviks isolated in a backward, largely peasant country, and therefore obliged to resort to some degree of "developmental dictatorship"; Trotsky advocated a hard, aggresively "industrializing" version of this policy, and Bukharin advanced the softer course of conciliating the peasants thereby "growing into socialism through the market." Unfortunately, both lost out to the man of brute power, Stalin, who produced a caricature of Leninist socialism with the crash industrialization and forced collectivization of that "revolution from above" called the First Five-Year Plan. Nonetheless, this school concludes, Stalin had at least put a modern "base" under the dangling "superstructure" of the Party, and so someday the new "urban, industrialized, and educated" Soviet society would democratize the Party, and thus, at last, create "socialism with a human face"[21] Matters, of course, were not put so baldly by the revisionists themselves, but this is what their discourse in fact comes down to.

A minority of the revisionists, however, most notably Sheila Fitzpatrick and the political scientist Jerry Hough, were more forthright and consequential in their acceptance of the harsh realities of "developmental dictatorship": if Stalin's rough methods were required to modernize Russia, then they, too, were part of the logic of Leninism and of the building of socialism under backward conditions. Indeed, this argument went, his "revolution from above" was a response to a "cultural revolution" against the "bourgeois" NEP launched from below by Party activists and class-conscious workers; and the resulting transformation of these workers into Stalin's cadres was a great feat of upward "social mobility." As for the peasants, they to be sure suffered greatly; but the most notable aspect of their story is that their resistance forced the regime to "negotiate," eventually even to surrend control of individual plots to their erstwhile owners. The purges of 1936–38, for their part, were no more than a "postscript," a "final bout of revolutionary fever," their victims numbering under a million (not the twenty million talked about by such cold warriors as Robert Conquest). Indeed, the meaningful course of the Revolution had really been completed, following the First Five-Year Plan, by the "Thermidorian stabilization" of 1934–36. For had not Crane Brinton shown that such a consolidation occurs in all revolutions?[22]

Now although a plausible Thermidor can be found in most revolutions before October, Brinton himself, in postwar editions of his classic, had second thoughts and tried to accommodate the obvious anomaly of the Russian case by calling it a "permanent revolution." Indeed, at the time of the supposed Soviet Thermidor the Bolshevik-Jacobins still had fifty-five more years of purge, Gulag, and totalitarian power ahead of them—all of which is enough to make the reader wonder who are the real Scythians of this fable, and who is singing to a "barbarian lyre."

As the grand implosion of 1989–91 indicates, however, neither school of revisionists got the dynamic of Soviet development right; and both, it must be concluded, failed because of their common premise that Soviet history was primarily the expression of socioeconomic forces acting from below. For this premise could only lead to an irresolvable paradox, which goes as follows: Although Russia made an authentic proletarian revolution, the backward peasant country unfortunately was "not yet ready for socialism," as the Mensheviks were the first to insist; yet since socialism was too good a goal to abandon, some measure of forced industrialization became a necessity to preserve the "conquests of the Revolution." Within this common Grand Paradigm, the various strains of revisionism would play at theme and variation.

In the majority current of revisionism, Trotsky, the proponent of a measured industrialization, was the first candidate for resolving this paradox in conformity with "true" socialism, and Bukharin, the defender of cooperation with the peasantry, was the second candidate; and when both lost, their legacies entered the historiography as putative continuations of October that would have permitted Russia to avoid Stalin. This position offered its partisans the consolations of belief in an ultimately democratic Leninism, but it also left them eternally waiting for Godot—until Gorbachev's failure showed that Godot did not in fact exist. The minority current of revisionism faced a reverse dilemma, for when Stalin actually "resolved" the paradox, the cost in coercion and terror turned out to be so great that his record could be incorporated into a Marxist developmentalism only selectively. Thus the first version of the common paradigm could not afford to confront real Soviet history in its culminating phase; and the second version could confront this phase only in truncated form. And so neither was positioned to account for the system's collapse in 1989–91, when the bill for ideologically driven, developmental dictatorship at last came due.

One way to explain the revisionists' failure to grasp the paradox of their position is that their Grand Paradigm was a legacy from successive losers of the Revolution—the Mensheviks, Trotsky, and Bukharin—as this legacy was elaborated by Western social-science refinement. Yet all these losers, despite their defeat, remained committed to that Revolution, and so also to the belief that the logic of history, and of democracy, led to socialism; in this perspective, therefore, the blame for the deformations of Soviet socialism, and the defeat of its "best" leaders, lay not with Marxist socialism as such but with Russian backwardness.

But this is only a priori "historiosophy" with a social-science face. For if socialism means, as it clearly does in the Marxist tradition, integral noncapitalism, to be achieved by the complete abolition of private property, profit, and the market, then there is no reason other than faith to believe that the logic of history culminates in such a clean sweep of existing society. Thus, if the maximalist socialist goal is not to be abandoned, the hand of history must be forced by a special political instrument—the Party—an agency defined, not by its social composition, but by its ideological commitment to achieving full Socialism. But forcing the hand of history by a permanent act of political will and in the name of an unattainable social goal is ultimately an impossible endeavor. So when the authoritarian Plan eventually led to economic decline, thereby unmasking the promises of the ideology to outproduce "capitalism," the system lost its means of legitimation. With this gone, the Party lost its will to coerce, and so the whole Soviet enterprise collapsed with stunning rapidity.

And this view from above does, indeed, account for the constant deformations and the ultimate failure of the Soviet adventure. The old-fashioned term for such a perspective is "totalitarianism," in the ideal-typical sense of the primacy of ideology and politics over economic and social forces: a primacy that did in fact exist in the Soviet Party-state, with its "command-administrative" economy, mandatory comprehensive ideology, and omnipresent political police. Thus the Soviet world can be understood only as an upside-down world, a "looking-glass" world as its dissidents used to say, in which the regime had in truth produced the society and not the other way around, as in normal national systems. American social-science historiography, however, by proceeding on the contrary assumption, wound up getting the Soviet world *really* upside down, and so failed ultimately to understand it.[23]

•

Consequently, when Gorbachev's perestroika unexpectedly brought the Soviet edifice tumbling down, the dominant Western social-history perspective so closely linked to it ought logically to have been called into question. Thus far, however, although there has been some vague talk of "reconfiguration" in the field, there is little sign of a reexamination of the crucial issue, namely, the social-history premises of the past quarter century and their record as applied to the explanation of the Communist "experiment." Rather, the main reaction of the profession so far has been to change the subject: the new avant-garde subjects of the field are the non-Russian nationalities of the former Soviet Union and local history within Russia itself.

Now this new direction is quite worth following in its own right, but it should not lead us to forget the enormous unfinished business at the heart of the field. For the Russian Empire and the Soviet-Party state remain, and will remain, the principal historical entities of their common geographical area; and the principal historiographical problems of that area remain, and will remain: why did the Russian Old Regime ultimately produce the Soviet "experiment"; and then why did that experiment work out so disastrously? Thus, someday Russian history in America will have to return from the nationalities on the periphery to the Russian center, and to its tragic fate. In the meantime, the field is living through what will probably be a prolonged interregnum.

This hiatus is all the more unfortunate since in Russia, too, history is living an interregnum; the scholarly profession, like everything else in the country, must be rebuilt. The old Soviet historical establishment, as typified by Volobuev, who is still editing books about the workers in 1917, by and large retains institutional power. Younger scholars, however, are beginning to produce monographic works in a positivistic, nonideological vein on limited subjects in both Old Regime and Soviet history; their methodological position is that the day for new, large-scale syntheses is as yet far off, and that in the meantime the principal task is to fill in the "blank spots" of the Soviet past. At the same time, these scholars often look to the West for models, just as, in the immediate wake of Communism's collapse, Russians generally looked westward for political and economic models. For the Soviet period of their history, unfortunately, these scholars will find abroad only too much of their own recent tradition, at least as matters now stand. For the history of the Old Regime, however, these scholars have the more promising recourse of building bridges back to their own prerevolutionary tradition; and in this process Western scholarship—political, intellectual, and social—on old Russia can play a role. Nonetheless, Russian historians themselves will eventually have to make up the largely lost seventy-odd years; and until this great gap is filled, Clio will remain a half-hostage to the Soviet Scythians.

As for Russian history in the West during the present interregnum, younger scholars start with advantages that were quite unknown to the first generation of the field, in the years following the Second World War. For these younger scholars, Russia is no longer a fearful or exotic enigma. They have usually made lengthy stays in the former Soviet Union; they know the language well and have extensive experience of the society. Nor is interaction with Russian historians, at least the younger among them, any longer a problem. And their research interests now range over the "FSU's" eleven time zones, from St. Petersburg to Vladivostok, in a manner inconceivable before 1991, let alone in the wake of 1945. As for those of them who have not turned from the center to the periphery, finally, they are no longer hung up on Communism's "reformability" or the sins of the Cold War, and so are beginning to produce studies that will, at last, permit us to dig the historiography of the Soviet period out "from under the rubble," in Solzhenitsyn's famous phrase regarding the Communist experience as a whole.

NOTES

1. The title of the first disabused overview of Soviet history: Mikhail Heller and Aleksandr Nekrich, *Utopia in Power: The History of the Soviet Union from 1917 to the Present*, trans. Phillis B. Carlos (New York, 1980).

2. This theme has been developed extensively by François Furet, *Le passé d'une illusion: essai sur l'idée communiste au XXème siècle* (Paris, 1995).

3. See John W. Baldwin, *The Government of Philip Augustus* (Berkeley, 1986); Robert Darnton, *The Business of Enlightenment* (Cambridge, 1979); and Robert Paxton, *Vichy France* (New York, 1972).

4. Anatole Leroy-Beaulieu, *L'empire des tsars et les russes*, 3 vols. (Paris, 1885); Alfred Rambaud, *Histoire de Russie* (Paris, 1886); Theodor Schiemann, *Geschichte Russlands unter Kaiser Nikolaus I*, 4 vols. (Berlin, 1904–19); and Otto Hoetzsch, *Katharina die Zweite von Russland*, first published in the Cambridge Modern History collection in English (Cambridge, 1909), and *Russland, eine Einführung auf Grund seiner Geschichte vom japonischen bis zum Weltkrieg* (Berlin, 1917).

5. B. D. Grekov, *Kiev Rus* (trans. in Moscow, 1959).

6. See especially Vasilii Kliuchevskii, *A History of Russia*, 3 vols. (London and New York, 1911–31), and Mikhail Rostovtseff, *Iranians and Greeks in South Russia* (Oxford, 1922). See also Terence Emmons, "Kliuchevskii's Pupils," in *California Slavic Studies*, vol. 14 (Berkeley, 1992).

7. See especially Sergei Platonov, *Histoire de Russie* (Paris, 1929), and *Time of Troubles: A Historical Study of the Internal Crisis and Social Struggle in 16th and 17th Century Muscovy* (Lawrence, 1970). P. Miliukov, L. Eisenmann, and Ch. Seignobos, *Histoire de Russie*, 3 vols. (Paris, 1932).

8. For the turn of the century down to 1914, however, there are important extra-academic works of history, usually produced by members of oppositional political parties. See A. A. Kornilov, *Modern Russia* (New York, 1916), first published 1912–13, and the Menshevik five-volume study of Russian society in 1905, *Obshchestvennoe dvizhenie v Rossii v nachale XX-go veka* (St. Petersburg: Obshchestvenaia pol'za, 1909–14).

9. For the beginnings of this "Karpovich generation," see George Fischer, Martin Malia, and Hugh McLean, eds., *Russian Thought and Politics*, Harvard Slavic Studies, vol. 4 (Cambridge, Mass., 1953).

10. Crane Brinton, *The Anatomy of Revolution* (New York, 1938).

11. A few of the works in this tradition are Nicholas V. Riasanovsky, *Nicholas I and Official Nationality in Russia, 1825–1855* (Berkeley, 1959); Richard Pipes, *Struve: Liberal on the Left, 1870–1905* (Cambridge, Mass., 1970); Marc Raeff, *Michael Speransky: Statesman of Imperial Russia* (The Hague, 1957); Martin Malia, *Alexander Herzen and the Birth of Russian Socialism, 1812–1855* (Cambridge, Mass., 1961); Terence Emmons, *The Russian Landed Gentry and the Peasant Emancipation of 1861* (Cambridge, 1967).

12. See, for example, P. V. Volobuev, *Proletariat i burzhuaziia Rossii v 1917 godu* (Moskva, 1964), and *Petrogradskii sovet rabochikh i soldatskikh deputatov* (Leningrad, 1991).

13. See for example, P. A. Zaionchkovskii, *The Abolition of Serfdom in Russia* (Gulf Breeze, Fla., 1978), and A. A. Zimin, *The Oprichnina of Ivan the Terrible*, in Russian (Moscow, 1964).

14. Robert Conquest, *The Great Terror* (New York, 1968; Oxford, 1990); and Richard Pipes, *Russia under the Old Regime* (New York, 1974), and *The Russian Revolution* (New York, 1990).

15. A few works in this tradition are Reginald Zelnik, *Labor and Society in Tsarist Russia: The Factory Workers of St. Petersburg* (Stanford, 1971); Alan Wildman, *The Making of a Workers' Revolution: Russian Social Democracy, 1891–1903* (Chicago and London, 1967); Wayne Vucinich, ed., *The Peasant in Nineteenth-Century Russia* (Stanford, 1968); Alan Wildman, *The End of the Russian Imperial Army*, 2 vols. (Princeton, 1980–87); John Bushnell, *Mutiny and Repression: Russian Soldiers in the Revolution of 1905–1906* (Bloomington, 1985); Gregory Freeze, *The Parish Clergy in Nineteenth-Century Russia: Crisis, Reform, Counter-reform* (Princeton, 1983), and *Description of the Clergy in Rural Russia* (Ithaca, 1985).

16. A few works in this tradition are Richard Stites, *The Women's Liberation Movement in Russia: Feminism, Nihilism, and Bolshevism, 1860–1930* (Princeton, 1978); Jeffrey Brooks, *When Russia Learned to Read* (Princeton, 1985); Laura Engelstein, *The Keys to Happiness: Sex and the Search for Modernity in Fin-de-Siècle Russia* (Ithaca, 1992).

17. The principal relevant works of Isaac Deutscher are *Stalin: A Political Biography* (1949, 1966); *The Prophet Armed: Trotsky, 1879–1921* (1954); *The Prophet Outcast: Trotsky, 1929–1940* (1963); all volumes published in New York by Oxford. The principal relevant works of E. H. Carr are *A History of Soviet Russia*, vol. 1: *The Bolshevik Revolution, 1917–1923*, 3 vols. (1951–53), vol. 2: *The Interregnum, 1923–1924* (1954), vol. 3: *Socialism in One Country, 1924–1926*, 3 vols. (1958), with R. W. Davies, vol. 4: *Foundations of a Planned Economy, 1926–1929*, 2 vols. (1969–79); all volumes published in New York by Macmillan. Carr's position is stated succinctly in his *The Russian Revolution: From Lenin to Stalin* (New York, 1979).

18. Leonard Schapiro, *The Origin of the Communist Autocracy* (Cambridge, Mass., 1955).

19. David Holloway, *Stalin and the Bomb* (New Haven, Conn., 1994).

20. A few of the key works on this subject are Leopold Haimson, "The Problem of Social Stability in Urban Russia, 1905–1917," *Slavic Review* 23 (1964): 619–42, and 24 (1965): 1–22; Daniel Kaiser, ed., *The Workers' Revolution in Russia, 1917: The View from Below* (Cambridge, Mass., 1987); and Alexander Rabinowitch, *The Bolsheviks Come to Power: The Revolution of 1917 in Petrograd* (New York, 1978).

21. The principal relevant works are Stephen F. Cohen, *Bukharin and the Bolshevik Revolution: A Political Biography, 1888–1938* (New York, 1973); Moshe Lewin, *The Making of the Soviet System: Essays in the Social History of Interwar Russia* (New York, 1985), and his *The Political Undercurrents of Soviet Economic Debates: From Bukharin to the Modern Reformers* (Princeton, 1974).

22. The principal relevant works of Sheila Fitzpatrick are Sheila Fitzpatrick, ed., *Cultural Revolution in Russia, 1928–1931* (Bloomington, 1988), especially the editor's introduction; *The Russian Revolution* (New York, 1982 & 1994), especially the final chapter; *Stalin's Peasants: Resistance and Survival in the Russian Village after Collectivization* (New York and Oxford, 1994). The principal relevant work of Jerry Hough is Jerry F. Hough and Merle Fainsod, *How the Soviet Union Is Governed* (Cambridge, 1979). This book turns on its head Merle Fainsod, *How Russia Is Ruled* (Cambridge, 1963), which offered the classic statement of the totalitarian model.

23. This critique of social-history revisionism is developed extensively in the author's *The Soviet Tragedy: A History of Socialism in Russia, 1917–1991* (New York, 1994). For a similar position, see Andrzej Walicki, *Marxism and the Leap to the Kingdom of Freedom: The Rise and Fall of the Communist Utopia* (Stanford, 1995).

CHAPTER 19

House of Mirrors

AMERICAN HISTORY-WRITING

ON JAPAN

CAROL GLUCK

CROSSED EXCEPTIONALISMS

In the geocultural scheme of things, here, I suppose, is the non-West. One might wonder at the inclusion of but a single chapter on what Barraclough once called "extra-European history" in a volume whose theme is presented as "the end of American exceptionalism." Perhaps it is not quite over. Apart from the national narrative, the normal nesting place for exceptionalism in every country, the essays here also reveal an expansive America-centrism, which was capable of co-opting large chunks of the world's past, from ancient Greece to the Renaissance, as part of a telos of History that led to these United States. Europe—as Americans imagined it—became part of America's past. It also constituted, until quite recently, most of what was taught as "world history" in the schools. The combination of a central enterprise in American history complemented by the study of its European antecedents and anti-models made perfect historical sense for a nation both proud and ambivalent about its newness. That American universities have long paid greater attention to extranational history than did their counterparts in places like France derives from this distinctive mix of conflicting national emotions. When it comes to history-writing, it seems that all cosmopolitanisms resemble one another, but each parochialism is parochial in its own way. And America's parochialism (like Japan's) often operated by seeing its national self in the reflection of others.

The European reflection was there from the earliest defining moment. Most of the rest of the world hove into American historical view much later and into the academy in a significant way only after the Second World War. Although it is institutionally customary to lump the histories of Asia, Africa, the Middle East, and often even Latin America into one great, undifferentiated "non-West," all "area studies" were not created equal. Because postwar history drove historiography, U.S. foreign relations made China and Japan loom larger than India, the Middle East more salient than Africa, and the Soviet Union more riveting than the for-decades-disappeared past of Eastern Europe. The regions also created their own differences. At a meeting of my assigned departmental subcommittee in the 1980s, I was asked which third world country I represented. Thinking of the then

triumphing Toyotas and the brand-name excesses of Tokyo's Gucci capitalism, I
sheepishly muttered "Japan"—and no one laughed. In this respect an essay on
Japanese history written in the United States cannot stand for other Others,
which despite commonalities of Cold War funding and disciplinary marginalization possessed historiographical characteristics of their own.[1]

Because these subjects took their place in the universities when America stood
at an unprecedentedly powerful, globally engaged moment in its history, their
teleological links to the United States often inverted the European narrative. If
Europe was America's past, America was Asia's future. The earlier transatlantic
movement of civilization would continue westward across the Pacific, its icons of
liberty and democracy now reframed in the twentieth-century language of economic and political development. Like a newly energized Hegelian world spirit,
American-style modernization appeared as the avatar of universal history, against
which the pasts of the not-yet-modern could be measured. As the export model
of U.S. exceptionalist history of the 1950s, modernization theory took the American exception and made it the world's rule.[2] And although this imperial historiography echoed earlier British and French views of the undercivilized, its mid-
twentieth-century field of operation was less magisterially absolute. The Japanese
had strong notions of their future and the way the past affected it, and they
possessed a contentious modern historiography, which had long wrestled with
the notion of modernity as a global phenomenon that must nonetheless find
authentic national inflection. In such a context American historians could not
write Japan without Japan writing back. The result was the meeting of two exceptionalisms, one American, the other Japanese.

The meeting did occur. Here perhaps lies another contrast to earlier American
historians of Europe, who often labored as if in adjacent vineyards to their counterparts in the countries that they studied. They may have shared the same stock
and made the same wine, but American vintages rarely made it to the high table
of another nation's historiography. For a long time the balance of footnote trade
weighed heavily in Europe's favor. With notable exceptions such as the oft noted
work of Robert Paxton on Vichy France and the greatly expanded transnational
interchange of the past two decades, American historians ran citation surpluses,
in which they were usually the quoters, seldom the quoted from. This is partly
because national histories tend by definition to be either uninterested in or im-
pervious to outside scholarship. Not so in Japan, which has fed its exceptionalism with an unrelenting interest in the opinions of foreigners. It is as if the American interest in Tocquevillean insights were raised to the tenth power, and then
doubled. As a result, the works of American historians frequently appear within
the frame of Japan's national history, published in Japanese translation and on
occasion generating heated controversy in the field. Indeed, in the 1960s Japanese historians working in the dominant Marxist tradition mounted a decade-
long defense against American "modernization theory." These progressives
formed an intellectual phalanx to prevent scholars like Edwin O. Reischauer and
John W. Hall from transforming modern Japanese history into a success story of
evolutionary change, thereby to their mind depriving Japan of all revolutionary

potential on its way to becoming like midcentury America. To this day "the challenge of modernization theory" figures prominently in accounts of history-writing in postwar Japan.

At the time this challenge seemed primarily a difference of Cold War politics. But of course the volatile relations between Japanese progressive and American liberal historians had colonial aspects as well. After the end of World War II, Japan and the United States found themselves locked in a relationship in which asymmetries of power had the usual consequences in asymmetries of knowledge. American historians showed no interest whatsoever in the way Japanese depicted American history. But Japanese historians, committed as most of them were to progressive politics, could not ignore the ideological challenge of American views that, in league with Japan's conservative establishment, seemed to them to be driving Japanese history in just the wrong direction. Thus a long-standing national sensitivity to foreign opinion combined with Japan's position in the American Cold War imperium to guarantee U.S. historians an audience for their books that was occasionally larger in Japan than it was at home. Until well into the 1980s, and sometimes beyond, many Americans regarded Japan as an exotic lotusland, a fanatic aggressor, or both, but remote in any case. For Japanese the United States was everything they both wanted and did not want to be, and they could not ignore its cultural and political presence, which loomed as large as a dinosaur in the front garden.

And so it seems that the transpacific asymmetries between Japan and America resembled the earlier transatlantic mixed feelings between America and Europe. Despite the difference in historical context and contacts, Japanese attitudes toward the United States betrayed the combination of attentiveness and ambivalence that had long characterized American views of Europe. Japan, like the United States, wielded comparison as a master technique in the production of national identity. Of the many possible routes to exceptionalism, both countries fashioned their historical incomparability not by dismissing other histories but by examining them first—and then dismissing them.[3] From the beginning of the professionalization of history, which occurred in Japan at roughly the same time as in the United States in the late 1880s and 1890s, Japanese universities also devoted considerable energy to the study of extranational histories. And while Americans studied what they would later call Western civilization, Japanese studied the same thing. In the mid-1890s the new academic discipline was divided into national history (Japan), Eastern history (Asia without Japan), and Western history (primarily Europe), a division that a century later remains anachronistically in place. The point of course was to highlight national distinctiveness by separating Japan from backward Asia and aligning it with the civilized West.[4] In the 1870s general "histories of civilization" had already reversed the Hegelian direction of history, making it move from West to East, from Rome to Japan. Now Japanese took the civilizational slights they suffered at the hands of the West and transferred the condescension to Asia. Japanese exceptionalism thus saw itself reflected in not one but two mirrors: Asia was its past, "Euro-America" its future, and Japanese history was imagined as connected to, but different from, them both.

This insistence on difference affects all writing about Japan, whether domestic or foreign, the one feeding the other in a seemingly endless loop of "Japaneseness." Part of it is cultural essentialism, like the Spanishness of Prescott's paradigm, except that it emanates (in both its good and bad senses) as much from inside Japan as from outside. A glance at any history of Japan in any language will reveal the ubiquity of the adjective "Japanese," as if historians were incapable of writing a sentence about peasants or capitalists without modifying them as *Japanese* peasants or *Japanese* capitalists. Another part of the insistence on difference emphasizes deviation from some universal norm, whether the distorted modernity stressed by Japan's Marxist historians or the distinctively smooth modernization admired by American historians in the 1960s. Sometimes this focus on difference amounts to an exemption from the processes of history. In his famous footnote claiming that Japanese feudalism gave "a much truer picture of the European Middle Ages than all our history books," Marx exempted Japan from the history of Asia as he saw it. In 1990 Eric Hobsbawm took the exemption further when he wrote that "Japan, though patently *sui generis*, could be considered an honorary western imperial power."[5] If one of our best historians considers Japan to be "in a class by itself," the chances for postexceptionalist history-writing might seem rather dim.

In fact, I think the world is turning. Historians everywhere are more aware of the ethnocentrisms they are subject or subjected to. Or at least they are talking about them, as is evidenced by the frequent allusions to exceptionalism in this book. A sketch of American history-writing on Japan may serve to test this change in the interaction between two strong national histories that have long honed their respective exceptionalisms in the reflection of others. Thrown together in a transpacific relationship that in the twentieth century took turn after turn for the worse, the United States and Japan emerged from World War II as allies, newly intertwined with the kind of intensity that former enmity sometimes confers. As a result Americans came to dominate the Western-language history-writing on Japan, outproducing and outpublishing nearly everyone except for the Japanese. Seen from Japan and Europe, the history they wrote was "very American," both in its politics and poetics, not to mention its "English-language imperialism." Was it any less American in the midnineties than it had been in the midfifties, or had the exceptionalisms crossed again but in a fashionably late-twentieth-century way?

THE CANONICAL CHRONOLOGY

A simple, rather too simple, chronology has become standard in nearly all Japanese (and some American) accounts of Japan studies in the United States. Japanese speak of "three generations," Americans prefer "three phases," and both have now to consider a fourth.[6] From the 1930s to the 1990s each generation/phase operated under the influence of multiple contemporary contexts.

The politics of Japanese-American relations established the historical foreground. Binational swings between hostility and amity drove the development of the field, with amity arousing scholarly interest but hostility having by far the greater institutional effect. War impelled much of the funding to train Americans in the study of Japan, first as wartime enemies, then as Cold War allies against a common communist foe, and later as rivals in a Japanese-American trade war. But the angle of interpretive sight was always refracted by where the historians stood in the domestic political landscape of their time, whether in the establishment or on the streets. Scholarly debates followed the fault lines of American politics, from the postwar myths of consensus through the 1960s experience of conflict to the identity politics of the 1990s. The scholars also, unsurprisingly, followed American historiographical trends, so that their postwar work looked positively positivistic to their committed Marxist counterparts in Japan. And this was no accident either, since American historians, who were always refining, rebutting, or exploiting Japanese historiography, for years wrote against Japanese Marxist scholarship, which had a politics and historical method of its own. As cultural nationalism waxed in Japan through the eighties, the Americans began to deconstruct the nation, now appearing to Japanese conservative historians as discourse revolutionaries and subversive multiculturalists. In each generation, phase, or age, American writing on Japanese history thus stood in a multiple optic, overdetermined by binational politics and historiography and seeing both itself and its subject reflected in the transpacific house of mirrors.

Since the 1870s a handful of American sojourners, missionaries, and the usual assortment of avid amateurs had written respectable histories of Japan. As the "mikado's empire" rose to power (war, especially the Russo-Japanese War of 1904–5, again providing the focus of attention), a few universities on the East and West Coasts appointed Japanese nationals to posts in Far Eastern history. The most notable was Asakawa Kan'ichi, who in 1906 began his long career at Yale, where he largely taught European feudalism for lack of student interest in his own subject, the feudal institutions of premodern Japan. The 1920s brought a period of relative amity marred by moments of acute hostility, in particular the exclusion of Japanese by the Immigration Act of 1924. That same year, in the liberal political mood of the time, the first chair of American history was established in Japan. Its holder, Takagi Yasaka, became active in the American-led international Institute of Pacific Relations (IPR), founded in 1925, and Japanese language programs began to appear at a small number of American universities.[7]

But to the United States, the Far East had always primarily meant China, now its "sister republic" across the sea. As Japan embarked on its aggressions of the 1930s, informed opinion, like the IPR itself, tilted politically toward China. The axiom of U.S. attitudes toward Asia holds that at a given moment Americans are drawn either to China or to Japan: when one is in, the other is politically, and emotionally, out. It comes as no surprise then that émigré scholars did not occupy the position of importance that Europeans did in developing European history in the United States. Racial exclusion combined with souring international relations, a general lack of interest in Asia, and when Asia, then China, to keep Japanese from transplanting their historical tradition into the American academy. When the first canonical generation of more or less professional Japanese historians emerged in the 1930s and '40s, they were all North American.

They were, however, a particular kind of North American, autobiographically impelled to the study of Japan by a prior, and deep, connection with the country. As missionary sons, Robert and Edwin Reischauer and the Canadian E. H. Norman were what was known as BIJ (born in Japan); Hugh Borton was a Quaker who had taught in Tokyo; and the British doyen of the field, Sir George Sansom, was a diplomat in Japan. These five figures constituted nearly the entire "first generation" of English-writing Japan historians. Their work transmitted the two main trends of Japanese scholarship of the 1930s: in Borton and Norman, the Marxist analyses of a peasantry oppressed by feudalism and of an incomplete revolution in 1868 that resulted in an authoritarian imperial state; in Sansom and the two Reischauers, the empirical and descriptive narratives of early Japanese history that characterized "positivist" historiography in Japan.

Because of the war, this tiny band had a profound effect on history itself. Turning from scholarship to what Edwin Reischauer later called "more immediately useful work in Washington," Borton and Reischauer participated in the State Department planning for the occupation of Japan.[8] Borton had a great deal to do with preventing the Japanese emperor from being deposed, or worse. And after the war Sansom, Norman, and Reischauer agreed, against strong opposition among the Allies and nearly everyone else, that the imperial institution should be retained. While Treasury Secretary Morgenthau was threatening to turn postwar Germany into farmland, the pacifist Quaker historian and one or two other Japan hands quietly planned for radical democratic reform to be carried out under the emperor. Products of liberal or left politics of the 1930s, the first-generation scholars both knew Japan and also believed that it could change. They intended to examine the structural pathology that underlay fascism and imperialism, whether in "the emergence of the modern state" or the "shame culture" of Japanese social psychology. For if one adds the anthropologist Ruth Benedict to this unlikely cast of scholarly characters, the premises of occupation reform are indeed complete. *The Chrysanthemum and the Sword*, her famous study of Japanese national character undertaken for the Office of War Information, exhibited both the anthropological culturalism of the day and the American faith that underneath the "patterns of culture," people everywhere were basically the same. Hence the Japanese, too, could change, and the Americans would be there to see to it that they did. True to the house of mirrors, Japanese progressive historians shared many of these same premises. In the immediate aftermath of war American and Japanese scholarly views of the imperial past sounded as if synchronized on issues like the feudal landlord system and the authoritarian state, though certainly not on the matter of retaining the emperor system, which the Japanese Left opposed. In a rare case of applied history the postwar reforms under the occupation were directly based on these views, which sought to make the future into the image of a harshly drawn anti-past.

Enter the second generation of Japan scholars. Trained in wartime military language schools for the sake of conquering the enemy, they then chose to study a country that fate had brought into their ken. By another autobiographical stroke, the group, including Japanese-Americans, who went to fight the Japanese came home to found a field. War and occupation produced a critical mass of Japan scholars who joined their predecessors, Borton, Sansom, and Rei-schauer, in entrenching the study of Japan in the American academy. Just as World War I had expanded the presence of "Western Civilization" in college curricula, World War II brought forth "area studies" as the institutional expression of the need for Americans to get up to global speed on the world they felt they now had to manage. Postwar times favored the efforts of historians like John King Fairbank and Edwin O. Reischauer, the patriarchs of Harvard's "rice paddies" course, to develop the East Asian field.[9] Between 1945 and 1960, funding from U.S. foundations and, later, from the government made it possible to develop Asian studies as an educational enclave, protected from the indifference of the mainstream disciplines and committed, in more ways than one, to the support of American–East Asian relations. In short, war generated the manpower, and postwar international relations supplied the mandate for the study of "foreign areas."

Because postwar was also Cold War, the founding generation of Japan historians has been roundly criticized both for the Americanism and anti-Marxism that characterized their approach to modernization and also for their support of the postwar Japanese-American alliance. These allegations, while not untrue, elide the formative political moment. Historians such as John Whitney Hall, Marius B. Jansen, Thomas C. Smith, and others who completed their dissertations in the late 1940s and 1950s were products less of the Cold War than of the Pacific War, or as some call it, the Japanese-American War. That is, they came of Japanological age during the postwar emergence of the "new Japan," and their own politics inclined most of them toward small-*l* liberal and small-*d* democratic ideals in the context of a fairly large-*A* Americanism. While this description fits many a cold warrior, it also captures the stance of the wartime and occupation cohort who believed in the virtue of America and the capacity of Japan to become virtuous in a similar direction.

These scholars were optimistic about Japan's future and consequently about its past as well. Their historiographical anti-Marxism derived not only from the "nonideological" language of postwar American social science carried in the ambient winds of the Cold War but also from their reluctance to fasten mainly on the failures of Japan's modern history. They considered Japanese progressive historians altogether too negative and doctrinaire about the possibilities of the past and its contribution to postwar peace and democracy. For fifteen years they contested E. H. Norman's left-liberal work on the origins of the Meiji state (which had been translated into Japanese in 1947 to the acclaim of progressive scholars), endeavoring to show in masterful detail that Japan's nineteenth-century "political leadership was less traditional, conservative, and oligarchic than Norman had implied."[10] Where Norman and the Japanese progressives concentrated on the causes of prewar catastrophe, the American historians sought the sources of postwar rebirth. Focusing on the modern period, they renamed the late feudal Tokugawa era (1600–1868) "early modern" and found in it the origins of political stability and economic growth.[11] In the Meiji Restoration of 1868 they saw not a failed bourgeois revolution but a successful systemic transformation.[12] In comparison to the "grand continental proportions" of China and the "influential religious traditions" of India, they encountered (or invented) "a story of modest but continuous political and social development, a development in fact that appeared increasingly parallel to that of Western societies the more it was studied."[13]

Here the teleology of postwar America-centrism—the world on its way to becoming "more like us"—joined the ideology of Cold War international relations. The United States was always already modern, whereas Japan, even Japan, was always modern*izing*, never fully modern. But it was at least modernizing in the right direction, as opposed to the socialist societies on the other side of the Cold War. By 1960, when some thirty Japanese and Western scholars of various political convictions gathered at Hakone to initiate what became known in the United States as the "modernization series" of conference volumes and in Japan as the "challenge of modernization theory," the rift between Japanese progressives and their American colleagues became an open controversy. Despite the diversity of position among the participants, the politics of the U.S. Japan field had become mainstream 1950s-style Americanism, with almost no Left left in it.[14] The Hakone conference took place the same summer as the violent Tokyo protests against the U.S.-Japan Security Treaty, which strained Japanese-American relations and marked a generation of young intellectuals in Japan in much the same way as 1968 did in Europe. When Reischauer, a participant at Hakone, was appointed ambassador to Japan in 1961, it seemed to many Japanese progressives that the link between American history-writing and Cold War politics was complete.

In their "attempt to devise a unified and objective conception of modernization," the American scholars at Hakone had hoped to uncouple modernization from Westernization. Japan's modernity could then be rendered as part of a worldwide process, without insisting on invidious comparisons with the West. In their definitional discussions the group met this worthy goal largely by replacing Marx with Weber and then suggesting the virtues of comparison, only to conclude that "the over-all pattern of Japan's modernization defies easy categorization (other than the very obvious one of being a late modernizer.)"[15] In the subsequent history written under the sign of modernization in the 1960s, Japanese exceptionalism often entailed a favorable comparison with China, which had "failed" where Japan had "succeeded" in response to the challenge of the West. Meanwhile, on the seesaw of general American attitudes toward Asia, Japan was up and China was down, its Maoism and Cultural Revolution less beguiling than the Tokyo Olympics and Japan's double-digit growth rates. Both fields of study grew during the 1960s, and by 1970 there were 110 historians teaching Japanese history in American colleges and universities.[16] Puny numbers perhaps, but considering that only 25 Ph.D.s were completed in the first postwar decade, the "second generation" of Japan historians had produced both an impressive body of scholarly work and also a new generation of students of Japan.

That generation, the third, proceeded to commit the intellectual parricide by which the scholarly world so often lurches from one received narrative to another. This group, my own, owed its emergence doubly to war, though not quite in the ways envisioned. Cold War anxieties of the post-*Sputnik* sort resulted in the National Defense Education Act of 1958, which funded a new generation of area-studies scholars who attended graduate school through the sixties and seventies. Politicization during the Vietnam War soon turned a number of them against the Cold War context that their knowledge had officially been intended to serve. They were in a sense the first self-selected cohort of Japan scholars, whose choice of field was not autobiographically determined by missionary parents or military service. Women began to appear in the Japanological preserve. An in-between group of slightly older historians who entered graduate school in the 1950s, some of whom had served in the Korean War, became masters to these younger apprentices, so that leading scholars like Tetsuo Najita, Harry D. Harootunian, and others first learned from the wartime generation and then taught those who criticized them.[17] Not that every Japan scholar trained in the 1960s was a historiographical rebel, any more than every one of their predecessors had been a practitioner of modernization theory. But as in other precincts of American history-writing, the rebels broke the postwar consensus and changed the angle of interpretation.

The immediate politics of the shift turned on the rejection of America's arrogation of Asia into its imperial sphere. The United States was charged with having treated the postwar Pacific as an "American lake" and Japan as its junior partner in Cold War geopolitics.[18] John W. Dower pointed out, more politely than some, that "much American scholarship on Japan has tended to be congruent with the objectives of the American Government," which he identified as "the twin pillars of counterrevolution and support of a capitalist mode of development."[19] This stance signified an American return to the Left, now newly New, in activist pursuit of change both in the government's objectives and in scholarship about Asia.[20] In this Asianist version of the revisionism that arose in American scholarship more generally, the main issues were U.S. imperialism, ethnocentrism, and the abuses of modernization theory. It also included the commitment to view the history of U.S.-Japan relations from both archival and political sides.[21] Japanese progressive historians, who had already reproduced themselves into the next generation, welcomed the unaccustomed political support from across the American lake. By the time the concerned Americans began to publish in the 1970s, Japan had already moved into its decade of deepening "conservatization," so that now Americans and Japanese often stood together against the trend of the political times.

In a telling political paradox, funding also began to shift from American to Japanese sources. Foundations like Ford and Rockefeller, which Japanese progressives regarded as the next thing to the CIA, had carried the field in the early postwar decades. The U.S. government, whose National Defense Foreign Language Fellowships once required students to sign a loyalty oath, invested heavily in the sixties and early seventies. And although these grants, minus the loyalty oath, still existed in the midnineties, their numbers were sharply reduced. In their stead, beginning in the 1970s Japanese monies began to come to the American academy from corporations and from the government-run Japan Foundation, which in one ten-million-dollar stroke in 1973 gave professorships in Japan studies to ten American universities (my own position among them). So it was that the cohort of scholars most critical of U.S. and Japanese Cold War policy flourished even as the money, which had earlier come from Washington, began to flow from Tokyo. By the 1990s, had it not been for Fulbright grants, American dissertation and postdoctoral research in Japan would have been funded almost entirely by Japanese sources. And those scholars who vocally continued to criticize this situation belonged, most of them, to the politically active "third generation."

Like their colleagues in other fields, this generation of Japan historians had responded to the sweeping winds that shifted the American political sands since the 1960s, which changed a great deal more than attitudes toward international relations. The critique of modernization history, for example—defined by its enemies and denied by those who were said to have practiced it—spread beyond the immediate political context that generated it to affect most American history-writing on Japan. During the 1970s and 1980s scholars questioned the linear teleology that had Japanese history moving toward a mirror of American modernity. They also objected to its extension in the notion of Japan as a model for the no longer "underdeveloped," now "developing," societies. In search of the "underside of modern Japan," they darkened the bright picture of a smooth and successful national transformation with the shadows of the costs of rapid modernization.[22] Where others had found consensus, they highlighted conflict, "the neglected tradition," producing a decade's worth of rigorous historical inquiry into social protest, political opposition, and ideological dissent.[23] The spate of "conflict volumes," as they came to be known, may have peaked in the mid-1980s, when, in a field that annually produces only scores of titles, four important monographs on peasant rebellions appeared within eighteen months.[24] In such books the label of "early modern" often reverted to the less teleological "Tokugawa era," as if to leave historical options open and not prematurely "modernize" the past. E. H. Norman's works were reprinted, and in studies by Harootunian and others, the Meiji Restoration became a revolution once again, a historical rupture rather than an evolutionary "transformation." Even when scholars cultivated the same historical ground as earlier they were clearly tilling with a different plow.

One sees the Western historiographical trends of the times in their work: history from below, the new social history, ideology as a cultural construction, the critique not only of modernization but of modernity itself. By the mideighties much of the radical politics of the early antimodernization arguments had moderated into a general "post-modernization" view of Japanese history without losing the emphasis on contestation and critique.[25] American historians now did most of their own scholarly slogging through the texts and the archives, no longer processing the work of their Japanese colleagues as had inevitably been the case in the early days of Borton and Norman and, to some extent, even in the collaborative American-Japanese projects of the second generation. But, ironically, the changes in both politics and historiography meant that their work often had more in common with the scholarship of the Japanese progressives than when their predecessors had strip-mined the empirical data from the Japanese secondary literature, taking care to leave the Marxist bedrock behind.

The greater irony, however, lay in the fact that the conservative turn among Japanese intellectuals since the 1970s brought the concept of modernization sudden respectability in some sectors of Japanese scholarship. Overturning any pretense of comparability, the new version of modernization history celebrated the Japanese past not only for its historical success but also for its national uniqueness. This historiographical crisscrossing in the transpacific house of mirrors raised a new challenge. Postwar historians like Hall and Reischauer had come to their arguments for the specialness of Japanese history from the basis of what they hoped was a definition of modernity (or feudalism, and so on) that was non-Marxist but still general enough to be common, even universal. After the 1980s historians felt themselves confronting a national(istic) narrative that would remove Japan to a realm all its own, an exceptionalism gone again to excess. At the same time Japanese-American trade relations made it increasingly popular in the United States to regard Japanese capitalism as utterly different from the "normal" kind, which is say, the American kind. Surrounded by exceptionalisms on both sides of the water, scholars who explained Japan in comparative context sometimes appeared to be defending it, earning them the mark of "Japanapologist" on their political foreheads. Historians who had trained themselves to think of Japan as an instance of historical modernity commensurate with other such instances, from Korea to France, found themselves walking a thin edge between the Orientalist cliffs of cultural condescension (which now encompassed any Euro-universal, including Marxism) and the abyss of a recidivist cultural essentialism, which explained things by labeling them genetically "Japanese." Godzilla meets Ruth Benedict: American history-writing on Japan seemed forever trapped in the particularities of the two countries' relationship with one another.

And yet the 1995 survey of Japan studies in the United States (funded of course by the Japan Foundation) reported dramatic growth in the field and something the American sociologist who compiled the data called "the loss of irrelevance." No longer an exotic field on the fringe of the academy, Japan had been "mainstreamed," implying that the field had escaped the protective enclave of area studies and moved into the real world of the disciplines and professions.[26] Considering the growing vocal antipathy toward "local knowledge" in departments of economics, sociology, and political science, this conclusion may seem dubious. But it was true in history and the social sciences that the term "Japanology" had become archaic among its practitioners and that most recent work was driven by disciplinary rather than area concerns. Although Japan historians in North America still numbered in the hundreds, they taught in, and identified themselves with, history departments, even if in some larger institutions they remained sequestered in the ghetto of the "non-West." The Japan Foundation report suggested that this change occurred because Japan had become "relevant" to the United States. Perhaps, but the younger cohort of Japan historians generally came to the field with the gleam of high-minded academic irrelevance shining in their eyes. Not yet identified as such in the Japanese media, it seems that the "fourth generation" had begun to appear. In college in the late seventies and eighties, its members learned of Japan as the risen economic superpower; many studied Japanese as their foreign language and spent time in Japan along the way. Theirs was, so to speak, a more normal course, neither autobiographically ordained nor funded wholesale for the sake of national defense and not all that concerned with contemporary U.S.-Japan relations. Some called it the maturation of the field; others saw in it the end of the peculiarly "Japamerican" cast in Japan studies in the United States. Whatever the label, it was apparent that the graduate students in Japanese history of the late 1980s and '90s looked quite like their colleagues in the French or American fields, which is to say, less postmodernization than postmodern.

Possibly because culturalism was so pronounced in considerations of Japan, European cultural theory and the so-called new cultural history had a generally salutary effect on writing in the Japan field. The newer history was skeptical of wielding familiar historical verities like the state, the emperor, the village, and most of all, "the Japanese," without subjecting them to appropriate deconstruction. In rethinking the history of the Tokugawa period scholars asked pointedly, "What is 'early modern' and 'Japanese' about early modern Japan?"[27] They edged sideways at the founding event of modern times, the Meiji Restoration of 1868, not to argue evolutionary continuity or revolutionary rupture but to pose longer-term questions about the unevenness of institutional change, the social relocations entailed in dismantling the hereditary status hierarchy, and the changes in visual culture from the wood-block print to the photograph.[28]

Wary of the modern, but made re-aware in the post–Cold War nationalist upsurge of the 1990s of the power of the nation-state, historians in the United States and Japan reviewed Japanese history in order to catch it in the modern act of "nationalizing" gender, language, culture, social relations, and the rest. They also, in the recent idioms of social and cultural history, sought "space" outside the nation-state, questioning its purported grip on the whole of Japanese history, from ancient times to the present. The tropes were familiar: borders and margins, the culture of everyday life, the places of memory. Attending to borders revealed the lateness of a territorially bounded "Japan," in fact a product of the nineteenth century retrojected back to the legendary age of the gods by ideologues of the modern nation-state. Pursuing people on the margins brought forth the cracks in the putatively tidy social order and mapped the sites of action not controlled by the state. Daily life offered a place to trace subjectivity and the social negotiations of the everyday. Reconstructing the remembered and retrieving the forgotten produced a counterhistory to the nationally created and sanctioned narrative.[29]

These subjects reflected the trends of social and cultural history in general, much as earlier studies of Japan's feudalism or economic development had responded to the scholarly concerns of their day. In themselves they thus provided no immunity from endemic exceptionalism. And yet one senses the vise of "Japaneseness" loosening, in part because poststructuralist conditioning, even at arm's length, had sensitized historians to the constructedness of such concepts. They set out to study modernity, memory, peripherality, feudalism, or Fordism *through* Japan rather than to find the adjectivalized Japanese version of these phenomena. This, I submit, made a huge interpretive difference. Some wrote history in the Foucauldian mode, that most American of genres which French historians find so curious. Others made the most of gender history, an area that Japanese scholars consider one of the most innovative and dynamic in recent U.S. historiography. Whether the "geography of power" in medieval social history, "cartographies of desire" in the history of male sexuality, a "historical ethnography of the nation-state" through the power and pageantry of the Meiji emperor, or "authenticating culture" in the aesthetic hothouse of interwar Japan, the fourth generation brought the boons of cultural theory to bear on some of the most nettlesome issues in Japanese history.[30]

Not only in cultural history but more generally, Japanese and American historians in the 1990s often shared theoretical touchstones and posed similar questions about Japan's past. To the extent that they were now working the same corridors in the house of mirrors, it was the politics of the post-age that were partly responsible. Post–Cold War, postcolonial, postmodern, these epithets meant different things to different people, but intellectuals around the world shared at least an acute sense of "afterness." In Japan the final demise of progressive historiography left a void on the left that some Japanese scholars thought might be filled by "cultural studies" (literally transliterated as *karuchuraru sutadiizu*) of the British and American sort. In the midnineties these historians turned to scholars like Naoki Sakai, who teaches Japanese history at Cornell and consciously practices self-translation of his own work for Japanese and English-language readers, for conceptual help in escaping the narcissism of the nation-state and thereby the paralysis of its politics.[31] In history-writing they sought to overcome the "negative particularism" that made Japanese history seem both different and deficient in comparison to the West.[32] This search had postcolonial overtones in its desire to free Japan's history from Western master narratives. American historians, now properly post-Orientalist, sympathized with this position and joined in the effort to frame Japan's past in its own terms. A tricky phrase, this, for who is to say whose "own terms" are whose. Still, in recent books on the history of "capitalism from within" or "revolution and subjectivity" in early postwar Japan, the authors worked to let the processes and the texts of the past speak for themselves—another epistemological impossibility that in these instances made for good history-writing nonetheless.[33]

If Japan was postcolonial in one direction, it bears pointing out that it was postimperial in the other, a fact that until recently had been more widely recognized than deeply studied by historians both in Japan and the United States.[34] But with the geopolitical shifts of the 1990s, the Japanese-American relationship, which had dominated for so long, receded a little at the same time that the importance of Asia grew a lot. Re-placing Japan in Asia became a political and intellectual challenge. Historians in both countries began to address issues of war and empire, often collaboratively, though less often collaborating with Japanese, Western, and Asian scholars all in the same room at the same time. The nearly mesmeric attraction that the subject of memory held for historians in the 1990s joined politics to history everywhere, but perhaps even more so in Japan, which had left so much of its memory work undone. During the occupation the Americans played a large role in fashioning the narrative of war and empire as a settled account of prewar aggression, corrected by postwar reform. And they also helped to focus the operations of memory on the Pacific War rather than the war in Asia. Throughout the Cold War, transpacific geopolitics and the U.S.-Japan alliance sanctioned this glaringly deficient story. Asian voices began to claim their rights of memory in the 1980s, and by the mid-1990s the claim became a clamor. Because a number of Japanese and American historians had both their own national and a shared common interest in these memory matters, they often worked in tandem on this issue, too.[35]

Although the image of commonality should not be overdrawn, the points of interaction do suggest a change in the broader political context of Japan scholarship. Since the United States still figured prominently, even dominantly, in Asian politics, it was not an out-of-sight, out-of-mind phenomenon of which one could say that the relationship between the two countries had become genuinely postcolonial. More likely, for American historians at least, the relationship had subsided in the size it occupied on their own political horizon, "normalized" perhaps. They studied Japan for many reasons, and they held diverse political views, which determined the history they wrote and also the Japanese historians they collaborated, or colluded, with. Indeed, distinctions of citizenship or national siting had less and less meaning in the marketplace of scholarship. Also, in contrast to the field of Chinese history, where current politics and a cohort of post-Tiananmen émigré scholars had significant effect in the United States, Japan in the 1990s lay in a lull of public interest. Of greater impact in Japanese history was American multiculturalism and identity politics, giving rise, for example, to interest among Asian-Americans in writing the history, not only of Asians in America, but of past links between the two.[36] This work resonated with research on minorities within Japan, including Koreans, the Ainu, and the Ryūkyūans on Oki nawa, peoples who had seldom appeared in the main national narrative. On these issues as well Japanese and Americans often shared what in Japanese is called the same "problem consciousness."

Whether the canonical generations—and the sketches here are drawn more from Japanese views of them than from self-descriptions, which in nearly every case would amount to self-denials at being included in such generational flattening—were so very canonical does not matter all that much. The chronology traced well enough the trajectory of growth and change in American history-writing on Japan across the shank of the twentieth century. But the characterizations omitted the diversity of scholarship that existed in each generation, to the point of paining my conscience at the many names (and friends) I have left out. They were also rather dismissive of "positivism," which after all constituted the mainstream of twentieth-century American historiography. This is because many, though certainly not all, postwar Japanese historians believed in and practiced politically committed history. And these observers were not wrong in spotting the commitment of American historians so often concealed in the comforting folds of their empiricist cloaks. Whatever one may say about Japanese history written in the United States, it was in that respect very American indeed.

THE WAY OUT

For those with ecumenical hopes for history, the present situation is less than inspiring. For while it points to a postexceptionalist future, it often acts like a collection of separate parochial presents. We live in a world of nation-states, each insisting on the specialness of its national history. And if nations did not make ideology out of their history, they would not need the institutional infrastructure that keeps the great number of historians in business. We cheerfully comply in the production and reproduction of our own limitations. When one studies the national history of someone else's country, the problems are doubled but are otherwise no different. America's Japan becomes our special preserve; at best we Japan scholars are (bi)national historians dedicated to the proposition that our own countrypeople ought—need—to know about the history of Japan. And why is that? Because it is (a) in the national interest,(b) relevant to or reflective of our condition, or (c) good for general education. None of the above, one wants to answer; it is history itself we are after, we just look for it in Japan. But that will not do either, for it begins to sound antiquarian, knowledge good for the soul but of no social or moral use. So instead we climb up from the bottom of our particular well to catch a glimpse of the wider sky and see whether we can do something more with national history than let it forever talk only to itself.

This horizon is promising, since so much history is experienced in common, a fact that is hard to keep in mind when one is working down at the bottom of the well. The first thing that becomes clear is the outline of one's own field. Indeed, were it not for the contrast with the European fields presented in this book, I might not have realized how closely intertwined American and Japanese historians have been in their respective and collaborative researches. The focus on the modern (and "early modern") periods is also striking, derived in part from the mid-twentieth-century context. In Japan as in Germany, because the war was considered a judgment on a modernity that had failed, modern times drew the concerned historical eye. In addition, the American postwar imperatives for Asia that it pursue a prescribed course toward economic and political development required an examination of the recent past, which might both impede and impel the processes of modernization. Despite this emphasis, the first three generations produced some fine work on earlier, especially medieval, Japan.[37] And yet, more recent scholars overwhelmingly chose to do modern history. They did not do so for instrumental or programmatic reasons but because in the late twentieth century intellectuals everywhere were rethinking modernity, and Japan was a conspicuous instance of the modern.

Two trends stand out in this rethought modernity. The first was the preoccupation with the state, which was as old as modern Japan itself. Japanese historians had long written top-down history, and even when they wrote from the bottom up, they posed the people against the state, which remained the protagonist in control of history. Japan's strong imperial state engendered this history-from-above, and American historians traced its course by examining the state and labor, the state and the mass media, the state and religion, intellectuals and the state, and "imperial democracy."[38] So while American social scientists were "bringing the state back in" in the 1980s, in Japan's case, it had never gone anywhere. Instead the paradigm had shifted to a state-society grid, in which interactions between the two provided the dynamic of change.[39]

But state and society were often treated as if they were two substantive antagonists ranged against one another, two "things" that stood separately with "interactions" or "responses" running thick between them. This thingification affected other notions such as the bureaucracy and the political parties, setting up a reified schematic that suggested it was always one against the other. In this way a lot of politics got lost, its small negotiations and sideslipping maneuvers too easily disappearing from view. Curiously enough, the concern with the state did not generate much of a historical literature on fascism. Compared to the attention American historians paid to national socialism in Germany and, to a lesser degree, fascism in Italy and Spain, this was a surprising lacuna. Nor did the concern with society produce a social history of fascism or, indeed, of the modern period in general. For that reason it remained difficult to know who supported whom and for what reasons during the so-called dark valley of the 1930s. This state-centered history possessed notable blank spots in the middle of it.

The second trend was the cultural turn that appeared across the historical board in the 1980s. In the case of Japan, it first galvanized the intellectual history of modernity and its critique. Studies of Marxist and mass culture, reactionary modernism and romantic antimodernism brought the cultural landscape of the interwar years to life.[40] If the social history of fascism was absent, not so its cultural history, which not only illuminated the struggle for an indigenous modernity but showed the modernist commonalities in Japan, Germany, France, Korea, and other places. Postmodern commonalities also began to receive similar attention.[41] As younger scholars followed the swerve to cultural history, its vibrancy left new absences in its wake. Economic history seemed virtually to have vanished, with a few exceptions; capitalism seemed not to dare to speak its name. Political history was in the doldrums, and for all the attention to memory of the war, few appeared interested in the causes of the conflict. None of this was peculiar to Japanese history, although in a small field the consequences of fashion were more pronounced; as one corner buzzed with excitement, large portions of the historyscape stood empty.

When it came to the poetics of history-writing, American historians may have shared, or sparred over, method and problem consciousness with their colleagues in Japan, but they practiced the historian's craft as professionalized in the United States. In brief, they wrote analytic narratives built around a (more or less) coherent argument on a single theme, standard procedure in American dissertations though not in Japan, where books grew by accumulating essays of article length. Japanese scholars often remarked that Americans chose bizarrely "big topics," whose generality was such as to be unresearchable. This expansive, or foolish, daring derived partly from the newness of the field, as John Hall later recalled of the 1950s: "One could take up any subject of research without fear of being crowded. One could write on almost any subject without being jumped on."[42] But later, long after a scholar could expect to be jumped on in at least two languages, American historians still grabbed for the thematic brass ring, tackling bigger themes than they might have had they been writing their own national history: the Meiji restoration, the rise of capitalism, the body in the nineteenth century, the occupation, each in a single book.

But if the field preferred big topics, it seldom produced big books. Granted such books are rare in any field. Yet writers who consider themselves historians first and Japan scholars second naturally wish to speak to the muse and not only to one another. In the recently revived debates over area studies, it was observed that Western studies of Japan had made almost no paradigmatic contribution to social science theory, except perhaps for the concept of the "capitalist development state." Southeast Asia, in contrast, had generated the moral economy versus the rational peasant, the nation as imagined community, and half the Geertzian repertoire of cultural anthropology. This aperçu of comparative social science provided, however, no explanation for either phenomenon. In history-writing, one wonders whether it was the books or the audience that kept Japanese history peripheral to centers of historical discourse. If scholars had produced titles like "Fin-de-siècle Tokyo," "Peasants into Japanese," "Festival in Shinano," or "Recasting Bourgeois Asia," would the books have been read, or was the deficit in interest in Japan too great? Perhaps because American historians interacted so closely with Japanese historiography they isolated themselves from the other histories. More likely, it was a matter of maturation on both sides: by the nineties, the Japan books had changed, addressing similar subjects with similar modes of analysis to those in the rest of the field, and the rest of the field was, if not exactly postparochial, at least more open to the insights of history from afar.

The main hurdles for Japan historians in any country remained the poetics and polarities of Otherness, which bifurcated things into East and West, Japan and non-Japan, and then insisted on the singularity of Japanese experience, resisting multiplicity and making Japan into an "absolute elsewhere." But there were promising signs of a simultaneous dejapanization and deamericanization of the historical narrative of modernity. Indeed, it began to seem possible to deterritorialize the modern, to recognize in analytic terms that modernity was a condition held in common in many places, East and West. Neither singular nor endlessly multiple, each society (or nation) inflected the modern differently and did so unevenly, both across societies and within them. The historian's task was to trace the inflections and the unevennesses, in such a way so as neither to flatten nor essentialize them. As for the longer past, it required both denationalizing, removing the anachronism of the nation from its prehistory, and demodernizing, suspending the telos of the future from considerations of ancient or medieval times.

These changes were not nearly as formidable as they sound; they demanded a shift in historiographical stance, not a revolution.

Elsewhere in this book, and in many other books, scholars recount a twentieth-century tale of history-writing that ends with a coming apart, not a coming together. In the epistemological narrative, scientific truth gave way to cultural construction, the Galilean paradigm to evidential conjecture, objectivism to subjectivity, reality to representation, the past-that-was-theirs to the story-that-is-ours. In the historiographical narrative, synthesis became specialization, wholeness became fragments, events became texts, reality became discourse, grand narratives became microhistories. In the political narrative, nation and state were set against race, gender, and ethnos, unity against identity, action against agency, self against other. Times, it was clear, had changed. Most placed the pivotal shift in the 1960s, the era of the great coming apart. Some thought discourse or theory the enemy, others runaway plurality and hybridity, still others recalcitrant grand narratives and functionalist paradigms. Whatever the diagnosis, it seemed as if the historical operation had been successful, but the patient, history, might yet die.

I don't think so. Without disputing the retrospective accounts, I would take a prospective view and argue that we have already entered a new phase. Like the 1880s when history was professionalized under the sign of the nation-state and the midtwentieth century when history looked forward from the ashes of war, the 1990s constitute another moment of historical opportunity. Rather than a crisis it is a conjuncture, a coming together of political, intellectual, and cultural change, and it is a conjuncture in common, as palpable in Japan as in Europe, India, or the United States. Far from being undone by theoretical ordeals or warped by the linguistic turn, we have benefited from them. With a heightened sense of historicity, a greater epistemological sensitivity, and an array of new methodological options, historians are better prepared to ask big questions without trumping them with prefabricated big answers. The grand narratives of the nineteenth century have finally whispered out, barely in time for the twenty-first century to begin. The lack of surety in the present world brings a (relative) absence of orthodoxy; heresy, whence innovation, is the order of the day. Meanwhile we have learned to disaggregate social nouns like the nation, women, and the working class and respect the negotiations that constitute experience in the everyday, which is where history actually happens. We have the opportunity, too, to write postnational history, even though we still live in nation-states. And refraining from fragments and macro-synopsis alike, we can manage middle-level syntheses in pursuing the processes of the past.

If this sounds like a phantasm, it is not. For a new kind of work is already underway among younger historians, historians much younger than anyone writing in this book. Theirs is the conjuncture of the 1990s; they did not make it, but they can make the most of it. It is an exciting time to be a historian, whether in Japan, of Japan, or anywhere else: no exceptions. It is as if the house of mirrors had become transparent, and we can see through it if we try.

NOTES

1. To be fair to the editors, a variety of reasons prevented the originally planned papers on China, Africa, and Latin America from being included in the volume.

2. See John W. Dower, "E. H. Norman, Japan and the Uses of History," in *Origins of the Modern Japanese State: Selected Writings of E. H. Norman* (New York: Pantheon Books, 1975), pp. 31–65.

3. See Daniel T. Rodgers, "Exceptionalism," chapter 1 in this volume.

4. See Stefan Tanaka, *Japan's Orient: Rendering Pasts into History* (Berkeley: University of California Press, 1993).

5. In Karl Marx, *Capital* (New York: Vintage Books, 1977) vol. 1, p. 878n; E. J. Hobsbawm, *Nations and Nationalism since 1780: Programme, Myth, Reality* (Cambridge: Cambridge University Press, 1990), p. 151.

6. See John Whitney Hall, "East, Southeast, and South Asia," in Michael Kammen, ed., *The Past before Us: Contemporary Historical Writing in the United States* (Ithaca: Cornell University Press, 1980), pp. 157–86; Marius B. Jansen, "History of Japanese Studies in the United States," in The Japan Foundation, ed., *Japanese Studies in the United States*, part I (Ann Arbor: The Association for Asian Studies, 1988), pp. 7–70; John W. Dower, "Nihon o hakaru: Eigoken in okeru Nihon kenkyū no rekishi jojutsu," *Shisō*, part 1 (Sept. 1995): 65–95; part 2 (Oct. 1995): 67–89.

7. Tadashi Aruga, "Japanese Scholarship and the Meaning of American History," *The Journal of American History* 79, 2 (Sept. 1992): 502–8; Paul F. Hooper, ed., *Rediscovering the IPR: Proceedings of the First International Research Conference on the Institute of Pacific Relations* (Honolulu: University of Hawaii, 1993).

8. Edwin O. Reischauer, *My Life between Japan and America* (New York: Harper & Row, 1986), p. xiii; Hugh Borton, *American Presurrender Planning for Postwar Japan* (New York: The East Asian Institute, 1967), pp. 15–16.

9. For the famous textbook that emerged from the rice-paddies course: John King Fairbank, Edwin O. Reischauer, and Albert M. Craig, *East Asia: The Great Tradition* and *East Asia: The Modern Transformation* (Boston: Houghton Mifflin, 1961, 1965).

10. Hall, "East, Southeast, and South Asia," p. 176.

11. E.g., Thomas C. Smith, *The Agrarian Origins of Modern Japan* (Stanford: Stanford University Press, 1959); the essays collected in John W. Hall and Marius B. Jansen, eds., *Studies in the Institutional History of Early Modern Japan* (Princeton: Princeton University Press, 1968); and, for a longer view, John W. Hall, *Government and Local Power 500 to 1700: A Study Based on Bizen Province* (Princeton: Princeton University Press, 1966).

12. E.g., Marius B. Jansen, *Sakamoto Ryōma and the Meiji Restoration* (Princeton: Princeton University Press, 1961); Albert M. Craig, *Choshu and the Meiji Restoration* (Cambridge: Harvard University Press, 1961).

13. Hall, "East, Southeast, and South Asia," p. 164.

14. Norman, then a diplomat, was hounded by McCarthyite forces to his suicide in 1959. See Roger Bowen, *Innocence Is Not Enough: The Life and Death of Herbert Norman* (Armonk: M. E. Sharpe, 1986).

15. John Whitney Hall, "Changing Conceptions of the Modernization of Japan," in Marius B. Jansen, *Changing Japanese Attitudes toward Modernization* (Princeton: Princeton University Press, 1965), pp. 7–41. This volume was followed by five others, all published by Princeton between 1965 and 1971.

16. Jansen, "History of Japanese Studies," p. 46, 51.

17. E.g., Tetsuo Najita, *Japan: The Intellectual Foundations of Modern Japanese Politics* (Chicago: University of Chicago Press, 1974), and *Visions of Virtue in Tokugawa Japan: The Kaitokudō Merchant Academy of Osaka* (Chicago: University of Chicago Press, 1987); H. D. Harootunian, *Toward Restoration: The Growth of Political Consciousness in Tokugawa Japan* (Berkeley: University of California Press, 1970), and *Things Seen and Unseen: Discourse and Ideology in Tokugawa Nativism* (Chicago: University of Chicago Press, 1988).

18. John W. Dower, "Occupied Japan and the American Lake, 1945–1950," in Edward Friedman and Mark Selden, eds., *America's Asia: Dissenting Essays on Asian-American Relations* (New York: Pantheon, 1971).

19. Dower, "E. H. Norman, Japan and the Uses of History," p. 33.

20. See the *Bulletin of Concerned Asian Scholars*, published since 1968 by the Committee of Concerned Asian Scholars, which was formed to protest U.S. policy in Southeast Asia.

21. E.g., John W. Dower, *War without Mercy: Race and Power in the Pacific War* (New York: Pantheon Books, 1986), and, from a different political but adjacent scholarly perspective, the works of Akira Iriye, including *Power and Culture: The Japanese-American War, 1941–1945* (Cambridge: Harvard University Press, 1981).

22. For a useful digest of Japanese scholarship along these lines, see Mikiso Hane, *Peasants, Rebels, & Outcastes: The Underside of Modern Japan* (New York: Pantheon Books, 1982).

23. Tetsuo Najita and J. Victor Koschmann, eds., *Conflict in Modern Japanese History: The Neglected Tradition* (Princeton: Princeton Univesity Press, 1982).

24. Herbert Bix, *Peasant Protest in Japan 1590–1884* (New Haven: Yale University Press, 1986); William W. Kelly, *Deference and Defiance in Nineteenth-Century Japan* (Princeton: Princeton University Press, 1985); Stephen Vlastos, *Peasant Protests and Uprisings in Tokugawa Japan* (Berkeley: University of California Press, 1986); Anne Walthall, *Social Protest and Popular Culture in Eighteenth Century Japan* (Tucson: University of Arizona Press, 1986).

25. I use "post-modernization" more broadly than Dower, who stresses those scholars (primarily social scientists) who emphasized Japan's divergence from, rather than convergence with, the American model. (Dower, "Nihon o hakaru," part 1). Here I mean history-writing that stood apart from the modernizationist narrative, which by the 1980s was nearly all of it. E.g., in regard to imperial Japan: Andrew Gordon, *The Evolution of Labor Relations in Japan: Heavy Industry, 1853–1955* (Cambridge: Council on East Asian Studies, 1985); Carol Gluck, *Japan's Modern Myths: Ideology in the Late Meiji Period* (Princeton: Princeton University Press, 1985); Sheldon Garon, *The State and Labor in Modern Japan* (Berkeley: University of California Press, 1987); Andrew Barshay, *State and Intellectual in Imperial Japan: The Public Man in Crisis* (Berkeley: University of California Press, 1988).

26. Patricia G. Steinhoff in *Japanese Studies in the United States: The 1990s* (Ann Arbor: The Japan Foundation, 1996), pp. 8–12.

27. A series of panels and conferences on this theme began in 1995 with future publications planned; participants included historians Ronald Toby, David Howell, Mary Elizabeth Berry, Kären Wigen, James Ketelaar, and others.

28. E.g., Helen Hardacre and Adam L. Kern, eds., *New Directions in the Study of Meiji Japan* (Leiden: Brill, 1997).

29. E.g., James Ketelaar's current research on the northern borders during the Tokuagawa period; Kären Wigen, *The Making of a Japanese Periphery, 1750–1920* (Berkeley: University of California Press, 1995); Jordan Sand's current work on house and home in modern Japan, etc.

30. Thomas Keirstead, *The Geography of Power in Medieval Japan* (Princeton: Princeton University Press, 1992); Gregory M. Pflugfelder, *Cartographies of Desire: Male-Male Sexuality in Japanese Discourse, 1600–1950* (Berkeley: University of California Press, forthcoming); T. Fujitani, *Splendid Monarchy: Power and Pageantry in Modern Japan* (Berkeley: University of California Press, 1996); Leslie Pincus: *Authenticating Culture in Imperial Japan: Kuki Shūzō and the Rise of National Aesthetics* (Berkeley: University of California Press, 1996).

31. E.g., Naoki Sakai, *Translation and Subjectivity: On Japan and Cultural Nationalism* (Minneapolis: University of Minnesota Press, 1997); also, *Voices of the Past: The Status of Language in Eighteenth-Century Japanese Discourse* (Ithaca: Cornell University Press, 1991).

32. The term is Narita Ryūichi's in "Historical Practice before the Dawn: 'Modern Japan' in Postwar History," *Iichiko*, no. 7 (1995): 115–26.

33. David L. Howell, *Capitalism from Within: Economy, Society, and the State in a Japanese Fishery* (Berkeley: University of California Press, 1995); J. Victor Koschmann, *Revolution and Subjectivity in Postwar Japan* (Chicago: University of Chicago Press, 1996).

34. E.g., Louise Young, *Japan's Total Empire: Manchuria and the Culture of Wartime Imperialism* (Berkeley: University of California Press, 1998); Peter Duus, *The Abacus and the Sword: The Japanese Penetration of Korea, 1895–1910* (Berkeley: University of Calfornia Press, 1995).

35. E.g., Lisa Yoneyama, *Hiroshima Traces: Time, Space and the Dialectics of Memory* (Berkeley: University of California Press, forthcoming); T. Fujitani, Geoffrey White, and Lisa Yoneyama, eds., *Perilous Memories: The Asia-Pacific War(s)* (in preparation); Laura Hein and Mark Selden, eds., *Living with the Bomb: American and Japanese Cultural Conflicts in the Nuclear Age* (Armonk: M. E. Sharpe, 1997); Carol Gluck, "The Past in the Present," in Andrew Gordon, ed., *Postwar Japan as History* (Berkeley: University of California Press, 1993), pp. 64–95.

36. E.g., T. Fujitani's current comparative work on ethnic and colonial soldiers in both the United States and Japan.

37. For "pre–early modern" history, e.g., the works of John W. Hall, Martin Collcutt, Mary Elizabeth Berry, Jeffrey P. Mass and his students, Hitomi Tonomura, Thomas Keirstead, Joan Piggott, Andrew Goble, and others.

38. Andrew Gordon, *Labor and Imperial Democracy in Prewar Japan* (Berkeley: University of California Press, 1991).

39. See Sheldon Garon, "Rethinking Modernization and Modernity in Japanese History: A Focus on State-Society Relations," *Journal of Asian Studies* 53, 2 (May 1994): 346–66, also his *Molding Japanese Minds: The State in Everyday Life* (Princeton: Princeton University Press, 1997).

40. E.g., Miriam Silverberg, *Changing Song: The Marxist Manifestos of Nakano Shigeharu* (Princeton: Princeton University Press, 1990); J. Thomas Rimer, ed., *Culture and Identity: Japanese Intellectuals during the Interwar Years* (Princeton: Princeton University Press, 1990); Kevin Michael Doak, *Dreams of Difference: The Japan Romantic School and the Crisis of Modernity* (Berkeley: University of California Press, 1994); Pincus, *Authenticating Culture*.

41. Masao Miyoshi and H. D. Harootunian, eds., *Postmodernism and Japan* (Durham: Duke University Press, 1989); Marilyn Ivy, *Discourses of the Vanishing: Modernity, Phantasm, Japan* (Chicago: University of Chicago Press, 1995).

42. John W. Hall, "100 Years of American Historiography on Japan," paper presented at the American Historical Association, Chicago, December 1984.

KEITH MICHAEL BAKER is the J. E. Wallace Sterling Professor in the Humanities and Professor of History at Stanford University, and the Anthony P. Meier Family Professor and Director of the Stanford Humanities Center. His publications include *Condorcet: From Natural Philosophy to Social Mathematics* (1975) and *Inventing the French Revolution* (1990), and he has edited *The French Revolution and the Creation of Modern Political Culture*, vol. 1, *The Political Culture of the Old Regime* (1987), and vol. 4, *The Terror* (1994). He was a coeditor of the *Journal of Modern History* from 1980 to 1988.

PHILIP BENEDICT is Professor of History at Brown University, author of *Rouen during the Wars of Religion* (1981) and many articles on the social and religious history of early modern France, and editor of *Cities and Social Change in Early Modern France* (1989) and the forthcoming *Reformation, Revolt, and Civil War in France and the Netherlands, 1555–1585*.

VOLKER BERGHAHN is the Seth Low Professor of History at Columbia University. His major publications are *Der Tirpitz-Plan* (1971), *Germany and the Approach of War in 1914* (1973), *Militarism* (1981), *The Americanisation of West German Industry, 1945–1973* (1986), and *Imperial Germany, 1871–1914* (1994).

GEORGE M. FREDRICKSON is Edgar E. Robinson Professor of United States History at Stanford University and president of the Organization of American Historians for 1997–98. He is the author of *The Inner Civil War* (1965), *The Black Image in the White Mind* (1971), *White Supremacy* (1981), *The Arrogance of Race* (1988), *Black Liberation* (1995), and *The Comparative Imagination* (1997).

PHILIP GLEASON is professor emeritus of history at the University of Notre Dame and president of the Immigration and Ethnic History Society. His particular interest is in the intersection of ethnic, religious, and intellectual history. His works include *The Conservative Reformers: German-American Catholics and the Social Order* (1968), *Keeping the Faith: American Catholicism Past and Present* (1987), *Speaking of Diversity: Language and Ethnicity in Twentieth-Century America* (1992), and *Contending with Modernity: Catholic Higher Education in the Twentieth Century* (1995).

CAROL GLUCK is the George Sansom Professor of History at Columbia University, author of *Japan's Modern Myths: Ideology in the Late Meiji Period* (1985), coeditor of *Showa: The Japan of Hirohito* (1992) and *Asia in Western and World History* (1997). Her *Versions of the Past: The Japanese and Their Modern History* is forthcoming.

THOMAS C. HOLT is the James Westfall Thompson Professor in American History at the University of Chicago. He is the author of *Black over White: Negro Political Leadership in South Carolina during Reconstruction* (1977) and *The Problem of Freedom: Race, Labor, and Politics in Jamaica and Britain, 1832–1938* (1992).

RICHARD L. KAGAN is Professor of History at the Johns Hopkins University. His publications include *Students and Society in Early Modern Spain* (1974), *Lawsuits and Litigants in Castile, 1500–1700* (1981), and *Lucrecia's Dreams* (1990). He has also edited *Spanish Cities of the Golden Age* (1987) and (with Geoffrey Parker) *Spain, Europe and the Atlantic World* (1995). His *Urban Images of the Hispanic World, 1493–1780* will be published by Yale

University Press in 1999. His essay in this volume forms part of a larger project on Spain and the American Imagination.

LINDA K. KERBER is May Brodbeck Professor in the Liberal Arts and Professor of History at the University of Iowa. She has served as president of the Organization of American Historians and the American Studies Association. Her most recent books are *Toward an Intellectual History of Women* (University of North Carolina Press, 1997) and *No Constitutional Right to Be Ladies: Women and the Obligations of Citizenship* (Hill & Wang, 1998). She is a member of the American Academy of Arts and Sciences.

NAOMI R. LAMOREAUX is Professor of Economics and History at the University of California, Los Angeles. She is the author of *The Great Merger Movement in American Business, 1895–1904* (Cambridge University Press, 1985) and *Insider Lending: Banks, Kinship Connections, and Economic Development in Industrial New England* (Cambridge University Press, 1994), as well as a number of articles in scholarly journals and collections. She served as coeditor of the *Journal of Economic History* from 1992 until 1996.

CHARLES MAIER is the Krupp Foundation Professor of History and director of the Center for European Studies at Harvard University. His major publications include *Recasting Bourgeois Europe* (1975), *The Unmasterable Past* (1988), and *Dissolution* (1997).

MARTIN MALIA is professor emeritus at the University of California, Berkeley. His fields of specialization are Russian history and modern European intellectual history, with a particular interest under both headings in the history of socialism. His principal publications are *Alexander Herzen and the Birth of Russian Socialism, 1812–1855* (Cambridge: Harvard University Press, 1961), *Comprendre la révolution russe* (Paris: Le Seuil, 1980), *The Soviet Tragedy: A History of Socialism in Russia, 1917–1991* (New York: Free Press, 1994). Forthcoming in 1999 with the Harvard University Press is *From the Bronze Horseman to the Lenin Mausoleum: Russia under Western Eyes*.

ANTHONY MOLHO is the David Herlihy University Professor and Professor of History at Brown University and codirector of the Centro di Studi Mediterranei in Naples, Italy. Most recently, he wrote *Marriage Alliance in Late Medieval Florence* (Harvard University Press, 1994) and coedited *Origini dello Stato: Processi de fomazione statale in Italia fra medioevo ed età moderna* (Bologna: Il Mulino, 1994).

JAMES T. PATTERSON is Ford Foundation Professor of History at Brown University. His recent publications include *America's Struggle against Poverty, 1900–1994* (Harvard University Press, 1995); *The Dread Disease: Cancer and Modern American Culture* (Harvard University Press, 1987); and *Grand Expectations: The United States, 1945–1974* (Oxford University Press, 1996), winner of a Bancroft Prize for American History. He is a member of the American Academy of Arts and Sciences.

DANIEL T. RODGERS is Professor of History at Princeton University, where he teaches American intellectual and cultural history. He is the author of *The Work Ethic in Industrial America* (1978), *Contested Truths: Keywords in American Politics since Independence* (1987), and *Atlantic Crossings: Social Politics in a Progressive Age* (1998).

DOROTHY ROSS is Arthur O. Lovejoy Professor of History at the Johns Hopkins University. She is the author of *G. Stanley Hall: The Psychologist as Prophet* (University of Chicago Press, 1972), *The Origins of American Social Science* (Cambridge University Press, 1991), and editor of *Modernist Impulses in the Human Sciences, 1870–1930* (Johns Hopkins University Press, 1993).

RICHARD SALLER is Edward L. Ryerson Distinguished Service Professor of History and Classics at the University of Chicago. His special research interests center on Roman imperial society. His books include *Personal Patronage under the early Empire* (1982), *Roman Empire: Economy, Society and Culture* (with Peter Garnsey, 1987), and *Patriarchy, Property and Death in the Roman Family* (1994).

GABRIELLE M. SPIEGEL is Professor of History at the Johns Hopkins University. She is the author of *The Chronicle Tradition of Saint-Denis: A Survey*, Medieval Classics: Texts and Studies, no. 10 (Leiden and Boston, 1978); *Romancing the Past: The Rise of Vernacular Prose Historiography in Thirteenth-Century France*, "The New Historicism" (University of California Press, Berkeley and Los Angeles, 1993); and *The Past as Text: The Theory and Practice of Medieval Historiography* (Johns Hopkins University Press, 1997). She is currently working on a book which will treat the tradition of medieval historical writing in North America from the revolutionary era to the present time.

EUGEN WEBER is the Joan Palevsky Professor of Modern European History at UCLA and author, among other works, of *A Modern History of Europe* and the PBS/WGBH series *The Western Tradition*.

GORDON S. WOOD is Alva O. Way University Professor and Professor of History at Brown University. He is the author of *The Creation of the American Republic, 1776–1787* and *The Radicalism of the American Revolution*.

JOSEPH ZIZEK received his Ph.D. in 1995 from the University of California, Berkeley, for a dissertation entitled "The Politics and Poetics of History during the French Revolution, 1787–1794." At Stanford University in 1995–97, he held a postdoctoral fellowship from the Social Sciences and Humanities Research Council of Canada; he is presently Visiting Assistant Professor at the Robert C. Clark Honors College of the University of Oregon. In July 1998 he will take up the post of Lecturer in History at the University of Auckland (New Zealand).